PROGRAMMING WITH
MICROSOFT® VISUAL BASIC® 2015

SEVENTH EDITION

PROGRAMMING WITH MICROSOFT® VISUAL BASIC® 2015

DIANE ZAK

CENGAGE
Learning®

Australia • Brazil • Mexico • Singapore • United Kingdom • United States

**Programming with Microsoft® Visual Basic®
2015, Seventh Edition**
Diane Zak

Product Director: Kathleen McMahon

Product Team Manager: Kristin McNary

Senior Product Manager: Jim Gish

Senior Content Developer: Alyssa Pratt

Product Assistant: Abigail Pufpaff

Marketing Manager: Eric LaScola

Senior Production Director:
Wendy Troeger

Production Director: Patty Stephan

Senior Content Project Manager:
Jennifer K. Feltri-George

Managing Art Director: Jack Pendleton

Cover image(s):
© Rudchenko Liliia/Shutterstock.com

Unless otherwise noted all screenshots are
courtesy of Microsoft Corporation

Open Clip art source: OpenClipArt

For product information and technology assistance, contact us at
Cengage Learning Customer & Sales Support, 1-800-354-9706
For permission to use material from this text or product, submit all
requests online at **www.cengage.com/permissions**
Further permissions questions can be emailed to
permissionrequest@cengage.com

Library of Congress Control Number: 2015940168
ISBN: 978-1-285-86026-8

Cengage Learning
20 Channel Center Street
Boston, MA 02210
USA

Cengage Learning is a leading provider of customized learning solutions
with employees residing in nearly 40 different countries and sales in more
than 125 countries around the world. Find your local representative at
www.cengage.com

Cengage Learning products are represented in Canada by
Nelson Education, Ltd.

For your course and learning solutions, visit **www.cengage.com**

Purchase any of our products at your local college store or at our
preferred online store **www.cengagebrain.com**

Notice to the Reader

Publisher does not warrant or guarantee any of the products described herein or
perform any independent analysis in connection with any of the product information contained herein. Publisher does not assume, and expressly disclaims, any
obligation to obtain and include information other than that provided to it by the
manufacturer. The reader is expressly warned to consider and adopt all safety
precautions that might be indicated by the activities described herein and to avoid
all potential hazards. By following the instructions contained herein, the reader
willingly assumes all risks in connection with such instructions. The publisher
makes no representations or warranties of any kind, including but not limited to,
the warranties of fitness for particular purpose or merchantability, nor are any such
representations implied with respect to the material set forth herein, and the
publisher takes no responsibility with respect to such material. The publisher shall
not be liable for any special, consequential, or exemplary damages resulting, in
whole or part, from the readers' use of, or reliance upon, this material.

Printed in the United States of America
Print Number: 01   Print Year: 2015

Brief Contents

Contents

CONTENTS

Preface

Programming with Microsoft Visual Basic 2015, Seventh Edition uses Visual Basic 2015, an object-oriented language, to teach programming concepts. This book is designed for a beginning programming course. However, it assumes students are familiar with basic Windows skills and file management.

Organization and Coverage

Programming with Microsoft Visual Basic 2015, Seventh Edition contains an Overview and 14 chapters that present hands-on instruction; it also contains five appendices (A through E). An additional appendix (Appendix F) covering multiple-form applications and the FontDialog, ColorDialog, and TabControl tools is available online at CengageBrain.com.

In the chapters, students with no previous programming experience learn how to plan and create their own interactive Windows applications. GUI design skills, OOP concepts, and planning tools (such as TOE charts, pseudocode, and flowcharts) are emphasized throughout the book. The chapters show students how to work with objects and write Visual Basic statements such as If...Then...Else, Select Case, Do...Loop, For...Next, and For Each...Next. Students also learn how to create and manipulate variables, constants, strings, sequential access files, structures, classes, and arrays. Chapter 12 shows students how to create both static and dynamic Web applications. In Chapter 13, students learn how to connect an application to a Microsoft Access database, and then use Language-Integrated Query (LINQ) to query the database. Chapter 14 continues the coverage of databases, introducing the student to more advanced concepts and Structured Query Language (SQL).

Appendix A, which can be covered after Chapter 3, teaches students how to locate and correct errors in their code. The appendix shows students how to step through their code and also how to create breakpoints. Appendix B recaps the GUI design guidelines mentioned in the chapters, and Appendix C lists the Visual Basic conversion functions. The Visual Basic 2015 Cheat Sheet contained in Appendix D summarizes important concepts covered in the chapters, such as the syntax of statements, methods, and so on. The Cheat Sheet provides a convenient place for students to locate the information they need as they are creating and coding their applications. Appendix E contains Case Projects that can be assigned after completing specific chapters in the book.

Approach

Programming with Microsoft Visual Basic 2015, Seventh Edition teaches programming concepts using a task-driven rather than a command-driven approach. By working through the chapters, which are each motivated by a realistic case, students learn how to develop applications they are likely to encounter in the workplace. This is much more effective than memorizing a list of commands out of context. The book motivates students by demonstrating why they need to learn the concepts and skills covered in each chapter.

Features

Programming with Microsoft Visual Basic 2015, Seventh Edition is an exceptional textbook because it also includes the following features:

READ THIS BEFORE YOU BEGIN This section is consistent with Cengage Learning's unequaled commitment to helping instructors introduce technology into the classroom. Technical considerations and assumptions about hardware, software, and default settings are listed in one place to help instructors save time and eliminate unnecessary aggravation.

YOU DO IT! BOXES These boxes provide simple applications that allow students to demonstrate their understanding of a concept before moving on to the next concept. The YOU DO IT! boxes are located almost exclusively in Lesson A of each chapter.

VISUAL STUDIO 2015 METHODS The book focuses on Visual Studio 2015 methods rather than on Visual Basic functions. Exceptions to this are the Val and Format functions, which are introduced in Chapter 2. These functions are covered in the book simply because it is likely that students will encounter them in existing Visual Basic programs. However, in Chapter 3, the student is taught to use the TryParse method and the Convert class methods rather than the Val function. Also in Chapter 3, the Format function is replaced with the ToString method.

OPTION STATEMENTS All programs include the Option Explicit, Option Strict, and Option Infer statements.

START HERE ARROWS These arrows indicate the beginning of a tutorial steps section in the book.

DATABASES, LINQ, AND SQL The book includes two chapters (Chapters 13 and 14) on databases. LINQ is covered in Chapter 13. SQL is covered in Chapter 14.

FIGURES Figures that introduce new statements, functions, or methods contain both the syntax and examples of using the syntax. Including the syntax in the figures makes the examples more meaningful, and vice versa.

CHAPTER CASES Each chapter begins with a programming-related problem that students could reasonably expect to encounter in business, followed by a demonstration of an application that could be used to solve the problem. Showing the students the completed application before they learn how to create it is motivational and instructionally sound. By allowing the students to see the type of application they will be able to create after completing the chapter, the students will be more motivated to learn because they can see how the programming concepts they are about to learn can be used and, therefore, why the concepts are important.

LESSONS Each chapter is divided into three lessons—A, B, and C. Lesson A introduces the programming concepts that will be used in the completed application. The concepts are illustrated with code examples and sample applications. The user interface for each sample application is provided to the student. Also provided are tutorial-style steps that guide the student on coding, running, and testing the application. Each sample application allows the student to observe how the current concept can be used before the next concept is introduced. In Lessons B and/or C, the student creates the application required to solve the problem specified in the Chapter Case.

APPENDICES Appendix A, which can be covered after Chapter 3, teaches students how to locate and correct errors (syntax, logic, and run time) in their code. The appendix shows students how to step through their code and also how to create breakpoints. Appendix B summarizes the GUI design guidelines taught in the chapters, making it easier for the student to follow the guidelines when designing an application's interface. Appendix C lists the Visual Basic conversion functions. Appendix D contains a Cheat Sheet that summarizes important concepts covered in the chapters, such as the syntax of statements, methods, and so on. The Cheat Sheet provides a convenient place for students to locate the information they need as they are creating and coding their applications. Appendix E contains Case Projects that can be assigned after completing specific chapters in the book. Appendix F, which is available online at CengageBrain.com, covers multiple-form applications and the FontDialog, ColorDialog, and TabControl tools.

GUI DESIGN TIP BOXES The GUI DESIGN TIP boxes contain guidelines and recommendations for designing applications that follow Windows standards. Appendix B provides a summary of the GUI design guidelines covered in the chapters.

 TIP These notes provide additional information about the current concept. Examples include alternative ways of writing statements or performing tasks, as well as warnings about common mistakes made when using a particular command and reminders of related concepts learned in previous chapters.

SUMMARY Each lesson contains a Summary section that recaps the concepts covered in the lesson.

KEY TERMS Following the Summary section in each lesson is a listing of the key terms introduced throughout the lesson, along with their definitions.

REVIEW QUESTIONS Each lesson contains Review Questions designed to test a student's understanding of the lesson's concepts.

EXERCISES The Review Questions in each lesson are followed by Exercises, which provide students with additional practice of the skills and concepts they learned in the lesson. The Exercises are designated as INTRODUCTORY, INTERMEDIATE, ADVANCED, DISCOVERY, and SWAT THE BUGS. The DISCOVERY Exercises encourage students to challenge and independently develop their own programming skills while exploring the capabilities of Visual Basic 2015. The SWAT THE BUGS Exercises provide an opportunity for students to detect and correct errors in an application's code.

New to This Edition!

 UPDATED VIDEOS These notes direct students to videos that accompany each chapter in the book. The videos explain and/or demonstrate one or more of the chapter's concepts. The videos have been revised from the previous edition and are available via the optional MindTap for this text.

NEW CHAPTER CASES, EXAMPLES, APPLICATIONS, REVIEW QUESTIONS, AND EXERCISES The chapters contain new Chapter Cases, code examples, sample applications, Review Questions, and Exercises.

CHAPTERS 2, 5, 6, AND 12 The Visible property is now introduced in Chapter 2 rather than in Chapter 5. Coverage of the priming and update reads was moved from Chapter 6's Lesson A to Chapter 6's Lesson B. The topics covered in Chapter 6's Lesson B are now covered in its Lesson C and vice versa. The Financial.Pmt function is covered in Chapter 6's Lesson B. Chapter 12, which covers Web applications, has been revamped.

Steps and Figures

The tutorial-style steps in the book assume you are using Microsoft Visual Studio Ultimate 2015 and a system running Microsoft Windows 8. The figures in the book reflect how your screen will look if you are using a Microsoft Windows 8 system. Your screen may appear slightly different in some instances if you are using a different version of Microsoft Windows.

Instructor Resources

The following teaching tools are available for download at our Instructor Companion Site. Simply search for this text at sso.cengage.com. An instructor login is required.

INSTRUCTOR'S MANUAL The Instructor's Manual that accompanies this textbook includes additional instructional material to assist in class preparation, including items such as Sample Syllabi, Chapter Outlines, Technical Notes, Lecture Notes, Quick Quizzes, Teaching Tips, Discussion Topics, and Additional Case Projects.

TEST BANK Cengage Learning Testing Powered by Cognero is a flexible, online system that allows you to:

- author, edit, and manage test bank content from multiple Cengage Learning solutions

- create multiple test versions in an instant

- deliver tests from your LMS, your classroom or wherever you want

POWERPOINT PRESENTATIONS This book offers Microsoft PowerPoint slides for each chapter. These are included as a teaching aid for classroom presentation, to make available to students on the network for chapter review, or to be printed for classroom distribution. Instructors can add their own slides for additional topics they introduce to the class.

SOLUTION FILES Solutions to the Lesson applications and the end-of-lesson Review Questions and Exercises are provided.

DATA FILES Data Files are necessary for completing the computer activities in this book. Data Files can also be downloaded by students at CengageBrain.com.

MindTap

MindTap is a personalized teaching experience with relevant assignments that guide students to analyze, apply, and improve thinking, allowing you to measure skills and outcomes with ease.

- Personalized Teaching: Becomes yours with a Learning Path that is built with key student objectives. Control what students see and when they see it. Use it as-is or match to your syllabus exactly—hide, rearrange, add and create your own content.

- Guide Students: A unique learning path of relevant readings, multimedia and activities that move students up the learning taxonomy from basic knowledge and comprehension to analysis and application.

- Promote Better Outcomes: Empower instructors and motivate students with analytics and reports that provide a snapshot of class progress, time in course, engagement and completion rates.

The MindTap for *Programming with Microsoft Visual Basic 2015* includes videos, study tools, and interactive quizzing, all integrated into a full eReader that contains the full content from the printed text.

Acknowledgments

Writing a book is a team effort rather than an individual one. I would like to take this opportunity to thank my team, especially Alyssa Pratt (Senior Content Developer), Heidi Aguiar (Full Service Project Manager), Serge Palladino and John Freitas (Quality Assurance), Jennifer Feltri-George (Senior Content Project Manager), and the compositors at GEX Publishing Services. Thank you for your support, enthusiasm, patience, and hard work. Last, but certainly not least, I want to thank the following reviewers for their invaluable ideas and comments: Cliff Brozo, Monroe College; Anthony Cameron, Fayetteville Technical Community College, and Tatyana Feofilaktova, ASA College. And a special thank you to Sally Douglas (College of Central Florida) for suggesting the YOU DO IT! boxes several editions ago.

Diane Zak

Read This Before You Begin

Technical Information

Data Files

You will need data files to complete the computer activities in this book. Your instructor may provide the data files to you. You may obtain the files electronically at CengageBrain.com and then navigating to the page for this book.

Each chapter in this book has its own set of data files, which are stored in a separate folder within the VB2015 folder. The files for Chapter 1 are stored in the VB2015\Chap01 folder. Similarly, the files for Chapter 2 are stored in the VB2015\Chap02 folder. Throughout this book, you will be instructed to open files from or save files to these folders.

You can use a computer in your school lab or your own computer to complete the steps and Exercises in this book.

Using Your Own Computer

To use your own computer to complete the computer activities in this book, you will need the following:

- A Pentium® 4 processor, 1.6 GHz or higher, personal computer running Microsoft Windows. This book was written using Microsoft Windows 8, and Quality Assurance tested using Microsoft Windows 10.

- Either Microsoft Visual Studio Ultimate 2015 or Visual Studio Community Edition installed on your computer. This book was written and Quality Assurance tested using Microsoft Visual Studio Ultimate 2015. At the time of this writing, you can download a free copy of the Community Edition at *https://www.visualstudio.com/en-us/downloads/ visual-studio-2015-downloads-vs*.

To control the display of filename extensions in Windows 8:

1. Press and hold down the Windows logo key on your keyboard as you tap the letter x. Click Control Panel, click Appearance and Personalization, click Folder Options, and then click the View tab.

2. Deselect the Hide extensions for known file types check box to show the extensions; or, select the check box to hide them. Click the OK button, and then close the Appearance and Personalization window.

To always display the underlined letters (called access keys) in Windows 8:

1. Press and hold down the Windows logo key on your keyboard as you tap the letter x. Click Control Panel, and then click Appearance and Personalization.

2. In the Ease of Access Center section, click Turn on easy access keys, and then select the Underline keyboard shortcuts and access keys check box. Click the OK button, and then close the Ease of Access Center window.

To start and configure Visual Studio to match the figures and tutorial steps in this book:

1. Use the steps on Page 11 to start Visual Studio.

2. Use the steps on Pages 12 and 13 to configure Visual Studio.

To install Microsoft Visual Basic PowerPacks 12.0:

1. Locate the vb_vbpowerpacks.exe file, which is contained in the VB2015\PowerPacks folder. Right-click the filename and then click Run as administrator. Click the Yes button.

2. Select the "I agree to the License Terms and Privacy Policy." check box. Either select or deselect the check box that asks if you want to join the Visual Studio Experience Improvement program. Click Install.

3. When the "Setup Successful!" message appears, click the Close button.

4. Start Visual Studio. Open the Toolbox window (if necessary) by clicking View on the menu bar and then clicking Toolbox. Right-click the Toolbox window and then click Add Tab. Type Visual Basic PowerPacks and press Enter.

5. Right-click the Visual Basic PowerPacks tab, and then click Choose Items. If necessary, click the .NET Framework Components tab in the Choose Toolbox Items dialog box.

6. In the Filter box, type PowerPacks. You may see one or more entries for the PrintForm control. Select Version 12's PrintForm control, as shown in Figure 1. (Although this book uses only the PrintForm control, you can also select Version 12's DataRepeater, LineShape, OvalShape, and RectangleShape controls.)

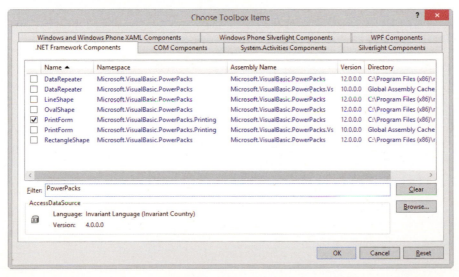

7. Click the OK button to close the Choose Toolbox Items dialog box. If the message "The following controls were successfully added to the toolbox but are not enabled in the active designer:" appears, click the OK button. The PrintForm control (as well as any other PowerPacks controls you selected) will not appear in the Toolbox window until you either create a new Visual Basic application or open an existing one. You will learn how to perform both of those tasks in Chapter 1.

Figures

The figures in this book reflect how your screen will look if you are using Microsoft Visual Studio Ultimate 2015 and a Microsoft Windows 8 system. Your screen may appear slightly different in some instances if you are using another version of either Microsoft Visual Studio or Microsoft Windows.

Visit Our Web Site

Additional materials designed for this textbook might be available at CengageBrain.com. Search this site for more details.

To the Instructor

To complete the computer activities in this book, your students must use a set of data files. These files can be obtained on the Instructor Companion Site or at CengageBrain.com.

The material in this book was written using Microsoft Visual Studio Ultimate 2015 on a Microsoft Windows 8 system. It was Quality Assurance tested using Microsoft Visual Studio Ultimate 2015 on a Microsoft Windows 10 system.

An Introduction to Programming

After studying the Overview, you should be able to:

◎ Define the terminology used in programming

◎ Explain the tasks performed by a programmer

◎ Understand the employment opportunities for programmers and software engineers

◎ Run a Visual Basic 2015 application

◎ Understand how to use the chapters effectively

Programming a Computer

In essence, the word **programming** means *giving a mechanism the directions to accomplish a task*. If you are like most people, you have already programmed several mechanisms, such as your digital video recorder (DVR), cell phone, or coffee maker. Like these devices, a computer also is a mechanism that can be programmed.

The directions (typically called instructions) given to a computer are called **computer programs** or, more simply, **programs**. The people who write programs are called **programmers**. Programmers use a variety of special languages, called **programming languages**, to communicate with the computer. Some popular programming languages are Visual Basic, C#, C++, and Java. In this book, you will use the Visual Basic programming language.

The Programmer's Job

When a company has a problem that requires a computer solution, typically it is a programmer who comes to the rescue. The programmer might be an employee of the company; or he or she might be a freelance programmer, which is a programmer who works on temporary contracts rather than for a long-term employer.

First the programmer meets with the user, who is the person (or people) responsible for describing the problem. In many cases, this person will also eventually use the solution. Depending on the complexity of the problem, multiple programmers may be involved, and they may need to meet with the user several times. Programming teams often contain subject matter experts, who may or may not be programmers. For example, an accountant might be part of a team working on a program that requires accounting expertise. The purpose of the initial meetings with the user is to determine the exact problem and to agree on a solution.

Overview-Programmers

After the programmer and user agree on the solution, the programmer begins converting the solution into a computer program. During the conversion phase, the programmer meets periodically with the user to determine whether the program fulfills the user's needs and to refine any details of the solution. When the user is satisfied that the program does what he or she wants it to do, the programmer rigorously tests the program with sample data before releasing it to the user, who will test it further to verify that it correctly solves the problem. In many cases, the programmer also provides the user with a manual that explains how to use the program. As this process indicates, the creation of a good computer solution to a problem—in other words, the creation of a good program—requires a great deal of interaction between the programmer and the user.

Employment Opportunities

Overview-Programmer
Qualities

When searching for a job in computer programming, you will encounter ads for "computer programmers" as well as for "computer software engineers." Although job titles and descriptions vary, computer software engineers typically are responsible for designing an appropriate solution to a user's problem, while computer programmers are responsible for translating the solution into a language that the computer can understand—a process called **coding**. Software engineering is a higher-level position that requires the ability to envision solutions. Using a construction analogy, software engineers are the architects, while programmers are the carpenters.

Keep in mind that depending on the employer as well as the size and complexity of the user's problem, the design and coding tasks may be performed by the same employee, no matter what his or her job title is. In other words, it is not unusual for a software engineer to code his or her solution or for a programmer to have designed the solution he or she is coding.

Programmers and software engineers need to have strong problem-solving and analytical skills, as well as the ability to communicate effectively with team members, end users, and other nontechnical personnel. Typically, computer software engineers are expected to have at least a bachelor's degree in software engineering, computer science, or mathematics, along with practical work experience, especially in the industry in which they are employed. Computer programmers usually need at least an associate's degree in computer science, mathematics, or information systems, as well as proficiency in one or more programming languages.

Computer programmers and software engineers are employed by companies in almost every industry, such as telecommunications companies, software publishers, financial institutions, insurance carriers, educational institutions, and government agencies. The U.S. Bureau of Labor Statistics predicts that employment of computer software engineers will increase by 22% from 2012 to 2022. The employment of computer programmers, on the other hand, will increase by 8% over the same period. In addition, consulting opportunities for freelance programmers and software engineers are expected to increase as companies look for ways to reduce their payroll expenses.

There is a great deal of competition for programming and software engineering jobs, so jobseekers need to keep up to date with the latest programming languages and technologies. A competitive edge may be gained by obtaining vendor-specific or language-specific certifications, as well as knowledge of a prospective employer's business. More information about computer programmers and computer software engineers can be found on the U.S. Bureau of Labor Statistics Web site at *www.bls.gov*.

Visual Basic 2015

In this book, you will learn how to create programs, called **applications**, using the Visual Basic 2015 programming language. Visual Basic 2015 is one of the languages built into Microsoft's newest integrated development environment: Visual Studio 2015. An **integrated development environment (IDE)** is an environment that contains all of the tools and features you need to create, run, and test your programs.

Visual Basic 2015 is an **object-oriented programming language**, which is a language that allows the programmer to use objects to accomplish a program's goal. An **object** is anything that can be seen, touched, or used. In other words, an object is nearly any *thing*. The objects in an object-oriented program can take on many different forms. Programs written for the Windows environment typically use objects such as check boxes, list boxes, and buttons. A payroll program, on the other hand, might utilize objects found in the real world, such as a time card object, an employee object, and a check object.

Every object in an object-oriented program is created from a **class**, which is a pattern that the computer uses to create the object. The class contains the instructions that tell the computer how the object should look and behave. An object created from a class is called an **instance** of the class and is said to be **instantiated** from the class. An analogy involving a cookie cutter and cookies is often used to describe a class and its objects: The class is the cookie cutter, and the objects instantiated from the class are the cookies. You will learn more about classes and objects throughout this book.

You can use Visual Basic to create applications for the Windows environment or for the Web. A Windows application has a Windows user interface and runs on a personal computer. A **user interface** is what the user sees and interacts with while an application is running. Examples of Windows applications include graphics programs, data-entry systems, and games. A Web application, on the other hand, has a Web user interface and runs on a server. You access a Web application using your computer's browser. Examples of Web applications include e-commerce applications available on the Internet and employee handbook applications accessible on a company's intranet. You can also use Visual Basic to create applications for tablet PCs and mobile devices, such as cell phones.

A Visual Basic 2015 Demonstration

In the following set of steps, you will run a Visual Basic 2015 application that shows you some of the objects you will learn about in the chapters. For now, it is not important for you to understand how these objects were created or why the objects perform the way they do. Those questions will be answered in the chapters.

START HERE **To run the Visual Basic 2015 application:**

You can also double-click the filename to run the application.

1. Use Windows to locate and then open the VB2015\Overview folder on your computer's hard disk or on the device designated by your instructor. Right-click **Monthly Payment Calculator (Monthly Payment Calculator.exe)** in the list of filenames and then click the **Open** button. (Depending on how Windows is set up on your computer, you may or may not see the .exe extension on the filename. Refer to the Overview's Summary section to learn how to show/hide filename extensions.)

2. After a few moments, the Monthly Payment Calculator application shown in Figure 1 appears on the screen. The interface contains a text box, a list box, buttons, radio buttons, and labels. You can use the application to calculate the monthly payment for a car loan.

Don't be concerned if some of the letters on your screen are not underlined. You can show/hide the underlined letters by pressing the Alt key.

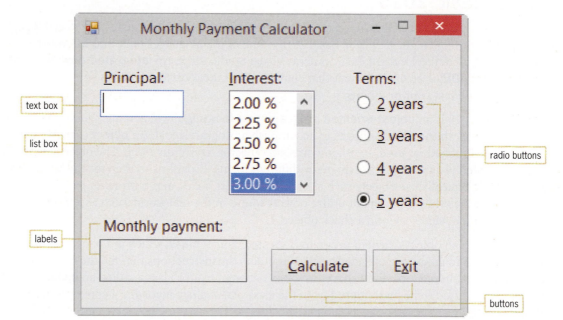

Figure 1 Monthly Payment Calculator application

3. Use the application to calculate the monthly payment for a $22,000 loan at 3.75% interest for five years. Type **22000** in the Principal text box. Scroll down the Interest list box and then click **3.75 %**. The radio button corresponding to the five-year term is already selected, so you just need to click the **Calculate** button to compute the monthly payment. The application indicates that your monthly payment would be $402.69. See Figure 2.

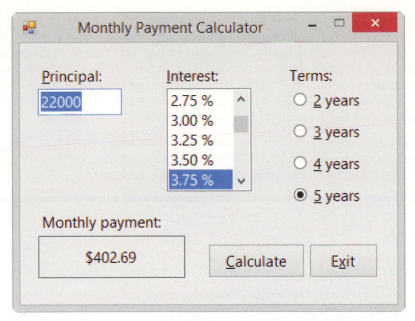

Figure 2   Computed monthly payment

4. Now determine what your monthly payment would be if you borrowed $5,000 at 4.5% interest for four years. Type **5000** in the Principal text box, click **4.50 %** in the Interest list box, click the **4 years** radio button, and then click the **Calculate** button. The Monthly payment box shows $114.02.

5. Click the **Exit** button to close the application.

Using the Chapters Effectively

This book is designed for a beginning programming course. However, it assumes students are familiar with basic Windows skills and file management. The chapters in this book will help you learn how to write programs using Microsoft Visual Basic 2015. The chapters are designed to be used at your computer. Begin by reading the text that explains the concepts. When you come to the numbered steps, follow the steps on your computer. Read each step carefully and completely before you try it. As you work, compare your screen with the figures to verify your results. The figures in this book reflect how your screen will look if you are using Visual Studio Ultimate 2015 and a Microsoft Windows 8 system. Your screen may vary in some instances if you are using a different edition of Visual Studio or if you are using another version of Microsoft Windows. Don't worry if your screen display differs slightly from the figures. The important parts of the screen display are labeled in each figure. Just be sure you have these parts on your screen.

Do not worry about making mistakes; that's part of the learning process. Tip notes identify common problems and explain how to get back on track. They also provide additional information about a procedure—for example, an alternative method of performing the procedure.

Tip notes are designated by the ᵠ icon.

Each chapter is divided into three lessons. You might want to take a break between lessons. Following each lesson is a Summary section that lists the important elements of the lesson. After the Summary section is a list of the key terms (including definitions) covered in the lesson. Following the Key Terms section are questions and exercises designed to review and reinforce the lesson's concepts. You should complete all of the end-of-lesson questions and several exercises before continuing to the next lesson. It takes a great deal of practice to acquire the skills needed to create good programs, and future chapters assume that you have mastered the information found in the previous chapters.

Some of the end-of-lesson exercises are Discovery exercises, which allow you to both "discover" the solutions to problems on your own and experiment with material that is not covered in the chapter. Some lessons also contain one or more Debugging exercises. In programming, the term **debugging** refers to the process of finding and fixing any errors, called bugs, in a program. Debugging exercises provide opportunities for you to find and correct the errors in existing applications. Appendix A, which can be covered after completing Chapter 3, guides you through the process of locating and correcting a program's errors (bugs).

Throughout the book, you will find GUI (graphical user interface) design tips. These tips contain guidelines and recommendations for designing applications. You should follow these guidelines and recommendations so that your applications conform to the Windows standards.

Summary

- Programs are the step-by-step instructions that tell a computer how to perform a task.

- Programmers use various programming languages to communicate with the computer.

- The creation of a good program requires a great deal of interaction between the programmer and the user.

- Programmers rigorously test a program with sample data before releasing the program to the user.

- It's not unusual for the same person to perform the duties of both a software engineer and a programmer.

- An object-oriented programming language, such as Visual Basic 2015, enables programmers to use objects to accomplish a program's goal. An object is anything that can be seen, touched, or used.

- Every object in an object-oriented program is instantiated (created) from a class, which is a pattern that tells the computer how the object should look and behave. An object is referred to as an instance of the class.

- The process of locating and correcting the errors (bugs) in a program is called debugging.

The Windows logo key looks like this  .

- To control the display of filename extensions, press and hold down the Windows logo key on your keyboard as you tap the letter x. Click Control Panel, click Appearance and Personalization, click Folder Options, and then click the View tab. Deselect the Hide extensions for known file types check box to show the extensions; or, select the check box to hide them.

Key Terms

Applications—programs created for the Windows environment, the Web, or mobile devices

Class—a pattern that the computer uses to create (instantiate) an object

Coding—the process of translating a solution into a language that the computer can understand

Computer programs—the directions given to computers; also called programs

Debugging—the process of locating and correcting the errors (bugs) in a program

IDE—integrated development environment

Instance—an object created (instantiated) from a class

Instantiated—the process of creating an object from a class

Integrated development environment—an environment that contains all of the tools and features you need to create, run, and test your programs; also called an IDE

Object—anything that can be seen, touched, or used

Object-oriented programming language—a programming language that allows the programmer to use objects to accomplish a program's goal

Programmers—the people who write computer programs

Programming—the process of giving a mechanism the directions to accomplish a task

Programming languages—languages used to communicate with a computer

Programs—the directions given to computers; also called computer programs

User interface—what the user sees and interacts with while an application is running

CHAPTER 1

An Introduction to Visual Basic 2015

Creating a Splash Screen

In this chapter, you will use Visual Basic 2015, Microsoft's newest version of the Visual Basic language, to create a splash screen for the Crighton Zoo. A splash screen is the first image that appears when an application is started. It is used to introduce the application and to hold the user's attention while the application is being read into the computer's internal memory.

Previewing the Splash Screen

Before you start the first lesson in this chapter, you will preview the completed splash screen contained in the VB2015\Chap01 folder.

To preview the completed splash screen:

START HERE

You can also double-click the filename to run the application.

1. Use Windows to locate and then open the VB2015\Chap01 folder on your computer's hard disk or on the device designated by your instructor. Right-click **Zoo Splash (Zoo Splash.exe)** in the list of filenames and then click the **Open** button. (Depending on how Windows is set up on your computer, you may or may not see the .exe extension on the filename. Refer to the Overview's Summary section to learn how to show/hide filename extensions.) After a few moments, the splash screen shown in Figure 1-1 appears on the screen. The splash screen closes when six seconds have elapsed.

Figure 1-1   Splash screen for the Crighton Zoo
Photos courtesy of the Nashville Zoo and Diane Zak

Chapter 1 is designed to help you get comfortable with the Visual Studio 2015 integrated development environment (IDE). As you learned in the Overview, an IDE is an environment that contains all of the tools and features you need to create, run, and test your programs. Like all the chapters in this book, Chapter 1 contains three lessons. You should complete a lesson in full and do all of the end-of-lesson questions and several exercises before continuing to the next lesson.

LESSON A

After studying Lesson A, you should be able to:

- Start and customize Visual Studio 2015

- Create a Visual Basic 2015 Windows application

- Manage the windows in the IDE

- Set the properties of an object

- Restore a property to its default setting

- Save a solution

- Close and open an existing solution

The Splash Screen Application

In this chapter, you will create a splash screen using Visual Basic 2015. The following set of steps will guide you in starting Visual Studio Ultimate 2015 from Windows 8. Your steps may differ slightly if you are using another edition of Visual Studio 2015.

To start Visual Studio Ultimate 2015:

1. If necessary, tap the **Windows logo** key to switch to the Windows 8 tile-based mode, and then click the **Visual Studio 2015** tile.

2. *If the Choose Default Environment Settings dialog box appears*, click **Visual Basic Development Settings** and then click **Start Visual Studio**.

   If the Choose Default Environment Settings dialog box does not appear, click **Tools** on the menu bar, click **Import and Export Settings**, select the **Reset all settings** radio button, click the **Next** button, select the **No, just reset settings, overwriting my current settings** radio button, click the **Next** button, click **Visual Basic**, and then click the **Finish** button. Click the **Close** button to close the Import and Export Settings Wizard dialog box.

3. Click **Window** on the menu bar, click **Reset Window Layout**, and then click the **Yes** button. When you start Visual Studio Ultimate 2015, your screen will appear similar to Figure 1-2. However, your menu bar may not contain underlined letters, called access keys. You will learn about access keys in Chapter 2. (You can show/hide the access keys by pressing the Alt key on your keyboard.)

START HERE

The Windows logo key looks like this .

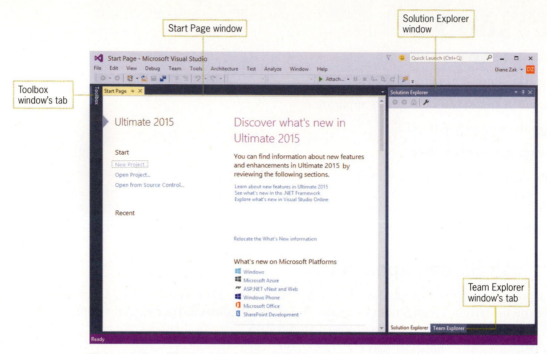

Figure 1-2   Microsoft Visual Studio Ultimate 2015 startup screen

Next, you will configure Visual Studio so that your screen and tutorial steps agree with the figures and tutorial steps in this book. As mentioned in the Overview, the figures reflect how your screen will look if you are using Visual Studio Ultimate 2015 and a Microsoft Windows 8 system. Your screen may vary in some instances if you are using a different edition of Visual Studio or if you are using another version of Microsoft Windows. Don't worry if your screen display differs slightly from the figures.

START HERE

To configure Visual Studio:

1. Click **Tools** on the menu bar and then click **Options** to open the Options dialog box. Click the **Projects and Solutions** node. Use the information shown in Figure 1-3 to select and deselect the appropriate check boxes.

The color of your dialog boxes depends on your computer's desktop theme.

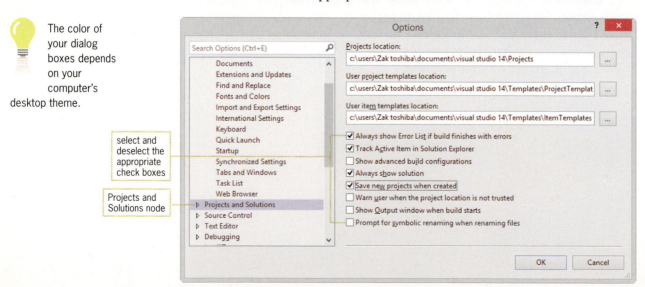

Figure 1-3   Options dialog box

2. Expand the **Text Editor** node and then expand the **All Languages** node. Click **CodeLens** and then deselect the **Enable CodeLens** check box.

3. Click the **Debugging** node and then deselect the **Step over properties and operators (Managed only)** check box. Also deselect the **Show elapsed time PerfTip while debugging** check box, which appears at the bottom of the list.

4. Click the **OK** button to close the Options dialog box.

   Note: If you change your default environment settings *after* performing the previous four steps, you will need to perform the steps again.

The splash screen will be a Windows application, which means it will have a Windows user interface and run on a desktop (or laptop) computer. Recall that a user interface is what the user sees and interacts with while an application is running. Windows applications in Visual Basic are composed of solutions, projects, and files. A solution is a container that stores the projects and files for an entire application. Although the solutions in this book contain only one project, a solution can contain several projects. A project is also a container, but it stores only the files associated with that particular project.

To create a Visual Basic 2015 Windows application:

START HERE

1. Click **File** on the menu bar and then click **New Project** to open the New Project dialog box. If necessary, click the **Visual Basic** node in the Installed Templates list, and then click **Windows Forms Application** in the middle column of the dialog box.

2. Change the name entered in the Name box to **Splash Project**.

3. Click the **Browse** button to open the Project Location dialog box. Locate and then click the **VB2015\Chap01** folder. Click the **Select Folder** button to close the Project Location dialog box.

4. If necessary, select the **Create directory for solution** check box in the New Project dialog box. Change the name entered in the Solution name box to **Splash Solution**. Figure 1-4 shows the completed New Project dialog box in Visual Studio Ultimate 2015. (Your dialog box may look slightly different if you are using another edition of Visual Studio. Do not be concerned if your dialog box shows a different version of the .NET Framework.)

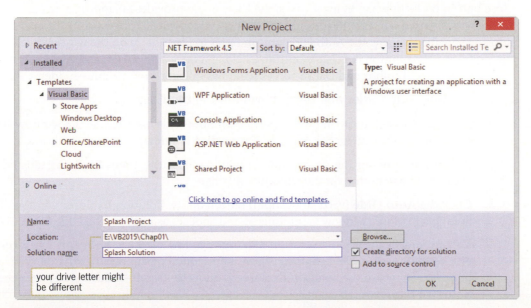

Figure 1-4   Completed New Project dialog box in Visual Studio Ultimate 2015

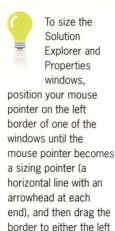

To size the Solution Explorer and Properties windows, position your mouse pointer on the left border of one of the windows until the mouse pointer becomes a sizing pointer (a horizontal line with an arrowhead at each end), and then drag the border to either the left or the right.

5. Click the **OK** button to close the New Project dialog box. The computer creates a solution and adds a Visual Basic project to the solution. The names of the solution and project, along with other information pertaining to the project, appear in the Solution Explorer window. See Figure 1-5. In addition to the windows shown earlier in Figure 1-2, three other windows appear in the IDE: Windows Form Designer, Properties, and Data Sources. (Don't be concerned if different properties appear in your Properties window.)

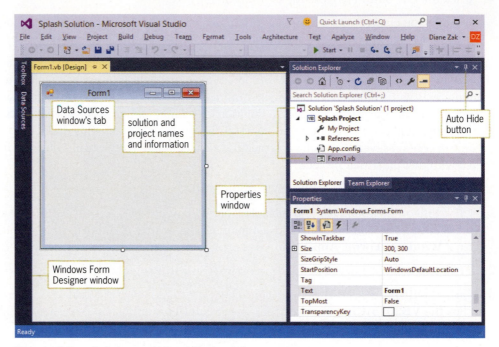

Figure 1-5   Solution and Visual Basic project

Managing the Windows in the IDE

In most cases, you will find it easier to work in the IDE if you either close or auto-hide the windows you are not currently using. The easiest way to close an open window is to click the Close button on its title bar. In most cases, the View menu provides an appropriate option for opening a closed window. In addition to closing a window, you can also auto-hide it. You auto-hide a window using the Auto Hide button (refer to Figure 1-5) on the window's title bar. The Auto Hide button is a toggle button: Clicking it once activates it, and clicking it again deactivates it. The Toolbox and Data Sources windows in Figure 1-5 are auto-hidden windows.

START HERE

To close, open, auto-hide, and display windows in the IDE:

1. Click the **Close** button on the Properties window's title bar to close the window. Then click **View** on the menu bar and click **Properties Window** to open the window.

2. If your IDE contains the Team Explorer window, click the **Team Explorer** tab and then click the **Close** button on the window's title bar.

3. Click the **Auto Hide** (vertical pushpin) button on the Solution Explorer window. The Solution Explorer window is minimized and appears as a tab on the edge of the IDE.

4. To temporarily display the Solution Explorer window, click the **Solution Explorer** tab. Notice that the Auto Hide button is now a horizontal pushpin rather than a vertical pushpin. To return the Solution Explorer window to its auto-hidden state, click the **Solution Explorer** tab again.

5. To permanently display the Solution Explorer window, click the **Solution Explorer** tab and then click the **Auto Hide** (horizontal pushpin) button on the window's title bar. The vertical pushpin replaces the horizontal pushpin on the button.

6. If necessary, close the Data Sources window.

7. If necessary, click **Form1.vb** in the Solution Explorer window. If the items in the Properties window do not appear in alphabetical order, click the **Alphabetical** button. (Refer to Figure 1-6 for the button's location.)

8. Figure 1-6 shows the current status of the windows in the IDE. Only the Windows Form Designer, Solution Explorer, and Properties windows are open; the Toolbox window is auto-hidden.

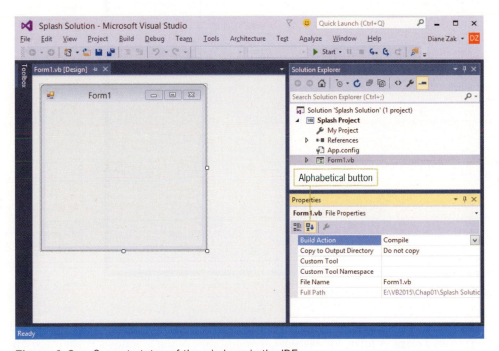

Figure 1-6   Current status of the windows in the IDE

To reset the window layout in the IDE, click Window on the menu bar, click Reset Window Layout, and then click the Yes button.

In the next several sections, you will take a closer look at the Windows Form Designer, Solution Explorer, and Properties windows. (The Toolbox window is covered in Lesson B.)

The Windows Form Designer Window

Figure 1-7 shows the **Windows Form Designer window**, where you create (or design) your application's graphical user interface, more simply referred to as a **GUI**. Only a Windows Form object appears in the designer window shown in the figure. A **Windows Form object**, or **form**, is the foundation for the user interface in a Windows application. You create the user interface by adding other objects, such as buttons and text boxes, to the form.

Notice that a title bar appears at the top of the form. The title bar contains a default caption (Form1) along with Minimize, Maximize, and Close buttons. At the top of the designer window is a tab labeled Form1.vb [Design]. Form1.vb is the name of the file (on your computer's hard disk or on another device) that contains the Visual Basic instructions associated with the form, and [Design] identifies the window as the designer window.

name of the disk file that
contains the instructions
associated with the form

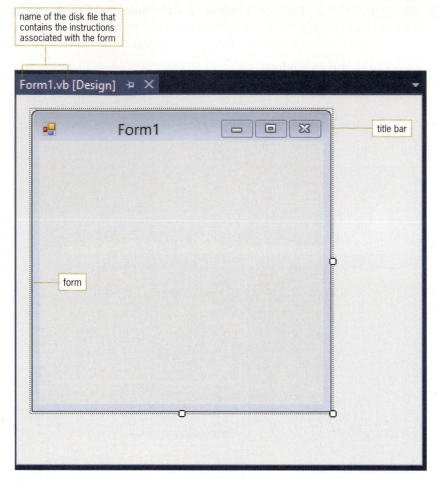

title bar

form

Figure 1-7   Windows Form Designer window

Recall that
a class is a
pattern that
the computer
uses to create
an object.

As you learned in the Overview, all objects in an object-oriented program are instantiated (created) from a class. A form, for example, is an instance of the Windows Form class. The form (an object) is automatically instantiated for you when you create a Windows application.

The Solution Explorer Window

The **Solution Explorer window** displays a list of the projects contained in the current solution and the items contained in each project. Figure 1-8 shows the Solution Explorer window for the Splash Solution, which contains one project named Splash Project. One of the items within the project is a file named Form1.vb. The .vb extension on the filename indicates that the file is a Visual Basic **source file**, which is a file that contains program instructions, called **code**. The Form1.vb file contains the code associated with the form displayed in the designer window. You can view the code using the Code Editor window, which you will learn about in Lesson B.

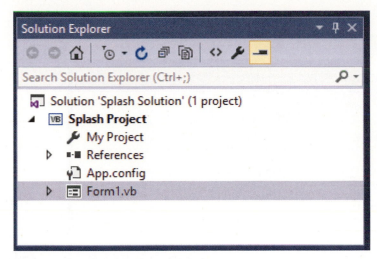

Figure 1-8   Solution Explorer window

The Form1.vb source file is referred to as a **form file** because it contains the code associated with a form. The code associated with the first form included in a project is automatically stored in a form file named Form1.vb. The code associated with the second form in the same project is stored in a form file named Form2.vb, and so on. Because a project can contain many forms and, therefore, many form files, it is a good practice to give each form file a more meaningful name. Doing this will help you keep track of the various form files in the project. You can use the Properties window to change the filename.

The Properties Window

Like everything in an object-oriented language, a file is an object. Each object has a set of attributes that determine its appearance and behavior. The attributes are called **properties** and are listed in the **Properties window**. When an object is created, a default value is assigned to each of its properties. The Properties window shown in Figure 1-9 lists the default values assigned to the properties of the selected object. (You do not need to size your Properties window to match Figure 1-9.)

The name of the selected object (in this case, the Form1.vb file) appears in the window's **Object box**. The window's **Properties list** has two columns. The left column displays the names of the selected object's properties, which can be viewed either alphabetically or by category. However, it's usually easier to work with the Properties window when the properties are listed in alphabetical order, as they are in Figure 1-9. The right column in the Properties list is called the **Settings box**, and it displays the current value (or setting) of each of the object's properties. A brief description of the selected property appears in the Description pane.

To display the properties of the Form1.vb form file, Form1.vb must be selected in the Solution Explorer window.

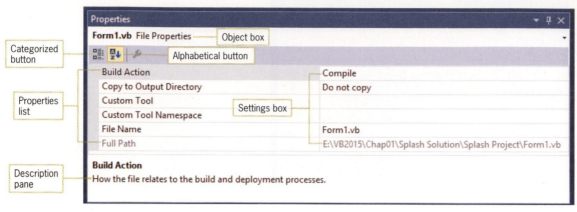

Figure 1-9   Properties window

START HERE

To use the Properties window to change the form file's name:

You can also change the File Name property by right-clicking Form1.vb in the Solution Explorer window and then clicking Rename on the context menu.

1. Form1.vb should be selected in the Solution Explorer window. Click **File Name** in the Properties list. Type **Splash Form.vb** and press **Enter**. (Be sure to include the .vb extension on the filename; otherwise, the computer will not recognize the file as a source file.) Splash Form.vb appears in the Solution Explorer and Properties windows and on the designer window's tab, as shown in Figure 1-10.

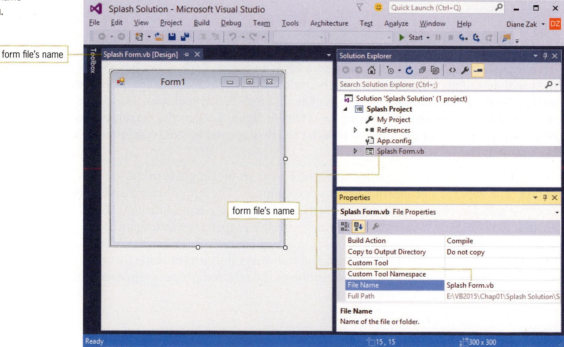

Figure 1-10   Form file's name shown in various locations

Properties of a Windows Form

Like a file, a Windows form also has a set of properties. The form's properties will appear in the Properties window when you select the form in the designer window.

To view the properties of the form:

START HERE

1. Click the **form** in the designer window. Figure 1-11 shows a partial listing of the properties of a Windows form.

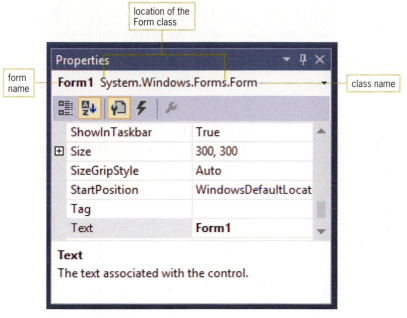

Figure 1-11 Properties window showing a partial listing of the form's properties

Notice that *Form1 System.Windows.Forms.Form* appears in the Object box in Figure 1-11. *Form1* is the name of the form. The name is automatically assigned to the form when the form is instantiated (created). In *System.Windows.Forms.Form, Form* is the name of the class used to instantiate the form. *System.Windows.Forms* is the namespace that contains the Form class definition. A **class definition** is a block of code that specifies (or defines) an object's appearance and behavior. All class definitions in Visual Basic 2015 are contained in namespaces, which you can picture as blocks of memory cells inside the computer. Each **namespace** contains the code that defines a group of related classes. The *System.Windows.Forms* namespace contains the definition of the Windows Form class. It also contains the class definitions for objects you add to a form, such as buttons and text boxes.

The period that separates each word in *System.Windows.Forms.Form* is called the **dot member access operator**. Similar to the backslash (\) in a folder path, the dot member access operator indicates a hierarchy, but of namespaces rather than folders. In other words, the backslash in the path *E:\VB2015\Chap01\Splash Solution\Splash Project\Splash Form.vb* indicates that the Splash Form.vb file is contained in (or is a member of) the Splash Project folder, which is a member of the Splash Solution folder, which is a member of the Chap01 folder, which is a member of the VB2015 folder, which is a member of the E: drive. Likewise, the name *System.Windows.Forms.Form* indicates that the Form class is a member of the Forms namespace, which is a member of the Windows namespace, which is a member of the System namespace. The dot member access operator allows the computer to locate the Form class in the computer's internal memory, similar to the way the backslash (\) allows the computer to locate the Splash Form.vb file on your computer's disk.

The Name Property

As you do to a form file, you should assign a more meaningful name to a Windows form because doing so will help you keep track of the various forms in a project. But unlike a form file, a Windows form has a Name property rather than a File Name property. You use the name entered in an object's Name property to refer to the object in code, so each object must have a unique name. The name you assign to an object must begin with a letter and contain only letters, numbers, and the underscore character. The name cannot include punctuation characters or spaces.

There are several conventions for naming objects in Visual Basic. In this book, you will use a naming convention called Hungarian notation. Names in Hungarian notation begin with an ID of three (or more) characters that represents the object's type, with the remaining characters in the name representing the object's purpose. For example, using Hungarian notation, you might assign the name frmSplash to the current form. The "frm" identifies the object as a form, and "Splash" reminds you of the form's purpose. Hungarian notation names are entered using **camel case**, which means you enter the ID characters in lowercase and then capitalize the first letter of each subsequent word in the name. Camel case refers to the fact that the uppercase letters appear as "humps" in the name because they are taller than the lowercase letters.

START HERE

To change the name of the form:

1. Drag the scroll box in the Properties window to the top of the vertical scroll bar. As you scroll, notice the various properties associated with a form. Also notice that the items within parentheses appear at the top of the Properties list.

2. Click **(Name)** in the Properties list. Type **frmSplash** and press **Enter**. The asterisk (*) that now appears on the designer window's tab indicates that the form has been changed since the last time it was saved.

The Text Property

In addition to changing the form's Name property, you should also change its Text property, which controls the text displayed in the form's title bar. Form1 is the default value assigned to the Text property of the first form in a project. In this case, "Crighton Zoo" would be a more descriptive value.

START HERE

To set the Text property of the form:

1. Locate the Text property in the Properties list. Click **Text**. Type **Crighton Zoo** and press **Enter**. The new text appears in the property's Settings box and also in the form's title bar.

The Name and Text properties of a Windows form should always be changed to more meaningful values. The Name property is used by the programmer when coding the application. The Text property, on the other hand, is read by the user while the application is running.

The StartPosition Property

When an application is started, the computer uses the form's StartPosition property to determine the form's initial position on the screen. The frmSplash form represents a splash screen, which typically appears in the middle of the screen.

To center a form on the screen when the application is started:
START HERE

1. Click **StartPosition** in the Properties list, click the **list arrow** in the Settings box, and then click **CenterScreen** in the list.

The Font Property

A form's Font property determines the type, style, and size of the font used to display the text on the form. A font is the general shape of the characters in the text. Segoe UI, Tahoma, and Microsoft Sans Serif are examples of font types. Font styles include regular, bold, and italic. The numbers 9, 12, and 18 are examples of font sizes, which typically are measured in points, with one **point** (pt) equaling 1/72 of an inch. The recommended font for applications created for systems running Windows 8 is Segoe UI because it offers improved readability. Segoe is pronounced "SEE-go," and UI stands for user interface. For most of the elements in the interface, you will use a 9pt font size. However, to make the figures in the book more readable, many of the interfaces created in this book will use a larger font size.

To set the form's Font property:
START HERE

1. Click **Font** in the Properties list and then click the **…** (ellipsis) button in the Settings box to open the Font dialog box.

2. Locate and then click the **Segoe UI** font in the Font box. Click **9** in the Size box and then click the **OK** button. (Do not be concerned if the size of the form changes.)

The Size Property

As you can with any Windows object, you can size a form by selecting it and then dragging the sizing handles that appear around it. You can also size an object by selecting it and then pressing and holding down the Shift key as you press the up, down, right, or left arrow key on your keyboard. In addition, you can set the object's Size property.

To set the form's Size property:
START HERE

1. Click **Size** in the Properties list. The first number in the Setting box represents the width of the form, measured in pixels. The second number represents the height, also measured in pixels. A pixel, which is short for "picture element," is one spot in a grid of thousands of such spots that form an image either produced on the screen by a computer or printed on a page by a printer.

2. Type **405, 340** and press **Enter**. Expand the Size property by clicking the **plus box** that appears next to the property. Notice that the first number listed in the property represents the width, and the second number represents the height. Click the **minus box** to collapse the property.

Setting and Restoring a Property's Value

In the next set of steps, you will practice setting and then restoring the value of the form's BackColor property, which determines the background color of the form.

To set and then restore the form's BackColor property value:
START HERE

1. Click **BackColor** in the Properties list, click the **list arrow**, click the **Custom** tab, and then click a **red square** to change the background color of the form to red.

2. Right-click **BackColor** in the Properties list and then click **Reset** on the context menu. The background color of the form returns to its default setting. Figure 1-12 shows the status of the form in the IDE.

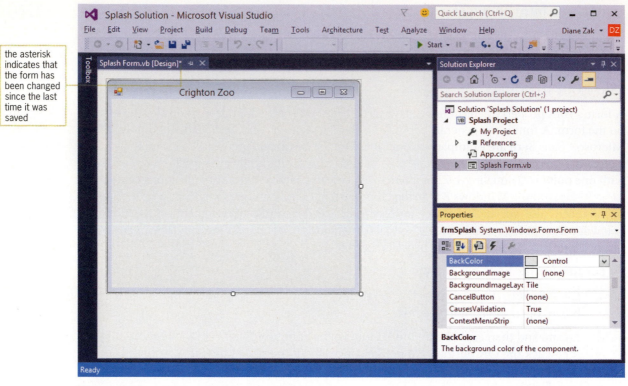

the asterisk indicates that the form has been changed since the last time it was saved

Figure 1-12   Status of the form in the IDE

Saving a Solution

The Save All button on the Standard toolbar looks like this: 💾.

The asterisk (*) that appears on the designer tab in Figure 1-12 indicates that a change was made to the form since the last time it was saved. It is a good idea to save the current solution every 10 or 15 minutes so that you will not lose a lot of your work if a power outage unexpectedly occurs. You can save the solution by clicking File on the menu bar and then clicking Save All. You can also click the Save All button on the Standard toolbar. When you save the solution, the computer saves any changes made to the files included in the solution. It also removes the asterisk that appears on the designer window's tab.

START HERE   **To save the current solution:**

1. Click **File** on the menu bar and then click **Save All**. The asterisk is removed from the designer window's tab, indicating that all changes made to the form have been saved.

Closing the Current Solution

When you are finished working on a solution, you should close it. Closing a solution closes all projects and files contained in the solution.

START HERE   **To close the Splash Solution:**

1. Click **File** on the menu bar. Notice that the menu contains a Close option and a Close Solution option. The Close option closes the designer window in the IDE; however, it does not close the solution itself. Only the Close Solution option closes the solution.

2. Click **Close Solution**. The Solution Explorer window indicates that no solution is currently open in the IDE.

Opening an Existing Solution

You can use the File menu to open an existing solution. The names of solution files end with .sln. If a solution is already open in the IDE, you will be given the option of closing it before another solution is opened.

To open the Splash Solution:

START HERE

1. Click **File** on the menu bar and then click **Open Project** to open the Open Project dialog box.

2. Locate and then open the VB2015\Chap01\Splash Solution folder. Click **Splash Solution (Splash Solution.sln)** in the list of filenames and then click the **Open** button. (Depending on how Windows is set up on your computer, you may or may not see the .sln extension on the filename. Refer to the Overview's Summary section to learn how to show/hide filename extensions.)

3. The Solution Explorer window indicates that the solution is open. If the designer window is not open, right-click **Splash Form.vb** in the Solution Explorer window and then click **View Designer**.

Exiting Visual Studio 2015

Finally, you will learn how to exit Visual Studio 2015. You will complete the splash screen in the remaining two lessons. You can exit Visual Studio using either the Close button on its title bar or the Exit option on its File menu.

To exit Visual Studio 2015:

START HERE

1. Click **File** on the menu bar and then click **Exit**.

Lesson A Summary

- To start Visual Studio 2015:

  Tap the Windows logo key (if necessary) to switch to the Windows 8 tile-based mode and then click the Visual Studio 2015 tile.

- To change the default environment settings:

  Click Tools, click Import and Export Settings, select the Reset all settings radio button, click the Next button, select the appropriate radio button, click the Next button, click the settings collection you want to use, click the Finish button, and then click the Close button to close the Import and Export Settings Wizard dialog box.

- To reset the window layout in the IDE:

  Click Window, click Reset Window Layout, and then click the Yes button.

- To configure Visual Studio:

  Click Tools, click Options, click the Projects and Solutions node, and then use the information shown earlier in Figure 1-3 to select and deselect the appropriate check boxes. Next, expand the Text Editor node, expand the All Languages node, click CodeLens, and then deselect the Enable CodeLens check box. Finally, click the Debugging node, deselect the Step over properties and operators (Managed only) check box, deselect the Show elapsed time PerfTip while debugging check box, and then click the OK button to close the Options dialog box.

- To create a Visual Basic 2015 Windows application:

  Start Visual Studio 2015. Click File, click New Project, click the Visual Basic node, and then click Windows Forms Application. Enter an appropriate name and location in the Name and Location boxes, respectively. Select the Create directory for solution check box. Enter an appropriate name in the Solution name box and then click the OK button.

- To close and open a window in the IDE:

  Close the window by clicking the Close button on its title bar. Use the appropriate option on the View menu to open the window.

- To auto-hide a window in the IDE:

  Click the Auto Hide (vertical pushpin) button on the window's title bar.

- To temporarily display an auto-hidden window in the IDE:

  Click the window's tab.

- To permanently display an auto-hidden window in the IDE:

  Click the window's tab to display the window, and then click the Auto Hide (horizontal pushpin) button on the window's title bar.

- To set the value of a property:

  Select the object whose property you want to set and then select the appropriate property in the Properties list. Type the new property value in the selected property's Settings box, or choose the value from the list, color palette, or dialog box.

- To give a more meaningful name to an object:

  Set the object's Name property.

- To control the text appearing in the form's title bar:

  Set the form's Text property.

- To specify the starting location of the form:

  Set the form's StartPosition property.

- To specify the type, style, and size of the font used to display text on the form:

  Set the form's Font property.

- To size a form:

  Drag the form's sizing handles. You can also set the form's Size, Height, and Width values in the Properties window. In addition, you can select the form and then press and hold down the Shift key as you press the up, down, left, or right arrow key on your keyboard.

- To change the background color of a form:

  Set the form's BackColor property.

- To restore a property to its default setting:

  Right-click the property in the Properties list and then click Reset.

- To save a solution:

  Click File on the menu bar and then click Save All. You can also click the Save All button on the Standard toolbar.

- To close a solution:

  Click File on the menu bar and then click Close Solution.

- To open an existing solution:

  Click File on the menu bar and then click Open Project. Locate and then open the application's solution folder. Click the solution filename, which ends with .sln. Click the Open button. If the designer window is not open, right-click the form file's name in the Solution Explorer window and then click View Designer.

- To exit Visual Studio 2015:

  Click the Close button on the Visual Studio 2015 title bar. You can also click File on the menu bar and then click Exit.

Lesson A Key Terms

Camel case—used when entering object names in Hungarian notation; the practice of entering the object's ID characters in lowercase and then capitalizing the first letter of each subsequent word in the name

Class definition—a block of code that specifies (or defines) an object's appearance and behavior

Code—program instructions

Dot member access operator—a period; used to indicate a hierarchy

Form—the foundation for the user interface in a Windows application; also called a Windows Form object

Form file—a file that contains the code associated with a Windows form

GUI—the acronym for graphical user interface

Namespace—a block of memory cells inside the computer; contains the code that defines a group of related classes

Object box—the section of the Properties window that contains the name of the selected object

Point—used to measure font size; 1/72 of an inch

Properties—the attributes that control an object's appearance and behavior

Properties list—the section of the Properties window that lists both the names and the values of the selected object's properties

Properties window—the window that lists an object's attributes (properties)

Settings box—the right column of the Properties list; displays each property's current value (setting)

Solution Explorer window—the window that displays a list of the projects contained in the current solution and the items contained in each project

Source file—a file that contains code

Windows Form Designer window—the window in which you create an application's GUI

Windows Form object—the foundation for the user interface in a Windows application; referred to more simply as a form

Lesson A Review Questions

1. When a form has been modified since the last time it was saved, what appears on its tab in the designer window?

   a. an ampersand (&)   c. a percent sign (%)

   b. an asterisk (*)   d. a plus sign (+)

2. Which window is used to set the characteristics that control an object's appearance and behavior?

   a. Characteristics   c. Properties

   b. Object   d. Toolbox

3. Which window lists the projects and files included in a solution?

   a. Object   c. Properties

   b. Project   d. Solution Explorer

4. What is the three-character extension appended to solution files in Visual Basic 2015?

   a. .prg   c. .src

   b. .sln   d. .vbs

5. Which of the following statements is true?

   a. You can auto-hide a window by clicking the Auto Hide (vertical pushpin) button on its title bar.

   b. An auto-hidden window appears as a tab on the edge of the IDE.

   c. You temporarily display an auto-hidden window by clicking its tab.

   d. all of the above

6. Which property controls the text displayed in a form's title bar?

   a. Caption   c. Title

   b. Text   d. TitleBar

7. Which property is used to give an object a more meaningful name?

   a. Application   c. Name

   b. Caption   d. Text

8. Which property determines the initial position of a form when the application is started?

   a. InitialLocation   c. StartLocation

   b. Location   d. StartPosition

9. Explain the difference between a form's Text property and its Name property.

10. Explain the difference between a form file and a form.

11. What does the dot member access operator indicate in the text *System.Windows.Forms. Label*?

Lesson A Exercises

1. If necessary, start Visual Studio 2015 and permanently display the Solution Explorer window. Use the File menu to open the VB2015\Chap01\Jackson Solution\Jackson Solution (Jackson Solution.sln) file. If necessary, right-click the form file's name in the Solution Explorer window and then click View Designer. Change the form file's name to Main Form.vb. Change the form's Name property to frmMain. Change the form's BackColor property to light purple. Change the form's Font property to Segoe UI, 9pt. Change the form's StartPosition property to CenterScreen. Change the form's Text property to Jackson Company. Click File on the menu bar and then click Save All to save the solution. Click File on the menu bar and then click Close Solution to close the solution.

INTRODUCTORY

2. If necessary, start Visual Studio 2015 and permanently display the Solution Explorer window. Create a Visual Basic Windows application. Use the following names for the solution and project, respectively: Merriton Solution and Merriton Project. Save the application in the VB2015\Chap01 folder. Change the form file's name to Main Form.vb. Change the form's name to frmMain. The form's title bar should say Merriton Township; set the appropriate property. The form should be centered on the screen when it first appears; set the appropriate property. Change the background color of the form to light pink. Any text on the form should appear in the Segoe UI, 12pt font; set the appropriate property. Save and then close the solution.

INTRODUCTORY

3. If necessary, start Visual Studio 2015 and permanently display the Solution Explorer window. Create a Visual Basic Windows application. Use the following names for the solution and project, respectively: Millers Solution and Millers Project. Save the solution in the VB2015\Chap01 folder. Change the form file's name to Main Form.vb. Change the form's name to frmMain. The form's title bar should say Millers Tires; set the appropriate property. The form should be centered on the screen when it first appears; set the appropriate property. Any text on the form should appear in the Segoe UI, 9pt font; set the appropriate property. Save and then close the solution.

INTRODUCTORY

LESSON B

After studying Lesson B, you should be able to:

- Add a control to a form
- Set the properties of a label, picture box, and button control
- Select multiple controls
- Change the layering order of controls
- Center controls on the form
- Open the Project Designer window
- Start and end an application
- Enter code in the Code Editor window
- Terminate an application using the `Me.Close()` instruction
- Run the project's executable file

The Ch01B video demonstrates most of the steps contained in Lesson B.

START HERE

The Toolbox Window

In Lesson A, you learned about the Windows Form Designer, Solution Explorer, and Properties windows. In this lesson, you will learn about the **Toolbox window**, referred to more simply as the toolbox. The **toolbox** contains the tools you use when creating your application's user interface. Each tool represents a class from which an object, such as a button or text box, can be instantiated. The instantiated objects, called **controls**, will appear on the form.

To open the Splash Solution from Lesson A and then display the Toolbox window:

1. If necessary, start Visual Studio 2015 and open the Solution Explorer window. Open the VB2015\Chap01\Splash Solution\Splash Solution (Splash Solution.sln) file. If necessary, open the designer window.

2. Permanently display the Properties and Toolbox windows, and then auto-hide the Solution Explorer window.

3. If necessary, expand the **Common Controls** node in the toolbox. Rest your mouse pointer on the word **Label** in the toolbox. The tool's purpose appears in a box. See Figure 1-13.

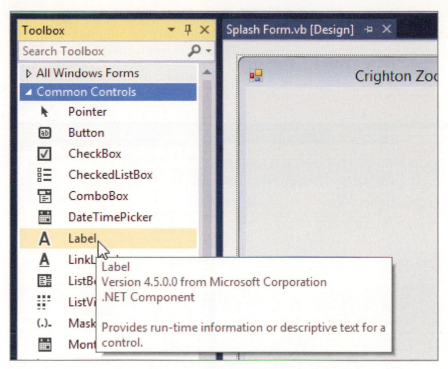

Figure 1-13 Toolbox window showing the purpose of the Label tool

The Label Tool

You use the Label tool to add a label control to a form. The purpose of a **label control** is to display text that the user is not allowed to edit while the application is running, such as the zoo's name or the "Come visit our residents!" message.

To use the Label tool to instantiate a label control:

START HERE

1. Click the **Label** tool in the toolbox, but do not release the mouse button. Hold down the mouse button as you drag the mouse pointer to the upper-left corner of the form. See Figure 1-14. The designer provides blue margin lines to assist you in spacing the controls properly on the form.

Figure 1-14 Label tool being dragged to the form

2. Release the mouse button. A label control appears on the form. See Figure 1-15. (If the wrong control appears on the form, right-click the control, click Delete, and then repeat Steps 1 and 2.) Notice that *Label1 System.Windows.Forms.Label* appears in the Object box in the Properties window. (You do not need to size your Properties

window to match Figure 1-15.) *Label1* is the default name assigned to the label control. *System.Windows.Forms.Label* indicates that the control is an instance of the *Label* class, which is defined in the *System.Windows.Forms* namespace.

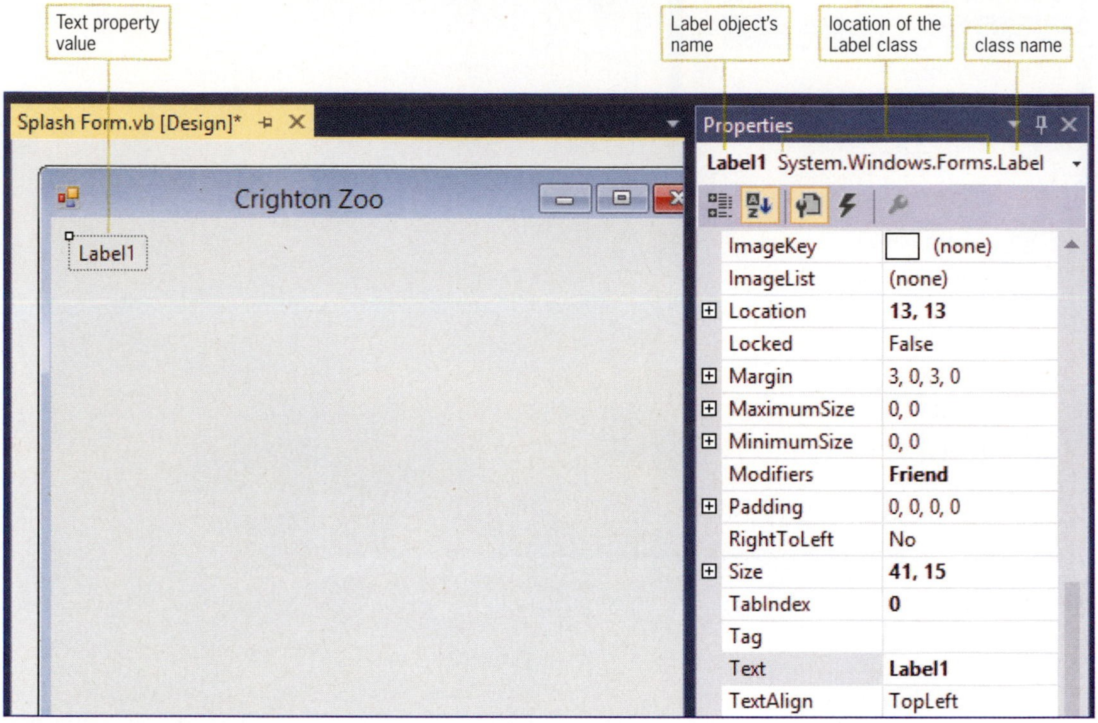

Figure 1-15   Label control added to the form

> You can also add a control to the form by clicking a tool and then clicking the form. In addition, you can click a tool, place the mouse pointer on the form, and then press the left mouse button and drag the mouse pointer until the control is the desired size. You can also double-click a tool.

Label1 is the default value assigned to the Text and Name properties of the first label control added to a form. The value of the Text property appears inside the label control, as indicated in Figure 1-15.

START HERE

To add another label control to the form:

1. Click the **Label** tool in the toolbox and then drag the mouse pointer to the form, positioning it below the existing label control. (Do not worry about the exact location.)

2. Release the mouse button. Label2 is assigned to the control's Text and Name properties.

Some programmers assign meaningful names to all of the controls in an interface, while others do so only for controls that are either coded or referred to in code. In subsequent chapters in this book, you will follow the latter convention. In this chapter, however, you will assign a meaningful name to each control in the interface. The three-character ID used for naming labels is lbl.

START HERE

To assign meaningful names to the label controls:

1. Click the **Label1** control on the form. This selects the control and displays its properties in the Properties window. Click **(Name)** in the Properties list. Type **lblName** and then press **Enter**.

2. Click the **Label2** control on the form. Change the control's name to **lblMsg** and then press **Enter**.

Setting the Text Property

As you learned earlier, a label control's Text property determines the value that appears inside the control. In this application, you want the words "Crighton Zoo" to appear in the lblName control, and the words "Come visit our residents!" to appear in the lblMsg control.

To set each label control's Text property:

START HERE

1. Currently, the lblMsg control is selected on the form. Click **Text** in the Properties list. Type **Come visit our residents!** and then press **Enter**. Because the default setting of a Label control's AutoSize property is set to True, the designer automatically sizes the lblMsg control to fit its current contents. (You can verify the setting by viewing the AutoSize property in the Properties window.)

2. Click the **lblName** control on the form. Change its Text property to **Crighton Zoo** and then press **Enter**. The lblName control stretches automatically to fit the contents of its Text property.

Setting the Location Property

You can move a control to a different location on the form by placing your mouse pointer on the control until it becomes a move pointer, and then dragging the control to the desired location. You can also select the control and then press and hold down the Control (Ctrl) key as you press the up, down, left, or right arrow key on your keyboard. In addition, you can set the control's Location property, which specifies the position of the upper-left corner of the control.

The move pointer is a horizontal line and a vertical line with an arrowhead at each of the four ends.

To set each label control's Location property:

START HERE

1. Click the **lblMsg** control to select it. Click **Location** in the Properties list. Expand the Location property by clicking its **plus box**. The X value specifies the number of pixels from the left border of the form to the left border of the control. The Y value specifies the number of pixels between the top border of the form and the top border of the control. In other words, the X value refers to the control's horizontal location on the form, whereas the Y value refers to its vertical location.

2. Type **180, 115** in the Location property and then press **Enter**. The lblMsg control moves to its new location. Click the **minus box** to collapse the property.

3. In addition to selecting a control by clicking it on the form, you can also select a control by clicking its entry (name and class) in the Object box in the Properties window. Click the **list arrow** in the Properties window's Object box, and then click **lblName System. Windows.Forms.Label** in the list. Set the control's Location property to **180, 70**.

Changing a Property for Multiple Controls

In Lesson A, you changed the form's Font property to Segoe UI, 9pt. When you add a control to the form, the control's Font property is set to the same value as the form's Font property. Using object-oriented programming terminology, the control "inherits" the Font attribute of the form. In this case, for example, the lblName and lblMsg controls inherit the form's Font property setting: Segoe UI, 9pt.

At times, you may want to use a different font type, style, or size for a control's text. One reason for doing this is to bring attention to a specific part of the screen. In the splash screen, for example, you can make the text in the two label controls more noticeable by increasing the size of the font used to display the text. You can change the font size for both controls at the same time by clicking one control and then pressing and holding down the Ctrl (Control) key as you click the other control on the form. You can use the Ctrl+click method to select as many controls as you want. To cancel the selection of one of the selected controls, press and hold down the Ctrl key as you click the control. To cancel the selection of all of the selected controls, release the Ctrl key and then click the form or any unselected control on the form.

To easily select a group of controls on a form, place the mouse pointer slightly above and to the left of the first control you want to select, and then press and hold down the left mouse button as you drag the mouse pointer. A dotted rectangle will appear as you drag. When all of the controls you want to select are within (or at least touched by) the dotted rectangle, release the mouse button. All of the controls surrounded or touched by the dotted rectangle will be selected.

START HERE ▶ **To select both label controls and then set their Font property:**

1. Verify that the lblName control is selected. Press and hold down the **Ctrl** (Control) key as you click the **lblMsg** control, and then release the Ctrl key. Both controls are selected, as shown in Figure 1-16.

Figure 1-16   Label controls selected on the form

2. Open the Font dialog box by clicking **Font** in the Properties list and then clicking the **…** (ellipsis) button in the Settings box. Click **12** in the Size box and then click the **OK** button. The text in the two label controls appears in the new font size.

3. Click the **form** to deselect the label controls.

4. Click the **lblName** control and then use its Font property to change its font style to **Bold**.

5. Click the **lblMsg** control and then use its Font property to change its font style to **Semibold Italic**.

6. Click the lblMsg control's **ForeColor** property. Click the **list arrow**, click the **Custom** tab, and then click a **red square** to change the font color to red.

7. Click the **form** to return to the designer window. Click **File** on the menu bar and then click **Save All** to save the solution.

Using the Format Menu's Order Option

The Format menu contains an Order option that allows you to control the layering of one or more controls on a form.

START HERE ▶ **To use the Format menu's Order option:**

1. Change the form's BackColor property to dark green.

2. Add another label control to the form. Set its BackColor property to pale green. Set its AutoSize property to **False** and its Location property to **10, 10**.

3. Place your mouse pointer on the sizing handle located in the lower-right corner of the label control. Drag the sizing handle until the control is the size shown in Figure 1-17 and then release the mouse button. As the figure shows, the lblName and lblMsg

controls are hidden by the Label1 control. This is because the designer places the Label1 control on the layer above the one occupied by the lblName and lblMsg controls.

Figure 1-17   New label on top of previous labels

4. Click the **Label1** control on the form. Click **Format** on the menu bar, point to **Order**, and then click **Send to Back**. Doing this sends the layer containing the Label1 control behind the one occupied by the lblName and lblMsg controls. See Figure 1-18.

 You can also right-click the Label1 control and then click Send to Back.

Figure 1-18   Result of sending Label1's layer to the back

5. Click the Label1 control's **Text** property in the Properties window. Press the **Backspace** key and then press **Enter** to remove the property's value.

6. Click the **lblName** control and then Ctrl+click the **lblMsg** control. Change the selected controls' BackColor property to the same pale green used for the Label1 control.

7. Click the **form's title bar** and then save the solution.

The PictureBox Tool

The splash screen you previewed at the beginning of the chapter showed two images. You can include an image on a form using a **picture box control**, which you instantiate using the PictureBox tool.

START HERE

To add two picture box controls to the form:

1. Click the **PictureBox** tool in the toolbox and then drag the mouse pointer to the upper-left corner of the Label1 control. Release the mouse button. The picture box control's properties appear in the Properties list, and a box containing a triangle appears in the upper-right corner of the control. The box is referred to as the task box because when you click it, it displays a list of tasks associated with the control. Each task in the list is associated with one or more properties. You can set the properties using the task list or the Properties window.

2. Click the **task box** on the PictureBox1 control. See Figure 1-19.

Figure 1-19 Open task list for a picture box

3. Click **Choose Image** to open the Select Resource dialog box. The Choose Image task is associated with the Image property in the Properties window.

4. To include the image file within the project itself, the Project resource file radio button must be selected in the dialog box. Verify that the radio button is selected, and then click the **Import** button to open the Open dialog box.

5. Open the VB2015\Chap01 folder. Click **Iguanas (Iguanas.jpg)** in the list of filenames and then click the **Open** button. See Figure 1-20.

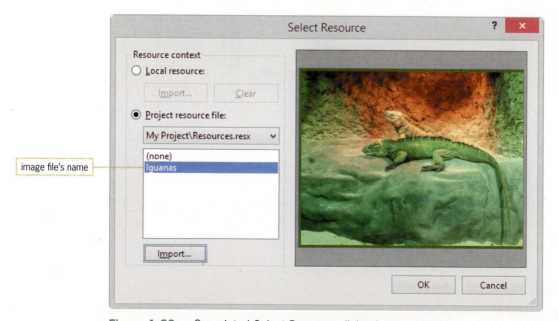

Figure 1-20 Completed Select Resource dialog box
Photo courtesy of the Nashville Zoo and Diane Zak

6. Click the **OK** button to close the dialog box. A small portion of the image appears in the picture box control on the form, and *Splash_Project.My.Resources.Resources.Iguanas* appears in the control's Image property in the Properties window.

7. If necessary, click the **task box** on the control to open the task list. Click the **list arrow** in the Size Mode box and then click **StretchImage** in the list. Click the **picture box** control to close the task list.

8. The three-character ID used when naming picture box controls is pic. Change the picture box's name to **picIguanas**.

9. On your own, add another picture box control to the form. Position the picture box below the lblMsg control. The picture box should display the image stored in the **Storks.jpg** file, which is contained in the VB2015\Chap01 folder. Change its size mode to **StretchImage** and its name to **picStorks**. Position and size the picture boxes as shown in Figure 1-21.

Figure 1-21   Picture boxes added to the form
Photo courtesy of the Nashville Zoo and Diane Zak

Using the Format Menu to Align and Size

The Format menu provides a Center in Form option for centering one or more controls either horizontally or vertically on the form. The menu also provides an Align option for aligning two or more controls by their left, right, top, or bottom borders. You can use the menu's Make Same Size option to make two or more controls the same width and/or height.

Before you can use the Format menu to change the alignment or size of two or more controls, you first must select the controls. You should always select the reference control first. The **reference control** is the one whose size and/or location you want to match. The reference control will have white sizing handles, whereas the other selected controls will have black sizing handles.

To experiment with the options on the Format menu, complete Discovery Exercise 4 at the end of this lesson.

START HERE

To size and align the picture boxes:

1. Click the **picIguanas** control (the reference control) and then Ctrl+click the **picStorks** control. Click **Format**, point to **Make Same Size**, and then click **Both**.

2. Click the **lblMsg** control (the reference control) and then Ctrl+click the **picStorks** control. Click **Format**, point to **Align**, and then click **Rights**.

3. Click the form's **title bar** and then save the solution.

The Button Tool

Every application should give the user a way to exit the program. Most Windows applications accomplish this task by using either an Exit option on the File menu or an Exit button. In this lesson, the splash screen will provide a button for ending the application. In Windows applications, a **button control** is commonly used to perform an immediate action when clicked. The OK and Cancel buttons are examples of button controls found in many Windows applications.

START HERE

To add a button control to the form:

1. Use the **Button** tool in the toolbox to add a button control to the form. Position the control in the upper-right corner of the pale green label control.

2. The three-character ID used when naming button controls is btn. Change the button control's name to **btnExit**.

3. The button control's Text property determines the text that appears on the button's face. Set the button control's Text property to **Exit**.

4. Save the solution.

Starting and Ending an Application

Now that the user interface is complete, you can start the splash screen application to see how it will appear to the user. Before you start an application for the first time, you should open the Project Designer window and verify the name of the **startup form**, which is the form that the computer automatically displays each time the application is started. You can open the Project Designer window by right-clicking My Project in the Solution Explorer window and then clicking Open on the context menu. Or, you can click Project on the menu bar and then click *<project name>* Properties on the menu.

START HERE

To verify the name of the startup form:

1. Auto-hide the Toolbox and Properties windows. Temporarily display the Solution Explorer window. Right-click **My Project** and then click **Open** to open the Project Designer window.

2. If necessary, click the **Application** tab to display the Application pane, which is shown in Figure 1-22. If frmSplash does not appear in the Startup form list box, click the **Startup form** list arrow and then click **frmSplash** in the list. (Do not be concerned if your Target framework list box shows a different value.)

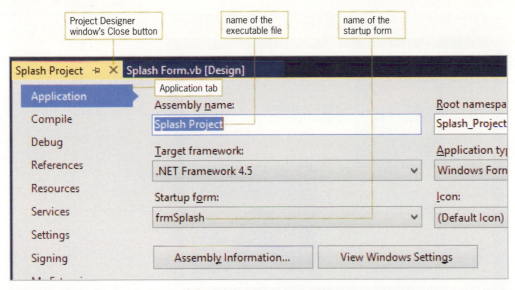

Figure 1-22 Application pane in the Project Designer window

You can start an application by clicking Debug on the menu bar and then clicking Start Debugging. You can also press the F5 key on your keyboard or click the Start button on the Standard toolbar.

When you start a Visual Basic application, the computer automatically creates a file that can be run outside of the IDE, like the The Zoo Splash.exe file you ran at the beginning of this chapter. The file is referred to as an **executable file**. The executable file's name is the same as the project's name, except it ends with .exe. The name of the executable file for the Splash Project, for example, is Splash Project.exe. However, you can use the Project Designer window to change the executable file's name.

The computer stores the executable file in the project's bin\Debug folder. In this case, the Splash Project.exe file is stored in the VB2015\Chap01\Splash Solution\Splash Project\bin\Debug folder. When you are finished with an application, you typically give the user only the executable file because it does not allow the user to modify the application's code. To allow someone to modify the code, you need to provide the entire solution.

To change the name of the executable file, and then start and end the application: START HERE

1. The Project Designer window should still be open. Change the filename in the Assembly name box to **Zoo Splash**. Save the solution and then close the Project Designer window by clicking its **Close** button. (Refer to Figure 1-22 for the location of the Close button.)

2. Click **Debug** on the menu bar and then click **Start Debugging** to start the application. See Figure 1-23. (Do not be concerned about any windows that appear at the bottom of the screen.)

startup form   form's Close button

Figure 1-23   Result of starting the splash screen application
Photo courtesy of the Nashville Zoo and Diane Zak

> The color of the form's title bar and borders depends on your computer's desktop theme.

3. Recall that the purpose of the Exit button is to allow the user to end the application. Click the **Exit** button on the splash screen. Nothing happens because you have not yet entered the instructions that tell the button how to respond when clicked.

4. Click the **Close** button on the form's title bar to stop the application. (You can also click the designer window to make it the active window, then click Debug on the menu bar, and then click Stop Debugging.)

The Code Editor Window

After creating your application's interface, you can begin entering the Visual Basic instructions (code) that tell the controls how to respond to the user's actions. Those actions—such as clicking, double-clicking, and scrolling—are called **events**. You tell an object how to respond to an event by writing an **event procedure**, which is a set of Visual Basic instructions that are processed only when the event occurs. You enter the procedure's code in the Code Editor window. In this lesson, you will write a Click event procedure for the Exit button, which should end the application when it is clicked.

START HERE

> The `Public` keyword in the Class statement indicates that the class can be used by code defined outside of the class.

To open the Code Editor window:

1. Right-click the **form** and then click **View Code** on the context menu. The Code Editor window opens in the IDE, as shown in Figure 1-24. The window contains the Class statement, which is used to define a class in Visual Basic. In this case, the Class statement begins with the `Public Class frmSplash` clause and ends with the `End Class` clause. Within the Class statement, you enter the code to tell the form and its objects how to react to the user's actions.

Figure 1-24 Code Editor window opened in the IDE

If the Code Editor window contains many lines of code, you might want to hide the sections of code that you are not presently working with or that you do not want to print. You hide a section (or region) of code by clicking the minus box that appears next to it. To unhide a region of code, you click the plus box that appears next to the code. Hiding and unhiding the code is also referred to as collapsing and expanding the code, respectively.

To collapse and expand a region of code in the Code Editor window:

START HERE

1. Click the **minus box** that appears next to the `Public Class frmSplash` clause in the Code Editor window. Doing this collapses the Class statement, as shown in Figure 1-25.

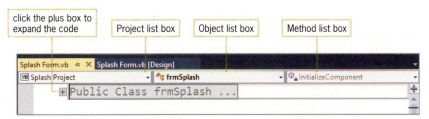

Figure 1-25 Code collapsed in the Code Editor window

2. Click the **plus box** to expand the code.

As Figure 1-25 indicates, the Code Editor window contains three dropdown list boxes named Project, Object, and Method. The Project box contains the name of the current project, Splash Project. The Object box lists the names of the objects included in the user interface, and the Method box lists the events to which the selected object is capable of responding. In object-oriented programming **(OOP)**, an event is considered a behavior of an object because it represents an action to which the object can respond. In the context of OOP, the Code Editor window "exposes" an object's behaviors to the programmer. You use the Object and Method list boxes to select the object and event, respectively, that you want to code. In this case, you will select btnExit in the Object list box, and you will select Click in the Method list box. This is because you want the application to end when the Exit button is clicked.

START HERE

To select the btnExit control's Click event:

1. Click the **Object** list arrow and then click **btnExit** in the list. Click the **Method** list arrow and then click **Click** in the list. A code template for the btnExit control's Click event procedure appears in the Code Editor window. See Figure 1-26.

Figure 1-26   btnExit control's Click event procedure

The Code Editor provides the code template to help you follow the rules of the Visual Basic language. The rules of a programming language are called its **syntax**. The first line in the code template is called the **procedure header**, and the last line is called the **procedure footer**. The procedure header begins with the keywords `Private Sub`. A **keyword** is a word that has a special meaning in a programming language. Keywords appear in a different color from the rest of the code. The `Private` keyword in Figure 1-26 indicates that the button's Click event procedure can be used only within the current Code Editor window. The `Sub` keyword is an abbreviation of the term **sub procedure**, which is a block of code that performs a specific task.

Following the `Sub` keyword is the name of the object, an underscore, the name of the event, and parentheses containing some text. For now, you do not have to be concerned with the text that appears between the parentheses. After the closing parenthesis is the following Handles clause: `Handles btnExit.Click`. This clause indicates that the procedure handles (or is associated with) the btnExit control's Click event. It tells the computer to process the procedure only when the btnExit control is clicked.

The code template ends with the procedure footer, which contains the keywords `End Sub`. You enter your Visual Basic instructions at the location of the insertion point, which appears between the Private Sub and End Sub clauses in Figure 1-26. The Code Editor automatically indents the line between the procedure header and footer. Indenting the lines within a procedure makes the instructions easier to read and is a common programming practice. In this case, the instruction you enter will tell the btnExit control to end the application when it is clicked.

The Me.Close() Instruction

The `Me.Close()` instruction tells the computer to close the current form. If the current form is the only form in the application, closing it terminates the entire application. In the instruction, `Me` is a keyword that refers to the current form, and `Close` is one of the methods available in Visual Basic. A **method** is a predefined procedure that you can call (or invoke) when needed. For example, if you want the computer to close the current form when the user clicks the Exit button, you enter the `Me.Close()` instruction in the button's Click event procedure. Notice the empty set of parentheses after the method's name in the instruction. The parentheses are required when calling some Visual Basic methods. However, depending on the method, the parentheses may or may not be empty. If you forget to enter the empty set of parentheses, the Code Editor will enter them for you when you move the insertion point to another line in the Code Editor window.

To code the btnExit_Click procedure:

START HERE

1. You can type the `Me.Close()` instruction on your own or use the Code Editor window's IntelliSense feature. In this set of steps, you will use the IntelliSense feature. Type **me.** (be sure to type the period, but don't press Enter). When you type the period, the IntelliSense feature displays a list of properties, methods, and so on from which you can select.

   Note: If the list of choices does not appear, the IntelliSense feature may have been turned off on your computer system. To turn it on, click Tools on the menu bar, click Options, expand the Text Editor node, click Basic, select the Auto list members check box, and then click the OK button.

2. Type **clo** (but don't press Enter). The IntelliSense feature highlights the Close method in the list. See Figure 1-27. For now, don't be concerned with the LightBulb indicator or the red jagged line (called a squiggle) below `Me.clo`; you will learn about those two features in Chapter 2.

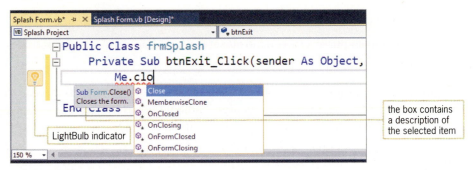

Figure 1-27 List displayed by the IntelliSense feature

3. Press **Tab** to include the Close method in the instruction and then press **Enter**. See Figure 1-28.

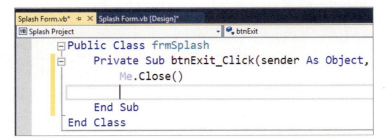

Figure 1-28 Completed btnExit_Click procedure

It's a good idea to test a procedure after you have coded it. By doing this, you'll know where to look if an error occurs. You can test the Exit button's Click event procedure by starting the application and then clicking the button. When the button is clicked, the computer will process the `Me.Close()` instruction contained in the procedure.

To test the btnExit_Click procedure and the executable file:

START HERE

1. Save the solution and then click the **Start** button on the Standard toolbar (or press the **F5** key) to start the application. The splash screen appears.

2. Click the **Exit** button to end the application. Close the Code Editor window and then close the solution.

 The Start button looks like this: ▶.

3. Use Windows to locate and then open the VB2015\Chap01\Splash Solution\Splash Project\bin\Debug folder. Right-click **Zoo Splash (Zoo Splash.exe)** and then click the **Open** button.

4. When the splash screen appears, click the **Exit** button.

Lesson B Summary

- To add a control to a form:

  Click a tool in the toolbox, but do not release the mouse button. Hold down the mouse button as you drag the tool to the form, and then release the mouse button. You can also click a tool and then click the form. In addition, you can click a tool, place the mouse pointer on the form, and then press the left mouse button and drag the mouse pointer until the control is the desired size. You can also double-click a tool in the toolbox.

- To display text that the user cannot edit while the application is running:

  Use the Label tool to instantiate a label control. Set the label control's Text property.

- To move a control to a different location on the form:

  Drag the control to the desired location. You can also set the control's Location property. In addition, you can select the control and then press and hold down the Ctrl (Control) key as you press the up, down, right, or left arrow key on your keyboard.

- To specify the type, style, and size of the font used to display text in a control:

  Set the control's Font property.

- To select multiple controls on a form:

  Click the first control you want to select, and then Ctrl+click each of the other controls you want to select. You can also select a group of controls on the form by placing the mouse pointer slightly above and to the left of the first control you want to select, and then pressing the left mouse button and dragging. A dotted rectangle appears as you drag. When all of the controls you want to select are within (or at least touched by) the dotted rectangle, release the mouse button. All of the controls surrounded or touched by the dotted rectangle will be selected.

- To cancel the selection of one or more controls:

  You cancel the selection of one control by pressing and holding down the Ctrl key as you click the control. You cancel the selection of all of the selected controls by releasing the Ctrl key and then clicking the form or any unselected control on the form.

- To specify the color of a control's text:

  Set the control's ForeColor property.

- To control the layering of a control:

  Select the control. Click Format on the menu bar, point to Order, and then click the appropriate option: either Send to Back or Bring to Front. You can also right-click the control and then click the appropriate option.

- To center one or more controls on the form:

  Select the controls you want to center. Click Format on the menu bar, point to Center in Form, and then click either Horizontally or Vertically.

- To align the borders of two or more controls on the form:

  Select the reference control and then select the other controls you want to align. Click Format on the menu bar, point to Align, and then click the appropriate option.

- To make two or more controls on the form the same size:

  Select the reference control and then select the other controls you want to size. Click Format on the menu bar, point to Make Same Size, and then click the appropriate option.

- To display a graphic in a control in the user interface:

  Use the PictureBox tool to instantiate a picture box control. Use the task box or Properties window to set the control's Image and SizeMode properties.

- To display a standard button that performs an action when clicked:

  Use the Button tool to instantiate a button control.

- To verify or change the names of the startup form and/or executable file:

  Use the Application pane in the Project Designer window. You can open the Project Designer window by right-clicking My Project in the Solution Explorer window, and then clicking Open on the context menu. Or, you can click Project on the menu bar and then click *<project name>* Properties on the menu.

- To start and stop an application:

  You can start an application by clicking Debug on the menu bar and then clicking Start Debugging. You can also press the F5 key on your keyboard or click the Start button on the Standard toolbar to start an application. You can stop an application by clicking the form's Close button. You can also first make the designer window the active window, then click Debug on the menu bar, and then click Stop Debugging to stop an application.

- To open the Code Editor window:

  Right-click the form and then click View Code on the context menu.

- To display an object's event procedure in the Code Editor window:

  Open the Code Editor window. Use the Object list box to select the object's name, and then use the Method list box to select the event.

- To allow the user to close the current form while an application is running:

  Enter the `Me.Close()` instruction in an event procedure.

- To run a project's executable file:

  Locate the .exe file in the project's bin\Debug folder. Right-click the filename and then click Open. You can also double-click the filename.

Lesson B Key Terms

Button control—the control commonly used to perform an immediate action when clicked

Controls—objects (such as a label, a picture box, or a button) added to a form

Event procedure—a set of Visual Basic instructions that tell an object how to respond to an event

Events—actions to which an object can respond; examples include clicking and double-clicking

Executable file—a file that can be run outside of the Visual Studio IDE; the file has the .exe extension on its filename

Keyword—a word that has a special meaning in a programming language

Label control—the control used to display text that the user is not allowed to edit while an application is running

Method—a predefined Visual Basic procedure that you can call (invoke) when needed

OOP—the acronym for object-oriented programming

Picture box control—the control used to display an image on a form

Procedure footer—the last line in a procedure

Procedure header—the first line in a procedure

Reference control—the first control selected in a group of controls; this is the control whose size and/or location you want the other selected controls to match

Startup form—the form that appears automatically when an application is started

Sub procedure—a block of code that performs a specific task

Syntax—the rules of a programming language

Toolbox—refers to the Toolbox window

Toolbox window—the window that contains the tools used when creating an interface (each tool represents a class); referred to more simply as the toolbox

Lesson B Review Questions

1. You use the _____ control to display text that the user is not allowed to edit while the application is running.

    a. Button

    b. DisplayBox

    c. Label

    d. PictureBox

2. The text displayed on a button's face is stored in which property?

    a. Caption

    b. Label

    c. Name

    d. Text

3. Which of the following can be accomplished using the Format menu?

    a. aligning the borders of two or more controls

    b. centering one or more controls horizontally on the form

    c. making two or more controls the same size

    d. all of the above

4. Which instruction terminates an application that contains only one form?

    a. `Me.Close()`

    b. `Me.Done()`

    c. `Me.Finish()`

    d. `Me.Stop()`

5. Define the term "syntax."

Lesson B Exercises

1. Create a Visual Basic Windows application. Use the following names for the solution and project, respectively: Warren Solution and Warren Project. Save the application in the VB2015\Chap01 folder.

   a. Change the form file's name to Main Form.vb.

   b. Change the form's name to frmMain. Change its Font property to Segoe UI, 9pt. The form's title bar should say Warren Fire Department; set the appropriate property. The form should be centered on the screen when it first appears; set the appropriate property.

   c. Add a label control to the form. The label should contain the text "We put out fires!" (without the quotation marks); set the appropriate property. Display the label's text in italics using the Segoe UI, 16pt font. The label should be located 20 pixels from the top of the form, and it should be centered horizontally on the form.

   d. Add a picture box control to the form. The control should display the image stored in the VB2015\Chap01\FireTruck.png file. (The image is provided courtesy of OpenClipArt.org/rdevries.) Set the picture box's size mode to StretchImage. Change the size of the picture box to 170, 140. Center the picture box on the form, both vertically and horizontally.

   e. Add a button control to the form. Position the button in the lower-right corner of the form. Change the button's name to btnExit. The button should display the text "Exit" (without the quotation marks); set the appropriate property.

   f. Open the Code Editor window. Enter the `Me.Close()` instruction in the btnExit control's Click event procedure.

   g. Display the Project Designer window. Verify that the name of the startup form is frmMain. Also, use the Assembly name box to change the executable file's name to Warren. Close the Project Designer window.

   h. Save the solution and then start the application. Use the Exit button to stop the application. Close the Code Editor window and then close the solution.

   i. Use Windows to open the project's bin\Debug folder, and then run the project's executable file.

2. Create a Visual Basic Windows application. Use the following names for the solution and project, respectively: Valley Solution and Valley Project. Save the application in the VB2015\Chap01 folder. Change the form file's name to Main Form.vb. Change the form's Font property to Segoe UI, 9pt. Create the user interface shown in Figure 1-29. The picture box should display the image stored in the VB2015\Chap01\Carnival.png file. You can use any font style, size, and color for the label controls. The form should be centered on the screen when the application is started. Code the Exit button so that it closes the application when it is clicked. Use the Project Designer window to verify that the name of the startup form is correct, and to change the executable file's name to Valley Park. Save the solution and then start the application. Use the Exit button to stop the application. Close the Code Editor window and then close the solution. Use Windows to open the project's bin\Debug folder, and then run the project's executable file.

Figure 1-29 User interface for the Valley Park application

INTERMEDIATE

3. Create a Visual Basic Windows application. Use the following names for the solution and project, respectively: Penguin Solution and Penguin Project. Save the application in the VB2015\Chap01 folder. Change the form file's name to Main Form.vb. Change the form's Font property to Segoe UI, 9pt. Create the user interface shown in Figure 1-30. You can use any font style, size, and color for the label control. The form should be centered on the screen when the application is started. Assign appropriate names to the form and button. The picture box should display the image stored in the VB2015\Chap01\Penguin.png file. Code the Exit button so that it closes the application when it is clicked. Change the executable file's name to Penguin. Save the solution and then start the application. Use the Exit button to stop the application. Close the Code Editor window and then close the solution. Use Windows to open the project's bin\Debug folder, and then run the project's executable file.

Figure 1-30   User interface for the Penguin Grille application

4. In this exercise, you learn about the Format menu's Align, Make Same Size, and Center   DISCOVERY
    in Form options.

    a. Open the VB2015\Chap01\Format Solution\Format Solution (Format Solution.sln)
        file. If necessary, open the designer window.

    b. Click the Button2 control, and then press and hold down the Ctrl (Control) key as
        you click the other two button controls. Release the Ctrl key. Notice that the sizing
        handles on the first button you selected (Button2) are white, while the sizing handles
        on the other two buttons are black. The Align and Make Same Size options on the
        Format menu use the control with the white sizing handles as the reference control
        when aligning and sizing the selected controls. First, you will practice with the Align
        option by aligning the three buttons by their left borders. Click Format, point to
        Align, and then click Lefts. The left borders of the Button1 and Button3 controls are
        aligned with the left border of the Button2 control, which is the reference control.

    c. The Make Same Size option makes the selected objects the same height or width,
        or both. Here again, the first object you select determines the size. Click the form to
        deselect the three buttons. Click Button1, Ctrl+click Button2, and then Ctrl+click
        Button3. Click Format, point to Make Same Size, and then click Both. The height
        and width of the Button2 and Button3 controls now match the height and width of
        the reference control (Button1).

    d. Click Format, point to Center in Form, and then click Horizontally to center the
        controls horizontally on the form.

    e. Click the form to deselect the buttons. Save and then close the solution.

▌ LESSON C

After studying Lesson C, you should be able to:

- Set the properties of a timer control
- Delete a control from the form
- Delete code from the Code Editor window
- Code a timer control's Tick event procedure
- Prevent the user from sizing a form
- Remove and/or disable a form's Minimize, Maximize, and Close buttons
- Print an application's code and interface

The Ch01C video demonstrates most of the steps contained in Lesson C.

START HERE

Using the Timer Tool

In Lesson B, you added an Exit button to the splash screen created for the Crighton Zoo. Splash screens usually do not contain an Exit button. Instead, they use a timer control to automatically remove themselves from the screen after a set period of time. In this lesson, you will remove the Exit button from the splash screen and replace it with a timer control.

To open the Splash Solution from Lesson B:

1. If necessary, start Visual Studio 2015 and open the Solution Explorer window. Open the VB2015\Chap01\Splash Solution\Splash Solution (Splash Solution.sln) file. If necessary, open the designer window.

2. Permanently display the Properties and Toolbox windows, and then auto-hide the Solution Explorer window.

You instantiate a timer control using the Timer tool, which is located in the Components section of the toolbox. When you drag the Timer tool to the form and then release the mouse button, the timer control will be placed in the component tray rather than on the form. The **component tray** is a special area of the IDE. Its purpose is to store controls that do not appear in the user interface during **run time**, which occurs while an application is running. In other words, the timer will not be visible to the user when the interface appears on the screen.

The Boolean values (True and False) are named after the English mathematician George Boole.

The purpose of a **timer control** is to process code at one or more regular intervals. The length of each interval is specified in milliseconds and entered in the timer's Interval property. A millisecond is 1/1000 of a second; in other words, there are 1,000 milliseconds in a second. The timer's state—either running or stopped—is determined by its Enabled property, which can be set to either the Boolean value True or the Boolean value False. When its Enabled property is set to True, the timer is running; when it is set to False (the default), the timer is stopped.

If the timer is running, its Tick event occurs each time an interval has elapsed. Each time the Tick event occurs, the computer processes any code contained in the Tick event procedure. If the timer is stopped, the Tick event does not occur and, therefore, any code entered in the Tick event procedure is not processed.

To add a timer control to the splash screen: START HERE

1. If necessary, expand the **Components** node in the toolbox. Click the **Timer** tool and then drag the mouse pointer to the form. (Do not worry about the exact location.) When you release the mouse button, a timer control appears in the component tray at the bottom of the IDE.

2. The three-character ID used when naming timer controls is tmr. Change the timer's name to **tmrExit**, and then set its Enabled property to **True**.

3. You will have the timer end the application after six seconds, which are equal to 6,000 milliseconds. Set the timer's Interval property to **6000** and press **Enter**. See Figure 1-31.

Figure 1-31 Timer control placed in the component tray
Photos courtesy of the Nashville Zoo and Diane Zak

You no longer need the Exit button, so you can delete it and its associated code. You then will enter the `Me.Close()` instruction in the timer's Tick event procedure.

To delete the Exit button and its code, and then code and test the timer: START HERE

1. Auto-hide the Toolbox and Properties windows. Click the **Exit** button to select it and then press **Delete** to delete the control from the form.

2. Deleting a control from the form does not delete the control's code, which remains in the Code Editor window. Open the Code Editor window. Select (highlight) the entire btnExit_Click procedure, as shown in Figure 1-32.

Figure 1-32 btnExit_Click procedure selected in the Code Editor window

3. Press **Delete** to delete the selected code from the Code Editor window.

4. Use the Object and Method list boxes to open the code template for the tmrExit control's Tick event procedure. Type **Me.Close()** and press **Enter**.

5. Save the solution and then start the application. The splash form appears on the screen.

> The horizontal sizing pointer is a horizontal line with an arrowhead at each end.

6. Place your mouse pointer on the form's right border until it becomes a horizontal sizing pointer, and then drag the form's border to the left. Notice that you can change the form's size during run time. Typically, a user is not allowed to change the size of a splash screen. You can prevent the user from sizing the form by changing the form's FormBorderStyle property, which you will do in the next section.

7. When six seconds have elapsed, the application ends and the splash form disappears. Click the **Splash Form.vb [Design]** tab to make the designer window the active window.

Setting the FormBorderStyle Property

A form's FormBorderStyle property determines the border style of the form. For most applications, you will leave the property at its default setting: Sizable. Doing this allows the user to change the form's size by dragging its borders while the application is running. When a form represents a splash screen, however, you typically set the FormBorderStyle property to either None or FixedSingle. The None setting removes the form's border, whereas the FixedSingle setting draws a fixed, thin line around the form.

START HERE

To change the FormBorderStyle property:

1. Click the **form's title bar** to select the form. Temporarily display the Properties window, and then set the FormBorderStyle property to **FixedSingle**.

2. Save the solution and then start the application. Try to size the form by dragging one of its borders. You will notice that you cannot size the form using its border.

3. When six seconds have elapsed, the application ends. Start the application again. Notice that the splash screen's title bar contains a Minimize button, a Maximize button, and a Close button. As a general rule, most splash screens do not contain these elements. You will learn how to remove the elements, as well as the title bar itself, in the next section. Again, the application ends after six seconds have elapsed.

The MinimizeBox, MaximizeBox, and ControlBox Properties

You can use a form's MinimizeBox property to disable the Minimize button that appears on the form's title bar. Similarly, you can use the MaximizeBox property to disable the Maximize button. You will experiment with both properties in the next set of steps.

START HERE

To experiment with the MinimizeBox and MaximizeBox properties:

1. If necessary, click the **form's title bar** to select the form. First, you will disable the Minimize button. Temporarily display the Properties window, and then set the form's MinimizeBox property to **False**. Notice that the Minimize button appears dimmed (grayed out) on the title bar. This indicates that the button is not available for use.

2. Next, you will enable the Minimize button and disable the Maximize button. Set the MinimizeBox property to **True**, and then set the MaximizeBox property to **False**. Now only the Maximize button appears dimmed (grayed out) on the title bar.

3. Observe what happens if both the MinimizeBox and MaximizeBox properties are set to False. Set the MinimizeBox property to **False**. (The MaximizeBox property is already

set to False.) Notice that when both properties are set to False, the buttons are not disabled; instead, they are removed from the title bar.

4. Now, return the buttons to their original state by setting the form's MinimizeBox and MaximizeBox properties to **True**.

Unlike most applications, splash screens typically do not contain a title bar. You can remove the title bar by setting the form's ControlBox property to False, and then removing the text from its Text property. You will try this next.

To remove the title bar from the splash screen:

START HERE

1. Set the form's ControlBox property to **False**. Doing this removes the title bar elements (icon and buttons) from the form; however, it does not remove the title bar itself. To remove the title bar, you must delete the contents of the form's Text property. Click the **Text** property, press the **Backspace** key, and then press **Enter**.

2. Save the solution and then start the application. The splash screen appears without a title bar. See Figure 1-33. The application ends after six seconds have elapsed.

Figure 1-33 Completed splash screen
Photos courtesy of the Nashville Zoo and Diane Zak

Printing the Application's Code and Interface

You should always print a copy of your application's code because the printout will help you understand and maintain the application in the future. To print the code, the Code Editor window must be the active (current) window. You should also print a copy of the application's user interface.

To print the splash screen's interface and code:

START HERE

1. Press the Windows logo key to switch to tile-based mode. Begin typing the words **snipping tool**. When you see Snipping Tool in the list of applications, click **Snipping Tool**.

2. Click the **New** button. Drag the cursor around the form and then release the mouse button.

3. Click **File** and then click **Save As**. Locate and then open the VB2015\Chap01\Splash Solution folder. If necessary, change the entry in the Save as type box to Portable Network Graphic file (PNG) (*.PNG). Type **Zoo Splash** in the File name box and then click the **Save** button. Close the Snipping Tool application.

4. If your computer is connected to a printer, use Windows to open the VB2015\Chap01\ Splash Solution folder. Right-click **Zoo Splash.PNG** and then click **Print** on the context menu. If necessary, select the appropriate printer in the Printer box. Click the **Print** button.

5. Click the **Splash Form.vb** tab to make the Code Editor window the active window. Click **File** on the menu bar, and then click **Print** to open the Print dialog box. See Figure 1-34. Notice that you can include line numbers in the printout. You can also choose to hide the collapsed regions of code. Currently, the Hide collapsed regions check box is grayed out because no code is collapsed in the Code Editor window.

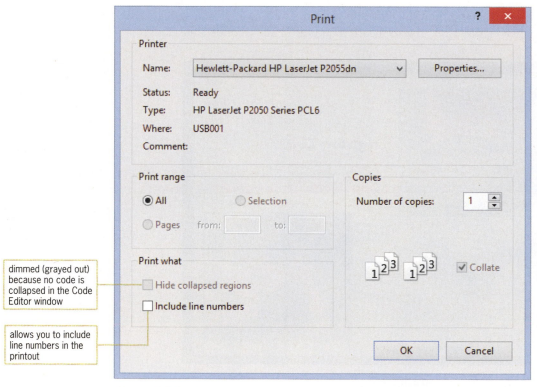

dimmed (grayed out) because no code is collapsed in the Code Editor window

allows you to include line numbers in the printout

Figure 1-34 Print dialog box

6. If your computer is connected to a printer, click the **OK** button to begin printing; otherwise, click the **Cancel** button. If you clicked the OK button, your printer prints the code.

7. Close the Code Editor window and then close the solution.

Lesson C Summary

- To process code at specified intervals of time:

  Use the Timer tool to instantiate a timer control. Set the timer's Interval property to the number of milliseconds for each interval. Turn on the timer by setting its Enabled property to True. Enter the timer's code in its Tick event procedure.

- To delete a control:

  Select the control you want to delete and then press Delete. If the control contains code, open the Code Editor window and delete the code contained in the control's event procedures.

- To control the border style of the form:

  Set the form's FormBorderStyle property.

- To enable/disable the Minimize button on the form's title bar:

  Set the form's MinimizeBox property.

- To enable/disable the Maximize button on the form's title bar:

  Set the form's MaximizeBox property.

- To control whether the icon and buttons appear in the form's title bar:

  Set the form's ControlBox property.

- To print the user interface:

  Make the designer window the active window. Open the Snipping Tool application. Click the New button. Drag the cursor around the form and then release the mouse button. Use the File menu to save the file as a PNG file, and then close the Snipping Tool application. Use Windows to locate the PNG file. Right-click the file's name and then click Print on the context menu. If necessary, select the appropriate printer in the Printer box. Click the Print button.

- To print the Visual Basic code:

  Make the Code Editor window the active window. Collapse any code you do not want to print. Click File on the menu bar and then click Print. If you don't want to print the collapsed code, select the Hide collapsed regions check box. If you want to print line numbers, select the Include line numbers check box. Click the OK button in the Print dialog box.

Lesson C Key Terms

Component tray—a special area in the IDE; stores controls that do not appear in the interface during run time

Run time—the state of an application while it is running

Timer control—the control used to process code at one or more regular intervals

Lesson C Review Questions

1. If a timer is running, the code in its _____ event procedure is processed each time an interval has elapsed.

   a. Interval   c. Timed

   b. Tick   d. Timer

2. Which of the following is false?

   a. When you add a timer control to a form, the control appears in the component tray.

   b. The user can see a timer control during run time.

   c. You stop a timer by setting its Enabled property to False.

   d. The number entered in a timer's Interval property represents the number of milliseconds for each interval.

3. To disable the Minimize button on a form's title bar, set the form's _____ property to False.

   a. ButtonMinimize
   b. Minimize
   c. MinimizeBox
   d. MinimizeButton

4. You can remove the Minimize, Maximize, and Close buttons from a form's title bar by setting the form's _____ property to False.

   a. ControlBox
   b. ControlButton
   c. TitleBar
   d. TitleBarElements

5. Explain how to delete a control that contains code.

Lesson C Exercises

INTRODUCTORY

1. In this exercise, you modify the Warren Fire Department application created in Lesson B's Exercise 1.

   a. Open the VB2015\Chap01\Warren Solution\Warren Solution (Warren Solution.sln) file. If necessary, open the designer window.
   b. Delete the Exit button from the form and then delete the button's code from the Code Editor window.
   c. Add a timer control to the form. Change the timer's name to tmrExit. Set the timer's Enabled property to True. The timer should end the application after eight seconds have elapsed; set the appropriate property. Enter the Me.Close() instruction in the appropriate event procedure in the Code Editor window.
   d. Save the solution and then start the application. When eight seconds have elapsed, the application ends.
   e. Add a label control to the form. Position the label below the picture box. Change the label's Text property to "Warren Fire Department" (without the quotation marks). Change its font size to 16pt. Center the label horizontally on the form.
   f. Set the form's FormBorderStyle property to FixedSingle. Also, remove the elements (icon and buttons) and text from the form's title bar.
   g. Save the solution and then start the application. Close the Code Editor window and then close the solution.

INTERMEDIATE

2. In this exercise, you modify the Valley Park application created in Lesson B's Exercise 2.

   a. Open the VB2015\Chap01\Valley Solution\Valley Solution (Valley Solution.sln) file. If necessary, open the designer window.
   b. Replace the Exit button with a timer control named tmrExit. The timer should end the application after six seconds have elapsed.
   c. Save the solution and then start the application. When six seconds have elapsed, the application ends.
   d. Change the label's text to "Come join the fun at Valley Park!" (without the quotation marks). Center the label horizontally on the form.
   e. Set the form's FormBorderStyle property to FixedSingle. Also, remove the elements (icon and buttons) and text from the form's title bar.
   f. Save the solution and then start the application. Close the Code Editor window and then close the solution.

3. Create a Visual Basic Windows application. Use the following names for the solution and project, respectively: Characters Solution and Characters Project. Save the application in the VB2015\Chap01 folder. Change the form file's name to Main Form.vb. Create the interface shown in Figure 1-35. The picture boxes should display the images stored in the Darth.png and Trooper.png files contained in the VB2015\ Chap01 folder. Include a timer that ends the application after five seconds have elapsed. Now, use the Project Designer window to change the executable file's name to Characters. Save the solution and then start the application. Close the Code Editor window and then close the solution. Use Windows to open the project's bin\Debug folder, and then run the project's executable file.

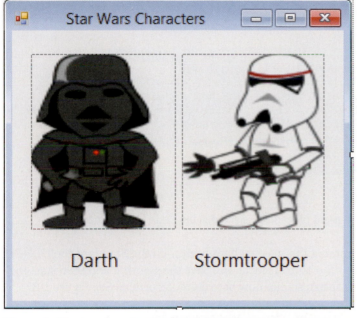

Figure 1-35 Interface for the Star Wars Characters application

4. Create a Visual Basic Windows application. Name the solution, project, and form file My Splash Solution, My Splash Project, and Splash Form.vb, respectively. Save the application in the VB2015\Chap01 folder. Create your own splash screen. Save the solution and then start the application. Close the Code Editor window and then close the solution.

5. The Internet contains a vast amount of code snippets that you can use in your Visual Basic applications. And in many cases, you can use the snippet without fully understanding each line of its code. In this exercise, you will use a code snippet that rounds the corners on a splash screen.

   a. Open the Rounded Corners Solution (Rounded Corners Solution.sln) file contained in the VB2015\Chap01\Rounded Corners Solution folder. If necessary, open the designer window. The image that appears on the form is displayed by the form's BackgroundImage property. The form's BackgroundImageLayout property is set to Stretch.

   b. For the code snippet to work properly, the splash screen cannot have a border. Therefore, change the form's FormBorderStyle property to None.

c. Save the application and then start the solution. Notice that the splash screen contains the standard corners, which are not rounded. Click the Exit button to end the application.

d. Open the Code Editor window. Select (highlight) the lines of code contained in the form's Load event procedure, which is processed when the application is run and the form is loaded into the computer's internal memory. See Figure 1-36.

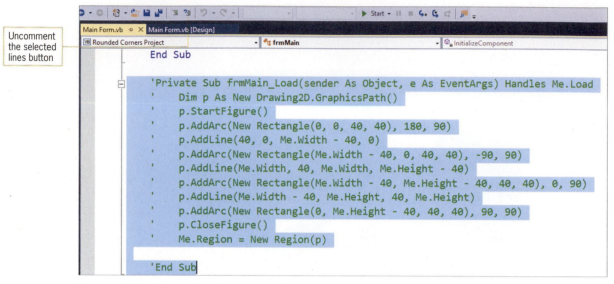

```
Uncomment                  Main Form.vb ⊡ ✕ Main Form.vb [Design]
the selected               VB Rounded Corners Project          ▾  frmMain                        ▾  InitializeComponent
lines button                              End Sub

                                  'Private Sub frmMain_Load(sender As Object, e As EventArgs) Handles Me.Load
                                  '    Dim p As New Drawing2D.GraphicsPath()
                                  '    p.StartFigure()
                                  '    p.AddArc(New Rectangle(0, 0, 40, 40), 180, 90)
                                  '    p.AddLine(40, 0, Me.Width - 40, 0)
                                  '    p.AddArc(New Rectangle(Me.Width - 40, 0, 40, 40), -90, 90)
                                  '    p.AddLine(Me.Width, 40, Me.Width, Me.Height - 40)
                                  '    p.AddArc(New Rectangle(Me.Width - 40, Me.Height - 40, 40, 40), 0, 90)
                                  '    p.AddLine(Me.Width - 40, Me.Height, 40, Me.Height)
                                  '    p.AddArc(New Rectangle(0, Me.Height - 40, 40, 40), 90, 90)
                                  '    p.CloseFigure()
                                  '    Me.Region = New Region(p)

                                  'End Sub
```

Figure 1-36   Form's Load event procedure selected in the Code Editor window

e. Click the Uncomment the selected lines button on the Standard toolbar. (Refer to Figure 1-36 for the button's location.) Save the solution and then start the application. The splash screen now has rounded corners. See Figure 1-37.

Figure 1-37   Splash screen with rounded corners
Photo courtesy of the Nashville Zoo and Diane Zak

f. Click the Exit button to end the application. Close the Code Editor window and then close the solution.

6. In this exercise, you will create a splash screen that has a transparent background. DISCOVERY

    a. Open the VB2015\Chap01\Transparency Solution\Transparency Solution
        (Transparency Solution.sln) file. If necessary, open the designer window.

    b. Click the form's title bar to select the form. Set the form's FormBorderStyle property
        to None.

    c. Click TransparencyKey in the Properties window. The TransparencyKey property
        determines the color that will appear transparent when the application is run. To
        make the form transparent, you set its TransparencyKey property to the same color
        as its BackColor property. Click the TransparencyKey property's list arrow, then click
        the System tab, and then click Control.

    d. Open the Code Editor window, which contains the `Me.Close()` instruction in the
        picHeart_Click event. Save the solution and then start the application. Because the
        color specified in the form's BackColor property is the same as the color specified in
        the TransparencyKey property, the form appears transparent. As a result, the splash
        screen shows only the image contained in the picture box. See Figure 1-38.

Figure 1-38 Splash screen with a transparent background

    e. Click the picture box to end the application. Close the Code Editor window and then
        close the solution.

7. In this exercise, you will learn how to display a splash screen followed by another form. DISCOVERY

    a. Open the Two Form Solution (Two Form Solution.sln) file contained in the
        VB2015\Chap01\Two Form Solution folder. If necessary, open the Solution
        Explorer and designer windows. Notice that the project contains one form named
        Splash Form.vb.

    b. Now you will add a new form to the project. Click Project on the menu bar, then
        click Add Windows Form, and then click the Add button. Change the new form
        file's name to Main Form.vb. Change the form's name to frmMain, and then set its
        StartPosition property to CenterScreen. Also set its Text property to Main Form.

c. Right-click My Project in the Solution Explorer window and then click Open. Change the entry in the Startup form box to frmMain. Change the entry in the Splash screen box to frmSplash. Close the Project Designer window.

d. Save the solution and then start the application. The splash screen (frmSplash) appears first. After a few seconds, the splash screen disappears automatically and the startup form (frmMain) appears. Click the Close button on the startup form's title bar, and then close the solution.

8. In this exercise, you learn how to display a tooltip. Open the VB2015\Chap01\ToolTip Solution\ToolTip Solution (ToolTip Solution.sln) file. If necessary, open the designer window. Click the ToolTip tool in the toolbox and then drag the tool to the form. Notice that a tooltip control appears in the component tray rather than on the form. Set the btnExit control's ToolTip on ToolTip1 property to "Ends the application" (without the quotation marks). Save the solution and then start the application. Hover your mouse pointer over the Exit button. The tooltip "Ends the application" appears in a tooltip box. Click the Exit button and then close the solution.

9. Open the VB2015\Chap01\Debug Solution\Debug Solution (Debug Solution.sln) file. If necessary, open the designer window. Start the application. The application is not working correctly because the splash screen does not disappear after four seconds have elapsed. Click Debug on the menu bar and then click Stop Debugging. Locate and then correct the error(s). Save the solution and then start the application again to verify that it is working correctly. Close the Code Editor window and then close the solution.

CHAPTER 2

Designing Applications

Creating the Meyer's Purple Bakery Application

In this chapter, you will create an application that prints a sales receipt for Meyer's Purple Bakery, a small bakery that sells a variety of doughnuts and muffins for $0.50 each. The application will allow the salesclerk to enter the current date and the number of doughnuts and muffins sold to a customer. It then will calculate and display the total number of items sold and the total sales amount.

Previewing the Meyer's Purple Bakery Application

Before you start the first lesson in this chapter, you will preview the completed application contained in the VB2015\Chap02 folder.

START HERE

To preview the completed application:

1. Use Windows to locate and then open the VB2015\Chap02 folder on your computer's hard disk or on the device designated by your instructor. Right-click **Bakery** (**Bakery.exe**) in the list of filenames and then click the **Open** button. The interface shown in Figure 2-1 appears on the screen. In addition to the picture box, label, and button controls that you learned about in Chapter 1, the interface contains three text boxes. A text box gives a user an area for entering data.

Figure 2-1   Meyer's Purple Bakery interface

Note: If the underlined letters, called access keys, do not appear on your screen, press the Alt key on your keyboard. You will learn about access keys in Lesson B.

2. The insertion point is located in the first text box. The label control to the left of the text box identifies the information the user should enter. Type **7/25/2016** as the date, and then press **Tab** twice to move the insertion point to the Muffins text box.

3. Type **2** and then press **Shift+Tab** (press and hold down the Shift key as you tap the Tab key) to move the insertion point to the Doughnuts text box.

4. Type **6** and then click the **Calculate** button. The button's Click event procedure calculates and displays the total number of items sold (8) and the total sales ($4.00).

5. Click the **Muffins** text box. Change the number 2 in the box to **3**, and then click the **Calculate** button. The button's Click event procedure recalculates the total number of items sold (9) and the total sales ($4.50). See Figure 2-2.

Figure 2-2   Completed sales receipt

6. Click the **Print Receipt** button. The sales receipt appears in the Print preview window. (It may take a few seconds for the window to open.) Click the **Zoom** button's list arrow, and then click **75%**. If necessary, size the Print preview window to view the entire sales receipt. See Figure 2-3.

Figure 2-3   Print preview window

7. If your computer is connected to a printer, click the **Print** button (the printer) on the Print preview window's toolbar to send the output to the printer.

8. Click the **Close** button on the Print preview window's toolbar.

9. Click the **Clear Screen** button to remove the sales information (except the date) from the interface, and then click the **Exit** button to end the application.

The Meyer's Purple Bakery application is an object-oriented program because it uses objects (such as buttons and text boxes) to accomplish its goal. In Lesson A, you will learn how a programmer plans an object-oriented program. You will create the application in Lessons B and C. Be sure to complete each lesson in full and do all of the end-of-lesson questions and several exercises before continuing to the next lesson.

LESSON A

After studying Lesson A, you should be able to:

- Plan an object-oriented Windows application in Visual Basic 2015
- Complete a TOE (Task, Object, Event) chart
- Follow the Windows standards regarding the layout and labeling of controls

Creating an Object-Oriented Application

As Figure 2-4 indicates, the process a programmer follows when creating an object-oriented (OO) application is similar to the process a builder follows when building a home. The planning step, which is Step 2 in the process, is covered in this lesson. Steps 3 through 6 are covered in Lessons B and C.

A builder's process	A programmer's process
1. Meet with the client.	1. Meet with the client.
2. Plan the home (blueprint).	2. Plan the application (TOE chart).
3. Build the frame.	3. Build the user interface.
4. Complete the home.	4. Code the application.
5. Inspect the home and fix any problems.	5. Test and debug the application.
6. Assemble the documentation.	6. Assemble the documentation.

Figure 2-4 Processes used by a builder and a programmer

Planning an Object-Oriented Application

As any builder will tell you, the most important aspect of a home is not its beauty. Rather, it is how well the home satisfies the buyer's wants and needs. The same is true of an OO application. For an application to fulfill the wants and needs of the user, it is essential for the programmer to plan the application jointly with the user. It cannot be stressed enough that the only way to guarantee the success of an application is to actively involve the user in the planning phase. The steps for planning an OO application are listed in Figure 2-5.

Planning an OO application
1. Identify the tasks the application needs to perform.
2. Identify the objects to which you will assign the tasks.
3. Identify the events required to trigger an object to perform its assigned tasks.
4. Draw a sketch of the user interface.

Figure 2-5 Steps for planning an OO application

You can use a TOE (Task, Object, Event) chart to record the application's tasks, objects, and events, which are identified in the first three steps of the planning phase. In the next section, you will begin completing a TOE chart for the Meyer's Purple Bakery application. The first step is to identify the application's tasks.

Identifying the Application's Tasks

Realizing that it is essential to involve the user when planning the application, you meet with the bakery's manager, Mr. Cortane, to determine his requirements. You ask Mr. Cortane to bring a sample of the bakery's current sales receipt; the sample is shown in Figure 2-6. Viewing the bakery's current forms and procedures will help you better understand the application you need to create. You can also use the current form as a guide when designing the user interface.

Meyer's Purple Bakery
Sales Receipt

Date: 10/9/2016

Doughnuts: 2
Muffins: 3

Total items: 5
Total sales: $2.50

Figure 2-6   Sample of the bakery's current sales receipt

When identifying the major tasks an application needs to perform, it is helpful to ask the questions italicized in the following bulleted items. The answers pertaining to the bakery application follow each question.

- *What information will the application need to display on the screen and/or print on the printer?* The application should display and also print the following information: the date, the number of doughnuts sold, the number of muffins sold, the total number of items sold, and the total sales amount.

- *What information will the user need to enter into the user interface to display and/or print the desired information?* The salesclerk (the user) must enter the date, the number of doughnuts sold, and the number of muffins sold.

- *What information will the application need to calculate to display and/or print the desired information?* The application needs to calculate the total number of items sold and the total sales amount.

- *How will the user end the application?* All applications should provide a way for the user to end the application. The bakery application will provide an Exit button.

- *Will previous information need to be cleared from the screen before new information is entered?* The previous customer's sales information will need to be cleared from the screen before the next customer's transaction begins.

Figure 2-7 shows the application's tasks listed in a TOE chart. The tasks do not need to be listed in any particular order. In this case, the data-entry tasks are listed first, followed by the calculation tasks, the display and printing tasks, the application-ending task, and the screen-clearing task.

You can draw a TOE chart by hand or use the table feature in a word processor.

Task	Object	Event

Get the following sales information from the user:
    Current date
    Number of doughnuts sold
    Number of muffins sold		

Calculate total items sold and total sales amount		

Display the following information:
    Current date
    Number of doughnuts sold
    Number of muffins sold
    Total items sold
    Total sales amount		

Print the sales receipt		
End the application		
Clear the screen for the next sale		

Figure 2-7   Tasks entered in a TOE chart

Identifying the Objects

After completing the Task column of the TOE chart, you then assign each task to an object in the user interface. For this application, the only objects you will use besides the Windows form itself are the button, label, and text box controls. As you already know, you use a label to display information that you do not want the user to change while the application is running, and you use a button to perform an action immediately after the user clicks it. You use a **text box** to give the user an area for entering data.

The first task listed in Figure 2-7 is to get the sales information from the user. Because you need to provide the salesclerk with areas in which to enter the information, you will assign the first task to three text boxes named txtDate, txtDonuts, and txtMuffins. The three-character ID used when naming text boxes is txt.

The second task listed in the TOE chart is to calculate the total number of items sold and the total sales amount. You will assign the task to a button named btnCalc so that the salesclerk can calculate both amounts at any time.

The third task listed in the TOE chart is to display five items of information. The first three items pertain to the sales information, which is displayed automatically when the user enters that information in the three text boxes. The last two items, however, are not entered by the user. Instead, those amounts are calculated by the btnCalc control. Because the user should not be allowed to change the calculated results, you will have the btnCalc control display the results in two label controls named lblTotalItems and lblTotalSales. If you look ahead to Figure 2-8, you will notice that "(from btnCalc)" was added to the last two display tasks in the Task column.

The last three tasks listed in the TOE chart will be assigned to three buttons named btnPrint, btnExit, and btnClear. Assigning the tasks to buttons will give the user control over when the tasks are performed. Figure 2-8 shows the TOE chart with the Task and Object columns completed.

Task	Object	Event
Get the following sales information from the user:		
Current date	txtDate	
Number of doughnuts sold	txtDonuts	
Number of muffins sold	txtMuffins	
Calculate total items sold and total sales amount	btnCalc	
Display the following information:		
Current date	txtDate	
Number of doughnuts sold	txtDonuts	
Number of muffins sold	txtMuffins	
Total items sold (from btnCalc)	lblTotalItems	
Total sales amount (from btnCalc)	lblTotalSales	
Print the sales receipt	btnPrint	
End the application	btnExit	
Clear the screen for the next sale	btnClear	

Figure 2-8   Tasks and objects entered in a TOE chart

Identifying the Events

After defining the application's tasks and assigning the tasks to objects in the interface, you then determine which event (if any) must occur in order for an object to carry out its assigned task. The three text boxes listed in the TOE chart in Figure 2-8 are assigned the tasks of getting and displaying the sales information. Text boxes accept and display information automatically, so no special event is necessary for them to do their assigned tasks. The two label controls listed in the TOE chart are assigned the task of displaying the two calculated amounts. Label controls automatically display their contents; so, here again, no special event needs to occur. (Recall that the label controls will get their values from the btnCalc control.) The remaining objects listed in the TOE chart are the four buttons. You will have the buttons perform their assigned tasks when the user clicks them. Figure 2-9 shows the completed TOE chart.

Task	Object	Event
Get the following sales information from the user:		
Current date	txtDate	None
Number of doughnuts sold	txtDonuts	None
Number of muffins sold	txtMuffins	None
Calculate total items sold and total sales amount	btnCalc	Click
Display the following information:		
Current date	txtDate	None
Number of doughnuts sold	txtDonuts	None
Number of muffins sold	txtMuffins	None
Total items sold (from btnCalc)	lblTotalItems	None
Total sales amount (from btnCalc)	lblTotalSales	None
Print the sales receipt	btnPrint	Click
End the application	btnExit	Click
Clear the screen for the next sale	btnClear	Click

Figure 2-9   Completed TOE chart ordered by task

If the application you are creating is small, like the bakery application, you can use the TOE chart in its current form to help you write the Visual Basic code. When the application is large, however, it is often helpful to rearrange the TOE chart so that it is ordered by object rather than by task. To do so, you list all of the objects in the Object column of a new TOE chart, being sure to list each object only once. You then list each object's tasks and events in the Task and Event columns, respectively. Figure 2-10 shows the rearranged TOE chart ordered by object rather than by task.

Task	Object	Event
1. Calculate total items sold and total sales amount 2. Display total items sold and total sales amount in lblTotalItems and lblTotalSales	btnCalc	Click
Print the sales receipt	btnPrint	Click
End the application	btnExit	Click
Clear the screen for the next sale	btnClear	Click
Display total items sold (from btnCalc)	lblTotalItems	None
Display total sales amount (from btnCalc)	lblTotalSales	None
Get and display the sales information	txtDate, txtDonuts, txtMuffins	None

Figure 2-10   Completed TOE chart ordered by object

After completing the TOE chart, the next step is to draw a rough sketch of the user interface.

Drawing a Sketch of the User Interface

A company's standards for interfaces used within the company supersede the Windows standards.

Although the TOE chart lists the objects to include in the interface, it does not indicate where the objects should be placed on the form. While the design of an interface is open to creativity, there are some guidelines to which you should adhere so that your interface is consistent with the Windows standards. This consistency will give your interface a familiar look, which will make your application easier for users to both learn and use. The guidelines are referred to as GUI (graphical user interface) guidelines.

The first GUI guideline covered in this book pertains to the organization of the controls in the interface. In Western countries, the user interface should be organized so that the information flows either vertically or horizontally, with the most important information always located in the upper-left corner of the interface. In a vertical arrangement, the information flows from top to bottom: The essential information is located in the first column of the interface, while secondary information is placed in subsequent columns. In a horizontal arrangement, on the other hand, the information flows from left to right: The essential information is placed in the first row of the interface, with secondary information placed in subsequent rows.

Ch02A-Containers

Related controls should be grouped together using either white (empty) space or one of the tools located in the Containers section of the toolbox. Examples of tools found in the Containers section include the GroupBox, Panel, and TableLayoutPanel tools.

Figures 2-11 and 2-12 show two different sketches of the bakery application's interface. In Figure 2-11, the information is arranged vertically, and white space is used to group related controls together. In Figure 2-12, the information is arranged horizontally, with related controls grouped together using a group box. Each box and button in both figures is labeled so the user knows its purpose. For example, the "Date:" label tells the user the type of information to enter in the box that appears to its right. Similarly, the "Calculate" caption on the first button indicates the action the button will perform when it is clicked.

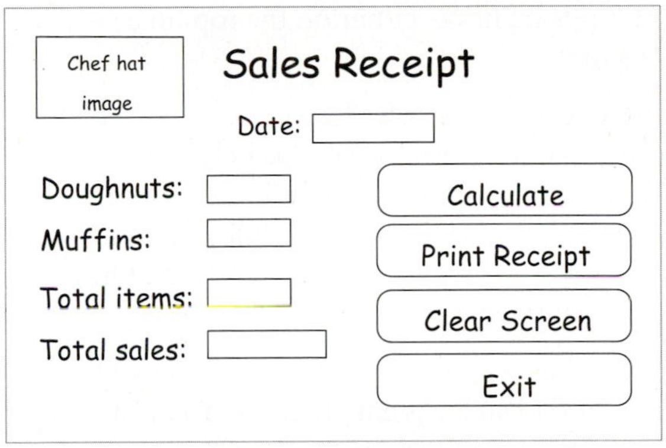

Figure 2-11   Vertical arrangement of the Meyer's Purple Bakery interface

Figure 2-12   Horizontal arrangement of the Meyer's Purple Bakery interface

Usually, program output (such as the result of calculations) is displayed in one or more label controls in the interface. Label controls that display program output should be labeled to make their contents obvious to the user. In the interfaces shown in Figures 2-11 and 2-12, the "Total items:" and "Total sales:" labels identify the contents of the lblTotalItems and lblTotalSales controls, respectively.

The text contained in a label control that identifies another control's contents should be meaningful and left-aligned within the label. In most cases, an identifying label should consist of one to three words only and appear on one line. In addition, the identifying label should be positioned either above or to the left of the control it identifies. An identifying label should end with a colon (:), which distinguishes it from other text in the user interface (such as the heading text "Sales Receipt"). Some assistive technologies, which are technologies that provide assistance to individuals with disabilities, rely on the colons to make this distinction. The Windows standard is to use sentence capitalization for identifying labels. **Sentence capitalization** means you capitalize only the first letter in the first word and in any words that are customarily capitalized.

As you learned in Chapter 1, buttons are identified by the text that appears on the button's face. The text is often referred to as the button's caption. The caption should be meaningful, consist of one to three words only, and appear on one line. A button's caption should be entered using **book title capitalization**, which means you capitalize the first letter in each word, except for articles, conjunctions, and prepositions that do not occur at either the beginning or end of the caption. If the buttons are stacked vertically, as they are in Figure 2-11, all the buttons should be the same height and width. If the buttons are positioned horizontally, as they are in Figure 2-12, all the buttons should be the same height, but their widths may vary if necessary. In a group of buttons, the most commonly used button typically appears first—either on the top (in a vertical arrangement) or on the left (in a horizontal arrangement).

When positioning the controls in the interface, place related controls close to each other and be sure to maintain a consistent margin from the edges of the form. Also, it is helpful to align the borders of the controls wherever possible to minimize the number of different margins appearing in the interface. Doing this allows the user to more easily scan the information. You can align the borders using the snap lines that appear as you are building the interface. Or, you can use the Format menu to align (and also size) the controls.

In this lesson, you learned some basic guidelines to follow when sketching a GUI. You will learn more GUI guidelines in the remaining lessons and in subsequent chapters. You can find a complete list of the GUI guidelines in Appendix B of this book.

GUI DESIGN TIP Layout and Organization of the User Interface

- Organize the user interface so that the information flows either vertically or horizontally, with the most important information always located in the upper-left corner of the interface.

- Group related controls together using either white (empty) space or one of the tools from the Containers section of the toolbox.

- Use a label to identify each text box in the user interface. Also use a label to identify other label controls that display program output. The label text should be meaningful, consist of one to three words only, and appear on one line. Left-align the text within the label and position the label either above or to the left of the control it identifies. Enter the label text using sentence capitalization, and insert a colon (:) following the label text.

- Display a meaningful caption on the face of each button. The caption should indicate the action the button will perform when clicked. Enter the caption using book title capitalization. Place the caption on one line and use from one to three words only.

- When a group of buttons are stacked vertically, all buttons in the group should be the same height and width. When a group of buttons are positioned horizontally, all buttons in the group should be the same height. In a group of buttons, the most commonly used button is typically placed first in the group.

- Align the borders of the controls wherever possible to minimize the number of different margins appearing in the interface.

Lesson A Summary

- To create an OO application:

  Follow these six steps in this order:

  1. Meet with the client.

  2. Plan the application.

  3. Build the user interface.

  4. Code the application.

  5. Test and debug the application.

  6. Assemble the documentation.

- To plan an OO application in Visual Basic:

  Perform these four steps in this order:

  1. Identify the tasks the application needs to perform.

  2. Identify the objects to which you will assign the tasks.

  3. Identify the events required to trigger an object to perform its assigned tasks.

  4. Draw a sketch of the user interface.

- To help you identify the major tasks an application needs to perform, ask the following questions:

  1. What information will the application need to display on the screen and/or print on the printer?

  2. What information will the user need to enter into the user interface in order to display and/or print the desired information?

  3. What information will the application need to calculate in order to display and/or print the desired information?

  4. How will the user end the application?

  5. Will prior information need to be cleared from the screen before new information is entered?

Lesson A Key Terms

Book title capitalization—the capitalization used for a button's caption; refers to capitalizing the first letter in each word, except for articles, conjunctions, and prepositions that do not occur at either the beginning or end of the caption

Sentence capitalization—the capitalization used for identifying labels; refers to capitalizing only the first letter in the first word and in any words that are customarily capitalized

Text box—a control that provides an area in the form for the user to enter data

Lesson A Review Questions

1. In which corner should the most important information be placed in a user interface?

    a. lower left
    b. lower right
    c. upper left
    d. upper right

2. A button's caption should be entered using which type of capitalization?

    a. book title
    b. sentence
    c. either book title or sentence

3. Which of the following statements is false?

    a. The text contained in identifying labels should be left-aligned within the label.

    b. An identifying label should be positioned either above or to the right of the control it identifies.

    c. Identifying labels should use sentence capitalization.

    d. Identifying labels should end with a colon (:).

4. Listed below are the four steps you should follow when planning an OO application. Put the steps in the proper order by placing a number (1 through 4) on the line to the left of the step.

    _____ Identify the objects to which you will assign the tasks.

    _____ Draw a sketch of the user interface.

    _____ Identify the tasks the application needs to perform.

    _____ Identify the events required to trigger an object to perform its assigned tasks.

5. Listed below are the six steps you should follow when creating an OO application. Put the steps in the proper order by placing a number (1 through 6) on the line to the left of the step.

    _____ Test and debug the application.

    _____ Build the user interface.

    _____ Code the application.

    _____ Assemble the documentation.

    _____ Plan the application.

    _____ Meet with the client.

Lesson A Exercises

INTRODUCTORY

1. The annual property tax in Richardson County is $1.50 for each $100 of a property's assessed value. The county clerk wants you to create an application that will display the property tax after he enters the property's assessed value. Prepare a TOE chart ordered by task, and then rearrange the TOE chart so that it is ordered by object. Be sure to include buttons that allow the user to both clear and print the screen. Draw a sketch of the user interface. (You will create the interface in Lesson B's Exercise 1 and then code the application in Lesson C's Exercise 1.)

2. All employees at Jordan Sports Store are paid based on an annual salary rather than an hourly wage. However, some employees are paid weekly, while others are paid every other week. Employees paid weekly receive 52 paychecks; employees paid every other week receive 26 paychecks. The payroll clerk wants you to create an application that allows her to enter an employee's annual salary. The application should display both the weekly gross pay and the biweekly gross pay. Prepare a TOE chart ordered by task, and then rearrange the TOE chart so that it is ordered by object. Be sure to include buttons that allow the user to both clear and print the screen. Draw a sketch of the user interface. (You will create the interface in Lesson B's Exercise 2 and then code the application in Lesson C's Exercise 2.)

INTRODUCTORY

3. Cranston Berries sells three types of berries: strawberries, blueberries, and raspberries. Sales have been booming this year and are expected to increase next year. The sales manager wants you to create an application that allows him to enter the projected increase (expressed as a decimal number) in berry sales for the following year. He will also enter the current year's sales for each type of berry. The application should display the projected sales total for each berry type. For example, if the projected increase in berry sales is .05 (the decimal equivalent of 5%) and the current sales amount for strawberries is $25,000, the projected sales total of strawberries for the following year is $26,250. Prepare a TOE chart ordered by task, and then rearrange the TOE chart so that it is ordered by object. Be sure to include buttons that allow the user to both clear and print the screen. (You will create the interface in Lesson B's Exercise 3 and then code the application in Lesson C's Exercise 3.)

INTRODUCTORY

LESSON B

After studying Lesson B, you should be able to:

- Build the user interface using your TOE chart and sketch
- Follow the Windows standards regarding the use of graphics, fonts, and color
- Set a control's BorderStyle, AutoSize, and TextAlign properties
- Add a text box to a form
- Lock the controls on the form
- Assign access keys to controls
- Set the TabIndex property

Building the User Interface

In Lesson A, you planned the Meyer's Purple Bakery application. Planning the application is the second of the six steps involved in creating an OO application. Now you are ready to tackle the third step, which is to build the user interface. You will use the TOE chart and sketch you created in the planning step as guides when building the interface, which involves placing the appropriate controls on the form and setting the applicable properties of the controls.

To save you time, the VB2015\Chap02\Bakery Solution folder contains a partially completed application for the bakery. When you open the solution, you will find that most of the user interface has been created and most of the properties have been set. You will complete the interface in this lesson.

START HERE

To open the partially completed application:

1. If necessary, start Visual Studio 2015 and open the Solution Explorer window. Open the Bakery Solution (Bakery Solution.sln) file contained in the VB2015\Chap02\Bakery Solution folder. If necessary, open the designer window.

2. Permanently display the Properties and Toolbox windows, and then auto-hide the Solution Explorer window. Figure 2-13 shows the partially completed interface, which resembles the sketch shown in Figure 2-11 in Lesson A.

Figure 2-13 Partially completed interface for the bakery application

The application's user interface follows the GUI guidelines covered in Lesson A. The information is arranged vertically, and the controls are aligned wherever possible. Each text box and button, as well as each label control that displays program output, is labeled so the user knows the control's purpose. The text contained in the identifying labels is entered using sentence capitalization. In addition, the text ends with a colon and is left-aligned within the label. The identifying labels are positioned to the left of the controls they identify. Each button's caption is entered using book title capitalization. The button captions and identifying labels appear on one line and do not exceed the three-word limit. Because the buttons are stacked in the interface, each button has the same height and width, and the most commonly used button (Calculate) is placed at the top of the button group.

When building the user interface, keep in mind that you want to create a screen that no one notices. Interfaces that contain a lot of different colors, fonts, and graphics may get "oohs" and "aahs" during their initial use, but they become tiresome after a while. The most important point to remember is that the interface should not distract the user from doing his or her work. The next three sections provide some guidelines to follow regarding the use of these elements in an interface.

The graphics, font, and color guidelines do not pertain to game applications.

Including Graphics in the User Interface

The human eye is attracted to pictures before text, so use graphics sparingly. Designers typically include graphics to either emphasize or clarify a portion of the screen. However, a graphic can also be used merely for aesthetic purposes, as long as it is small and placed in a location that does not distract the user. The small graphic in the Meyer's Purple Bakery interface is included for aesthetics only. The graphic is purposely located in the upper-left corner of the interface, which is where you want the user's eye to be drawn first anyway. (Remember that the most important information usually begins there.) The graphic adds a personal touch to the sales receipt form without distracting the user.

GUI DESIGN TIP Adding Graphics

- Use graphics sparingly. If the graphic is used solely for aesthetics, use a small graphic and place it in a location that will not distract the user.

Selecting Fonts for the Interface

As you learned in Chapter 1, an object's Font property determines the type, style, and size of the font used to display the object's text. You should use only one font type (typically Segoe UI) for all of the text in the interface, and use no more than two different font sizes. In addition, avoid using italics and underlining in an interface because both font styles make text difficult to read. The use of bold text should be limited to titles, headings, and key items that you want to emphasize.

Adding Color to the Interface

The human eye is attracted to color before black and white; therefore, use color sparingly in an interface. It is a good practice to build the interface using black, white, and gray first, and then add color only if you have a good reason to do so. Keep the following three points in mind when deciding whether to include color in an interface:

1. People who have some form of either color blindness or color confusion will have trouble distinguishing colors.

2. Color is very subjective: A color that looks pretty to you may be hideous to someone else.

3. A color may have a different meaning in a different culture.

Usually, it is best to use black text on a white, off-white, or light gray background because dark text on a light background is the easiest to read. You should never use a dark color for the background or a light color for the text. This is because a dark background is hard on the eyes, and light-colored text can appear blurry.

If you are going to include color in an interface, limit the number of colors to three, not including white, black, and gray. Be sure that the colors you choose complement each other. Although color can be used to identify an important element in the interface, you should never use it as the only means of identification. In the bakery application's interface, for example, the colored box helps the salesclerk quickly locate the total sales amount. However, color is not the only means of identifying the contents of that box; the box also has an identifying label (Total sales:).

The BorderStyle, AutoSize, and TextAlign Properties

A control's border is determined by its **BorderStyle property**, which can be set to None, FixedSingle, or Fixed3D. Controls with a BorderStyle property set to None have no border. Setting the BorderStyle property to FixedSingle surrounds the control with a thin line, and setting it to Fixed3D gives the control a three-dimensional appearance. In most cases, a text box's BorderStyle property should be left at the default setting: Fixed3D. The BorderStyle property for each text box in the bakery application's interface follows this convention.

The appropriate setting for a label control's BorderStyle property depends on the control's purpose. Label controls that identify other controls (such as those that identify text boxes) should have a BorderStyle property setting of None, which is the default setting. Label controls that display program output, such as the result of a calculation, typically have a BorderStyle property setting of FixedSingle. You should avoid setting a label control's BorderStyle property to Fixed3D because in Windows applications, a control with a three-dimensional appearance implies that it can accept user input.

A label control's **AutoSize property** determines whether the control automatically sizes to fit its current contents. The appropriate setting depends on the label's purpose. Label controls that identify other controls use the default setting: True. However, you typically use False for the AutoSize property of label controls that display program output.

A label control's **TextAlign property** determines the alignment of the text within the label. The TextAlign property can be set to nine different values, such as TopLeft, MiddleCenter, and BottomRight.

In the next set of steps, you will change the AutoSize, BorderStyle, and TextAlign properties of the lblTotalSales control. (The AutoSize, BorderStyle, and TextAlign properties of the other label that displays program output have already been set.) You will also delete the contents of the control's Text property and then size the control to match the height of the lblTotalItems control.

To change the properties of the lblTotalSales control and then size the control: START HERE

1. Click the **lblTotalSales** control. Set the AutoSize and BorderStyle properties to **False** and **FixedSingle**, respectively.

2. Click **TextAlign** in the Properties list and then click the **list arrow** in the Settings box. Click the center button to change the property's setting to MiddleCenter.

3. Click **Text** in the Properties list, press the **Backspace** key, and then press **Enter**.

4. Click the **lblTotalItems** control and then Ctrl+click the **lblTotalSales** control. Click **Format** on the menu bar, point to **Make Same Size**, and then click **Height**.

5. Click the **form** to deselect the two labels.

GUI DESIGN TIP Setting the BorderStyle Property of a Text Box or Label

- Keep the BorderStyle property of text boxes at the default setting: Fixed3D.

- Keep the BorderStyle property of identifying labels at the default setting: None.

- Use FixedSingle for the BorderStyle property of labels that display program output, such as the result of a calculation.

- Avoid setting a label control's BorderStyle property to Fixed3D because in Windows applications, a control with a three-dimensional appearance implies that it can accept user input.

GUI DESIGN TIP Setting the AutoSize and TextAlign Properties of a Label

- Keep the AutoSize property of identifying labels at the default setting: True.

- In most cases, use False for the AutoSize property of label controls that display program output.

- Use the TextAlign property to specify the alignment of the text within the label.

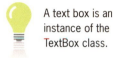

A text box is an instance of the TextBox class.

Adding a Text Box to the Form

As mentioned earlier, a text box provides an area in the form in which the user can enter data. Missing from the bakery application's interface is the text box for entering the number of muffins sold. You will add the missing text box in the next set of steps.

START HERE

To add the missing text box to the form:

1. Use the TextBox tool to add a text box to the form. Position the text box immediately below the txtDonuts control. Change the text box's name to **txtMuffins** and press **Enter**.

2. Click the **txtDonuts** control and then Ctrl+click the **txtMuffins** control. Click **Format**, point to **Make Same Size**, and then click **Both**.

3. You can align the txtMuffins control using either the Format menu or the snap lines. You will use the snap lines. Click the **form** to deselect the text boxes. Place your mouse pointer on the txtMuffins control, and then press and hold down the left mouse button as you drag the control to the location shown in Figure 2-14. The blue snap lines help you align the txtMuffins control with the txtDonuts control. The pink snap line allows you to align the text in the txtMuffins control with the text in its identifying label.

Figure 2-14   Snap lines shown in the interface

4. When the txtMuffins control is in the correct location, release the mouse button.

Locking the Controls on a Form

After placing all of the controls in their appropriate locations, it is a good idea to lock the controls on the form. Locking the controls prevents them from being moved inadvertently as you work in the IDE. You can lock the controls by clicking the form (or any control on the form) and then clicking the Lock Controls option on the Format menu; you can follow the same procedure to unlock the controls. You can also lock and unlock the controls by right-clicking the form (or any control on the form) and then clicking Lock Controls on the context menu. When a control is locked, a small lock appears in the upper-left corner of the control.

 A locked control can be deleted. It can also be moved by setting its Location property.

To lock the controls on the form and then save the solution:

START HERE

1. Right-click the **form** and then click **Lock Controls**. A small lock appears in the upper-left corner of the form.

2. Save the solution. Try dragging one of the controls to a different location on the form. You will not be able to do so.

Assigning Access Keys

In Figure 2-14, the text in many of the controls contains an underlined letter. The underlined letter is called an **access key**, and it allows the user to select an object using the Alt key in combination with a letter or number. For example, you can select the Exit button in the bakery application's interface by pressing Alt+x because the letter x is the Exit button's access key. Access keys are not case sensitive. Therefore, you can select the Exit button by pressing either Alt+x or Alt+X. If you do not see the underlined access keys while an application is running, you can show them temporarily by pressing the Alt key. (To always display access keys, see the Summary section at the end of this lesson.)

In an interface, you should assign access keys to each control that can accept user input, such as text boxes and buttons. This is because the user can enter information in a text box and click a button. The only exceptions to this rule are the OK and Cancel buttons, which typically do not have access keys in Windows applications. It is important to assign access keys for the following reasons:

• They allow users to work with the application even when their mouse becomes inoperative.

• They allow users who are fast typists to keep their hands on the keyboard.

• They allow people who cannot work with a mouse, such as people with disabilities, to use the application.

You assign an access key by including an ampersand (&) in the control's caption or identifying label. If the control is a button, you include the ampersand in the button's Text property, which is where a button's caption is stored. If the control is a text box, you include the ampersand in the Text property of its identifying label. (As you will learn later in this lesson, you must also set the TabIndex properties of the text box and its identifying label appropriately.) You enter the ampersand to the immediate left of the character you want to designate as the access key.

Each access key in an interface should be unique. The first choice for an access key is the first letter of the caption or identifying label, unless another letter provides a more meaningful association. For example, the letter x is the access key for an Exit button because it provides a more meaningful association than does the letter E. If you can't use the first letter (perhaps because it is already used as the access key for another control) and no other letter provides a more meaningful association, then use a distinctive consonant in the caption or label. The last choices for an access key are a vowel or a number.

Missing from the interface shown in Figure 2-14 are the access keys for the Calculate button and Date text box. You will assign those access keys in the next set of steps. However, notice that the Total items: and Total sales: labels also do not have access keys. This is because those labels do not identify controls that accept user input; rather, they identify other label controls (lblTotalItems and lblTotalSales). Recall that users cannot access label controls while an application is running, so it is inappropriate to assign an access key to their identifying labels.

START HERE ▶

To assign access keys to the Calculate button and Date text box:

1. Click the **Calculate** button. Change the button's Text property to **&Calculate** and then press **Enter**. The letter C in the button's caption is now underlined.

2. Next, change the Date: label's Text property to **Da&te:** and then press **Enter**.

GUI DESIGN TIP Assigning Access Keys

- Assign a unique access key to each control that can accept user input.

- When assigning an access key to a control, use the first letter of the control's caption or identifying label, unless another letter provides a more meaningful association. If you can't use the first letter and no other letter provides a more meaningful association, then use a distinctive consonant. As a last resort, use a vowel or a number.

Controlling the Tab Order

When a text box has the focus, an insertion point appears inside it. When a button has the focus, a dotted rectangle appears inside its darkened border.

While you are creating the interface, each control's **TabIndex property** contains a number that represents the order in which the control was added to the form. The first control added to a form has a TabIndex value of 0, the second control has a TabIndex value of 1, and so on. The TabIndex values determine the **tab order**, which is the order in which each control receives the **focus** when the user either presses the Tab key or employs an access key while an application is running. A control whose TabIndex is 2 will receive the focus immediately after the control whose TabIndex is 1, and so on. When a control has the focus, it can accept user input. Not all controls have a TabIndex property; a PictureBox control, for example, does not have a TabIndex property.

Most times, you will need to reset the TabIndex values for an interface. This is because controls rarely are added to a form in the desired tab order. To determine the appropriate TabIndex values, you first make a list of the controls that can accept user input. The list should reflect the order in which the user will want to access the controls. In the bakery application's interface, the user typically will want to access the txtDate control first, followed by the txtDonuts control, the txtMuffins control, the btnCalc control, and so on.

If a control that accepts user input is identified by a label control, you also include the label control in the list. (A text box is an example of a control that accepts user input and is identified by a label control.) You place the name of the label control immediately above the name of the control it identifies in the list. In the bakery application's interface, the Label2 control (which contains Date:) identifies the txtDate control. Therefore, Label2 should appear immediately above txtDate in the list.

The names of controls that do not accept user input and are not used to identify controls that do should be placed at the bottom of the list; these names do not need to appear in any specific order. After listing the control names, you then assign a TabIndex value to each control in the list, beginning with the number 0. If a control does not have a TabIndex property, you do not assign it a TabIndex value in the list. You can tell whether a control has a TabIndex property by viewing its Properties list.

Figure 2-15 shows the list of controls and TabIndex values for the bakery application's interface. Notice that the TabIndex value assigned to each text box's identifying label is one number less than the value assigned to the text box itself. This is necessary for a text box's access key (which is defined in its identifying label) to work correctly.

Controls that accept user input, along with their identifying labels	TabIndex value
Label2 (Date:)	0
txtDate	1
Label3 (Doughnuts:)	2
txtDonuts	3
Label4 (Muffins:)	4
txtMuffins	5
btnCalc	6
btnPrint	7
btnClear	8
btnExit	9
Other controls	
Label1 (Sales Receipt)	10
Label5 (Total items:)	11
Label6 (Total sales:)	12
lblTotalItems	13
lblTotalSales	14
PictureBox1	N/A

Figure 2-15 List of controls and TabIndex values

You can set each control's TabIndex property using either the Properties window or the Tab Order option on the View menu. The Tab Order option is available only when the designer window is the active window.

To set the TabIndex values and then verify the tab order:

START HERE

1. Click the **form** to make the designer window the active window. Click **View** on the menu bar and then click **Tab Order**. The current TabIndex values appear in blue boxes on the form. (The picture box does not have a TabIndex property.)

2. According to Figure 2-15, the first control in the tab order should be the Label2 control, which displays the Date: text. Click the **blue box that contains the number 1**. (You can also click the Label2 control directly.) The number 0 replaces the number 1 in the box, and the color of the box changes from blue to white to indicate that you have set the control's TabIndex value.

3. The second control in the tab order should be the txtDate control, which currently has a TabIndex value of 6. Click the **blue box that contains the number 6**. The number 1 replaces the number 6 in the box, and the color of the box changes from blue to white.

4. Use the information shown in Figure 2-16 to set the TabIndex properties for the remaining controls, which have TabIndex values of 2 through 14. Be sure to set the values in numerical order. If you make a mistake, press the Esc key to remove the TabIndex boxes from the form, and then repeat Steps 1 through 4. When you have finished setting all of the TabIndex values, the color of the boxes will automatically change from white to blue, as shown in Figure 2-16.

Figure 2-16   TabIndex boxes showing the correct TabIndex values

5. Press **Esc** (or click **View** and then click **Tab Order**) to remove the TabIndex boxes from the form.

6. Save the solution, and then start the application. If the access keys do not appear in the interface, press the **Alt** key. When you start an application, the computer sends the focus to the control whose TabIndex is 0. In the bakery application's interface, that control is the Label2 (Date:) control. However, because label controls cannot receive the focus, the computer sends the focus to the next control in the tab order sequence (txtDate). The blinking insertion point indicates that the text box has the focus and is ready to receive input from you. See Figure 2-17.

Figure 2-17   Result of starting the bakery application

7. Type **7/25/2016** in the Date text box. The information you entered is recorded in the text box's Text property.

8. In Windows applications, the Tab key moves the focus forward, and the Shift+Tab key combination moves the focus backward. Press **Tab** to move the focus to the Doughnuts text box, and then press **Shift+Tab** to move the focus back to the Date text box.

9. Now use the Tab key to verify the tab order of the controls in the interface. Press **Tab**, slowly, three times. The focus moves to the Doughnuts text box, then to the Muffins text box, and then to the Calculate button. Notice that when a button has the focus, a dotted rectangle appears inside its darkened border. Press **Tab**, slowly, three more times. The focus moves to the Print Receipt button, then to the Clear Screen button, and finally to the Exit button.

10. Pressing the Enter key when a button has the focus invokes the button's Click event, causing the computer to process any code contained in the Click event procedure. Press **Enter** to have the computer process the btnExit_Click procedure, which contains the `Me.Close()` instruction. The application ends.

11. You can also move the focus using a text box's access key. Start the application. If the access keys do not appear in the interface, press the **Alt** key to display them. Next, press **Alt+m** to move the focus to the Muffins text box. Then press **Alt+t** to move the focus to the Date text box. Finally, press **Alt+d** to move the focus to the Doughnuts text box.

12. Unlike pressing a text box's access key, which moves the focus, pressing a button's access key invokes the button's Click event. Press **Alt+x** to invoke the Exit button's Click event, which ends the application.

13. Close the solution.

GUI DESIGN TIP Using the TabIndex Property to Control the Focus

- Assign a TabIndex value (starting with 0) to each control in the interface, except for controls that do not have a TabIndex property. The TabIndex values should reflect the order in which the user will want to access the controls.

- To allow users to access a text box using the keyboard, assign an access key to the text box's identifying label. Set the identifying label's TabIndex property to a value that is one number less than the value stored in the text box's TabIndex property.

Lesson B Summary

- To use appropriate graphics, fonts, and colors in an interface:

  Refer to the GUI guidelines listed in Appendix B for this chapter's lesson.

- To specify a control's border:

  Set the control's BorderStyle property.

- To specify whether a label control should automatically size to fit its current contents:

  Set the label control's AutoSize property.

- To specify the alignment of the text within a label control:

  Set the label control's TextAlign property.

- To lock/unlock the controls on the form:

  Right-click the form or any control on the form, and then select Lock Controls on the context menu. You can also click the Lock Controls option on the Format menu.

- To assign an access key to a control:

  Type an ampersand (&) in the Text property of the control or identifying label. The ampersand should appear to the immediate left of the character that you want to designate as the access key.

- To provide keyboard access to a text box:

  Assign an access key to the text box's identifying label. Set the identifying label's TabIndex property to a value that is one number less than the text box's TabIndex value.

- To employ an access key:

  If necessary, press the Alt key to display the access keys, and then release the key. Press and hold down the Alt key as you tap the access key.

- To set the tab order:

  Set each control's TabIndex property to a number (starting with 0) that represents the order in which the control should receive the focus. You can set the TabIndex property using either the Properties window or the Tab Order option on the View menu.

- To always display access keys:

  Open the Windows Control Panel, and then click Appearance and Personalization. In the Ease of Access Center section, click Turn on easy access keys. Select the Underline keyboard shortcuts and access keys check box, and then click the OK button. Close the Control Panel window.

Lesson B Key Terms

Access key—the underlined character in an object's identifying label or caption; allows the user to select the object using the Alt key in combination with the underlined character

AutoSize property—determines whether a control automatically sizes to fit its current contents

BorderStyle property—determines the appearance of a control's border

Focus—indicates that a control is ready to accept user input

Tab order—the order in which each control receives the focus when the user either presses the Tab key or employs an access key while an application is running

TabIndex property—specifies a control's position in the tab order

TextAlign property—determines the alignment of the text within a control

Lesson B Review Questions

1. Which property determines the tab order for the controls in an interface?

    a. SetOrder

    b. SetTab

    c. TabIndex

    d. TabOrder

2. Which letter should always be used for the Exit button's access key?

    a. E

    b. x

    c. i

    d. t

3. A control's access key is specified in which of its properties?

    a. Access

    b. Caption

    c. Key

    d. Text

4. Which of the following specifies the letter D as the access key?

    a. &Display

    b. #Display

    c. ^Display

    d. D&isplay

5. Explain the method for providing keyboard access to a text box.

Lesson B Exercises

1. In this exercise, you will continue creating the Richardson County application from Lesson A's Exercise 1. Open the VB2015\Chap02\Richardson Solution\Richardson Solution (Richardson Solution.sln) file. If necessary, open the designer window. Figure 2-18 shows the completed interface. Add the missing txtAssessed and lblTax controls to the form. Set the lblTax control's TextAlign property to MiddleCenter. Lock the controls on the form. Assign the access keys (shown in the figure) to the text box and buttons. Set the TabIndex values appropriately. Save the solution and then start the application. Verify that the tab order is correct. Also verify that the access keys work appropriately. Use the Exit button to end the application. (You will code the Calculate, Print, and Clear Screen buttons in Lesson C's Exercise 1.)

INTRODUCTORY

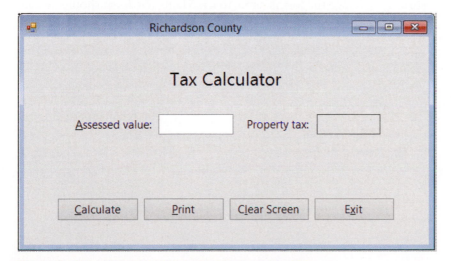

Figure 2-18   Richardson County application's interface

2. In this exercise, you will continue creating the Jordan Sports Store application from Lesson A's Exercise 2. Create a Visual Basic Windows application. Use the following names for the solution and project, respectively: Jordan Solution and Jordan Project. Save the application in the VB2015\Chap02 folder. Change the form file's name to Main Form.vb. Change the form's name to frmMain. The form should be centered on the screen when it first appears; set the appropriate property. Create the interface shown in Figure 2-19. Use the following names for the text box, labels, and buttons: txtAnnual, lblWeekly, lblBiweekly, btnCalc, btnPrint, btnClear, and btnExit. (Or, use the names from the TOE chart you created in Lesson A's Exercise 2.) The contents of the lblWeekly and lblBiweekly controls should be centered; set the appropriate property. Lock the controls on the form. Set the TabIndex values appropriately. The Exit button should end the application when it is clicked; code the appropriate event procedure. Save the solution, and then start the application. Verify that the tab order is correct. Also verify that the access keys work properly. Use the Exit button to end the application. (You will code the Calculate, Print, and Clear buttons in Lesson C's Exercise 2.)

Figure 2-19 Jordan Sports Store application's interface

3. In this exercise, you will continue creating the Cranston Berries application from Lesson A's Exercise 3. Create a Visual Basic Windows application. Use the following names for the solution and project, respectively: Cranston Solution and Cranston Project. Save the application in the VB2015\Chap02 folder. Change the form file's name to Main Form.vb. Change the form's name to frmMain. The form should be centered on the screen when it first appears; set the appropriate property. Create the interface shown in Figure 2-20. Use the following names for the text boxes, labels, and buttons: txtProjIncrease, txtStraw, txtBlue, txtRasp, lblStraw, lblBlue, lblRasp, btnCalc, btnPrint, btnClear, and btnExit. (Or, use the names from the TOE chart you created in Lesson A's Exercise 3.) The contents of the three label controls that display the projected sales should be right-aligned; set the appropriate property. Lock the controls on the form. Set the TabIndex values appropriately. The Exit button should end the application when it is clicked; code the appropriate event procedure. Save the solution and then start the application. Verify that the tab order is correct. Also verify that the access keys work properly. Use the Exit button to end the application. (You will code the Calculate, Print, and Clear buttons in Lesson C's Exercise 3.)

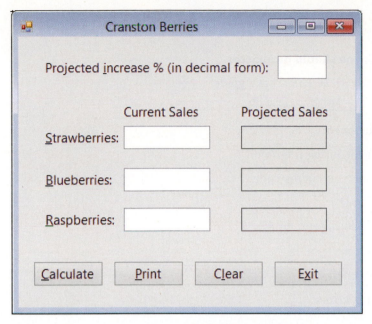

Figure 2-20   Cranston Berries application's interface

INTRODUCTORY

4. Open the Age Solution (Age Solution.sln) file contained in the VB2015\Chap02\Age Solution folder. If necessary, open the designer window. The application allows you to enter the year you were born and the current year. When it is coded, the Calculate button will calculate your age by subtracting your birth year from the current year. Lay out and organize the interface so that it follows all of the GUI design guidelines you have learned so far. (Refer to Appendix B for a listing of the guidelines covered in Chapter 1 and in Lessons A and B of Chapter 2.) Lock the controls on the form. Code the Exit button's Click event procedure so it ends the application. Save the solution and then start the application. Verify that the tab order is correct. Also verify that the access keys work properly. Use the Exit button to end the application. Close the solution. (You will code the Calculate and Print buttons in Lesson C's Exercise 4.)

LESSON C

After studying Lesson C, you should be able to:

- Code an application using its TOE chart as a guide
- Plan an object's code using either pseudocode or a flowchart
- Write an assignment statement
- Send the focus to a control during run time
- Include internal documentation in the code
- Print an interface from code
- Show and hide a control during run time
- Write arithmetic expressions
- Use the Val and Format functions
- Locate and correct syntax errors

Coding the Application

In Lessons A and B, you created a TOE chart and user interface for the Meyer's Purple Bakery application. The user interface and TOE chart are shown in Figures 2-21 and 2-22, respectively.

Figure 2-21   Bakery application's interface from Lesson B

Task	Object	Event
1. Calculate total items sold and total sales amount 2. Display total items sold and total sales amount in lblTotalItems and lblTotalSales	btnCalc	Click
Print the sales receipt	btnPrint	Click
End the application	btnExit	Click
Clear the screen for the next sale	btnClear	Click
Display total items sold (from btnCalc)	lblTotalItems	None
Display total sales amount (from btnCalc)	lblTotalSales	None
Get and display the sales information	txtDate, txtDonuts, txtMuffins	None

Figure 2-22   TOE chart (ordered by object) for the bakery application

After planning an application and building its user interface, you then can begin coding the application. You code an application so that the objects in the interface perform their assigned tasks when the appropriate event occurs. The objects and events that need to be coded, as well as the tasks assigned to each object and event, are listed in the application's TOE chart. The TOE chart in Figure 2-22 indicates that only the four buttons require coding; they are the only objects with an event listed in the third column of the chart.

Before you begin coding an object's event procedure, you should plan it. Many programmers use planning tools such as pseudocode and flowcharts. You do not need to create both a flowchart and pseudocode for a procedure; you need to use only one of these planning tools. The tool you use is really a matter of personal preference. For simple procedures, pseudocode works just fine. When a procedure becomes more complex, however, the procedure's steps may be easier to understand in a flowchart. The programmer uses either the procedure's pseudocode or its flowchart as a guide when coding the procedure.

Using Pseudocode to Plan a Procedure

Pseudocode uses short phrases to describe the steps a procedure must take to accomplish its goal. Even though the word *pseudocode* might be unfamiliar to you, you have already written pseudocode without even realizing it. Consider the last time you gave written directions to someone. You wrote each direction down on paper, in your own words; your directions were a form of pseudocode.

Figure 2-23 shows the pseudocode for the procedures that need to be coded in the bakery application. Notice that the btnClear control's Click event procedure doesn't clear the date entered in the txtDate control, and it sends the focus to the txtDonut control rather than to the txtDate control. This is because after the salesclerk enters the date for the first sale of the day, there is no reason to have him or her enter it again for subsequent sales made on the same day.

<u>btnExit Click event procedure</u>
end the application

<u>btnCalc Click event procedure</u>
1. calculate total items sold = doughnuts sold + muffins sold
2. calculate total sales = total items sold * item price
3. display total items sold and total sales in lblTotalItems and lblTotalSales

<u>btnPrint Click event procedure</u>
print the sales receipt

<u>btnClear Click event procedure</u>
1. clear the contents of the txtDonuts and txtMuffins text boxes
2. clear the contents of the lblTotalItems and lblTotalSales controls
3. send the focus to the txtDonuts control so the user can begin entering the next sale

Figure 2-23 Pseudocode for the bakery application

Using a Flowchart to Plan a Procedure

Unlike pseudocode, which consists of short phrases, a **flowchart** uses standardized symbols to show the steps a procedure must follow to reach its goal. Figure 2-24 shows the flowcharts for the procedures that need to be coded in the bakery application. The logic illustrated in the flowcharts is the same as the logic shown in the pseudocode in Figure 2-23.

The flowcharts contain three different symbols: an oval, a rectangle, and a parallelogram. The oval symbol is called the **start/stop symbol**. The start and stop ovals indicate the beginning and end, respectively, of the flowchart. The rectangles are called **process symbols**. You use the process symbol to represent tasks such as making assignments and calculations. The parallelogram in a flowchart is called the **input/output symbol**, and it is used to represent input tasks (such as getting information from the user) and output tasks (such as displaying information). The parallelograms in Figure 2-24 represent output tasks. The lines connecting the symbols in a flowchart are called **flowlines**.

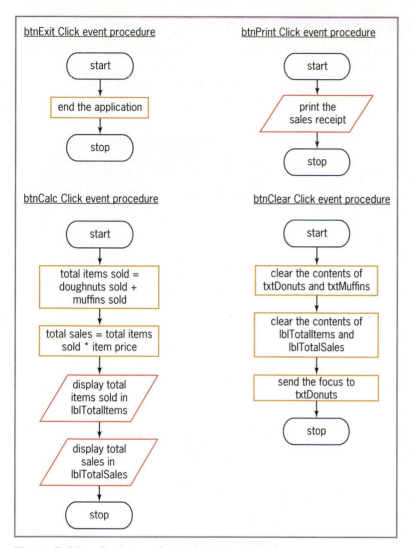

Figure 2-24 Flowcharts for the bakery application

Coding the btnClear_Click Procedure

According to its pseudocode and flowchart, the btnClear_Click procedure should clear the Text property of two of the text boxes and two of the labels in the interface. It then should send the focus to the txtDonuts control. You can clear the Text property of an object by assigning a zero-length string to it. A **string** is defined as zero or more characters enclosed in quotation marks. The word "Jones" is a string. Likewise, "45" is a string, but 45 (without the quotes) is a number. "Jones" is a string with a length of five because there are five characters between the quotation marks. "45" is a string with a length of two because there are two characters between the quotation marks. Following this logic, a **zero-length string**, also called an **empty string**, is a set of quotation marks with nothing between them, like this: "". Assigning a zero-length string to the Text property of an object during run time removes the contents of the object. You can also clear an object's Text property by assigning the value **String.Empty** to it while an application is running. When you do this, the computer assigns an empty string to the Text property, thereby removing its contents.

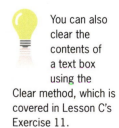

You can also clear the contents of a text box using the Clear method, which is covered in Lesson C's Exercise 11.

Assigning a Value to a Property During Run Time

In Chapter 1, you learned how to use the Properties window to set an object's properties during design time, which is when you are building the interface. You can also set an object's properties during run time by using an assignment statement. An **assignment statement** is one of many different types of Visual Basic instructions. Its purpose is to assign a value to something (such as to the property of an object) while an application is running.

The syntax of an assignment statement is shown in Figure 2-25 along with examples of using the syntax. In the syntax, *object* and *property* are the names of the object and property, respectively, to which you want the value of the *expression* assigned. The expression can be a string, a keyword, a number, or a calculation. You use a period to separate the object name from the property name. Recall that the period is the dot member access operator. In this case, the operator indicates that the *property* is a member of the *object*. You use an equal sign between the *object.property* information and the *expression*. The equal sign in an assignment statement is called the **assignment operator**. When the computer processes an assignment statement, it assigns the value of the expression that appears on the right side of the assignment operator to the object and property that appear on the left side of the assignment operator.

Assigning a Value to a Property During Run Time

Syntax
object.*property* = *expression*

Examples

`txtCity.Text = "Akron"`	assigns the string "Akron" to the txtCity's Text property
`lblSum.Text = String.Empty`	assigns the empty string to the lblSum's Text property
`picLogo.Visible = False`	assigns the Boolean value False to the picLogo's Visible property
`lblDue.Width = 120`	assigns the number 120 to the lblDue's Width property
`lblTax.Text = 100 * .05`	multiplies 100 by .05 and then assigns the result to the lblTax's Text property

---

Figure 2-25   Syntax and examples of assigning a value to a property during run time

You will use assignment statements to code the btnClear_Click procedure. According to its pseudocode and flowchart (shown earlier in Figures 2-23 and 2-24, respectively), the procedure should clear the contents of the txtDonuts and txtMuffins text boxes. You can do this by using either the *textbox*.`Text = String.Empty` instruction or the *textbox*.`Text = ""` instruction, where *textbox* is the name of the appropriate text box.

START HERE ▶ **To begin coding the btnClear_Click procedure:**

1. If necessary, start Visual Studio 2015 and open the Solution Explorer window. Open the Bakery Solution (Bakery Solution.sln) file from Lesson B.

2. Auto-hide the Solution Explorer window. If necessary, auto-hide the Properties and Toolbox windows.

3. Open the Code Editor window, which contains the btnExit_Click procedure. Open the code template for the btnClear_Click procedure. Press **Enter** to insert a blank line below the procedure header.

4. You will use the Code Editor's IntelliSense feature to enter the `txtDonuts.Text = String.Empty` assignment statement in the procedure. Type the five letters **txtdo** to

highlight txtDonuts in the list of choices, and then press **Tab** to enter txtDonuts in the assignment statement.

5. Now type **.** (a period) to display a listing of the properties and methods of the txtDonuts control. Type **te** to highlight Text in the list. At this point, you can either press the Tab key to enter the Text property in the assignment statement, or you can type the character that follows Text in the statement. In this case, the next character is the assignment operator. Type = to enter the Text property and the assignment operator in the statement.

6. Next, type **stri** to highlight String in the list, and then type **.e** to highlight Empty. Press **Enter**. See Figure 2-26.

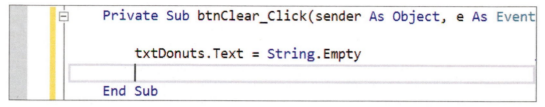

```
    Private Sub btnClear_Click(sender As Object, e As Event

        txtDonuts.Text = String.Empty

    End Sub
```

Figure 2-26   First assignment statement entered in the procedure

When entering code, you can type the names of commands, objects, and properties in lowercase letters. When you move to the next line in the Code Editor window, the Code Editor automatically changes your code to reflect the proper capitalization of those elements. This provides a quick way of verifying that you entered an object's name and property correctly, and that you entered the code using the correct syntax. If the capitalization does not change, it means that the Code Editor does not recognize the object, command, or property. In subsequent steps in this book, you will always be given the complete instruction to enter, including the appropriate capitalization. Keep in mind that you can either type the instruction on your own or use the IntelliSense feature to enter the instruction.

To continue coding the btnClear_Click procedure: START HERE

1. Type **txtMuffins.Text = String.Empty** and press **Enter**.

2. Next, the procedure should clear the contents of the lblTotalItems and lblTotalSales controls. Enter the following two assignment statements. Press **Enter** twice after typing the last statement.

   lblTotalItems.Text = String.Empty
   lblTotalSales.Text = String.Empty

The last step in the procedure's pseudocode and flowchart is to send the focus to the txtDonuts control. You can accomplish this task using the Focus method. Recall that a method is a predefined Visual Basic procedure that you can call (or invoke) when needed.

Using the Focus Method

You can use the **Focus method** to move the focus to a specified control while an application is running. As you learned in Lesson B, a control that has the focus can accept user input. The Focus method's syntax is *object*.Focus(), in which *object* is the name of the object to which you want the focus sent.

To enter the Focus method in the btnClear_Click procedure: START HERE

1. Type **txtDonuts.Focus()** and press **Enter**. Then save the solution.

Internally Documenting the Program Code

It is a good practice to include comments, called internal documentation, as reminders in the Code Editor window. Programmers use comments to indicate a procedure's purpose and also to explain various sections of a procedure's code. Including comments in your code will make the code more readable and easier to understand by anyone viewing it. You create a comment in Visual Basic by placing an apostrophe (') before the text that represents the comment. The computer ignores everything that appears after the apostrophe on that line. Although it is not required, some programmers use a space to separate the apostrophe from the comment text; you will follow that convention in this book.

START HERE

To add comments to the btnClear_Click procedure:

1. Click the **blank line** above the first assignment statement. Type ' **prepare screen for the next sale** (be sure to type the apostrophe followed by a space) and press **Enter**. Notice that comments appear in a different color from the rest of the code.

2. Click the **blank line** above the statement containing the Focus method. Type ' **send the focus to the Doughnuts box** and then click the **blank line** above the procedure's End Sub clause. See Figure 2-27.

```
Private Sub btnClear_Click(sender As Object, e As Event
    ' prepare screen for the next sale

    txtDonuts.Text = String.Empty
    txtMuffins.Text = String.Empty
    lblTotalItems.Text = String.Empty
    lblTotalSales.Text = String.Empty
    ' send the focus to the Doughnuts box
    txtDonuts.Focus()


End Sub
```

Figure 2-27   btnClear_Click procedure

It is a good idea to test a procedure after you have coded it because, by doing so, you will know where to look if an error occurs.

START HERE

To test the btnClear_Click procedure:

1. Save the solution and then start the application. Type **5** in each of the three text boxes. You haven't coded the Calculate button yet, so the Total items and Total sales boxes are empty at this point. Therefore, you will only be able to observe whether the Clear Screen button clears the Doughnuts and Muffins text boxes and moves the focus appropriately. You will need to test the Clear Screen button again after the Calculate button is coded.

2. Click the **Clear Screen** button to process the instructions contained in its Click event procedure. The instructions remove the contents of the Doughnuts and Muffins text boxes (and also the contents of the two labels, which are currently empty) and then send the focus to the Doughnuts box. Click the **Exit** button to end the application.

Many programmers also use comments to document the project's name and purpose, the programmer's name, and the date the code was either created or modified. Such comments are placed above the Public Class clause in the Code Editor window. The area above the Public Class clause is called the **General Declarations section**.

START HERE

To include comments in the General Declarations section:

1. Click **before the letter P** in the `Public Class frmMain` line and then press **Enter** to insert a blank line. Now, click the **blank line**.

2. Type the comments shown in Figure 2-28 and then save the solution. In the comments, replace <your name> and <current date> with your name and the current date, respectively.

enter these four comments in the General Declarations section

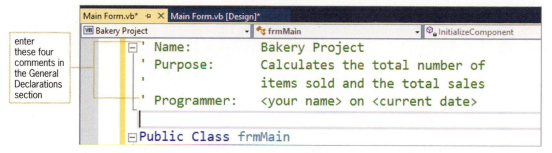

```
Main Form.vb* + X   Main Form.vb [Design]*
[VB] Bakery Project          ▾  ⁑ frmMain              ▾  🛠 InitializeComponent

          ⊟  ' Name:        Bakery Project
             ' Purpose:     Calculates the total number of
             '              items sold and the total sales
             ' Programmer:  <your name> on <current date>

          ⊟ Public Class frmMain
```

Figure 2-28 Comments entered in the General Declarations section

Coding the btnPrint_Click Procedure

Visual Basic provides the **PrintForm tool** for printing an interface from code. The tool is contained in the Visual Basic PowerPacks section of the toolbox. When you drag the PrintForm tool to a form, the instantiated print form control appears in the component tray. You can use the control to send the printout to a file or the Print preview window, or directly to the printer. You will have the Print Receipt button send the sales receipt to the Print preview window so that the user will have more control over when the receipt is printed.

To add a print form control to the application:

START HERE

1. Click the **designer window's tab** to make the designer window the active window.

2. Temporarily display the toolbox. Scroll down the toolbox until you see the Visual Basic PowerPacks section. If necessary, expand the section's node. See Figure 2-29. (Your Visual Basic PowerPacks section may contain additional tools.)

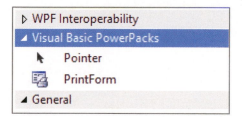

```
▷ WPF Interoperability
◢ Visual Basic PowerPacks
    ▸   Pointer
    🖼   PrintForm
◢ General
```

Figure 2-29 Visual Basic PowerPacks section in the toolbox

Note: If your toolbox does not contain the Visual Basic PowerPacks section, refer to the Read This Before You Begin page in this book.

3. Click **PrintForm** and then drag your mouse pointer to the form. When you release the mouse button, a print form control appears in the component tray.

4. In the Properties window, set the control's PrintAction property to **PrintToPreview**.

5. Return to the Code Editor window. Open the code template for the btnPrint_Click procedure. Type **' print the sales receipt** and press **Enter** twice. Then type **PrintForm1.Print()** and press **Enter**.

6. Save the solution and then start the application. Click the **Print Receipt** button. A printout of the interface appears in the Print preview window. (It may take a few seconds for the window to open.) Click the **Zoom** button's list arrow and then click **75%**. See Figure 2-30. Notice that the four buttons appear on the sales receipt. You will fix that problem in the next set of steps.

Figure 2-30   Print preview window

7. You won't need to print the sales receipt, so click the **Close** button on the Print preview window's toolbar, and then click the **Exit** button in the interface.

You can prevent the buttons from appearing on the printed receipt by hiding them on the form *before* the receipt is printed and then showing them again *after* the receipt is printed.

Showing and Hiding a Control

A control's **Visible property**, which can be set to either True or False, determines whether the control is visible (True) or hidden (False) while an application is running.

START HERE

To finish coding the btnPrint_Click procedure:

1. Enter the eight assignment statements indicated in Figure 2-31.

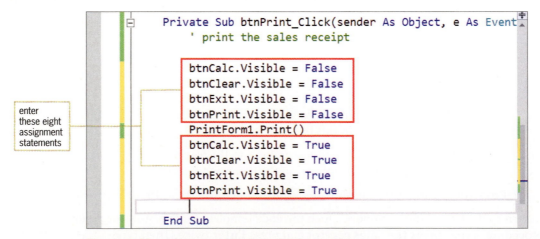

Figure 2-31   Completed btnPrint_Click procedure

2. Save the solution and then start the application. Click the **Print Receipt** button to display the sales receipt in the Print preview window. Notice that the four buttons do not appear on the sales receipt.

3. If your computer is connected to a printer, click the **Print** button (the printer) on the Print preview window's toolbar.

4. Click the **Close** button on the Print preview window's toolbar, and then click the **Exit** button in the interface.

Before you can code the btnCalc_Click procedure, you need to learn how to write arithmetic expressions in Visual Basic.

Note: You have learned a lot so far in this lesson. You may want to take a break at this point before continuing.

Writing Arithmetic Expressions

Most applications require the computer to perform at least one calculation. You instruct the computer to perform a calculation by writing an arithmetic expression, which is an expression that contains one or more arithmetic operators. Figure 2-32 lists the most commonly used arithmetic operators available in Visual Basic, along with their precedence numbers. The precedence numbers indicate the order in which the computer performs the operation in an expression. Operations with a precedence number of 1 are performed before operations with a precedence number of 2, and so on. However, you can use parentheses to override the order of precedence because operations within parentheses are always performed before operations outside parentheses.

Operator	Operation	Precedence number
^	exponentiation (raises a number to a power)	1
–	negation (reverses the sign of a number)	2
*, /	multiplication and division	3
\	integer division	4
Mod	modulus (remainder) arithmetic	5
+, –	addition and subtraction	6

Figure 2-32   Most commonly used arithmetic operators

Although the negation and subtraction operators listed in Figure 2-32 use the same symbol (a hyphen), there is a difference between them: the negation operator is *unary*, whereas the subtraction operator is *binary*. *Unary* and *binary* refer to the number of operands required by the operator. Unary operators require one operand. The expression –10, for example, uses the unary negation operator to turn its one operand (the positive number 10) into a negative number. Binary operators, on the other hand, require two operands. The expression 8 – 2, for instance, uses the binary subtraction operator to subtract its second operand (the number 2) from its first operand (the number 8).

Two of the arithmetic operators listed in Figure 2-32 might be less familiar to you: the integer division operator (\) and the modulus (remainder) operator (Mod). You use the **integer division operator** to divide two integers (whole numbers) and then return the result as an integer. For instance, the expression 211 \ 4 results in 52, which is the integer result of dividing 211 by 4. (If you use the standard division operator [/] to divide 211 by 4, the result is 52.75 rather than 52.) You might use the integer division operator in a program that determines the number of quarters, dimes, and nickels to return as change to a customer. For example, if a customer should receive 53 cents in change, you could use the expression 53 \ 25 to determine the number of quarters to return; the expression evaluates to 2.

The **modulus operator** (sometimes referred to as the remainder operator) is also used to divide two numbers, but the numbers do not have to be integers. After dividing the numbers, the modulus operator returns the remainder of the division. For instance, 211 Mod 4 equals 3, which is the remainder of 211 divided by 4. A common use for the modulus operator is to determine whether a number is even or odd. If you divide the number by 2 and the remainder is 0, the number is even; if the remainder is 1, however, the number is odd. Figure 2-33 shows several examples of using the integer division and Mod operators.

Examples	Results
211 \ 4	52
211 Mod 4	3
53 \ 25	2
53 Mod 25	3
75 \ 2	37
75 Mod 2	1
100 \ 2	50
100 Mod 2	0

Figure 2-33   Examples of the integer division and Mod (remainder) operators

You may have noticed that some of the operators listed in Figure 2-32, such as the addition and subtraction operators, have the same precedence number. When an expression contains more than one operator having the same priority, those operators are evaluated from left to right. In the expression 7 − 8 / 2 + 5, for instance, the division (/) is performed first, then the subtraction (−), and then the addition (+). The result of the expression is the number 8, as shown in Example 1 in Figure 2-34. You can use parentheses to change the order in which the operators in an expression are evaluated. As Example 2 shows, the expression 7 − (8 / 2 + 5) evaluates to −2 rather than to 8. This is because the parentheses tell the computer to perform the division first, then the addition, and then the subtraction.

Ch02C-Arithmetic
Operators

Example 1	
Original expression	7 − 8 / 2 + 5
The division is performed first	7 − 4 + 5
The subtraction is performed next	3 + 5
The addition is performed last	8
Example 2	
Original expression	7 − (8 / 2 + 5)
The division is performed first	7 − (4 + 5)
The addition is performed next	7 − 9
The subtraction is performed last	−2

Figure 2-34   Expressions containing more than one operator having the same precedence

When entering an arithmetic expression in code, you do not enter a comma or special characters, such as the dollar sign or percent sign. If you want to include a percentage in an arithmetic expression, you do so by using its decimal equivalent; for example, you enter .05 rather than 5%.

Coding the btnCalc_Click Procedure

According to its pseudocode and flowchart (shown earlier in Figures 2-23 and 2-24), the btnCalc_Click procedure should calculate the total number of items sold by adding together the number of doughnuts sold and the number of muffins sold. The number of doughnuts sold is recorded in the txtDonuts control's Text property as the user enters that information in the interface. Likewise, the number of muffins sold is recorded in the txtMuffins control's Text property. You can use an assignment statement to first add together the Text property of the two text boxes and then assign the sum to the Text property of the lblTotalItems control. The total items sold calculation is illustrated in Figure 2-35.

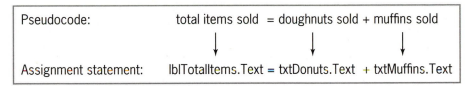

Pseudocode:	total items sold = doughnuts sold + muffins sold
Assignment statement:	lblTotalItems.Text = txtDonuts.Text + txtMuffins.Text

Figure 2-35   Illustration of the total items sold calculation

Next, the procedure should calculate the total sales by multiplying the total number of items sold (which is recorded in the lblTotalItems control) by the item price ($0.50). The total sales should be displayed in the lblTotalSales control. The total sales calculation is illustrated in Figure 2-36.

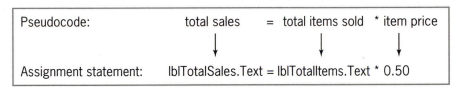

Pseudocode:	total sales = total items sold * item price
Assignment statement:	lblTotalSales.Text = lblTotalItems.Text * 0.50

Figure 2-36   Illustration of the total sales calculation

Finally, the procedure should display the total items sold and the total sales amount in the appropriate label controls. The assignment statements shown in Figures 2-35 and 2-36 accomplish this task.

To code the btnCalc_Click procedure and then test it:

START HERE

1. Open the code template for the btnCalc_Click procedure. Type **' calculate number of items sold and total sales** and press **Enter** twice.

2. Next, enter the following two assignment statements:

   lblTotalItems.Text = txtDonuts.Text + txtMuffins.Text
   lblTotalSales.Text = lblTotalItems.Text * .5

3. Save the solution and then start the application. Click the **Doughnuts** text box. Type **6** and then press **Tab**. Type **2** as the number of muffins sold and then click the **Calculate** button. The button's Click event procedure calculates the total number of items sold and total sales, displaying the results in the two label controls. As Figure 2-37 indicates, the displayed results are incorrect. Instead of mathematically adding the two sales quantities together, giving 8, the second sales quantity was appended to the first sales quantity, giving 62. When the total items sold amount is incorrect, the total sales will also be incorrect because the total items sold amount is used in the total sales calculation.

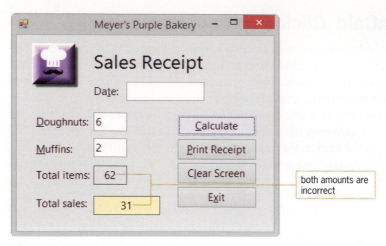

Figure 2-37 Interface showing the incorrect results of the calculations

4. Click the **Exit** button to end the application.

Even though you do not see the quotation marks around the value, a value stored in the Text property of an object is treated as a string rather than as a number. Adding strings together does not give you the same result as adding numbers together. Adding the string "2" to the string "5" results in the string "25", whereas adding the number 2 to the number 5 results in the number 7. To add together the contents of two text boxes, you need to tell the computer to treat the contents as numbers rather than as strings. The easiest way, although not one of the preferred ways, is to use the Val function. However, because this lesson's topics are difficult for many beginning programmers, you will use the Val function in this lesson (and only in this lesson) so as not to complicate those topics.

The Val Function

A **function** is a predefined procedure that performs a specific task and then returns a value after completing the task. The **Val function**, for instance, temporarily converts a string to a number and then returns the number. The number is stored in the computer's internal memory only while the function is processing.

The syntax of the Val function is shown in Figure 2-38. The item within the parentheses is called an argument and represents information that the function needs to perform its task. In this case, the *string* argument represents the string you want treated as a number. Because the Val function must be able to interpret the string as a numeric value, the string cannot include a letter, a comma, or a special character (such as the dollar sign or percent sign); it can, however, include a period or a space. When the Val function encounters an invalid character in its *string* argument, it stops converting the string to a number at that point. Figure 2-38 shows some examples of how the Val function converts various strings.

```
Val Function

Syntax
Val(string)

Example                    Numeric result
Val("456")                    456
Val("24,500")                  24
Val("123X")                   123
Val("25%")                     25
Val("  12   34   ")          1234
Val("$56.88")                   0
Val("Abc")                      0
Val("")                         0
```

Figure 2-38   Syntax and examples of the Val function

To include the Val function in the btnCalc_Click procedure:

START HERE

1. Make the modifications highlighted in Figure 2-39.

```
Private Sub btnCalc_Click(sender As Object, e As EventArgs) Handles
    ' calculate number of items sold and total sales

    lblTotalItems.Text = Val(txtDonuts.Text) + Val(txtMuffins.Text)
    lblTotalSales.Text = Val(lblTotalItems.Text) * 0.5

End Sub
```

Figure 2-39   Val function entered in the assignment statements

2. Save the solution and then start the application. Type **6** in the Doughnuts box and **2** in the Muffins box. Click the **Calculate** button. The application correctly calculates and displays the total number of items sold (8) and total sales amount (4). See Figure 2-40.

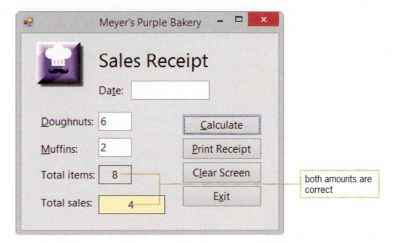

Figure 2-40   Interface showing the correct results of the calculations

3. In the next section, you will improve the appearance of the total sales amount by including a dollar sign, a thousands separator (if appropriate), and two decimal places. Click the **Exit** button.

The Format Function

You can use the **Format function** to improve the appearance of numbers in an interface. The function's syntax is shown in Figure 2-41. The *expression* argument specifies the number, date, time, or string whose appearance you want to format. The *style* argument can be a predefined Visual Basic format style; some of these styles are explained in the figure. The *style* argument can also be a string containing special symbols that indicate how you want the expression displayed. (You can display the Help screen for the Format function to learn more about these special symbols.) In this case, you will use one of the predefined format styles.

Format Function

Syntax
Format(expression**,** style**)**

Format style	Description
Currency	Formats the number with a dollar sign, two decimal places, and (if appropriate) a thousands separator; negative numbers are enclosed in parentheses
Fixed	Formats the number with at least one digit to the left of the decimal point and two digits to the right of the decimal point
Standard	Formats the number with at least one digit to the left of the decimal point, two digits to the right of the decimal point, and (if appropriate) a thousands separator
Percent	Multiplies the number by 100 and then formats the result with a percent sign and two digits to the right of the decimal point

---

Figure 2-41   Format function's syntax and some of the predefined format styles

START HERE

To format the total sales amount:

1. Enter the additional assignment statement highlighted in Figure 2-42.

> You can also include the Format function in the calculation statement, like this:
> ```
> lblTotalSales.
> Text = Format(Val
> (lblTotalItems.
> Text) * 0.5,
> "currency").
> ```

```
Private Sub btnCalc_Click(sender As Object, e As EventArgs) Handles
    ' calculate number of items sold and total sales

    lblTotalItems.Text = Val(txtDonuts.Text) + Val(txtMuffins.Text)
    lblTotalSales.Text = Val(lblTotalItems.Text) * 0.5
    lblTotalSales.Text = Format(lblTotalSales.Text, "currency")

End Sub
```

Figure 2-42   Format function entered in the procedure

2. Save the solution and then start the application. Type **11/23/2016** in the Date box, **12** in the Doughnuts box, and **3** in the Muffins box. Click the **Calculate** button. See Figure 2-43.

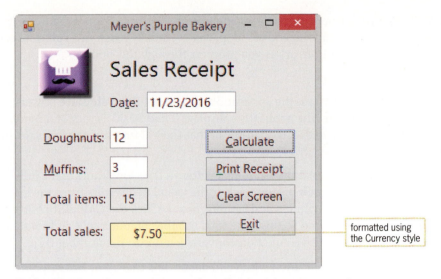

Figure 2-43   Formatted total sales amount shown in the interface

3. Click the **Exit** button.

You have completed the first four of the six steps involved in creating an OO application: meeting with the client, planning the application, building the user interface, and coding the application. The fifth step is to test and debug the application.

Testing and Debugging the Application

You test an application by starting it and entering some sample data. The sample data should include both valid and invalid data. **Valid data** is data that the application is expecting the user to enter, whereas **invalid data** is data that the application is *not* expecting the user to enter. The bakery application expects the user to enter a numeric value in the Doughnuts box; it does not expect the user to enter a letter. In most cases, invalid data is a result of a typing error made by the user. You should test an application as thoroughly as possible to ensure that it displays the correct output when valid data is entered and does not end abruptly when invalid data is entered.

Debugging refers to the process of locating and correcting the errors, called **bugs**, in a program. Program bugs are typically categorized as syntax errors, logic errors, or run time errors. As you learned in Chapter 1, the term *syntax* refers to the set of rules you must follow when using a programming language. A **syntax error** occurs when you break one of the language's rules. Most syntax errors are a result of typing errors that occur when entering instructions, such as typing `Me.Clse()` instead of `Me.Close()`. The Code Editor detects most syntax errors as you enter the instructions.

Logic errors, on the other hand, are much more difficult to find because the Code Editor cannot detect them for you. A **logic error** can occur for a variety of reasons, such as forgetting to enter an instruction or entering the instructions in the wrong order. Some logic errors occur as a result of calculation statements that are correct syntactically but incorrect mathematically. Consider the statement `lblSquared.Text = Val(txtNum.Text) + Val(txtNum.Text)`, which is supposed to square the number entered in the txtNum control. The statement's syntax is correct; however, the statement is incorrect mathematically because you square a value by multiplying it by itself, not by adding it to itself.

A **run time error** is an error that occurs while an application is running. A procedure that continues to run, because it contains an endless loop, will eventually result in a run time error. You will learn more about run time errors as you progress through this book.

START HERE

To test the bakery application:

1. Start the application. First, test the application by clicking the **Calculate** button without entering any data. The application displays 0 and $0.00 as the total number of items sold and total sales, respectively. (Recall that the Val function converts the empty string to the number 0.)

2. Next, you will test the application by typing a letter in the Doughnuts and Muffins boxes. Click the **Clear Screen** button to clear the calculated results from the label controls. Type **p** in the Doughnuts and Muffins boxes. Click the **Calculate** button. The application displays 0 and $0.00 as the total number of items sold and total sales, respectively. (Recall that the Val function converts a letter to the number 0.)

3. Finally, you will test the application with valid data. Click the **Clear Screen** button. Type **2/28/2016** in the Date box, **6** in the Doughnuts box, and **3** in the Muffins box. Click the **Calculate** button. The application correctly calculates and displays the total number of items sold (9) and total sales amount ($4.50).

4. Click the **Print Receipt** button. If your computer is connected to a printer, print the sales receipt. Close the Print preview window.

5. Click the **Clear Screen** button and then practice with other entries to see how the application responds. When you are finished testing the application, click the **Exit** button to end the application.

In the following set of steps, you will introduce syntax errors in the application's code. You will also learn how to locate and correct the errors.

START HERE

To introduce syntax errors in the code and also debug the code:

1. Change the statement in the btnExit_Click procedure to **Me.Clse()** and then click the **blank line** above the procedure header. The jagged line, called a squiggle, below the statement indicates that the statement contains a syntax error. Hover your mouse pointer over the statement. See Figure 2-44.

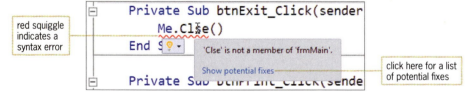

red squiggle indicates a syntax error

click here for a list of potential fixes

Figure 2-44   Result of hovering the mouse pointer over the statement containing the syntax error

2. Click **Show potential fixes** (or click the lightbulb's list arrow) and then click **Change 'Clse' to 'Close'.** in the list. Doing this changes the statement to Me.Close() and also removes the red squiggle.

3. In this step, you will observe what happens when you start an application whose code contains a syntax error. First, delete the ending parenthesis in the last assignment statement in the btnCalc_Click procedure. A red squiggle appears after the closing

quotation mark in the statement. Click the **blank line** below the statement. Save the solution and then start the application. The message dialog box shown in Figure 2-45 appears.

Figure 2-45   Message dialog box

4. Click the **No** button. The Error List window shown in Figure 2-46 opens at the bottom of the IDE. The window indicates that the code contains one error, and it provides both a description and the location of the error in the Code Editor window.

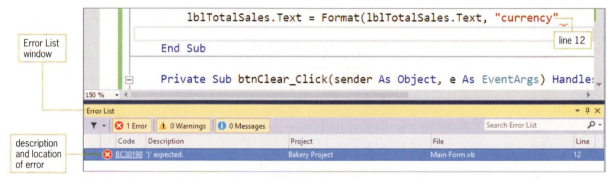

Figure 2-46   Error List window in the IDE

5. Double-click the **error message** in the Error List window. Doing this positions the insertion point at the end of the statement that contains the syntax error. Type **)** (the missing ending parentheses). The Code Editor removes both the red squiggle from the end of the statement and the error message from the Error List window.

6. Close the Error List window. Save the solution and then start the application. Test the application to verify that it works correctly, and then click the **Exit** button to end the application.

7. Close the Code Editor window and then close the solution.

Assembling the Documentation

After you have tested an application thoroughly, you can move to the last step involved in creating an OO application: assemble the documentation. Assembling the documentation refers to putting your planning tools and a printout of the application's interface and code in a safe place so you can refer to them if you need to change the application in the future. Your planning tools include the TOE chart, a sketch of the user interface, and either the flowcharts or the pseudocode.

The code for the bakery application is shown in Figure 2-47. If you want to display line numbers in the Code Editor window, click Tools on the menu bar, click Options, expand the Text Editor node, click Basic, select the Line numbers check box, and then click the OK button.

```vbnet
 1 ' Name:         Bakery Project
 2 ' Purpose:      Calculates the total number of
 3 '               items sold and the total sales
 4 ' Programmer:   <your name> on <current date>
 5
 6 Public Class frmMain
 7     Private Sub btnCalc_Click(sender As Object,
       e As EventArgs) Handles btnCalc.Click
 8         ' calculate number of items sold and total sales
 9
10         lblTotalItems.Text = Val(txtDonuts.Text) +
             Val(txtMuffins.Text)
11         lblTotalSales.Text = Val(lblTotalItems.Text) * 0.5
12         lblTotalSales.Text =
             Format(lblTotalSales.Text, "currency")
13
14     End Sub
15
16     Private Sub btnClear_Click(sender As Object,
       e As EventArgs) Handles btnClear.Click
17         ' prepare screen for the next sale
18
19         txtDonuts.Text = String.Empty
20         txtMuffins.Text = String.Empty
21         lblTotalItems.Text = String.Empty
22         lblTotalSales.Text = String.Empty
23         ' send the focus to the Doughnuts box
24         txtDonuts.Focus()
25
26     End Sub
27
28     Private Sub btnExit_Click(sender As Object,
       e As EventArgs) Handles btnExit.Click
29         Me.Close()
30     End Sub
31
32     Private Sub btnPrint_Click(sender As Object,
       e As EventArgs) Handles btnPrint.Click
33         ' print the sales receipt
34
35         btnCalc.Visible = False
36         btnClear.Visible = False
37         btnExit.Visible = False
38         btnPrint.Visible = False
39         PrintForm1.Print()
40         btnCalc.Visible = True
41         btnClear.Visible = True
42         btnExit.Visible = True
43         btnPrint.Visible = True
44
45     End Sub
46 End Class
```

Figure 2-47   Meyer's Purple Bakery application's code

Lesson C Summary

- To plan an object's code:

  Use pseudocode or a flowchart.

- To clear the Text property of an object while an application is running:

  Assign either the `String.Empty` value or the empty string ("") to the property.

- To assign a value to an object's property while an application is running:

  Use an assignment statement that follows the syntax *object.property = expression*.

- To move the focus to an object while an application is running:

  Use the Focus method. The method's syntax is *object*.`Focus()`.

- To show or hide an object during run time:

  Set the object's Visible property.

- To create a comment in Visual Basic:

  Begin the comment text with an apostrophe (`'`).

- To divide two integers and then return the result as an integer:

  Use the integer division operator (\).

- To divide two numbers and then return the remainder:

  Use the modulus (remainder) operator (Mod).

- To print the interface from code:

  Use the PrintForm tool to instantiate a print form control. The tool is located in the Visual Basic PowerPacks section of the toolbox.

- To temporarily convert a string to a number:

  Use the Val function. The function's syntax is `Val`(*string*).

- To improve the appearance of numbers in the user interface:

  Use the Format function. The function's syntax is `Format`(*expression*, *style*).

- To display line numbers in the Code Editor window:

  Click Tools on the menu bar, click Options, expand the Text Editor node, click Basic, select the Line numbers check box, and then click the OK button.

Lesson C Key Terms

Assignment operator—the equal sign in an assignment statement

Assignment statement—an instruction that assigns a value to something, such as to the property of an object

Bugs—the errors in a program

Debugging—the process of locating and correcting the bugs (errors) in a program

Empty string—a set of quotation marks with nothing between them (""); also called a zero-length string

Flowchart—a planning tool that uses standardized symbols to show the steps a procedure must take to accomplish its goal

Flowlines—the lines connecting the symbols in a flowchart

Focus method—moves the focus to a specified control during run time

Format function—used to improve the appearance of numbers in an interface

Function—a procedure that processes a specific task and returns a value

General Declarations section—the area above the Public Class clause in the Code Editor window

Input/output symbol—the parallelogram in a flowchart; used to represent input and output tasks

Integer division operator—represented by a backslash (\); divides two integers and then returns the quotient as an integer

Invalid data—data that an application is not expecting the user to enter

Logic error—occurs when you neglect to enter an instruction or enter the instructions in the wrong order; also occurs as a result of calculation statements that are correct syntactically but incorrect mathematically

Modulus operator—represented by the keyword Mod; divides two numbers and returns the remainder of the division

PrintForm tool—used to instantiate a print form control; located in the Visual Basic PowerPacks section of the toolbox

Process symbols—the rectangle symbols in a flowchart; used to represent assignment and calculation tasks

Pseudocode—a planning tool that uses phrases to describe the steps a procedure must take to accomplish its goal

Run time error—an error that occurs while an application is running; an example is an expression that attempts to divide by 0

Start/stop symbol—the oval symbol in a flowchart; used to indicate the beginning and end of the flowchart

String—zero or more characters enclosed in quotation marks

String.Empty—the value that represents the empty string in Visual Basic

Syntax error—occurs when an instruction in an application's code breaks one of a programming language's rules

Val function—temporarily converts a string to a number and then returns the number

Valid data—data that an application is expecting the user to enter

Visible property—determines whether a control is visible in the interface during run time

Zero-length string—a set of quotation marks with nothing between them (""); also called an empty string

Lesson C Review Questions

1. Which of the following assignment statements will not calculate correctly?

    a. `lblTotal.Text = Val(txtSales1.Text) + Val(txtSales2.Text)`

    b. `lblTotal.Text = 4 - Val(txtSales1.Text)`

    c. `lblTotal.Text = Val(txtQuantity.Text + 3)`

    d. All of the above assignment statements will calculate correctly.

2. Which function temporarily converts a string to a number and then returns the number?

    a. Format   c. StringToNumber

    b. FormatNumber   d. Val

3. Which symbol is used in a flowchart to represent an output task?

    a. circle   c. parallelogram

    b. oval   d. rectangle

4. What value is assigned to the lblNum control when the `lblNum.Text = 99 \ 25` instruction is processed by the computer?

5. What value is assigned to the lblNum control when the `lblNum.Text = 99 Mod 25` instruction is processed by the computer?

Lesson C Exercises

Note: In several exercises in this lesson, you perform the second through sixth steps involved in creating an OO application. Recall that the six steps are:

---

1. Meet with the client.
2. Plan the application. (Prepare a TOE chart that is ordered by object, and then draw a sketch of the user interface.)
3. Build the user interface. (Refer to Appendix B for a listing of the GUI guidelines you have learned so far. To help you remember the names of the controls as you are coding, print the application's interface and then write the names next to each object.)
4. Code the application. (Write pseudocode for each of the objects that will be coded. Include appropriate comments in the code.)
5. Test and debug the application.
6. Assemble the documentation (your planning tools and a printout of the interface and code).

---

1. In this exercise, you complete the Richardson County application from Exercise 1 in both Lesson A and Lesson B. Open the VB2015\Chap02\Richardson Solution\ Richardson Solution (Richardson Solution.sln) file.

    INTRODUCTORY

    a. The Calculate button should display the annual property tax, which is $1.50 for each $100 of a property's assessed value. Code the button's Click event procedure using the Val function. Use the Format function to display the tax with a dollar sign, a thousands separator, and two decimal places.

    b. Code the Clear Screen button. Send the focus to the Assessed value text box.

    c. Add a print form control to the application. The control should send the printout to the Print preview window. Code the Print button, being sure to hide the buttons before printing, and then display them after printing.

d. Add appropriate comments in the General Declarations section and in the coded procedures.

e. Save the solution and then start the application. Test the application using 120500 as the assessed value. The tax should be $1,807.50. If your computer is connected to a printer, print the interface.

f. Clear the screen. Now test the application using invalid data. More specifically, test it without entering any data. Then test it using a letter as the assessed value.

INTRODUCTORY

2. In this exercise, you complete the Jordan Sports Store application from Exercise 2 in both Lesson A and Lesson B. Open the VB2015\Chap02\Jordan Solution\Jordan Solution (Jordan Solution.sln) file.

a. The Calculate button should display two amounts: the weekly gross pay and the biweekly gross pay. Employees paid weekly receive 52 paychecks; employees paid biweekly receive 26 paychecks. Code the button's Click event procedure using the Val function. Use the Format function to display the gross pay amounts with a dollar sign, a thousands separator, and two decimal places.

b. Code the Clear button. Send the focus to the Annual salary text box.

c. Add a print form control to the application. The control should send the printout to the Print preview window. Code the Print button, being sure to hide the buttons before printing, and then display them after printing.

d. Add appropriate comments in the General Declarations section and in the coded procedures.

e. Save the solution and then start the application. Test the application using 75000 as the annual salary. The gross pay amounts should be $1,442.31 and $2,884.62. If your computer is connected to a printer, print the interface.

f. Clear the screen. Now test the application using invalid data. More specifically, test it without entering any data. Then test it using a letter as the annual salary.

INTRODUCTORY

3. In this exercise, you complete the Cranston Berries application from Exercise 3 in both Lesson A and Lesson B. Open the VB2015\Chap02\Cranston Solution\Cranston Solution (Cranston Solution.sln) file.

a. The Calculate button should display the projected sales for each type of berry. Code the button's Click event procedure using the Val function. Use the Format function to display the projected sales amounts with a dollar sign, a thousands separator, and two decimal places.

b. Code the Clear button. Send the focus to the projected increase's text box.

c. Add a print form control to the application. The control should send the printout to the Print preview window. Code the Print button, being sure to hide the buttons before printing, and then display them after printing.

d. Add appropriate comments in the General Declarations section and in the coded procedures.

e. Save the solution and then start the application. Test the application using .05 (the decimal equivalent of 5%) as the projected increase, 25000 as the strawberry sales, 20200 as the blueberry sales, and 16750 as the raspberry sales. The projected sales amounts should be $26,250.00, $21,210.00, and $17,587.50. If your computer is connected to a printer, print the interface.

f. Clear the screen. Now test the application using invalid data. More specifically, test it without entering any data. Then test it using letters as the projected increase and sales amounts.

4. In this exercise, you complete the application from Lesson B's Exercise 4. Open the VB2015\Chap02\Age Solution\Age Solution (Age Solution.sln) file. The Calculate button should calculate your age by subtracting your birth year from the current year. Code the Calculate button using the Val function. Add a print form control to the application. The control should send the printout to the Print preview window. Code the Print button so that it prints the interface with the buttons. Add appropriate comments in the General Declarations section and in the coded procedures. Save the solution and then start the application. Test the application using your birth year and the current year. Also test it without entering any data. Finally, test it using a dollar sign ($) for the birth year and a percent sign (%) for the current year.

5. Jefferson Sales wants you to create an application that displays a salesperson's monthly commission, given his or her monthly sales and commission rate (entered in decimal form). The commission is calculated by multiplying the monthly sales by the commission rate.

   a. Perform the steps involved in creating an OO application. (See the Note at the beginning of the Exercises section.) Include a button for clearing the screen.

   b. Create an application, using the following names for the solution and project, respectively: Jefferson Solution and Jefferson Project. Save the application in the VB2015\Chap02 folder. Change the form file's name to Main Form.vb. Change the form's name to frmMain. Code the application using the Val and Format functions. Add appropriate comments in the General Declarations section and in the coded procedures.

   c. Test the application using 5600 as the monthly sales amount and 10% as the commission rate. Then test it without entering any data. Also test it using a letter as the sales amount and commission rate.

6. Your science teacher has asked you to create an application that displays how much a person would weigh on the following planets: Venus, Mars, and Jupiter. The application's interface should allow the user to enter the person's weight on Earth.

   a. Perform the steps involved in creating an OO application. (See the Note at the beginning of the Exercises section.) Include a button for clearing the screen.

   b. Create an application, using the following names for the solution and project, respectively: Planet Solution and Planet Project. Save the application in the VB2015\Chap02 folder. Change the form file's name to Main Form.vb. Change the form's name to frmMain. Code the application using the Val and Format functions. One pound on Earth is equal to 0.91, 0.38, and 2.53 pounds on Venus, Mars, and Jupiter, respectively. Add appropriate comments in the General Declarations section and in the coded procedures. Test the application using both valid and invalid data.

7. In this exercise, you modify the bakery application from the chapter. Use Windows to make a copy of the Bakery Solution folder contained in the VB2015\Chap02 folder. Rename the copy Modified Bakery Solution. Open the Bakery Solution (Bakery Solution.sln) file contained in the Modified Bakery Solution folder. Open the designer window. Modify the interface so that it allows the user to enter the item price. Also modify the application's code. The Clear Screen button should not clear the item price's text box. Save the solution and then start the application. Test the application using .65, 5, and 7 as the item price, number of doughnuts, and number of muffins, respectively.

8. Create an application that displays the average of three test scores entered by the user. Use the following names for the solution and project, respectively: Average Solution and Average Project. Save the application in the VB2015\Chap02 folder. Change the form file's name to Main Form.vb. Change the form's name to frmMain. Display the average with two decimal places. Code the application using the Val and Format functions. Add appropriate comments in the General Declarations section and in the coded procedures. Test the application using both valid and invalid data.

9. A group of people needs to be transported to a concert. If an SUV can accommodate seven people, how many SUVs will be completely full and how many people will still need transportation? Create an application that displays the answers. The user will enter the number of people in the group. You can assume that the group will always contain at least seven people. Use the following names for the solution and project, respectively: Transportation Solution and Transportation Project. Save the application in the VB2015\Chap02 folder. Change the form file's name to Main Form.vb. Change the form's name to frmMain. Code the application using the Val function. Add appropriate comments in the General Declarations section and in the coded procedures. Test the application using 73 as the number of people going to the concert. Also test it using invalid data.

10. The payroll clerk at Photo Workshop has asked you to create an application that displays an employee's net pay. The application should allow the payroll clerk to enter the employee's name, hours worked, and rate of pay. For this application, you do not have to worry about overtime because this company does not allow anyone to work more than 40 hours. The application should calculate and display the gross pay, federal withholding tax (FWT), Social Security tax (FICA), state income tax, and net pay. The FWT, FICA tax, and state income tax are 20%, 8% and 3% of the gross pay, respectively. First, perform the steps involved in creating an OO application. (See the Note at the beginning of the Exercises section.) Then, create an application, using the following names for the solution and project, respectively: Photo Solution and Photo Project. Save the application in the VB2015\Chap02 folder. Change the form file's name to Main Form.vb. Change the form's name to frmMain. Code the application. Format the calculated amounts using the Standard format style. Test the application using both valid and invalid data.

11. In this exercise, you learn about a text box's Clear method, which can be used to remove the contents of the text box during run time. Use Windows to make a copy of the Bakery Solution folder from the chapter. Rename the copy Discovery Bakery Solution. Open the Bakery Solution (Bakery Solution.sln) file contained in the Discovery Bakery Solution folder. Open the designer window. The Clear method's syntax is *textbox*.`Clear()`. Use the Clear method in the btnClear_Click procedure to remove the contents of the txtDonuts and txtMuffins controls. (You cannot use the Clear method to remove the contents of label controls.) Save the solution and then start the application. Enter any date and sales amounts, and then click the Calculate button. Click the Clear Screen button to verify that the Clear method worked correctly.

12. Open the VB2015\Chap02\Debug Solution\Debug Solution (Debug Solution.sln) file. Locate and then correct the syntax errors in the Code Editor window. Save the solution, and then start and test the application.

CHAPTER 3

Using Variables and Constants

Revising the Meyer's Purple Bakery Application

In this chapter, you will modify the bakery application from Chapter 2. The modified application will calculate a 2% sales tax and then display the result in the interface. It will also display the name of the salesclerk who entered the sales information.

Previewing the Modified Bakery Application

Before you start the first lesson in this chapter, you will preview the completed application contained in the VB2015\Chap03 folder.

START HERE

To preview the completed application:

1. Use Windows to locate and then open the VB2015\Chap03 folder on your computer's hard disk or on the device designated by your instructor. Right-click **Bakery** (**Bakery.exe**) in the list of filenames and then click the **Open** button. A sales receipt similar to the one created in Chapter 2 appears on the screen.

2. Type **11/8/2016** in the Date box, type **4** in the Doughnuts box, and type **3** in the Muffins box.

3. Although the Calculate button does not have the focus, you can select it by pressing the Enter key because it is the default button in the interface. You will learn how to designate a default button in Lesson B. Press **Enter**. The Name Entry dialog box appears and requests the salesclerk's name, as shown in Figure 3-1.

Figure 3-1   Name Entry dialog box

4. Type **Melinda Hazelton** and then press **Enter** to select the dialog box's OK button. The completed sales receipt is shown in Figure 3-2. The application uses string concatenation, which is covered in Lesson B, to display the sales tax amount and the salesclerk's name on the receipt.

if the underlined letters do not appear in your interface, press the Alt key

Figure 3-2   Completed sales receipt

5. Change the number of muffins sold to **12**. The application clears the contents of the label controls that display the total number of items sold, the total sales amount, and the message. In Lesson C, you will learn how to clear the contents of a control when a change is made to the value stored in a different control.

6. Click the **Calculate** button. The Name Entry dialog box appears and displays the salesclerk's name. Press **Enter** to select the dialog box's OK button. The application recalculates the appropriate amounts and then displays the information on the sales receipt.

7. Click the **Clear Screen** button to clear the sales information (except the date) from the form, and then click the **Exit** button to end the application.

In Lesson A, you will learn how to store information temporarily in memory locations inside the computer. Then you will modify the bakery application in Lessons B and C. Be sure to complete each lesson in full and do all of the end-of-lesson questions and several exercises before continuing to the next lesson.

Ch03A-Variables

LESSON A

After studying Lesson A, you should be able to:

- Declare variables and named constants
- Assign data to an existing variable
- Convert string data to a numeric data type using the TryParse method
- Convert numeric data to a different data type using the Convert class methods
- Explain the scope and lifetime of variables and named constants
- Explain the purpose of Option Explicit, Option Infer, and Option Strict

Using Variables to Store Information

In the bakery application from Chapter 2, all of the sales information is temporarily stored in the properties of the controls on the sales receipt form. For example, the numbers of doughnuts and muffins sold are stored in the Text properties of the txtDonuts and txtMuffins controls, respectively. Recall that the btnCalc_Click procedure uses the Text properties of those controls to calculate the total number of items sold, like this: `lblTotalItems.Text = Val(txtDonuts.Text) + Val(txtMuffins.Text)`. The procedure then uses the lblTotalItems control's Text property to calculate the total sales amount, like this: `lblTotalSales.Text = Val(lblTotalItems.Text) * 0.5`.

Besides storing data in the properties of controls, a programmer can also temporarily store data in memory locations inside the computer. The memory locations are called **variables** because the contents of the locations can change (vary) as the application is running. It may be helpful to picture a variable as a small box inside the computer. You can enter and store data in the box, but you cannot actually see the box. One use for a variable is to hold information that is not stored in a control on the form. For example, if you didn't need to display the total number of items sold on the bakery's sales receipt, you could eliminate the lblTotalItems control from the form and store the total number of items sold in a variable instead. You then would use the value stored in the variable, rather than the value stored in the control's Text property, in the total sales calculation.

You can also use a variable to store the data contained in a control's property, such as the data contained in a control's Text property. Programmers typically do this when the data is a numeric amount that will be used in a calculation. As you will learn in the next section, assigning numeric data to a variable allows you to control the preciseness of the data. It also makes your code run more efficiently because the computer can process data stored in a variable much faster than it can process data stored in the property of a control.

Every variable has a data type, name, scope, and lifetime. First, you will learn how to select an appropriate data type for a variable.

Selecting a Data Type for a Variable

Each variable used in an application should be assigned a data type by the programmer. The **data type** determines the type of data the variable can store. Figure 3-3 describes most of the basic data types available in Visual Basic 2015. Each data type is a class, which means that each is a pattern from which one or more objects—in this case, variables—are instantiated (created).

Data Type	Stores	Memory Required
Boolean	a logical value (True, False)	2 bytes
Char	one Unicode character	2 bytes
Date	date and time information Date range: January 1, 0001 to December 31, 9999 Time range: 0:00:00 (midnight) to 23:59:59	8 bytes
Decimal	a number with a decimal place Range with no decimal place: +/–79,228,162,514,264,337,593,543,950,335 Range with a decimal place: +/–7.9228162514264337593543950335	16 bytes
Double	a number with a decimal place Range: +/–$4.94065645841247 \times 10^{-324}$ to +/–$1.79769313486231 \times 10^{308}$	8 bytes
Integer	integer Range: –2,147,483,648 to 2,147,483,647	4 bytes
Long	integer Range: –9,223,372,036,854,775,808 to 9,223,372,036,854,775,807	8 bytes
Object	data of any type	4 bytes
Short	integer Range: –32,768 to 32,767	2 bytes
Single	a number with a decimal place Range: +/–1.401298×10^{-45} to +/–3.402823×10^{38}	4 bytes
String	text; 0 to approximately 2 billion characters	

Figure 3-3   Basic data types in Visual Basic

Don't be overwhelmed by the number of data types listed in Figure 3-3. This book will use only the Boolean, Decimal, Double, Integer, and String data types.

As Figure 3-3 indicates, variables assigned the Integer, Long, or Short data type can store integers (whole numbers), which are positive or negative numbers that do not have any decimal places. These three data types differ in the range of integers each can store and the amount of memory each needs to store the integer.

Decimal, Double, and Single variables can store numbers containing a decimal place. Here again, these three data types differ in the range of numbers each can store and the amount of memory each needs to store the numbers. However, calculations involving Decimal variables are not subject to the small rounding errors that may occur when using Double or Single variables. In most cases, these errors do not create any problems in an application. One exception to this is when the application contains complex equations involving money, where you need accuracy to the penny. In those cases, you should use the Decimal data type.

The Char data type can store one Unicode character, while the String data type can store from zero to approximately 2 billion Unicode characters. **Unicode** is the universal coding scheme for characters. It assigns a unique numeric value to each character used in the written languages of the world. (For more information, see The Unicode Consortium Web site at *http://unicode.org*.)

Also listed in Figure 3-3 are the Boolean, Date, and Object data types. You use a Boolean variable to store a Boolean value (either True or False) and a Date variable to store date and time information. The Object data type can store any type of data. However, your application will pay a price for this flexibility: It will run more slowly because the computer must determine the type of data currently stored in an Object variable. It is best to avoid using the Object data type.

The applications in this book will use the Integer data type for variables that will store integers used in calculations, even when the integers are small enough to fit into a Short variable. This is because a calculation containing Integer variables takes less time to process than the equivalent calculation containing Short variables. Either the Decimal data type or the Double data type will be used for numbers that contain decimal places and are used in calculations. The applications will use the String data type for variables that contain either text or numbers not used in calculations and the Boolean data type to store Boolean values (either True or False).

Selecting a Name for a Variable

A variable's name, also called its identifier, should describe its contents. A good variable name is meaningful right after you finish a program and also years later when you (or perhaps a co-worker) need to modify the program. There are several conventions for naming variables in Visual Basic. This book uses Hungarian notation, which is the same naming convention used for controls. Each variable name will begin with a three-character ID that represents the variable's data type. The three-character IDs for the most commonly used data types are listed in Figure 3-4 along with examples of variable names. Like control names, variable names are entered using camel case, which means you lowercase the ID and then uppercase the first letter of each word in the name.

Data type	ID	Example
Boolean	bln	blnInsured
Decimal	dec	decGrossPay
Double	dbl	dblSales
Integer	int	intNumSold
String	str	strFirstName

Figure 3-4   Three-character IDs and examples

Figure 3-5 lists the rules for naming variables and includes examples of valid and invalid variable names.

Rules for Naming Variables

1. The name must begin with a letter or an underscore.
2. The name can contain only letters, numbers, and the underscore character. No punctuation characters, special characters, or spaces are allowed in the name.
3. Although the name can contain thousands of characters, 32 characters is the recommended maximum number to use.
4. The name cannot be a reserved word, such as Sub or Double.

Valid names
intQuantity, decSales2016, dblStore_43, strName, blnIsValid

Invalid names	Problem
4thQuarter	The name must begin with a letter or an underscore.
dblWest Region	The name cannot contain a space.
strFirst.Name	The name cannot contain punctuation.
decSales$East	The name cannot contain a special character.

Figure 3-5   Variable naming rules and examples

Declaring a Variable

Once you have chosen its data type and name, you can declare the variable in code. Declaring a variable tells the computer to set aside a small section of its internal memory, and it allows you to refer to the section by the variable's name. The size of the section is determined by the variable's data type. You declare a variable using a declaration statement. Figure 3-6 shows the syntax of a declaration statement and includes examples of declaring variables. The {Dim | Private | Static} portion of the syntax indicates that you can select only one of the keywords appearing within the braces. In most instances, you declare a variable using the Dim keyword. (You will learn about the Private and Static keywords later in this lesson.)

> Dim comes from the word *dimension*, which is how programmers in the 1960s referred to the process of allocating the computer's memory. *Dimension* refers to the size of something.

Variable Declaration Statement

Syntax
{**Dim | Private | Static**} *variableName* **As** *dataType* [= *initialValue*]

Example 1
```
Dim intQuantity As Integer
Dim dblDiscountRate As Double
```
declares an Integer variable named intQuantity and a Double variable named dblDiscountRate; the variables are automatically initialized to 0

Example 2
```
Dim decSales As Decimal
```
declares a Decimal variable named decSales; the variable is automatically initialized to 0

Example 3
```
Dim blnInsured As Boolean = True
```
declares a Boolean variable named blnInsured and initializes it using the keyword True

Example 4
```
Dim strMsg As String = "Total due: "
```
declares a String variable named strMsg and initializes it using the string "Total due: "

Figure 3-6   Syntax and examples of a variable declaration statement

As mentioned earlier, a variable is considered an object in Visual Basic and is an instance of the class specified in the *dataType* information. The Dim intQuantity As Integer statement, for example, uses the Integer class to create a variable (object) named intQuantity.

In the syntax, *initialValue* is the value you want stored in the variable when it is created in the computer's internal memory. The square brackets in the syntax indicate that the "= *initialValue*" part of a variable declaration statement is optional. If you do not assign an initial value to a variable when it is declared, the computer stores a default value in the variable. The default value depends on the variable's data type. A variable declared using one of the numeric data types is automatically initialized to—in other words, given a beginning value of—the number 0. The computer automatically initializes a Boolean variable using the keyword False and a Date variable to 1/1/0001 12:00:00 AM. Object and String variables are automatically initialized using the keyword Nothing. Variables initialized to Nothing do not actually contain the word *Nothing*; rather, they contain no data at all.

Assigning Data to an Existing Variable

In Chapter 2, you learned how to use an assignment statement to assign a value to a control's property during run time. An assignment statement is also used to assign a value to a variable during run time; the syntax for doing this is shown in Figure 3-7. In the syntax, *expression* can contain items such as literal constants, object properties, variables, keywords, and arithmetic operators. A **literal constant** is an item of data whose value does not change while the application is running; examples include the string literal constant "Mary" and the numeric literal constant 500. When the computer processes an assignment statement, it assigns the value of the expression that appears on the right side of the assignment operator (=) to the variable (memory location) whose name appears on the left side of the assignment operator. In other words, the computer evaluates the expression first and then stores the result in the variable.

Assigning a Value to a Variable During Run Time

Syntax
variableName = *expression*

Note: In each of the following examples, the data type of the expression assigned to the variable is the same as the data type of the variable itself.

Example 1
`intYear = 2017`
assigns the integer 2017 to the `intYear` variable

Example 2
`strCity = "Boise"`
assigns the string "Boise" to the `strCity` variable

Example 3
`strState = txtState.Text`
assigns the string contained in the txtState control's Text property to the `strState` variable

Example 4
`dblRate = 0.25`
assigns the Double number 0.25 to the `dblRate` variable

Example 5
`decRaiseRate = 0.03D`
converts the Double number 0.03 to Decimal and then assigns the result to the `decRaiseRate` variable

Example 6
`dblNewPay = dblCurrentPay * 1.03`
multiplies the contents of the `dblCurrentPay` variable by the Double number 1.03 and then assigns the result to the `dblNewPay` variable

---

Figure 3-7 Syntax and examples of assigning a value to a variable during run time

The data type of the expression assigned to a variable should be the same data type as the variable itself; this is the case in all of the examples included in Figure 3-7. The assignment statement in Example 1 stores the numeric literal constant 2017 (an integer) in an Integer variable named `intYear`. Similarly, the assignment statement in Example 2 stores the string literal constant "Boise" in a String variable named `strCity`. Notice that string literal constants are enclosed in quotation marks, but numeric literal constants and variable names are not. The quotation marks differentiate a string from both a number and a variable name. In other words, "2017" is a string, but 2017 is a number. Similarly, "Boise" is a string, but Boise (without the quotation marks) would be interpreted by the computer as the name of a variable. When the computer processes an assignment statement that assigns a string to a String variable, it assigns only the characters that appear between the quotation marks; it does not assign the quotation marks themselves.

The assignment statement in Example 3 assigns the string contained in the txtState control's Text property to a String variable named `strState`. (Recall that the value stored in the Text property of an object is always treated as a string.) The assignment statement in Example 4 assigns the Double number 0.25 to a Double variable named `dblRate`. This is because a numeric literal constant that has a decimal place is automatically treated as a Double number in Visual Basic. When entering a numeric literal constant, you do not enter a comma or special characters, such as the dollar sign or percent sign. If you want to include a percentage in an assignment statement, you do so using its decimal equivalent; for example, you enter 0.25 rather than 25%. (If you enter .25 in the Code Editor window, the editor will change the number to 0.25 when you move the insertion point to a different line.)

The `decRaiseRate = 0.03D` statement in Example 5 shows how you convert a numeric literal constant of the Double data type to the Decimal data type, and then assign the result to a Decimal variable. The D that follows the number 0.03 in the statement is one of the literal type characters in Visual Basic. A **literal type character** forces a literal constant to assume a data type other than the one its form indicates. In this case, the D forces the Double number 0.03 to assume the Decimal data type.

You will learn about another literal type character, the letter C, in Chapter 8.

Finally, the `dblNewPay = dblCurrentPay * 1.03` statement in Example 6 multiplies the contents of the `dblCurrentPay` variable by the Double number 1.03 and then assigns the result to the `dblNewPay` variable. When an assignment statement's expression contains the name of a variable, the computer uses the value stored inside the variable to evaluate the expression. Notice that the calculation appearing on the right side of the assignment operator is performed first, and then the result is assigned to the variable whose name appears on the left side of the assignment operator.

A variable can store only one value at any one time. When you use an assignment statement to assign another value to the variable, the new value replaces the existing value, as illustrated in Figure 3-8.

```
Private Sub btnCalc_Click(sender As Obj
    Dim intNum As Integer                    initializes the
                                             variable to 0

    intNum = 100                             replaces 0 with 100
    intNum = intNum * 3                      replaces 100 with 300
End Sub
```

Figure 3-8 Assignment statements entered in the btnCalc_Click procedure

In all of the assignment statements shown in Figures 3-7 and 3-8, the expression's data type is the same as the variable's data type. At times, however, you may need to store a value of a different data type in a variable. You can change the value's data type to match the variable's data type using either the TryParse method or one of the methods in the Convert class.

The TryParse Method

Like the Val function, which you learned about in Chapter 2, the **TryParse method** converts a string to a number. However, unlike the Val function, which returns a Double number, the TryParse method allows the programmer to specify the number's data type; for this reason, most programmers prefer to use the TryParse method. Every numeric data type in Visual Basic has a TryParse method that converts a string to that particular data type.

Figure 3-9 shows the basic syntax of the TryParse method and includes examples of using the method. In the syntax, *dataType* is one of the numeric data types available in Visual Basic. The dot member access operator in the syntax indicates that the method is a member of the *dataType* class. The method's arguments (*string* and *numericVariableName*) represent information that the method needs to perform its task. The *string* argument is the string you want converted to a number of the *dataType* type. The *string* argument is typically either the Text property of a control or the name of a String variable. The *numericVariableName* argument is the name of a numeric variable that the TryParse method can use to store the number. The numeric variable must have the same data type as specified in the *dataType* portion of the syntax. For example, when using the TryParse method to convert a string to a Double number, you need to provide the method with the name of a Double variable in which to store the number.

The TryParse method parses its *string* argument to determine whether the string can be converted to a number. In this case, the term *parse* means to look at each character in the string. If the string can be converted, the TryParse method converts the string to a number and then stores the number in the variable specified in the *numericVariableName* argument. If the TryParse method determines that the string cannot be converted to the appropriate data type, it assigns the number 0 to the variable.

You will learn more about the TryParse method in Chapter 5.

TryParse Method

Basic syntax
dataType.**TryParse**(*string*, *numericVariableName*)

Example 1
`Double.TryParse(txtPaid.Text, dblPaid)`
If the string contained in the txtPaid control's Text property can be converted to a Double number, the TryParse method converts the string and then stores the result in the `dblPaid` variable; otherwise, it stores the number 0 in the variable.

Example 2
`Decimal.TryParse(txtTotal.Text, decTotal)`
If the string contained in the txtTotal control's Text property can be converted to a Decimal number, the TryParse method converts the string and then stores the result in the `decTotal` variable; otherwise, it stores the number 0 in the variable.

Example 3
`Integer.TryParse(strQuantity, intQuantity)`
If the string contained in the `strQuantity` variable can be converted to an Integer number, the TryParse method converts the string and then stores the result in the `intQuantity` variable; otherwise, it stores the number 0 in the variable.

Figure 3-9   Basic syntax and examples of the TryParse method

Figure 3-10 shows how the TryParse method of the Double, Decimal, and Integer data types would convert various strings. As the figure indicates, the three methods can convert a string that contains only numbers. They can also convert a string that contains a leading sign as well as one that contains leading or trailing spaces. In addition, the Double.TryParse and Decimal.TryParse methods can convert a string that contains a decimal point or a comma. However, none of the three methods can convert a string that contains a dollar sign, a percent sign, a letter, a space within the string, or an empty string.

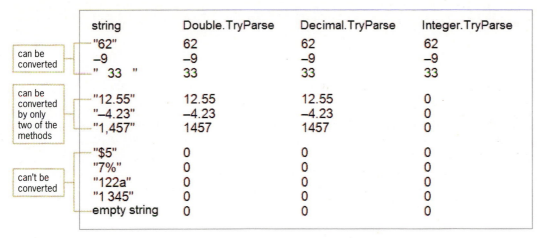

	string	Double.TryParse	Decimal.TryParse	Integer.TryParse
can be converted	"62"	62	62	62
	–9	–9	–9	–9
	" 33 "	33	33	33
can be converted by only two of the methods	"12.55"	12.55	12.55	0
	"–4.23"	–4.23	–4.23	0
	"1,457"	1457	1457	0
can't be converted	"$5"	0	0	0
	"7%"	0	0	0
	"122a"	0	0	0
	"1 345"	0	0	0
	empty string	0	0	0

Figure 3-10   Results of the TryParse method for the Double, Decimal, and Integer data types

The Convert Class

At times, you may need to convert a number (rather than a string) from one data type to another. Visual Basic provides several ways of accomplishing this task. One way is to use the Visual Basic conversion functions, which are listed in Appendix C in this book. You can also use one of the methods defined in the **Convert class**. In this book, you will use the Convert class methods because they can be used in any of the languages built into Visual Studio. The conversion functions, on the other hand, can be used only in the Visual Basic language. The more commonly used methods in the Convert class are the ToDecimal, ToDouble, ToInt32, and ToString methods. The methods convert a value to the Decimal, Double, Integer, and String data types, respectively.

The syntax for using the Convert class methods is shown in Figure 3-11 along with examples of using the methods. The dot member access operator in the syntax indicates that the *method* is a member of the Convert class. In most cases, the *value* argument is a numeric value that you want converted either to the String data type or to a different numeric data type (for example, from Double to Decimal). Although you can use the Convert methods to convert a string to a numeric data type, the TryParse method is the recommended method to use for that task. This is because, unlike the Convert methods, the TryParse method does not produce an error when it tries to convert an empty string. Instead, the TryParse method assigns the number 0 to its *numericVariableName* argument.

Convert Class Methods

<u>Syntax</u>
Convert.*method***(***value***)**

<u>Example 1</u>
`decRate = Convert.ToDecimal(0.15)`
converts the Double number 0.15 to Decimal and then assigns the result to the `decRate` variable

<u>Example 2</u>
`lblQuantity.Text = Convert.ToString(intQuantity)`
converts the integer stored in the `intQuantity` variable to String and then assigns the result to the lblQuantity control's Text property

<u>Example 3</u>
`decBonus = decSales * Convert.ToDecimal(0.05)`
converts the Double number 0.05 to Decimal, then multiplies the result by the contents of the `decSales` variable, and then assigns that result to the `decBonus` variable

---

Figure 3-11   Syntax and examples of the Convert class methods

In the statement shown in Example 1, the Convert.ToDecimal method converts the Double number 0.15 to Decimal. (Recall that a number with a decimal place is automatically treated as a Double number in Visual Basic.) The statement then assigns the result to the **decRate** variable. You could also write the statement as **decRate = 0.15D**. However, some programmers would argue that using the Convert.ToDecimal method, rather than the literal type character D, makes the code clearer.

In Example 2's statement, the Convert.ToString method converts the integer stored in the **intQuantity** variable to String before the statement assigns the result to the lblQuantity control's Text property. The statement in Example 3 uses the Convert.ToDecimal method to convert the Double number 0.05 to Decimal. The statement multiplies the result by the contents of the **decSales** variable and then assigns the product to the **decBonus** variable. You could also write this statement as **decBonus = decSales * 0.05D**.

YOU DO IT 1!

Create an application named YouDoIt 1 and save it in the VB2015\Chap03 folder. Add a text box, a label, and a button to the form. The button's Click event procedure should store the contents of the text box in a Double variable named **dblCost**. It then should display the variable's contents in the label. Code the procedure. Save the solution, and then start and test the application. Close the solution.

Note: You have learned a lot so far in this lesson. You may want to take a break at this point before continuing.

The Scope and Lifetime of a Variable

Besides a name, a data type, and an initial value, every variable also has a scope and a lifetime. A variable's **scope** indicates where the variable can be used in an application's code, and its **lifetime** indicates how long the variable remains in the computer's internal memory. Variables can have class scope, procedure scope, or block scope. However, most of the variables used in an application will have procedure scope. This is because fewer unintentional errors occur in applications when the variables are declared using the minimum scope needed, which usually is procedure scope.

A variable's scope and lifetime are determined by where you declare the variable. Typically, you enter the declaration statement either in a procedure (such as an event procedure) or in the Declarations section of a form. A form's Declarations section is not the same as the General Declarations section, which you learned about in Chapter 2. The General Declarations section is located above the Public Class clause in the Code Editor window, whereas the **form's Declarations section** is located between the Public Class and End Class clauses.

Variables declared in a form's Declarations section have class scope. Variables declared in a procedure, on the other hand, have either procedure scope or block scope, depending on where in the procedure they are declared. In the next two sections, you will learn about procedure scope variables and class scope variables. Variables with block scope are covered in Chapter 4.

Variables with Procedure Scope

When you declare a variable in a procedure, the variable is called a **procedure-level variable**. Procedure-level variables have **procedure scope** because they can be used only by the procedure in which they are declared. Procedure-level variables are typically declared at the beginning of a procedure, and they remain in the computer's internal memory only while the procedure is running. Procedure-level variables are removed from memory when the procedure in which they are declared ends. In other words, a procedure-level variable has the same lifetime as the procedure that declares it. As mentioned earlier, most of the variables in your applications will be procedure-level variables.

The Commission Calculator application that you will view next illustrates the use of procedure-level variables. As the interface shown in Figure 3-12 indicates, the application displays the amount of a salesperson's commission. The commission is calculated by multiplying the salesperson's sales by the appropriate commission rate: either 8% or 10%.

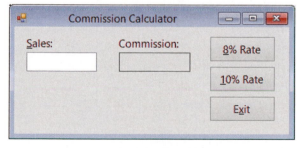

Figure 3-12   User interface for the Commission Calculator application

Figure 3-13 shows the Click event procedures for the 8% Rate and 10% Rate buttons. The comments in the figure indicate the purpose of each line of code. When each procedure ends, its procedure-level variables are removed from the computer's memory. The variables will be created again the next time the user clicks the button.

ChO3A-Scope and Lifetime

Variables can also have namespace scope and are referred to as namespace variables, global variables, or public variables. Such variables can lead to unintentional errors in a program and should be avoided, if possible. For this reason, they are not covered in this book.

Procedure-level variables are also called local variables and their scope is often referred to as local scope.

In the *Static Variables* section of this chapter, you will learn how to declare a procedure-level variable that remains in the computer's memory even when the procedure in which it is declared ends.

```
Private Sub btnRate8_Click(sender As Object, e As EventArgs)
Handles btnRate8.Click
    ' calculates and displays an 8% commission

    ' the Dim statements declare two procedure-level
    ' variables that can be used only within the
    ' btnRate8_Click procedure
    Dim dblSales As Double          removed from memory
    Dim dblComm8 As Double          when the btnRate8_Click
                                    procedure ends

    ' the TryParse method converts the contents of the
    ' txtSales control to Double and then stores the
    ' result in the procedure-level dblSales variable
    Double.TryParse(txtSales.Text, dblSales)

    ' the assignment statement multiplies the value
    ' stored in the procedure-level dblSales variable
    ' by the Double number 0.08 and then assigns the
    ' result to the procedure-level dblComm8 variable
    dblComm8 = dblSales * 0.08

    ' the Convert method converts the value stored in
    ' the procedure-level dblComm8 variable to String,
    ' and the assignment statement assigns the result
    ' to the lblComm control's Text property
    lblComm.Text = Convert.ToString(dblComm8)
End Sub


Private Sub btnRate10_Click(sender As Object, e As EventArgs)
Handles btnRate10.Click
    ' calculates and displays a 10% commission

    ' the Dim statements declare two procedure-level
    ' variables that can be used only within the
    ' btnRate10_Click procedure
    Dim dblSales As Double          removed from memory
    Dim dblComm10 As Double         when the btnRate10_Click
                                    procedure ends

    ' the TryParse method converts the contents of the
    ' txtSales control to Double and then stores the
    ' result in the procedure-level dblSales variable
    Double.TryParse(txtSales.Text, dblSales)

    ' the assignment statement multiplies the value
    ' stored in the procedure-level dblSales variable
    ' by the Double number 0.1 and then assigns the
    ' result to the procedure-level dblComm10 variable
    dblComm10 = dblSales * 0.1

    ' the Convert method converts the value stored in
    ' the procedure-level dblComm10 variable to String,
    ' and the assignment statement assigns the result
    ' to the lblComm control's Text property
    lblComm.Text = Convert.ToString(dblComm10)
End Sub
```

Figure 3-13   Click event procedures using procedure-level variables

Notice that both procedures in Figure 3-13 declare a variable named `dblSales`. When you use the same name to declare a variable in more than one procedure, each procedure creates its own variable when the procedure is invoked. Each procedure also destroys its own variable when the procedure ends. In other words, although both procedures declare a variable named `dblSales`, each `dblSales` variable will refer to a different section in the computer's internal memory, and each will be both created and destroyed independently from the other.

To code and then test the Commission Calculator application:

START HERE

1. If necessary, start Visual Studio 2015. Open the Commission Solution (Commission Solution.sln) file contained in the VB2015\Chap03\Commission Solution-Procedure-level folder. The user interface shown earlier in Figure 3-12 appears on the screen.

2. Open the Code Editor window. See Figure 3-14. For now, do not be concerned about the three Option statements that appear in the window. You will learn about them later in this lesson. Replace <your name> and <current date> in the comments with your name and the current date, respectively.

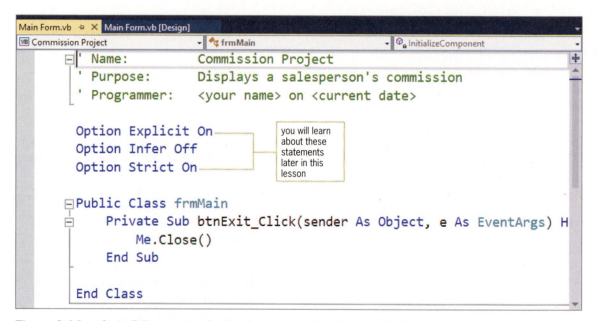

Figure 3-14   Code Editor window for the Commission Calculator application

3. Open the code templates for the btnRate8_Click and btnRate10_Click procedures. In the procedures, enter the comments and code shown earlier in Figure 3-13.

4. Save the solution and then start the application. If necessary, press **Alt** to display the access keys in the interface.

    Note: The figures in this book usually show the interface's access keys. However, from now on, you will not be instructed to press Alt to display the access keys. Instead, you can choose whether or not to display them.

5. First, calculate and display an 8% commission on $55,000. Type **55000** in the Sales box and then click the **8% Rate** button. The number 4400 appears in the Commission box, as shown in Figure 3-15.

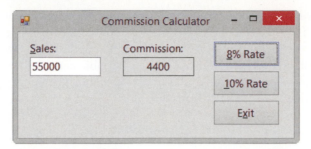

Figure 3-15   Commission shown in the interface

6. Next, test the btnRate8_Click procedure using an invalid sales amount. Change the sales amount to the letter **a** and then click the **8% Rate** button. The number 0 appears in the Commission box.

7. Change the sales amount to **15000** and then click the **10% Rate** button. The number 1500 appears in the Commission box.

8. Now test the btnRate10_Click procedure using an invalid sales amount. Change the sales amount to **$5999** (be sure to type the dollar sign) and then click the **10% Rate** button. The number 0 appears in the Commission box.

9. Click the **Exit** button. Close the Code Editor window and then close the solution.

Variables with Class Scope

In addition to declaring a variable in a procedure, you can also declare a variable in the form's Declarations section, which begins with the Public Class clause and ends with the End Class clause. When you declare a variable in the form's Declarations section, the variable is called a **class-level variable** and it has **class scope**. Class-level variables can be used by all of the procedures in the form, including the procedures associated with the controls contained on the form. Class-level variables retain their values and remain in the computer's internal memory until the application ends. In other words, a class-level variable has the same lifetime as the application itself.

 Although you can also use the Dim keyword to declare a class-level variable, most Visual Basic programmers use the Private keyword so that the scope is more obvious to anyone reading the code.

Unlike a procedure-level variable, which is declared using the Dim keyword, you declare a class-level variable using the Private keyword. You typically use a class-level variable when you need more than one procedure in the same form to use the same variable. However, a class-level variable can also be used when a procedure needs to retain a variable's value after the procedure ends. The Total Scores application, which you will view next, illustrates this use of a class-level variable. The application's interface is shown in Figure 3-16. As the interface indicates, the application calculates and displays the total of the scores entered by the user.

Figure 3-16   User interface for the Total Scores application

Figure 3-17 shows most of the Total Scores application's code. The code uses a class-level variable named `decTotal` to accumulate (add together) the scores entered by the user. Class-level variables are declared after the Public Class clause, but before the first Private Sub clause, in the form's Declarations section.

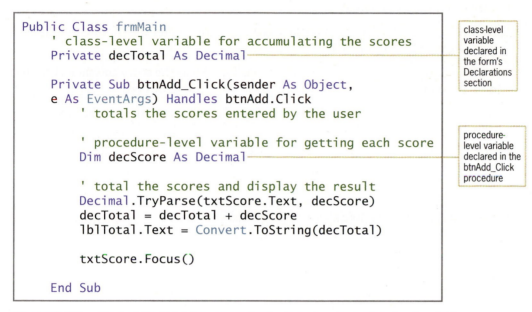

```
Public Class frmMain
    ' class-level variable for accumulating the scores
    Private decTotal As Decimal

    Private Sub btnAdd_Click(sender As Object,
    e As EventArgs) Handles btnAdd.Click
        ' totals the scores entered by the user

        ' procedure-level variable for getting each score
        Dim decScore As Decimal

        ' total the scores and display the result
        Decimal.TryParse(txtScore.Text, decScore)
        decTotal = decTotal + decScore
        lblTotal.Text = Convert.ToString(decTotal)

        txtScore.Focus()

    End Sub
```

class-level variable declared in the form's Declarations section

procedure-level variable declared in the btnAdd_Click procedure

Figure 3-17   Most of the Total Scores application's code using a class-level variable

When the user starts the Total Scores application, the computer will process the `Private decTotal As Decimal` statement first. The statement creates and initializes the class-level `decTotal` variable. The variable is created and initialized only once, when the application starts. It remains in the computer's internal memory until the application ends.

Each time the user clicks the Add to Total button, the button's Click event procedure creates and initializes a procedure-level variable named `decScore`. The TryParse method then converts the contents of the txtScore control to Decimal, storing the result in the `decScore` variable. The first assignment statement in the procedure adds the contents of the procedure-level `decScore` variable to the contents of the class-level `decTotal` variable. At this point, the `decTotal` variable contains the sum of all of the scores entered so far. The last assignment statement in the procedure converts the contents of the `decTotal` variable to String and then assigns the result to the lblTotal control. The procedure then sends the focus to the txtScore control. When the procedure ends, the computer removes the procedure-level `decScore` variable from its memory. However, it does not remove the class-level `decTotal` variable. The `decTotal` variable is removed from the computer's memory only when the application ends.

To code and then test the Total Scores application:

START HERE

1. Open the Total Scores Solution (Total Scores Solution.sln) file contained in the Total Scores Solution-Class-level folder. The user interface shown earlier in Figure 3-16 appears on the screen.

2. Open the Code Editor window. Replace <your name> and <current date> in the comments with your name and the current date, respectively.

3. First, declare the class-level `decTotal` variable in the form's Declarations section. Enter the following comment and declaration statement in the blank line below the Public Class clause:

' class-level variable for accumulating the scores
Private decTotal As Decimal

4. Open the code template for the btnAdd_Click procedure. Enter the comments and code shown earlier in Figure 3-17.

5. Save the solution and then start the application. Type **89** as the score and then click the **Add to Total** button. The number 89 appears in the Total scores box.

6. Change the score to **75** and then click the **Add to Total** button. The number 164 appears in the Total scores box.

7. Change the score to **100** and then click the **Add to Total** button. The number 264 appears in the Total scores box, as shown in Figure 3-18.

Figure 3-18   Interface showing the total of the scores you entered

8. Click the **Exit** button. Close the Code Editor window and then close the solution.

Static Variables

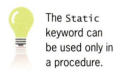

The `Static` keyword can be used only in a procedure.

A **static variable** is a procedure-level variable that remains in memory and also retains its value, even when the procedure in which it is declared ends. Like a class-level variable, a static variable is not removed from the computer's internal memory until the application ends. However, unlike a class-level variable, which can be used by all of the procedures in a form, a static variable can be used only by the procedure in which it is declared. In other words, a static variable has a narrower (or more restrictive) scope than does a class-level variable. As mentioned earlier, you can prevent many unintentional errors from occurring in an application by declaring the variables using the minimum scope needed.

In the previous section, you viewed the interface and code for the Total Scores application, which uses a class-level variable to accumulate the scores entered by the user. Rather than using a class-level variable for that purpose, you can also use a static variable, as shown in the code in Figure 3-19.

```
Public Class frmMain

    Private Sub btnAdd_Click(sender As Object,
    e As EventArgs) Handles btnAdd.Click
        ' totals the scores entered by the user

        ' procedure-level variable for getting each score
        Dim decScore As Decimal
        ' static variable for accumulating the scores
        Static decTotal As Decimal ─────────────

        ' total the scores and display the result
        Decimal.TryParse(txtScore.Text, decScore)
        decTotal = decTotal + decScore
        lblTotal.Text = Convert.ToString(decTotal)

        txtScore.Focus()

    End Sub
```

static variable
declared in the
btnAdd_Click
procedure

Figure 3-19   Most of the Total Scores application's code using a static variable

The first time the user clicks the Add to Total button, the button's Click event procedure creates and initializes (to 0) a procedure-level variable named **decScore** and a static variable named **decTotal**. The TryParse method then converts the contents of the txtScore control to Decimal, storing the result in the **decScore** variable. The first assignment statement in the procedure adds the contents of the **decScore** variable to the contents of the static **decTotal** variable. The last assignment statement in the procedure converts the contents of the **decTotal** variable to String and assigns the result to the lblTotal control. The procedure then sends the focus to the txtScore control. When the procedure ends, the computer removes the variable declared using the **Dim** keyword (**decScore**) from its internal memory. But it does not remove the variable declared using the **Static** keyword (**decTotal**).

Each subsequent time the user clicks the Add to Total button, the computer re-creates and re-initializes the **decScore** variable declared in the btnAdd_Click procedure. However, it does not re-create or re-initialize the static **decTotal** variable because that variable, as well as its current value, is still in the computer's memory. After re-creating and re-initializing the **decScore** variable, the computer processes the remaining instructions contained in the button's Click event procedure. Here again, each time the procedure ends, the **decScore** variable is removed from the computer's internal memory. The **decTotal** variable is removed only when the application ends.

To use a static variable in the Total Scores application:

START HERE

1. Open the Total Scores Solution (Total Scores Solution.sln) file contained in the Total Scores Solution-Static folder. The user interface shown earlier in Figure 3-16 appears on the screen.

2. Open the Code Editor window. Replace <your name> and <current date> in the comments with your name and the current date, respectively.

3. Delete the comment and the Private declaration statement entered in the form's Declarations section.

4. Modify the btnAdd_Click procedure so that it uses a static variable rather than a class-level variable. Use the code shown in Figure 3-19 as a guide.

5. Save the solution and then start the application.

6. Use the application to total the following three scores: **89**, **75**, and **100**. Be sure to click the **Add to Total** button after typing each score. Also be sure to delete the previous score before entering the next score. When you are finished entering the scores, the number 264 appears in the Total scores box, as shown earlier in Figure 3-18.

7. Click the **Exit** button. Close the Code Editor window and then close the solution.

YOU DO IT 2!

Create an application named YouDoIt 2 and save it in the VB2015\Chap03 folder. Add a label and a button to the form. The button's Click event procedure should add the number 1 to the contents of a class-level Integer variable named `intNumber` and then display the variable's contents in the label. Code the application. Save the solution, and then start and test the application. Next, change the class-level variable to a static variable. Save the solution, and then start and test the application. Close the solution.

Named Constants

In addition to using literal constants and variables in your code, you can also use named constants. Like a variable, a **named constant** is a memory location inside the computer. However, unlike the value stored in a variable, the value stored in a named constant cannot be changed while the application is running. You declare a named constant using the **Const statement**. The statement's syntax is shown in Figure 3-20. In the syntax, *expression* is the value you want stored in the named constant when it is created in the computer's internal memory. The expression's value must have the same data type as the named constant. The expression can contain a literal constant, another named constant, or an arithmetic operator; however, it cannot contain a variable or a method.

Declaring a Named Constant

Syntax
[**Private**] **Const** constantName **As** dataType = expression

Example 1
`Const dblPI As Double = 3.141593`
declares `dblPI` as a Double named constant and initializes it to the Double number 3.141593

Example 2
`Const intMAX_SPEED As Integer = 70`
declares `intMAX_SPEED` as an Integer named constant and initializes it to the integer 70

Example 3
`Const strTITLE As String = "Vice President of Sales"`
declares `strTITLE` as a String named constant and initializes it to the string "Vice President of Sales"

Example 4
`Private Const decRATE As Decimal = 0.05D` ———— changes the number's type from Double to Decimal
declares `decRATE` as a Decimal named constant and initializes it to the Decimal number 0.05

Figure 3-20   Syntax and examples of the Const statement

To differentiate the name of a constant from the name of a variable, many programmers lowercase the three-character ID that represents the constant's data type and then uppercase the remaining characters in the name, as shown in the examples in Figure 3-20. When entered in a procedure, the Const statements shown in the first three examples create procedure-level named constants. To create a class-level named constant, you precede the **Const** keyword with the **Private** keyword, as shown in Example 4. In addition, you enter the Const statement in the form's Declarations section. Notice that Example 4 uses the literal type character D to convert the Double number 0.05 to Decimal. The Convert.ToDecimal method was not used for this purpose because, as mentioned earlier, the expression assigned to a named constant cannot contain a method.

Named constants make code more self-documenting and easier to modify because they allow you to use meaningful words in place of values that are less clear. The named constant `dblPI`, for example, is much more meaningful than the number 3.141593, which is the value of pi rounded to six decimal places. Once you create a named constant, you then can use the constant's name, rather than its value, in the application's code. Unlike the value stored in a variable, the value stored in a named constant cannot be inadvertently changed while the application is running. Using a named constant to represent a value has another advantage: If the value changes in the future, you will need to modify only the Const statement in the program rather than all of the program statements that use the value.

The Area Calculator application that you will view next illustrates the use of a named constant. As the interface shown in Figure 3-21 indicates, the application displays a circle's area, given its radius. The formula for calculating the area of a circle is πr^2, where π stands for pi (3.141593).

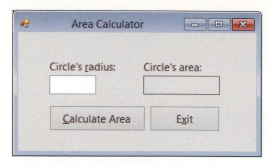

Figure 3-21   User interface for the Area Calculator application

Figure 3-22 shows the code for the Calculate Area button's Click event procedure. The declaration statements declare and initialize a named constant and two variables. The TryParse method converts the contents of the txtRadius control to Double, storing the result in the `dblRadius` variable. The first assignment statement calculates the circle's area using the values stored in the `dblPI` named constant and the `dblRadius` variable; it then assigns the result to the `dblArea` variable. In the second assignment statement, the Format function (which returns a string) formats the contents of the `dblArea` variable. The assignment statement then displays the resulting string in the lblArea control. When the procedure ends, the computer removes the named constant and two variables from its internal memory.

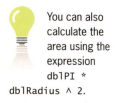
You can also calculate the area using the expression dblPI * dblRadius ^ 2.

```
Private Sub btnCalc_Click(sender As Object,
e As EventArgs) Handles btnCalc.Click
    ' calculates and displays the area of a circle

    ' declare named constant and variables
    Const dblPI As Double = 3.141593
    Dim dblRadius As Double
    Dim dblArea As Double

    ' calculate and display area
    Double.TryParse(txtRadius.Text, dblRadius)
    dblArea = dblPI * dblRadius * dblRadius
    lblArea.Text = Format(dblArea, "standard")

End Sub
```

named constant declaration statement

assignment statement containing the named constant

Figure 3-22   Calculate Area button's Click event procedure

START HERE

To code and then test the Area Calculator application:

1. Open the Area Calculator Solution (Area Calculator Solution.sln) file contained in the Area Calculator Solution folder. The user interface shown earlier in Figure 3-21 appears on the screen.

2. Open the Code Editor window. Replace <your name> and <current date> in the comments with your name and the current date, respectively.

3. Open the code template for the btnCalc_Click procedure, and then enter the comments and code shown earlier in Figure 3-22.

4. Save the solution and then start the application. Type **10** in the Circle's radius box and then click the **Calculate Area** button. The number 314.16 appears in the Circle's area box, as shown in Figure 3-23.

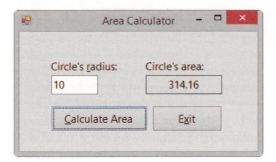

Figure 3-23   Interface showing the circle's area

5. Click the **Exit** button. Close the Code Editor window and then close the solution.

Option Statements

Finally, you will learn about the three Option statements shown earlier in Figure 3-14. The Option statements appeared in the Code Editor window for all of the applications you viewed in this lesson. You will learn about the Option Explicit and Option Infer statements first.

Option Explicit and Option Infer

It is important to declare every variable used in your code. This means every variable should appear in a declaration statement, such as a Dim, Static, or Private statement. The declaration statement is important because it allows you to control the variable's data type. Declaration statements also make your code more self-documenting. A word of caution is in order at this point: In Visual Basic, you can create variables "on the fly." This means that if a statement in your code refers to an undeclared variable, Visual Basic will create the variable for you and assign the Object data type to it. Recall that the Object type is not a very efficient data type, and its use should be limited.

Because it is so easy to forget to declare a variable—and so easy to misspell a variable's name while coding, thereby inadvertently creating an undeclared variable—Visual Basic provides a statement that tells the Code Editor to flag any undeclared variables in your code: `Option Explicit On`. You enter the statement in the General Declarations section (located above the Public Class clause) of the Code Editor window. When you also enter the `Option Infer Off` statement in the General Declarations section, the Code Editor ensures that every variable and named constant is declared with a data type. In other words, the statement tells the computer not to infer (or assume) a memory location's data type based on the data assigned to the memory location.

Option Strict

As you learned earlier, the data type of the value assigned to a memory location should be the same as the data type of the memory location itself. If the value's data type does not match the memory location's data type, the computer uses a process called **implicit type conversion** to convert the value to fit the memory location. For example, when processing the statement `Dim dblLength As Double = 9`, the computer converts the integer 9 to the Double number 9.0 before storing the value in the `dblLength` variable. When a value is converted from one data type to another data type that can store either larger numbers or numbers with greater precision, the value is said to be **promoted**. In this case, if the `dblLength` variable is used subsequently in a calculation, the results of the calculation will not be adversely affected by the implicit promotion of the number 9 to the number 9.0.

On the other hand, if you inadvertently assign a Double number to a memory location that can store only integers, the computer converts the Double number to an integer before storing the value in the memory location. It does this by rounding the number to the nearest whole number and then truncating (dropping off) the decimal portion of the number. When processing the statement `Dim intScore As Integer = 78.4`, for example, the computer converts the Double number 78.4 to the integer 78 before storing the integer in the `intScore` variable. When a value is converted from one data type to another data type that can store only smaller numbers or numbers with less precision, the value is said to be **demoted**. If the `intScore` variable is used subsequently in a calculation, the implicit demotion of the number 78.4 to the number 78 will probably cause the calculated results to be incorrect.

With implicit type conversions, data loss can occur when a value is converted from one data type to a narrower data type, which is a data type with less precision or smaller capacity. You can eliminate the problems that occur as a result of implicit type conversions by entering the `Option Strict On` statement in the General Declarations section of the Code Editor window. When the `Option Strict On` statement appears in an application's code, the computer uses the type conversion rules listed in Figure 3-24. The figure also includes examples of these rules.

Type Conversion Rules

1. Strings will not be implicitly converted to numbers. The Code Editor will display a warning message when a statement attempts to use a string where a number is expected.

   ```
   Incorrect:      dblRadius = txtRadius.Text
   Correct:        Double.TryParse(txtRadius.Text, dblRadius)
   ```

2. Numbers will not be implicitly converted to strings. The Code Editor will display a warning message when a statement attempts to use a number where a string is expected.

   ```
   Incorrect:      lblArea.Text = dblArea
   Correct:        lblArea.Text = Convert.ToString(dblArea)
   Correct:        lblArea.Text = Format(dblArea, "standard")
   ```

3. Wider data types will not be implicitly demoted to narrower data types. The Code Editor will display a warning message when a statement attempts to use a wider data type where a narrower data type is expected.

   ```
   Incorrect:      Dim decRate As Decimal = 0.05
   Correct:        Dim decRate As Decimal = 0.05D
   Correct:        Dim decRate As Decimal = Convert.ToDecimal(0.05)
   ```

4. Narrower data types will be implicitly promoted to wider data types.

   ```
   Correct:        dblAverage = dblTotal / intNum
   ```

Figure 3-24 Rules and examples of type conversions

According to the first rule, the computer will not implicitly convert a string to a number. As a result, the Code Editor will issue the warning message "Option Strict On disallows implicit conversions from 'String' to 'Double'" when your code contains the statement `dblRadius = txtRadius.Text`. As you learned earlier, you should use the TryParse method to explicitly convert a string to the Double data type before assigning it to a Double variable. The appropriate TryParse method to use in this case is shown in Figure 3-24.

According to the second rule, the computer will not implicitly convert a number to a string. Therefore, the Code Editor will issue an appropriate warning message when your code contains the statement `lblArea.Text = dblArea`. You can use either the Convert class methods or the Format function to explicitly convert a number to the String data type, as shown in Figure 3-24.

The third rule states that wider data types will not be implicitly demoted to narrower data types. A data type is wider than another data type if it can store either larger numbers or numbers with greater precision. Because of this rule, a Double number will not be implicitly demoted to the Decimal or Integer data types. If your code contains the statement `Dim decRate As Decimal = 0.05`, the Code Editor will issue an appropriate warning message because the statement assigns a Double number to a Decimal variable. You can use either the literal type character D or the Convert.ToDecimal method to convert a Double number to the Decimal data type, as shown in Figure 3-24.

According to the last rule listed in Figure 3-24, the computer will implicitly promote narrower data types to wider data types. This means that when processing the statement `dblAverage = dblTotal / intNum`, the computer will implicitly promote the integer stored in the `intNum` variable to Double before dividing it into the contents of the `dblTotal` variable. The result, a Double number, will be assigned to the `dblAverage` variable.

Figure 3-25 shows the three Option statements entered in the General Declarations section of the Code Editor window. If a project contains more than one form, the statements must be entered in each form's Code Editor window.

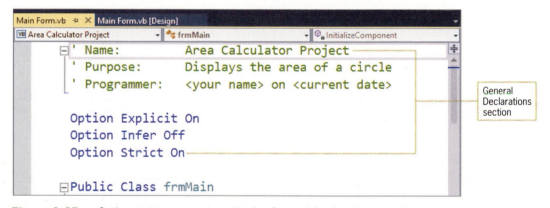

Figure 3-25   Option statements entered in the General Declarations section

Rather than entering the Option statements in the Code Editor window, you can set the options using either the Project Designer window or the Options dialog box. However, it is strongly recommended that you enter the Option statements in the Code Editor window because doing so makes your code more self-documenting and ensures that the options are set appropriately. The steps for setting the options in the Project Designer window and the Options dialog box are listed in Lesson A's Summary section.

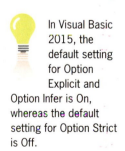

In Visual Basic 2015, the default setting for Option Explicit and Option Infer is On, whereas the default setting for Option Strict is Off.

YOU DO IT 3!

Create an application named YouDoIt 3 and save it in the VB2015\Chap03 folder. Add a text box, a label, and a button to the form. In the General Declarations section of the Code Editor window, enter the following three Option statements: `Option Explicit On`, `Option Strict Off`, and `Option Infer Off`. In the button's Click event procedure, declare a Double variable named `dblNum`. Use an assignment statement to assign the contents of the text box to the Double variable. Then, use an assignment statement to assign the contents of the Double variable to the label. Save the solution, and then start and test the application. Stop the application. Finally, change the `Option Strict Off` statement to `Option Strict On` and make the necessary modifications to the code. Save the solution, and then start and test the application. Close the solution.

Lesson A Summary

- To declare a variable:

  The syntax of a variable declaration statement is {`Dim` | `Private` | `Static`} *variableName* `As` *dataType* [= *initialValue*]. Use camel case for a variable's name.

- To declare a procedure-level variable:

  Enter the variable declaration statement in a procedure. Use the `Dim` keyword to declare a procedure-level variable that will be removed from the computer's internal memory when the procedure ends. Use the `Static` keyword to declare a procedure-level variable that remains in the computer's internal memory and also retains its value until the application ends.

- To declare a class-level variable:

  Enter the variable declaration statement in a form's Declarations section. Use the `Private` keyword.

- To use an assignment statement to assign data to an existing variable:

  Use the syntax *variableName* = *expression*.

- To force a Double literal constant to assume the Decimal data type:

  Append the letter D to the end of the Double literal constant.

- To convert a string to a numeric data type:

  Use the TryParse method. The method's syntax is *dataType*.`TryParse`(*string*, *numericVariableName*).

- To convert a numeric value to a different data type:

  Use one of the Convert methods. Each method's syntax is `Convert`.*method*(*value*).

- To declare a named constant:

  Use the Const statement. The statement's syntax is [`Private`] `Const` *constantName* `As` *dataType* = *expression*. Enter the three-character ID in lowercase, and enter the remainder of the name in uppercase.

- To declare a procedure-level named constant:

  Enter the Const statement (without the `Private` keyword) in a procedure.

- To declare a class-level named constant:

  Enter the Const statement, preceded by the keyword `Private`, in a form's Declarations section.

- To prevent the computer from creating an undeclared variable:

  Enter the `Option Explicit On` statement in the General Declarations section of the Code Editor window.

- To prevent the computer from inferring a variable's data type:

  Enter the `Option Infer Off` statement in the General Declarations section of the Code Editor window.

- To prevent the computer from making implicit type conversions that may result in a loss of data:

  Enter the `Option Strict On` statement in the General Declarations section of the Code Editor window.

- To use the Project Designer window to set Option Explicit, Option Strict, and Option Infer for an entire project:

  Open the solution that contains the project. Right-click My Project in the Solution Explorer window and then click Open to open the Project Designer window. Click the Compile tab. Use the Option explicit, Option strict, and Option infer boxes to set the options. Save the solution and then close the Project Designer window.

- To use the Options dialog box to set Option Explicit, Option Strict, and Option Infer for all of the projects you create:

  Click Tools on the Visual Studio menu bar and then click Options. When the Options dialog box opens, expand the Projects and Solutions node and then click VB Defaults. Use the Option Explicit, Option Strict, and Option Infer boxes to set the options. Click the OK button to close the Options dialog box.

Lesson A Key Terms

Class scope—the scope of a class-level variable or named constant; refers to the fact that the memory location can be used by any procedure in the form

Class-level variable—a variable declared in a form's Declarations section; it has class scope and should be declared using the `Private` keyword

Const statement—the statement used to create a named constant

Convert class—contains methods that return the result of converting a value to a specified data type

Data type—indicates the type of data a memory location (variable or named constant) can store

Demoted—the process of converting a value from one data type to another data type that can store only smaller numbers or numbers with less precision

Form's Declarations section—located between the Public Class and End Class clauses in the Code Editor window; the section of the Code Editor window where class-level variables and class-level named constants are declared

Implicit type conversion—the process by which a value is automatically converted to fit the memory location to which it is assigned

Lifetime—indicates how long a variable or named constant remains in the computer's internal memory

Literal constant—an item of data whose value does not change during run time

Literal type character—a character (such as the letter D) appended to a literal constant for the purpose of forcing the literal constant to assume a different data type (such as Decimal)

Named constant—a computer memory location whose contents cannot be changed during run time; declared using the Const statement

Procedure scope—the scope of a procedure-level variable or named constant; refers to the fact that the memory location can be used only by the procedure in which it is declared

Procedure-level variable—a variable declared in a procedure; the variable has procedure scope

Promoted—the process of converting a value from one data type to another data type that can store either larger numbers or numbers with greater precision

Scope—indicates where a memory location (variable or named constant) can be used in an application's code

Static variable—a procedure-level variable that remains in memory and retains its value until the application (rather than the declaring procedure) ends

TryParse method—used to convert a string to a number of a specified data type

Unicode—the universal coding scheme that assigns a unique numeric value to each character used in the written languages of the world

Variables—computer memory locations where programmers can temporarily store data, as well as change the data, while an application is running

Lesson A Review Questions

1. Which of the following keywords is used to declare a class-level variable?

   a. `Class`   c. `Global`

   b. `Dimension`   d. `Private`

2. Which of the following is a data item whose value does not change during run time?

   a. literal constant   c. named constant

   b. literal variable   d. variable

3. Which of the following statements declares a procedure-level variable that remains in the computer's memory until the application ends?

   a. `Dim Static intScore As Integer`

   b. `Private Static intScore As Integer`

   c. `Static intScore As Integer`

   d. both b and c

4. Which of the following keywords can be used to declare a variable within a procedure?

   a. `Dim`   c. `Static`

   b. `Procedure`   d. both a and c

5. Which of the following statements declares a class-level variable?

    a. `Class intNum As Integer`

    b. `Private intNum As Integer`

    c. `Private Class intNum As Integer`

    d. `Private Dim intNum As Integer`

6. Which of the following declares a procedure-level String variable?

    a. `Dim String strCity`   c. `Private strCity As String`

    b. `Dim strCity As String`   d. both b and c

7. Which of the following are computer memory locations that can temporarily store information?

    a. literal constants   c. variables

    b. named constants   d. both b and c

8. If Option Strict is set to On, which of the following statements will assign the contents of the txtSales control to a Double variable named `dblSales`?

    a. `dblSales = txtSales.Text`

    b. `dblSales = txtSales.Text.Convert.ToDouble`

    c. `Double.TryParse(txtSales.Text, dblSales)`

    d. `TryParse.Double(txtSales.Text, dblSales)`

9. Which of the following declares a named constant having the Double data type?

    a. `Const dblRATE As Double = 0.09`

    b. `Const dblRATE As Double`

    c. `Constant dblRATE = 0.09`

    d. both a and b

10. If Option Strict is set to On, which of the following statements assigns the sum of two Integer variables to the Text property of the lblTotal control?

    a. `lblTotal.Text = Convert.ToInteger(intN1 + intN2)`

    b. `lblTotal.Text = Convert.ToInt32(intN1 + intN2)`

    c. `lblTotal.Text = Convert.ToString(intN1) + Convert.ToString(intN2)`

    d. none of the above

11. Which of the following statements prevents data loss due to implicit type conversions?

    a. `Option Explicit On`   c. `Option Implicit Off`

    b. `Option Strict On`   d. `Option Convert Off`

12. A static variable has the same _____ as a procedure-level variable but the same _____ as a class-level variable.

    a. lifetime, scope

    b. scope, lifetime

Lesson A Exercises

INTRODUCTORY 1. A procedure needs to store a salesperson's name and bonus amount (which may have decimal places). Write the appropriate Dim statements to declare the necessary procedure-level variables.

INTRODUCTORY 2. A procedure needs to store a person's height and weight. The height may have a decimal place; the weight will always be a whole number. Write the appropriate Dim statements to declare the necessary procedure-level variables.

INTRODUCTORY 3. A procedure needs to store the name of a business, the number of its employees at the beginning of the current year, the number of new employees hired during the current year, the number of employees who left the business during the current year, and the number of its employees at the end of the current year. Write the appropriate Dim statements to declare the necessary procedure-level variables.

INTRODUCTORY 4. Write an assignment statement that assigns Georgia to a String variable named strState.

INTRODUCTORY 5. Write an assignment statement that assigns the name Carol Jones to a String variable named strEmployee. Also write assignment statements that assign the numbers 34 and 15.99 to variables named intAge and dblPayRate, respectively.

INTRODUCTORY 6. Write the statement to declare the procedure-level decINTEREST_RATE named constant whose value is 0.075.

INTRODUCTORY 7. Write the statement to store the contents of the txtAge control in an Integer variable named intAge.

INTRODUCTORY 8. Write the statement to assign the contents of the dblTotalSales variable to the lblTotal control.

INTRODUCTORY 9. Write a Private statement to declare a class-level variable named dblGrandTotal.

INTRODUCTORY 10. Write an assignment statement that subtracts the contents of the dblExpenses variable from the contents of the dblIncome variable and then assigns the result to the dblNet variable.

INTRODUCTORY 11. Open the VB2015\Chap03\Mileage Solution\Mileage Solution (Mileage Solution.sln) file. The application displays the miles per gallon, given the miles driven and gallons used. In the General Declarations section of the Code Editor window, enter your name, the current date, and the three Option statements. Use variables and the TryParse method to code the btnCalc_Click procedure. Use the Format function to display the miles per gallon with two decimal places. Save the solution and then start the application. Enter 324 and 17 as the miles driven and gallons used, respectively. The miles per gallon should be 19.06. Clear the screen. Now test the application using invalid data. More specifically, test it without entering any data, and then test it using letters as the input. When invalid data is entered, the Miles per gallon box will say either NaN (which stands for *Not a Number*) or Infinity. Both messages are a result of the miles per gallon calculation attempting to divide a Double number by the number 0. In Chapter 4, you will learn how to prevent these error mesages by using a selection structure.

INTRODUCTORY 12. Open the VB2015\Chap03\Tax Solution\Tax Solution (Tax Solution.sln) file. The application displays a 5% sales tax on the purchase amount entered by the user. In the General Declarations section of the Code Editor window, enter your name, the current date, and the three Option statements. Use variables and the TryParse method to code the Calculate button. Declare a named constant for the sales tax rate, which will be 5%. Use the Format function to display the sales tax with a dollar sign and two decimal places. Save the solution and then start the application. Test the application without entering any data. Then test it using 100.57 as the purchase amount. Finally, test it using $67.98 for the purchase amount.

13. Write an assignment statement that increases the contents of the `decPrice` variable by 2%.   ⟨ INTERMEDIATE

14. Write an assignment statement that adds together the values stored in the `decDomestic` and `decInternational` variables and then assigns the result to a String variable named `strIncome`.   ⟨ INTERMEDIATE

15. Write the statement to declare a Double variable that can be used by two procedures in the same form. Name the variable `dblNetIncome`. Also specify where you will need to enter the statement in the Code Editor window and whether the variable is a procedure-level or class-level variable.   ⟨ INTERMEDIATE

16. Open the VB2015\Chap03\Floor Solution\Floor Solution (Floor Solution.sln) file. The application displays the area of a floor in square yards, given its length and width (both measured in feet). In the General Declarations section of the Code Editor window, enter your name, the current date, and the three Option statements. Use variables and the TryParse method to code the Calculate button. Use the Format function to display the calculated results using the Standard format style. Save the solution and then start the application. Test the application using 20 as the length and 15 as the width. Next, test the application using invalid data. More specifically, test it without entering any data, and then test it using letters as the input.   ⟨ INTERMEDIATE

17. Open the VB2015\Chap03\Width Solution\Width Solution (Width Solution.sln) file. The application calculates a rectangle's width, given its perimeter and length. In the General Declarations section of the Code Editor window, enter your name, the current date, and the three Option statements. Use variables and the TryParse method to code the Calculate button. Use the Format function to display the width with two decimal places. Save the solution and then start the application. Test the application using 100 and 24 as the perimeter and the length, respectively. The width should be 26. Test the application without entering any data. Also test it using letters as the input.   ⟨ INTERMEDIATE

18. In this exercise, you experiment with procedure-level and class-level variables. Open the VB2015\Chap03\Scope Solution\Scope Solution (Scope Solution.sln) file. The application allows the user to calculate either a 5% or 10% commission on a sales amount. It displays the sales and commission amounts in the lblSales and lblCommission controls, respectively.   ⟨ DISCOVERY

a. Open the Code Editor window and then open the code template for the btnSales_ Click procedure. Code the procedure so that it performs the following three tasks: declares a variable named `dblSales`, uses an assignment statement to assign the number 500 to the variable, and displays the contents of the variable in the lblSales control.

b. Save the solution and then start the application. Click the Display Sales button. What does the btnSales_Click procedure display in the lblSales control? When the procedure ends, what happens to the `dblSales` variable? Click the Exit button.

c. Open the code template for the btnComm5_Click procedure. In the procedure, enter an assignment statement that multiplies a variable named `dblSales` by 0.05, assigning the result to the lblCommission control. When you press Enter after typing the assignment statement, a red squiggle appears below dblSales in the instruction. The red squiggle indicates that the code contains a syntax error. To determine the problem, rest your mouse pointer on the variable name, dblSales. The message in the box indicates that the variable is not declared. In other words, the btnComm5_Click procedure cannot locate the variable's declaration statement, which you previously entered in the btnSales_Click procedure. As you learned in Lesson A, only the procedure in which a variable is declared can use the variable. No other procedure is even aware that the variable exists.

d. Now observe what happens when you use the same name to declare a variable in more than one procedure. Insert a blank line above the assignment statement in the btnComm5_Click procedure. In the blank line, type a statement that declares the dblSales variable, and then click the assignment statement to move the insertion point away from the current line. Notice that the red squiggle disappears from the assignment statement. Save the solution and then start the application. Click the Display Sales button. The value stored in the dblSales variable declared in the btnSales_Click procedure (500) appears in the lblSales control. Click the 5% Commission button. Why does the number 0 appear in the lblCommission control? What happens to the dblSales variable declared in the btnComm5_Click procedure when the procedure ends? Click the Exit button. As this example shows, when you use the same name to declare a variable in more than one procedure, each procedure creates its own procedure-level variable. Although the variables have the same name, each refers to a different location in memory.

e. Next, you use a class-level variable in the application. Insert a blank line below the Public Class clause. Enter a statement that declares a class-level variable named dblSales.

f. Delete the Dim statement from the btnSales_Click procedure. Also delete the Dim statement from the btnComm5_Click procedure.

g. Open the code template for the btnComm10_Click procedure. In the procedure, enter an assignment statement that multiplies the dblSales variable by 0.1, assigning the result to the lblCommission control.

h. Save the solution and then start the application. The variable declaration statement in the form's Declarations section creates the class-level dblSales variable and initializes it to 0. Click the Display Sales button. The button's Click event procedure stores the number 500 in the class-level variable and then displays the contents of the variable (500) in the lblSales control. Click the 5% Commission button. The button's Click event procedure multiplies the contents of the class-level variable (500) by 0.05 and then displays the result (25) in the lblCommission control. Click the 10% Commission button. The button's Click event procedure multiplies the contents of the class-level variable (500) by 0.1 and then displays the result (50) in the lblCommission control. As this example shows, any procedure in the form can use a class-level variable. Click the Exit button. What happens to the class-level dblSales variable when the application ends?

19. Open the VB2015\Chap03\Debug Solution-Lesson A\Debug Solution (Debug Solution.sln) SWAT THE BUGS
file. The application is supposed to display the number of times the Count button is pressed,
but it is not working correctly.

   a. Start the application. Click the Count button. The message indicates that
       you have pressed the Count button once, which is correct. Click the Count
       button several more times. The message still displays the number 1. Click the
       Exit button.

   b. Open the Code Editor window and study the code. What are two ways to
       correct the code? Which way is the preferred way? Modify the code using
       the preferred way. Save the solution and then start the application. Click the
       Count button several times. Each time you click the Count button, the message
       should change to indicate the number of times the button was pressed. Click the
       Exit button.

▌ LESSON B

After studying Lesson B, you should be able to:

- Include procedure-level and class-level variables in an application

- Concatenate strings

- Get user input by using the InputBox function

- Include the ControlChars.NewLine constant in code

- Designate the default button for a form

- Format numbers using the ToString method

Modifying the Meyer's Purple Bakery Application

Your task in this chapter is to modify the bakery application created in Chapter 2. The modified application will calculate and display a 3% sales tax. It will also display the name of the salesclerk who entered the sales information. Before making modifications to an application's existing code, you should review the application's documentation and revise the necessary documents. In this case, you need to revise the application's TOE chart and also the pseudocode for the Calculate button. The revised TOE chart is shown in Figure 3-26. The changes made to the original TOE chart from Chapter 2 are shaded in the figure. (You will view the revised pseudocode for the Calculate button later in this lesson.)

Task	Object	Event
1. Calculate total items sold and total sales amount	btnCalc	Click
2. Display total items sold and total sales amount in lblTotalItems and lblTotalSales		
3. Calculate the sales tax		
4. Display sales tax and salesclerk's name in lblMsg		
Print the sales receipt	btnPrint	Click
End the application	btnExit	Click
Clear the screen for the next sale	btnClear	Click
Display total items sold (from btnCalc)	lblTotalItems	None
Display total sales amount (from btnCalc)	lblTotalSales	None
Get and display the sales information	txtDate, txtDonuts, txtMuffins	None
Get the salesclerk's name	frmMain	Load
Display sales tax and salesclerk's name (from btnCalc)	lblMsg	None

Figure 3-26   Revised TOE chart for the bakery application

Notice that the revised TOE chart includes two additional objects (the form and a label control) as well as an additional event (Load). A form's **Load event** occurs when the application is started and the form is displayed the first time. According to the TOE chart, the Load event is responsible for getting the salesclerk's name. Also notice that the btnCalc control's Click event procedure now has two additional tasks: It must calculate the sales tax and also display the sales tax and the salesclerk's name in the lblMsg control.

START HERE

To open the bakery application:

1. If necessary, start Visual Studio 2015. Open the VB2015\Chap03\Bakery Solution\ Bakery Solution (Bakery Solution.sln) file. See Figure 3-27.

Figure 3-27   Bakery application's modified interface

Two modifications were made to the application created in Chapter 2: The lblMsg control was added to the interface, and the statement `lblMsg.Text = String.Empty` was added to the btnClear_Click procedure. The statement will remove the contents of the lblMsg control when the user clicks the Clear Screen button.

Modifying the Calculate Button's Code

Currently, the Calculate button uses the Val function and the Text properties of controls to make the necessary calculations. In this lesson, you will modify the button's code to use the TryParse method and variables.

START HERE

To begin modifying the application's code:

1. Open the Code Editor window. Replace <your name> and <current date> with your name and the current date, respectively.

2. The code will contain variables, so you will enter the three Option statements in the Code Editor window. Click the **blank line** above the Public Class clause, and then press **Enter** to insert another blank line. Enter the following three statements:

   Option Explicit On
   Option Infer Off
   Option Strict On

3. If necessary, scroll down the Code Editor window until the entire btnCalc_Click procedure is visible. Notice that red squiggles appear below the expressions in the two calculations. The squiggles indicate that the expressions contain one or more syntax errors.

4. Position your mouse pointer on the first squiggle, as shown in Figure 3-28. An error message appears in a box. (Don't be concerned if your error message contains additional information.) The error message says "Option Strict On disallows implicit conversions from 'Double' to 'String.'" You received this error message because the expression on the right side of the assignment operator results in a Double number, and the assignment statement is attempting to assign that Double number to the Text property of a control. (Recall that the Val function returns a Double number, and the Text property of a control is a string.)

```
                                               mouse pointer

Private Sub btnCalc_Click(sender As Object, e As EventArgs) Handles btnCalc
        ' calculate number of items sold and total sales


      lblTotalItems.Text = Val(txtDonuts.Text) + Val(txtMuffins.Text)
      lblTotalSales.Text = Val(lblTotalI    Option Strict On disallows implicit conversions from 'Double' to 'String'.
      lblTotalSales.Text = Format(lblTot....

End Sub
```

Figure 3-28   A red squiggle indicates a syntax error

5. Highlight (select) the three lines of code and the blank line that appears below them, as shown in Figure 3-29. Press **Delete** to remove the highlighted (selected) lines from the procedure.

```
     Private Sub btnCalc_Click(sender As Object, e As EventArgs) Handles bt
             ' calculate number of items sold and total sales


           lblTotalItems.Text = Val(txtDonuts.Text) + Val(txtMuffins.Text)
           lblTotalSales.Text = Val(lblTotalItems.Text) * 0.5
           lblTotalSales.Text = Format(lblTotalSales.Text, "currency")

         End Sub
```

highlight (select) these lines and then press Delete

Figure 3-29   Lines to delete from the procedure

Figure 3-30 shows the revised pseudocode and flowchart for the btnCalc_Click procedure. Changes made to the original pseudocode and flowchart from Chapter 2 are shaded in the figure. The procedure includes two additional calculations: one for the subtotal and one for the sales tax. The subtotal is computed by multiplying the total number of items sold by the item price. The sales tax is computed by multiplying the subtotal by the sales tax rate. Notice that the total sales expression has changed; it now adds the subtotal to the sales tax. Last, the procedure displays the sales tax and the salesclerk's name in the lblMsg control.

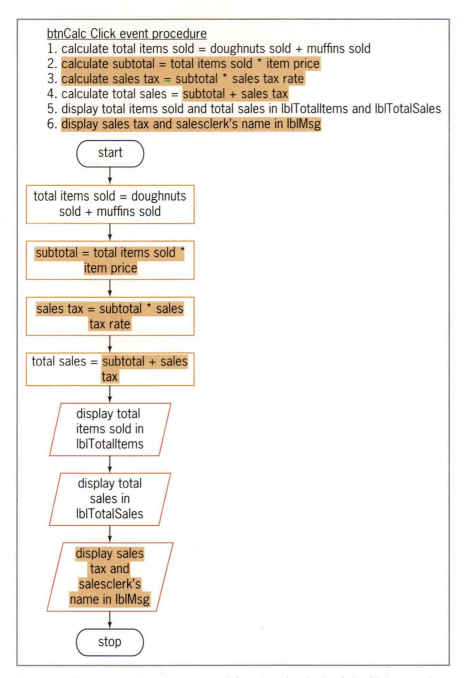

btnCalc Click event procedure
1. calculate total items sold = doughnuts sold + muffins sold
2. calculate subtotal = total items sold * item price
3. calculate sales tax = subtotal * sales tax rate
4. calculate total sales = subtotal + sales tax
5. display total items sold and total sales in lblTotalItems and lblTotalSales
6. display sales tax and salesclerk's name in lblMsg

start

total items sold = doughnuts sold + muffins sold

subtotal = total items sold * item price

sales tax = subtotal * sales tax rate

total sales = subtotal + sales tax

display total items sold in lblTotalItems

display total sales in lblTotalSales

display sales tax and salesclerk's name in lblMsg

stop

Figure 3-30   Revised pseudocode and flowchart for the btnCalc_Click procedure

Before you begin coding a procedure, you first study the procedure's pseudocode (or flowchart) to determine the variables and named constants (if any) the procedure will use. When determining the named constants, look for items whose value should be the same each time the procedure is invoked. In the btnCalc_Click procedure, the item price and sales tax rate will always be $0.50 and 0.02 (the decimal equivalent of 2%), respectively; therefore, you will assign both values to Decimal named constants.

When determining a procedure's variables, look in the pseudocode (or flowchart) for items whose value is allowed to change each time the procedure is processed. In the btnCalc_Click procedure, the numbers of doughnuts and muffins sold will likely be different each time the procedure is processed. As a result, the total number of items sold, subtotal, sales tax, and total sales amounts will also vary because they are based on the numbers of doughnuts and muffins sold. Therefore, you will assign those six values to variables. Integer variables are a good choice for storing the number of doughnuts sold, the number of muffins sold, and the total number of items sold because a customer can buy only a whole number of items. You will use Decimal variables to store the subtotal, sales tax, and total price because these amounts may contain a decimal place. Figure 3-31 lists the names and data types of the two named constants and six variables you will use in the procedure.

Named constants	Data type	Value
decITEM_PRICE	Decimal	0.5D
decTAX_RATE	Decimal	0.02D
Variables	Data type	
intDonuts	Integer	
intMuffins	Integer	
intTotalItems	Integer	
decSubtotal	Decimal	
decSalesTax	Decimal	
decTotalSales	Decimal	

Figure 3-31   List of named constants and variables for the btnCalc_Click procedure

When declaring named constants and variables in the Code Editor window, be sure to enter the name using the exact capitalization you want. Then, any time you want to refer to the named constant or variable in the code, you can enter its name using any case. The Code Editor will automatically adjust the name to match the case used in the declaration statement.

START HERE

To declare the named constants and variables:

1. The insertion point should be located in the blank line above the End Sub clause in the btnCalc_Click procedure. If necessary, press **Tab** until the blinking insertion point is aligned with the apostrophe in the comment.

2. First, you will declare the named constants. Enter the following declaration statements. (For now, don't be concerned about the green squiggle that appears below each statement after you press Enter.)

   Const decITEM_PRICE As Decimal = 0.5D
   Const decTAX_RATE As Decimal = 0.02D

3. Next, enter the following six variable declaration statements. Press **Enter** twice after typing the last statement.

   Dim intDonuts As Integer
   Dim intMuffins As Integer
   Dim intTotalItems As Integer
   Dim decSubtotal As Decimal
   Dim decSalesTax As Decimal
   Dim decTotalSales As Decimal

4. Place your mouse pointer on the green squiggle that appears below the last Dim statement. A warning message appears in a box, as shown in Figure 3-32. The message alerts you that the `decTotalSales` variable has been declared but has not been used yet. In other words, the variable name does not appear in any other statement in the code. The squiggle will disappear when you include the variable name in another statement in the procedure.

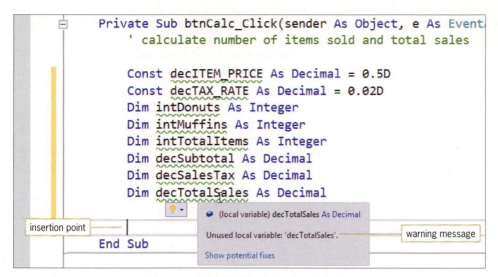

Figure 3-32   Const and Dim statements entered in the procedure

After declaring the named constants and variables, you can begin coding either each step in the procedure's pseudocode or each symbol (other than the start and stop ovals) in its flowchart. Keep in mind that some steps and symbols may require more than one line of code. You will use the pseudocode shown earlier in Figure 3-30 to code the procedure. The first step in the pseudocode calculates the total number of items sold by adding the number of doughnuts sold to the number of muffins sold. The numbers of doughnuts and muffins sold are stored in the Text properties of the txtDonuts and txtMuffins controls, respectively. You will use the TryParse method to convert the Text properties to integers and then store the results in the `intDonuts` and `intMuffins` variables. You then will use an assignment statement to add together the contents of both variables, assigning the sum to the `intTotalItems` variable.

To continue coding the btnCalc_Click procedure:

START HERE

1. The insertion point should be positioned as shown earlier in Figure 3-32. Enter the following comment and TryParse methods. When you press Enter after typing each TryParse method, the Code Editor removes the green squiggle from the respective variable's Dim statement.

   ' calculate total number of items sold
   Integer.TryParse(txtDonuts.Text, intDonuts)
   Integer.TryParse(txtMuffins.Text, intMuffins)

2. Next, type the following assignment statement and then press **Enter** twice. (Notice that all of the variables in the assignment statement have the same data type: Integer.)

   intTotalItems = intDonuts + intMuffins

3. The second step in the pseudocode calculates the subtotal by multiplying the total number of items sold by the item price. You will assign the subtotal to the `decSubtotal` variable. When processing the assignment statement, the computer will implicitly convert the integer stored in the `intTotalItems` variable to Decimal before multiplying it by the Decimal number stored in the `decITEM_PRICE` constant. It then will assign the result to the `decSubtotal` variable. Enter the following comment and assignment statement. Press **Enter** twice after typing the assignment statement.

   ' calculate the subtotal
   decSubtotal = intTotalItems * decITEM_PRICE

4. The third step in the pseudocode calculates the sales tax by multiplying the subtotal by the sales tax rate. You will assign the sales tax to the `decSalesTax` variable. Enter the following comment and assignment statement. Press **Enter** twice after typing the assignment statement. (Notice that the variables and named constant in the assignment statement have the same data type: Decimal.)

' calculate the sales tax
decSalesTax = decSubtotal * decTAX_RATE

5. The fourth step in the pseudocode calculates the total sales by adding together the subtotal and the sales tax. You will assign the result to the `decTotalSales` variable. Enter the following comment and assignment statement. Press **Enter** twice after typing the assignment statement. (Notice that all of the variables in the assignment statement have the same data type: Decimal.)

' calculate the total sales
decTotalSales = decSubtotal + decSalesTax

6. Step 5 in the pseudocode displays the total number of items sold and the total sales in their respective label controls. The total number of items sold and the total sales are stored in the `intTotalItems` and `decTotalSales` variables, respectively. Because both variables have a numeric data type, you will need to convert their contents to the String data type before assigning the contents to the label controls. You can use the Convert class's ToString method to make the conversions. Enter the following comment and assignment statements. Press **Enter** twice after typing the last assignment statement.

' display total amounts
lblTotalItems.Text = Convert.ToString(intTotalItems)
lblTotalSales.Text = Convert.ToString(decTotalSales)

7. The last step in the pseudocode displays both the sales tax and the salesclerk's name in the lblMsg control. For now, you will display only the sales tax. Enter the following comment and assignment statement:

' display tax and salesclerk's name
lblMsg.Text = Convert.ToString (decSalesTax)

8. Save the solution. Figure 3-33 shows the code entered in the btnCalc_Click procedure.

```
Private Sub btnCalc_Click(sender As Object,
e As EventArgs) Handles btnCalc.Click
    ' calculate number of items sold and total sales

    Const decITEM_PRICE As Decimal = 0.5D
    Const decTAX_RATE As Decimal = 0.02D
    Dim intDonuts As Integer
    Dim intMuffins As Integer
    Dim intTotalItems As Integer
    Dim decSubtotal As Decimal
    Dim decSalesTax As Decimal
    Dim decTotalSales As Decimal

    ' calculate total number of items sold
    Integer.TryParse(txtDonuts.Text, intDonuts)
    Integer.TryParse(txtMuffins.Text, intMuffins)
    intTotalItems = intDonuts + intMuffins
```

Figure 3-33 Code entered in the btnCalc_Click procedure *(continues)*

(continued)

```
    ' calculate the subtotal
    decSubtotal = intTotalItems * decITEM_PRICE

    ' calculate the sales tax
    decSalesTax = decSubtotal * decTAX_RATE

    ' calculate the total sales
    decTotalSales = decSubtotal + decSalesTax

    ' display total amounts
    lblTotalItems.Text = Convert.ToString(intTotalItems)
    lblTotalSales.Text = Convert.ToString(decTotalSales)

    ' display tax and salesclerk's name
    lblMsg.Text = Convert.ToString(decSalesTax)

End Sub
```

Figure 3-33   Code entered in the btnCalc_Click procedure

To start and then test the application:

START HERE

1. Start the application. Type **3/23/2016** in the Date box, type **12** in the Doughnuts box, and type **2** in the Muffins box. Click the **Calculate** button. The total number of items sold, total sales, and sales tax appear in the interface, as shown in Figure 3-34. Although the calculated results are correct, the total sales and sales tax amounts should be formatted to show two decimal places rather than three decimal places. You will fix this problem in the next section.

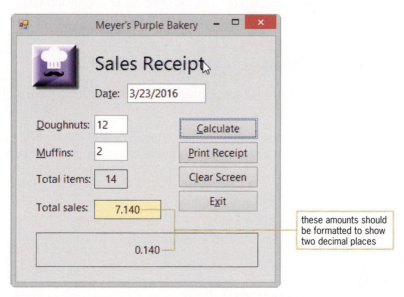

Figure 3-34   Calculated amounts shown in the interface

2. Click the **Clear Screen** button to clear the sales receipt (except for the date), and then click the **Exit** button.

Using the ToString Method to Format Numbers

Numbers representing monetary amounts are usually displayed with either zero or two decimal places and may include a dollar sign and a thousands separator. Similarly, numbers representing percentage amounts are displayed with zero or more decimal places and a percent sign. Specifying the number of decimal places and the special characters to display in a number is called **formatting**. In Chapter 2, you learned how to use the Format function to format a number for output as a string. Although you can still use the Format function, many programmers now use the ToString method because it can be used in any language built into Visual Studio.

The ToString method's syntax is shown in Figure 3-35. In the syntax, *numericVariableName* is the name of a numeric variable. The **ToString method** formats the number stored in the numeric variable and then returns the result as a string. The *formatString* argument in the syntax specifies the format you want to use. The *formatString* argument must take the form "*Axx*", where *A* is an alphabetic character called the format specifier and *xx* is a sequence of digits called the precision specifier. The format specifier must be one of the built-in format characters. The most commonly used format characters are listed in Figure 3-35. Notice that you can use either an uppercase letter or a lowercase letter as the format specifier. When used with one of the format characters listed in the figure, the precision specifier controls the number of digits that will appear after the decimal point in the formatted number. Also included in Figure 3-35 are examples of using the ToString method.

Using the ToString Method to Format a Number

Syntax
numericVariableName.**ToString(***formatString***)**

Format specifier (Name)	Description
C or c (Currency)	displays the string with a dollar sign and includes a thousands separator (if appropriate); negative values are enclosed in parentheses
N or n (Number)	similar to the Currency format but does not include a dollar sign and negative values are preceded by a minus sign
F or f (Fixed-point)	same as the Number format but does not include a thousands separator
P or p (Percent)	multiplies the numeric variable's value by 100 and formats the result with a percent sign; negative values are preceded by a minus sign

Example 1
```
intSales = 75000
lblSales.Text = intSales.ToString("C2")
```
assigns the string "$75,000.00" to the lblSales control's Text property

Example 2
```
decTotal = 4599.639D
lblTotal.Text = decTotal.ToString("N2")
```
assigns the string "4,599.64" to the lblTotal control's Text property

---

Figure 3-35   Syntax and examples of the ToString method *(continues)*

(continued)

Example 3
```
dblRate = 0.15
lblRate.Text = dblRate.ToString("P0")
```
assigns the string "15 %" to the lblRate control's Text property

Figure 3-35   Syntax and examples of the ToString method

To format the total sales and sales tax amounts:

START HERE

1. Change the statement that displays the total sales amount as follows:

   lblTotalSales.Text = decTotalSales.ToString("C2")

2. Next, change the statement that displays the sales tax amount as follows:

   lblMsg.Text = decSalesTax.ToString("C2")

3. Save the solution and then start the application. Type **12** in the Doughnuts box and type **2** in the Muffins box. Click the **Calculate** button. The formatted amounts appear in the interface, as shown in Figure 3-36. However, it's not obvious to the user that $0.14 is the sales tax. You can fix this problem by displaying the message "The sales tax was" before the sales tax amount. However, before you can accomplish this task, you must learn how to concatenate (link together) strings. String concatenation is covered in the next section.

4. Click the **Exit** button.

Figure 3-36   Formatted amounts shown in the interface

Concatenating Strings

You use the **concatenation operator**, which is the ampersand (**&**), to concatenate (connect or link together) strings. For the Code Editor to recognize the ampersand as the concatenation operator, the ampersand must be both preceded and followed by a space. Figure 3-37 shows some examples of string concatenation.

 You can also use the plus sign (+) to concatenate strings. However, for clarity in your programs, you should use the plus sign for addition and the ampersand for concatenation.

Concatenating Strings

Variables	Contents
strCity	Nashville
strState	Tennessee
intPop	43500

Concatenated string	Result
strCity & strState	NashvilleTennessee
strState & " " & strCity	Tennessee Nashville
strCity & ", " & strState	Nashville, Tennessee
"He lives in " & strCity & "."	He lives in Nashville.
"Population: " & Convert.ToString(intPop)	Population: 43500

Figure 3-37   Examples of string concatenation

You will use the concatenation operator to concatenate the following three strings: "The sales tax was ", the contents of the **decSalesTax** variable after it has been converted to a string, and ".". Using the examples shown in Figure 3-37 as a guide, the correct assignment statement is `lblMsg.Text = "The sales tax was " & decSalesTax.ToString("C2") & ".".`

The assignment statement is rather long and, depending on the size of the font used in your Code Editor window, you may not be able to view the entire statement without scrolling the window. Fortunately, the Code Editor allows you to break a line of code into two or more physical lines as long as the break comes either before a closing parenthesis or after one of the following: a comma, an opening parenthesis, or an operator (arithmetic, assignment, comparison, logical, or concatenation). If you want to break a line of code anywhere else, you will need to use the **line continuation character**, which is an underscore (_) that is immediately preceded by a space. However, if you use the line continuation character, it must appear at the end of a physical line of code. In this case, you will break the assignment statement after the first concatenation operator.

START HERE

To concatenate the strings and then test the code:

1. Change the last assignment statement in the procedure as shown in Figure 3-38. The modifications are shaded in the figure.

```
' display total amounts
lblTotalItems.Text = Convert.ToString(intTotalItems)
lblTotalSales.Text = decTotalSales.ToString("C2")

' display tax and salesclerk's name            space
lblMsg.Text = "The sales tax was " &           modify this
    decSalesTax.ToString("C2") & "."           assignment
                                               statement

End Sub
```

Figure 3-38   String concatenation included in the assignment statement

2. Save the solution and then start the application. Type **5** in the Doughnuts box and type **4** in the Muffins box. Click the **Calculate** button. The lblMsg control contains the sentence "The sales tax was $0.09.", as shown in Figure 3-39.

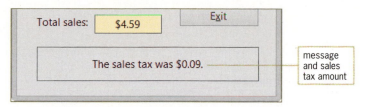

Figure 3-39   Concatenated strings displayed in the lblMsg control

3. Click the **Exit** button.

You also need to display the salesclerk's name in the lblMsg control. You can use the InputBox function to obtain the name from the user.

The InputBox Function

The **InputBox function** displays an input dialog box, which is one of the standard dialog boxes available in Visual Basic. An example of an input dialog box is shown in Figure 3-40. The message in the dialog box should prompt the user to enter the appropriate information in the input area. The user closes the dialog box by clicking the OK button, Cancel button, or Close button. The value returned by the InputBox function depends on the button the user chooses. If the user clicks the OK button, the function returns the value contained in the input area of the dialog box; the return value is always treated as a string. If the user clicks either the Cancel button in the dialog box or the Close button on the dialog box's title bar, the function returns an empty (or zero-length) string.

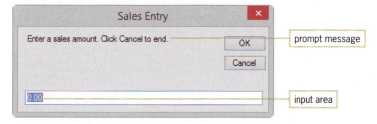

Figure 3-40   Example of an input dialog box

Figure 3-41 shows the basic syntax of the InputBox function. The *prompt* argument contains the message to display inside the dialog box. The optional *title* and *defaultResponse* arguments control the text that appears in the dialog box's title bar and input area, respectively. If you omit the *title* argument, the project name appears in the title bar. If you omit the *defaultResponse* argument, a blank input area appears when the dialog box opens. The *prompt*, *title*, and *defaultResponse* arguments can be string literal constants, String named constants, or String variables. The Windows standard is to use sentence capitalization for the prompt but book title capitalization for the title. The capitalization (if any) you use for the defaultResponse depends on the text itself. In most cases, you assign the value returned by the InputBox function to a String variable, as shown in the first three examples in Figure 3-41.

Using the InputBox Function

Note: The InputBox function's syntax also includes optional *XPos* and *YPos* arguments for specifying the dialog box's horizontal and vertical positions, respectively. If both arguments are omitted, the dialog box appears centered on the screen.

Basic syntax
InputBox(*prompt*[, *title*][, *defaultResponse*]**)**

Example 1
```
strSales =
   InputBox("Enter a sales amount. Click Cancel to end.",
   "Sales Entry", "0.00")
```
Displays the input dialog box shown in Figure 3-40. When the user closes the dialog box, the assignment statement assigns the function's return value to the strSales variable.

Example 2
```
strCity = InputBox("City name:", "City")
```
Displays an input dialog box that shows "City name:" as the prompt, "City" in the title bar, and an empty input area. When the user closes the dialog box, the assignment statement assigns the function's return value to the strCity variable.

Example 3
```
Const strPROMPT As String = "Enter the discount rate:"
Const strTITLE As String = "Discount Rate"
strRate = InputBox(strPROMPT, strTITLE, ".00")
```
Displays an input dialog box that shows the contents of the strPROMPT constant as the prompt, the contents of the strTITLE constant in the title bar, and .00 in the input area. When the user closes the dialog box, the assignment statement assigns the function's return value to the strRate variable.

Example 4
```
Integer.TryParse(InputBox("How old are you?",
    "Discount Verification"), intAge)
```
Displays an input dialog box that shows "How old are you?" as the prompt, "Discount Verification" in the title bar, and an empty input area. When the user closes the dialog box, the TryParse method converts the function's return value from String to Integer and then stores the result in the intAge variable.

Figure 3-41   Basic syntax and examples of the InputBox function

GUI DESIGN TIP InputBox Function's Prompt and Title Capitalization

• Use sentence capitalization for the prompt but book title capitalization for the title.

You will use the InputBox function to prompt the salesclerk to enter his or her name. The function should be entered in the form's Load event procedure because that procedure is responsible for getting the name. Recall that a form's Load event occurs before the form appears on the screen. After the Load event procedure obtains the salesclerk's name, you will have the btnCalc_Click procedure concatenate the name to the message displayed in the lblMsg control.

Before entering the InputBox function in the Load event procedure, you must decide where to declare the String variable that will store the function's return value. In other words, should the variable have procedure scope or class scope? When deciding, consider the fact that the form's Load event procedure needs to store a value in the variable, and the btnCalc_Click procedure needs to display the variable's value in the lblMsg control. Recall from Lesson A that when two procedures in the same form need access to the same variable, you declare the variable as a class-level variable by entering its declaration statement in the form's Declarations section.

To continue coding the bakery application:

START HERE

1. Scroll to the top of the Code Editor window. Insert two blank lines immediately below the Public Class clause. First, you will declare a class-level String variable named strClerk. Enter the comment and declaration statement shown in Figure 3-42.

```
Public Class frmMain

    ' class-level variable for storing salesclerk's name
    Private strClerk As String
```

enter this comment and declaration statement

Figure 3-42 Class-level variable declared in the form's Declarations section

2. Next, you will enter the InputBox function in the form's Load event procedure. You access the form's procedures by selecting (frmMain Events) in the Object list box. Click the **Object** list arrow and then click **(frmMain Events)** in the list. Click the **Method** list arrow to view a list of the form's events. Scroll down the list, and then click **Load** to open the code template for the frmMain_Load procedure.

3. To make the assignment statement that contains the InputBox function shorter and easier to understand, you will create named constants for the function's *prompt* and *title* arguments, and then you will use the named constants (rather than the longer strings) in the function. You use named constants rather than variables because the prompt and title will not change as the application is running. Enter the comments and code shown in Figure 3-43.

```
Private Sub frmMain_Load(sender As Object, e As EventAr
    ' get the salesclerk's name

    Const strPROMPT As String = "Salesclerk's name:"
    Const strTITLE As String = "Name Entry"
    ' assign name to class-level variable
    strClerk = InputBox(strPROMPT, strTITLE)

End Sub
```

enter these comments and lines of code

Figure 3-43 frmMain_Load procedure

4. Next, you will concatenate the strClerk variable to the message assigned to the lblMsg control. Locate the btnCalc_Click procedure. Click **immediately after the closing quotation mark** in the "." entry. Press the **Spacebar** to enter a space character, and then type **&** and press **Enter**. Finally, type **strClerk** and then click the **blank line** above the End Sub clause.

5. Save the solution and then start the application. The Name Entry dialog box created by the InputBox function appears first. See Figure 3-44.

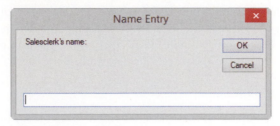

Figure 3-44 Dialog box created by the InputBox function

6. Type your name in the input area of the dialog box and then click the **OK** button. The sales receipt appears. Type **4** in the Doughnuts box and then click the **Calculate** button. Notice that your name appears much too close to the period in the lblMsg control. You can correct the spacing problem by replacing the period in the assignment statement with a period and two spaces (". "). Or, you can use the ControlChars.NewLine constant to display the salesclerk's name on the next line in the lblMsg control. Click the **Exit** button.

The ControlChars.NewLine Constant

The **ControlChars.NewLine constant** instructs the computer to advance the insertion point to the next line in a control. (You can also use it to advance the insertion point in a file or on a document sent to the printer.) Whenever you want to start a new line, you simply enter the constant at the appropriate location in your code. In this case, you want to advance to a new line after displaying the period—in other words, before displaying the salesclerk's name.

START HERE

To display the salesclerk's name on a separate line:

> The Control-Chars.NewLine constant is an intrinsic constant, which is a named constant built into Visual Basic.

1. Modify the last assignment statement in the btnCalc_Click procedure as indicated in Figure 3-45. The modifications are shaded in the figure.

```
' display tax and salesclerk's name
lblMsg.Text = "The sales tax was " &
    decSalesTax.ToString("C2") & "." &
    ControlChars.NewLine & strClerk
```
make the shaded modifications

End Sub

Figure 3-45 Modified assignment statement

2. Save the solution and then start the application. The Name Entry dialog box shown in Figure 3-46 appears. The blinking insertion point indicates that the dialog box's input area has the focus. However, notice that the OK button in the dialog box has a darkened border even though it does not have the focus. In Windows terminology, a button that has a darkened border when it does not have the focus is called the default button. You can select a default button by pressing Enter at any time.

Figure 3-46 Name Entry input dialog box

the default button has a darkened border

the input area has the focus

3. Type **Jasmine Chou** and then press **Enter**. The sales receipt appears.

4. Type **16** in the Doughnuts box. Click the **Calculate** button. The salesclerk's name now appears on a separate line in the lblMsg control, as shown in Figure 3-47.

Total sales: $8.16   Exit

The sales tax was $0.16.
Jasmine Chou

the salesclerk's name appears on a separate line

Figure 3-47 Salesclerk's name shown on the sales receipt

5. Click the **Exit** button.

Designating a Default Button

As you already know from using Windows applications, you can select a button either by clicking it or by pressing the Enter key when the button has the focus. If you make a button the **default button**, you can also select it by pressing the Enter key even when the button does not have the focus. When a button is selected, the computer processes the code contained in the button's Click event procedure.

An interface does not have to have a default button. However, if one is used, it should be the button that is most often selected by the user, except in cases where the tasks performed by the button are both destructive and irreversible. For example, a button that deletes information should not be designated as the default button unless the application provides a way for the information to be restored. If you assign a default button in an interface, it typically is the first button on the left when the buttons are positioned horizontally but the first button on the top when they are stacked vertically. A form can have only one default button. You specify the default button (if any) by setting the form's AcceptButton property to the name of the button.

 Forms also have a CancelButton property, which is covered in Lesson B's Exercise 12.

GUI DESIGN TIP Assigning a Default Button

- The default button should be the button that is most often selected by the user, except in cases where the tasks performed by the button are both destructive and irreversible. If a form contains a default button, it typically is the first button.

START HERE
To make the Calculate button the default button:

1. Return to the designer window and set the form's AcceptButton property to **btnCalc**. A darkened border appears around the Calculate button.

2. Save the solution and then start the application. Type your name in the Name Entry dialog box and press **Enter**. The sales receipt appears.

3. Type any date in the Date box, type **5** in the Doughnuts box, and type **12** in the Muffins box. Press **Enter** to select the Calculate button. The btnCalc_Click procedure calculates and displays the total number of items sold (17) and the total sales ($8.67). In addition, the message "The sales tax was $0.17." and your name appear in the lblMsg control. Click the **Exit** button. Close the Code Editor window and then close the solution. See Figure 3-48.

```
1 ' Name:          Bakery Project
2 ' Purpose:       Calculates the total number of
3 '                items sold and the total sales
4 ' Programmer:    <your name> on <current date>
5
6 Option Explicit On
7 Option Infer Off
8 Option Strict On
9
10 Public Class frmMain
11
12    ' class-level variable for storing salesclerk's name
13    Private strClerk As String
14
15    Private Sub btnCalc_Click(sender As Object,
      e As EventArgs) Handles btnCalc.Click
16       ' calculate number of items sold and total sales
17
18       Const decITEM_PRICE As Decimal = 0.5D
19       Const decTAX_RATE As Decimal = 0.02D
20       Dim intDonuts As Integer
21       Dim intMuffins As Integer
22       Dim intTotalItems As Integer
23       Dim decSubtotal As Decimal
24       Dim decSalesTax As Decimal
25       Dim decTotalSales As Decimal
26
27       ' calculate total number of items sold
28       Integer.TryParse(txtDonuts.Text, intDonuts)
29       Integer.TryParse(txtMuffins.Text, intMuffins)
30       intTotalItems = intDonuts + intMuffins
31
32       ' calculate the subtotal
33       decSubtotal = intTotalItems * decITEM_PRICE
34
35       ' calculate the sales tax
36       decSalesTax = decSubtotal * decTAX_RATE
37
38       ' calculate the total sales
39       decTotalSales = decSubtotal + decSalesTax
40
41       ' display total amounts
42       lblTotalItems.Text = Convert.ToString(intTotalItems)
```

Figure 3-48   Bakery application's code at the end of Lesson B *(continues)*

(continued)

```vbnet
43          lblTotalSales.Text = decTotalSales.ToString("C2")
44
45      ' display tax and salesclerk's name
46      lblMsg.Text = "The sales tax was " &
47          decSalesTax.ToString("C2") & "." &
48          ControlChars.NewLine & strClerk
49
50  End Sub
51
52  Private Sub btnClear_Click(sender As Object,
    e As EventArgs) Handles btnClear.Click
53      ' prepare screen for the next sale
54
55      txtDonuts.Text = String.Empty
56      txtMuffins.Text = String.Empty
57      lblTotalItems.Text = String.Empty
58      lblTotalSales.Text = String.Empty
59      lblMsg.Text = String.Empty
60      ' send the focus to the Doughnuts box
61      txtDonuts.Focus()
62
63  End Sub
64
65  Private Sub btnExit_Click(sender As Object,
    e As EventArgs) Handles btnExit.Click
66      Me.Close()
67  End Sub
68
69  Private Sub btnPrint_Click(sender As Object,
    e As EventArgs) Handles btnPrint.Click
70      ' print the sales receipt
71
72      btnCalc.Visible = False
73      btnClear.Visible = False
74      btnExit.Visible = False
75      btnPrint.Visible = False
76      PrintForm1.Print()
77      btnCalc.Visible = True
78      btnClear.Visible = True
79      btnExit.Visible = True
80      btnPrint.Visible = True
81
82  End Sub
83
84  Private Sub frmMain_Load(sender As Object,
    e As EventArgs) Handles Me.Load
85      ' get the salesclerk's name
86
87      Const strPROMPT As String = "Salesclerk's name:"
88      Const strTITLE As String = "Name Entry"
89      ' assign name to class-level variable
90      strClerk = InputBox(strPROMPT, strTITLE)
91
92  End Sub
93 End Class
```

Figure 3-48 Bakery application's code at the end of Lesson B

Lesson B Summary

- To format a number for output as a string:

  Use the ToString method. The method's syntax is *numericVariableName*`.ToString` (*formatString*).

- To concatenate strings:

  Use the concatenation operator (&). Be sure to include a space before and after the ampersand.

- To display an input dialog box:

  Use the InputBox function. The function's syntax is `InputBox(`*prompt*[`,` *title*] [`,` *defaultResponse*]`)`. The *prompt*, *title*, and *defaultResponse* arguments can be string literal constants, String named constants, or String variables. Use sentence capitalization for the prompt but book title capitalization for the title.

  If the user clicks the OK button, the InputBox function returns the value contained in the input area of the dialog box. The return value is always treated as a string. If the user clicks either the dialog box's Cancel button or its Close button, the InputBox function returns an empty string.

- To advance the insertion point to the next line:

  Use the ControlChars.NewLine constant in code.

- To break up a long instruction into two or more physical lines in the Code Editor window:

  Break the line after a comma, after an opening parenthesis, before a closing parenthesis, or after an operator (arithmetic, assignment, comparison, logical, or concatenation). You can also use the line continuation character, which is an underscore (_). The line continuation character must be immediately preceded by a space and appear at the end of a physical line of code.

- To make a button the default button:

  Set the form's AcceptButton property to the name of the button.

Lesson B Key Terms

&—the concatenation operator

Concatenation operator—the ampersand (&); used to concatenate strings; must be both preceded and followed by a space character

ControlChars.NewLine constant—used to advance the insertion point to the next line

Default button—a button that can be selected by pressing the Enter key even when the button does not have the focus

Formatting—specifying the number of decimal places and the special characters to display in a number

InputBox function—a Visual Basic function that displays an input dialog box containing a message, OK and Cancel buttons, and an input area

Line continuation character—an underscore that is immediately preceded by a space and located at the end of a physical line of code; used to split a long instruction into two or more physical lines in the Code Editor window

Load event—an event associated with a form; occurs when the application is started and the form is displayed the first time

ToString method—formats a number stored in a numeric variable and then returns the result as a string

Lesson B Review Questions

1. The name of a form's default button is specified in the _____ property.

   a. button's AcceptButton
   b. button's DefaultButton
   c. form's AcceptButton
   d. form's DefaultButton

2. The InputBox function displays a dialog box containing which of the following?

   a. input area
   b. OK and Cancel buttons
   c. prompt
   d. all of the above

3. Which of the following is the concatenation operator?

   a. @
   b. &
   c. $
   d. #

4. Which of the following Visual Basic constants advances the insertion point to the next line?

   a. Advance
   b. ControlChars.Advance
   c. ControlChars.NewLine
   d. none of the above

5. The `strWord1` and `strWord2` variables contain the strings "Input" and "Box", respectively. Which of the following will display the string "InputBox" (one word) in the lblWord control?

   a. `lblWord.Text = strWord1 & strWord2`
   b. `lblWord.Text = "strWord1" & "strWord2"`
   c. `lblWord.Text = strWord1 @ strWord2`
   d. `lblWord.Text = strWord1 # strWord2`

6. The `strCity` and `strState` variables contain the strings "Louisville" and "KY", respectively. Which of the following will display the string "Louisville, KY" (the city, a comma, a space, and the state) in the lblCityState control?

   a. `lblCityState.Text = strCity & ', ' & strState`
   b. `lblCityState.Text = strCity & ", " & strState`
   c. `lblCityState.Text = "strCity" & ", " & "strState"`
   d. none of the above

7. Which of the following statements correctly assigns the InputBox function's return value to a Double variable named `dblNum`?

   a. `Double.TryParse(InputBox(strMSG, "Number"), dblNum)`

   b. `dblNum = Double.TryParse(InputBox(strMSG, "Number"))`

   c. `dblNum = InputBox(strMSG, "Number")`

   d. `TryParse.Double(InputBox(strMSG, "Number"), dblNum)`

8. Which of the following statements correctly assigns the InputBox function's return value to a String variable named `strCity`?

   a. `String.TryParse(InputBox(strMSG, "City"), strCity)`

   b. `strCity = String.TryParse(InputBox(strMSG, "City"))`

   c. `strCity = InputBox(strMSG, "City")`

   d. none of the above

9. The InputBox function's prompt argument should be entered using which type of capitalization?

   a. book title

   b. sentence

10. If the `decPay` variable contains the number 1200.76, which of the following statements displays the number as 1,200.76?

    a. `lblPay.Text = decPay.ToString("C2")`

    b. `lblPay.Text = decPay.ToString("F2")`

    c. `lblPay.Text = decPay.ToString("D2")`

    d. `lblPay.Text = decPay.ToString("N2")`

Lesson B Exercises

INTRODUCTORY

1. This exercise assumes you have completed the Richardson County application from Exercise 1 in each of Chapter 2's lessons. Use Windows to copy the Richardson Solution folder from the VB2015\Chap02 folder to the VB2015\Chap03 folder, and then open the Richardson Solution (Richardson Solution.sln) file. Open the Code Editor window and enter the three Option statements in the General Declarations section. Modify the application's code to use variables and the TryParse and ToString methods rather than the Val and Format functions. Save the solution, and then start and test the application.

INTRODUCTORY

2. This exercise assumes you have completed the Jordan Sports Store application from Exercise 2 in each of Chapter 2's lessons. Use Windows to copy the Jordan Solution folder from the VB2015\Chap02 folder to the VB2015\Chap03 folder, and then open the Jordan Solution (Jordan Solution.sln) file. Open the Code Editor window and enter the three Option statements in the General Declarations section. Modify the application's code to use variables and the TryParse and ToString methods rather than the Val and Format functions. Save the solution, and then start and test the application.

3. This exercise assumes you have completed the Cranston Berries application from Exercise 3 in each of Chapter 2's lessons. Use Windows to copy the Cranston Solution folder from the VB2015\Chap02 folder to the VB2015\Chap03 folder, and then open the Cranston Solution (Cranston Solution.sln) file. Open the Code Editor window and enter the three Option statements in the General Declarations section. Modify the application's code to use variables and the TryParse and ToString methods rather than the Val and Format functions. Save the solution, and then start and test the application. INTRODUCTORY

4. Open the VB2015\Chap03\Bonus Solution\Bonus Solution (Bonus Solution.sln) file. The application displays a salesperson's total sales and bonus amounts. The bonus is calculated by multiplying the total sales by 10%. Make the Calculate button the default button. Open the Code Editor window and enter your name, the current date, and the three Option statements in the General Declarations section. Code the application using variables, a named constant for the bonus rate, and the TryParse and ToString methods. Display the total sales and bonus amounts with a dollar sign, two decimal places, and a thousands separator (if appropriate). Save the solution and then start the application. Test the application by calculating the bonus for a salesperson whose sales are $2000, $4550.89, and $5650.99. INTRODUCTORY

5. In this exercise, you modify the bonus application from Exercise 4. Use Windows to make a copy of the Bonus Solution folder. Rename the copy Modified Bonus Solution. Open the Bonus Solution (Bonus Solution.sln) file contained in the Modified Bonus Solution folder. Code the frmMain_Load event so that it asks the user for the bonus rate. Then, use the bonus rate entered by the user in the btnCalc_Click procedure. Save the solution and then start the application. Test the application by calculating a 10% bonus for a salesperson whose sales are $2000, $4550.89, and $5650.99. Stop the application, and then test it again using a 5% bonus rate and sales of $12,200, $14,300, and $13,000. INTRODUCTORY

6. In this exercise, you modify the bakery application from this lesson. Use Windows to make a copy of the Bakery Solution folder. Rename the copy Modified Bakery Solution-Lesson B. Open the Bakery Solution (Bakery Solution.sln) file contained in the Modified Bakery Solution-Lesson B folder. Modify the application's code to allow the user to enter the item price each time the application is started. Save the solution, and then start and test the application. INTRODUCTORY

7. The **strFirst** and **strLast** variables contain the strings "Kate" and "Juarez", respectively. Write an assignment statement to display the string "Kate Juarez" in the lblName control. INTRODUCTORY

8. The **strCity** and **strState** variables contain the strings "Scottsdale" and "AZ", respectively. Write an assignment statement to display the string "They live in Scottsdale, AZ." in the lblMsg control. INTRODUCTORY

9. The **strFirst**, **strMiddle**, **strLast**, and **strNickname** variables contain the strings "Addison", "Grace", "Carson", and "Addi G", respectively. Write an assignment statement that will display the string "My name is Addison Grace Carson, but you can call me Addi G." in the lblMsg control. INTERMEDIATE

INTERMEDIATE

10. K & L Clothiers wants you to create an application that prints a customer's sales receipt. A sample receipt is shown in Figure 3-49. Use the following names for the solution and project, respectively: Clothiers Solution and Clothiers Project. Save the application in the VB2015\Chap03 folder. Change the form file's name to Main Form.vb. Change the form's name to frmMain. The interface you design does not have to match exactly the one shown in Figure 3-49, but it should include all of the information shown on the receipt. (To display an ampersand in a label control, you will need to include two ampersands in its Text property, like this: K && L.) Before coding the procedure that calculates and displays the discount amount and balance due, write the procedure's pseudocode. Be sure to use variables and the TryParse method in the code. (Do not use the Val function.) Also be sure to enter the three Option statements in the General Declarations section. Save the solution, and then test the application using the data shown in Figure 3-49. Then test it again using your own data.

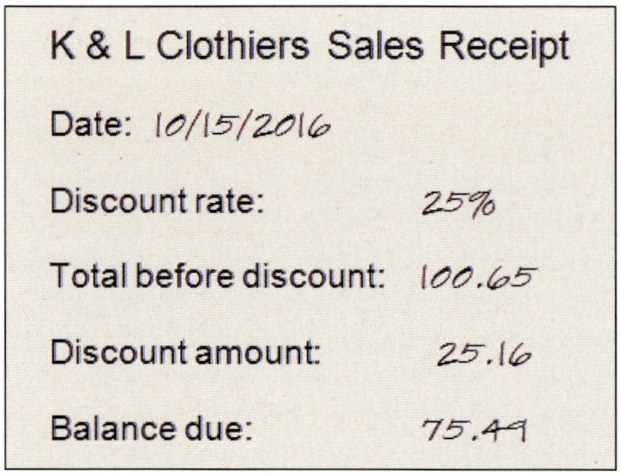

K & L Clothiers Sales Receipt

Date: 10/15/2016

Discount rate: 25%

Total before discount: 100.65

Discount amount: 25.16

Balance due: 75.49

Figure 3-49   Sample sales receipt for K & L Clothiers

INTERMEDIATE

11. Create an application that displays a circle's area and circumference, given its radius. Use the following names for the solution and project, respectively: Circle Solution and Circle Project. Save the application in the VB2015\Chap03 folder. Change the form file's name to Main Form.vb. Change the form's name to frmMain. Be sure to use variables, a named constant for the value of pi (3.14), and the TryParse method in the code. (Do not use the Val function.) Also be sure to enter the three Option statements in the General Declarations section. Display the area and circumference with two decimal places. Save the solution and then test the application.

DISCOVERY

12. In this exercise, you will learn about a form's CancelButton property, which specifies the button whose Click event procedure is processed when the user presses the Esc key. Open the VB2015\Chap03\Cancel Solution\Cancel Solution (Cancel Solution.sln) file.

   a. Open the Code Editor window and review the existing code. Start the application. Type your first name in the text box and then press Enter to select the Clear button, which is the form's default button. The Clear button removes your name from the text box. Click the Undo button. Your name reappears in the text box. Click the Exit button.

   b. Return to the designer window. Set the form's CancelButton property to btnUndo. Doing this tells the computer to process the btnUndo_Click procedure when the user presses the Esc key. Save the solution and then start the application. Type your first name in the text box and then press Enter to select the Clear button. Press Esc to select the Undo button. Your name reappears in the text box.

LESSON C

After studying Lesson C, you should be able to:

- Include a static variable in code
- Code the TextChanged event procedure
- Create a procedure that handles more than one event

Modifying the Load and Click Event Procedures

Currently, the Meyer's Purple Bakery application allows the user to enter the salesclerk's name only when the application first starts. In this lesson, you will modify the code so that it asks for the name each time the Calculate button is clicked. This will allow another salesclerk to enter his or her name on the sales receipt without having to start the application again.

As you learned in Lesson B, you should review an application's documentation and revise the necessary documents before making modifications to the code. Figure 3-50 shows the revised TOE chart. Changes made to the TOE chart from Lesson B are shaded in the figure. Notice that the Calculate button's Click event procedure, rather than the form's Load event procedure, is now responsible for getting the salesclerk's name.

Task	Object	Event
1. Get the salesclerk's name	btnCalc	Click
2. Calculate total items sold and total sales amount		
3. Display total items sold and total sales amount in lblTotalItems and lblTotalSales		
4. Calculate the sales tax		
5. Display sales tax and salesclerk's name in lblMsg		
Print the sales receipt	btnPrint	Click
End the application	btnExit	Click
Clear the screen for the next sale	btnClear	Click
Display total items sold (from btnCalc)	lblTotalItems	None
Display total sales amount (from btnCalc)	lblTotalSales	None
Get and display the sales information	txtDate, txtDonuts txtMuffins	None
Get the salesclerk's name	frmMain	Load
Display sales tax and salesclerk's name (from btnCalc)	lblMsg	None

Figure 3-50 Revised TOE chart for the bakery application in Lesson C

Figure 3-51 shows the revised pseudocode for the Calculate button's Click event procedure. Changes made to the pseudocode from Lesson B are shaded in the figure.

```
btnCalc Click event procedure
1. get the salesclerk's name
2. calculate total items sold = doughnuts sold + muffins sold
3. calculate subtotal = total items sold * item price
4. calculate sales tax = subtotal * sales tax rate
5. calculate total sales = subtotal + sales tax
6. display total items sold and total sales in lblTotalItems and lblTotalSales
7. display sales tax and salesclerk's name in lblMsg
```

Figure 3-51   Revised pseudocode for the Calculate button in Lesson C

First, you will open the bakery application from Lesson B and move the code contained in the frmMain_Load procedure to the btnCalc_Click procedure.

START HERE

To open the bakery application and then move some of the code:

1. If necessary, start Visual Studio 2015. Open the Bakery Solution (Bakery Solution.sln) file from Lesson B.

2. Open the Code Editor window and locate the frmMain_Load procedure. Highlight (select) the two Const statements in the procedure, and then press **Ctrl+x** to cut the statements from the procedure.

3. Locate the btnCalc_Click procedure. Click the **blank line** above the first Const statement in the procedure, and then press **Enter** to insert a new blank line. With the insertion point in the new blank line, press **Ctrl+v** to paste the two Const statements in the procedure. (Don't be concerned about the squiggles that appear below the two Const statements. They will disappear when you use the constants in another statement within the procedure.)

4. Return to the frmMain_Load procedure. Highlight the second comment and the assignment statement, and then press **Ctrl+x** to remove the selected lines from the procedure.

5. Return to the btnCalc_Click procedure. Click the **blank line** below the last Dim statement, and then press **Enter** to insert a new blank line. With the insertion point in the new blank line, press **Ctrl+v** to paste the comment and assignment statement in the procedure, and then press **Enter** to insert a new blank line below the assignment statement. Change the pasted comment to ' **assign name to variable**.

6. Return to the frmMain_Load procedure, and then delete the entire procedure from the Code Editor window.

Now that you have moved the InputBox function from the frmMain_Load procedure to the btnCalc_Click procedure, only one procedure—the btnCalc_Click procedure—needs to use the strClerk variable. Therefore, you should change the variable from a class-level variable to a procedure-level variable. You can do this by moving the variable's declaration statement from the form's Declarations section to the btnCalc_Click procedure and then changing the keyword in the declaration statement from Private to Dim.

START HERE

To move the declaration statement and then modify it:

1. First, delete the comment from the form's Declarations section. Next, highlight the **Private strClerk As String** statement, and then press **Ctrl+x** to cut the statement from the Declarations section.

2. Click the **blank line** below the last Dim statement in the btnCalc_Click procedure. Press **Ctrl+v** to paste the Private statement in the procedure, and then press **Enter** to insert a blank line below the statement.

3. The red squiggle below the `Private` keyword indicates that the statement contains a syntax error. Rest your mouse pointer on the `Private` keyword. The error message indicates that the keyword is not valid on a local variable declaration. Change `Private` in the variable declaration statement to **Dim**.

4. Save the solution and then start the application. Click the **Calculate** button. Type your name in the Name Entry dialog box and then press **Enter**. The message "The sales tax was $0.00." and your name appear in the lblMsg control.

5. Click the **Calculate** button again. Notice that the Name Entry dialog box requires the user to enter the salesclerk's name again. It would be more efficient for the user if the name appeared as the default response the second and subsequent times the Calculate button is clicked.

6. Click the **Cancel** button in the dialog box. The InputBox function returns an empty string, so no name appears in the lblMsg control. Click the **Exit** button.

To display the salesclerk's name in the dialog box when the Calculate button is clicked the second and subsequent times, you can declare the `strClerk` variable as either a class-level variable or a static variable and then use the variable as the *defaultResponse* argument in the InputBox function. In this case, a static variable is a better choice because static variables have a lesser (more restrictive) scope than class-level variables. Recall that a static variable is really just a special type of procedure-level variable. As you learned in Lesson A, fewer unintentional errors occur in applications when variables are declared using the minimum scope needed. In this case, the minimum scope required for the `strClerk` variable is procedure scope because only one procedure needs to use the variable.

To modify the btnCalc_Click procedure:

START HERE

1. In the btnCalc_Click procedure, change the `Dim` in the `Dim strClerk As String` statement to **Static**.

2. Next, change the statement that contains the InputBox function as follows, and then click the **blank line** below the statement:

strClerk = InputBox(strPROMPT, strTITLE, strClerk)

3. Save the solution and then start the application. Type any date in the Date box, type **5** in the Doughnuts box, and type **1** in the Muffins box. Press **Enter**. Type your name in the Name Entry dialog box and then press **Enter**. The application calculates and displays the total items sold (6) and total sales ($3.06). In addition, the message "The sales tax was $0.06." and your name appear in the lblMsg control.

4. Change the number of muffins sold to **4**. At this point, the calculated amounts on the sales receipt are incorrect because they do not reflect the change in the number of muffins sold. To display the correct amounts, you will need to recalculate the amounts by selecting the Calculate button. Press **Enter** to select the Calculate button. Your name appears highlighted in the input area of the Name Entry dialog box.

5. Press **Enter** to select the dialog box's OK button. The application calculates and displays the total items sold (9) and total sales ($4.59). The message "The sales tax was $0.09." and your name appear in the lblMsg control. Click the **Exit** button.

Having the previously calculated amounts remain on the screen when a change is made to the interface could be misleading. A better approach is to clear the amounts when a change is made to either the number of doughnuts sold or the number of muffins sold.

Coding the TextChanged Event Procedure

A control's **TextChanged event** occurs when a change is made to the contents of the control's Text property. This can happen as a result of either the user entering data into the control or the application's code assigning data to the control's Text property. In the next set of steps, you will code the txtDonuts_TextChanged procedure so that it clears the contents of the lblTotalItems, lblTotalSales, and lblMsg controls when the user changes the number of doughnuts sold.

START HERE

To code the txtDonuts_TextChanged procedure:

1. Open the code template for the txtDonuts_TextChanged procedure. Type the following comment and then press **Enter** twice:

    ' clear the total items, total sales, and message

2. Enter the following three assignment statements:

    lblTotalItems.Text = String.Empty
    lblTotalSales.Text = String.Empty
    lblMsg.Text = String.Empty

3. Save the solution and then start the application. Type any date in the Date box, type **3** in the Doughnuts box, and type **2** in the Muffins box. Press **Enter**. Type your name in the Name Entry dialog box and then press **Enter**. The application displays the calculated amounts and your name.

4. Change the number of doughnuts sold to **4**. When you make this change, the txtDonuts_TextChanged procedure clears the total items sold, total sales, and message information from the form. Click the **Exit** button.

Recall that you also want to clear the calculated amounts when a change is made to the number of muffins sold. One way of accomplishing this is to copy the code from the txtDonuts_TextChanged procedure to the txtMuffins_TextChanged procedure; you then would have two procedures with the exact same code. However, another way is to create one procedure for the computer to process when the TextChanged event of either of the two controls occurs.

Associating a Procedure with Different Objects and Events

The Handles clause in an event procedure's header indicates the object and event associated with the procedure. The Handles clause in Figure 3-52, for example, indicates that the procedure is associated with the TextChanged event of the txtDonuts control. As a result, the procedure will be processed when the txtDonuts control's TextChanged event occurs.

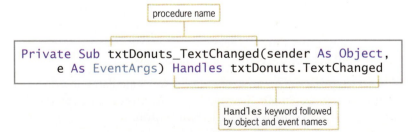

Figure 3-52 TextChanged event procedure associated with the txtDonuts control

Although an event procedure's name contains the names of its associated object and event separated by an underscore, that is not a requirement. You can change the name of an event procedure to almost anything you like as long as the name follows the same rules for naming variables. Unlike variable names, however, procedure names are usually entered using **Pascal case**, which means you capitalize the first letter in the name and the first letter of each subsequent word in the name. For example, you can change the name of the procedure in Figure 3-52 from txtDonuts_TextChanged to ClearLabels and the procedure will still work correctly. This is because the Handles clause, rather than the event procedure's name, determines when the procedure is invoked.

You can associate a procedure with more than one object and event as long as each event contains the same parameters in its procedure header. To do so, you list each object and event in the procedure's Handles clause. You separate the object and event with a period, like this: *object.event*. You use a comma to separate each *object.event* from the next *object.event*. In the next set of steps, you will change the name of the txtDonuts_TextChanged procedure to ClearLabels and then associate the procedure with the txtDonuts.TextChanged and txtMuffins.TextChanged events.

To change the procedure's name and then associate it with different objects and events: START HERE

1. In the procedure header, change `txtDonuts_TextChanged` to **ClearLabels**.

2. Next, click **immediately before the letter H** in the keyword `Handles`. Type _ (an underscore, which is the line continuation character). Be sure there is a space between the ending parenthesis and the underscore. Then press **Enter** to move the Handles clause to the next line in the procedure.

3. In the Handles clause, click **immediately after TextChanged**. The ClearLabels procedure is already associated with the txtDonuts.TextChanged event. You just need to associate it with the txtMuffins.TextChanged event. Type **,** (a comma) and then press the **Spacebar**. Scroll the list of object names until you see txtMuffins. Click **txtMuffins** in the list, and then press **Tab** to enter the object name in the Handles clause.

4. Type **.** (a period). Scroll the list of event names until you see TextChanged. Click **TextChanged**, press **Tab**, and then click the **blank line** below the comment. Figure 3-53 shows the completed ClearLabels procedure.

```
Private Sub ClearLabels(sender As Object, e As EventArgs) _      ⟵ line continuation
    Handles txtDonuts.TextChanged, txtMuffins.TextChanged            character
        ' clear the total items, total sales, and message
        |

    lblTotalItems.Text = String.Empty
    lblTotalSales.Text = String.Empty
    lblMsg.Text = String.Empty


    End Sub
```

Handles clause ⟵

Figure 3-53 Completed ClearLabels procedure

5. Save the solution and then start the application. Type **2/23/2016** in the Date box, type **13** in the Doughnuts box, and type **7** in the Muffins box. Press **Enter**. Type your name in the Name Entry dialog box and then press **Enter**. The application displays the calculated amounts and message.

6. Change the number of doughnuts sold to **2**. The ClearLabels procedure clears the calculated amounts and message from the form.

7. Press **Enter** to select the Calculate button, and then press **Enter** again to select the OK button in the Name Entry dialog box. The application displays the new calculated amounts and message.

8. Change the number of muffins sold to **4**. The ClearLabels procedure clears the calculated amounts and message from the form.

9. Press **Enter** to select the Calculate button. Type **Peter Harrison** in the Name Entry dialog box, and then press **Enter** to select the OK button. See Figure 3-54.

Figure 3-54   Completed sales receipt

10. Click the **Exit** button. Close the Code Editor window and then close the solution. Figure 3-55 shows the bakery application's code at the end of Lesson C.

```
 1 ' Name:          Bakery Project
 2 ' Purpose:       Calculates the total number of
 3 '                items sold and the total sales
 4 ' Programmer:    <your name> on <current date>
 5
 6 Option Explicit On
 7 Option Infer Off
 8 Option Strict On
 9
10 Public Class frmMain
11
12    Private Sub btnCalc_Click(sender As Object,
      e As EventArgs) Handles btnCalc.Click
13        ' calculate number of items sold and total sales
14
15        Const strPROMPT As String = "Salesclerk's name:"
16        Const strTITLE As String = "Name Entry"
17        Const decITEM_PRICE As Decimal = 0.5D
```

Figure 3-55   Bakery application's code at the end of Lesson C *(continues)*

(continued)

```
18          Const decTAX_RATE As Decimal = 0.02D
19          Dim intDonuts As Integer
20          Dim intMuffins As Integer
21          Dim intTotalItems As Integer
22          Dim decSubtotal As Decimal
23          Dim decSalesTax As Decimal
24          Dim decTotalSales As Decimal
25          Static strClerk As String
26
27          ' assign name to variable
28          strClerk = InputBox(strPROMPT, strTITLE, strClerk)
29
30          ' calculate total number of items sold
31          Integer.TryParse(txtDonuts.Text, intDonuts)
32          Integer.TryParse(txtMuffins.Text, intMuffins)
33          intTotalItems = intDonuts + intMuffins
34
35          ' calculate the subtotal
36          decSubtotal = intTotalItems * decITEM_PRICE
37
38          ' calculate the sales tax
39          decSalesTax = decSubtotal * decTAX_RATE
40
41          ' calculate the total sales
42          decTotalSales = decSubtotal + decSalesTax
43
44          ' display total amounts
45          lblTotalItems.Text = Convert.ToString(intTotalItems)
46          lblTotalSales.Text = decTotalSales.ToString("C2")
47
48          ' display tax and salesclerk's name
49          lblMsg.Text = "The sales tax was " &
50              decSalesTax.ToString("C2") & "." &
51              ControlChars.NewLine & strClerk
52
53      End Sub
54
55      Private Sub btnClear_Click(sender As Object,
        e As EventArgs) Handles btnClear.Click
56          ' prepare screen for the next sale
57
58          txtDonuts.Text = String.Empty
59          txtMuffins.Text = String.Empty
60          lblTotalItems.Text = String.Empty
61          lblTotalSales.Text = String.Empty
62          lblMsg.Text = String.Empty
63          ' send the focus to the Doughnuts box
64          txtDonuts.Focus()
65
66      End Sub
67
68      Private Sub btnExit_Click(sender As Object,
        e As EventArgs) Handles btnExit.Click
69          Me.Close()
70      End Sub
```

Figure 3-55 Bakery application's code at the end of Lesson C *(continues)*

(continued)

```
71
72    Private Sub btnPrint_Click(sender As Object,
      e As EventArgs) Handles btnPrint.Click
73        ' print the sales receipt
74
75        btnCalc.Visible = False
76        btnClear.Visible = False
77        btnExit.Visible = False
78        btnPrint.Visible = False
79        PrintForm1.Print()
80        btnCalc.Visible = True
81        btnClear.Visible = True
82        btnExit.Visible = True
83        btnPrint.Visible = True
84
85    End Sub
86
87    Private Sub ClearLabels(sender As Object, e As EventArgs) _
88    Handles txtDonuts.TextChanged, txtMuffins.TextChanged
89        ' clear the total items, total sales, and message
90
91        lblTotalItems.Text = String.Empty
92        lblTotalSales.Text = String.Empty
93        lblMsg.Text = String.Empty
94
95    End Sub
96 End Class
```

Figure 3-55   Bakery application's code at the end of Lesson C

Lesson C Summary

- To create a procedure-level variable that remains in memory and also retains its value until the application ends:

  Declare the variable in a procedure using the **Static** keyword.

- To process code when a change is made to the contents of a control's Text property:

  Enter the code in the control's TextChanged event procedure.

- To associate a procedure with more than one object or event:

  List each object and event (using the syntax *object.event*) after the **Handles** keyword in the procedure header. Use a comma to separate each object and event from the previous object and event.

Lesson C Key Terms

Pascal case—used when entering procedure names; the process of capitalizing the first letter in the name and the first letter of each subsequent word in the name

TextChanged event—occurs when a change is made to the contents of a control's Text property

Lesson C Review Questions

1. Which of the following events occurs when a change is made to the contents of a text box?

   a. Change   c. TextChanged

   b. Changed   d. TextChange

2. A _____ variable is a procedure-level variable that retains its value after the procedure in which it is declared ends.

   a. constant   c. stationary

   b. static   d. term

3. Which of the following clauses associates a procedure with the TextChanged event of the txtMid and txtFinal controls?

   a. `Associates txtMid_TextChanged, txtFinal_TextChanged`

   b. `Handled txtMid_TextChanged, txtFinal_TextChanged`

   c. `Controls txtMid.TextChanged And txtFinal.TextChanged`

   d. `Handles txtMid.TextChanged, txtFinal.TextChanged`

4. Which of the following statements declares a procedure-level variable that is removed from the computer's memory when the procedure ends?

   a. `Const intCounter As Integer`

   b. `Dim intCounter As Integer`

   c. `Local intCounter As Integer`

   d. `Static intCounter As Integer`

5. Which of the following statements declares a procedure-level variable that retains its value after the procedure in which it is declared ends?

   a. `Const intCounter As Integer`

   b. `Dim intCounter As Constant`

   c. `Dim intCounter As Integer`

   d. `Static intCounter As Integer`

Lesson C Exercises

1. In this exercise, you modify the bakery application from this lesson. Use Windows to make a copy of the Bakery Solution folder. Rename the copy Modified Bakery Solution-Lesson C-Intro. Open the Bakery Solution (Bakery Solution.sln) file contained in the Modified Bakery Solution-Lesson C-Intro folder. An hour before the bakery closes, the price of the doughnuts and muffins drops to $0.35. Modify the btnCalc_Click procedure to allow the user to enter the item price. Save the solution, and then start and test the application.

   `INTRODUCTORY`

2. Create an application using the following names for the solution and project, respectively: Chopkins Solution and Chopkins Project. Save the application in the VB2015\Chap03 folder. Change the form file's name to Main Form.vb. Change the

   `INTRODUCTORY`

form's name to frmMain. Create the interface shown in Figure 3-56. The application displays the total number of packs ordered and the total price of the order. The prices of a 12 pack, 5 pack, and 2 pack are $14.99, $6.99, and $2.50, respectively. Be sure to use variables, named constants, and the TryParse method in your code. Also be sure to enter the three Option statements in the General Declarations section. The total sales amount should be displayed with a dollar sign and two decimal places. Clear the calculated amounts when a change is made to the number of 12 packs, 5 packs, or 2 packs. Save the solution, and then start and test the application.

Figure 3-56   Interface for Chopkins Toys

INTRODUCTORY

3. Create an application using the following names for the solution and project, respectively: Tile Solution and Tile Project. Save the application in the VB2015\Chap03 folder. Change the form file's name to Main Form.vb. Change the form's name to frmMain. The manager of Tile Unlimited wants you to create an application that displays the area of a rectangular floor (in square feet) and the total cost of tiling the floor. Use text boxes to get the floor's length and width measurements (in feet). Use the InputBox function to get the price of a square foot of tile. The price may vary, so it will need to be entered before each calculation. Be sure to use variables and the TryParse method in your code. Also be sure to enter the three Option statements in the General Declarations section. Display the total cost amount with a dollar sign and two decimal places. Display the area with two decimal places. Clear the calculated amounts when a change is made to the floor measurements. Save the solution, and then start and test the application.

INTERMEDIATE

4. In this exercise, you modify the bakery application from this lesson. Use Windows to make a copy of the Bakery Solution folder. Rename the copy Modified Bakery Solution-Lesson C-Intermediate. Open the Bakery Solution (Bakery Solution.sln) file contained in the Modified Bakery Solution-Lesson C-Intermediate folder. Recently, the bakery has had to increase the price of its muffins. Modify the btnCalc_Click procedure to allow the user to enter the doughnut price and also the muffin price. Save the solution, and then start and test the application.

INTERMEDIATE

5. Create an application using the following names for the solution and project, respectively: Van Solution and Van Project. Save the application in the VB2015\Chap03 folder. Change the form file's name to Main Form.vb. Change the form's name to frmMain. Rent-A-Van wants you to create an application that calculates the total cost of renting a van. Customers pay a base fee plus a charge per mile driven. The user will enter the base fee and the charge

per mile driven when the application is started. Use text boxes to get the customer's name, the mileage at the beginning of the rental period, and the mileage at the end of the rental period. Use labels to display the base fee, the charge per mile driven, the number of miles driven, and the total rental cost. Be sure to use variables and the TryParse method in your code. Also be sure to enter the three Option statements in the General Declarations section. The total rental cost should be displayed with a dollar sign and two decimal places. Clear the calculated amounts when a change is made to the beginning or ending mileage. Save the solution, and then start and test the application.

6. Create an application using the following names for the solution and project, respectively: Retirement Solution and Retirement Project. Save the application in the VB2015\Chap03 folder. Change the form file's name to Main Form.vb. Change the form's name to frmMain. Pamela receives 52 weekly paychecks each year. Each week, she contributes a specific percentage of her gross weekly pay to her retirement plan at work. Her employer also contributes to her retirement plan but at a different rate. Create an interface that allows Pamela to enter the amount of her gross weekly pay, her contribution rate, and her employer's contribution rate. The interface should display her annual contribution, her employer's annual contribution, and the total annual contribution. Be sure to use variables and the TryParse method in your code. Also be sure to enter the three Option statements in the General Declarations section. The contribution amounts should be displayed with a dollar sign and two decimal places. Clear the calculated amounts when a change is made to any of the input items. Save the solution, and then start and test the application.

INTERMEDIATE

7. In this exercise, you modify the Chopkins Toys application from Exercise 2. Use Windows to make a copy of the Chopkins Solution folder. Rename the copy Modified Chopkins Solution. Open the Chopkins Solution (Chopkins Solution.sln) file contained in the Modified Chopkins Solution folder. Modify the interface as shown in Figure 3-57. The interface will now display the sale totals for each of the different packs. For example, if the customer purchased five 12 packs, the label that appears next to the associated text box should display 74.95 (5 * 14.99). Modify the btnCalc_Click procedure appropriately. The procedure should also allow the user to enter the shipping charge, which should be added to the total sale amount. Save the solution, and then start and test the application.

INTERMEDIATE

Figure 3-57   Modified interface for Chopkins Toys

8. Create an application using the following names for the solution and project, respectively: Pennies Solution and Pennies Project. Save the application in the VB2015\ Chap03 folder. Change the form file's name to Main Form.vb. Change the form's name to frmMain. Create an interface that allows the user to enter the number of pennies saved in a jar. The application should display the number of dollars, quarters, dimes, nickels, and pennies the user will receive when the pennies are cashed in at a bank. (It might be helpful to review the information in Figures 2-32 and 2-33 in Chapter 2.) Clear the calculated amounts when a change is made to the number of pennies entered by the user. Be sure to use variables and the TryParse method in your code. Also be sure to enter the three Option statements in the General Declarations section. Save the solution and then start the application. Test the application twice using the following data: 653 pennies and 250 pennies.

9. Create an application using the following names for the solution and project, respectively: Credit Card Solution and Credit Card Project. Save the application in the VB2015\ Chap03 folder. Change the form file's name to Main Form.vb. Change the form's name to frmMain. Create an interface that allows the user to enter the total amount charged to his or her credit card for each of the following six expense categories: Merchandise, Restaurants, Gasoline, Travel/Entertainment, Services, and Supermarkets. Use text boxes to get the six input items. The application should display the total charged to the credit card and the percentage that each category contributed to the total amount charged. Be sure to use variables and the TryParse method in your code. Also be sure to enter the three Option statements in the General Declarations section. Display each category's percentage with a percent sign and one decimal place. Save the solution, and then start and test the application.

10. Create an application using the following names for the solution and project, respectively: Pink Elephant Solution and Pink Elephant Project. Save the application in the VB2015\Chap03 folder. Change the form file's name to Main Form.vb. Change the form's name to frmMain. The application's interface should allow the owner of the Pink Elephant Photo Studio to enter the studio's quarterly sales amount. The application should display the amount of state, county, and city sales tax the studio must pay. It should also display the total sales tax. The sales tax rates for the state, county, and city are 2.5%, 0.5%, and 0.25%, respectively. Each sales tax is calculated by multiplying the appropriate rate by the quarterly sales amount. Be sure to use variables, named constants, and the TryParse method in your code. Also be sure to enter the three Option statements in the General Declarations section. Display the sales taxes with a dollar sign and two decimal places. Save the solution, and then start and test the application.

11. Open the VB2015\Chap03\Debug Solution-Lesson C\Debug Solution (Debug Solution. sln) file. Start and then test the application. Locate and correct any errors.

CHAPTER 4

The Selection Structure

Creating the Treeline Resort Application

In this chapter, you will create a reservation application for Treeline Resort. The application should allow the user to enter the following information: the number of rooms to reserve, the length of stay (in nights), the number of adult guests, and the number of child guests. Each room can accommodate a maximum of six guests. The resort charges $225.50 per room per night. It also charges a 16.25% sales and lodging tax, which is based on the room charge. In addition, there is a $12.50 resort fee per room per night. The application should display the total room charge, the sales and lodging tax, the total resort fee, and the total due.

Previewing the Treeline Resort Application

Before you start the first lesson in this chapter, you will preview the completed application contained in the VB2015\Chap04 folder.

START HERE

To preview the completed application:

1. Use Windows to locate and then open the VB2015\Chap04 folder. Right-click **Treeline** (**Treeline.exe**) and then click the **Open** button. The application's user interface appears on the screen.

2. Type **1** in the Rooms box, type **3** in the Nights box, type **2** in the Adults box, and type **3** in the Children box. Click the **Calculate** button. See Figure 4-1.

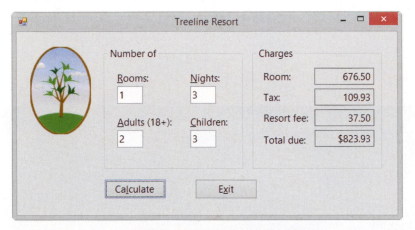

Figure 4-1   Interface showing the calculated amounts

3. Recall that only six guests are allowed in a room. Change the number of adults to **4** and then click the **Calculate** button. The message box shown in Figure 4-2 appears on the screen. You will learn how to create a message box in Lesson B.

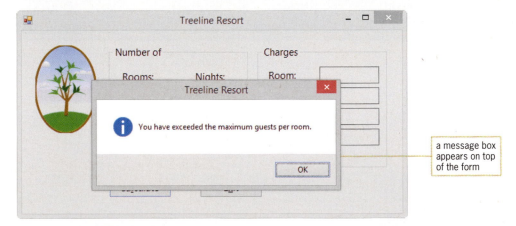

a message box appears on top of the form

Figure 4-2   Message box

4. Click the **OK** button to close the message box. Try to type a **$** in the Nights box. Notice that the text box does not accept the entry. You will learn how to prevent a text box from accepting unwanted characters in Lesson C.

5. Change the number of nights and the number of adults to **1** and **2**, respectively. Also change the number of children to **2**. Click the **Calculate** button. See Figure 4-3.

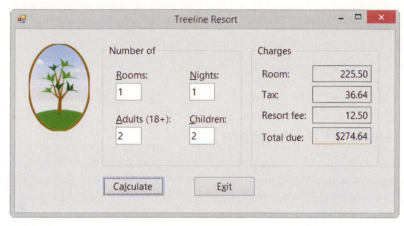

Figure 4-3   New charges shown in the interface

6. Click the **Exit** button to end the application.

The Treeline Resort application uses the selection structure, which you will learn about in Lesson A. In Lesson B, you will complete the application's interface and also begin coding the application. You will finish coding the application in Lesson C. Be sure to complete each lesson in full and do all of the end-of-lesson questions and several exercises before continuing to the next lesson.

LESSON A

After studying Lesson A, you should be able to:

- Write pseudocode for the selection structure
- Create a flowchart to help you plan an application's code
- Write an If...Then...Else statement
- Include comparison operators in a selection structure's condition
- Include logical operators in a selection structure's condition
- Change the case of a string

Making Decisions in a Program

All of the procedures in an application are written using one or more of three basic control structures: sequence, selection, and repetition. The procedures in the previous three chapters used the sequence structure only. When one of the procedures was invoked during run time, the computer processed its instructions sequentially—in other words, in the order the instructions appeared in the procedure. Every procedure you write will contain the sequence structure.

Many times, however, a procedure will need the computer to make a decision before selecting the next instruction to process. A procedure that calculates an employee's gross pay, for example, typically has the computer determine whether the number of hours an employee worked is greater than 40. The computer then would select either an instruction that computes regular pay only or an instruction that computes regular pay plus overtime pay. Procedures that need the computer to make a decision require the use of the selection structure (also called the decision structure).

ChO4A-Selection

The **selection structure** indicates that a decision (based on some condition) needs to be made, followed by an appropriate action derived from that decision. But how does a programmer determine whether a problem's solution requires a selection structure? The answer is by studying the problem specification.

The first problem specification you will examine in this lesson involves an evil scientist named Dr. N. The problem specification and an illustration of the problem are shown in Figure 4-4 along with a solution to the problem. The solution, which is written in pseudocode, requires only the sequence structure.

Problem Specification

Dr. N is sitting in a chair in his lair, facing a control deck and an electronic screen. At times, visitors come to the door located at the rear of the lair. Before pressing the blue button on the control deck to open the door, Dr. N likes to view the visitor on the screen. He can do so by pressing the orange button on the control deck. Write the instructions that direct Dr. N to view the visitor first and then open the door and say "Welcome".

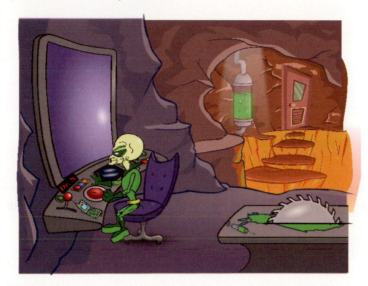

Solution
1. press the orange button on the control deck to view the visitor on the screen
2. press the blue button on the control deck to open the door
3. say "Welcome"

Figure 4-4   A problem that requires the sequence structure only
Image by Diane Zak; created with Reallusion CrazyTalk Animator

Now we'll make a slight change to the problem specification from Figure 4-4. In this case, Dr. N should open the door only if the visitor knows the secret password. The modified problem specification and solution are shown in Figure 4-5. The solution contains both the sequence and selection structures. The selection structure's condition directs Dr. N to make a decision about the visitor's password. More specifically, he needs to determine whether the visitor's password matches the secret password. The **condition** in a selection structure must be phrased so that it evaluates to an answer of either true or false. In this case, either the visitor's password matches the secret password (true) or it doesn't match the secret password (false). Only if both passwords are the same does Dr. N need to follow the two indented instructions. The selection structure in Figure 4-5 is referred to as a **single-alternative selection structure** because it requires one or more actions to be taken *only* when its condition evaluates to true. Other examples of single-alternative selection structures include "if it's raining, take an umbrella" and "if you are driving your car at night, turn your car's headlights on".

> In pseudocode, use the words *if* and *end if* to denote the beginning and end, respectively, of a selection structure. Also indent the instructions within the structure.

Figure 4-5   A problem that requires the sequence structure and a single-alternative selection structure

Figure 4-6 shows a modified version of the previous problem specification. In this version, Dr. N will say "Sorry, you are wrong" and then destroy the visitor if the passwords do not match. Also shown in Figure 4-6 are two possible solutions to the problem; both solutions produce the same result. The condition in Solution 1's selection structure determines whether the visitor's password is *correct*, whereas the condition in Solution 2's selection structure determines whether it is *incorrect*.

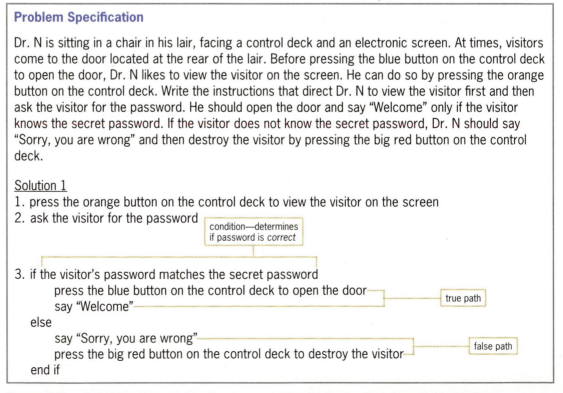

Figure 4-6   A problem that requires the sequence structure and a dual-alternative selection structure *(continues)*

(continued)

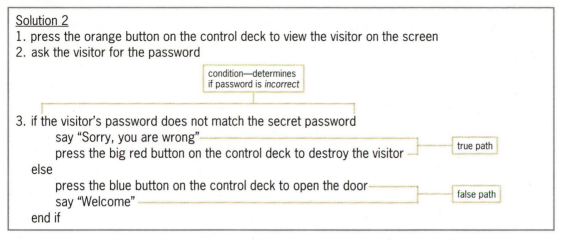

Solution 2
1. press the orange button on the control deck to view the visitor on the screen
2. ask the visitor for the password

condition—determines
if password is *incorrect*

3. if the visitor's password does not match the secret password
        say "Sorry, you are wrong"
        press the big red button on the control deck to destroy the visitor — true path
    else
        press the blue button on the control deck to open the door — false path
        say "Welcome"
    end if

Figure 4-6   A problem that requires the sequence structure and a dual-alternative selection structure

Unlike the selection structure in Figure 4-5, which provides instructions for Dr. N to follow *only* when the selection structure's condition is true, the selection structures in Figure 4-6 require Dr. N to perform one set of instructions when the condition is true and a different set of instructions when the condition is false. The instructions to follow when the condition evaluates to true are called the **true path**. The true path begins with the instruction immediately below the *if* and ends with either the *else* (if there is one) or the *end if*. The instructions to follow when the condition evaluates to false are called the **false path**. The false path begins with the instruction immediately below the *else* and ends with the *end if.* For clarity, the instructions in each path should be indented as shown in Figure 4-6. Selection structures that contain instructions in both paths, like the ones in Figure 4-6, are referred to as **dual-alternative selection structures**.

Flowcharting a Selection Structure

As you learned in Chapter 2, many programmers use flowcharts (rather than pseudocode) when planning solutions to problems. Figure 4-7 shows a problem specification along with two correct solutions in flowchart form. The diamond in a flowchart is called the **decision symbol** because it is used to represent the condition (decision) in both the selection and repetition structures. The diamonds in Figure 4-7 represent the conditions in selection structures. Flowchart A contains a single-alternative selection structure because it requires a set of actions to be taken only when its condition evaluates to true. Flowchart B contains a dual-alternative selection structure because it requires two different sets of actions: one to be taken only when its condition evaluates to true, and the other to be taken only when its condition evaluates to false.

Problem Specification

Create an application that displays an employee's weekly gross pay, given the number of hours worked and hourly pay rate. Employees working more than 40 hours are paid their hourly rate plus an additional one-half of their hourly rate for each hour worked over 40.

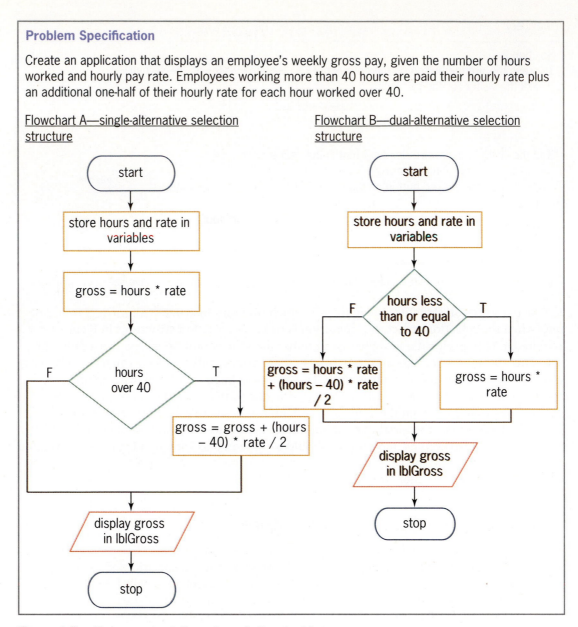

Figure 4-7   Two correct solutions shown in flowchart form

Notice that the conditions in both diamonds evaluate to either true or false only. Also notice that both diamonds have one flowline entering the symbol and two flowlines leaving the symbol. One of the flowlines leading out of a diamond in a flowchart should be marked with a T (for true) and the other should be marked with an F (for false). The T flowline points to the next instruction to be processed when the condition evaluates to true. In Flowchart A, the next instruction calculates the gross pay with overtime; in Flowchart B, it calculates the gross pay without any overtime. The F flowline points to the next instruction to be processed when the condition evaluates to false. In Flowchart A, that instruction displays the gross pay; in Flowchart B, it calculates the gross pay with overtime. You can also mark the flowlines leading out of a diamond with a Y and an N (for yes and no, respectively).

Coding Selection Structures in Visual Basic

Visual Basic provides the **If...Then...Else statement** for coding single-alternative and dual-alternative selection structures. The statement's syntax is shown in Figure 4-8. The square brackets in the syntax indicate that the Else portion, referred to as the Else clause, is optional. The boldfaced items in the syntax are required; however, the `Else` keyword is necessary only in a dual-alternative selection structure.

Italicized items in the syntax indicate where the programmer must supply information. In the If...Then...Else statement, the programmer must supply the *condition* that the computer needs to evaluate before further processing can occur. The condition must be a Boolean expression, which is an expression that results in a Boolean value (True or False). Besides providing the condition, the programmer must provide the statements to be processed in the true path and (optionally) in the false path. The set of statements contained in each path is referred to as a **statement block**. (In Visual Basic, a statement block is a set of statements terminated by an Else, End If, Loop, or Next clause. You will learn about the Loop and Next clauses in Chapters 6 and 7.)

The examples in Figure 4-8 illustrate how to use the If...Then...Else statement to code the selection structures shown earlier in Figure 4-7. The examples use comparison operators (> and <=) to compare the hours worked to the number 40. Comparison operators are covered in the next section.

If...Then...Else Statement

<u>Syntax</u>
If *condition* **Then**
    statement block to be processed when the condition is true
[Else
    statement block to be processed when the condition is false]
End If

<u>Example 1</u>
```
Private Sub btnCalc_Click(sender As Object, e As EventArgs
) Handles btnCalc.Click
    ' calculate gross pay

    Dim decHours As Decimal
    Dim decRate As Decimal
    Dim decGross As Decimal

    Decimal.TryParse(txtHours.Text, decHours)
    Decimal.TryParse(txtRate.Text, decRate)

    ' regular pay
    decGross = decHours * decRate
    ' add overtime, if appropriate
    If decHours > 40 Then
        decGross = decGross +
            (decHours - 40) * decRate / 2        single-alternative
    End If                                        selection structure

    lblGross.Text = decGross.ToString("c2")
End Sub
```

Figure 4-8   Syntax and examples of the If...Then...Else statement *(continues)*

(continued)

```
Example 2
Private Sub btnCalc_Click(sender As Object, e As EventArgs
) Handles btnCalc.Click
    ' calculate gross pay

    Dim decHours As Decimal
    Dim decRate As Decimal
    Dim decGross As Decimal

    Decimal.TryParse(txtHours.Text, decHours)
    Decimal.TryParse(txtRate.Text, decRate)

    If decHours <= 40 Then
        ' regular pay
        decGross = decHours * decRate
    Else
        ' regular pay with overtime
        decGross = decHours * decRate +
            (decHours - 40) * decRate / 2
    End If

    lblGross.Text = decGross.ToString("c2")
End Sub
```

dual-alternative selection structure

Figure 4-8   Syntax and examples of the If...Then...Else statement

START HERE

To code and then test the Gross Pay Calculator application:

1. If necessary, start Visual Studio 2015. Open the Gross Solution (Gross Solution.sln) file contained in the VB2015\Chap04\Gross Solution-Single folder. Open the Code Editor window. Replace <your name> and <current date> in the comments with your name and the current date, respectively.

2. Locate the btnCalc_Click procedure, and then enter the single-alternative selection structure shown in Example 1 in Figure 4-8.

3. Save the solution and then start the application. First, calculate the gross pay using **40** and **10** as the hours worked and the hourly rate, respectively. The gross pay is $400.00. See Figure 4-9.

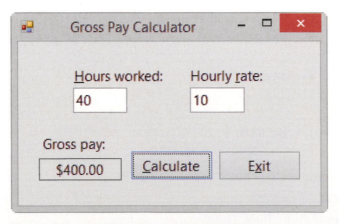

Figure 4-9   Interface showing the gross pay

4. Next, calculate the gross pay using **45** as the hours worked and **11.65** as the hourly rate. $553.38 appears in the Gross pay box.

5. Click the **Exit** button. Close the Code Editor window and then close the solution.

6. Open the Gross Solution (Gross Solution.sln) file contained in the VB2015\Chap04\ Gross Solution-Dual folder. Open the Code Editor window. Replace <your name> and <current date> in the comments with your name and the current date, respectively.

7. Locate the btnCalc_Click procedure, and then enter the dual-alternative selection structure shown in Example 2 in Figure 4-8.

8. Save the solution and then start the application. First, calculate the gross pay using **40** and **10** as the hours worked and the hourly rate, respectively. $400.00 appears in the Gross pay box.

9. Next, calculate the gross pay using **45** as the hours worked and **11.65** as the hourly rate. $553.38 appears in the Gross pay box.

10. Click the **Exit** button. Close the Code Editor window and then close the solution.

YOU DO IT 1!

Create an application named YouDoIt 1 and save it in the VB2015\Chap04 folder. Add a text box, a label, and a button to the form. The button's Click event procedure should display the string "Over 100" in the label when the value in the text box is greater than the number 100; otherwise, it should display the string "Not Over 100". Code the procedure. Save the solution, and then start and test the application. Close the solution.

As mentioned earlier, an If...Then...Else statement's condition must be a Boolean expression, which is an expression that evaluates to either True or False. The expression can contain variables, constants, properties, methods, keywords, arithmetic operators, comparison operators, and logical operators. You already know about variables, constants, properties, methods, keywords, and arithmetic operators. You will learn about comparison operators and logical operators in this lesson. We'll begin with comparison operators.

Comparison Operators

Figure 4-10 lists the most commonly used **comparison operators** in Visual Basic. Comparison operators (also referred to as relational operators) are used in expressions to compare two values. When making comparisons, keep in mind that equal to (=) is the opposite of not equal to (<>), greater than (>) is the opposite of less than or equal to (<=), and less than (<) is the opposite of greater than or equal to (>=). Expressions containing a comparison operator always evaluate to a Boolean value: either True or False. Also included in Figure 4-10 are examples of using comparison operators in an If...Then...Else statement's condition.

Comparison Operators

Operator	Operation
=	equal to
>	greater than
>=	greater than or equal to
<	less than
<=	less than or equal to
<>	not equal to

Example 1
```
If strState = "IL" Then
```
The condition evaluates to True when the strState variable contains the string "IL"; otherwise, it evaluates to False.

Example 2
```
If decHours > 40 Then
```
The condition evaluates to True when the value stored in the decHours variable is greater than 40; otherwise, it evaluates to False.

Example 3
```
If decMax >= 75.65D Then
```
The condition evaluates to True when the value stored in the decMax variable is greater than or equal to 75.65; otherwise, it evaluates to False. You can also write the condition as decMax >= Convert.ToDecimal(75.65).

Example 4
```
If intOnHand < intOrdered Then
```
The condition evaluates to True when the value stored in the intOnHand variable is less than the value stored in the intOrdered variable; otherwise, it evaluates to False.

Example 5
```
If dblTotal <= 999.99 Then
```
The condition evaluates to True when the value stored in the dblTotal variable is less than or equal to 999.99; otherwise, it evaluates to False.

Example 6
```
If strContinue <> "N" Then
```
The condition evaluates to True when the strContinue variable does not contain the string "N"; otherwise, it evaluates to False.

Figure 4-10 Listing and examples of commonly used comparison operators

Unlike arithmetic operators, comparison operators in Visual Basic do not have an order of precedence. When an expression contains more than one comparison operator, the computer evaluates the comparison operators from left to right in the expression. Comparison operators are evaluated after any arithmetic operators. For example, when processing the expression $14 / 2 < 15 - 2 * 3$, the computer will evaluate the three arithmetic operators before it evaluates the comparison operator. The result of the expression is the Boolean value True, as shown in Figure 4-11. Also included in the figure are the evaluation steps for two other expressions that contain arithmetic and comparison operators.

Evaluation steps	Result
Original expression	14 / 2 < 15 – 2 * 3
The division is performed first.	7 < 15 – 2 * 3
The multiplication is performed next.	7 < 15 – 6
The subtraction is performed next.	7 < 9
The < comparison is performed last.	True
Original expression	6 * 2 + 3 >= 5 * 4
The first multiplication is performed first.	12 + 3 >= 5 * 4
The remaining multiplication is performed next.	12 + 3 >= 20
The addition is performed next.	15 >= 20
The >= comparison is performed last.	False
Original expression	12 + 4 * 3 * 2 – 2 > 65
The first multiplication is performed first.	12 + 12 * 2 – 2 > 65
The remaining multiplication is performed next.	12 + 24 – 2 > 65
The addition is performed next.	36 – 2 > 65
The subtraction is performed next.	34 > 65
The > comparison is performed last.	False

Figure 4-11   Evaluation steps for expressions containing arithmetic and comparison operators

YOU DO IT 2!

On a piece of paper, write down the answers to the following four expressions:

4 + 3 * 2 > 2 * 10 – 11

8 + 3 – 6 + 85 < 5 * 26

10 / 5 + 3 – 6 * 2 > 0

75 / 25 + 2 * 5 * 6 <= 8 * 8

Next, create an application named YouDoIt 2 and save it in the VB2015\Chap04 folder. Add four labels and a button to the form. The button's Click event procedure should display the results of the four expressions shown here. Code the procedure. Save the solution, and then start and test the application. Compare the application's results with your answers. Close the solution.

In the next two sections, you will view two procedures that contain a comparison operator in an If...Then...Else statement's condition. The first procedure uses a single-alternative selection structure, and the second procedure uses a dual-alternative selection structure.

Using Comparison Operators: Swapping Numeric Values

Figure 4-12 shows a sample run of an application that displays the lowest and highest of two scores entered by the user. Figure 4-13 shows the pseudocode and flowchart for the Display button's Click event procedure. The procedure contains a single-alternative selection structure whose condition determines whether the first score entered by the user is greater than the second score. If it is, the selection structure's true path takes the appropriate action.

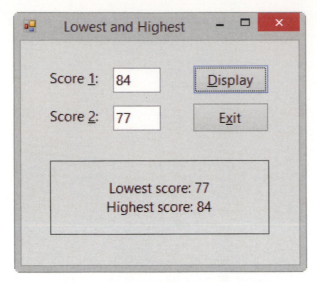

Figure 4-12   Sample run of the Lowest and Highest application

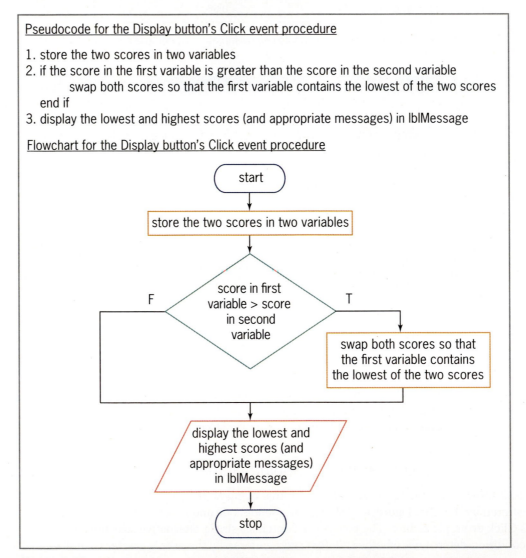

Pseudocode for the Display button's Click event procedure

1. store the two scores in two variables
2. if the score in the first variable is greater than the score in the second variable
        swap both scores so that the first variable contains the lowest of the two scores
   end if
3. display the lowest and highest scores (and appropriate messages) in lblMessage

Flowchart for the Display button's Click event procedure

Figure 4-13   Pseudocode and flowchart containing a single-alternative selection structure

Figure 4-14 shows the code entered in the Display button's Click event procedure. The condition in the If clause compares the contents of the intScore1 variable with the contents of the intScore2 variable. If the value in the intScore1 variable is greater than the value in the intScore2 variable, the condition evaluates to True and the four instructions in the If... Then...Else statement's true path swap both values. Swapping the values places the smaller number in the intScore1 variable and places the larger number in the intScore2 variable. If the condition evaluates to False, on the other hand, the true path instructions are skipped over because the intScore1 variable already contains a number that is smaller than (or possibly equal to) the number stored in the intScore2 variable.

```vb
Private Sub btnDisplay_Click(sender As Object, e As EventArgs
) Handles btnDisplay.Click
    ' display the lowest and highest scores

    Dim intScore1 As Integer
    Dim intScore2 As Integer

    Integer.TryParse(txtScore1.Text, intScore1)
    Integer.TryParse(txtScore2.Text, intScore2)

    ' swap scores, if necessary                    comparison
    If intScore1 > intScore2 Then                  operator
        Dim intTemp As Integer
        intTemp = intScore1                    single-alternative
        intScore1 = intScore2                  selection structure
        intScore2 = intTemp
    End If

    ' display lowest and highest scores
    lblMessage.Text = "Lowest score: " &
        Convert.ToString(intScore1) & ControlChars.NewLine &
        "Highest score: " & Convert.ToString(intScore2)
End Sub
```

Figure 4-14 Display button's Click event procedure

The first instruction in the If...Then...Else statement's true path declares and initializes a variable named intTemp. Like a variable declared at the beginning of a procedure, a variable declared within a statement block—referred to as a **block-level variable**—remains in memory until the procedure ends. However, unlike a variable declared at the beginning of a procedure, block-level variables have block scope rather than procedure scope.

A variable that has **block scope** can be used only within the statement block in which it is declared. More specifically, it can be used only below its declaration statement within the statement block. In this case, the procedure-level intScore1 and intScore2 variables can be used anywhere below their Dim statements within the btnDisplay_Click procedure, but the block-level intTemp variable can be used only after its Dim statement within the If...Then...Else statement's true path.

You may be wondering why the intTemp variable was not declared at the beginning of the procedure along with the other variables. Although there is nothing wrong with declaring the variable in that location, there is no reason to create it until it is needed, which (in this case) is only when a swap is necessary.

The second instruction in the If...Then...Else statement's true path assigns the `intScore1` variable's value to the `intTemp` variable. If you do not store that value in the `intTemp` variable, it will be lost when the computer processes the next statement, `intScore1 = intScore2`, which replaces the contents of the `intScore1` variable with the contents of the `intScore2` variable. Finally, the `intScore2 = intTemp` instruction assigns the `intTemp` variable's value to the `intScore2` variable; this completes the swap. Figure 4-15 illustrates the concept of swapping, assuming the user enters the numbers 84 and 77 in the Score 1 and Score 2 boxes, respectively.

ChO4A-Swapping

	intScore1	intScore2	intTemp
values stored in the variables immediately before the `intTemp = intScore1` statement is processed	84	77	0
result of the `intTemp = intScore1` statement	84	77	84
result of the `intScore1 = intScore2` statement	77	77	84
result of the `intScore2 = intTemp` statement	77	84	84

the values were swapped

Figure 4-15   Illustration of the swapping concept

START HERE

To code and then test the Lowest and Highest application:

1. Open the Lowest and Highest Solution (Lowest and Highest Solution.sln) file contained in the VB2015\Chap04\Lowest and Highest Solution folder. Open the Code Editor window. Replace <your name> and <current date> in the comments with your name and the current date, respectively.

2. Locate the btnDisplay_Click procedure, and then enter the single-alternative selection structure shown earlier in Figure 4-14.

3. Save the solution and then start the application. Type **84** in the Score 1 box and then type **77** in the Score 2 box. Click the **Display** button. The button's Click event procedure displays the lowest and highest scores, as shown earlier in Figure 4-12.

4. Click the **Exit** button. Close the Code Editor window and then close the solution.

Using Comparison Operators: Displaying Net Income or Loss

Figure 4-16 shows two sample runs of an application that displays either the net income using a black font or the net loss using a red font. Figure 4-17 shows the pseudocode, flowchart, and code for the Calculate button's Click event procedure, which contains a dual-alternative selection structure.

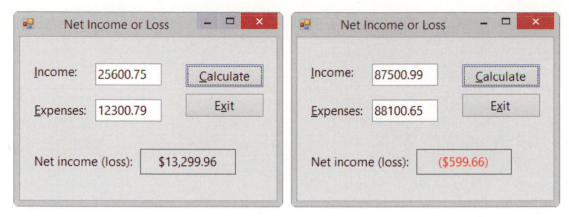

Figure 4-16 Sample runs of the Net Income or Loss application

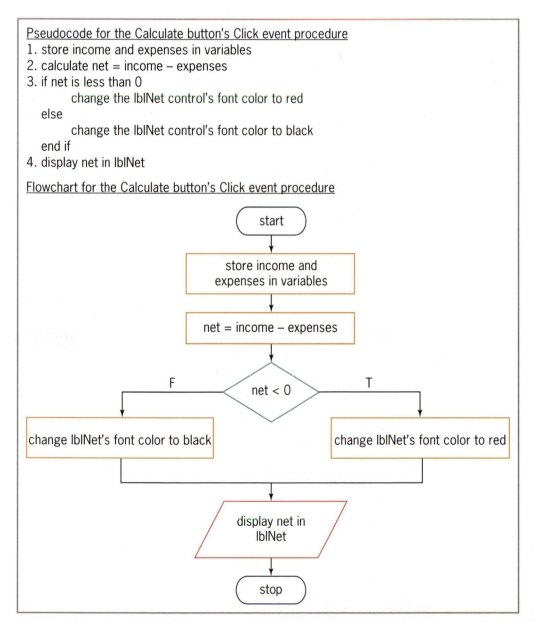

Pseudocode for the Calculate button's Click event procedure
1. store income and expenses in variables
2. calculate net = income – expenses
3. if net is less than 0
       change the lblNet control's font color to red
  else
       change the lblNet control's font color to black
  end if
4. display net in lblNet

Flowchart for the Calculate button's Click event procedure

Figure 4-17 Pseudocode, flowchart, and code containing a dual-alternative selection structure (*continues*)

(continued)

```
Private Sub btnCalc_Click(sender As Object, e As EventArgs
) Handles btnCalc.Click
    ' calculate net income or net loss

    Dim decIncome As Decimal
    Dim decExpenses As Decimal
    Dim decNet As Decimal

    Decimal.TryParse(txtIncome.Text, decIncome)
    Decimal.TryParse(txtExpenses.Text, decExpenses)

    decNet = decIncome - decExpenses
    If decNet < 0 Then                          comparison operator
        lblNet.ForeColor = Color.Red
    Else
        lblNet.ForeColor = Color.Black
    End If
    lblNet.Text = decNet.ToString("c2")
End Sub
```

dual-alternative
selection structure

Figure 4-17   Pseudocode, flowchart, and code containing a dual-alternative selection structure

START HERE

To code and then test the Net Income or Loss application:

1. Open the VB2015\Chap04\Net Solution\Net Solution (Net Solution.sln) file. Open the Code Editor window. Replace <your name> and <current date> in the comments with your name and the current date, respectively.

2. Locate the btnCalc_Click procedure, and then enter the dual-alternative selection structure shown in Figure 4-17.

3. Save the solution and then start the application. Test the application twice, using the income and expense amounts shown earlier in Figure 4-16.

4. Click the **Exit** button. Close the Code Editor window and then close the solution.

YOU DO IT 3!

Create an application named YouDoIt 3 and save it in the VB2015\Chap04 folder. Add a text box, a label, and a button to the form. If the user enters a number that is greater than or equal to 100 in the text box, the button's Click event procedure should display the result of multiplying the number by the number 5; otherwise, it should display the result of dividing the number by the number 5. Code the procedure. Save the solution, and then start and test the application. Close the solution.

Create an application named YouDoIt 4 and save it in the VB2015\Chap04 folder. Add two text boxes, a label, and a button to the form. The button's Click event procedure should assign the contents of the text boxes to Double variables named dblNum1 and dblNum2. It then should divide the dblNum1 variable's value by the dblNum2 variable's value, assigning the result to a Double variable named dblAnswer. Display the answer in the label. Code the procedure. Save the solution and then start the application. Test the application using the numbers 6 and 2; the number 3 appears in the label control. Now test it using the numbers 6 and 0. The word *Infinity* appears in the label control because, as in math, division by 0 is not possible. Add a selection structure to the procedure. The selection structure should perform the division only if the value in the dblNum2 variable is not 0. Save the solution, and then start and test the application. Close the solution.

Note: You have learned a lot so far in this lesson. You may want to take a break at this point before continuing.

Logical Operators

An If...Then...Else statement's condition can also contain logical operators, which are always evaluated after any arithmetic or comparison operators in an expression. Visual Basic provides the six logical operators listed in Figure 4-18. All of the **logical operators**, with the exception of the Not operator, allow you to combine two or more conditions, called subconditions, into one compound condition. The compound condition will always evaluate to either True or False, which is why logical operators are often referred to as Boolean operators. Even though this book only uses the Not, AndAlso, and OrElse operators, you should familiarize yourself with the And, Or, and Xor operators because you may encounter them when modifying another programmer's code. Also included in Figure 4-18 are examples of using logical operators in the If...Then...Else statement's condition.

Logical Operators

Operator	Operation	Precedence number
Not	reverses the truth-value of the condition; True becomes False, and False becomes True	1
And	all subconditions must be true for the compound condition to evaluate to True	2
AndAlso	same as the And operator, except performs short-circuit evaluation	2
Or	only one of the subconditions needs to be true for the compound condition to evaluate to True	3
OrElse	same as the Or operator, except performs short-circuit evaluation	3
Xor	only one of the subconditions can be true for the compound condition to evaluate to True	4

Figure 4-18 Listing and examples of logical operators *(continues)*

(continued)

Example 1
```
If Not blnSenior Then
```
The condition evaluates to True when the `blnSenior` variable contains the Boolean value False; otherwise, it evaluates to False. The clause also could be written more clearly as `If blnSenior = False Then`.

Example 2
```
If dblRate > 0 AndAlso dblRate < 0.15 Then
```
The compound condition evaluates to True when the value in the `dblRate` variable is greater than 0 and, at the same time, less than 0.15; otherwise, it evaluates to False.

Example 3
```
If strCode = "1" AndAlso decSales > 4999.99D Then
```
The compound condition evaluates to True when the `strCode` variable contains the string "1" and, at the same time, the value in the `decSales` variable is greater than 4999.99; otherwise, it evaluates to False.

Example 4
```
If strCode = "1" OrElse decSales > 4999.99D Then
```
The compound condition evaluates to True when the `strCode` variable contains the string "1" or when the value in the `decSales` variable is greater than 4999.99; otherwise, it evaluates to False.

Example 5
```
If strCoupon1 = "USE" Xor strCoupon2 = "USE" Then
```
The compound condition evaluates to True when only one of the variables contains the string "USE"; otherwise, it evaluates to False.

Figure 4-18   Listing and examples of logical operators

You already are familiar with logical operators because you use them on a daily basis. Examples of this include the following:

- if you finished your homework *and* you studied for tomorrow's exam, watch a movie

- if your cell phone rings *and* (it's your spouse calling *or* it's your child calling), answer the phone

- if you are driving your car *and* (it's raining *or* it's foggy *or* there is bug splatter on your windshield), turn your car's wipers on

As mentioned earlier, all expressions containing a logical operator evaluate to either True or False only. The tables shown in Figure 4-19, called **truth tables**, summarize how the computer evaluates the logical operators in an expression.

Truth Tables for the Logical Operators Used in This Book

Not operator

value of *condition*	value of Not *condition*
True	False
False	True

AndAlso operator

subcondition1	subcondition2	subcondition1 AndAlso subcondition2
True	True	True
True	False	False
False	(not evaluated)	False

OrElse operator

subcondition1	subcondition2	subcondition1 OrElse subcondition2
True	(not evaluated)	True
False	True	True
False	False	False

Truth Tables for the Logical Operators Not Used in This Book

And operator

subcondition1	subcondition2	subcondition1 And subcondition2
True	True	True
True	False	False
False	True	False
False	False	False

Or operator

subcondition1	subcondition2	subcondition1 Or subcondition2
True	True	True
True	False	True
False	True	True
False	False	False

Xor operator

subcondition1	subcondition2	subcondition1 Xor subcondition2
True	True	False
True	False	True
False	True	True
False	False	False

Figure 4-19 Truth tables for the logical operators

As the figure indicates, the **Not operator** reverses the truth-value of the *condition*. If the value of the *condition* is True, then the value of Not *condition* is False. Likewise, if the value of the *condition* is False, then the value of Not *condition* is True.

When you use either the **And operator** or the **AndAlso operator** to combine two subconditions, the resulting compound condition evaluates to True only when both subconditions are True. If either subcondition is False or if both subconditions are False, then the compound condition evaluates to False. The difference between the And and AndAlso operators is that the And operator always evaluates both subconditions, while the AndAlso operator performs a **short-circuit evaluation**, which means it does not always evaluate subcondition2. Because both subconditions combined with the AndAlso operator need to be True for the compound condition to evaluate to True, the AndAlso operator does not evaluate subcondition2 when subcondition1 is False; this makes the AndAlso operator more efficient than the And operator.

When you combine two subconditions using either the **Or operator** or the **OrElse operator**, the compound condition evaluates to True when either one or both of the subconditions is True. The compound condition will evaluate to False only when both subconditions are False. The difference between the Or and OrElse operators is that the Or operator always evaluates both subconditions, while the OrElse operator performs a short-circuit evaluation. In this case, because only one of the subconditions combined with the OrElse operator needs to be True for the compound condition to evaluate to True, the OrElse operator does not evaluate subcondition2 when subcondition1 is True. As a result, the OrElse operator is more efficient than the Or operator.

Finally, when you combine conditions using the Xor operator, the compound condition evaluates to True when only one of the subconditions is True. If both subconditions are True or both subconditions are False, then the compound condition evaluates to False. In the next section, you will use the truth tables to determine which logical operator to use in an If...Then... Else statement's condition.

Using the Truth Tables

An application needs to display an employee's weekly gross pay, given the number of hours worked and the hourly pay rate. The number of hours worked must be at least 0 but not more than 40. Before making the gross pay calculation, the application should verify that the number of hours is within the expected range. Programmers refer to the process of verifying the input data as **data validation**. If the number of hours is valid, the application should calculate and display the gross pay; otherwise, it should display the message "N/A" (for "Not Available"). Figure 4-20 shows the problem specification and two partially completed If clauses that could be used to verify the number of hours. Missing from each If clause is the appropriate logical operator.

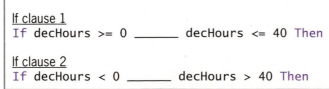

Problem Specification

Create an application that displays an employee's weekly gross pay, given the number of hours worked and the hourly pay rate. The number of hours worked must be at least 0 but not more than 40. If the number of hours worked is not valid, the application should display the string "N/A" (for "Not Available").

If clause 1
```
If decHours >= 0 _____ decHours <= 40 Then
```

If clause 2
```
If decHours < 0 _____ decHours > 40 Then
```

Figure 4-20   Problem specification and partially completed If clauses

The first If clause contains two subconditions that determine whether the number of hours is *within* the expected range of 0 through 40. For the number of hours to be valid, both subconditions must be True at the same time. In other words, the number of hours must be greater than or equal to 0 and also less than or equal to 40. If both subconditions are not True, it means that the number of hours is *outside* the expected range. Which logical operator should you use to combine both subconditions into one compound condition? Looking at the AndAlso and OrElse truth tables, you will notice that only the AndAlso operator evaluates the compound condition as True when both subconditions are True, while evaluating the compound condition as False when at least one of the subconditions is False. Therefore, the correct compound condition to use here is `decHours >= 0 AndAlso decHours <= 40`.

The second If clause in Figure 4-20 contains two subconditions that determine whether the number of hours is *outside* the expected range of 0 through 40. For the number of hours to be invalid, at least one of the subconditions must be True. In other words, the number of hours must be either less than 0 or greater than 40. If both subconditions are False, it means that the number of hours is *within* the expected range. Which logical operator should you use to combine both subconditions into one compound condition? According to the AndAlso and OrElse truth tables, only the OrElse operator evaluates the compound condition as True when at least one of the subconditions is True, while evaluating the compound condition as False when both subconditions are False. Therefore, the correct compound condition to use here is `decHours < 0 OrElse decHours > 40`.

The dual-alternative selection structures shown in Figure 4-21 contain the completed If clauses. Both selection structures produce the same result and simply represent two different ways of performing the same task.

Problem Specification

Create an application that displays an employee's weekly gross pay, given the number of hours worked and the hourly pay rate. The number of hours worked must be at least 0 but not more than 40. If the number of hours worked is not valid, the application should display the string "N/A" (for "Not Available").

Dual-alternative selection structure 1
```
If decHours >= 0 AndAlso decHours <= 40 Then
    decGross = decHours * decRate
    lblGross.Text = decGross.ToString("c2")
Else
    lblGross.Text = "N/A"
End If
```

Dual-alternative selection structure 2
```
If decHours < 0 OrElse decHours > 40 Then
    lblGross.Text = "N/A"
Else
    decGross = decHours * decRate
    lblGross.Text = decGross.ToString("c2")
End If
```

Figure 4-21 Problem specification and dual-alternative selection structures

START HERE

To code and then test the dual-alternative selection structures:

1. Open the Gross Solution (Gross Solution.sln) file contained in the VB2015\Chap04\ Gross Solution-Logical folder. Open the Code Editor window. Replace <your name> and <current date> in the comments with your name and the current date, respectively.

2. Locate the btnAndAlso_Click procedure, and then click the **blank line** above the End Sub clause. Enter the first dual-alternative selection structure shown in Figure 4-21.

3. Locate the btnOrElse_Click procedure, and then click the **blank line** above the End Sub clause. Enter the second dual-alternative selection structure shown in Figure 4-21.

4. Save the solution and then start the application. Type **10** and **8** in the Hours worked and Hourly rate boxes, respectively. Click the **Calculate-AndAlso** button. See Figure 4-22.

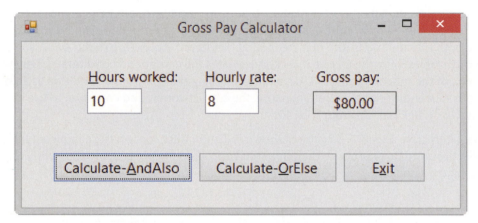

Figure 4-22   Sample run of the application using valid data

5. Change the number of hours worked to **43** and then click the **Calculate-AndAlso** button. See Figure 4-23.

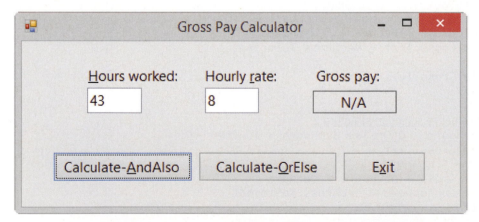

Figure 4-23   Sample run of the application using invalid data

6. Type **10** in the Hours worked box and then click the **Calculate-OrElse** button. The gross pay is $80.00, as shown earlier in Figure 4-22. Change the number of hours worked to **43** and then click the **Calculate-OrElse** button. The "N/A" message appears in the Gross pay box, as shown earlier in Figure 4-23.

7. Click the **Exit** button.

If you are unsure whether to use AndAlso or OrElse in an If clause, test the selection structure using both operators; only the correct operator will give you the expected results. For example, let's see what happens if you switch the logical operators in the dual-alternative selection structures.

To test the selection structures with different logical operators: START HERE

1. In the btnAndAlso_Click procedure, change AndAlso to **OrElse**. Save the solution and then start the application. Type **10** and **8** in the Hours worked and Hourly rate boxes, respectively. Click the **Calculate-AndAlso** button. $80.00 appears in the Gross pay box, which is correct.

2. Next, change the number of hours worked to **43** and then click the **Calculate-AndAlso** button. $344.00, rather than the "N/A" message, appears in the Gross pay box, which is incorrect.

Always be sure to use data that will test both paths in a selection structure.

3. Click the **Exit** button. In the btnAndAlso_Click procedure, change OrElse to **AndAlso**.

4. In the btnOrElse_Click procedure, change OrElse to **AndAlso**. Save the solution and then start the application. Type **10** and **8** in the Hours worked and Hourly rate boxes, respectively. Click the **Calculate-OrElse** button. $80.00 appears in the Gross pay box, which is correct.

5. Finally, change the number of hours worked to **43** and then click the **Calculate-OrElse** button. $344.00, rather than the "N/A" message, appears in the Gross pay box, which is incorrect.

6. Click the **Exit** button. In the btnOrElse_Click procedure, change AndAlso to **OrElse**.

7. Close the Code Editor window and then close the solution.

YOU DO IT 5!

Create an application named YouDoIt 5 and save it in the VB2015\Chap04 folder. Add a text box, a label, and a button to the form. If the user enters a number that is either less than 0 or greater than 100, the button's Click event procedure should display the string "Invalid number" in the label; otherwise, it should display the string "Valid number". Code the procedure. Save the solution and then start and test the application. Close the solution.

Comparing Strings Containing One or More Letters

A procedure needs to display the message "Senior discount" when the user enters the letter Y in the txtAtLeast65 control, and the message "No discount" when the user enters anything else. Figure 4-24 shows five ways of writing the code to display the appropriate message.

Comparing Strings Containing One or More Letters

Example 1 – using the OrElse operator

```
Dim strSenior As String
strSenior = txtAtLeast65.Text
If strSenior = "Y" OrElse strSenior = "y" Then
    lblMsg.Text = "Senior discount"
Else
    lblMsg.Text = "No discount"
End If
```

Example 2 – using the AndAlso operator

```
Dim strSenior As String
strSenior = txtAtLeast65.Text
If strSenior <> "Y" AndAlso strSenior <> "y" Then
    lblMsg.Text = "No discount"
Else
    lblMsg.Text = "Senior discount"
End If
```

Example 3 – inefficient solution

```
Dim strSenior As String
strSenior = txtAtLeast65.Text
If strSenior = "Y" OrElse strSenior = "y" Then
    lblMsg.Text = "Senior discount"
End If
```
unnecessary evaluation ───
```
If strSenior <> "Y" AndAlso strSenior <> "y" Then
    lblMsg.Text = "No discount"
End If
```

Example 4 – using the ToUpper method

```
Dim strSenior As String
strSenior = txtAtLeast65.Text
If strSenior.ToUpper = "Y" Then
    lblMsg.Text = "Senior discount"
Else
    lblMsg.Text = "No discount"
End If
```

Example 5 – using the ToLower method

```
Dim strSenior As String
strSenior = txtAtLeast65.Text.ToLower
If strSenior = "y" Then
    lblMsg.Text = "Senior discount"
Else
    lblMsg.Text = "No discount"
End If
```

Figure 4-24   Examples of string comparisons containing one or more letters

The compound condition in Example 1's dual-alternative selection structure determines whether the value stored in the **strSenior** variable is either the uppercase letter Y or the lowercase letter y. When the variable contains one of those two letters, the compound condition evaluates to True and the selection structure's true path displays the message "Senior discount" on the screen; otherwise, its false path displays the message "No discount". You may be wondering why you need to compare the contents of the variable with both the uppercase and lowercase forms of the letter Y. As is true in many programming languages, string comparisons in Visual Basic are case sensitive, which means that the uppercase version of a letter and its lowercase counterpart are not interchangeable. So, although a human recognizes Y and y as being the same letter, a computer does not; to a computer, a Y is different from a y. The reason for this differentiation is that each character on the computer keyboard is stored using a different Unicode character in the computer's internal memory.

In Example 2's dual-alternative selection structure, the compound condition determines whether the value stored in the `strSenior` variable is not equal to the uppercase letter Y and also not equal to the lowercase letter y. When the variable does not contain either of those two letters, the compound condition evaluates to True and the selection structure's true path displays the words "No discount" on the screen; otherwise, its false path displays the words "Senior discount".

Example 3 uses two single-alternative selection structures rather than one dual-alternative selection structure. Although Example 3's code produces the same results as the code in Examples 1 and 2, it does so less efficiently. For instance, if the `strSenior` variable contains the letter Y, the compound condition in the first selection structure in Example 3 will evaluate to True, and the structure's true path will display the "Senior discount" message. Although the appropriate message already appears in the interface, the procedure will still evaluate the second selection structure's compound condition to determine whether to display the "No discount" message. The second evaluation is unnecessary and makes Example 3's code less efficient than the code shown in Examples 1 and 2.

The dual-alternative selection structures in Examples 4 and 5 in Figure 4-24 also contain a string comparison in their condition. However, notice that the conditions do not use a logical operator. Instead, Example 4's condition uses the ToUpper method, and Example 5's condition uses the ToLower method. You will learn about the ToUpper and ToLower methods in the next section.

Converting a String to Uppercase or Lowercase

As already mentioned, string comparisons in Visual Basic are case sensitive, which means that the string "Yes" is not the same as either the string "YES" or the string "yes". Because of this, a problem may occur when comparing strings that are entered by the user, who may enter the string using any combination of uppercase and lowercase letters. Although you can change a text box's **CharacterCasing property** from its default value of Normal to either Upper (which converts the user's entry to uppercase) or Lower (which converts the user's entry to lowercase), you may not want to change the case of the user's entry as he or she is typing it. To fix the comparison problem, you can use either the **ToUpper method** or the **ToLower method** to temporarily convert the string to either uppercase or lowercase, respectively, and then use the converted string in the comparison.

You will use the CharacterCasing property in Exercise 19 at the end of this lesson.

Figure 4-25 shows the syntax of the ToUpper and ToLower methods and includes examples of using the methods. In each syntax, *string* is usually either the name of a String variable or the Text property of an object. Both methods copy the contents of the *string* to a temporary location in the computer's internal memory. The methods convert the temporary string to the appropriate case (if necessary) and then return the temporary string. Keep in mind that the ToUpper and ToLower methods do not change the contents of the *string*; they change the contents of the temporary location only. In addition, the ToUpper and ToLower methods affect only letters of the alphabet, which are the only characters that have uppercase and lowercase forms.

ToUpper and ToLower Methods

Syntax
string.**ToUpper**
string.**ToLower**

Example 1
`If strSenior.ToUpper = "Y" Then`
temporarily converts the contents of the `strSenior` variable to uppercase and then compares the result with the uppercase letter Y

Example 2
`If strName1.ToLower = strName2.ToLower Then`
temporarily converts the contents of the `strName1` and `strName2` variables to lowercase and then compares both results

Example 3
`lblState.Text = strState.ToUpper`
temporarily converts the contents of the `strState` variable to uppercase and then assigns the result to the lblState control's Text property

Example 4
`strName = strName.ToUpper`
`txtState.Text = txtState.Text.ToLower`
changes the contents of the `strName` variable to uppercase and changes the contents of the txtState control's Text property to lowercase

Figure 4-25   Syntax and examples of the ToUpper and ToLower methods

When using the ToUpper method in a comparison, be sure that everything you are comparing is uppercase, as shown in Example 1 in Figure 4-25; otherwise, the comparison will not evaluate correctly. For instance, the clause `If strSenior.ToUpper = "y" Then` is not correct. The condition will always evaluate to False because the uppercase version of a letter will never be equal to its lowercase counterpart. Likewise, when using the ToLower method in a comparison, be sure that everything you are comparing is lowercase, as shown in Example 2. The statement in Example 3 temporarily converts the contents of the `strState` variable to uppercase and then assigns the result to the lblState control. As Example 4 indicates, you can also use the ToUpper and ToLower methods to permanently convert the contents of either a String variable or a control's Text property to uppercase or lowercase, respectively.

Using the ToUpper and ToLower Methods: Displaying a Message

Figure 4-26 shows the problem specification for the Mount Rushmore application. It also shows a sample run of the application and two ways of writing the code for the Display button's Click event procedure.

Problem Specification

An application needs to display the message "On Mount Rushmore" when the user enters the name of any of the four Mount Rushmore presidents; otherwise, it should display the message "Not on Mount Rushmore".

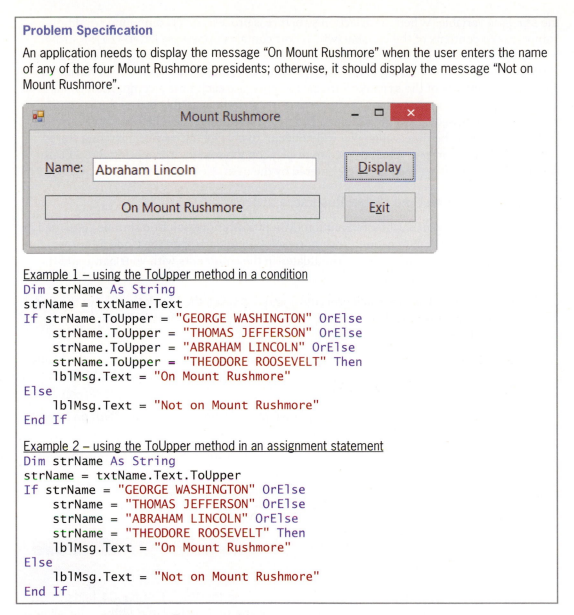

Example 1 – using the ToUpper method in a condition
```
Dim strName As String
strName = txtName.Text
If strName.ToUpper = "GEORGE WASHINGTON" OrElse
    strName.ToUpper = "THOMAS JEFFERSON" OrElse
    strName.ToUpper = "ABRAHAM LINCOLN" OrElse
    strName.ToUpper = "THEODORE ROOSEVELT" Then
    lblMsg.Text = "On Mount Rushmore"
Else
    lblMsg.Text = "Not on Mount Rushmore"
End If
```

Example 2 – using the ToUpper method in an assignment statement
```
Dim strName As String
strName = txtName.Text.ToUpper
If strName = "GEORGE WASHINGTON" OrElse
    strName = "THOMAS JEFFERSON" OrElse
    strName = "ABRAHAM LINCOLN" OrElse
    strName = "THEODORE ROOSEVELT" Then
    lblMsg.Text = "On Mount Rushmore"
Else
    lblMsg.Text = "Not on Mount Rushmore"
End If
```

Figure 4-26   Problem specification, sample run, and code

When the computer processes the compound condition in Example 1, it temporarily converts the contents of the `strName` variable to uppercase and then compares the result to the string "GEORGE WASHINGTON". If the comparison evaluates to False, the computer again temporarily converts the contents of the variable to uppercase, this time comparing the result to the string "THOMAS JEFFERSON". Each time the comparison evaluates to False, the computer must temporarily convert the `strName` variable's contents to uppercase before comparing the result to the next string. Depending on the result of each subcondition, the computer might need to temporarily convert the contents of the `strName` variable to uppercase four times.

Example 2 in Figure 4-26 provides a more efficient way of writing Example 1's code. The `strName = txtName.Text.ToUpper` statement in Example 2 temporarily converts the contents of the txtName control's Text property to uppercase and then assigns the result to the strName variable. When the selection structure is processed, its compound condition compares the contents of the variable (which now contains uppercase letters) to the string "GEORGE WASHINGTON". If the comparison evaluates to False, the computer compares the variable's contents to the string "THOMAS JEFFERSON", and so on. Rather than having to convert the contents of the strName variable to uppercase each time a comparison is made, as in Example 1, Example 2 stores the uppercase letters in the variable before the selection structure is processed. However, although Example 2's code is more efficient than Example 1's code, there may be times when you will not want to change the case of the string stored in a variable. For example, you may need to display (on the screen or in a printed report) the variable's contents using the exact case entered by the user.

START HERE ▶

To code and then test the Mount Rushmore application:

1. Open the Mount Rushmore Solution (Mount Rushmore Solution.sln) file contained in the VB2015\Chap04\Mount Rushmore Solution folder. Open the Code Editor window. Replace <your name> and <current date> in the comments with your name and the current date, respectively.

2. Locate the btnDisplay_Click procedure, and then click the **blank line** above the End Sub clause. Enter the dual-alternative selection structure shown in Example 2 in Figure 4-26.

3. Save the solution and then start the application. Type **thomas jefferson** in the Name box, and then press **Enter** to select the Display button. The message "On Mount Rushmore" appears in the interface.

4. Change the name to **john adams** and then press **Enter**. The message "Not on Mount Rushmore" appears in the interface.

5. On your own, test the code using the names of the other three presidents on Mount Rushmore. When you are finished testing the code, click the **Exit** button. Close the Code Editor window and then close the solution.

YOU DO IT 6!

Create an application named YouDoIt 6 and save it in the VB2015\Chap04 folder. Add a text box, a label, and a button to the form. If the user enters the letter A (in either uppercase or lowercase), the button's Click event procedure should display the string "Addition" in the label; otherwise, it should display the string "Subtraction". Code the procedure. Save the solution, and then start and test the application. Close the solution.

Ch04A-Operators

Summary of Operators

Figure 4-27 shows the order of precedence for the arithmetic, concatenation, comparison, and logical operators you have learned so far. Recall that when an expression contains more than one operator with the same precedence number, those operators are evaluated from left to right. The figure also shows the evaluation steps for an expression that contains two arithmetic operators, two comparison operators, and one logical operator. Notice that the arithmetic operators are evaluated first, followed by the comparison operators and then the logical operator. (Keep in mind that you can use parentheses to override the order of precedence.)

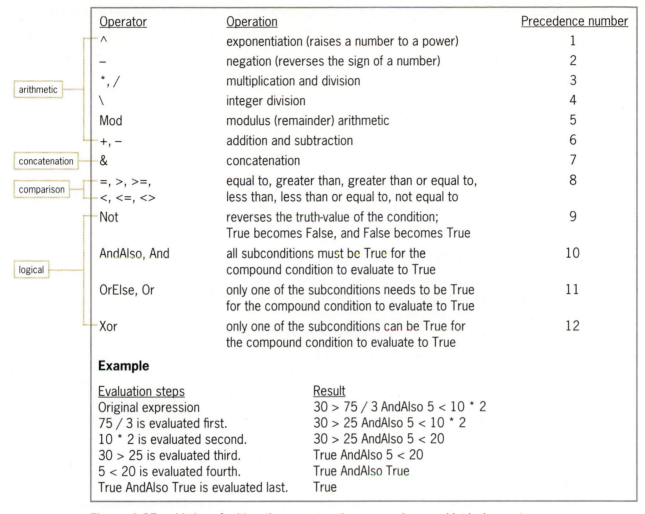

Operator	Operation	Precedence number
^	exponentiation (raises a number to a power)	1
−	negation (reverses the sign of a number)	2
*, /	multiplication and division	3
\	integer division	4
Mod	modulus (remainder) arithmetic	5
+, −	addition and subtraction	6
&	concatenation	7
=, >, >=, <, <=, <>	equal to, greater than, greater than or equal to, less than, less than or equal to, not equal to	8
Not	reverses the truth-value of the condition; True becomes False, and False becomes True	9
AndAlso, And	all subconditions must be True for the compound condition to evaluate to True	10
OrElse, Or	only one of the subconditions needs to be True for the compound condition to evaluate to True	11
Xor	only one of the subconditions can be True for the compound condition to evaluate to True	12

arithmetic — ^, −, *, /, \, Mod, +, −
concatenation — &
comparison — =, >, >=, <, <=, <>
logical — Not, AndAlso And, OrElse Or, Xor

Example

Evaluation steps	Result
Original expression	30 > 75 / 3 AndAlso 5 < 10 * 2
75 / 3 is evaluated first.	30 > 25 AndAlso 5 < 10 * 2
10 * 2 is evaluated second.	30 > 25 AndAlso 5 < 20
30 > 25 is evaluated third.	True AndAlso 5 < 20
5 < 20 is evaluated fourth.	True AndAlso True
True AndAlso True is evaluated last.	True

Figure 4-27 Listing of arithmetic, concatenation, comparison, and logical operators

Lesson A Summary

- To code single-alternative and dual-alternative selection structures:

  Use the If...Then...Else statement. The statement's syntax is shown in Figure 4-8.

- To compare two values:

  Use the comparison operators listed in Figure 4-10.

- To swap the values contained in two variables:

  Assign the first variable's value to a temporary variable. Assign the second variable's value to the first variable, and then assign the temporary variable's value to the second variable. An illustration of the swapping concept is shown in Figure 4-15.

- To create a compound condition:

  Use the logical operators and truth tables listed in Figures 4-18 and 4-19, respectively.

- To convert the user's text box entry to either uppercase or lowercase as the user is typing the text:

  Change the text box's CharacterCasing property from Normal to either Upper or Lower.

- To temporarily convert a string to uppercase:

  Use the ToUpper method. The method's syntax is *string*.`ToUpper`.

- To temporarily convert a string to lowercase:

  Use the ToLower method. The method's syntax is *string*.`ToLower`.

- To evaluate an expression containing arithmetic, comparison, and logical operators:

  Evaluate the arithmetic operators first, followed by the comparison operators and then the logical operators. Figure 4-27 shows the order of precedence for the arithmetic, concatenation, comparison, and logical operators you have learned so far.

Lesson A Key Terms

And operator—one of the logical operators; same as the AndAlso operator, but less efficient because it does not perform a short-circuit evaluation

AndAlso operator—one of the logical operators; when used to combine two subconditions, the resulting compound condition evaluates to True only when both subconditions are True, and it evaluates to False only when one or both of the subconditions are False; same as the And operator but more efficient because it performs a short-circuit evaluation

Block scope—the scope of a variable declared within a statement block; a variable with block scope can be used only within the statement block in which it is declared and only after its declaration statement

Block-level variable—a variable declared within a statement block; the variable has block scope

CharacterCasing property—controls the case of the text entered in a text box

Comparison operators—operators used to compare values in an expression; also called relational operators

Condition—specifies the decision you are making and must be phrased so that it evaluates to an answer of either true or false

Data validation—the process of verifying that a program's input data is within the expected range

Decision symbol—the diamond in a flowchart; used to represent the condition in selection and repetition structures

Dual-alternative selection structure—a selection structure that requires one set of actions to be performed when the structure's condition evaluates to True and requires a different set of actions to be performed when the structure's condition evaluates to False

False path—contains the instructions to be processed when a selection structure's condition evaluates to False

If...Then...Else statement—used to code single-alternative and dual-alternative selection structures in Visual Basic

Logical operators—operators used to combine two or more subconditions into one compound condition; also called Boolean operators

Not operator—one of the logical operators; reverses the truth-value of a condition

Or operator—one of the logical operators; same as the OrElse operator but less efficient because it does not perform a short-circuit evaluation

OrElse operator—one of the logical operators; when used to combine two subconditions, the resulting compound condition evaluates to True when at least one of the subconditions is True and evaluates to False only when both subconditions are False; same as the Or operator but more efficient because it performs a short-circuit evaluation

Selection structure—one of the three basic control structures; tells the computer to make a decision based on some condition and then select the appropriate action; also called the decision structure

Short-circuit evaluation—refers to the way the computer evaluates two subconditions connected by either the AndAlso or OrElse operator (for example, when the AndAlso operator is used, the computer does not evaluate subcondition2 if subcondition1 is False; when the OrElse operator is used, the computer does not evaluate subcondition2 if subcondition1 is True)

Single-alternative selection structure—a selection structure that requires a special set of actions to be performed only when the structure's condition evaluates to True

Statement block—in a selection structure, the set of statements terminated by an Else or End If clause

ToLower method—temporarily converts a string to lowercase

ToUpper method—temporarily converts a string to uppercase

True path—contains the instructions to be processed when a selection structure's condition evaluates to True

Truth tables—tables that summarize how the computer evaluates the logical operators in an expression

Lesson A Review Questions

1. An If...Then...Else statement in the btnCalc_Click procedure declares a variable in its false path. Where can the variable be used?

   a. in the entire Code Editor window
   b. in the entire btnCalc_Click procedure
   c. in both paths in the If...Then...Else statement
   d. only in the false path in the If...Then...Else statement

2. Which of the following compound conditions can be used to determine whether the value in the `intQuantity` variable is *outside* the range of 0 through 500?

   a. `intQuantity < 0 OrElse intQuantity > 500`
   b. `intQuantity > 0 AndAlso intQuantity < 500`
   c. `intQuantity <= 0 OrElse intQuantity >= 500`
   d. `intQuantity < 0 AndAlso intQuantity > 500`

3. Which of the following If clauses should you use to compare the string contained in the txtId control with the state abbreviation CA?

   a. `If txtId.Text = ToUpper("CA") Then`
   b. `If txtId.Text = ToLower("ca") Then`
   c. `If txtId.Text.ToUpper = "CA" Then`
   d. `If ToUpper(txtId.Text) = "CA" Then`

4. The six logical operators are listed below. Indicate their order of precedence by placing a number (1, 2, and so on) on the line to the left of the operator. If two or more operators have the same precedence, assign the same number to each.

    _____ Xor
    _____ And
    _____ Not
    _____ Or
    _____ AndAlso
    _____ OrElse

5. An expression can contain arithmetic, comparison, and logical operators. Indicate the order of precedence for the three types of operators by placing a number (1, 2, or 3) on the line to the left of the operator type.

    _____ Arithmetic
    _____ Logical
    _____ Comparison

6. The expression `6 > 12 OrElse 4 < 5` evaluates to _____.

    a. True
    b. False

7. The expression `6 + 3 > 7 AndAlso 11 > 2 * 5` evaluates to _____.

    a. True
    b. False

8. The expression `8 >= 4 + 6 OrElse 5 > 6 AndAlso 4 < 7` evaluates to _____.

    a. True
    b. False

9. The expression `7 + 3 * 2 > 5 * 3 AndAlso True` evaluates to _____.

    a. True
    b. False

10. The expression `5 * 4 > 6 ^ 2` evaluates to _____.

    a. True
    b. False

11. The expression `5 * 4 > 6 ^ 2 AndAlso True OrElse False` evaluates to _____.

    a. True
    b. False

Lesson A Exercises

1. Write an If...Then...Else statement that displays the string "Columbia" in the lblCapital control when the txtState control contains the string "SC" (in any case).   INTRODUCTORY

2. Write an If...Then...Else statement that displays the string "Please enter ZIP code" in the lblMsg control when the txtZip control does not contain any data.   INTRODUCTORY

3. Write an If...Then...Else statement that displays the string "Incorrect quantity" in the lblMsg control when the `intQuantity` variable contains a number that is less than 0; otherwise, display the string "Valid quantity".   INTRODUCTORY

4. Write an If...Then...Else statement that displays the string "Time to reorder" in the lblMsg control when the `intInStock` variable contains a number that is less than 250; otherwise, display the string "We have enough in stock".   INTRODUCTORY

5. Write an If...Then...Else statement that assigns the number 35 to the `intCommission` variable when the `decSales` variable contains a number that is less than or equal to $250; otherwise, assign the number 50.   INTRODUCTORY

6. Write an If...Then...Else statement that displays the value 25 in the lblShipping control when the `strState` variable contains the string "Alaska" (in any case); otherwise, display the value 15.   INTRODUCTORY

7. Write an If...Then...Else statement that displays the string "Cat" in the lblAnimal control when the `strAnimal` variable contains the letter "C" (in any case); otherwise, display the string "Dog". Also draw the flowchart.   INTRODUCTORY

8. A procedure should calculate a 2.5% commission when the `strCommType` variable contains the string "Prime" (in any case); otherwise, it should calculate a 2% commission. The commission is calculated by multiplying the commission rate by the contents of the `dblSales` variable. Display the commission in the lblComm control. Draw the flowchart and then write the Visual Basic code.   INTRODUCTORY

9. In this exercise, you modify one of the Gross Pay Calculator applications from the lesson. Use Windows to make a copy of the Gross Solution-Single folder. Rename the copy Modified Gross Solution-Single. Open the Gross Solution (Gross Solution.sln) file contained in the Modified Gross Solution-Single folder. Locate the btnCalc_Click procedure in the Code Editor window. Change the selection structure's true path as indicated in Figure 4-28. Save the solution, and then start and test the application.   INTRODUCTORY

```
1. store hours and rate in variables
2. gross = hours * rate
3. if hours are greater than 40
       overtime = (hours − 40) * rate / 2
       gross = gross + overtime
   end if
4. display gross in lblGross
```

Figure 4-28   Pseudocode for Exercise 9

INTRODUCTORY

10. In this exercise, you modify the Net Income or Loss application from the lesson. Use Windows to make a copy of the Net Solution folder. Rename the copy Modified Net Solution. Open the Net Solution (Net Solution.sln) file contained in the Modified Net Solution folder. Locate the btnCalc_Click procedure in the Code Editor window. Change the selection structure's condition so that it tests for the opposite of what it does now, and then make the necessary modifications to the structure's paths. Save the solution, and then start and test the application.

INTERMEDIATE

11. In this exercise, you modify one of the Gross Pay Calculator applications from the lesson. Use Windows to make a copy of the Gross Solution-Dual folder. Rename the copy Modified Gross Solution-Dual. Open the Gross Solution (Gross Solution.sln) file contained in the Modified Gross Solution-Dual folder. Locate the btnCalc_Click procedure in the Code Editor window. Change the selection structure as indicated in Figure 4-29. You will need to provide the overtime calculation. Save the solution, and then start and test the application.

```
1. store hours and rate in variables
2. if hours are less than or equal to 40
       gross = hours * rate
   else
       gross = 40 * rate
       overtime = _____      ·········  you will need to provide the
       gross = gross + overtime                  overtime calculation
   end if
3. display gross in lblGross
```

Figure 4-29   Pseudocode for Exercise 11

INTERMEDIATE

12. Sam's Paper Shoppe wants you to create an application that allows a salesclerk to enter an item's price and the quantity purchased by a customer. When the quantity purchased is greater than 5, the customer is given a 15% discount. The application should display the total amount the customer owes. Use the following names for the solution and project, respectively: Sam Solution and Sam Project. Save the application in the VB2015\Chap04 folder. Test the application using 10 and 5 as the price and quantity purchased, respectively; the total owed is $50.00. Then test the application using 9 and 6 as the price and quantity purchased, respectively; the total owed is $45.90.

INTERMEDIATE

13. Create an application that displays a salesperson's annual bonus amount, given his or her annual sales amount. The bonus rate is 10% when the sales amount is at least $25,000; otherwise, the bonus rate is 8%. Use the following names for the solution and project, respectively: Bonus Solution and Bonus Project. Save the application in the VB2015\Chap04 folder. Test the application appropriately.

INTERMEDIATE

14. Create an application that determines whether a customer is entitled to free shipping when ordering from Savannah's Web site. Savannah's does not charge shipping when the customer uses his or her Savannah's credit card to pay for an order totaling $100 or more. Customers who do not meet these two requirements are charged $9 for shipping. The application should display the appropriate shipping charge: either $0 or $9. Use the following names for the solution and project, respectively: Savannah Solution and Savannah Project. Save the application in the VB2015\Chap04 folder. Test the application appropriately.

15. Create an application that determines whether a customer is entitled to free shipping when ordering from JimJoe's Web site. JimJoe's does not charge shipping on any order when the customer belongs to the JimJoe's Free Shipping Club. It also doesn't charge shipping for any order totaling $100 or more. The application should display one of the following messages: "Your shipping is free!" or "You will be charged for shipping." Use the following names for the solution and project, respectively: JimJoe Solution and JimJoe Project. Save the application in the VB2015\Chap04 folder. Test the application appropriately.

INTERMEDIATE

16. In this exercise, you modify the Sam's Paper Shoppe application from Exercise 12. Use Windows to make a copy of the Sam Solution folder. Rename the copy Modified Sam Solution. Open the Sam Solution (Sam Solution.sln) file contained in the Modified Sam Solution folder. Change the code to give a 15% discount when the quantity purchased is at least 10 and a 5% discount when the quantity purchased is less than 10. Test the application appropriately.

INTERMEDIATE

17. Create an application that displays a salesperson's monthly commission amount, given his or her monthly sales amount and commission ID. Salespeople who have one of the following commission IDs receive a 15% commission: A1, B2, C3. All other salespeople receive a 12% commission. Use the following names for the solution and project, respectively: Commission Solution and Commission Project. Save the application in the VB2015\Chap04 folder. Test the application appropriately.

INTERMEDIATE

18. In this exercise, you modify the commission application from Exercise 17. Use Windows to make a copy of the Commission Solution folder. Rename the copy Modified Commission Solution. Open the Commission Solution (Commission Solution.sln) file contained in the Modified Commission Solution folder. The requirements for a 15% commission have changed: In addition to having one of the three IDs mentioned in Exercise 17, the salesperson's monthly sales must be at least $25,000. Salespeople who do not meet these requirements receive a 12% commission. Modify the code to reflect these changes. Test the application appropriately.

ADVANCED

19. In this exercise, you learn how to use a text box's CharacterCasing property. Open the VB2015\Chap04\CharCase Solution\CharCase Solution (CharCase Solution.sln) file.

DISCOVERY

    a. Open the Code Editor window and study the code contained in the btnDisplay_Click procedure. The code compares the contents of the txtId control with the strings "AB12", "XY59", and "TV45". However, it does not convert the contents of the text box to uppercase. Start the application. Enter ab12 as the ID and then click the Display button. The button's Click event procedure displays the "Invalid ID" message, which is incorrect. Click the Exit button.

    b. Use the Properties window to change the txtId control's CharacterCasing property to Upper. Save the solution and then start the application. Enter ab12 as the ID. Notice that the letters appear in uppercase in the text box. Click the Display button. The button's Click event procedure displays the "Valid ID" message, which is correct. Click the Exit button.

LESSON B

After studying Lesson B, you should be able to:

- Group objects using a GroupBox control
- Create a message box using the MessageBox.Show method
- Determine the value returned by a message box

Creating the Treeline Resort Application

Recall that your task in this chapter is to create a reservation application for Treeline Resort. The application will allow the user to enter the following information: the number of rooms to reserve, the length of stay (in nights), the number of adults, and the number of children. Each room can accommodate a maximum of six people. The resort charges $225.50 per room per night. It also charges a 16.25% sales and lodging tax, which is based on the room charge. In addition, there is a $12.50 resort fee per room per night. The application should display the total room charge, the sales and lodging tax, the total resort fee, and the total due.

START HERE

To open the partially completed Treeline Resort application:

1. If necessary, start Visual Studio VB2015. Open the VB2015\Chap04\Treeline Solution\ Treeline Solution (Treeline Solution.sln) file. See Figure 4-30. In the next section, you will add a second group box to the interface.

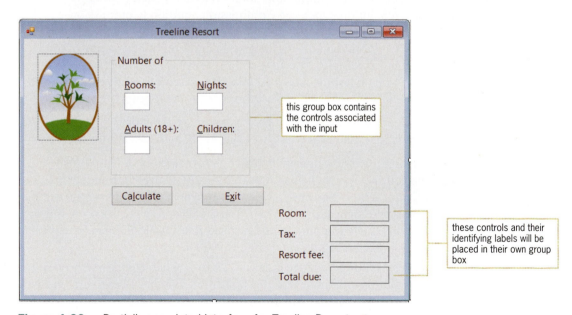

Figure 4-30   Partially completed interface for Treeline Resort

Adding a Group Box to the Form

You use the GroupBox tool, which is located in the Containers section of the toolbox, to add a group box to the interface. A **group box** serves as a container for other controls and is typically used to visually separate related controls from other controls on the form. You can include an identifying label on a group box by setting the group box's Text property. Labeling a group box is optional; but if you do label it, the label should be entered using sentence capitalization. A group box and its controls are treated as one unit. Therefore, when you move or delete a group box, the controls inside the group box are also moved or deleted, respectively.

START HERE

GUI DESIGN TIP Labeling a Group Box

- Use sentence capitalization for the optional identifying label, which is entered in the group box's Text property.

To add a group box to the interface:

1. If necessary, expand the Containers node in the toolbox. Click the **GroupBox** tool and then drag the mouse pointer to the form. You do not need to worry about the exact location. Release the mouse button. The GroupBox2 control appears on the form.

2. Change the group box's Text property to **Charges**, and then position and size the group box as shown in Figure 4-31.

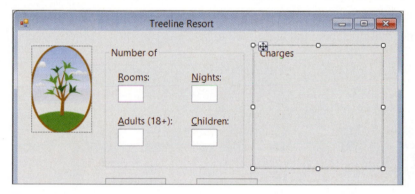

Figure 4-31   Interface showing the location and size of the additional group box

3. Next, you will drag the eight controls related to the calculated amounts into the Charges group box. You then will center the controls within the group box. Place your mouse pointer slightly above and to the left of the Room: label. Press and hold down the left mouse button as you drag the mouse pointer down and to the right. A dotted rectangle appears as you drag. Continue to drag until the dotted rectangle surrounds the eight controls, as shown in Figure 4-32.

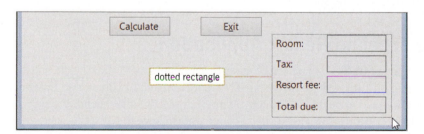

Figure 4-32   Dotted rectangle surrounding the eight controls

The move pointer mentioned in Step 4 looks like this:

4. When the dotted rectangle surrounds the eight controls, release the mouse button to select them. Place your mouse pointer on one of the selected controls. The mouse pointer turns into the move pointer. Press and hold down the left mouse button as you drag the selected controls into the Charges group box, and then release the mouse button.

5. Use the Format menu's Center in Form option to center the selected controls both horizontally and vertically in the group box.

6. Click the form to deselect the controls. Use the sizing handle to move the form's bottom border closer to the buttons (you can look ahead to Figure 4-33 and use it as a guide), and then lock the controls on the form.

7. Click **View** on the menu bar and then click **Tab Order**. Notice that the TabIndex values of the controls contained within each group box begin with the TabIndex value of the group box itself. This indicates that the controls belong to the group box rather than to the form. As mentioned earlier, if you move or delete the group box, the controls that belong to the group box will also be moved or deleted. The numbers that appear after the period in the TabIndex values indicate the order in which each control was added to the group box.

8. Use the information shown in Figure 4-33 to set each control's TabIndex value.

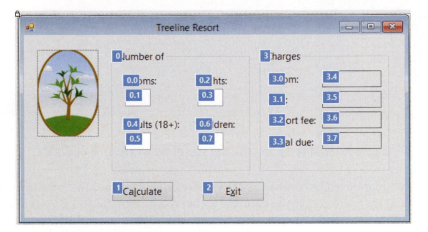

Figure 4-33   Correct TabIndex values for the interface

9. When you are finished setting the TabIndex values, press **Esc** to remove the TabIndex boxes, and then save the solution.

Coding the Treeline Resort Application

According to the application's TOE chart, which is shown in Figure 4-34, the Click event procedures for the two buttons need to be coded. The TextChanged, KeyPress, and Enter events for the four text boxes also need to be coded. When you open the Code Editor window, you will notice that the btnExit_Click procedure has already been coded and so have the TextChanged event procedures for the four text boxes. In this lesson, you will code only the btnCalc_Click procedure. You will code the KeyPress and Enter event procedures for the four text boxes in Lesson C.

Task	Object	Event
1. Calculate the total room charge, tax, total resort fee, and total due	btnCalc	Click
2. Display the calculated amounts in lblRoomChg, lblTax, lblResortFee, and lblTotalDue		
End the application	btnExit	Click
Display the total room charge (from btnCalc)	lblRoomChg	None
Display the tax (from btnCalc)	lblTax	None
Display the total resort fee (from btnCalc)	lblResortFee	None
Display the total due (from btnCalc)	lblTotalDue	None
Get and display the number of rooms reserved, number of nights, number of adults, and number of children	txtRooms, txtNights, txtAdults, txtChildren	None
Clear the contents of lblRoomChg, lblTax, lblResortFee, and lblTotalDue	txtRooms, txtNights, txtAdults, txtChildren	TextChanged
Allow the text box to accept only numbers and the Backspace key	txtRooms, txtNights, txtAdults, txtChildren	KeyPress
Select the contents of the text box	txtRooms, txtNights, txtAdults, txtChildren	Enter

Figure 4-34   TOE chart for the Treeline Resort application

Coding the btnCalc Control's Click Event Procedure

The btnCalc_Click procedure is responsible for calculating and displaying the total room charge, tax, total resort fee, and total due. The procedure's pseudocode is shown in Figure 4-35.

btnCalc Click event procedure
1. store user input (numbers of rooms reserved, nights, adults, and children) in variables
2. calculate the total number of guests = number of adult guests + number of child guests
3. calculate the number of rooms required = total number of guests / maximum number of guests per room, which is 6
4. if the number of rooms reserved < number of rooms required
      display the message "You have exceeded the maximum guests per room."
  else
      calculate total room charge = number of rooms reserved * number of nights * daily room charge of $225.50
      calculate tax = total room charge * tax rate of 16.25%
      calculate total resort fee = number of rooms reserved * number of nights * daily resort fee of $12.50
      calculate total due = total room charge + tax + total resort fee
      display total room charge, tax, total resort fee, and total due
  end if

Figure 4-35   Pseudocode for the btnCalc_Click procedure

START HERE

To begin coding the btnCalc_Click procedure:

1. Open the Code Editor window. Replace <your name> and <current date> in the comments with your name and the current date, respectively.

2. Open the code template for the btnCalc_Click procedure. Type the comments shown in Figure 4-36, and then position the insertion point as shown in the figure.

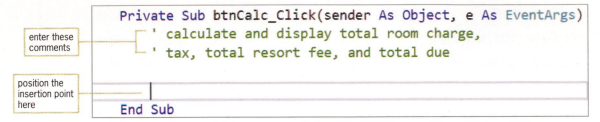

```
Private Sub btnCalc_Click(sender As Object, e As EventArgs)
    ' calculate and display total room charge,
    ' tax, total resort fee, and total due


End Sub
```

enter these comments

position the insertion point here

Figure 4-36 Comments entered in the procedure

Now, study the procedure's pseudocode to determine any named constants or variables the procedure will use. When determining the named constants, look for items whose value should remain the same each time the procedure is invoked. In the btnCalc_Click procedure, those items are the maximum number of guests per room, the daily room charge, the tax rate, the daily resort fee, and the message. Figure 4-37 shows the named constants that the procedure will use for these items. The named constants will make the code easier to understand, and they will allow you (or another programmer) to quickly locate those values should they need to be changed in the future.

Named constants	Values
intMAX_PER_ROOM	6
dblDAILY_ROOM_CHG	225.50
dblTAX_RATE	0.1625 (the decimal equivalent of 16.25%)
dblDAILY_RESORT_FEE	12.50
strMSG	"You have exceeded the maximum guests per room."

Figure 4-37 Listing of named constants and their values

When determining the procedure's variables, look in the pseudocode for items whose value is allowed to change each time the procedure is processed. The btnCalc_Click procedure has 10 such items: the four input items and the six calculated items. Figure 4-38 shows the variables that the procedure will use.

Variable names	Stores
intRoomsReserved	the number of rooms reserved
intNights	the number of nights
intAdults	the number of adult guests
intChildren	the number of child guests
intNumGuests	the total number of guests, which is calculated by adding together the number of adult guests and the number of child guests
dblRoomsRequired	the number of rooms required, which is calculated by dividing the total number of guests by the maximum number of guests per room (may contain a decimal place)
dblTotalRoomChg	the total room charge, which is calculated by multiplying the number of rooms reserved by the number of nights and then multiplying the result by the daily room charge
dblTax	the tax, which is calculated by multiplying the total room charge by the tax rate
dblTotalResortFee	the total resort fee, which is calculated by multiplying the number of rooms reserved by the number of nights and then multiplying the result by the daily resort fee
dblTotalDue	the total due, which is calculated by adding together the total room charge, tax, and total resort fee

Figure 4-38   Listing of variables and what each stores

To continue coding the btnCalc_Click procedure:

START HERE

1. Enter the Const and Dim statements shown in Figure 4-39, and then position the insertion point as shown in the figure.

```
Const intMAX_PER_ROOM As Integer = 6
Const dblDAILY_ROOM_CHG As Double = 225.5
Const dblTAX_RATE As Double = 0.1625
Const dblDAILY_RESORT_FEE As Double = 12.5
Const strMSG As String = "You have exceeded the maximum guests per room."
Dim intRoomsReserved As Integer
Dim intNights As Integer
Dim intAdults As Integer
Dim intChildren As Integer
Dim intNumGuests As Integer
Dim dblRoomsRequired As Double
Dim dblTotalRoomChg As Double
Dim dblTax As Double
Dim dblTotalResortFee As Double
Dim dblTotalDue As Double



End Sub
```

position the insertion point here

Figure 4-39   Const and Dim statements entered in the procedure

Using a blank line to separate related blocks of code in the Code Editor window makes the code easier to read and understand.

2. Step 1 in the pseudocode is to store the input items in variables. Enter the following comment and TryParse methods. Press **Enter** twice after typing the last TryParse method.

' store input in variables
Integer.TryParse(txtRooms.Text, intRoomsReserved)
Integer.TryParse(txtNights.Text, intNights)
Integer.TryParse(txtAdults.Text, intAdults)
Integer.TryParse(txtChildren.Text, intChildren)

3. Step 2 in the pseudocode calculates the total number of guests by adding together the number of adult guests and the number of child guests. Enter the following comment and assignment statement:

' calculate total number of guests
intNumGuests = intAdults + intChildren

4. Step 3 in the pseudocode calculates the number of rooms required by dividing the total number of guests by the maximum number of guests per room. Enter the following comment and assignment statement. Press **Enter** twice after typing the assignment statement.

' calculate number of rooms required
dblRoomsRequired = intNumGuests / intMAX_PER_ROOM

5. Step 4 in the pseudocode is a selection structure that determines whether the number of rooms reserved is adequate for the number of guests. If the number of reserved rooms is less than the number of required rooms, the selection structure's true path displays an appropriate message. In the next section, you will learn how to display the message in a message box. For now, enter the following comments and If clause. When you press Enter after typing the If clause, the Code Editor will automatically enter the End If clause for you.

' determine whether number of reserved rooms is
' adequate and then either display a message or
' calculate and display the charges
If intRoomsReserved < dblRoomsRequired Then

6. Save the solution.

The MessageBox.Show Method

At times, an application may need to communicate with the user during run time. One means of doing this is through a message box. You display a message box using the **MessageBox.Show method**. The message box contains text, one or more buttons, and an icon. Figure 4-40 shows the method's syntax and lists the meaning of each argument. The figure also includes examples of using the method. Figures 4-41 and 4-42 show the message boxes created by the two examples.

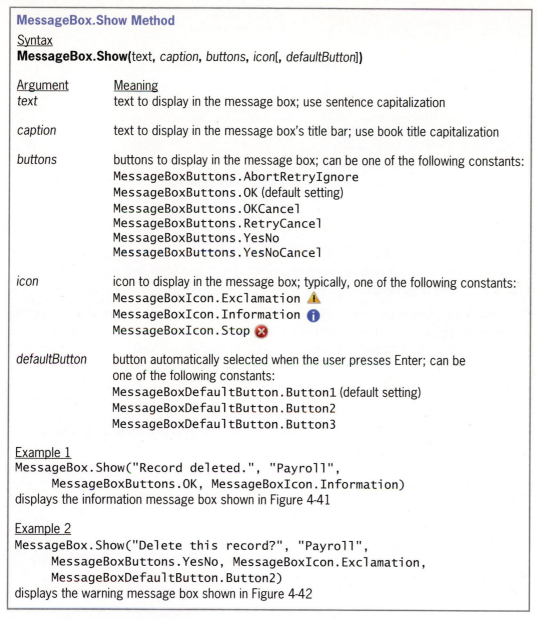

MessageBox.Show Method

<u>Syntax</u>
MessageBox.Show(text, *caption*, *buttons*, *icon*[, *defaultButton*]**)**

<u>Argument</u>	<u>Meaning</u>
text	text to display in the message box; use sentence capitalization
caption	text to display in the message box's title bar; use book title capitalization
buttons	buttons to display in the message box; can be one of the following constants: MessageBoxButtons.AbortRetryIgnore MessageBoxButtons.OK (default setting) MessageBoxButtons.OKCancel MessageBoxButtons.RetryCancel MessageBoxButtons.YesNo MessageBoxButtons.YesNoCancel
icon	icon to display in the message box; typically, one of the following constants: MessageBoxIcon.Exclamation ⚠ MessageBoxIcon.Information ⓘ MessageBoxIcon.Stop ⊗
defaultButton	button automatically selected when the user presses Enter; can be one of the following constants: MessageBoxDefaultButton.Button1 (default setting) MessageBoxDefaultButton.Button2 MessageBoxDefaultButton.Button3

<u>Example 1</u>
```
MessageBox.Show("Record deleted.", "Payroll",
     MessageBoxButtons.OK, MessageBoxIcon.Information)
```
displays the information message box shown in Figure 4-41

<u>Example 2</u>
```
MessageBox.Show("Delete this record?", "Payroll",
     MessageBoxButtons.YesNo, MessageBoxIcon.Exclamation,
     MessageBoxDefaultButton.Button2)
```
displays the warning message box shown in Figure 4-42

Figure 4-40 Syntax and examples of the MessageBox.Show method

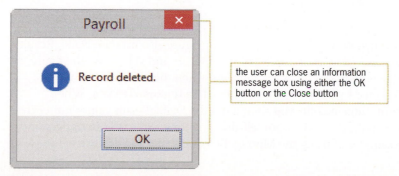

the user can close an information message box using either the OK button or the Close button

Figure 4-41 Message displayed by the code in Example 1 in Figure 4-40

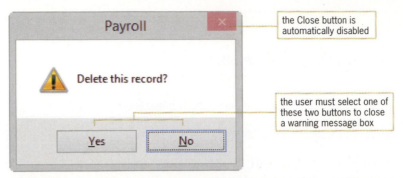

Figure 4-42   Message displayed by the code in Example 2 in Figure 4-40

GUI DESIGN TIP MessageBox.Show Method

- Use sentence capitalization for the *text* argument, but use book title capitalization for the *caption* argument.

- Display the Exclamation icon to alert the user that he or she must make a decision before the application can continue. You can phrase the message as a question. Message boxes that contain the Exclamation icon typically contain more than one button.

- Display the Information icon along with an OK button in a message box that displays an informational message.

- Display the Stop icon to alert the user of a serious problem that must be corrected before the application can continue.

- The default button in the message box should represent the user's most likely action as long as that action is not destructive.

After displaying the message box, the MessageBox.Show method waits for the user to choose one of the buttons. It then closes the message box and returns an integer indicating the button chosen by the user. Sometimes you are not interested in the value returned by the MessageBox.Show method. This is the case when the message box is for informational purposes only, such as the message box shown in Figure 4-41. Many times, however, the button selected by the user determines the next task performed by the application. Selecting the Yes button in the message box shown in Figure 4-42 tells the application to delete the record; selecting the No button tells it *not* to delete the record.

Figure 4-43 lists the integer values returned by the MessageBox.Show method. Each value is associated with a button that can appear in a message box. The figure also lists the DialogResult values assigned to each integer as well as the meaning of the integers and values. As the figure indicates, the MessageBox.Show method returns the integer 6 when the user selects the Yes button. The integer 6 is represented by the DialogResult value `DialogResult.Yes`. When referring to the method's return value in code, you should use the DialogResult values rather than the integers because the values make the code more self-documenting and easier to understand. Figure 4-43 also shows two examples of using the MessageBox.Show method's return value.

```
MessageBox.Show Method's Return Values
Integer        DialogResult value              Meaning
1              DialogResult.OK                 user chose the OK button
2              DialogResult.Cancel             user chose the Cancel button
3              DialogResult.Abort              user chose the Abort button
4              DialogResult.Retry              user chose the Retry button
5              DialogResult.Ignore             user chose the Ignore button
6              DialogResult.Yes                user chose the Yes button
7              DialogResult.No                 user chose the No button

Example 1
Dim dlgButton As DialogResult
dlgButton =
      MessageBox.Show("Delete this record?", "Payroll",
      MessageBoxButtons.YesNo, MessageBoxIcon.Exclamation,
      MessageBoxDefaultButton.Button2)
If dlgButton = DialogResult.Yes Then
      instructions to delete the record
End If

Example 2
If MessageBox.Show("Play another game?", "Math Monster",
      MessageBoxButtons.YesNo, MessageBoxIcon.Exclamation) =
      DialogResult.Yes Then
      instructions to start another game
Else    ' No button
      instructions to close the game application
End If
```

Figure 4-43   Values returned by the MessageBox.Show method

In the first example in Figure 4-43, the MessageBox.Show method's return value is assigned to a DialogResult variable named `dlgButton`. The selection structure in the example compares the contents of the `dlgButton` variable with the `DialogResult.Yes` value. In the second example, the method's return value is not stored in a variable. Instead, the method appears in the selection structure's condition, where its return value is compared with the `DialogResult.Yes` value. The selection structure in Example 2 performs one set of tasks when the user selects the Yes button in the message box, and it performs a different set of tasks when the user selects the No button. Many programmers document the Else portion of the selection structure as shown in Example 2 because it clearly states that the Else portion is processed only when the user selects the No button.

In the next set of steps, you will use the MessageBox.Show method to display the appropriate message when the number of reserved rooms is less than the number of required rooms. The message box is for informational purposes only. Therefore, it should contain the Information icon and the OK button, and you do not need to be concerned with its return value.

START HERE

To add the MessageBox.Show method to the btnCalc_Click procedure:

1. The insertion point should be positioned in the blank line above the End If clause. Enter the following lines of code:

```
MessageBox.Show(strMSG, "Treeline Resort",
        MessageBoxButtons.OK,
        MessageBoxIcon.Information)
```

Completing the btnCalc_Click Procedure

Recall that Step 4 in the btnCalc_Click procedure's pseudocode is a selection structure that determines whether the number of rooms reserved is adequate for the number of guests. In the previous section, you completed the selection structure's true path. You will complete the false path in this section. According to the pseudocode, the false path should calculate and display the total room charge, tax, total resort fee, and total due.

START HERE

To complete the btnCalc_Click procedure and then test it:

1. In the blank line above the End If clause, type **else** and press **Enter**.

2. The total room charge is calculated by first multiplying the number of rooms reserved by the number of nights and then multiplying the result by the daily room charge. Enter the following comment and assignment statement:

```
' calculate charges
dblTotalRoomChg = intRoomsReserved *
    intNights * dblDAILY_ROOM_CHG
```

3. The tax is calculated by multiplying the total room charge by the tax rate. Enter the following assignment statement:

```
dblTax = dblTotalRoomChg * dblTAX_RATE
```

4. The total resort fee is calculated by first multiplying the number of rooms reserved by the number of nights and then multiplying the result by the daily resort fee. Enter the following assignment statement:

```
dblTotalResortFee = intRoomsReserved *
    intNights * dblDAILY_RESORT_FEE
```

5. The total due is calculated by adding together the total room charge, tax, and total resort fee. Enter the following assignment statement:

```
dblTotalDue = dblTotalRoomChg +
    dblTax + dblTotalResortFee
```

6. Finally, you will display the calculated amounts in the interface. Press **Enter** to insert another blank line below the last assignment statement. Enter the following comment and assignment statements:

```
' display charges
lblRoomChg.Text = dblTotalRoomChg.ToString("n2")
lblTax.Text = dblTax.ToString("n2")
lblResortFee.Text = dblTotalResortFee.ToString("n2")
lblTotalDue.Text = dblTotalDue.ToString("c2")
```

7. If necessary, delete the blank line above the End If clause.

8. Save the solution and then start the application. Type **1** in the Rooms box, type **2** in the Nights box, type **4** in the Adults box, and type **4** in the Children box. Click the **Calculate** button. The message box shown in Figure 4-44 opens.

Figure 4-44 Message box created by the MessageBox.Show method

9. Click the **OK** button to close the message box. Change the number of adults to **2**. Also change the number of children to **2**. Click the **Calculate** button. See Figure 4-45.

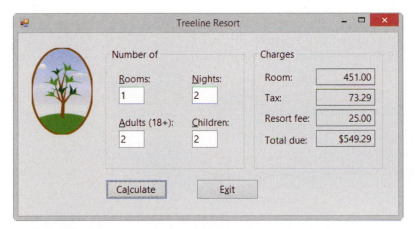

Figure 4-45 Calculated amounts shown in the interface

10. Click the **Exit** button.

Figure 4-46 shows the application's code at the end of Lesson B.

```
 1 ' Name:          Treeline Project
 2 ' Purpose:       Display the total room charge, tax,
 3 '                total resort fee, and total due
 4 ' Programmer:    <your name> on <current date>
 5
 6 Option Explicit On
 7 Option Strict On
 8 Option Infer Off
 9
10 Public Class frmMain
11     Private Sub btnCalc_Click(sender As Object, e As EventArgs
       ) Handles btnCalc.Click
12         ' calculate and display total room charge,
13         ' tax, total resort fee, and total due
14
15         Const intMAX_PER_ROOM As Integer = 6
16         Const dblDAILY_ROOM_CHG As Double = 225.5
17         Const dblTAX_RATE As Double = 0.1625
18         Const dblDAILY_RESORT_FEE As Double = 12.5
19         Const strMSG As String =
               "You have exceeded the maximum guests per room."
20         Dim intRoomsReserved As Integer
21         Dim intNights As Integer
22         Dim intAdults As Integer
23         Dim intChildren As Integer
24         Dim intNumGuests As Integer
25         Dim dblRoomsRequired As Double
26         Dim dblTotalRoomChg As Double
27         Dim dblTax As Double
28         Dim dblTotalResortFee As Double
29         Dim dblTotalDue As Double
30
31         ' store input in variables
32         Integer.TryParse(txtRooms.Text, intRoomsReserved)
33         Integer.TryParse(txtNights.Text, intNights)
34         Integer.TryParse(txtAdults.Text, intAdults)
35         Integer.TryParse(txtChildren.Text, intChildren)
36
37         ' calculate total number of guests
38         intNumGuests = intAdults + intChildren
39         ' calculate number of rooms required
40         dblRoomsRequired = intNumGuests / intMAX_PER_ROOM
41
42         ' determine whether number of reserved rooms is
43         ' adequate and then either display a message or
44         ' calculate and display the charges
45         If intRoomsReserved < dblRoomsRequired Then
46             MessageBox.Show(strMSG, "Treeline Resort",
47                             MessageBoxButtons.OK,
48                             MessageBoxIcon.Information)
49         Else
50             ' calculate charges
```

Figure 4-46   Treeline Resort application's code at the end of Lesson B (continues)

(continued)

```
51                dblTotalRoomChg = intRoomsReserved *
52                    intNights * dblDAILY_ROOM_CHG
53                dblTax = dblTotalRoomChg * dblTAX_RATE
54                dblTotalResortFee = intRoomsReserved *
55                    intNights * dblDAILY_RESORT_FEE
56                dblTotalDue = dblTotalRoomChg +
57                    dblTax + dblTotalResortFee
58
59                ' display charges
60                lblRoomChg.Text = dblTotalRoomChg.ToString("n2")
61                lblTax.Text = dblTax.ToString("n2")
62                lblResortFee.Text = dblTotalResortFee.ToString("n2")
63                lblTotalDue.Text = dblTotalDue.ToString("c2")
64        End If
65    End Sub
66
67    Private Sub btnExit_Click(sender As Object, e As EventArgs
      ) Handles btnExit.Click
68        Me.Close()
69    End Sub
70
71    Private Sub ClearLabels(sender As Object, e As EventArgs) _
72        Handles txtRooms.TextChanged, txtNights.TextChanged,
73        txtAdults.TextChanged, txtChildren.TextChanged
74        ' clear calculated amounts
75
76        lblRoomChg.Text = String.Empty
77        lblTax.Text = String.Empty
78        lblResortFee.Text = String.Empty
79        lblTotalDue.Text = String.Empty
80    End Sub
81 End Class
```

Figure 4-46   Treeline Resort application's code at the end of Lesson B

Lesson B Summary

- To group controls together using a group box:

  Use the GroupBox tool to add a group box to the form. Drag controls from either the form or the toolbox into the group box. To include an optional identifying label on a group box, set the group box's Text property. The TabIndex value of a control contained within a group box is composed of two numbers separated by a period. The number to the left of the period is the TabIndex value of the group box itself. The number to the right of the period indicates the order in which the control was added to the group box.

- To display a message box that contains text, one or more buttons, and an icon:

  Use the MessageBox.Show method. The method's syntax is shown in Figure 4-40, and its return values are explained in Figure 4-43.

Lesson B Key Terms

Group box—a control that is used to contain other controls; instantiated using the GroupBox tool, which is located in the Containers section of the toolbox

MessageBox.Show method—displays a message box that contains text, one or more buttons, and an icon; allows an application to communicate with the user while the application is running

Lesson B Review Questions

1. Which of the following statements is false?

   a. When you delete a group box, the controls contained within the group box are also deleted.

   b. Moving a group box also moves all of the controls contained within the group box.

   c. A group box's Label property specifies its identifying label.

   d. You can drag a control from the form into a group box.

2. What is the TabIndex value of the first control added to a group box whose TabIndex value is 3?

   a. 3

   b. 3.0

   c. 3.1

   d. none of the above

3. You use the _____ constant to include the Exclamation icon in a message box.

   a. `MessageBox.Exclamation`

   b. `MessageBox.IconExclamation`

   c. `MessageBoxIcon.Exclamation`

   d. `MessageBox.WarningIcon`

4. If a message is for informational purposes only and does not require the user to make a decision, the message box should display which of the following?

   a. an OK button and the Information icon

   b. an OK button and the Exclamation icon

   c. a Yes button and the Information icon

   d. any button and the Information icon

5. If the user clicks the Yes button in a message box, the message box returns the number 6, which is equivalent to which value?

   a. `DialogResultButton.Yes`

   b. `DialogResult.Yes`

   c. `DialogResult.YesButton`

   d. none of the above

Lesson B Exercises

1. Create an application that converts American dollars to the three currencies indicated in Figure 4-47. Use the following names for the solution and project, respectively: Converter Solution and Converter Project. Save the application in the VB2015\Chap04 folder. Make the Convert button the default button. Use the Internet to determine the current conversion rates. Display the output with two decimal places. Clear the output when a change is made to the number of American dollars. Use a selection structure to verify that the American dollar box is not empty. If the box is empty, use the MessageBox.Show method to display an appropriate message. Test the application appropriately.

Figure 4-47   Interface for Exercise 1

2. In this exercise, you modify the Net Income or Loss application from Lesson A. Use Windows to make a copy of the Net Solution folder. Rename the copy Net Solution-Print. Open the Net Solution (Net Solution.sln) file contained in the Net Solution-Print folder. Locate the btnCalc_Click procedure in the Code Editor window. After displaying the output, use the MessageBox.Show method to ask the user whether he or she wants to print the interface. If the user wants to print the interface, send the printout to the Print preview window. (Use the examples shown earlier in Figure 4-43 as a guide.) Test the application appropriately.

3. Tea Time Company wants you to create an application that allows a clerk to enter the number of pounds of tea ordered, the price per pound, and whether the customer should be charged a $15 shipping fee. The application should calculate and display the total amount the customer owes. Use the following names for the solution and project, respectively: Tea Time Solution and Tea Time Project. Save the application in the VB2015\Chap04 folder. The total amount owed should be removed from the interface when a change is made to the contents of a text box in the interface. Use the MessageBox.Show method to determine whether the user should be charged for shipping. (Use the examples shown earlier in Figure 4-43 as a guide.) Test the application appropriately.

INTERMEDIATE

4. Triple County Electric wants you to create an application that calculates a customer's monthly electric bill, given the customer's name and his or her current and previous meter readings. If the current reading is less than the previous reading, use the MessageBox.Show method to display an appropriate message. The charge per unit of electricity is $0.13. Use the following names for the solution and project, respectively: Triple County Solution and Triple County Project. Save the application in the VB2015\Chap04 folder. The total charge for the month should be removed from the interface when a change is made to the contents of a text box in the interface. Test the application appropriately.

ADVANCED

5. Create an application that displays the result of dividing the larger of two numbers entered by the user by the smaller one, as indicated in Figure 4-48. Use the following names for the solution and project, respectively: Division Solution and Division Project. Save the application in the VB2015\Chap04 folder. If the smaller number is 0, the application should display the message "Cannot divide by 0" in a message box. Test the application by entering 150.72 and 3 in the First and Second boxes, respectively. Then test it by entering 4 and 100 in the First and Second boxes, respectively. Also test it using 0 and 5, and then test it again using 0 and –3.

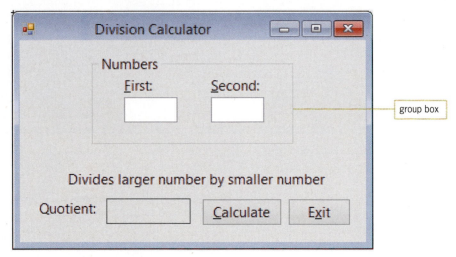

Figure 4-48   Interface for Exercise 5

LESSON C

After studying Lesson C, you should be able to:

● Prevent the entry of unwanted characters in a text box

● Select the existing text in a text box

Coding the KeyPress Event Procedures

To complete the Treeline Resort application, you need to code the KeyPress and Enter event procedures for the four text boxes. You will code the KeyPress event procedures first.

To open the Treeline Resort application: ◀ START HERE

1. If necessary, start Visual Studio 2015. Open the Treeline Solution (Treeline Solution.sln) file from Lesson B.

The application provides text boxes for the user to enter the numbers of rooms, nights, adults, and children. The user should enter those items using only numbers. The items should not contain any letters, spaces, punctuation marks, or special characters. Unfortunately, you can't stop the user from trying to enter an inappropriate character into a text box. However, you can prevent the text box from accepting the character by coding the text box's KeyPress event procedure.

To view the code template for the txtRooms_KeyPress procedure: ◀ START HERE

1. Open the Code Editor window, and then open the code template for the txtRooms_KeyPress procedure. See Figure 4-49.

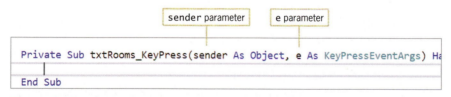

Figure 4-49   Code template for the txtRooms_KeyPress procedure

A control's **KeyPress event** occurs each time the user presses a key while the control has the focus. The procedure associated with the KeyPress event has two parameters, which appear within the parentheses in the procedure header: `sender` and `e`. A **parameter** represents information that is passed to the procedure when the event occurs. When the KeyPress event occurs, a character corresponding to the pressed key is sent to the event's `e` parameter. For example, when the user presses the period (.) while entering data into a text box, the text box's KeyPress event occurs and a period is sent to the event's `e` parameter. Similarly, when the Shift key along with a letter is pressed, the uppercase version of the letter is sent to the `e` parameter.

To prevent a text box from accepting an inappropriate character, you first use the `e` parameter's **KeyChar property** to determine the pressed key. (*KeyChar* stands for *key character*.) You then use the `e` parameter's **Handled property** to cancel the key if it is an inappropriate one. You cancel the key by setting the Handled property to True, like this: `e.Handled = True`.

Figure 4-50 shows examples of using the KeyChar and Handled properties in the KeyPress event procedure. The condition in Example 1's selection structure compares the contents of the KeyChar property with a dollar sign. If the condition evaluates to True, the `e.Handled = True`

The KeyPress event automatically allows the use of the Delete key for editing.

instruction in the selection structure's true path cancels the $ key before it is entered in the txtSales control. You can use the selection structure in Example 2 to allow the text box to accept only numbers and the Backspace key (which is used for editing). You refer to the Backspace key on your keyboard using Visual Basic's **ControlChars.Back constant**.

Controlling the Characters Accepted by a Text Box

Example 1
```
Private Sub txtSales_KeyPress(sender As Object, e As KeyPressEventArgs
) Handles txtSales.KeyPress
    ' prevents the text box from accepting the dollar sign

    If e.KeyChar = "$" Then
        e.Handled = True
    End If
End Sub
```

Example 2
```
Private Sub txtAge_KeyPress(sender As Object, e As KeyPressEventArgs
) Handles txtAge.KeyPress
    ' allows the text box to accept only numbers and the Backspace key

    If (e.KeyChar < "0" OrElse e.KeyChar > "9") AndAlso
        e.KeyChar <> ControlChars.Back Then
        e.Handled = True
    End If
End Sub
```

Figure 4-50   Examples of using the KeyChar and Handled properties in the KeyPress event procedure

According to the application's TOE chart, each text box's KeyPress event procedure should allow the text box to accept only numbers and the Backspace key. All other keys should be canceled. (The TOE chart is shown in Figure 4-34 in Lesson B.)

START HERE

To code and then test the KeyPress event procedures:

1. Change txtRooms_KeyPress in the procedure header to **CancelKeys**.

2. Place the insertion point **immediately before the)** (closing parenthesis) in the procedure header, and then press **Enter** to move the parenthesis and the Handles clause to the next line in the procedure. (You can look ahead to Figure 4-51 and use it as a guide.)

3. Place the insertion point **at the end of the Handles clause**. Type the following text and press **Enter**. (Be sure to type the comma before and after txtNights.KeyPress.)

    , txtNights.KeyPress,

4. Now type the following text and press **Enter**:

    txtAdults.KeyPress, txtChildren.KeyPress

5. Enter the comments and code shown in Figure 4-51.

```
Private Sub CancelKeys(sender As Object, e As KeyPressEventArgs
                    ) Handles txtRooms.KeyPress, txtNights.KeyPress,
                    txtAdults.KeyPress, txtChildren.KeyPress
    ' allows the text box to accept only numbers and the Backspace

    If (e.KeyChar < "0" OrElse e.KeyChar > "9") AndAlso
            e.KeyChar <> ControlChars.Back Then
        ' cancel the key
        e.Handled = True
    End If
End Sub
```

the procedure is associated with each text box's KeyPress event

Figure 4-51   CancelKeys procedure

6. Save the solution and then start the application. Try to enter a letter in the Rooms box, and then try to enter a dollar sign. Type **10** in the Rooms box and then press **Backspace** to delete the 0. The Rooms box now contains only the number 1.

7. Try to enter a letter in the Nights box, and then try to enter a percent sign. Type **21** in the Nights box and then press **Backspace** to delete the 1. The Nights box now contains only the number 2.

8. Try to enter a letter in the Adults box, and then try to enter an ampersand. Type **20** in the Adults box and then press **Backspace** to delete the 0. The Adults box now contains only the number 2.

9. Try to enter a letter in the Children box, and then try to enter a period. Type **13** in the Children box and then press **Backspace** to delete the 3. The Children box now contains only the number 1.

10. Click the **Calculate** button to display the calculated amounts in the interface.

11. Press **Tab** twice to move the focus to the Rooms box. Notice that the insertion point appears at the end of the number 1. It is customary in Windows applications to have a text box's existing text selected (highlighted) when the text box receives the focus. You will learn how to select the existing text in the next section. Click the **Exit** button to end the application.

Coding the Enter Event Procedures

To complete the Treeline Resort application, you just need to code the Enter event procedures for the four text boxes. A text box's **Enter event** occurs when the text box receives the focus, which can happen as a result of the user tabbing to the control or using the control's access key. It also occurs when the Focus method is used to send the focus to the control. In the current application, the Enter event procedure for each text box is responsible for selecting (highlighting) the contents of the text box. When the text is selected in a text box, the user can remove the text simply by pressing a key on the keyboard, such as the letter n; the pressed key—in this case, the letter n—replaces the selected text.

Visual Basic provides the **SelectAll method** for selecting a text box's existing text. The method's syntax is shown in Figure 4-52 along with an example of using the method. In the syntax, *textbox* is the name of the text box whose contents you want to select.

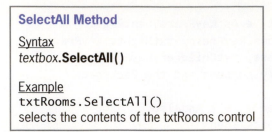

SelectAll Method

Syntax
textbox.**SelectAll()**

Example
`txtRooms.SelectAll()`
selects the contents of the txtRooms control

Figure 4-52   Syntax and an example of the SelectAll method

START HERE

To code and then test each text box's Enter event procedure:

1. Open the code template for the txtRooms_Enter procedure. Type the following comment and then press **Enter** twice:

    ' select contents when text box receives focus

2. Type **txtRooms.SelectAll()** and then click the **blank line** below the comment.

3. Open the code template for the txtNights_Enter procedure. Copy the comment and the SelectAll method from the txtRooms_Enter procedure to the txtNights_Enter procedure. Change txtRooms in the SelectAll method to **txtNights** and then click the **blank line** below the comment.

4. Open the code templates for the txtAdults_Enter and txtChildren_Enter procedures. On your own, enter the appropriate comment and SelectAll method in each procedure.

5. Save the solution and then start the application. Type **1** in the Rooms box, type **1** in the Nights box, type **2** in the Adults box, and type **2** in the Children box. Click the **Calculate** button to display the calculated amounts in the interface.

6. Press **Tab** twice to move the focus to the Rooms box. The txtRooms_Enter procedure selects the contents of the text box, as shown in Figure 4-53.

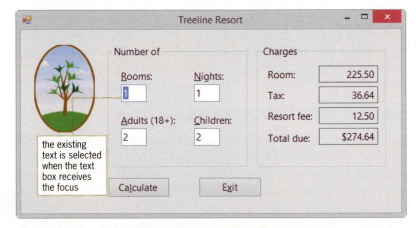

Figure 4-53   Existing text selected in the txtRooms control

7. Press **Tab** three times, slowly, to move the focus to each of the other three text boxes. Each text box's Enter event procedure selects the contents of the text box.

8. Click the **Exit** button. Close the Code Editor window and then close the solution.

Figure 4-54 shows the application's code at the end of Lesson C.

```vb
 1 ' Name:          Treeline Project
 2 ' Purpose:       Display the total room charge, tax,
 3 '                total resort fee, and total due
 4 ' Programmer:    <your name> on <current date>
 5
 6 Option Explicit On
 7 Option Strict On
 8 Option Infer Off
 9
10 Public Class frmMain
11     Private Sub btnCalc_Click(sender As Object, e As EventArgs
       ) Handles btnCalc.Click
12         ' calculate and display total room charge,
13         ' tax, total resort fee, and total due
14
15         Const intMAX_PER_ROOM As Integer = 6
16         Const dblDAILY_ROOM_CHG As Double = 225.5
17         Const dblTAX_RATE As Double = 0.1625
18         Const dblDAILY_RESORT_FEE As Double = 12.5
19         Const strMSG As String =
             "You have exceeded the maximum guests per room."
20         Dim intRoomsReserved As Integer
21         Dim intNights As Integer
22         Dim intAdults As Integer
23         Dim intChildren As Integer
24         Dim intNumGuests As Integer
25         Dim dblRoomsRequired As Double
26         Dim dblTotalRoomChg As Double
27         Dim dblTax As Double
28         Dim dblTotalResortFee As Double
29         Dim dblTotalDue As Double
30
31         ' store input in variables
32         Integer.TryParse(txtRooms.Text, intRoomsReserved)
33         Integer.TryParse(txtNights.Text, intNights)
34         Integer.TryParse(txtAdults.Text, intAdults)
35         Integer.TryParse(txtChildren.Text, intChildren)
36
37         ' calculate total number of guests
38         intNumGuests = intAdults + intChildren
39         ' calculate number of rooms required
40         dblRoomsRequired = intNumGuests / intMAX_PER_ROOM
41
42         ' determine whether number of reserved rooms is
43         ' adequate and then either display a message or
44         ' calculate and display the charges
45         If intRoomsReserved < dblRoomsRequired Then
46             MessageBox.Show(strMSG, "Treeline Resort",
47                             MessageBoxButtons.OK,
48                             MessageBoxIcon.Information)
49         Else
50             ' calculate charges
51             dblTotalRoomChg = intRoomsReserved *
52                 intNights * dblDAILY_ROOM_CHG
```

Figure 4-54   Treeline Resort application's code at the end of Lesson C *(continues)*

(continued)

```
53              dblTax = dblTotalRoomChg * dblTAX_RATE
54              dblTotalResortFee = intRoomsReserved *
55                  intNights * dblDAILY_RESORT_FEE
56              dblTotalDue = dblTotalRoomChg +
57                  dblTax + dblTotalResortFee
58
59              ' display charges
60              lblRoomChg.Text = dblTotalRoomChg.ToString("n2")
61              lblTax.Text = dblTax.ToString("n2")
62              lblResortFee.Text = dblTotalResortFee.ToString("n2")
63              lblTotalDue.Text = dblTotalDue.ToString("c2")
64          End If
65      End Sub
66
67      Private Sub btnExit_Click(sender As Object, e As EventArgs
        ) Handles btnExit.Click
68          Me.Close()
69      End Sub
70
71      Private Sub ClearLabels(sender As Object, e As EventArgs) _
72          Handles txtRooms.TextChanged, txtNights.TextChanged,
73          txtAdults.TextChanged, txtChildren.TextChanged
74          ' clear calculated amounts
75
76          lblRoomChg.Text = String.Empty
77          lblTax.Text = String.Empty
78          lblResortFee.Text = String.Empty
79          lblTotalDue.Text = String.Empty
80      End Sub
81
82      Private Sub CancelKeys(sender As Object, e As KeyPressEventArgs
83                  ) Handles txtRooms.KeyPress, txtNights.KeyPress,
84                  txtAdults.KeyPress, txtChildren.KeyPress
85          ' allows the text box to accept only numbers and the Backspace
86
87          If (e.KeyChar < "0" OrElse e.KeyChar > "9") AndAlso
88                  e.KeyChar <> ControlChars.Back Then
89              ' cancel the key
90              e.Handled = True
91          End If
92      End Sub
93
94      Private Sub txtRooms_Enter(sender As Object, e As EventArgs
        ) Handles txtRooms.Enter
95          ' select contents when text box receives focus
96
97          txtRooms.SelectAll()
98      End Sub
99
100     Private Sub txtNights_Enter(sender As Object, e As EventArgs
        ) Handles txtNights.Enter
101         ' select contents when text box receives focus
102
103         txtNights.SelectAll()
104     End Sub
```

Figure 4-54   Treeline Resort application's code at the end of Lesson C *(continues)*

(continued)

```
105
106     Private Sub txtAdults_Enter(sender As Object, e As EventArgs
        ) Handles txtAdults.Enter
107         ' select contents when text box receives focus
108
109         txtAdults.SelectAll()
110     End Sub
111
112     Private Sub txtChildren_Enter(sender As Object, e As EventArgs
        ) Handles txtChildren.Enter
113         ' select contents when text box receives focus
114
115         txtChildren.SelectAll()
116     End Sub
117 End Class
```

Figure 4-54   Treeline Resort application's code at the end of Lesson C

Lesson C Summary

- To allow a text box to accept only certain keys:

  Code the text box's KeyPress event procedure. The key the user pressed is stored in the e.KeyChar property. You use the `e.Handled = True` statement to cancel the key pressed by the user.

- To select the existing text in a text box:

  Use the SelectAll method. The method's syntax is *textbox*.`SelectAll()`.

- To process code when a control receives the focus:

  Enter the code in the control's Enter event procedure.

Lesson C Key Terms

ControlChars.Back constant—the Visual Basic constant that represents the Backspace key on your keyboard

Enter event—occurs when a control receives the focus, which can happen as a result of the user either tabbing to the control or using the control's access key; also occurs when the Focus method is used to send the focus to the control

Handled property—a property of the KeyPress event procedure's e parameter; when assigned the value True, it cancels the key pressed by the user

KeyChar property—a property of the KeyPress event procedure's e parameter; stores the character associated with the key pressed by the user

KeyPress event—occurs each time the user presses a key while a control has the focus

Parameter—an item contained within parentheses in a procedure header; represents information passed to the procedure when the procedure is invoked

SelectAll method—used to select all of the text contained in a text box

Lesson C Review Questions

1. When entering data in a text box, each key the user presses invokes the text box's _____ event.

   a. Focus

   b. Key

   c. KeyFocus

   d. KeyPress

2. When entered in the appropriate event procedure, which of the following statements cancels the key pressed by the user?

   a. `e.Cancel = True`

   b. `e.Cancel = False`

   c. `e.Handled = True`

   d. `e.Handled = False`

3. Which of the following If clauses determines whether the user pressed the Backspace key?

   a. `If e.KeyChar = ControlChars.Back Then`

   b. `If e.KeyChar = Backspace Then`

   c. `If e.KeyChar = ControlChars.Backspace Then`

   d. `If ControlChars.BackSpace = True Then`

4. Which of the following If clauses determines whether the user pressed the % key?

   a. `If ControlChars.PercentSign = True Then`

   b. `If e.KeyChar.ControlChars = "%" Then`

   c. `If e.KeyChar = Chars.PercentSign Then`

   d. `If e.KeyChar = "%" Then`

5. When a user tabs to a text box, the text box's _____ event occurs.

   a. Access

   b. Enter

   c. TabOrder

   d. TabbedTo

6. Which of the following tells the computer to highlight all of the text contained in the txtName control?

   a. `txtName.SelectAll()`

   b. `txtName.HighlightAll()`

   c. `Highlight(txtName)`

   d. `SelectAll(txtName.Text)`

7. The statement `txtHours.Focus()` invokes the txtHours _____ event.

   a. Click

   b. Enter

   c. Focus

   d. SetFocus

Lesson C Exercises

1. Create an application that displays a person's maximum heart rate, given his or her age. The maximum heart rate is calculated by subtracting the person's age from the number 220. The application should also display the person's target heart rate zone, which is 50% to 85% of the maximum heart rate. Use the following names for the solution and project, respectively: Heart Solution and Heart Project. Save the application in the VB2015\Chap04 folder. Create the interface shown in Figure 4-55. The image of the heart is stored in the VB2015\Chap04\Heart.png file. The Age text box should accept only numbers and the Backspace key. When the Age text box receives the focus, its existing text should be selected. Test the application with both valid data (numbers and the Backspace key) and invalid data (letters and special characters).

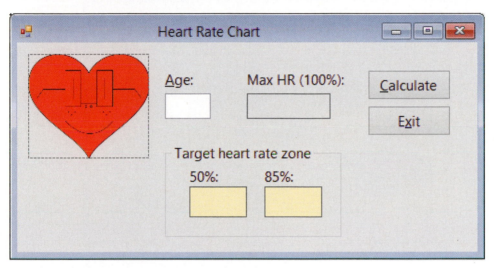

Figure 4-55   Interface for Exercise 1

2. In this exercise, you modify the bakery application from Chapter 3. Use Windows to copy the Bakery Solution folder from the VB2015\Chap03 folder to the VB2015\Chap04 folder, and then open the Bakery Solution (Bakery Solution.sln) file. When a text box in the interface receives the focus, its existing text should be selected. The Date text box should accept only numbers, the slash (/), the hyphen (-), and the Backspace key. The Doughnuts and Muffins boxes should accept only numbers and the Backspace key. Modify the code to reflect these changes. Test the application appropriately.

3. Open the MessageBox Value Solution (MessageBox Value Solution.sln) file contained in the VB2015\Chap04\MessageBox Value Solution folder. Open the Code Editor window. When the Hours worked text box receives the focus, its existing text should be selected. The text box should accept only numbers, the period, and the Backspace key. Before displaying the gross pay, the btnCalc_Click procedure should ask whether the user wants to include a dollar sign in the gross pay amount. Use the MessageBox.Show method with Yes and No buttons. If the user clicks the Yes button, the procedure should display the gross pay amount using the "C2" format; otherwise, the amount should be displayed using the "N2" format. Test the application appropriately.

4. Create an application, using the following names for the solution and project, respectively: Dahlia Solution and Dahlia Project. Save the application in the VB2015\ Chap04 folder. Create the interface shown in Figure 4-56. The interface provides text boxes for the salesclerk to enter the numbers of DVDs and Blu-rays purchased by a

customer. All DVDs sell for $9.99 each; all Blu-rays are $11.99 each. The sales tax rate is 6.5%. In addition to displaying the subtotal, sales tax, and total due, the application should display a message indicating the amount of Dahlia Cash the customer earned; however, it should leave the message area blank when the customer hasn't earned any Dahlia Cash. Customers earn $10 in Dahlia Cash for every $50 he or she spends, not including the sales tax. The DVDs and Blu-rays text boxes should accept only numbers and the Backspace key. Clear the calculated amounts and the message when a change is made to the number of either DVDs or Blu-rays. When a text box receives the focus, select its existing text. Test the application appropriately.

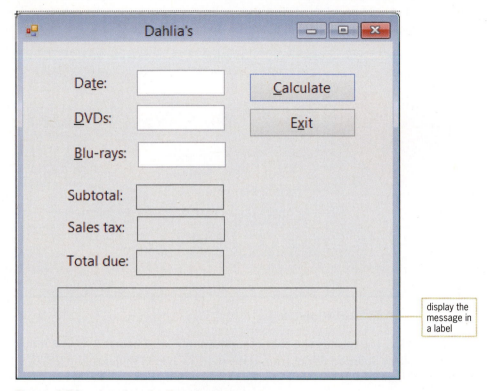

Figure 4-56   Interface for Exercise 4

INTERMEDIATE   5.   Marcy's Department store is having a BoGoHo (Buy One, Get One Half Off) sale. The store manager wants an application that allows the salesclerk to enter the prices of two items. The application should calculate and display the total amount the customer owes. The half-off should always be applied to the item that has the lowest price. Use the MessageBox.Show method to display the amount the customer saved. For example, if the two items cost $24.99 and $10.00, the half-off would be applied to the $10.00 item, and the message box would indicate that the customer saved $5.00. Use the following names for the solution and project, respectively: Marcy Solution and Marcy Project. Save the application in the VB2015\Chap04 folder. The total amount owed should be removed from the interface when a change is made to the contents of a text box in the interface. When a text box receives the focus, its existing text should be selected. Each text box should accept only numbers, the period, and the Backspace key. Test the application appropriately.

INTERMEDIATE   6.   In this exercise, you create an application for Beachwood Industries. Use the following names for the solution and project, respectively: Beachwood Solution and Beachwood Project. Save the application in the VB2015\Chap04 folder.

The application's interface should provide text boxes for the user to enter two values: the quantity of an item ordered and the item's price. The application should calculate the discount (if any) and total due. Before calculating the discount, the application should use the MessageBox.Show method to determine whether the customer is a wholesaler because all wholesalers receive a 15% discount. The discount and total due should be removed from the interface when a change is made to the contents of a text box in the interface. When a text box receives the focus, its existing text should be selected. The text box that contains the quantity ordered should accept only numbers and the Backspace key. The text box that contains the price should accept only numbers, the period, and the Backspace key. Test the application appropriately.

7. Create an application that can be used to teach the Italian words for the colors red, yellow, and green. Use the following names for the solution and project, respectively: Colors Solution and Colors Project. Save the application in the VB2015\Chap04 folder. Create the interface shown in Figure 4-57. The interface contains three text boxes, five buttons, and one label. Use the Internet to research the appropriate Italian words. After entering the Italian word corresponding to a button's color, the user will need to click the button to verify the entry. If the Italian word is correct, the button's Click event procedure should change the color of the text box to match the button's color. (Hint: Assign the button's BackColor property to the text box's BackColor property.) Otherwise, the Click event procedure should display the appropriate Italian word in a message box. The Clear button should change each text box's background color to white and clear the contents of each text box. Test the application appropriately.

INTERMEDIATE

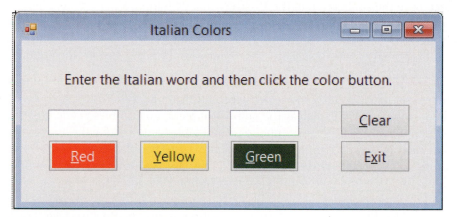

Figure 4-57   Interface for Exercise 7

8. Patti Garcia owns two cars, referred to as Car 1 and Car 2. She wants to drive one of the cars to her vacation destination, but she's not sure which one (if any) would cost her the least amount in gas. Use the following names for the solution and project, respectively: Car Solution and Car Project. Save the application in the VB2015\Chap04 folder.

INTERMEDIATE

a. The application's interface should provide text boxes for Patti to enter the following five items: the total miles she will drive, Car 1's miles per gallon, Car 2's miles per gallon, Car 1's cost per gallon of gas, and Car 2's cost per gallon of gas. (The cost per gallon of gas must be entered separately for each car because one car uses regular gas and the other uses premium gas.) The interface should display the total cost of the gas if she takes Car 1 as well as the total cost of the gas if she takes Car 2. It should also display a message that indicates which car she should take and approximately how much she will save by taking that car (show the savings with no decimal places).

Display the message in either a label or a message box. If the total cost of gas would be the same for both cars, Patti should take Car 1 because that's her favorite car.

b. The three text boxes that get the trip miles and the miles per gallon should accept only numbers and the Backspace key. The two text boxes that get the cost per gallon should accept only numbers, the period, and the Backspace key.

c. When a text box receives the focus, its existing text should be selected.

d. The calculated amounts and message (if you are using a label) should be cleared when a change is made to the contents of a text box in the interface.

e. Test the application using 1200, 28, 35, 3.69, and 3.38 as the trip miles, Car 1's miles per gallon, Car 2's miles per gallon, Car 1's cost per gallon, and Car 2's cost per gallon, respectively. (Hint: The total costs for Car 1 and Car 2 are $158.14 and $115.89, respectively. By taking Car 2, Patti will save approximately $42.)

f. Now, change Car 1's miles per gallon to 35. Also change Car 2's miles per gallon to 28. Which car should Patti take, and how much (approximately) will she save?

g. Next, change Car 1's miles per gallon and cost per gallon to 28 and 3.38, respectively. Which car should Patti take, and how much (approximately) will she save?

INTERMEDIATE

9. Create an application that displays the number of round tables needed to seat only the guests at a wedding reception. (In other words, the bridal party does not need to be included in this calculation.) Each round table can accommodate a maximum of 8 guests. The interface should provide a text box for the user to enter the total number of guests who need to be seated. Display the number of tables in a label. Use the following names for the solution and project, respectively: Wedding Solution and Wedding Project. Save the application in the VB2015\Chap04 folder. When the text box receives the focus, its existing text should be selected. The text box should accept only numbers and the Backspace key. The output should be cleared when a change is made to the contents of the text box. Test the application appropriately. (Hint: If the number of guests is 235, the number of required tables is 30.)

INTERMEDIATE

10. In this exercise, you modify the wedding reception application from Exercise 9. The modified application will display the number of rectangular tables needed to seat the bridal party as well as the number of round tables required for the guests. Each rectangular table can accommodate a maximum of 10 people. As in Exercise 9, a maximum of 8 guests can fit at each round table. Use Windows to make a copy of the Wedding Solution folder. Rename the copy Modified Wedding Solution. Open the Wedding Solution (Wedding Solution.sln) file contained in the Modified Wedding Solution folder. In addition to entering the number of guests, the interface should now allow the user to also enter the number of people in the bridal party. Test the application appropriately.

ADVANCED

11. Create an application, using the following names for the solution and project, respectively: Jerome Solution and Jerome Project. Save the application in the VB2015\Chap04 folder. Create the interface shown in Figure 4-58. The Calculate button's Click event procedure should add the item price to the total of the prices already entered; this amount represents the subtotal owed by the customer. The procedure should display the subtotal on the form. It also should display a 5% sales tax, the shipping charge, and the grand total owed by the customer. The grand total is calculated by adding together the subtotal, the 5% sales tax, and a $6.50 shipping charge. For example, if the user enters 15.75 as the price and then clicks the Calculate button, the button's Click event procedure should display 15.75 as the subtotal, 0.79 as the sales tax, 6.50 as the shipping charge, and 23.04 as the total due. If the user subsequently enters 10 as the price and

then clicks the Calculate button, the button's Click event procedure should display 25.75 as the subtotal, 1.29 as the sales tax, 6.50 as the shipping charge, and 33.54 as the total due. However, when the subtotal is at least $100, the shipping charge is 0.00. Test the application appropriately.

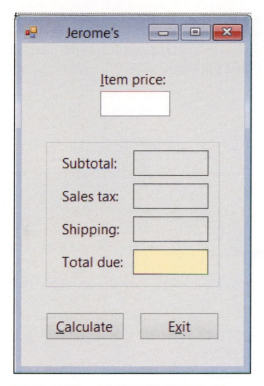

Figure 4-58   Interface for Exercise 11

DISCOVERY

12. In this exercise, you learn how to specify the maximum number of characters that can be entered in a text box. Open the VB2015\Chap04\Zip Solution\Zip Solution (Zip Solution.sln) file. Click the txtZip control, and then search the Properties list for a property that allows you to specify the maximum number of characters that can be entered in the text box. When you locate the property, set its value to 10. Save the solution and then start the application. Test the application by trying to enter more than 10 characters in the text box.

SWAT THE BUGS

13. Open the VB2015\Chap04\Debug Solution\Debug Solution (Debug Solution.sln) file. Open the Code Editor window and review the existing code. The btnCalc_Click procedure should calculate a 5% commission when the code entered by the user is 1, 2, or 3 and, at the same time, the sales amount is greater than $5,000; otherwise, the commission rate is 3%. Also, the CancelKeys procedure should allow the two text boxes to accept only numbers, the period, and the Backspace key.

a. Start the application. Type the number 1 in the Code box and then press the Backspace key. Notice that the Backspace key is not working correctly. Stop the application and then make the appropriate change to the CancelKeys procedure.

b. Save the solution and then start the application. Type the number 12 in the Code box and then press the Backspace key to delete the 2. The Code box now contains the number 1.

c.   Type 2000 in the Sales amount box and then click the Calculate button. A message box appears and indicates that the commission amount is $100.00 (5% of $2,000), which is incorrect; it should be $60.00 (3% of $2,000). Close the message box. Stop the application and then make the appropriate change to the btnCalc control's Click event procedure.

d.   Save the solution and then start the application. Type the number 1 in the Code box. Type 2000 in the Sales amount box and then click the Calculate button. The message box should indicate that the commission amount is $60.00. Close the message box.

e.   Test the application using the data shown in Figure 4-59.

Code	Sales amount
1	7000
2	5000
2	5000.75
3	175.55
3	9000.65
4	2000
4	6700

Figure 4-59   Test data for Exercise 13

CHAPTER 5

More on the Selection Structure

Revising the Treeline Resort Application

In this chapter, you will modify the Treeline Resort application from Chapter 4. In addition to the previous input data, the application's interface will now allow the user to select the number of beds (either two queen beds or one king bed), the view (either standard or atrium), and whether the guest should be charged a vehicle parking fee. The resort charges a nightly fee of $225.50 for two queen beds with a standard view, $275 for two queen beds with an atrium view, $245.50 for one king bed with a standard view, and $325 for one king bed with an atrium view. The vehicle parking fee is $8.50 per night. In addition to displaying the total room charge, the sales and lodging tax, the resort fee, and the total due, the application should now also display the total parking fee.

Previewing the Modified Treeline Resort Application

Before you start the first lesson in this chapter, you will preview the completed application contained in the VB2015\Chap05 folder.

START HERE

To preview the completed application:

1. Use Windows to locate and then open the VB2015\Chap05 folder. Right-click **Treeline** (**Treeline.exe**) and then click the **Open** button. The application's user interface appears on the screen. Type **1**, **1**, **2**, and **2** in the Rooms, Nights, Adults, and Children boxes, respectively. Click the **Calculate** button. See Figure 5-1.

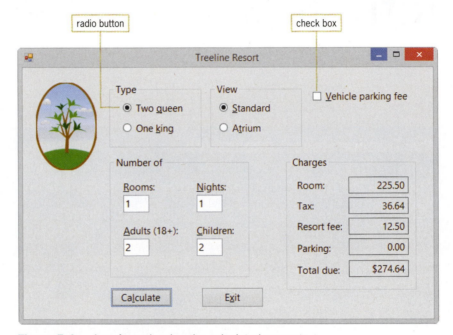

Figure 5-1   Interface showing the calculated amounts

2. The interface contains radio buttons and a check box. These controls are covered in Lesson B. Click the **One king** and **Atrium** radio buttons to select both. Also click the **Vehicle parking fee** check box to select it. Click the **Calculate** button. See Figure 5-2.

Figure 5-2   Recalculated amounts shown in the interface

3. Click the **Exit** button to end the application.

The modified Treeline Resort application uses nested selection structures, which you will learn about in Lesson A. You will also learn about multiple-alternative selection structures. In Lesson B, you will add a radio button and a check box to the Treeline Resort application's interface, and also modify the application's code. In Lesson C, you will learn how to use the TryParse method for data validation. You will also learn how to generate random integers. Be sure to complete each lesson in full and do all of the end-of-lesson questions and several exercises before continuing to the next lesson.

▌ LESSON A

After studying Lesson A, you should be able to:

• Include a nested selection structure in pseudocode and in a flowchart

• Code a nested selection structure

• Desk-check an algorithm

• Recognize common logic errors in selection structures

• Include a multiple-alternative selection structure in pseudocode and in a flowchart

• Code a multiple-alternative selection structure

Nested Selection Structures

Both the true and false paths in a selection structure can include instructions that declare variables, perform calculations, and so on. Both paths can also include other selection structures. When either a selection structure's true path or its false path contains another selection structure, the inner selection structure is referred to as a **nested selection structure** because it is contained (nested) entirely within the outer selection structure.

ChO5A-Nested Selection

A programmer determines whether a problem's solution requires a nested selection structure by studying the problem specification. The first problem specification you will examine in this chapter involves a basketball player named Maleek. The problem specification and an illustration of the problem are shown in Figure 5-3 along with an appropriate solution. The solution requires a selection structure but not a nested one. This is because only one decision—whether the basketball went through the hoop—is necessary.

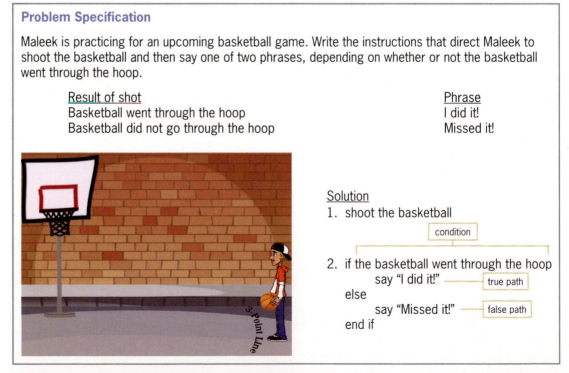

Problem Specification

Maleek is practicing for an upcoming basketball game. Write the instructions that direct Maleek to shoot the basketball and then say one of two phrases, depending on whether or not the basketball went through the hoop.

Result of shot	Phrase
Basketball went through the hoop	I did it!
Basketball did not go through the hoop	Missed it!

Solution
1. shoot the basketball

                                        condition

2. if the basketball went through the hoop
          say "I did it!" ——— true path
     else
          say "Missed it!" ——— false path
     end if

Figure 5-3   A problem that requires the selection structure
Image by Diane Zak; created with Reallusion CrazyTalk Animator; OpenClipArt.org/Tom Kolter/tawm1972

Now we'll make a slight change to the problem specification. This time, Maleek should say either one or two phrases, depending not only on whether or not the ball went through the hoop, but also on where he was standing when he made the basket. Figure 5-4 shows the modified problem specification and solution. The modified solution contains an outer dual-alternative selection structure and a nested dual-alternative selection structure. The outer selection structure begins with "if the basketball went through the hoop", and it ends with the last "end if". The last "else" belongs to the outer selection structure and separates the structure's true path from its false path. Notice that the instructions in both paths are indented within the outer selection structure. Indenting in this manner clearly indicates the instructions to be followed when the basketball went through the hoop, as well as the ones to be followed when the basketball did not go through the hoop.

The nested selection structure in Figure 5-4 appears in the outer selection structure's true path. The nested selection structure begins with "if Maleek was either inside or on the 3-point line", and it ends with the first "end if". The indented "else" belongs to the nested selection structure and separates the nested structure's true path from its false path. For clarity, the instructions in the nested selection structure's true and false paths are indented within the structure. For a nested selection structure to work correctly, it must be contained entirely within either the outer selection structure's true path or its false path. The nested selection structure in Figure 5-4 appears entirely within the outer selection structure's true path.

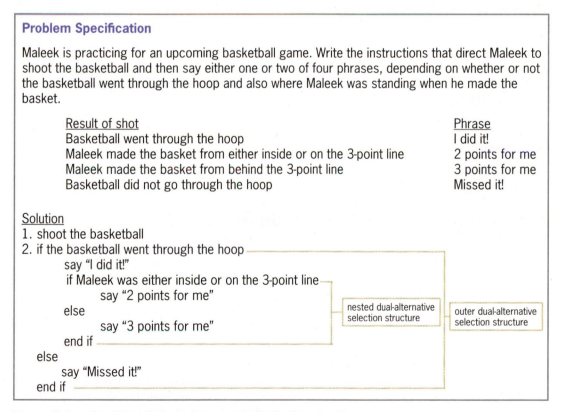

Problem Specification

Maleek is practicing for an upcoming basketball game. Write the instructions that direct Maleek to shoot the basketball and then say either one or two of four phrases, depending on whether or not the basketball went through the hoop and also where Maleek was standing when he made the basket.

Result of shot	Phrase
Basketball went through the hoop	I did it!
Maleek made the basket from either inside or on the 3-point line	2 points for me
Maleek made the basket from behind the 3-point line	3 points for me
Basketball did not go through the hoop	Missed it!

Solution
1. shoot the basketball
2. if the basketball went through the hoop
    say "I did it!"
    if Maleek was either inside or on the 3-point line
        say "2 points for me"
    else
        say "3 points for me"
    end if
  else
    say "Missed it!"
  end if

nested dual-alternative selection structure

outer dual-alternative selection structure

Figure 5-4   A problem that requires a nested selection structure

Figure 5-5 shows a modified version of the previous problem specification, along with the modified solution. In this version of the problem, Maleek should still say "Missed it!" when the basketball misses its target. However, if the basketball hits the rim, he should also say "So close". In addition to the nested dual-alternative selection structure from the previous solution, the modified solution also contains a nested single-alternative selection structure, which appears in the outer selection structure's false path. The nested single-alternative selection structure begins with "if the basketball hit the rim", and it ends with the second "end if". Notice that the nested single-alternative selection structure is contained entirely within the outer selection structure's false path.

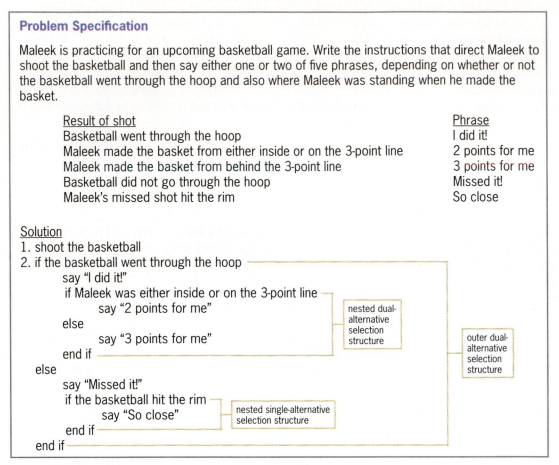

Problem Specification

Maleek is practicing for an upcoming basketball game. Write the instructions that direct Maleek to shoot the basketball and then say either one or two of five phrases, depending on whether or not the basketball went through the hoop and also where Maleek was standing when he made the basket.

Result of shot	Phrase
Basketball went through the hoop	I did it!
Maleek made the basket from either inside or on the 3-point line	2 points for me
Maleek made the basket from behind the 3-point line	3 points for me
Basketball did not go through the hoop	Missed it!
Maleek's missed shot hit the rim	So close

Solution
1. shoot the basketball
2. if the basketball went through the hoop
        say "I did it!"
        if Maleek was either inside or on the 3-point line
                say "2 points for me"
        else
                say "3 points for me"
        end if
    else
        say "Missed it!"
        if the basketball hit the rim
                say "So close"
        end if
    end if

nested dual-alternative selection structure

outer dual-alternative selection structure

nested single-alternative selection structure

Figure 5-5   A problem that requires two nested selection structures

Flowcharting a Nested Selection Structure

Figure 5-6 shows a problem specification for a voter eligibility application. The application determines whether a person can vote and then displays one of three messages. The appropriate message depends on the person's age and voter registration status. If the person is younger than 18 years old, the application should display the message "You are too young to vote." However, if the person is at least 18 years old, it should display one of two messages. The correct message to display is determined by the person's voter registration status. If the person is registered, then the appropriate message is "You can vote."; otherwise, it is "You must register before you can vote." Notice that determining the person's voter registration status is important only *after* his or her age is determined. Because of this, the decision regarding the age is considered the primary decision, while the decision regarding the registration status is considered the secondary decision because whether it needs to be made depends on the result of the primary decision. A primary decision is always made by an outer selection structure, while a secondary decision is always made by a nested selection structure.

Also included in Figure 5-6 is a correct solution to the problem in flowchart form. The first diamond in the flowchart represents the outer selection structure's condition, which checks whether the age entered by the user is greater than or equal to 18. If the condition evaluates to False, it means that the person is not old enough to vote. In that case, the outer structure's false path will display the "You are too young to vote." message before the outer structure ends. However, if the outer selection structure's condition evaluates to True, it means that the person *is* old enough to vote. Before displaying the appropriate message, the outer structure's true path gets the registration status from the user. After that, it uses a nested selection structure first to determine whether the person is registered and then to take the appropriate action. The nested structure's condition is represented by the second diamond in Figure 5-6. If the person is registered, the nested structure's true path displays the "You can vote." message; otherwise, its false path displays the "You must register before you can vote." message. After the appropriate message is displayed, the nested and outer selection structures end. Notice that the nested structure is processed only when the outer structure's condition evaluates to True.

Problem Specification

Create an application that displays one of three messages, as shown here. The application's interface will provide a text box for entering the person's age. It will use a message box to ask the user whether the person is registered to vote.

Messages	Criteria
You are too young to vote.	person is younger than 18 years old
You can vote.	person is at least 18 years old and is registered to vote
You must register before you can vote.	person is at least 18 years old but is not registered to vote

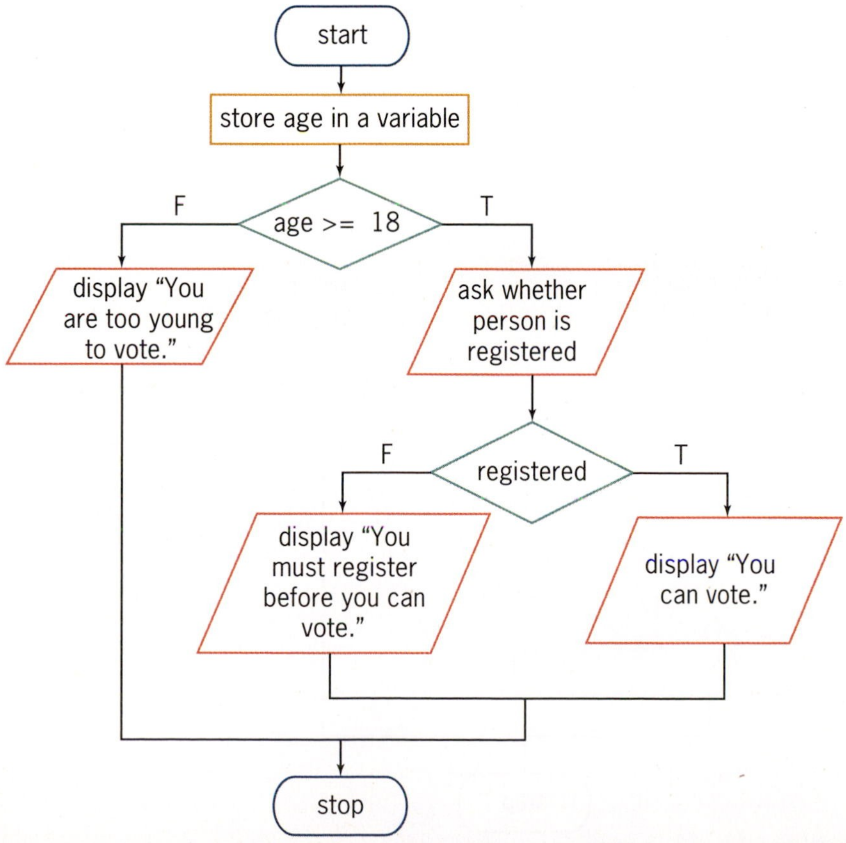

Figure 5-6 Problem specification and a correct solution for the voter eligibility problem

Even small problems can have more than one solution. Figure 5-7 shows another correct solution, also in flowchart form, for the voter eligibility problem. As in the previous solution, the outer selection structure in this solution determines the age (the primary decision), and the nested selection structure determines the voter registration status (the secondary decision). In this solution, however, the outer structure's condition is the opposite of the one in Figure 5-6: It checks whether the person's age is less than 18 rather than checking if it is greater than or equal to 18. (Recall that *less than* is the opposite of *greater than or equal to*.) In addition, the nested structure appears in the outer structure's false path in this solution, which means it will be processed only when the outer structure's condition evaluates to False. The solutions in Figures 5-6 and 5-7 produce the same results. Neither solution is better than the other; each simply represents a different way of solving the same problem.

Problem Specification

Create an application that displays one of three messages, as shown here. The application's interface will provide a text box for entering the person's age. It will use a message box to ask the user whether the person is registered to vote.

Messages	Criteria
You are too young to vote.	person is younger than 18 years old
You can vote.	person is at least 18 years old and is registered to vote
You must register before you can vote.	person is at least 18 years old but is not registered to vote

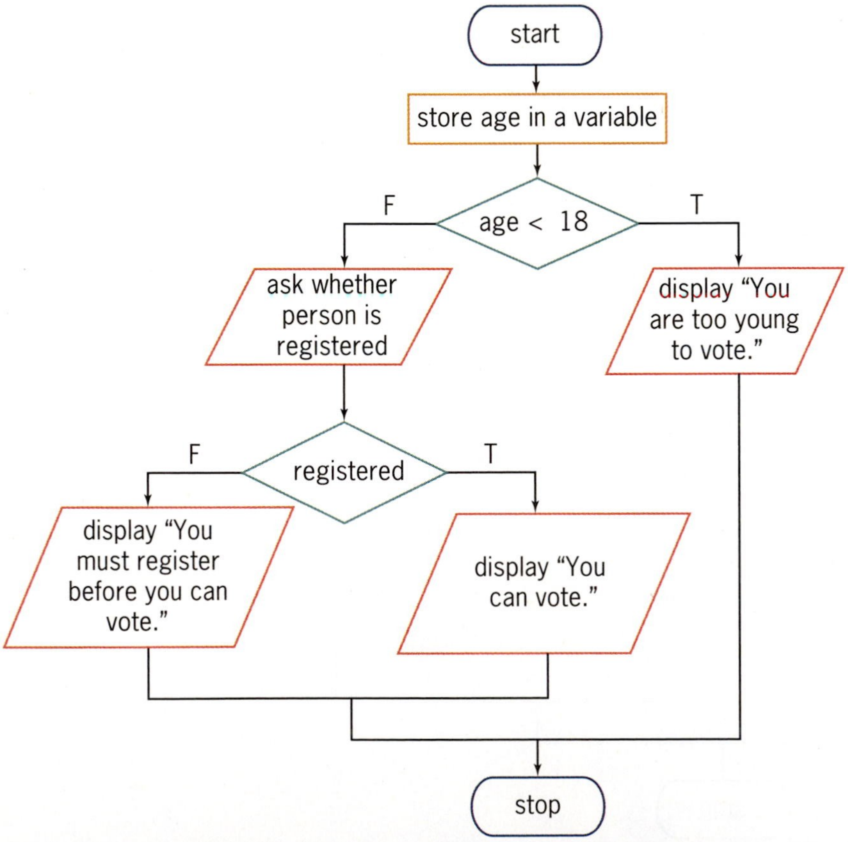

Figure 5-7 Another correct solution for the voter eligibility problem

Coding a Nested Selection Structure

Figure 5-8 shows examples of code that could be used for the voter eligibility application. The first example corresponds to the flowchart in Figure 5-6, and the second example corresponds to the flowchart in Figure 5-7.

```vb
Example 1: Code for the flowchart in Figure 5-6
Const strTOO_YOUNG As String = "You are too young to vote."
Const strMUST_REGISTER As String =
    "You must register before you can vote."
Const strCAN_VOTE As String = "You can vote."
Const strPROMPT As String = "Are you registered to vote?"
Dim intAge As Integer
Dim dlgButton As DialogResult

Integer.TryParse(txtAge.Text, intAge)

If intAge >= 18 Then
    dlgButton = MessageBox.Show(strPROMPT,
                "Voter Eligibility",
                MessageBoxButtons.YesNo,
                MessageBoxIcon.Exclamation)
    If dlgButton = DialogResult.Yes Then
        lblMsg.Text = strCAN_VOTE
    Else
        lblMsg.Text = strMUST_REGISTER
    End If
Else
    lblMsg.Text = strTOO_YOUNG
End If

Example 2: Code for the flowchart in Figure 5-7
Const strTOO_YOUNG As String = "You are too young to vote."
Const strMUST_REGISTER As String =
    "You must register before you can vote."
Const strCAN_VOTE As String = "You can vote."
Const strPROMPT As String = "Are you registered to vote?"
Dim intAge As Integer
Dim dlgButton As DialogResult
```

Figure 5-8   Code for the flowcharts in Figures 5-6 and 5-7 (continues)

(continued)

```
Integer.TryParse(txtAge.Text, intAge)

If intAge < 18 Then
    lblMsg.Text = strTOO_YOUNG
Else
    dlgButton = MessageBox.Show(strPROMPT,
                "Voter Eligibility",
                MessageBoxButtons.YesNo,
                MessageBoxIcon.Exclamation)
    If dlgButton = DialogResult.Yes Then
        lblMsg.Text = strCAN_VOTE
    Else
        lblMsg.Text = strMUST_REGISTER
    End If
End If
```

Figure 5-8   Code for the flowcharts in Figures 5-6 and 5-7

START HERE ▶

To code and then test the Voter Eligibility application:

1. If necessary, start Visual Studio 2015. Open the VB2015\Chap05\Voter Solution\Voter Solution (Voter Solution.sln) file. Open the Code Editor window. Replace <your name> and <current date> in the comments with your name and the current date, respectively.

2. Locate the btnDisplay_Click procedure. Enter the selection structures shown in either of the examples in Figure 5-8.

3. Save the solution and then start the application. Type **27** in the Enter age box and then press **Enter**. A message box opens and displays the "Are you registered to vote?" message. Click the **No** button. See Figure 5-9.

Figure 5-9   Sample run of the Voter Eligibility application

4. Click the **Display Message** button, and then press **Enter** to select the Yes button in the message box. The "You can vote." message appears in the lblMsg control.

5. Change the age to **17** and then press **Enter**. The "You are too young to vote." message appears in the lblMsg control.

6. Click the **Exit** button. Close the Code Editor window and then close the solution.

YOU DO IT 1!

Create an application named YouDoIt 1 and save it in the VB2015\Chap05 folder. Add a label and two buttons to the form. The application should display the price of a CD (compact disc) in the label. The prices are shown below. Code the first button's Click event procedure using a nested selection structure in the outer selection structure's true path. Code the second button's Click event procedure using a nested selection structure in the outer selection structure's false path. In both Click event procedures, use a message box with Yes and No buttons to determine whether the customer has a coupon. If the customer has a coupon, use a message box with Yes and No buttons to determine whether they have the $2 coupon. (A customer can use only one coupon.) Save the solution, and then start and test the application. Close the solution.

Prices	Criteria
$12	customer does not have a coupon
$10	customer has a $2 coupon
$ 8	customer has a $4 coupon

Logic Errors in Selection Structures

In the next few sections, you will observe some of the common logic errors made when writing selection structures. Being aware of these errors will help you avoid making them. In most cases, logic errors in selection structures are a result of one of the following four mistakes:

1. using a compound condition rather than a nested selection structure

2. reversing the decisions in the outer and nested selection structures

3. using an unnecessary nested selection structure

4. including an unnecessary comparison in a condition

It's easier to understand these four logic errors by viewing them in a procedure. We will present the first three errors using a procedure that displays the daily fee for renting a car, and we'll illustrate the last error using a procedure that displays an item's price. Let's begin with the daily car rental fee procedure. The procedure's problem specification along with a correct algorithm (written in pseudocode) are shown in Figure 5-10. An **algorithm** is the set of step-by-step instructions for accomplishing a task.

Problem Specification

Sam's Car Rental wants an application that displays the daily fee for renting a car. The daily fee is $55; however, there is an additional charge for renting a luxury car. The additional charge depends on whether the customer belongs to Sam's Car Rental Club, as indicated in the chart shown here:

Daily fee:	$55
Additional daily charge for luxury car:	
Club member	$20
Nonmember	$30

Correct algorithm
1. daily fee = 55
2. if luxury car
      if club member
          add 20 to the daily fee
      else
          add 30 to the daily fee
      end if
   end if
3. display the daily fee

Figure 5-10 Problem specification and a correct algorithm for Sam's Car Rental

Notice that the car's classification determines whether the renter is charged an additional amount. If the car is classified as a luxury vehicle, then whether the customer is a club member determines the appropriate additional amount. In this case, the decision regarding the car's classification is the primary decision, while the decision regarding the customer's membership status is the secondary decision.

The Ch05A-Rental Correct Desk-Check

You can verify that the algorithm in Figure 5-10 works correctly by desk-checking it. **Desk-checking** refers to the process of reviewing the algorithm while seated at your desk rather than in front of the computer. Desk-checking is also called **hand-tracing** because you use a pencil and paper to follow each of the algorithm's instructions by hand. You desk-check an algorithm to verify that it is not missing any instructions and that the existing instructions are correct and in the proper order.

Before you begin the desk-check, you first choose a set of sample data for the input values, which you then use to manually compute the expected output values. Figure 5-11 shows the input values you will use to desk-check Figure 5-10's algorithm four times; it also includes the expected output values.

Desk-check	Car classification	Membership status	Expected daily fee
1	standard	member	$55
2	standard	nonmember	$55
3	luxury	member	$75
4	luxury	nonmember	$85

Figure 5-11 Sample data and expected results for the algorithm shown in Figure 5-10

In Figure 5-11, the first set of test data is for a club member renting a standard vehicle. Step 1 in Figure 5-10's algorithm assigns $55 as the daily fee. Next, the condition in the outer selection structure determines whether the car is a luxury vehicle. The condition evaluates to False; as a result, the outer selection structure ends without processing the nested selection structure. This is because the membership information is not important when the car is not a luxury vehicle. The last step in the algorithm displays the expected daily fee of $55.

Next, we'll desk-check the algorithm using the second set of test data: standard vehicle and nonmember. The algorithm begins by assigning $55 as the daily fee. The condition in the outer selection structure then determines whether the car is a luxury vehicle. The condition evaluates to False; as a result, the outer selection structure ends. The last step in the algorithm displays the expected daily fee, $55.

Next, we'll desk-check the algorithm using the third set of test data: luxury vehicle and club member. First, the algorithm assigns $55 as the daily fee. Then the condition in the outer selection structure determines whether the car is a luxury vehicle. In this case, the condition evaluates to True, so the nested selection structure's condition checks whether the customer is a club member. This condition also evaluates to True, so the nested structure's true path adds $20 to the daily fee, giving $75; after doing this, both selection structures end. The last step in the algorithm displays the expected daily fee, $75.

Finally, we'll desk-check the algorithm using the fourth set of test data: luxury vehicle and nonmember. Step 1 assigns $55 as the daily fee. The condition in the outer selection structure determines whether the car is a luxury vehicle. The condition evaluates to True, so the nested selection structure's condition checks whether the customer is a club member. This condition evaluates to False, so the nested structure's false path adds $30 to the daily fee, giving $85; after doing this, both selection structures end. The last step in the algorithm displays the expected daily fee of $85. The results of desk-checking the algorithm using the data from Figure 5-11 agree with the expected values, as indicated in Figure 5-12.

Desk-check	Car classification	Membership status	Expected daily fee	Actual result
1	standard	member	$55	$55 (correct)
2	standard	nonmember	$55	$55 (correct)
3	luxury	member	$75	$75 (correct)
4	luxury	nonmember	$85	$85 (correct)

Figure 5-12 Actual results included in the desk-check chart

First Logic Error: Using a Compound Condition Rather than a Nested Selection Structure

A common error made when writing selection structures is to use a compound condition in the outer selection structure when a nested selection structure is needed. Figure 5-13 shows an example of this error in the car rental algorithm. The correct algorithm is included in the figure for comparison. Notice that the incorrect algorithm uses one selection structure rather than two selection structures and that the selection structure contains a compound condition. Consider why the selection structure in the incorrect algorithm cannot be used in place of the selection structures in the correct one. In the correct algorithm, the outer and nested structures indicate that a hierarchy exists between the car classification and membership status decisions: The car classification decision is always made first, followed by the membership status decision (if necessary). In the incorrect algorithm, the compound condition indicates that no hierarchy exists between the classification and membership decisions. Consider how this difference changes the algorithm.

```
Correct algorithm                          Incorrect algorithm (first logic error)
1. daily fee = 55                          1. daily fee = 55
2. if luxury car                           2. if luxury car and club member ──────  uses a compound
       if club member                             add 20 to the daily fee             condition instead
             add 20 to the daily fee       else                                       of a nested
       else                                        add 30 to the daily fee            selection structure
             add 30 to the daily fee       end if
       end if                              3. display the daily fee
   end if
3. display the daily fee
```

Figure 5-13   Correct algorithm and an incorrect algorithm containing the first logic error

The Ch05A-First Logic Error Desk-Check

To understand why the incorrect algorithm in Figure 5-13 will not work correctly, we will desk-check it using the same test data used to desk-check the correct algorithm. Step 1 in the incorrect algorithm assigns $55 as the daily fee. Next, the compound condition in Step 2 determines whether the car is classified as a luxury vehicle and, at the same time, whether the renter is a club member. Using the first set of test data (standard and member), the compound condition evaluates to False because the car is not a luxury vehicle. As a result, the selection structure's false path adds $30 to the daily fee, giving $85, and then the selection structure ends. The last step in the incorrect algorithm displays $85 as the daily fee, which is not correct; the correct fee is $55, as shown earlier in Figure 5-12.

Next, we'll desk-check the incorrect algorithm using the second set of test data: standard and nonmember. The algorithm begins by assigning $55 as the daily fee. The compound condition then determines whether the car is a luxury vehicle and, at the same time, whether the renter is a club member. The compound condition evaluates to False, so the selection structure's false path adds $30 to the daily fee, giving $85, and then the selection structure ends. The last step in the incorrect algorithm displays $85 as the daily fee, which is not correct; the correct fee is $55, as shown earlier in Figure 5-12.

Next, we'll desk-check the incorrect algorithm using the third set of test data: luxury and member. First, the algorithm assigns $55 as the daily fee. The compound condition then determines whether the car is a luxury vehicle and, at the same time, whether the renter is a club member. In this case, the compound condition evaluates to True, so the selection structure's true path adds $20 to the daily fee, giving $75, and then the selection structure ends. The last step in the incorrect algorithm displays the expected daily fee, $75. Even though its selection structure is phrased incorrectly, the incorrect algorithm produces the same result as the correct algorithm using the third set of test data.

Finally, we'll desk-check the incorrect algorithm using the fourth set of test data: luxury and nonmember. Step 1 assigns $55 as the daily fee. Next, the compound condition determines whether the car is a luxury vehicle and, at the same time, whether the renter is a club member. The compound condition evaluates to False because the renter is not a club member. As a result, the selection structure's false path adds $30 to the daily fee, giving $85, and then the selection structure ends. The last step in the incorrect algorithm displays $85 as the daily fee, which is correct. Here, too, even though its selection structure is phrased incorrectly, the incorrect algorithm produces the same result as the correct algorithm using the fourth set of test data.

Figure 5-14 shows the desk-check table for the incorrect algorithm from Figure 5-13. As indicated in the figure, only the results of the third and fourth desk-checks are correct.

Desk-check	Car classification	Membership status	Expected rental fee	Actual result
1	standard	member	$55	$85 (incorrect)
2	standard	nonmember	$55	$85 (incorrect)
3	luxury	member	$75	$75 (correct)
4	luxury	nonmember	$85	$85 (correct)

Figure 5-14   Results of desk-checking the incorrect algorithm from Figure 5-13

We cannot overemphasize the importance of desk-checking an algorithm several times using different data. For example, if we had used only the last two sets of data to desk-check the incorrect algorithm, we would not have discovered that the algorithm did not work as intended.

Second Logic Error: Reversing the Outer and Nested Decisions

Another common error made when writing selection structures is to reverse the order of the decisions made by the outer and nested structures. Figure 5-15 shows an example of this error in the car rental algorithm. The correct algorithm is included in the figure for comparison. Unlike the selection structures in the correct algorithm, which determine the car classification before determining the membership status, the selection structures in the incorrect algorithm determine the membership status before determining the car classification.

Consider how this difference changes the algorithm. In the correct algorithm, the selection structures indicate that only renters of luxury cars pay an additional amount. The selection structures in the incorrect algorithm, on the other hand, indicate that the additional amount is paid by club members only. Figure 5-16 shows the result of desk-checking the incorrect algorithm from Figure 5-15. As indicated in the figure, only two of the four results are correct.

The Ch05A-Second Logic Error Desk-Check

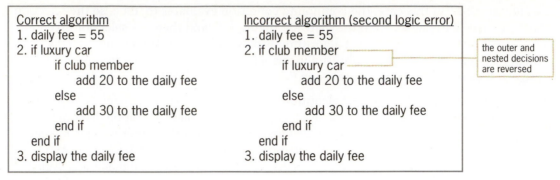

```
Correct algorithm                          Incorrect algorithm (second logic error)
1. daily fee = 55                          1. daily fee = 55
2. if luxury car                           2. if club member
       if club member                             if luxury car
             add 20 to the daily fee                   add 20 to the daily fee
       else                                       else
             add 30 to the daily fee                   add 30 to the daily fee
       end if                                     end if
   end if                                     end if
3. display the daily fee                   3. display the daily fee
```

the outer and nested decisions are reversed

Figure 5-15   Correct algorithm and an incorrect algorithm containing the second logic error

Desk-check	Car classification	Membership status	Expected rental fee	Actual result
1	standard	member	$55	$85 (incorrect)
2	standard	nonmember	$55	$55 (correct)
3	luxury	member	$75	$75 (correct)
4	luxury	nonmember	$85	$55 (incorrect)

Figure 5-16   Results of desk-checking the incorrect algorithm from Figure 5-15

Third Logic Error: Using an Unnecessary Nested Selection Structure

Another common error made when writing selection structures is to include an unnecessary nested selection structure. In most cases, a selection structure containing this error will still produce the correct results. However, it will do so less efficiently than selection structures that are properly structured.

The Ch05A-Third Logic Error Desk-Check

Figure 5-17 shows an example of this error in the car rental algorithm. The correct algorithm is included in the figure for comparison. Unlike the correct algorithm, which contains two selection structures, the inefficient algorithm contains three selection structures. The condition in the third selection structure determines whether the renter is *not* a member of the rental club and is processed only when the second selection structure's condition evaluates to False. In other words, it is processed only when the procedure has already determined that the renter is *not* a club member. Therefore, the third selection structure is unnecessary. Figure 5-18 shows the results of desk-checking the inefficient algorithm. Although the results of the four desk-checks are correct, the result of the last desk-check is obtained in a less efficient manner.

```
Correct algorithm                          Inefficient algorithm (third logic error)
1. daily fee = 55                          1. daily fee = 55
2. if luxury car                           2. if luxury car
       if club member                             if club member
             add 20 to the daily fee                   add 20 to the daily fee
       else                                       else
             add 30 to the daily fee                   if nonmember
       end if                                           add 30 to the daily fee
   end if                                           end if
3. display the daily fee                         end if
                                              end if
                                           3. display the daily fee
```

unnecessary nested selection structure

Figure 5-17   Correct algorithm and an inefficient algorithm containing the third logic error

Desk-check	Car classification	Membership status	Expected daily fee	Actual result
1	standard	member	$55	$55 (correct)
2	standard	nonmember	$55	$55 (correct)
3	luxury	member	$75	$75 (correct)
4	luxury	nonmember	$85	$85 (correct)

result obtained in a less efficient manner

Figure 5-18   Results of desk-checking the inefficient algorithm from Figure 5-17

Fourth Logic Error: Including an Unnecessary Comparison in a Condition

Another common error made when writing selection structures is to include an unnecessary comparison in a condition. Like selection structures containing the third logic error, selection structures containing this error also produce the correct results in an inefficient way. We'll demonstrate this error using a procedure that displays an item's price, which is based on the quantity purchased. Figure 5-19 shows the problem specification, a correct algorithm, and an inefficient algorithm that contains the fourth logic error.

The Ch05A-Fourth Logic Error Desk-Check

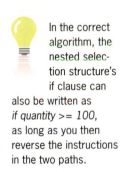

In the correct algorithm, the nested selection structure's if clause can also be written as *if quantity >= 100*, as long as you then reverse the instructions in the two paths.

Problem Specification

Create an application that displays the price of an item. The price depends on the quantity purchased, as shown here:

Quantity purchased	Price per item ($)
Less than or equal to 0	0.0
1–99	9.50
Greater than 99	7.75

Correct algorithm
```
1. if quantity <= 0
        price = 0
   else
        if quantity < 100
            price = 9.50
        else
            price = 7.75
        end if
   end if
2. display the price
```

Inefficient algorithm
```
1. if quantity <= 0
        price = 0                    unnecessary
   else                              comparison
        if quantity > 0 and quantity < 100
            price = 9.50
        else
            price = 7.75
        end if
   end if
2. display the price
```

Figure 5-19   Problem specification, a correct algorithm, and an inefficient algorithm

---

Unlike the nested selection structure in the correct algorithm, the nested structure in the inefficient algorithm contains a compound condition that compares the quantity to both 0 and 100. Consider why the comparison to 0 in the compound condition is unnecessary. If the quantity *is* less than or equal to 0, the outer selection structure's condition will evaluate to True. As a result, the outer selection structure's true path will assign the number 0 as the price before the outer structure ends. In other words, a quantity that is either less than or equal to 0 will be handled by the outer structure's true path. The nested selection structure's condition will be evaluated only when the quantity is greater than 0. Therefore, the comparison to 0 is unnecessary in the compound condition. Figure 5-20 shows the results of desk-checking the correct and inefficient algorithms. Although the results of the three desk-checks for the inefficient algorithm are correct, the results of the second and third desk-checks are obtained in a less efficient manner.

Correct Algorithm

Desk-check	Quantity	Expected price	Actual result
1	−2	0	0 (correct)
2	83	9.50	9.50 (correct)
3	105	7.75	7.75 (correct)

Inefficient Algorithm

Desk-check	Quantity	Expected price	Actual result
1	−2	0	0 (correct)
2	83	9.50	9.50 (correct) — results obtained in a less efficient manner
3	105	7.75	7.75 (correct) —

Figure 5-20   Results of desk-checking the algorithms from Figure 5-19

Note: You have learned a lot so far in this lesson. You may want to take a break at this point before continuing.

Multiple-Alternative Selection Structures

Figure 5-21 shows the problem specification for the Snowboard Shop application. The application's solution requires a selection structure that can choose from several different item codes. As the figure indicates, when the code is 12, the application should display "Tennessee" as the warehouse location. When the code is 36, it should display "Kentucky". And when the code is either 40 or 43, it should display "Louisiana". Finally, when the code is not 12, 36, 40, or 43, it should display the "Invalid code" message. Selection structures containing several alternatives are referred to as **multiple-alternative selection structures** or **extended selection structures**.

Problem Specification

Each item sold by the Snowboard Shop has a code that identifies the location of the warehouse in which it is stored. Create an application that displays the location corresponding to the code entered by the user. The valid codes and their corresponding warehouse locations are shown here. If the item code entered by the user is not listed here, the application should display the "Invalid code" message.

Item code	Warehouse location
12	Tennessee
36	Kentucky
40, 43	Louisiana

Figure 5-21   Problem specification for the Snowboard Shop application

Figure 5-22 shows the pseudocode and flowchart for a procedure that displays the appropriate output. The diamond in the flowchart represents the condition in the multiple-alternative selection structure. Recall that the diamond is also used to represent the condition in both the single-alternative and dual-alternative selection structures. However, unlike the diamond in both of those selection structures, the diamond in a multiple-alternative selection structure has several flowlines (rather than only two flowlines) leading out of the symbol. Each flowline represents a possible path and must be marked appropriately, indicating the value or values necessary for the path to be chosen.

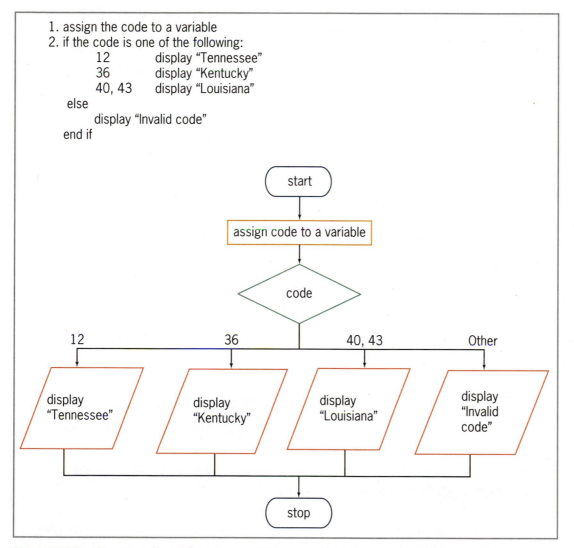

```
1. assign the code to a variable
2. if the code is one of the following:
        12          display "Tennessee"
        36          display "Kentucky"
        40, 43      display "Louisiana"
   else
        display "Invalid code"
   end if
```

Figure 5-22   Pseudocode and flowchart containing a multiple-alternative selection structure

Figure 5-23 shows two versions of the code corresponding to the multiple-alternative selection structure from Figure 5-22; both versions use If...Then...Else statements. Although both versions produce the same result, Version 2 provides a more convenient way of coding a multiple-alternative selection structure.

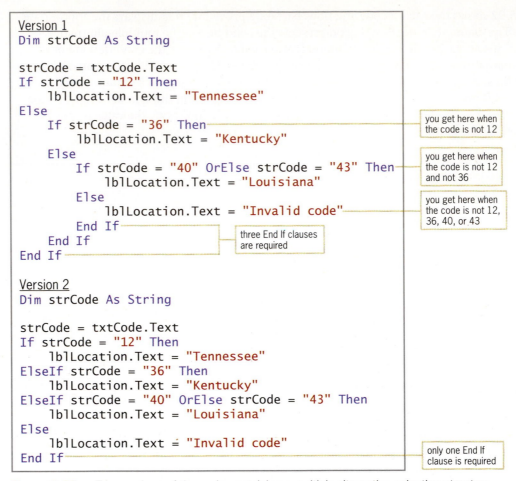

```
Version 1
Dim strCode As String

strCode = txtCode.Text
If strCode = "12" Then
    lblLocation.Text = "Tennessee"
Else
    If strCode = "36" Then
        lblLocation.Text = "Kentucky"
    Else
        If strCode = "40" OrElse strCode = "43" Then
            lblLocation.Text = "Louisiana"
        Else
            lblLocation.Text = "Invalid code"
        End If
    End If
End If
```

you get here when the code is not 12

you get here when the code is not 12 and not 36

you get here when the code is not 12, 36, 40, or 43

three End If clauses are required

```
Version 2
Dim strCode As String

strCode = txtCode.Text
If strCode = "12" Then
    lblLocation.Text = "Tennessee"
ElseIf strCode = "36" Then
    lblLocation.Text = "Kentucky"
ElseIf strCode = "40" OrElse strCode = "43" Then
    lblLocation.Text = "Louisiana"
Else
    lblLocation.Text = "Invalid code"
End If
```

only one End If clause is required

Figure 5-23   Two versions of the code containing a multiple-alternative selection structure

START HERE

To code and then test the Snowboard Shop application:

1. Open the Snowboard Solution (Snowboard Solution.sln) file contained in the VB2015\Chap05\Snowboard Solution-If folder. Open the Code Editor window. Replace <your name> and <current date> in the comments with your name and the current date, respectively.

2. Locate the btnDisplay_Click procedure. Beginning in the blank line below the assignment statement, enter the multiple-alternative selection structure shown in Version 2 in Figure 5-23.

3. Save the solution and then start the application. Type **40** and then click the **Display** button. See Figure 5-24.

Figure 5-24   Louisiana message shown in the interface

4. On your own, test the application using the following codes: **12**, **36**, **43**, and **7**. When you are finished testing, click the **Exit** button. Close the Code Editor window and then close the solution.

YOU DO IT 2!

Create an application named YouDoIt 2 and save it in the VB2015\Chap05 folder. Add a text box, a label, and a button to the form. The button's Click event procedure should display (in the label) either the price of a concert ticket or the N/A message. The ticket price is based on the code entered in the text box, as shown below. Code the procedure. Save the solution, and then start and test the application. Close the solution.

Code	Ticket price
1	$15
2	$15
3	$25
4	$35
5	$37
Other	N/A

The Select Case Statement

When a multiple-alternative selection structure has many paths from which to choose, it is often simpler and clearer to code the selection structure using the **Select Case statement** rather than several If...Then...Else statements. The Select Case statement's syntax is shown in Figure 5-25. The figure also shows how you can use the statement to code the multiple-alternative selection structure from Figure 5-23.

Select Case Statement

Syntax
Select Case *selectorExpression*
    Case *expressionList1*
       instructions for the first Case
    [**Case** *expressionList2*
       instructions for the second Case]
    [**Case** *expressionListN*
       instructions for the Nth Case]
    [**Case Else**
       instructions for when the selectorExpression does not match any of the expressionLists]
End Select

Example
```
Dim strCode As String

strCode = txtCode.Text
Select Case strCode
    Case "12"
        lblLocation.Text = "Tennessee"
    Case "36"
        lblLocation.Text = "Kentucky"
    Case "40", "43"
        lblLocation.Text = "Louisiana"
    Case Else
        lblLocation.Text = "Invalid code"
End Select
```

the *selectorExpression* needs to match only one of these values

Figure 5-25   Syntax and an example of the Select Case statement

The Select Case statement begins with the keywords `Select Case`, followed by a *selectorExpression*. The selectorExpression can contain any combination of variables, constants, keywords, functions, methods, operators, and properties. In the example in Figure 5-25, the selectorExpression is a String variable named `strCode`. The Select Case statement ends with the End Select clause. Between the Select Case and End Select clauses are the individual Case clauses. Each Case clause represents a different path that the computer can follow. It is customary to indent each Case clause and the instructions within each Case clause, as shown in the figure. You can have as many Case clauses as necessary in a Select Case statement. However, if the Select Case statement includes a Case Else clause, the Case Else clause must be the last clause in the statement.

Each of the individual Case clauses except the Case Else clause must contain an *expressionList*, which can include one or more expressions. To include more than one expression in an expressionList, you separate each expression with a comma, like this: `Case "40", "43"`. The selectorExpression needs to match only one of the expressions listed in an expressionList. The data type of the expressions must be compatible with the data type of the selectorExpression. If the selectorExpression is numeric, the expressions in the Case clauses should be numeric. Likewise, if the selectorExpression is a string, the expressions should be strings. In the example in Figure 5-25, the selectorExpression (`strCode`) is a string, and so are the expressions `"12"`, `"36"`, `"40"`, and `"43"`.

The Select Case statement looks more complicated than it really is. When processing the statement, the computer simply compares the value of the selectorExpression with the value or values listed in each of the Case clauses, one Case clause at a time beginning with the first. If the selectorExpression matches at least one of the values listed in a Case clause, the computer processes only the instructions contained in that Case clause. After the Case clause instructions are processed, the Select Case statement ends and the computer skips to the instruction following the End Select clause. For instance, if the `strCode` variable in the example shown in Figure 5-25 contains the string "12", the computer will display the "Tennessee" message and then skip to the instruction following the End Select clause. Similarly, if the variable contains the string "40", the computer will display the "Louisiana" message and then skip to the instruction following the End Select clause. Keep in mind that if the selectorExpression matches a value in more than one Case clause, only the instructions in the first match's Case clause are processed.

The Ch05A-Select Case

If the selectorExpression does *not* match any of the values listed in any of the Case clauses, the next instruction processed depends on whether the Select Case statement contains a Case Else clause. If there *is* a Case Else clause, the computer processes the instructions in that clause and then skips to the instruction following the End Select clause. (Recall that the Case Else clause and its instructions immediately precede the End Select clause.) If there *isn't* a Case Else clause, the computer just skips to the instruction following the End Select clause.

To use the Select Case statement in the Snowboard Shop application:

START HERE

1. Open the Snowboard Solution (Snowboard Solution.sln) file contained in the VB2015\Chap05\Snowboard Solution-Select Case folder. Open the Code Editor window. Replace <your name> and <current date> in the comments with your name and the current date, respectively.

2. Locate the btnDisplay_Click procedure. Beginning in the blank line below the assignment statement, enter the Select Case statement shown in Figure 5-25.

3. Save the solution and then start the application. Type **40** and then click the **Display** button. The "Louisiana" message appears in the interface, as shown earlier in Figure 5-24.

4. On your own, test the application using the following codes: **12**, **36**, **43**, and **7**. When you are finished testing, click the **Exit** button. Close the Code Editor window and then close the solution.

Specifying a Range of Values in a Case Clause

In addition to specifying one or more discrete values in a Case clause, you can also specify a range of values, such as the values 1 through 4 or values greater than 10. You do this using either the keyword To or the keyword Is. You use the To keyword when you know both the upper and lower values in the range. The Is keyword is appropriate when you know only one end of the range (either the upper or lower end).

Figure 5-26 shows the syntax for using the Is and To keywords in a Case clause. It also contains an example of a Select Case statement that assigns a price based on the number of items ordered.

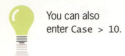

You can also enter `Case > 10`.

Specifying a Range of Values in a Case Clause

<u>Syntax</u>
Case *smallest value in the range* **To** *largest value in the range*
Case Is *comparisonOperator value*

Note: Be sure to test your code thoroughly because the computer will not display an error message when the value preceding To in a Case clause is greater than the value following To. Instead, the Select Case statement will not give the correct results.

<u>Example</u>
The ABC Corporation's price chart is shown here:

<u>Quantity ordered</u>	<u>Price per item</u>
1–5	$25
6–10	$23
More than 10	$20
Fewer than 1	$0

```
Select Case intQuantity
    Case 1 To 5
        intPrice = 25
    Case 6 To 10
        intPrice = 23
    Case Is > 10
        intPrice = 20
    Case Else
        intPrice = 0
End Select
```

Figure 5-26 Syntax and an example of specifying a range of values

According to the price chart shown in the figure, the price for 1 to 5 items is $25 each. Using discrete values, the first Case clause would look like this: `Case 1, 2, 3, 4, 5`. However, a more convenient way of writing that range of numbers is to use the `To` keyword, like this: `Case 1 To 5`. The expression `1 To 5` specifies the range of numbers from 1 to 5, inclusive. The expression `6 To 10` in the second Case clause in the example specifies the range of numbers from 6 through 10. Notice that both Case clauses state both the lower (1 and 6) and upper (5 and 10) values in each range.

The third Case clause, `Case Is > 10`, contains the `Is` keyword rather than the `To` keyword. Recall that you use the `Is` keyword when you know only one end of the range of values. In this case, you know only the lower end of the range, 10. The `Is` keyword is always used in combination with one of the following comparison operators: =, <, <=, >, >=, <>. The `Case Is > 10` clause specifies all numbers greater than the number 10. Because `intQuantity` is an Integer variable, you can also write this Case clause as `Case Is >= 11`. The Case Else clause in the example in Figure 5-26 is processed only when the `intQuantity` variable contains a value that is not included in any of the previous Case clauses.

To code and then test the ABC Corporation application:

1. Open the VB2015\Chap05\ABC Solution\ABC Solution (ABC Solution.sln) file. Open the Code Editor window. Replace <your name> and <current date> in the comments with your name and the current date, respectively.

2. Locate the btnDisplay_Click procedure. Beginning in the blank line below the second comment, enter the Select Case statement shown in Figure 5-26.

3. Save the solution and then start the application. Type **7** in the Quantity ordered box and then press **Enter**. See Figure 5-27.

Figure 5-27   Price per item shown in the interface

4. On your own, test the application using **4**, **11**, and **0** as the quantity ordered. When you are finished testing, click the **Exit** button. Close the Code Editor window and then close the solution.

YOU DO IT 3!

Create an application named YouDoIt 3 and save it in the VB2015\Chap05 folder. Add a text box, a label, and a button to the form. The button's Click event procedure should display (in the label) either the price of a concert ticket or the N/A message. The ticket price is based on the code entered in the text box, as shown here. Code the procedure using the Select Case statement. Save the solution, and then start and test the application. Close the solution.

Code	Ticket price
1	$15
2	$15
3	$25
4	$35
5	$37
Other	N/A

Lesson A Summary

- To create a selection structure that evaluates both a primary and a secondary decision:

  Place (nest) the secondary decision's selection structure entirely within either the true or false path of the primary decision's selection structure.

- To verify that an algorithm works correctly:

  Desk-check (hand-trace) the algorithm.

- To code a multiple-alternative selection structure:

  Use either If...Then...Else statements or the Select Case statement.

- To specify a range of values in a Select Case statement's Case clause:

  Use the To keyword when you know both the upper and lower values in the range. Use the Is keyword when you know only one end of the range. The Is keyword is used in combination with one of the following comparison operators: =, <, <=, >, >=, <>.

Lesson A Key Terms

Algorithm—a set of step-by-step instructions for accomplishing a task

Desk-checking—the process of using sample data to manually walk through the steps in an algorithm; also called hand-tracing

Extended selection structures—another name for multiple-alternative selection structures

Hand-tracing—another term for desk-checking

Multiple-alternative selection structures—selection structures that contain several alternatives; also called extended selection structures; can be coded using either If...Then...Else statements or the Select Case statement

Nested selection structure—a selection structure that is wholly contained (nested) within either the true or false path of another selection structure

Select Case statement—used to code a multiple-alternative selection structure in Visual Basic

Lesson A Review Questions

Use the code shown in Figure 5-28 to answer Review Questions 1 through 4.

```
If dblSales <= 0 Then
    dblRate = 0
ElseIf dblSales < 460 Then
    dblRate = 0.05
ElseIf dblSales < 1000 Then
    dblRate = 0.1
Else
    dblRate = 0.15
End If
```

Figure 5-28   Code for Review Questions 1 through 4

1. What will the code in Figure 5-28 assign to the **dblRate** variable when the **dblSales** variable contains the number 459.99?

    a. 0   c. 0.1
    b. 0.05   d. 0.15

2. What will the code in Figure 5-28 assign to the **dblRate** variable when the **dblSales** variable contains the number 0?

    a. 0   c. 0.1
    b. 0.05   d. 0.15

3. What will the code in Figure 5-28 assign to the **dblRate** variable when the **dblSales** variable contains the number 999.75?

    a. 0   c. 0.1
    b. 0.05   d. 0.15

4. What will the code in Figure 5-28 assign to the **dblRate** variable when the **dblSales** variable contains the number 1000?

    a. 0   c. 0.1
    b. 0.05   d. 0.15

Use the code shown in Figure 5-29 to answer Review Questions 5 through 8.

```
If strLevel = "1" OrElse strLevel = "2" Then
    lblStatus.Text = "Bronze"
ElseIf strLevel = "3" OrElse strLevel = "4" Then
    lblStatus.Text = "Silver"
ElseIf strLevel = "5" Then
    lblStatus.Text = "Gold"
Else
    lblStatus.Text = "Platinum"
End If
```

Figure 5-29   Code for Review Questions 5 through 8

5. What will the code in Figure 5-29 assign to the lblStatus control when the **strLevel** variable contains the string "2"?

    a. Bronze   c. Platinum
    b. Gold   d. Silver

6. What will the code in Figure 5-29 assign to the lblStatus control when the **strLevel** variable contains the string "5"?

    a. Bronze   c. Platinum
    b. Gold   d. Silver

7. What will the code in Figure 5-29 assign to the lblStatus control when the **strLevel** variable contains the string "10"?

    a. Bronze   c. Platinum
    b. Gold   d. Silver

8. What will the code in Figure 5-29 assign to the lblStatus control when the `strLevel` variable contains the string "3"?

    a. Bronze

    b. Gold

    c. Platinum

    d. Silver

9. A nested selection structure can appear _____.

    a. only in an outer selection structure's false path

    b. only in an outer selection structure's true path

    c. in either an outer selection structure's true path or its false path

10. Which of the following Case clauses is valid in a Select Case statement whose selectorExpression is an Integer variable named `intCode`?

    a. `Case Is > 7`

    b. `Case 3, 5`

    c. `Case 1 To 4`

    d. all of the above

Use the code shown in Figure 5-30 to answer Review Questions 11 through 14.

```
Select Case intLevel
    Case 1, 2
        strStatus = "Bronze"
    Case 3 To 5
        strStatus = "Silver"
    Case 6, 7
        strStatus = "Gold"
    Case Else
        strStatus = "Platinum"
End Select
```

Figure 5-30   Code for Review Questions 11 through 14

11. What will the code in Figure 5-30 assign to the `strStatus` variable when the `intLevel` variable contains the number 4?

    a. Bronze

    b. Gold

    c. Platinum

    d. Silver

12. What will the code in Figure 5-30 assign to the `strStatus` variable when the `intLevel` variable contains the number 8?

    a. Bronze

    b. Gold

    c. Platinum

    d. Silver

13. What will the code in Figure 5-30 assign to the `strStatus` variable when the `intLevel` variable contains the number 7?

    a. Bronze

    b. Gold

    c. Platinum

    d. Silver

14. What will the code in Figure 5-30 assign to the `strStatus` variable when the `intLevel` variable contains the number 1?

    a. Bronze

    b. Gold

    c. Platinum

    d. Silver

15. List the four errors commonly made when writing selection structures. Which errors produce the correct results but in a less efficient way?

16. Explain the meaning of the term *desk-checking*.

Lesson A Exercises

1. Travis is standing in front of two containers: one marked Trash and the other marked Recycle. In his right hand, he is holding a bag that contains either trash or recyclables. Travis needs to lift the lid from the appropriate container (if necessary), then drop the bag in the container, and then put the lid back on the container. Write an appropriate algorithm using only the instructions listed in Figure 5-31. (An instruction can be used more than once.)

INTRODUCTORY

```
else
end if
drop the bag of recyclables in the Recycle container
drop the bag of trash in the Trash container
if the bag contains trash
if the lid is on the Recycle container
if the lid is on the Trash container
lift the Recycle container's lid using your left hand
lift the Trash container's lid using your left hand
put the lid back on the Recycle container using your left hand
put the lid back on the Trash container using your left hand
```

Figure 5-31   Instructions for Exercise 1

2. Caroline is at a store's checkout counter. She'd like to pay for her purchase using either her credit card or her debit card, but preferably her credit card. However, she is not sure whether the store accepts either card. If the store doesn't accept either card, she will need to pay cash for the items. Write an appropriate algorithm using only the instructions listed in Figure 5-32. (An instruction can be used more than once.)

INTRODUCTORY

```
else
end if
pay for your items using your credit card
pay for your items using your debit card
pay for your items using cash
if the store accepts your credit card
if the store accepts your debit card
ask the store clerk whether the store accepts your credit card
ask the store clerk whether the store accepts your debit card
```

Figure 5-32   Instructions for Exercise 2

3. What is wrong with the algorithm shown in Figure 5-33?

INTRODUCTORY

```
1. shoot the basketball
2. if the basketball went through the hoop
        say "I did it!"
    else
        if the basketball did not go through the hoop
            say "Missed it!"
        end if
    end if
```

Figure 5-33   Algorithm for Exercise 3

INTRODUCTORY

4. Write the Visual Basic code for the algorithm shown in Figure 5-10 in this lesson. The car classification (either S for standard or L for luxury) is stored, in uppercase, in a variable named **strClass**. The club membership information (either M for member or N for nonmember) is stored, in uppercase, in a variable named **strClub**. Assign the fee to a variable named **intDailyFee**. Display the fee in the lblFee control.

INTRODUCTORY

5. Write the Visual Basic code that displays the message "Use the Kanton room" when the number of seminar participants is at least 75. When the number is 40 through 74, display the message "Use the Harris room". When the number is 10 through 39, display the message "Use the small conference room". When the number is less than 10, display the message "Cancel the seminar". The number of participants is stored in the **intParticipants** variable. Display the appropriate message in the lblMsg control. Code the multiple-alternative selection structure using the If...Then...Else statement.

INTRODUCTORY

6. Rewrite the code from Exercise 5 using the Select Case statement.

INTRODUCTORY

7. Open the Movie Ticket Solution (Movie Ticket Solution.sln) file contained in the VB2015\Chap05\Movie Ticket Solution folder. If necessary, open the designer window. Use the If...Then...Else statement to code the If...Then...Else button's Click event procedure. Use the Select Case statement to code the Select Case button's Click event procedure. Both procedures should display the appropriate ticket price, which is based on the customer's age as shown below. Test each button's Click event procedure five times, using the numbers 1, 3, 64, 65, and 70.

Age	Price ($)
Under 3	0
3 to 64	9
65 and over	6

INTERMEDIATE

8. Does the algorithm in Figure 5-34 produce the same results as the solution shown in Figure 5-4 in this lesson? If not, why not?

```
1. shoot the basketball
2. if the basketball went through the hoop and Maleek was either inside or on the 3-point line
        say "I did it!"
        say "2 points for me"
   else
        if Maleek was behind the 3-point line
              say "I did it!"
              say "3 points for me"
        else
              say "Missed it!"
        end if
   end if
```

Figure 5-34   Algorithm for Exercise 8

INTERMEDIATE

9. Does the algorithm in Figure 5-35 produce the same results as the solution shown in Figure 5-4 in this lesson? If not, why not?

```
1. shoot the basketball
2. if the basketball did not go through the hoop
        say "Missed it!"
   else
        say "I did it!"
        if Maleek was either inside or on the 3-point line
                say "2 points for me"
        else
                say "3 points for me"
        end if
   end if
```

Figure 5-35   Algorithm for Exercise 9

10. Does the algorithm in Figure 5-36 produce the same results as the solution shown in Figure 5-5 in this lesson? If not, why not?

INTERMEDIATE

```
1. shoot the basketball
2. if the basketball hit the rim
        say "So close"
   else
        if the basketball went through the hoop
                say "I did it!"
                if Maleek was outside the 3-point line
                        say "3 points for me"
                else
                        say "2 points for me"
                end if
        else
                say "Missed it!"
        end if
   end if
```

Figure 5-36   Algorithm for Exercise 10

11. Does the algorithm in Figure 5-37 produce the same results as the solution shown in Figure 5-5 in this lesson? If not, why not?

INTERMEDIATE

```
1. shoot the basketball
2. if the basketball did not go through the hoop
        say "Missed it!"
        if the basketball hit the rim
                say "So close"
        end if
   else
        say "I did it!"
        if Maleek was outside the 3-point line
                say "3 points for me"
        else
                say "2 points for me"
        end if
   end if
```

Figure 5-37   Algorithm for Exercise 11

INTERMEDIATE

12. Open the VB2015\Chap05\Bonus Solution\Bonus Solution (Bonus Solution.sln) file. Use the Select Case statement to finish coding the Calculate button's Click event procedure. Use the partial flowchart shown in Figure 5-38 as a guide. Test the application appropriately.

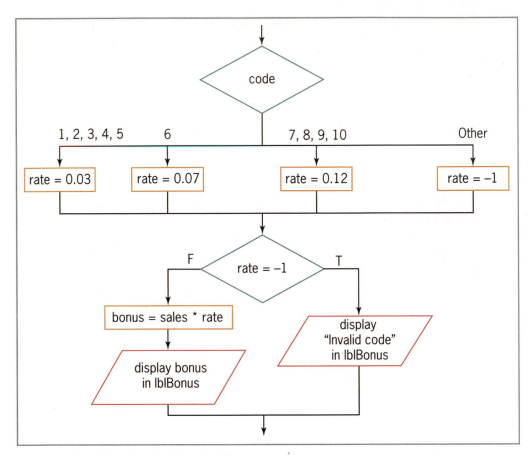

Figure 5-38   Flowchart for Exercise 12

INTERMEDIATE

13. Open the VB2015\Chap05\Carillo Solution\Carillo Solution (Carillo Solution.sln) file. The txtSales control should accept only numbers, the period, and the Backspace key; code the appropriate procedure. The btnCalc_Click procedure calculates a 3.5% commission when the annual sales are greater than $165,000; otherwise, it calculates a 2.5% commission. Modify the procedure to use the commission rates shown below. Use the If...Then...Else statement to code the multiple-alternative selection structure. Test the application seven times, using 125000, 165000, 15000, 165000.99, 200000, 50000, and 50000.01 as the annual sales.

Annual sales ($)	Commission rate
0–50,000	1.5%
50,000.01–75,000	2.0%
75,000.01–165,000	2.5%
Over 165,000	3.5%

14. In this exercise, you modify the Carillo application from Exercise 13. Use Windows to make a copy of the Carillo Solution folder. Rename the copy Modified Carillo Solution. Open the Carillo Solution (Carillo Solution.sln) file contained in the Modified Carillo Solution folder. In the btnCalc_Click procedure, code the multiple-alternative selection structure using the Select Case statement rather than the If...Then...Else statement. Test the application seven times, using 125000, 165000, 15000, 165000.99, 200000, 50000, and 50000.01 as the annual sales. **INTERMEDIATE**

15. Open the VB2015\Chap05\Jetters Solution\Jetters Solution (Jetters Solution.sln) file. The txtPrice control should accept only numbers, the period, and the Backspace key; code the appropriate procedure. The txtQuantity control should accept only numbers and the Backspace key; code the appropriate procedure. Jetters now uses the discount rates shown below. Make the appropriate modifications to the btnCalc_Click procedure. Test the application appropriately. **INTERMEDIATE**

Quantity purchased	Discount rate
0–10	0
11–15	2%
16–20	2.5%
Over 20	3%

16. Open the VB2015\Chap05\Canton Solution\Canton Solution (Canton Solution.sln) file. Canton Ltd. sells economic development software to cities around the country. The company is having its annual users' forum next month. The price per person depends on the number of people a user registers. The first 5 people a user registers are charged $90 per person. Registrants 6 through 11 are charged $70 per person. Registrants 12 through 20 are charged $60 per person. Registrants over 20 are charged $40 per person. For example, if a user registers 13 people, then the total amount owed is $990. The $990 is calculated by first multiplying 5 by 90, giving 450. You then multiply 6 by 70, giving 420. Then, you multiply 2 by 60, giving 120. Finally, you add together the numbers 450, 420, and 120, giving 990. Display the total amount owed in the lblTotal control. Use the Select Case statement to complete the Calculate button's Click event procedure. Test the application appropriately. **ADVANCED**

17. Open the Golf Solution (Golf Solution.sln) file contained in the VB2015\Chap04\Golf Solution-Ex17 folder. Test the application using the data shown in Figure 5-39. Modify the code to produce the correct results. **SWAT THE BUGS**

Desk-check	Membership status	Day information	Expected golf fee
1	member	weekday	$25
2	member	weekend	$25
3	nonmember	weekday	$40
4	nonmember	weekend	$45

    Figure 5-39   Test data for Exercises 17 and 18

18. Open the Golf Solution (Golf Solution.sln) file contained in the VB2015\Chap04\Golf Solution-Ex18 folder. Test the application using the data shown in Exercise 17's Figure 5-39. Modify the code to produce the correct results. **SWAT THE BUGS**

LESSON B

After studying Lesson B, you should be able to:

- Include a group of radio buttons in an interface
- Designate a default radio button
- Include a check box in an interface
- Compare Boolean values

Modifying the Treeline Resort Application

Your task in this chapter is to modify the Treeline Resort application from Chapter 4. In addition to the previous input data, the application's interface will now allow the user to select the number of beds (either two queen beds or one king bed), the view (either standard or atrium), and whether the guest should be charged a vehicle parking fee of $8.50 per night. In addition to displaying the total room charge, the sales and lodging tax, the resort fee, and the total due, the application should now also display the total parking fee. Figure 5-40 shows the application's revised TOE chart. The changes made to the original TOE chart from Chapter 4 are shaded in the figure.

Task	Object	Event
1. Calculate the total room charge, tax, total resort fee, total parking fee, and total due 2. Display the calculated amounts in lblRoomChg, lblTax, lblResortFee, lblParkingFee, and lblTotalDue	btnCalc	Click
End the application	btnExit	Click
Display the total room charge (from btnCalc)	lblRoomChg	None
Display the tax (from btnCalc)	lblTax	None
Display the total resort fee (from btnCalc)	lblResortFee	None
Display the total parking fee (from btnCalc)	lblParkingFee	None
Display the total due (from btnCalc)	lblTotalDue	None
Specifies whether the guest should be charged the vehicle parking fee	chkParkingFee	None
Get and display the number of rooms reserved, number of nights, number of adults, and number of children	txtRooms, txtNights, txtAdults, txtChildren	None
Get number of beds	radQueen, radKing	None
Get room view	radStandard, radAtrium	None

Figure 5-40   Revised TOE chart for the Treeline Resort application *(continues)*

(continued)

Task	Object	Event
Clear the contents of lblRoomChg, lblTax, lblResortFee, lblParkingFee, and lblTotalDue	txtRooms, txtNights, txtAdults, txtChildren	TextChanged
	radQueen, radKing, radStandard, radAtrium, chkParkingFee	CheckedChanged
Allow the text box to accept only numbers and the Backspace key	txtRooms, txtNights, txtAdults, txtChildren	KeyPress
Select the contents of the text box	txtRooms, txtNights, txtAdults, txtChildren	Enter

Figure 5-40   Revised TOE chart for the Treeline Resort application

The revised TOE chart indicates that the interface will now include six additional controls: a label, a check box, and four radio buttons. The additional label will display the total parking fee. The check box will specify whether the vehicle parking fee is applicable to the guest. Two of the four radio buttons pertain to the number of beds, while the other two pertain to the room view.

To open the Treeline Resort application:

START HERE

1. If necessary, start Visual Studio 2015. Open the VB2015\Chap05\Treeline Solution\ Treeline Solution (Treeline Solution.sln) file. See Figure 5-41.

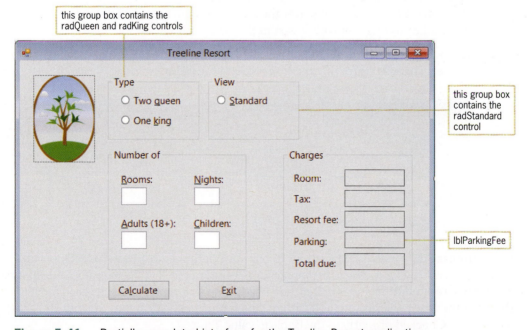

Figure 5-41   Partially completed interface for the Treeline Resort application

Four of the additional six controls listed in the TOE chart have already been added to the interface, as shown in Figure 5-41. The interface also includes two group boxes that will serve as containers for the radio buttons. (Controls whose purpose is to contain other controls do not need to be listed in the TOE chart.) Missing from the interface are the Atrium radio button and the Vehicle parking fee check box.

Ch05B-RadioButtons

Adding a Radio Button to the Interface

You create a radio button using the RadioButton tool in the toolbox. **Radio buttons** allow you to limit the user to only one choice from a group of two or more related but mutually exclusive options. Each radio button in an interface should be labeled so the user knows the choice it represents. You enter the label using sentence capitalization in the radio button's Text property. Each radio button should also have a unique access key that allows the user to select the button using the keyboard. The three-character ID for a radio button's name is rad.

The Treeline Resort interface will use two groups of radio buttons: one for selecting the number of beds and one for selecting the room view. To include two groups of radio buttons in an interface, at least one of the groups must be placed within a container, such as a group box. Otherwise, the radio buttons are considered to be in the same group and only one can be selected at any one time. In this case, the radio buttons pertaining to the number of beds are contained in the Type group box, and the radio buttons pertaining to the room view are contained in the View group box. Placing each group of radio buttons in a separate group box allows the user to select one button from each group. During run time, you can determine whether a radio button is selected or unselected by looking at the value in its **Checked property**. If the property contains the Boolean value True, the radio button is selected. If it contains the Boolean value False, the radio button is not selected.

The minimum number of radio buttons in a group is two. This is because the only way to deselect a radio button is to select another radio button. The recommended maximum number of radio buttons in a group is seven. In the next set of steps, you will add the missing Atrium radio button to the View group box.

START HERE

To add the Atrium radio button to the View group box:

1. Click the **RadioButton** tool in the toolbox, and then drag the mouse pointer into the View group box, placing it below the Standard radio button. Release the mouse button. The RadioButton1 control appears in the group box.

2. Change the RadioButton1 control's name to **radAtrium**, and then change its Text property to **A&trium**. If necessary, position the radio button as shown in Figure 5-42.

Figure 5-42   Atrium radio button added to the View group box

It is customary in Windows applications to have one of the radio buttons in each group already selected when the user interface first appears. The automatically selected radio button is called the **default radio button** and is either the radio button that represents the user's most likely choice or the first radio button in the group. You designate the default radio button by setting the button's Checked property to the Boolean value True.

START HERE

To designate a default radio button in each group:

1. Click the **Two queen** radio button, and then use the Properties window to set the radio button's Checked property to **True**. When you do this, a colored dot appears inside the button's circle to indicate that the button is selected.

2. Set the Standard radio button's Checked property to **True**.

GUI DESIGN TIP Radio Button Standards

- Use radio buttons to limit the user to one choice in a group of related but mutually exclusive options.

- The minimum number of radio buttons in a group is two, and the recommended maximum number is seven.

- The label in the radio button's Text property should be entered using sentence capitalization.

- Assign a unique access key to each radio button in an interface.

- Use a container (such as a group box) to create separate groups of radio buttons. Only one button in each group can be selected at any one time.

- Designate a default radio button in each group of radio buttons.

Adding a Check Box to the Interface

You create a check box using the CheckBox tool in the toolbox. Like radio buttons, check boxes can be either selected or deselected. Also like radio buttons, you can determine whether a check box is selected by looking at the value in its Checked property during run time: A True value indicates that the check box is selected, whereas a False value indicates that it is not selected. However, unlike radio buttons, **check boxes** provide one or more independent and nonexclusive items from which the user can choose. Whereas only one button in a group of radio buttons can be selected at any one time, any number of check boxes on a form can be selected at the same time. Each check box in an interface should be labeled to make its purpose obvious. You enter the label using sentence capitalization in the check box's Text property. Each check box should also have a unique access key that allows the user to select it by using the keyboard. The three-character ID for a check box's name is chk.

To add a check box to the interface:

START HERE

1. Click the **CheckBox** tool in the toolbox, and then drag the mouse pointer onto the form. Position it to the right of the View group box, and then release the mouse button.

2. Change the CheckBox1 control's name to **chkParkingFee**, and then change its Text property to **&Vehicle parking fee**. If necessary, position the check box as shown in Figure 5-43.

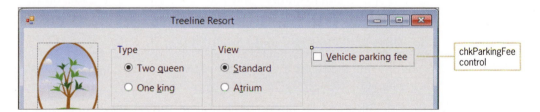

Figure 5-43   Vehicle parking fee check box added to the interface

> **GUI DESIGN TIP** Check Box Standards
>
> • Use check boxes to allow the user to select any number of choices from a group of one or more independent and nonexclusive options.
>
> • The label in the check box's Text property should be entered using sentence capitalization.
>
> • Assign a unique access key to each check box in an interface.

Now that you have completed the user interface, you can lock the controls in place and then set each control's TabIndex property.

START HERE

To lock the controls and then set each control's TabIndex property:

1. Lock the controls on the form, and then use the information shown in Figure 5-44 to set the TabIndex values for the controls. (As you learned in Chapter 2, picture boxes do not have a TabIndex property.) When you are finished, press **Esc** to remove the TabIndex boxes from the form.

Figure 5-44   Correct TabIndex values

Next, you will start the application to observe how you select and deselect radio buttons and check boxes.

START HERE

To select and deselect radio buttons and check boxes:

1. Save the solution and then start the application. Notice that the first radio button in each group is already selected.

2. You can select a different radio button by clicking it. You can click either the circle or the text that appears inside the radio button. Click the **One king** radio button. The computer selects the One king radio button as it deselects the Two queen radio button. This is because both radio buttons belong to the same group, and only one radio button in a group can be selected at any one time.

3. Click the **Atrium** radio button. The computer selects the Atrium radio button as it deselects the Standard radio button. Here again, the radio buttons associated with the room view belong to the same group, so selecting one deselects the other.

4. You can select a check box by clicking either the square or the text that appears inside the control. Click the **Vehicle parking fee** check box to select it. A check mark appears inside the check box to indicate that the check box is selected. Now, click the **Vehicle parking fee** check box again. The check box is deselected, as the absence of the check mark indicates. Click the **Exit** button.

Modifying the Calculate Button's Code

According to the application's TOE chart (shown earlier in Figure 5-40), the btnCalc control's Click event procedure will now need to calculate and display the total parking fee. However, that is not the only modification you will need to make to the procedure. You will also need to change the way it calculates the total room charge because the daily room charge now depends on both the number of beds and the room view. Figure 5-45 shows the modified pseudocode, with the changes made to the original pseudocode from Chapter 4 shaded in the figure.

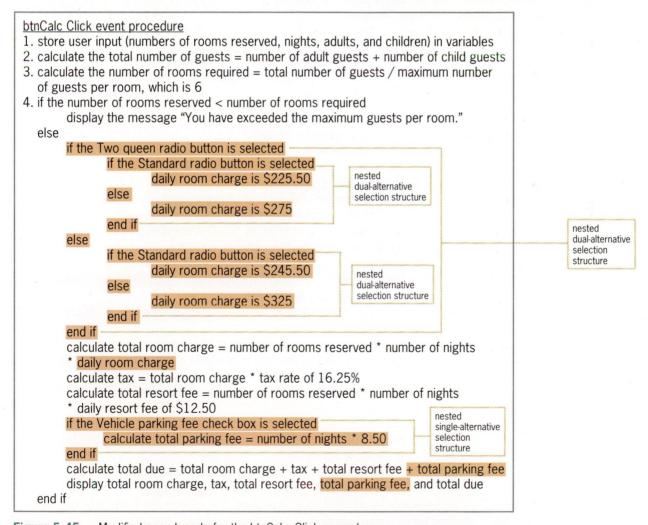

Figure 5-45   Modified pseudocode for the btnCalc_Click procedure

Notice that the outer selection structure's false path in Figure 5-45 now includes a nested dual-alternative selection structure and a nested single-alternative selection structure. Each path in the nested dual-alternative selection structure also contains a nested dual-alternative selection structure.

Figure 5-46 contains a list of the modified procedure's named constants and variables. The changes made to the list from Chapter 4 are shaded in the figure. As the figure indicates, the dblDaily_Room_Chg named constant has been replaced with four named constants, each representing one of the four different daily room charges. The fifth new named constant, dblDAILY_PARKING_FEE, will store the daily vehicle parking fee. The two additional variables in the list will store the total parking fee and the appropriate daily room charge.

Named constants	Values
intMAX_PER_ROOM	6
~~dblDAILY_ROOM_CHG~~	~~225.50~~
dblDAILY_ROOM_CHG_QUEEN_STAND	225.50
dblDAILY_ROOM_CHG_QUEEN_ATRIUM	275.00
dblDAILY_ROOM_CHG_KING_STAND	245.50
dblDAILY_ROOM_CHG_KING_ATRIUM	325.00
dblDAILY_PARKING_FEE	8.50
dblTAX_RATE	0.1625 (the decimal equivalent of 16.25%)
dblDAILY_RESORT_FEE	12.50
strMSG	"You have exceeded the maximum guests per room."

Variable names	Stores
intRoomsReserved	the number of rooms reserved
intNights	the number of nights
intAdults	the number of adult guests
intChildren	the number of child guests
intNumGuests	the total number of guests, which is calculated by adding together the number of adult guests and the number of child guests
dblRoomsRequired	the number of rooms required, which is calculated by dividing the total number of guests by the maximum number of guests per room (may contain a decimal place)
dblParkingFee	the total parking fee, which is calculated by multiplying the number of nights by the daily parking fee
dblDailyRoomChg	the daily room charge, which depends on the number of beds and room view
dblTotalRoomChg	the total room charge, which is calculated by multiplying the number of rooms reserved by the number of nights and then multiplying the result by the daily room charge
dblTax	the tax, which is calculated by multiplying the total room charge by the tax rate
dblTotalResortFee	the total resort fee, which is calculated by multiplying the number of rooms reserved by the number of nights and then multiplying the result by the daily resort fee
dblTotalDue	the total due, which is calculated by adding together the total room charge, tax, total resort fee, and total parking fee

Figure 5-46   Modified list of named constants and variables

To begin modifying the btnCalc_Click procedure:

1. Open the Code Editor window. Replace <your name> and <current date> in the comments with your name and the current date, respectively.

2. Locate the btnCalc_Click procedure. Delete the Const statement that declares the `dblDAILY_ROOM_CHG` constant, and then enter the five Const statements indicated in Figure 5-47.

```
Const intMAX_PER_ROOM As Integer = 6
Const dblDAILY_ROOM_CHG_QUEEN_STAND As Double = 225.5
Const dblDAILY_ROOM_CHG_QUEEN_ATRIUM As Double = 275
Const dblDAILY_ROOM_CHG_KING_STAND As Double = 245.5
Const dblDAILY_ROOM_CHG_KING_ATRIUM As Double = 325
Const dblDAILY_PARKING_FEE As Double = 8.5
Const dblTAX_RATE As Double = 0.1625
Const dblDAILY_RESORT_FEE As Double = 12.5
Const strMSG As String = "You have exceeded the maximum
Dim intRoomsReserved As Integer
```
enter these Const statements

Figure 5-47   Named constants added to the procedure

3. Insert a blank line below the Dim statement that declares the `dblRoomsRequired` variable, and then enter the two Dim statements indicated in Figure 5-48.

```
Dim dblRoomsRequired As Double
Dim dblParkingFee As Double
Dim dblDailyRoomCharge As Double
Dim dblTotalRoomChg As Double
Dim dblTax As Double
```
enter these Dim statements

Figure 5-48   Variables added to the procedure

According to the procedure's pseudocode, you need to add three nested dual-alternative selection structures to the outer selection structure's false path. The conditions in the nested structures will determine whether the Two queen and Standard radio buttons are selected. As you learned earlier, you can determine the status of a radio button by looking at the value in its Checked property. If the property contains the Boolean value True, the radio button is selected. If it contains the Boolean value False, the radio button is not selected.

Comparing Boolean Values

In addition to comparing numbers and strings, you can also compare Boolean values in If...Then... Else and Select Case statements. Examples of such comparisons are shown in Figure 5-49.

Comparing Boolean Values

<u>Example 1</u>
```
If blnIsInsured Then
```
The condition evaluates to True when the `blnIsInsured` variable contains the Boolean value True; otherwise, it evaluates to False. You can also write the If clause like this: `If blnIsInsured = True Then`.

<u>Example 2</u>
```
If Not blnIsInsured Then
```
As you learned in Chapter 4, the Not operator reverses the truth-value of a condition. Therefore, the condition evaluates to True when the `blnIsInsured` variable contains the Boolean value False; otherwise, it evaluates to True. You can also write the If clause like this: `If blnIsInsured = False Then`.

<u>Example 3</u>
```
If chkParkingFee.Checked Then
```
The condition evaluates to True when the chkParkingFee check box is selected; otherwise, it evaluates to False. You can also write the If clause like this: `If chkParkingFee.Checked = True Then`.

<u>Example 4</u>
```
Select Case chkParkingFee.Checked
    Case True
        instructions to process when the check box is selected
    Case False
        instructions to process when the check box is not selected
End Select
```
The instructions in the first Case clause will be processed when the chkParkingFee check box is selected. The instructions in the second Case clause will be processed when the check box is not selected. Because a check box's Checked property can only be either True or False, you can replace the `Case False` clause with `Case Else`.

<u>Example 5</u>
```
Select Case True
    Case radStandard.Checked
        instructions to process when the radStandard radio button is selected
    Case radAtrium.Checked
        instructions to process when the radAtrium radio button is selected
End Select
```
The instructions in the first Case clause will be processed when the radStandard radio button is selected. The instructions in the second Case clause will be processed when the radAtrium radio button is selected. Because the Standard and Atrium radio buttons are the only radio buttons in their group, you can replace the second case clause with `Case Else`.

Figure 5-49   Examples of comparing Boolean values

To finish modifying the btnCalc_Click procedure:

1. First, you'll enter the three nested dual-alternative selection structures. Insert a blank line below the `' calculate charges` comment, and then enter the nested structures indicated in Figure 5-50. The nested structures determine the selected radio buttons and then assign the appropriate daily room charge to the `dblDailyRoomChg` variable.

```
Else
    ' calculate charges
    If radQueen.Checked Then
        If radStandard.Checked Then
            dblDailyRoomCharge = dblDAILY_ROOM_CHG_QUEEN_STAND
        Else
            dblDailyRoomCharge = dblDAILY_ROOM_CHG_QUEEN_ATRIUM
        End If
    Else
        If radStandard.Checked Then
            dblDailyRoomCharge = dblDAILY_ROOM_CHG_KING_STAND
        Else
            dblDailyRoomCharge = dblDAILY_ROOM_CHG_KING_ATRIUM
        End If
    End If
    dblTotalRoomChg = intRoomsReserved *
        intNights * dblDAILY_ROOM_CHG
    dblTax = dblTotalRoomChg * dblTAX_RATE
```

enter these selection structures

Figure 5-50   Nested dual-alternative selection structures entered in the procedure

> You can also write the If clauses as If radQueen. Checked = True Then and If rad-Standard.Checked = True Then.

2. In the assignment statement below the nested selection structures, change db1DAILY_ROOM_CHG to **dblDailyRoomChg**.

3. You also need to include a single-alternative selection structure that determines whether the check box is selected. If it is, the procedure should calculate the total parking fee by multiplying the number of nights by the daily parking fee. Insert a blank line above the statement that calculates the total due, and then enter the selection structure indicated in Figure 5-51.

```
    dblTotalResortFee = intRoomsReserved *
        intNights * dblDAILY_RESORT_FEE
    If chkParkingFee.Checked Then
        dblParkingFee = intNights * dblDAILY_PARKING_FEE
    End If
    dblTotalDue = dblTotalRoomChg +
        dblTax + dblTotalResortFee
```

enter this selection structure

Figure 5-51   Nested single-alternative selection structure entered in the procedure

> You can also write the If clause as If chkParking-Fee.Checked = True Then.

4. Finally, you need to add the total parking fee to the total due and also display the total parking fee in the lblParkingFee control. Make the modifications indicated in Figure 5-52.

```
                dblTotalDue = dblTotalRoomChg +
                    dblTax + dblTotalResortFee + dblParkingFee

enter this          ' display charges
code                lblRoomChg.Text = dblTotalRoomChg.ToString("n2")
                    lblTax.Text = dblTax.ToString("n2")
                    lblResortFee.Text = dblTotalResortFee.ToString("n2")
enter this          lblParkingFee.Text = dblParkingFee.ToString("n2")
statement           lblTotalDue.Text = dblTotalDue.ToString("c2")
                End If
```

Figure 5-52   Final modifications made to the procedure

5. Save the solution and then start the application. Type **1**, **1**, and **2** in the Rooms, Nights, and Adults boxes, respectively, and then click the **Calculate** button. See Figure 5-53.

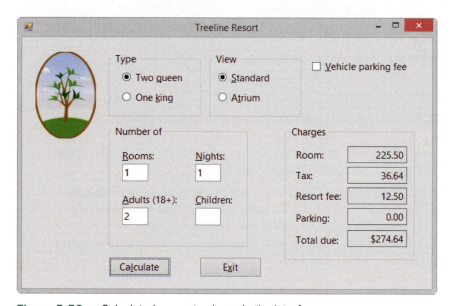

Figure 5-53   Calculated amounts shown in the interface

6. Click the **Atrium** radio button. Notice that the calculated amounts still appear in the interface. You will fix that problem in the next section.

7. Change the number of nights to **2** and then click the **Calculate** button. The total due is now $664.38.

8. Click the **Vehicle parking fee** check box and then click the **Calculate** button. The total due is now $681.38.

9. Click the **Exit** button.

Modifying the ClearLabels Procedure

According to the application's TOE chart (shown earlier in Figure 5-40), the CheckedChanged events of the radio buttons and check box need to be coded. The **CheckedChanged event** occurs when the value in a control's Checked property changes. For example, when you select a check box, its Checked property changes from False to True and its CheckedChanged event occurs. Deselecting a check box changes its Checked property from True to False, thereby invoking its CheckedChanged event. Similarly, when you select a radio button, its Checked property changes from False to True and its CheckedChanged event occurs. In addition, the Checked property of the previously selected radio button in the same group changes from True to False, thereby invoking that radio button's CheckedChanged event.

The TOE chart indicates that the CheckedChanged events should clear the contents of five label controls in the interface. The ClearLabels procedure that you created in Chapter 4 will perform that task. All you need to do is add the `lblParkingFee.Text = String.Empty` statement to the procedure, and then include the CheckedChanged events for the radio buttons and check box in the procedure's Handles cause.

To modify and then test the ClearLabels procedure:

START HERE

1. Locate the ClearLabels procedure, and then make the modifications indicated in Figure 5-54. (Be sure to type the comma after `txtChildren.TextChanged` in the Handles clause.)

```
Private Sub ClearLabels(sender As Object, e As EventArgs) _
    Handles txtRooms.TextChanged, txtNights.TextChanged,
    txtAdults.TextChanged, txtChildren.TextChanged,          be sure to type
    radQueen.CheckedChanged, radKing.CheckedChanged,          the comma
    radStandard.CheckedChanged, radAtrium.CheckedChanged,    enter this code
    chkParkingFee.CheckedChanged
    ' clear calculated amounts

    lblRoomChg.Text = String.Empty
    lblTax.Text = String.Empty
    lblResortFee.Text = String.Empty
    lblParkingFee.Text = String.Empty          enter this statement
    lblTotalDue.Text = String.Empty
End Sub
```

Figure 5-54   Modified ClearLabels procedure

2. Save the solution and then start the application. Type **1**, **1**, and **2** in the Rooms, Nights, and Adults boxes, respectively, and then click the **Calculate** button. The total due is $274.64, as shown earlier in Figure 5-53.

3. Click the **Atrium** radio button. The ClearLabels procedure removes the calculated amounts from the interface. Click the **Calculate** button. The total due is now $332.19.

4. Click the **Vehicle parking fee** check box. The ClearLabels procedure removes the calculated amounts from the interface. Click the **Calculate** button. The total due is now $340.69.

5. On your own, verify that the ClearLabels procedure removes the calculated amounts when the One king radio button is clicked and also when the Standard radio button is clicked.

6. Click the **Exit** button. Close the Code Editor window and then close the solution.

Figure 5-55 shows the application's code at the end of Lesson B.

```
 1 ' Name:          Treeline Project
 2 ' Purpose:       Display the total room charge, tax,
 3 '                total resort fee, and total due
 4 ' Programmer:    <your name> on <current date>
 5
 6 Option Explicit On
 7 Option Strict On
 8 Option Infer Off
 9
10 Public Class frmMain
11     Private Sub btnCalc_Click(sender As Object, e As EventArgs
       ) Handles btnCalc.Click
12         ' calculate and display total room charge,
13         ' tax, total resort fee, and total due
14
15         Const intMAX_PER_ROOM As Integer = 6
16         Const dblDAILY_ROOM_CHG_QUEEN_STAND As Double = 225.5
17         Const dblDAILY_ROOM_CHG_QUEEN_ATRIUM As Double = 275
18         Const dblDAILY_ROOM_CHG_KING_STAND As Double = 245.5
19         Const dblDAILY_ROOM_CHG_KING_ATRIUM As Double = 325
20         Const dblDAILY_PARKING_FEE As Double = 8.5
21         Const dblTAX_RATE As Double = 0.1625
22         Const dblDAILY_RESORT_FEE As Double = 12.5
23         Const strMSG As String =
             "You have exceeded the maximum guests per room."
24         Dim intRoomsReserved As Integer
25         Dim intNights As Integer
26         Dim intAdults As Integer
27         Dim intChildren As Integer
28         Dim intNumGuests As Integer
29         Dim dblRoomsRequired As Double
30         Dim dblParkingFee As Double
31         Dim dblDailyRoomCharge As Double
32         Dim dblTotalRoomChg As Double
33         Dim dblTax As Double
34         Dim dblTotalResortFee As Double
35         Dim dblTotalDue As Double
36
37         ' store input in variables
38         Integer.TryParse(txtRooms.Text, intRoomsReserved)
39         Integer.TryParse(txtNights.Text, intNights)
40         Integer.TryParse(txtAdults.Text, intAdults)
41         Integer.TryParse(txtChildren.Text, intChildren)
42
43         ' calculate total number of guests
44         intNumGuests = intAdults + intChildren
45         ' calculate number of rooms required
46         dblRoomsRequired = intNumGuests / intMAX_PER_ROOM
47
48         ' determine whether number of reserved rooms is
49         ' adequate and then either display a message or
50         ' calculate and display the charges
51         If intRoomsReserved < dblRoomsRequired Then
52             MessageBox.Show(strMSG, "Treeline Resort",
53                             MessageBoxButtons.OK,
54                             MessageBoxIcon.Information)
55         Else
56             ' calculate charges
```

Figure 5-55 Completed Treeline Resort application's code (*continues*)

(continued)

```
57                  If radQueen.Checked Then
58                      If radStandard.Checked Then
59                          dblDailyRoomCharge =
                                dblDAILY_ROOM_CHG_QUEEN_STAND
60                      Else
61                          dblDailyRoomCharge =
                                dblDAILY_ROOM_CHG_QUEEN_ATRIUM
62                      End If
63                  Else
64                      If radStandard.Checked Then
65                          dblDailyRoomCharge =
                                dblDAILY_ROOM_CHG_KING_STAND
66                      Else
67                          dblDailyRoomCharge =
                                dblDAILY_ROOM_CHG_KING_ATRIUM
68                      End If
69                  End If
70                  dblTotalRoomChg = intRoomsReserved *
71                      intNights * dblDailyRoomCharge
72                  dblTax = dblTotalRoomChg * dblTAX_RATE
73                  dblTotalResortFee = intRoomsReserved *
74                      intNights * dblDAILY_RESORT_FEE
75                  If chkParkingFee.Checked Then
76                      dblParkingFee = intNights * dblDAILY_PARKING_FEE
77                  End If
78                  dblTotalDue = dblTotalRoomChg +
79                      dblTax + dblTotalResortFee + dblParkingFee
80
81                  ' display charges
82                  lblRoomChg.Text = dblTotalRoomChg.ToString("n2")
83                  lblTax.Text = dblTax.ToString("n2")
84                  lblResortFee.Text = dblTotalResortFee.ToString("n2")
85                  lblParkingFee.Text = dblParkingFee.ToString("n2")
86                  lblTotalDue.Text = dblTotalDue.ToString("c2")
87          End If
88      End Sub
89
90      Private Sub btnExit_Click(sender As Object, e As EventArgs
        ) Handles btnExit.Click
91          Me.Close()
92      End Sub
93
94      Private Sub ClearLabels(sender As Object, e As EventArgs) _
95          Handles txtRooms.TextChanged, txtNights.TextChanged,
96          txtAdults.TextChanged, txtChildren.TextChanged,
97          radQueen.CheckedChanged, radKing.CheckedChanged,
98          radStandard.CheckedChanged, radAtrium.CheckedChanged,
99          chkParkingFee.CheckedChanged
100         ' clear calculated amounts
101
102         lblRoomChg.Text = String.Empty
103         lblTax.Text = String.Empty
104         lblResortFee.Text = String.Empty
105         lblParkingFee.Text = String.Empty
106         lblTotalDue.Text = String.Empty
107     End Sub
108
```

Figure 5-55 Completed Treeline Resort application's code *(continues)*

(continued)

```
109     Private Sub CancelKeys(sender As Object,
        e As KeyPressEventArgs
110         ) Handles txtRooms.KeyPress, txtNights.KeyPress,
111         txtAdults.KeyPress, txtChildren.KeyPress
112         ' allows the text box to accept only numbers
        and the Backspace
113
114         If (e.KeyChar < "0" OrElse e.KeyChar > "9") AndAlso
115             e.KeyChar <> ControlChars.Back Then
116             ' cancel the key
117             e.Handled = True
118         End If
119     End Sub
120
121     Private Sub txtRooms_Enter(sender As Object,
        e As EventArgs) Handles txtRooms.Enter
122         ' select contents when text box receives focus
123
124         txtRooms.SelectAll()
125     End Sub
126
127     Private Sub txtNights_Enter(sender As Object,
        e As EventArgs) Handles txtNights.Enter
128         ' select contents when text box receives focus
129
130         txtNights.SelectAll()
131     End Sub
132
133     Private Sub txtAdults_Enter(sender As Object,
        e As EventArgs) Handles txtAdults.Enter
134         ' select contents when text box receives focus
135
136         txtAdults.SelectAll()
137     End Sub
138
139     Private Sub txtChildren_Enter(sender As Object,
        e As EventArgs) Handles txtChildren.Enter
140         ' select contents when text box receives focus
141
142         txtChildren.SelectAll()
143     End Sub
144 End Class
```

Figure 5-55   Completed Treeline Resort application's code

Lesson B Summary

- To limit the user to only one choice in a group of two or more related but mutually exclusive options:

  Use the RadioButton tool to add two or more radio buttons to the form. To include two groups of radio buttons on a form, at least one of the groups must be placed within a container, such as a group box.

- To allow the user to select any number of choices from a group of one or more independent and nonexclusive options:

  Use the CheckBox tool to add one or more check box controls to the form.

- To determine whether a radio button or check box is selected or unselected:

  Use the Checked property of the radio button or check box. The property will contain the Boolean value True if the control is selected; otherwise, it will contain the Boolean value False.

- To process code when the value in the Checked property of a radio button or check box changes:

  Enter the code in the radio button's or check box's CheckedChanged event procedure.

Lesson B Key Terms

Check boxes—controls used to offer the user one or more independent and nonexclusive choices

Checked property—the property of radio button and check box controls that indicates whether or not the control is selected; contains either the Boolean value True or the Boolean value False

CheckedChanged event—an event associated with radio buttons and check boxes; occurs when the value in a control's Checked property changes

Default radio button—the radio button that is automatically selected when an interface first appears

Radio buttons—controls used to limit the user to only one choice from a group of two or more related but mutually exclusive options

Lesson B Review Questions

1. What is the minimum number of radio buttons in a group?

   a. one

   b. two

   c. three

   d. There is no minimum number of radio buttons.

2. If a check box is not selected, what value is contained in its Checked property?

   a. True

   b. Unchecked

   c. False

   d. Unselected

3. Which capitalization should be used for the text appearing in check boxes and radio buttons?

   a. sentence capitalization
   b. book title capitalization
   c. either book title capitalization or sentence capitalization

4. It is customary in Windows applications to designate a default check box.

   a. True

   b. False

5. A form contains six radio buttons. Three of the radio buttons are located in a group box. How many of the radio buttons on the form can be selected at the same time?

   a. one

   b. two

   c. three

   d. six

6. A form contains six check boxes. Three of the check boxes are located in a group box. How many of the check boxes on the form can be selected at the same time?

    a. one   c. three

    b. two   d. six

7. If a radio button is selected, its _____ property contains the Boolean value True.

    a. Checked   c. Selected

    b. On   d. Selection

8. Which of the following If clauses will evaluate to True when the Bonus check box is selected?

    a. `If chkBonus.Check = True Then`

    b. `If chkBonus.Checked Then`

    c. `If chkBonus.Selected = True Then`

    d. `If chkBonus.Selected Then`

9. Which of the following events occurs when a check box is clicked?

    a. Check   c. CheckedChange

    b. Checked   d. CheckedChanged

10. If the `blnSenior` variable contains the Boolean value False, then the `Not blnSenior` condition will evaluate to_____.

    a. True

    b. False

Lesson B Exercises

INTRODUCTORY

1. In this exercise, you modify the Treeline Resort application from this lesson. Use Windows to make a copy of the Treeline Solution folder. Rename the copy Treeline Solution-Select Case. Open the Treeline Solution (Treeline Solution.sln) file contained in the Treeline Solution-Select Case folder. In the btnCalc_Click procedure, replace the If...Then...Else statement that determines the number of beds with the Select Case statement. Test the application appropriately.

INTRODUCTORY

2. In this exercise, you create an application for Brazilian Tea, which sells both hot and iced tea in three different cup sizes. Use the following names for the solution and project, respectively: Tea Solution and Tea Project. Save the application in the VB2015\Chap05 folder. The application's interface, which is shown in Figure 5-56, provides radio buttons for selecting the cup size. The check box is used to specify whether the customer is ordering iced tea. The price for each cup size is shown in the interface; however, the store must also charge a 4% sales tax. The Calculate button should calculate the total price of a cup of tea. It then should display (in the label control) a message that indicates the cup size, the total price, and whether the tea is hot or iced. Use the If...Then...Else statement to code the multiple-alternative selection structure. The CheckedChanged event procedures for the radio buttons and check box should clear the message from the label control. Test the application appropriately.

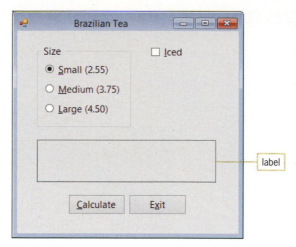

Figure 5-56   Interface for Exercise 2

3. In this exercise, you modify the Brazilian Tea application from Exercise 2. Use Windows to make a copy of the Tea Solution folder. Rename the copy Modified Tea Solution. Open the Tea Solution (Tea Solution.sln) file contained in the Modified Tea Solution folder. Use the Select Case statement (rather than the If...Then...Else statement) to code the multiple-alternative selection structure. Test the application appropriately.   <kbd>INTRODUCTORY</kbd>

4. In this exercise, you code an application that allows the user to select one radio button from each of two groups: an English group and a Spanish group. Open the VB2015\Chap05\Language Solution\Language Solution (Language Solution.sln) file. When a radio button is selected, its CheckedChanged event procedure should clear the contents of the lblMsg control. The Verify Answer button's Click event procedure should verify that the selected English word is the proper translation for the selected Spanish word. If it is, the procedure should display the message "Correct"; otherwise, it should display the message "Incorrect". Code the procedure using one dual-alternative selection structure. Test the application appropriately.   <kbd>INTRODUCTORY</kbd>

5. Willow Hill Athletic Club offers personal training sessions to its members. The sessions are either 30 or 60 minutes in length, and members can sign up to meet either two or three times per week. The application's interface is shown in Figure 5-57. Each 30-minute session costs $17.50; each 60-minute session costs $30. However, members who sign up for three 60-minute sessions per week receive a 10% discount. Additionally, members who are at least 60 years old receive a senior discount, which is an additional 5% off the total cost. Use the following names for the solution and project, respectively: Willow Solution and Willow Project. Save the application in the VB2015\Chap05 folder. The application should display the total cost for four weeks of personal training. Test the application appropriately. (Hint: The monthly cost for a member who signs up for three 60-minute sessions per week is $324.00. If the member is entitled to the senior discount, the cost is $307.80.)   <kbd>INTERMEDIATE</kbd>

Figure 5-57   Interface for Exercise 5

INTERMEDIATE   6. In this exercise, you modify the Treeline Resort application from this lesson. Use Windows to make a copy of the Treeline Solution folder. Rename the copy Modified Treeline Solution. Open the Treeline Solution (Treeline Solution.sln) file contained in the Modified Treeline Solution folder.

a. Currently, the application calculates the total parking fee by multiplying the daily parking fee by the number of nights. However, this calculation is based on the assumption that the guest will have only one vehicle to park, when it is entirely possible that he or she (or other members of the guest's party) may have two or more vehicles. Add a label control and a text box to the form, positioning both below the check box. Change the label's Text property to N&umber of vehicles: (including the colon). The user will enter the number of vehicles in this new text box. When the user selects the check box, display the number 1 in the text box. When the user deselects the check box, clear the contents of the text box. (Hint: A check box also has a Click event.)

b. Modify the code so it now calculates the total parking fee by multiplying the daily parking fee by the number of nights, and then multiplying that result by the number of vehicles. As is currently done, the parking fee should be charged only when the check box is selected. Clear the calculated amounts when a change is made to the number of vehicles. Make the appropriate modifications to the code. Test the application appropriately.

ADVANCED   7. Shopper Stoppers wants you to create an application that displays the number of reward points a customer earns each month. The reward points are based on the customer's membership type and total monthly purchase amount, as shown in Figure 5-58. Use the following names for the solution and project, respectively: Shopper Solution and Shopper Project. Save the application in the VB2015\Chap05 folder. Create a suitable interface, using radio buttons to get the membership type. Display the reward points as whole numbers. Test the application appropriately.

Membership type	Total monthly purchase ($)	Reward points
Basic	Less than 100	0
	100–249.99	5% of the total monthly purchase
	250 and over	6% of the total monthly purchase
Standard	Less than 50	2% of the total monthly purchase
	50 and over	7% of the total monthly purchase
Premium	Less than 200	7% of the total monthly purchase
	200 and over	9% of the total monthly purchase

Figure 5-58   Reward points for Exercise 7

8. Create an application, using the following names for the solution and project, respectively: Songs Solution and Songs Project. Save the application in the VB2015\Chap05 folder.

DISCOVERY

   a. Create the interface shown in Figure 5-59. The four radio buttons contain song titles. The Artist Name button's Click event procedure should display the name of the artist associated with the selected radio button. The names of the artists are Andrea Bocelli, Michael Jackson, Beyonce, and Josh Groban. Code the application, and then test it appropriately.

   b. Remove the Artist Name button from the interface. Also remove the button's code from the Code Editor window. Code the application so that the artist name automatically appears when a radio button is selected. Save the solution and then start the application. The name "Andrea Bocelli" should appear in the Artist box because the Because We Believe radio button is selected. Click the Billie Jean radio button. The name "Michael Jackson" should appear in the Artist box. Test the remaining radio buttons.

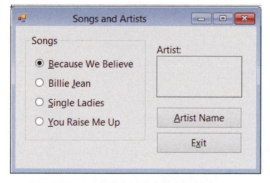

Figure 5-59   Interface for Exercise 8

■ LESSON C

After studying Lesson C, you should be able to:

- Validate data using the TryParse method

- Generate random numbers

Using the TryParse Method for Data Validation

In Chapter 3, you learned how to use the TryParse method to convert a string to a number of a specific data type. Recall that if the conversion is successful, the TryParse method stores the number in the variable specified in the method's *numericVariableName* argument; otherwise, it stores the number 0 in the variable. What you didn't learn in Chapter 3 was that in addition to storing a number in the variable, the TryParse method also returns a Boolean value that indicates whether the conversion was successful (True) or unsuccessful (False). You can assign the value returned by the TryParse method to a Boolean variable, as shown in the syntax and example in Figure 5-60. You then can use a selection structure to take the appropriate action based on the result of the conversion. For example, you might want a selection structure's true path to calculate an employee's gross pay only when the user's input (hours worked and pay rate) can be converted to numbers; otherwise, its false path should display an "Input Error" message.

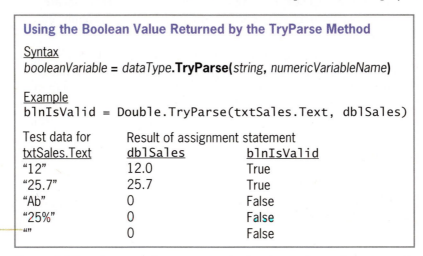

Using the Boolean Value Returned by the TryParse Method

Syntax
booleanVariable = *dataType*.**TryParse(***string***,** *numericVariableName***)**

Example
blnIsValid = Double.TryParse(txtSales.Text, dblSales)

Test data for txtSales.Text	Result of assignment statement dblSales	blnIsValid
"12"	12.0	True
"25.7"	25.7	True
"Ab"	0	False
"25%"	0	False
empty string — ""	0	False

Figure 5-60 Syntax and an example of using the Boolean value returned by the TryParse method

The TryParse method in the assignment statement in Figure 5-60 will attempt to convert the string stored in the txtSales control's Text property to a Double number. If the conversion is successful, the method stores the Double number in the dblSales variable and also returns the Boolean value True. If the conversion is not successful, the method stores the number 0 in the dblSales variable and returns the Boolean value False. The assignment statement assigns the TryParse method's return value (either True or False) to the blnIsValid variable.

START HERE

To use the Boolean value returned by the TryParse method:

1. If necessary, start Visual Studio 2015. Open the New Pay Solution (New Pay Solution.sln) file contained in the VB2015\Chap05\New Pay Solution folder. Open the Code Editor window. Replace <your name> and <current date> in the comments with your name and the current date, respectively.

2. Locate the btnCalc_Click procedure. Before modifying the code to use the Boolean value returned by the TryParse method, you will observe how the procedure currently

works. Start the application. Type **10** in the Old pay box and then click the **Calculate** button. Rather than alerting the user that the Raise rate box is empty, the procedure displays the old pay amount ($10.00) in the New pay box.

3. Type **a** in the Raise rate box and then click the **Calculate** button. Even though the raise rate is invalid, the procedure displays the old pay amount ($10.00) in the New pay box. See Figure 5-61.

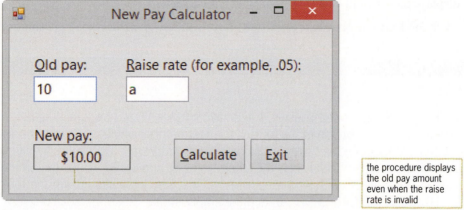

the procedure displays the old pay amount even when the raise rate is invalid

Figure 5-61   Sample run of the original btnCalc_Click procedure

4. Change the raise rate to **.05** and then click the **Calculate** button. The procedure displays $10.50 in the New pay box, which is correct. Click the **Exit** button.

5. Use the code shown in Figure 5-62 to modify the btnCalc_Click procedure. The modifications are shaded in the figure.

```vb
Private Sub btnCalc_Click(sender As Object, e As EventArgs
) Handles btnCalc.Click
    ' calculates and displays the new pay

    Dim dblOld As Double
    Dim dblRate As Double
    Dim dblNew As Double
    Dim blnIsOldOk As Boolean
    Dim blnIsRateOk As Boolean

    ' convert the input to numbers
    blnIsOldOk = Double.TryParse(txtOld.Text, dblOld)
    blnIsRateOk = Double.TryParse(txtRate.Text, dblRate)

    ' determine whether the conversions were successful
    If blnIsOldOk AndAlso blnIsRateOk Then
        ' calculate and display the new pay
        dblNew = dblOld + dblOld * dblRate
        lblNew.Text = dblNew.ToString("C2")
    Else
        lblNew.Text = "Invalid data"
    End If

    ' set the focus
    txtOld.Focus()
End Sub
```

Figure 5-62   Modified btnCalc_Click procedure

6. Save the solution and then start the application. Type **10** in the Old pay box and then click the **Calculate** button. Because no raise rate was entered, the procedure displays the "Invalid data" message in the New pay box.

7. Type **.05** in the Raise rate box and then click the **Calculate** button. The procedure calculates and displays $10.50 as the new pay amount, which is correct.

8. Change the old pay to the letter **a** and then click the **Calculate** button. The procedure displays the "Invalid data" message, which is correct.

9. Click the **Exit** button. Close the Code Editor window and then close the solution.

YOU DO IT 4!

Create an application named YouDoIt 4 and save it in the VB2015\Chap05 folder. Add a text box, a label, and a button to the form. If the user enters a value that can be converted to the Integer data type, the button's Click event procedure should display the integer in the label; otherwise, it should display the string "Can't be converted". Code the procedure. Save the solution and then start the application. Test the application using the following values: 12, 12.75, 2, $45, 3, 5%, 6, and the empty string. Close the solution.

Generating Random Integers

Many computer game programs use random numbers. The numbers can be integers or real numbers, which are numbers containing a decimal place. In this section, you will learn how to generate random integers. If you want to learn how to generate random real numbers, refer to Exercise 11 at the end of this lesson.

Most programming languages provide a **pseudo-random number generator**, which is a mathematical algorithm that produces a sequence of numbers that, although not completely random, are sufficiently random for practical purposes. The pseudo-random number generator in Visual Basic is represented by an object whose data type is Random.

Figure 5-63 shows the syntax for generating random integers in Visual Basic, and it includes examples of using the syntax. As the figure indicates, you first create a **Random object** to represent the pseudo-random number generator in your application's code. You create the Random object by declaring it in a Dim statement, which you enter in the procedure that will use the number generator. After the Random object is created, you can use the object's Random. Next method to generate random integers. In the method's syntax, *randomObjectName* is the name of the Random object. The *minValue* and *maxValue* arguments must be integers, and minValue must be less than maxValue. The **Random.Next method** returns an integer that is greater than or equal to minValue but less than maxValue. You will use random integers to code the Roll 'Em Game application, which simulates the rolling of two dice.

Generating Random Integers

<u>Syntax</u>
Dim *randomObjectName* **As New Random**
randomObjectName.**Next**(*minValue, maxValue*)

<u>Example 1</u>
```
Dim randGen As New Random
intNum = randGen.Next(1, 51)
```
The Dim statement creates a Random object named `randGen`. The `randGen.Next(1, 51)` expression generates a random integer that is greater than or equal to 1 but less than 51. The assignment statement assigns the random integer to the `intNum` variable.

<u>Example 2</u>
```
Dim randGen As New Random
intNum = randGen.Next(-10, 0)
```
The Dim statement creates a Random object named `randGen`. The `randGen.Next(-10, 0)` expression generates a random integer that is greater than or equal to –10 but less than 0. The assignment statement assigns the random integer to the `intNum` variable.

Figure 5-63   Syntax and examples of generating random integers

To open the Roll 'Em Game application:

START HERE

1. Open the Roll Em Solution (Roll Em Solution.sln) file contained in the VB2015\Chap05\Roll Em Solution folder. See Figure 5-64.

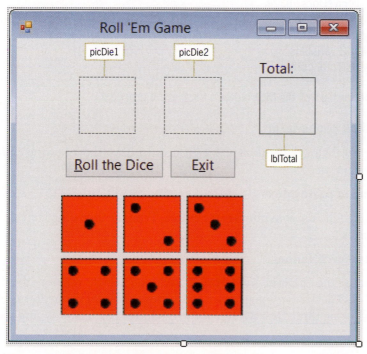

Figure 5-64   Roll 'Em Game application's interface

2. Open the Code Editor window. Replace <your name> and <current date> in the comments with your name and the current date, respectively.

When the user clicks the Roll the Dice button, the button's Click event procedure will generate two random integers from 1 through 6. It will use the random integers to select one of the images located below the buttons in the interface. The images are named picOneDot, picTwoDots, picThreeDots, picFourDots, picFiveDots, and picSixDots. The procedure will display the selected images in the picDie1 and picDie2 controls. It will also total the number of dots appearing on both dice and then display the total in the lblTotal control. Figure 5-65 shows the procedure's pseudocode.

btnRoll Click event procedure
1. generate a random integer from 1 through 6 and assign to a variable named intNum1
2. generate a random integer from 1 through 6 and assign to a variable named intNum2
3. use the intNum1 variable's value to display the appropriate image in the picDie1 control
   if intNum1 contains:
   1   display the picOneDot image
   2   display the picTwoDots image
   3   display the picThreeDots image
   4   display the picFourDots image
   5   display the picFiveDots image
   6   display the picSixDots image
4. use the intNum2 variable's value to display the appropriate image in the picDie2 control
   if intNum2 contains:
   1   display the picOneDot image
   2   display the picTwoDots image
   3   display the picThreeDots image
   4   display the picFourDots image
   5   display the picFiveDots image
   6   display the picSixDots image
5. calculate the total number of dots on both dice by adding together the integers stored in the intNum1 and intNum2 variables
6. display the total in the lblTotal control

Figure 5-65   Pseudocode for the Roll the Dice button's Click event procedure

START HERE

To code the btnRoll_Click procedure:

1. Open the code template for the btnRoll_Click procedure. Type the following comment and then press **Enter** twice:

   ' simulates a game of rolling dice

2. First, you will declare the random number generator. Type the following Dim statement and then press **Enter**:

   Dim randGen As New Random

3. Next, you will declare the intNum1 and intNum2 variables, which will store the random integers. You will also declare an Integer variable to store the total of the dots on both dice. Enter the following three Dim statements. Press **Enter** twice after typing the last Dim statement.

   Dim intNum1 As Integer
   Dim intNum2 As Integer
   Dim intTotal As Integer

4. The first two steps in the pseudocode generate two random integers from 1 through 6 and assign them to the `intNum1` and `intNum2` variables. To generate integers in that range, you will need to use 1 for the Random.Next method's *minValue* argument and 7 for its *maxValue* argument. Enter the following comment and two assignment statements. Press **Enter** twice after typing the second assignment statement.

   ' assign random integer from 1 through 6
   intNum1 = randGen.Next(1, 7)
   intNum2 = randGen.Next(1, 7)

5. Step 3 in the pseudocode uses the `intNum1` variable's value to display the appropriate image in the picDie1 control. Enter the following comment and Select Case statement:

   ' display appropriate image in picDie1

   Select Case intNum1
       Case 1
           picDie1.Image = picOneDot.Image
       Case 2
           picDie1.Image = picTwoDots.Image
       Case 3
           picDie1.Image = picThreeDots.Image
       Case 4
           picDie1.Image = picFourDots.Image
       Case 5
           picDie1.Image = picFiveDots.Image
       Case 6
           picDie1.Image = picSixDots.Image
   End Select

6. Similarly, Step 4 uses the `intNum2` variable's value to display the appropriate image in the picDie2 control. Insert another blank line above the End Sub clause, and then enter the following comment and Select Case statement:

   ' display appropriate image in picDie2
   Select Case intNum2
       Case 1
           picDie2.Image = picOneDot.Image
       Case 2
           picDie2.Image = picTwoDots.Image
       Case 3
           picDie2.Image = picThreeDots.Image
       Case 4
           picDie2.Image = picFourDots.Image
       Case 5
           picDie2.Image = picFiveDots.Image
       Case 6
           picDie2.Image = picSixDots.Image
   End Select

7. The last two steps in the pseudocode calculate the total number of dots on both dice and then display the result in the lblTotal control. Insert another blank line above the End Sub clause, and then enter the following comment and assignment statements:

' calculate and display total number of dots
intTotal = intNum1 + intNum2
lblTotal.Text = intTotal.ToString

8. Save the solution and then start the application. Click the **Roll the Dice** button. See Figure 5-66. Because random numbers are used to select the appropriate images for the picDie1 and picDie2 controls, your dice and total might be different from the dice and total shown in the figure.

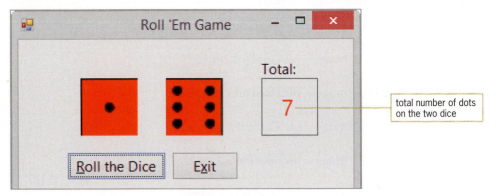

total number of dots on the two dice

Figure 5-66   Result of clicking the Roll the Dice button

9. Click the **Roll the Dice** button several more times to verify that different images appear in the picDie1 and picDie2 controls. Also verify that the number in the Total box is correct. When you are finished testing the application, click the **Exit** button, and then close the Code Editor window.

YOU DO IT 5!

Close the Roll Em Solution file. Create an application named YouDoIt 5 and save it in the VB2015\Chap05 folder. Add a label and a button to the form. The button's Click event procedure should display an integer from 1 through 10 in the label. Code the procedure. Save the solution, and then start and test the application. Close the solution.

Completing the Roll 'Em Game Application

The six picture boxes located at the bottom of the form should not appear while the application is running. As you learned in Chapter 2, you can hide a control during run time by changing its Visible property from True to False.

To hide the six picture boxes and then resize the form:

1. If necessary, open the Roll Em Solution (Roll Em Solution.sln) file. Select the six picture boxes located at the bottom of the form, and then use the Properties window to change the Visible property to **False**. Click the **form** to deselect the picture boxes.

2. Drag the form's bottom sizing handle up until the form is approximately the size shown in Figure 5-67.

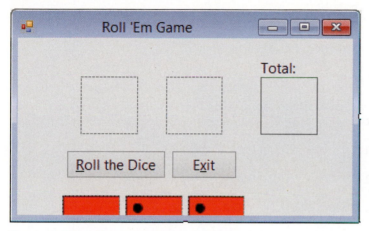

Figure 5-67   Resized form

3. Lock the controls on the form. Save the solution and then start the application. Click the **Roll the Dice** button. See Figure 5-68. Notice that the picture boxes located at the bottom of the form are hidden from view.

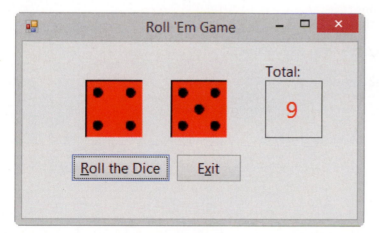

Figure 5-68   Interface with six of the picture boxes hidden

4. Click the **Exit** button and then close the solution.

Figure 5-69 shows the code entered in the btnRoll_Click procedure.

```vb
Private Sub btnRoll_Click(sender As Object, e As EventArgs
) Handles btnRoll.Click
    ' simulates a game of rolling dice

    Dim randGen As New Random
    Dim intNum1 As Integer
    Dim intNum2 As Integer
    Dim intTotal As Integer

    ' assign random integer from 1 through 6
    intNum1 = randGen.Next(1, 7)
    intNum2 = randGen.Next(1, 7)

    ' display appropriate image in picDie1
    Select Case intNum1
        Case 1
            picDie1.Image = picOneDot.Image
        Case 2
            picDie1.Image = picTwoDots.Image
        Case 3
            picDie1.Image = picThreeDots.Image
        Case 4
            picDie1.Image = picFourDots.Image
        Case 5
            picDie1.Image = picFiveDots.Image
        Case 6
            picDie1.Image = picSixDots.Image
    End Select

    ' display appropriate image in picDie2
    Select Case intNum2
        Case 1
            picDie2.Image = picOneDot.Image
        Case 2
            picDie2.Image = picTwoDots.Image
        Case 3
            picDie2.Image = picThreeDots.Image
        Case 4
            picDie2.Image = picFourDots.Image
        Case 5
            picDie2.Image = picFiveDots.Image
        Case 6
            picDie2.Image = picSixDots.Image
    End Select

    ' calculate and display total number of dots
    intTotal = intNum1 + intNum2
    lblTotal.Text = intTotal.ToString

End Sub
```

Figure 5-69   Roll the Dice button's Click event procedure

Lesson C Summary

- To determine whether the TryParse method converted a string to a number of the specified data type:

  Use the syntax *booleanVariable = dataType.***TryParse**(*string, numericVariableName*). The TryParse method returns the Boolean value True when the string can be converted to the numeric *dataType*; otherwise, it returns the Boolean value False.

- To generate random integers:

  Create a Random object to represent the pseudo-random number generator. Then use the object's Random.Next method to generate a random integer. Refer to the syntax and examples shown earlier in Figure 5-63.

Lesson C Key Terms

Pseudo-random number generator—a mathematical algorithm that produces a sequence of random numbers; in Visual Basic, the pseudo-random generator is represented by an object whose data type is Random

Random object—represents the pseudo-random number generator in Visual Basic

Random.Next method—used to generate a random integer that is greater than or equal to a minimum value but less than a maximum value

Lesson C Review Questions

1. If the txtPrice control contains the value 75, what value will the `Decimal.TryParse(txtPrice.Text, decPrice)` method return?

    a. False
    b. True
    c. 75
    d. 75.00

2. Which of the following statements will hide the picCar control?

    a. `picCar.Hide`
    b. `picCar.Hide = True`
    c. `picCar.Invisible = True`
    d. `picCar.Visible = False`

3. Which of the following statements declares an object to represent the pseudo-random number generator in a procedure?

    a. `Dim randGen As New RandomNumber`
    b. `Dim randGen As New Generator`
    c. `Dim randGen As New Random`
    d. `Dim randGen As New RandomObject`

4. Which of the following statements generates a random integer from 1 to 25, inclusive?

   a. `intNum = randGen.Next(1, 25)`
   b. `intNum = randGen.Next(1, 26)`
   c. `intNum = randGen(1, 25)`
   d. `intNum = randGen.NextNumber(1, 26)`

5. If the txtAge control is empty, the `blnIsOk = Integer.TryParse(txtAge.Text, intAge)` statement will store _____ in the `intAge` variable and also assign _____ to the `blnIsOk` variable.

   a. 0, True
   b. 0, False

   c. False, the empty string
   d. the empty string, False

Lesson C Exercises

INTRODUCTORY

1. Open the VB2015\Chap05\Riley Solution\Riley Solution (Riley Solution.sln) file. The btnCalc_Click procedure should display the message "Please enter the price." in a message box when the contents of the txtPrice control cannot be converted to a Double number. Otherwise, it should display the 25% discount and new price amounts. Make the appropriate modifications to the procedure's code. Test the application appropriately.

INTRODUCTORY

2. Create an application, using the following names for the solution and project, respectively: Lottery Solution and Lottery Project. Save the application in the VB2015\Chap05 folder. Create the interface shown in Figure 5-70. The image for the picture box is stored in the VB2015\Chap05\BagOfMoney.png file. The Select Numbers button should display six lottery numbers. Each lottery number can range from 1 through 54 only. An example of six lottery numbers would be: 4 8 35 15 20 3. For now, do not worry if the lottery numbers are not unique. You will learn how to display unique numbers in Chapter 9. Test the application appropriately.

Figure 5-70   Interface for Exercise 2

3. Create an application, using the following names for the solution and project, respectively: Zander Solution and Zander Project. Save the application in the VB2015\
Chap05 folder. Create the interface shown in Figure 5-71. The text box should accept only numbers, the period, and the Backspace key. It also should have its existing text selected when it receives the focus. The amounts in the Shipping and Total due boxes should be cleared when a change is made to any of the input items (i.e., price, region, or delivery). The application should display the appropriate shipping charge and total due. The shipping charges are included in Figure 5-71. The total due is calculated by adding together the price and the shipping charge. Only calculate the shipping charge and total due when the contents of the text box can be converted to a number; otherwise, display an appropriate message. (Hint: Although you are allowing the text box to accept only numbers, the period, and the Backspace key, the user might inadvertently enter more than one period in the price. An entry that contains more than one period cannot be converted to a number.) Test the application appropriately.

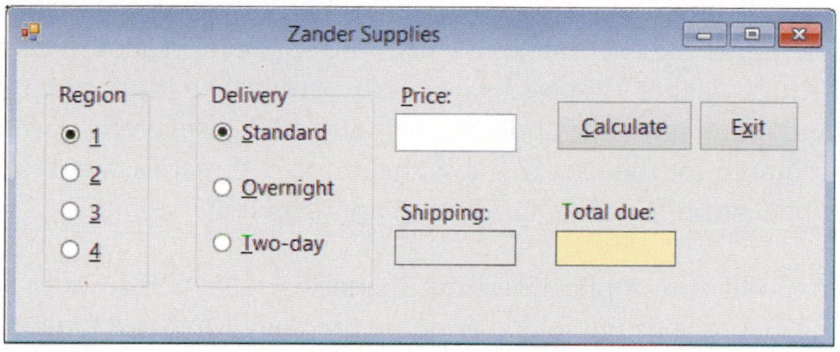

Region	Standard delivery charge ($)
1	4.99
2	6.99
3	7.99
4	2.99

Overnight delivery:	add $10 to the standard delivery charge
Two-day delivery:	add $5 to the standard delivery charge

Figure 5-71   Interface and shipping information for Exercise 3

4. Create a Visual Basic Windows application. Use the following names for the solution and project, respectively: Concert Solution and Concert Project. Save the application in the VB2015\Chap05 folder. Create the interface shown in Figure 5-72. The three text boxes should be invisible when the application starts. When the user selects a check box, its corresponding text box should appear in the interface and remain visible until the user deselects the check box. The user will enter the number of tickets he or she wants to purchase in the appropriate text box. Allow only numbers and the Backspace key. When the user deselects a check box, the contents of its corresponding text box should be cleared. Keep in mind that the user can purchase any combination of tickets, such as 3 box tickets and 5 lawn tickets, or 2 pavilion tickets, 1 box ticket, and 2 lawn tickets. The application should display the total number of tickets purchased and the total due. The tickets for box, pavilion, and lawn seats are $97.50, $55.50, and $21, respectively. The 10% check box in the interface allows the user to specify whether the customer is entitled to a 10% discount on the total due. Test the application appropriately.

Figure 5-72   Interface for Exercise 4

INTERMEDIATE ▶

5. Create an application, using the following names for the solution and project, respectively: Guessing Game Solution and Guessing Game Project. Save the application in the VB2015\Chap05 folder. The application should generate a random integer from 1 through 30, inclusive. It then should give the user as many chances as necessary to guess the integer. Each time the user makes a guess, the application should display one of three messages: "Guess higher", "Guess lower", or "Correct. The random integer is x.", where x is the random integer. The application should also display the number of chances that were required for the user to guess the number. Create a suitable interface, and then code the application. Test the application appropriately.

INTERMEDIATE ▶

6. In this exercise, you modify the application from Exercise 5. Use Windows to make a copy of the Guessing Game Solution folder. Rename the copy Modified Guessing Game Solution. Open the Guessing Game Solution (Guessing Game Solution.sln) file contained in the Modified Guessing Game Solution folder. The application should allow the user to make only five incorrect guesses. When the user has made the fifth incorrect guess, display the random integer. Modify the code to reflect these changes. Test the application appropriately.

INTERMEDIATE ▶

7. Create an application, using the following names for the solution and project, respectively: MacroTech Solution and MacroTech Project. Save the application in the VB2015\Chap05 folder. Create the interface shown in Figure 5-73. MacroTech sells a software package that is available in three editions. The application should display the price of the edition a customer wants to purchase. The retail prices for the Ultimate, Professional, and Student editions are $775.99, $499.99, and 149.99, respectively. Some customers may have a coupon worth 10% off the price of the Ultimate edition, while others may have a coupon worth 20% off the price of the Student edition. Test the application appropriately.

Figure 5-73   Interface for Exercise 7

INTERMEDIATE

8. Create an application, using the following names for the solution and project, respectively: Kerry Cable Solution and Kerry Cable Project. Save the application in the VB2015\Chap05 folder. Kerry Cable Company wants you to create an application that displays a customer's monthly cable bill, which is based on the information shown in Figure 5-74. Use radio buttons for the different packages, and use check boxes for the additional features. Test the application appropriately.

Packages	Monthly charge ($)
Basic	39.99
Silver	45.99
Gold	74.99
Diamond	99.99
Additional features	Monthly charge ($)
Cinnematic movie channels	10.50
HBI movie channels	10.50
Showtimer movie channels	11.50
Local stations	5.00

Figure 5-74   Information for Exercise 8

ADVANCED

9. Create an application, using the following names for the solution and project, respectively: Marshall Solution and Marshall Project. Save the application in the VB2015\Chap05 folder. Create the interface shown in Figure 5-75. Each salesperson at Marshall Sales Corporation receives a commission based on the amount of his or her sales. The commission rates are included in Figure 5-75. If the salesperson has worked at the company for more than 10 years, he or she receives an additional $500. If the salesperson is classified as a traveling salesperson, he or she receives an additional $700. The text box should accept only numbers, the period, and the Backspace key, and its text should be selected when it receives the focus. Make the appropriate calculations only when the sales amount can be converted to a Double number; otherwise, display an appropriate message. (Hint: Although you are allowing the text box to accept only numbers, the period, and the Backspace key, the user might inadvertently enter more than one period in the sales amount. An entry that contains more than one period cannot be converted to a number.) The calculated amounts should be cleared when a change is made to any of the input items. Test the application appropriately.

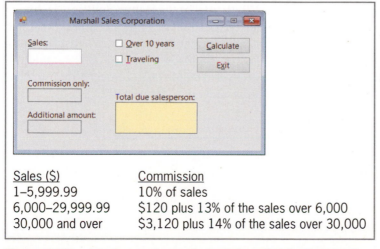

Sales ($)	Commission
1–5,999.99	10% of sales
6,000–29,999.99	$120 plus 13% of the sales over 6,000
30,000 and over	$3,120 plus 14% of the sales over 30,000

Figure 5-75   Interface and commission information for Exercise 9

ADVANCED

10. In this exercise, you create an application for Sunnyside Products. The application displays the price of an order based on the number of units ordered and the customer's status (either wholesaler or retailer). The price per unit is shown in Figure 5-76. Create an application, using the following names for the solution and project, respectively: Sunnyside Solution and Sunnyside Project. Save the application in the VB2015\Chap05 folder. Create a suitable interface. Use radio buttons to determine the customer's status. Code the application, and then test it appropriately.

Wholesaler		Retailer	
Number of units	Price per unit ($)	Number of units	Price per unit ($)
1–100	19	1–50	25
101–200	17	Over 50	20
Over 200	13		

Figure 5-76 Pricing chart for Exercise 10

DISCOVERY

11. This exercise will show you how to generate and display random numbers containing decimal places. Open the Random Double Solution (Random Double Solution.sln) file contained in the VB2015\Chap05\Random Double Solution folder.

a. Open the Code Editor window. You can use the Random.NextDouble method to return a random number that is greater than or equal to 0.0 but less than 1.0. The syntax of the Random.NextDouble method is *randomObjectName*.**NextDouble**. Code the btnDisplay_Click procedure so that it displays a random number in the lblNumber control. Save the solution and then start the application. Click the Display Random Number button several times. Each time you click the button, a random number that is greater than or equal to 0.0 but less than 1.0 appears in the lblNumber control.

b. You can use the following formula to generate random numbers within a specified range: (*maxValue* − *minValue* + 1) * *randomObjectName*.**NextDouble** + *minValue*. For example, if the Random object's name is `randGen`, the formula `(10 − 1 + 1) * randGen.NextDouble + 1` generates random numbers that are greater than or equal to 1.0 but less than 11.0. Modify the btnDisplay_Click procedure to display a random number that is greater than or equal to 25.0 but less than 51.0. Display two decimal places in the number. Test the application several times.

SWAT THE BUGS

12. The purpose of this exercise is to demonstrate the importance of testing an application thoroughly. Open the VB2015\Chap05\Debug Solution\Debug Solution (Debug Solution.sln) file. The application displays a shipping charge that is based on the total price entered by the user, as shown in Figure 5-77. Test the application using the following total prices: 100, 501, 1500, 500.75, 30, 1000.33, and 2000. Notice that the application does not always display the correct shipping charge. Correct the application's code, and then test it appropriately.

Total price	Shipping
At least $100 but less than $501	$10
At least $501 but less than $1,001	$ 7
At least $1,001	$ 5
Less than $100	$13

Figure 5-77 Shipping charges for Exercise 12

CHAPTER 6

The Repetition Structure

Creating the Monthly Payment Application

In this chapter, you create an application that displays the monthly payments on a mortgage loan using terms of 15, 20, 25, and 30 years. The term is the number of years the borrower has to pay off the loan. The user will enter the loan amount, called the principal, in a text box. He or she will select the interest rate from a list box that displays rates from 2.0% to 7.0% in increments of 0.5%.

Previewing the Monthly Payment Application

Before you start the first lesson in this chapter, you will preview the completed application contained in the VB2015\Chap06 folder.

START HERE

To preview the completed application:

1. Use Windows to locate and then open the VB2015\Chap06 folder. Right-click **Payment** (**Payment.exe**) and then click the **Open** button. The application's interface contains a list box. List box controls are covered in Lesson B.

2. Type **120000** in the Principal box, and then click **2.5** in the Rate list box. Click the **Calculate** button. The monthly payments for the different terms appear in the Monthly payment box. See Figure 6-1.

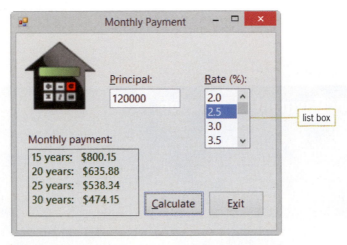

Figure 6-1   Monthly payments shown in the interface

3. Click the **Exit** button to end the application.

The Monthly Payment application uses the repetition structure, which is covered in this chapter. You will code the application in Lesson B. Be sure to complete each lesson in full and do all of the end-of-lesson questions and several exercises before continuing to the next lesson.

LESSON A

After studying Lesson A, you should be able to:

- Differentiate between a looping condition and a loop exit condition
- Explain the difference between a pretest loop and a posttest loop
- Include pretest and posttest loops in pseudocode and in a flowchart
- Write a Do...Loop statement
- Stop an infinite loop
- Utilize counters and accumulators
- Abbreviate assignment statements using the arithmetic assignment operators
- Code a counter-controlled loop using the For...Next statement

Repeating Program Instructions

Programmers use the **repetition structure**, referred to more simply as a **loop**, when they need the computer to repeatedly process one or more program instructions. The loop contains a condition that controls whether the instructions are repeated. In many programming languages, the condition can be phrased in one of two ways: It can either specify the requirement for repeating the instructions or specify the requirement for *not* repeating them. The requirement for repeating the instructions is referred to as the **looping condition** because it indicates when the computer should continue "looping" through the instructions. The requirement for *not* repeating the instructions is referred to as the **loop exit condition** because it tells the computer when to exit (or stop) the loop. Every looping condition has an opposing loop exit condition; one is the opposite of the other.

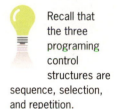

Recall that the three programing control structures are sequence, selection, and repetition.

Some examples may help illustrate the difference between the looping condition and the loop exit condition. You may have heard the old adage "Make hay while the sun shines." The "while the sun shines" part is the looping condition because it tells you when to *continue* making hay. The adage could also be phrased as "Make hay until the sun is no longer shining." In this case, the "until the sun is no longer shining" part is the loop exit condition because it indicates when you should *stop* making hay. Figure 6-2 contains two other examples of looping and loop exit conditions. As mentioned earlier, the looping and loop exit conditions are the opposite of each another.

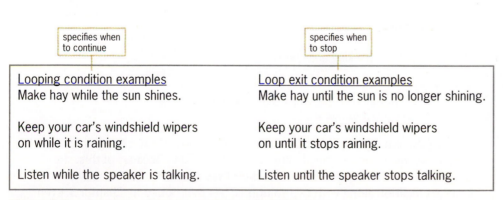

Figure 6-2   Examples of looping and loop exit conditions

Ch06A-Repetition

The programmer determines whether a problem's solution requires a loop by studying the problem specification. The first problem specification you will examine in this chapter involves a superheroine named Sahirah. The problem specification and an illustration of the problem are shown in Figure 6-3, along with a correct solution written in pseudocode. The solution uses only the sequence and selection structures because no instructions need to be repeated.

Problem Specification

A superheroine named Sahirah must prevent a poisonous yellow spider from attacking King Khafra and Queen Rashida. Sahirah has one weapon at her disposal: a laser beam that shoots out from her right hand. Unfortunately, Sahirah gets only one shot at the spider, which is flying around the palace looking for the king and queen. Before taking the shot, she needs to position both her right arm and her right hand toward the spider. After taking the shot, she should return her right arm and right hand to their original positions. In addition, if the laser beam hit the spider, she should say "You are safe now. The spider is dead."; otherwise, she should say "Run for your lives, my king and queen!"

Solution
1. position both your right arm and your right hand toward the spider
2. shoot a laser beam at the spider
3. return your right arm and your right hand to their original positions
4. if the laser beam hit the spider
        say "You are safe now. The spider is dead."
    else
        say "Run for your lives, my king and queen!"
    end if

Figure 6-3   A problem that requires the sequence and selection structures
Image by Diane Zak; created with Reallusion CrazyTalk Animator

Now, let's change the problem specification slightly. This time, rather than taking only one shot, Sahirah can take as many shots as needed to destroy the spider. Because of this, she will never need to tell the king and queen to run for their lives again. Figure 6-4 shows the modified problem specification along with two solutions. (As mentioned in Chapter 5, even small problems can have more than one solution.) Both solutions contain the sequence and repetition structures. The repetition structure in Solution 1 begins with the "repeat while the laser beam did not hit the spider" clause and ends with the "end repeat while" clause. The repetition structure in Solution 2, on the other hand, begins with the "repeat until the laser beam hits the spider" clause and ends with the "end repeat until" clause. The instructions between both clauses are called the **loop body**, and they are indented to indicate that they are part of the repetition structure.

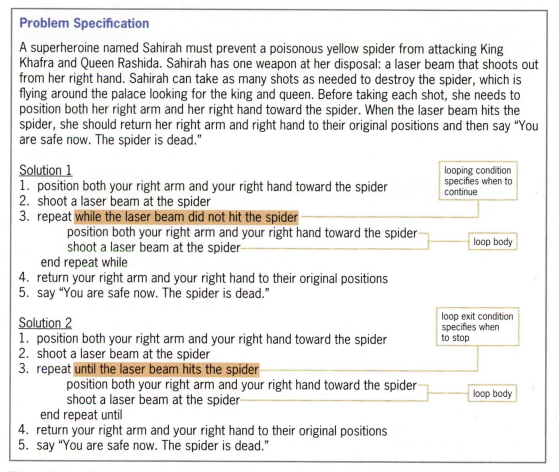

Problem Specification

A superheroine named Sahirah must prevent a poisonous yellow spider from attacking King Khafra and Queen Rashida. Sahirah has one weapon at her disposal: a laser beam that shoots out from her right hand. Sahirah can take as many shots as needed to destroy the spider, which is flying around the palace looking for the king and queen. Before taking each shot, she needs to position both her right arm and her right hand toward the spider. When the laser beam hits the spider, she should return her right arm and right hand to their original positions and then say "You are safe now. The spider is dead."

Solution 1
1. position both your right arm and your right hand toward the spider
2. shoot a laser beam at the spider
3. repeat while the laser beam did not hit the spider
    position both your right arm and your right hand toward the spider
    shoot a laser beam at the spider
   end repeat while
4. return your right arm and your right hand to their original positions
5. say "You are safe now. The spider is dead."

                                                              looping condition specifies when to continue

loop body

Solution 2
1. position both your right arm and your right hand toward the spider
2. shoot a laser beam at the spider
3. repeat until the laser beam hits the spider
    position both your right arm and your right hand toward the spider
    shoot a laser beam at the spider
   end repeat until
4. return your right arm and your right hand to their original positions
5. say "You are safe now. The spider is dead."

loop exit condition specifies when to stop

loop body

Figure 6-4   A problem that requires the sequence and repetition structures

The shaded portion in each solution in Figure 6-4 specifies the repetition structure's condition. The condition in Solution 1 is phrased as a looping condition because it tells Sahirah when to *continue* repeating the instructions. In this case, she should repeat the instructions as long as (or while) the laser beam did not hit the spider. The condition in Solution 2 is phrased as a loop exit condition because it tells Sahirah when to *stop* repeating the instructions. In this case, she should stop when the laser beam hits the spider. Notice that the loop exit condition is the opposite of the looping condition. Whether you use a looping condition or a loop exit condition, the condition must evaluate to a Boolean value (either True or False).

YOU DO IT 1!

Using only the seven instructions shown here, write two solutions for printing the pages in a document that contains at least one page. Use a looping condition in the first solution. Use a loop exit condition in the second solution.

end repeat until
end repeat while
print the next page
print the first page
repeat until there are no more pages to print
repeat while there is another page to print
say "Done printing"

The Projected Sales Application

Figure 6-5 shows the next problem specification you will examine in this chapter, along with the pseudocode and code for the Calculate Projected Sales button's Click event procedure. The procedure requires only the sequence structure. It does not need a selection structure or a loop because no decisions need to be made and no instructions need to be repeated to display the projected sales amount for the following year.

Problem Specification

Create an application that displays the amount of a company's projected sales for the following year, using a 3% growth rate per year.

Pseudocode for the Calculate Projected Sales button's Click event procedure
1. store current sales in sales variable
2. increase = sales * growth rate
3. sales = sales + increase
4. display sales

Code for the Calculate Projected Sales button's Click event procedure
```
Const dblGROWTH_RATE As Double = 0.03
Dim dblSales As Double
Dim dblIncrease As Double

Double.TryParse(txtCurrentSales.Text, dblSales)
dblIncrease = dblSales * dblGROWTH_RATE
dblSales = dblSales + dblIncrease
lblProjSales.Text = "Projected sales for next year: " &
    dblSales.ToString("c0")
```

Figure 6-5   Problem specification, pseudocode, and code for the Projected Sales application

To run the Projected Sales application:

1. If necessary, start Visual Studio 2015. Open the VB2015\Chap06\Sales Solution\Sales Solution (Sales Solution.sln) file. Open the Code Editor window. Replace <your name> and <current date> in the comments with your name and the current date, respectively.

2. Locate the btnCalc_Click procedure, which contains the code shown in Figure 6-5. Save the solution and then start the application. Type **92000** in the Current sales box and then click the **Calculate Projected Sales** button. See Figure 6-6.

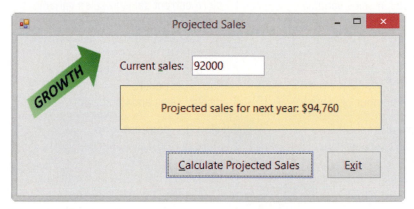

Figure 6-6   Sample run of the Projected Sales application

3. Click the **Exit** button.

Now, we'll make a slight change to the problem specification from Figure 6-5. The application will now need to display the number of years required for the projected sales to reach at least $150,000. It will also need to display the projected sales amount at that time. Consider the changes you will need to make to the Calculate Projected Sales button's original pseudocode.

The first step in the original pseudocode is to store the current sales amount in a variable; the modified pseudocode will still need this step. Steps 2 and 3 calculate the projected increase and projected sales, respectively, for the following year. The modified pseudocode will need to repeat both steps either while the projected sales amount is less than $150,000 (looping condition) or until it is greater than or equal to $150,000 (loop exit condition). Here, too, notice that the loop exit condition is the opposite of the looping condition. The loop in the modified pseudocode will also need to keep track of the number of times the instructions in Steps 2 and 3 are processed because each time represents a year. The last step in the original pseudocode displays the projected sales amount. The modified pseudocode will need to display the projected sales amount as well as the number of years.

The modified problem specification is shown in Figure 6-7 along with four versions of the modified pseudocode for the Calculate Projected Sales button's Click event procedure. (Here again, notice that even small procedures can have many solutions.) Only the loop is different in each version.

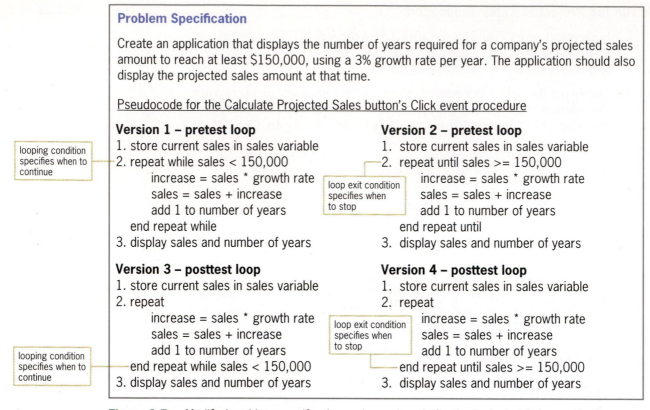

looping condition specifies when to continue

loop exit condition specifies when to stop

looping condition specifies when to continue

loop exit condition specifies when to stop

Figure 6-7   Modified problem specification and pseudocode for the Projected Sales application

Pretest and posttest loops are also called top-driven and bottom-driven loops, respectively.

The loops in Versions 1 and 2 are pretest loops. In a **pretest loop**, the condition appears at the beginning of the loop, indicating that it is evaluated *before* the instructions within the loop are processed. The condition in Version 1 is a looping condition because it tells the computer when to continue repeating the loop instructions. Version 2's condition, on the other hand, is a loop exit condition because it tells the computer when to stop repeating the instructions. Depending on the result of the evaluation, the instructions in a pretest loop may never be processed. For example, if the sales amount entered by the user is greater than or equal to 150,000, the "while sales < 150,000" looping condition in Version 1 will evaluate to False and the loop instructions will be skipped over. Similarly, the "until sales >= 150,000" loop exit condition in Version 2 will evaluate to True, causing the loop instructions to be bypassed.

The loops in Versions 3 and 4 in Figure 6-7, on the other hand, are posttest loops. In a **posttest loop**, the condition appears at the end of the loop, indicating that it is evaluated *after* the instructions within the loop are processed. The condition in Version 3 is a looping condition, whereas the condition in Version 4 is a loop exit condition. Unlike the instructions in a pretest loop, the instructions in a posttest loop will always be processed at least once before the loop ends. Posttest loops should be used only when you are certain that the loop instructions should be processed one or more times.

The Visual Basic language provides three different statements for coding loops: Do...Loop, For...Next, and For Each...Next. The Do...Loop statement can be used to code both pretest and posttest loops, whereas the For...Next and For Each...Next statements are used only for pretest loops. You will learn about the Do...Loop and For...Next statements in this lesson. The For Each...Next statement is covered in Chapter 9.

The Do...Loop Statement

Figure 6-8 shows two versions of the syntax for the **Do...Loop statement**: one for coding a pretest loop and the other for coding a posttest loop. The {While | Until} portion in each syntax indicates that you can select only one of the keywords appearing within the braces. You follow the keyword with a *condition*, which can be phrased as either a looping condition or a loop exit condition. You use the `While` keyword in a looping condition to specify that the loop body should be processed *while* (in other words, as long as) the condition is true. You use the `Until` keyword in a loop exit condition to specify that the loop body should be processed *until* the condition becomes true, at which time the loop should stop. Like the condition in an If...Then... Else statement, the condition in a Do...Loop statement can contain variables, constants, properties, methods, keywords, and operators; it also must evaluate to a Boolean value. The condition is evaluated with each repetition of the loop and determines whether the computer processes the loop body. Notice that the keyword (either `While` or `Until`) and the condition appear in the Do clause in a pretest loop, but they appear in the Loop clause in a posttest loop.

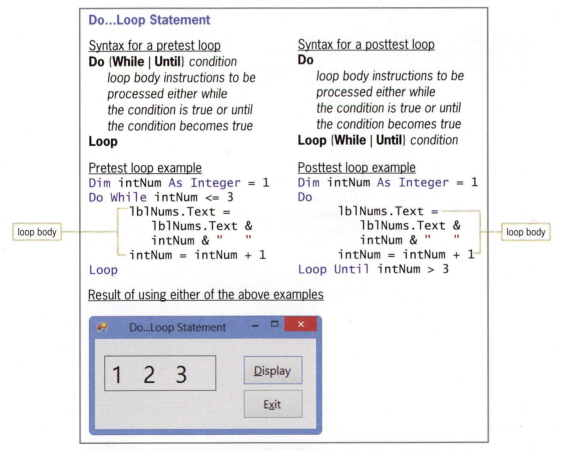

You can use the `Exit Do` statement to exit the Do... Loop statement before the loop has finished processing. You may need to do this if the computer encounters an error when processing the loop instructions.

Figure 6-8 Syntax versions and examples of the Do...Loop statement

Figure 6-8 also shows examples of using both syntax versions to display the numbers 1, 2, and 3 in a label control, and it includes a sample run of an application that contains either example. Figure 6-9 describes the way the computer processes the code shown in the examples.

Ch06A-Do Loop

Processing steps for the pretest loop example

1. The `intNum` variable is created and initialized to 1.
2. The Do clause checks whether the value in the `intNum` variable (1) is less than or equal to 3. It is, so the loop body instructions display the number 1 in the lblNums control and then add 1 to the contents of the `intNum` variable, giving 2.
3. The Loop clause returns processing to the Do clause (the beginning of the loop).
4. The Do clause checks whether the value in the `intNum` variable (2) is less than or equal to 3. It is, so the loop body instructions display the numbers 1 and 2 (separated by spaces) in the lblNums control and then add 1 to the contents of the `intNum` variable, giving 3.
5. The Loop clause returns processing to the Do clause (the beginning of the loop).
6. The Do clause checks whether the value in the `intNum` variable (3) is less than or equal to 3. It is, so the loop body instructions display the numbers 1, 2, and 3 (separated by spaces) in the lblNums control and then add 1 to the contents of the `intNum` variable, giving 4.
7. The Loop clause returns processing to the Do clause (the beginning of the loop).
8. The Do clause checks whether the value in the `intNum` variable (4) is less than or equal to 3. It isn't, so the loop ends. Processing will continue with the statement following the Loop clause.

Processing steps for the posttest loop example

1. The `intNum` variable is created and initialized to 1.
2. The Do clause marks the beginning of the posttest loop.
3. The loop body instructions display the number 1 in the lblNums control and then add 1 to the contents of the `intNum` variable, giving 2.
4. The Loop clause checks whether the value in the `intNum` variable (2) is greater than 3. It isn't, so processing returns to the Do clause (the beginning of the loop).
5. The loop body instructions display the numbers 1 and 2 (separated by spaces) in the lblNums control and then add 1 to the contents of the `intNum` variable, giving 3.
6. The Loop clause checks whether the value in the `intNum` variable (3) is greater than 3. It isn't, so processing returns to the Do clause (the beginning of the loop).
7. The loop body instructions display the numbers 1, 2, and 3 (separated by spaces) in the lblNums control and then add 1 to the contents of the `intNum` variable, giving 4.
8. The Loop clause checks whether the value in the `intNum` variable (4) is greater than 3. It is, so the loop ends. Processing will continue with the statement following the Loop clause.

Figure 6-9   Processing steps for the loop examples from Figure 6-8

Although both examples in Figure 6-8 produce the same results, pretest and posttest loops are not always interchangeable. For instance, if the `intNum` variable in the pretest loop in Figure 6-8 is initialized to 10 rather than to 1, the instructions in the pretest loop will not be processed because the `intNum <= 3` condition (which is evaluated before the instructions are processed) evaluates to False. However, if the `intNum` variable in the posttest loop is initialized to 10 rather than to 1, the instructions in the posttest loop will be processed one time because the `intNum > 3` condition is evaluated after (rather than before) the loop instructions are processed.

It's often easier to understand loops by viewing them in flowchart form. Figure 6-10 shows the flowcharts associated with the loop examples from Figure 6-8. The diamond in each flowchart indicates the beginning of a repetition structure (loop). Like the diamond in a selection structure, the diamond in a repetition structure contains a condition that evaluates to either True or False only. The condition determines whether the instructions within the loop are processed. Also, like the diamond in a selection structure, the diamond in a repetition structure has one flowline entering the symbol and two flowlines leaving the symbol. The two flowlines leading out of the diamond should be marked so that anyone reading the flowchart can distinguish the true path from the false path. Typically, the flowlines are marked with a T (for true) and an F (for false); however, they can also be marked with a Y (for yes) and an N (for no).

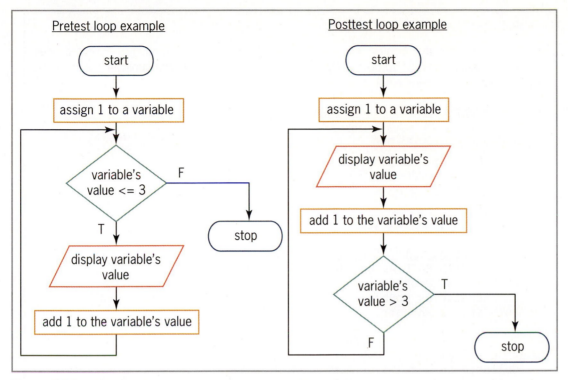

Figure 6-10 Flowcharts for the loop examples from Figure 6-8

In the pretest loop's flowchart in Figure 6-10, a circle or loop is formed by the flowline entering the diamond combined with the diamond itself and the symbols and flowlines within the true path. In the posttest loop's flowchart, the loop (circle) is formed by all of the symbols in the false path. It is this loop (circle) that distinguishes the repetition structure from the selection structure in a flowchart.

YOU DO IT 2!

Close the Projected Sales application's solution, if necessary. Create an application named YouDoIt 2 and save it in the VB2015\Chap06 folder. Add two buttons to the form. Both buttons should display the following numbers in message boxes: 1, 3, 5, and 7. Code the first button's Click event procedure using a pretest loop. Code the second button's Click event procedure using a posttest loop. Save the solution, and then start and test the application. Close the solution.

Coding the Modified Projected Sales Application

Figure 6-11 shows the modified pseudocode from Version 1 in Figure 6-7. It also shows the corresponding Visual Basic code. The changes made to the original pseudocode and code, which were shown earlier in Figure 6-5, are shaded in Figure 6-11. The looping condition in the Do...Loop statement tells the computer to repeat the loop body as long as (or while) the number in the **dblSales** variable is less than 150000. You can also use a loop exit condition in the Do clause, like this: Do Until dblSales >= 150000. (Recall that >= is the opposite of <.)

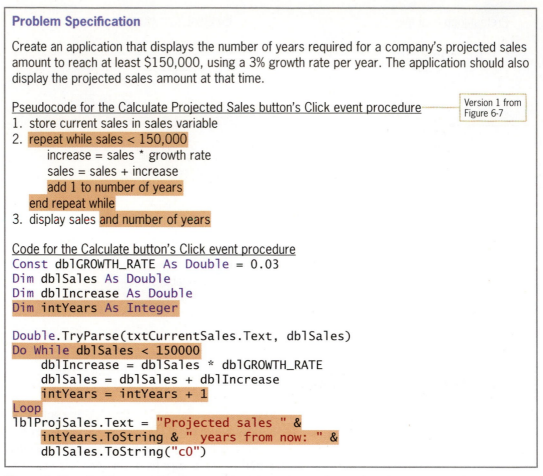

Problem Specification

Create an application that displays the number of years required for a company's projected sales amount to reach at least $150,000, using a 3% growth rate per year. The application should also display the projected sales amount at that time.

Pseudocode for the Calculate Projected Sales button's Click event procedure — Version 1 from Figure 6-7
1. store current sales in sales variable
2. repeat while sales < 150,000
   increase = sales * growth rate
   sales = sales + increase
   add 1 to number of years
   end repeat while
3. display sales and number of years

Code for the Calculate button's Click event procedure
```
Const dblGROWTH_RATE As Double = 0.03
Dim dblSales As Double
Dim dblIncrease As Double
Dim intYears As Integer

Double.TryParse(txtCurrentSales.Text, dblSales)
Do While dblSales < 150000
    dblIncrease = dblSales * dblGROWTH_RATE
    dblSales = dblSales + dblIncrease
    intYears = intYears + 1
Loop
lblProjSales.Text = "Projected sales " &
    intYears.ToString & " years from now: " &
    dblSales.ToString("c0")
```

Figure 6-11   Problem specification, pseudocode, and code for the modified Projected Sales application

START HERE

To modify the Projected Sales application:

1. If necessary, open the VB2015\Chap06\Sales Solution\Sales Solution (Sales Solution.sln) file. Open the Code Editor window and then locate the btnCalc_Click procedure. Make the modifications shaded in Figure 6-11 to the procedure's code.

2. Save the solution and then start the application. Type **92000** in the Current sales box and then click the **Calculate Projected Sales** button. See Figure 6-12.

Figure 6-12   Sample run of the modified Projected Sales application

3. Delete the contents of the Current sales box, and then click the **Calculate Projected Sales** button. After a short period of time, a run time error occurs and the error message box shown in Figure 6-13 appears on the screen. (It may take as long as 30 seconds for the error message box to appear.) Place your mouse pointer on `intYears`, as shown in the figure.

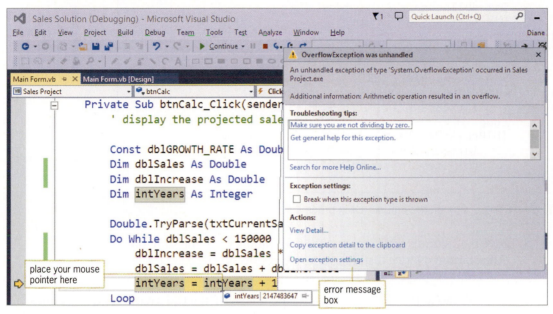

Figure 6-13   Screen showing the error message box

The error message informs you that an arithmetic operation—in this case, adding 1 to the `intYears` variable—resulted in an overflow. An **overflow error** occurs when the value assigned to a memory location is too large for the location's data type. (An overflow error is similar to trying to fill an 8-ounce glass with 10 ounces of water.) In this case, the `intYears` variable already contains the highest value that can be stored in an Integer variable (2,147,483,647 according to Figure 3-3 in Chapter 3). Therefore, when the `intYears = intYears + 1` statement attempts to increase the variable's value by 1, an overflow error occurs.

But why does the `intYears` variable contain 2,147,483,647? In this case, because you didn't provide an initial value for the current sales amount, the loop's condition (`dblSales < 150000`) always evaluated to True; it never evaluated to False, which is required for stopping the loop. A loop that has no way to end is called an **infinite loop** or an **endless loop**. You can stop a program that has an infinite loop by clicking Debug on the menu bar and then clicking Stop Debugging. Or, you can click the Stop Debugging button (the red square) on the Standard toolbar.

To modify and then test the btnCalc_Click procedure:

START HERE

1. Click **Debug** on the menu bar, and then click **Stop Debugging**.

2. In the btnCalc_Click procedure, change the condition in the Do While clause to a compound condition, as indicated in Figure 6-14.

```
Private Sub btnCalc_Click(sender As Object, e As EventArgs
) Handles btnCalc.Click
    ' display the projected sales

    Const dblGROWTH_RATE As Double = 0.03
    Dim dblSales As Double
    Dim dblIncrease As Double
    Dim intYears As Integer

    Double.TryParse(txtCurrentSales.Text, dblSales)
    Do While dblSales > 0 AndAlso dblSales < 150000
        dblIncrease = dblSales * dblGROWTH_RATE
        dblSales = dblSales + dblIncrease
        intYears = intYears + 1
    Loop
    lblProjSales.Text = "Projected sales " &
        intYears.ToString & " years from now: " &
        dblSales.ToString("c0")
End Sub
```

make the shaded modification

Figure 6-14   Completed btnCalc_Click procedure

3. Save the solution and then start the application. Click the **Calculate Projected Sales** button. Notice that no overflow error occurs. Instead, the button's Click event procedure displays the "Projected sales 0 years from now: $0" message.

4. Type **92000** in the Current sales box, and then click the **Calculate Projected Sales** button. The button's Click event procedure displays the message shown earlier in Figure 6-12.

5. On your own, test the application using different sales amounts. When you are finished, click the **Exit** button. Close the Code Editor window and then close the solution.

The Click event procedure shown in Figure 6-14 uses a counter (intYears) to keep track of the number of years. It also uses an accumulator (dblSales) to keep track of the projected sales amount. Counters and accumulators are covered in the next section.

Counters and Accumulators

Some procedures require you to calculate a subtotal, a total, or an average. You make these calculations using a loop that includes a counter, an accumulator, or both. A **counter** is a numeric variable used for counting something, such as the number of employees paid in a week. An **accumulator** is a numeric variable used for accumulating (adding together) something, such as the total dollar amount of a week's payroll. The intYears variable in the code shown earlier in Figure 6-14 is a counter because it keeps track of the number of years required for the projected sales amount to reach $150,000. The dblSales variable in the code is an accumulator because it adds together the projected increase amounts.

Two tasks are associated with counters and accumulators: initializing and updating. **Initializing** means assigning a beginning value to the counter or accumulator. Typically, counters and accumulators are initialized to the number 0. However, they can be initialized to any number depending on the value required by the procedure's code. The initialization task is performed before the loop is processed because it needs to be performed only once.

Updating refers to the process of either adding a number to (called **incrementing**) or subtracting a number from (called **decrementing**) the value stored in the counter or accumulator. The number can be either positive or negative, integer or non-integer. A counter is always updated by a constant amount—typically the number 1. An accumulator, on the other hand, is usually updated by an amount that varies. Accumulators are usually updated by incrementing rather than by decrementing. The assignment statement that updates a counter or an accumulator is placed in the body of a loop. This is because the update task must be performed each time the loop instructions are processed.

Game programs make extensive use of counters and accumulators. The partial game program shown in Figure 6-15, for example, uses a counter to keep track of the number of smiley faces that Eddie (the character in the figure) destroys. After he destroys three smiley faces and then jumps through the manhole, he advances to the next level in the game, as shown in the figure.

ChO6A-Eddie

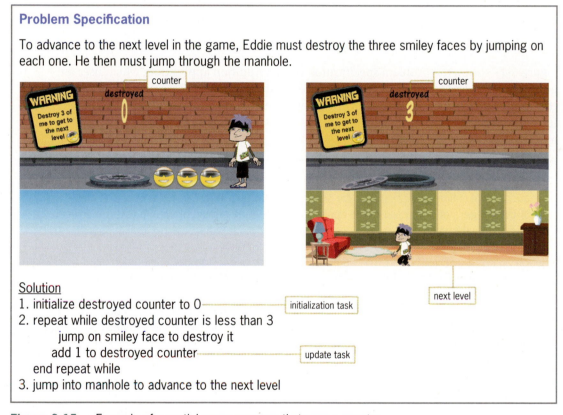

Figure 6-15   Example of a partial game program that uses a counter
Image by Diane Zak; created with Reallusion CrazyTalk Animator

Figure 6-16 shows the syntax used for updating counters and accumulators; it also includes examples of using each syntax. (You can also use arithmetic assignment operators to update counters and accumulators. You will learn about those operators in the *Arithmetic Assignment Operators* section.) In the syntax for counters, notice that *counterVariable* appears on both sides of the assignment operator (=). The syntax tells the computer to add the *constantValue* to (or subtract the *constantValue* from) the *counterVariable* first and then place the result back in the *counterVariable*. In the syntax for accumulators, *accumulatorVariable* appears on both sides of the assignment operator (=). This syntax tells the computer to add the *value* to (or subtract the *value* from) the *accumulatorVariable* first and then place the result back in the *accumulatorVariable*.

Updating Counters and Accumulators

Syntax
counterVariable = counterVariable {+ | −} constantValue
accumulatorVariable = accumulatorVariable {+ | −} value

Counter examples
```
intYears = intYears + 1
intStudents = intStudents + 1
intEvenNum = intEvenNum + 2
```

Accumulator examples
```
dblSales = dblSales + dblIncrease
intSum = intSum + intNum
decTotal = decTotal + decScore
```

Figure 6-16   Syntax and examples of update statements for counters and accumulators

The Addition Application

Figure 6-17 shows the problem specification for the Addition application, which uses an accumulator to add together (accumulate) the numbers entered by the user. In this application, the accumulator is a class-level variable named intSum. The figure also shows the pseudocode for the Add and Start Over buttons' Click event procedures as well as a sample run of the application.

Problem Specification

Create an application that calculates the sum of the integers entered by the user and also displays a list of the integers and their sum. The application's interface should provide a text box for entering the integers and another text box for displaying the list of integers entered. It also should provide a label for displaying the sum. In addition to an Exit button, the interface should provide an Add button and a Start Over button. The Add button should perform the calculation and display tasks, using an accumulator to total the integers. The accumulator should be a class-level Integer variable. The Start Over button should reset the accumulator to 0 and also clear the existing data from the screen. Use the following names for the controls in the interface: txtNumber, txtList, lblSum, btnAdd, btnStartOver, and btnExit. Use the following names for the variables: intNum and intSum (accumulator).

Pseudocode for the Add button's Click event procedure
1. display (in the txtList control) the integer entered by the user
2. add the integer entered by the user to the intSum accumulator
3. display the intSum accumulator's value in the lblSum control
4. send the focus to the txtNumber control and select its existing text

Pseudocode for the Start Over button's Click event procedure
1. reset the intSum accumulator to 0
2. clear the contents of the txtNumber, txtList, and lblSum controls
3. send the focus to the txtNumber control

Figure 6-17   Problem specification, pseudocode, and a sample run for the Addition application *(continues)*

(continued)

Sample run

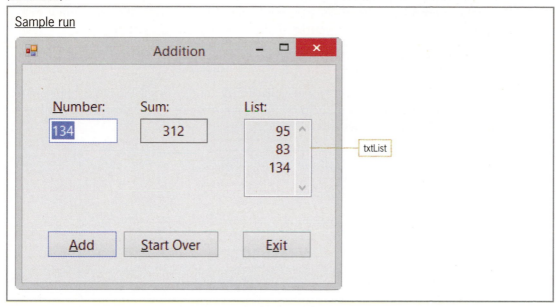

Figure 6-17   Problem specification, pseudocode, and a sample run for the Addition application

The txtList control in the interface has its Multiline and ReadOnly properties set to True and its ScrollBars property set to Vertical. When a text box's **Multiline property** is set to True, the text box can both accept and display multiple lines of text; otherwise, only one line of text can be entered in the text box. Changing a text box's **ReadOnly property** from its default value (False) to True prevents the user from changing the contents of the text box during run time. A text box's **ScrollBars property** specifies whether the text box has no scroll bars (the default), a horizontal scroll bar, a vertical scroll bar, or both horizontal and vertical scroll bars. The txtList control also has its TextAlign property set to Right.

To code and then test the btnAdd_Click procedure:

START HERE

1. Open the VB2015\Chap06\Addition Solution\Addition Solution (Addition Solution.sln) file. Open the Code Editor window. Replace <your name> and <current date> in the comments with your name and the current date, respectively.

2. First, you will declare the `intSum` accumulator variable, which should be a class-level Integer variable. A class-level variable is appropriate in this case because the variable will need to be used by two different procedures: btnAdd_Click and btnStartOver_Click.

3. In the blank line before the ' `class-level accumulator` comment, type the following Private statement and then press **Enter**:

   Private intSum As Integer

4. Next, locate the btnAdd_Click procedure. In the blank line above the End Sub clause, type the following Dim statement and then press **Enter** twice:

   Dim intNum As Integer

5. Step 1 in the Add button's pseudocode is to display (in the txtList control) the integer entered by the user. Enter the following comment and assignment statement. Press **Enter** twice after typing the assignment statement.

   ' display number in the list
   txtList.Text = txtList.Text &
       txtNumber.Text & ControlChars.NewLine

6. Step 2 adds the integer entered by the user to the intSum accumulator. Before you can enter the appropriate assignment statement, you need to convert the user's input to a number. Enter the following TryParse method and assignment statement:

Integer.TryParse(txtNumber.Text, intNum)
intSum = intSum + intNum

7. The last two steps in the pseudocode display the accumulator's value in the appropriate label control, send the focus to the txtNumber control, and then select its existing text. Enter the comment and lines of code indicated in Figure 6-18.

```
Private Sub btnAdd_Click(sender As Object, e As EventArgs
) Handles btnAdd.Click
    ' accumulate the numbers entered by the user

    Dim intNum As Integer

    ' display number in the list
    txtList.Text = txtList.Text &
        txtNumber.Text & ControlChars.NewLine

    Integer.TryParse(txtNumber.Text, intNum)
    intSum = intSum + intNum
    lblSum.Text = intSum.ToString
    ' send focus and select text
    txtNumber.Focus()
    txtNumber.SelectAll()
End Sub
```

enter this comment and three lines of code

Figure 6-18   Completed btnAdd_Click procedure

8. Save the solution and then start the application. Type the following three numbers, pressing **Enter** after typing each one: **95**, **83**, and **134**. The three numbers appear in the txtList control, and 312 appears in the Sum box, as shown earlier in Figure 6-17.

9. Type the following three numbers, pressing **Enter** after typing each one: **4**, **76**, and **2**. The number 394 appears in the Sum box, and a scroll box appears on the txtList control. The scroll box allows you to view the numbers that are not currently displayed in the control. See Figure 6-19.

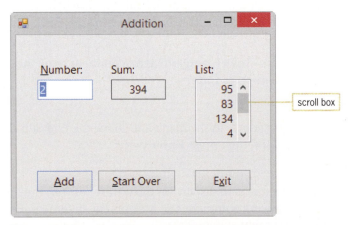

Figure 6-19   Scroll box on the txtList control

10. Use the scroll box to scroll through the list of numbers contained in the txtList control, and then click the **Exit** button.

Next, you will complete the Addition application by coding its Start Over button's Click event procedure. According to its pseudocode (shown earlier in Figure 6-17), the procedure should reset the accumulator variable to 0. It should also clear the contents of the two text boxes and the lblSum control, and then send the focus to the txtNumber control.

To code and then test the btnStartOver_Click procedure:

START HERE

1. Open the code template for the btnStartOver_Click procedure. Enter the comment and five lines of code indicated in Figure 6-20.

```
Private Sub btnStartOver_Click(sender As Object, e As EventArgs
) Handles btnStartOver.Click
    ' reset accumulator, clear screen, set focus

    intSum = 0
    txtNumber.Text = String.Empty
    txtList.Text = String.Empty
    lblSum.Text = String.Empty
    txtNumber.Focus()
End Sub
```

enter this comment and five lines of code

Figure 6-20 Completed btnStartOver_Click procedure

2. Save the solution and then start the application. Type any three numbers, pressing **Enter** after typing each one, and then click the **Start Over** button. The button's Click event procedure clears the contents of the txtNumber, txtList, and lblSum controls.

3. Recall that the button's Click event procedure also resets the intSum accumulator variable to 0. To verify that fact, type the following two numbers, pressing **Enter** after typing each one: **2** and **5**. The correct sum, 7, appears in the Sum box.

4. Click the **Exit** button. Close the Code Editor window and then close the solution.

YOU DO IT 3!

Create an application named YouDoIt 3 and save it in the VB2015\Chap06 folder. Add a label and two buttons to the form. The first button's Click event procedure should keep track of the number of times the button is clicked while always displaying the current count in the label. The second button's Click event procedure should clear the label's contents and also allow the user to start counting from 0 again. Code each button's Click event procedure. Save the solution, and then start and test the application. Close the solution.

Arithmetic Assignment Operators

In addition to the standard arithmetic operators listed in Figure 2-32 in Chapter 2, Visual Basic provides several arithmetic assignment operators. You can use the **arithmetic assignment operators** to abbreviate an assignment statement that contains an arithmetic operator. However, the assignment statement must have the following format, in which *variableName* on both sides of the equal sign is the name of the same variable: *variableName = variableName arithmeticOperator value*. For example, you can use the addition assignment operator (+=)

to abbreviate the statement `intYears = intYears + 1` as follows: `intYears += 1`. Both statements tell the computer to add the number 1 to the contents of the `intYears` variable and then store the result in the variable.

Figure 6-21 shows the syntax for using arithmetic assignment operators, and it includes examples of using them. Notice that each arithmetic assignment operator consists of an arithmetic operator followed immediately by the assignment operator (=). The arithmetic assignment operators do not contain a space; including a space in an arithmetic assignment operator is a common syntax error. To abbreviate an assignment statement, you simply remove the variable name that appears on the left side of the assignment operator and then put the assignment operator immediately after the arithmetic operator.

Arithmetic Assignment Operators

<u>Syntax</u>
variableName arithmeticAssignmentOperator value

<u>Operator</u>	<u>Purpose</u>
+=	addition assignment
−=	subtraction assignment
*=	multiplication assignment
/=	division assignment

<u>Example 1</u>
Original statement: `intYears = intYears + 1`
Abbreviated statement: `intYears += 1`
Both statements add 1 to the number stored in the `intYears` variable and then assign the result to the variable.

<u>Example 2</u>
Original statement: `decPrice = decPrice - decDiscount`
Abbreviated statement: `decPrice -= decDiscount`
Both statements subtract the number stored in the `decDiscount` variable from the number stored in the `decPrice` variable and then assign the result to the `decPrice` variable.

<u>Example 3</u>
Original statement: `dblPrice = dblPrice * 1.05`
Abbreviated statement: `dblPrice *= 1.05`
Both statements multiply the number stored in the `dblPrice` variable by 1.05 and then assign the result to the variable.

<u>Example 4</u>
Original statement: `dblNum = dblNum / 2`
Abbreviated statement: `dblNum /= 2`
Both statements divide the number stored in the `dblNum` variable by 2 and then assign the result to the variable.

Figure 6-21   Syntax and examples of the arithmetic assignment operators

START HERE ▶

To use an arithmetic assignment operator in the Addition application:

1. Use Windows to make a copy of the Addition Solution folder. Rename the copy Modified Addition Solution. Open the Addition Solution (Addition Solution.sln) file contained in the Modified Addition Solution folder.

2. Open the Code Editor window. In the btnAdd_Click procedure, change the statement that accumulates the numbers to **intSum += intNum**.

3. Save the solution and then start the application. Type the following three numbers, pressing **Enter** after typing each one: **95**, **83**, and **134**. The three numbers appear in the txtList control, and 312 appears in the Sum box, as shown earlier in Figure 6-17.

4. Click the **Exit** button. Close the Code Editor window and then close the solution.

Note: You have learned a lot so far in this lesson. You may want to take a break at this point before continuing.

The For...Next Statement

Unlike the Do...Loop statement, which can be used to code both pretest and posttest loops, the **For...Next statement** can be used to code only a specific type of pretest loop, called a counter-controlled loop. A **counter-controlled loop** is a loop whose processing is controlled by a counter. You use a counter-controlled loop when you want the computer to process the loop instructions a precise number of times. Although you can also use the Do...Loop statement to code a counter-controlled loop, the For...Next statement provides a more compact and convenient way of writing that type of loop.

Figure 6-22 shows the For...Next statement's syntax and includes examples of using the statement. It also shows the tasks performed by the computer when processing the statement. You enter the loop body, which contains the instructions you want the computer to repeat, between the statement's For and Next clauses. The *counterVariableName* that appears in both clauses is the name of a numeric variable that the computer will use to keep track of (in other words, count) the number of times the loop body instructions are processed. Although, technically, you do not need to specify the name of the counter variable in the Next clause, doing so is highly recommended because such self-documentation makes your code easier to understand.

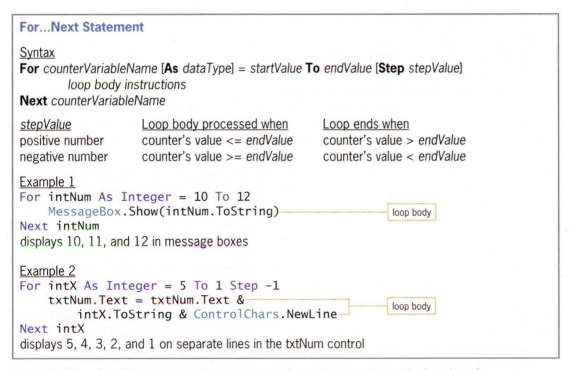

For...Next Statement

Syntax
For *counterVariableName* [**As** *dataType*] = *startValue* **To** *endValue* [**Step** *stepValue*]
    loop body instructions
Next *counterVariableName*

stepValue	Loop body processed when	Loop ends when
positive number	counter's value <= *endValue*	counter's value > *endValue*
negative number	counter's value >= *endValue*	counter's value < *endValue*

Example 1
```
For intNum As Integer = 10 To 12
    MessageBox.Show(intNum.ToString)          loop body
Next intNum
```
displays 10, 11, and 12 in message boxes

Example 2
```
For intX As Integer = 5 To 1 Step -1
    txtNum.Text = txtNum.Text &
        intX.ToString & ControlChars.NewLine     loop body
Next intX
```
displays 5, 4, 3, 2, and 1 on separate lines in the txtNum control

 You can use the Exit For statement to exit the For...Next statement before the loop has finished processing. You may need to do this if the computer encounters an error when processing the loop instructions.

Figure 6-22 For...Next statement's syntax, examples, and processing tasks *(continues)*

(continued)

Example 3

```
Dim dblRate As Double
For dblRate = 0.05 To 0.1 Step 0.01
    lblRates.Text = lblRates.Text &
        dblRate.ToString("P0") &
        ControlChars.NewLine
Next dblRate
```
⎯⎯ loop body

displays 5 %, 6 %, 7 %, 8 %, 9 %, and 10 % on separate lines in the lblRates control

Processing tasks
1. If the counter variable is declared in the For clause, the variable is created and then initialized to the *startValue*; otherwise, it is just initialized to the *startValue*. The initialization task is done only once, at the beginning of the loop.
2. The counter's value is compared with the *endValue* to determine whether the loop should end. If the *stepValue* is a positive number, the comparison determines whether the counter's value is greater than the *endValue*. If the *stepValue* is a negative number, the comparison determines whether the counter's value is less than the *endValue*. Notice that the computer evaluates the loop condition before processing the instructions within the loop.
3. If the comparison from Step 2 evaluates to True, the loop ends and processing continues with the statement following the Next clause. Otherwise, the loop body instructions are processed and then Task 4 is performed.
4. Task 4 is performed only when the comparison from Task 2 evaluates to False. In this task, the *stepValue* is added to the counter's value, and then Tasks 2, 3, and 4 are repeated until the loop condition evaluates to True.

Figure 6-22   For...Next statement's syntax, examples, and processing tasks

You can use the As *dataType* portion of the For clause to declare the counter variable, as shown in the first two examples in Figure 6-22. When you declare a variable in the For clause, the variable has block scope and can be used only within the For...Next loop. Alternatively, you can declare the counter variable in a Dim statement, as shown in Example 3. As you know, a variable declared in a Dim statement at the beginning of a procedure has procedure scope and can be used within the entire procedure. When deciding where to declare the counter variable, keep in mind that if the variable is needed only by the For...Next loop, then it is a better programming practice to declare the variable in the For clause. As mentioned in Chapter 3, fewer unintentional errors occur in applications when the variables are declared using the minimum scope needed. Block-level variables have the smallest scope, followed by procedure-level variables and then class-level variables. You should declare the counter variable in a Dim statement only when its value is required by statements outside the For...Next loop in the procedure.

The *startValue*, *endValue*, and *stepValue* items in the For clause control the number of times the loop body is processed. The startValue and endValue tell the computer where to begin and end counting, respectively. The stepValue tells the computer how much to count by—in other words, how much to add to the counter variable each time the loop body is processed. If you omit the stepValue, a stepValue of positive 1 is used. In Example 1 in Figure 6-22, the startValue is 10, the endValue is 12, and the stepValue (which is omitted) is 1. Those values tell the computer to start counting at 10 and, counting by 1s, stop at 12—in other words, count 10, 11, and 12. The computer will process the instructions in Example 1's loop body three times.

The startValue, endValue, and stepValue items must be numeric and can be either positive or negative, integer or non-integer. As indicated in Figure 6-22, if the stepValue is a positive number, the startValue must be less than or equal to the endValue for the loop instructions to be processed. For instance, the `For intNum As Integer = 10 To 12` clause is correct, but the `For intNum As Integer = 12 To 10` clause is not correct because you cannot count from 12 (the startValue) to 10 (the endValue) by adding increments of 1 (the stepValue). If, on the other hand, the stepValue is a negative number, then the startValue must be greater than or equal to the endValue for the loop instructions to be processed. As a result, the `For intX As Integer = 5 To 1 Step -1` clause is correct, but the `For intX As Integer = 1 To 5 Step -1` clause is not correct because you cannot count from 1 to 5 by adding increments of negative 1. Adding increments of a negative 1 is the same as decrementing by 1.

Figure 6-23 describes the tasks the computer performs when processing the loop shown in Example 1 in Figure 6-22. As Task 2 indicates, the loop's condition is evaluated *before* the loop body is processed. This is because the loop created by the For...Next statement is a pretest loop. Notice that the `intNum` variable contains the number 13 when the For...Next statement ends. The number 13 is the first integer that is greater than the loop's endValue of 12.

ChO6A-For Next

Processing Tasks for Example 1

1. The For clause creates the `intNum` variable and initializes it to 10.
2. The For clause compares the `intNum` value (10) with the endValue (12) to determine whether the loop should end. 10 is not greater than 12, so the MessageBox.Show method displays the number 10 in a message box, and then the For clause increments `intNum` by 1, giving 11.
3. The For clause compares the `intNum` value (11) with the endValue (12) to determine whether the loop should end. 11 is not greater than 12, so the MessageBox.Show method displays the number 11 in a message box, and then the For clause increments `intNum` by 1, giving 12.
4. The For clause compares the `intNum` value (12) with the endValue (12) to determine whether the loop should end. 12 is not greater than 12, so the MessageBox.Show method displays the number 12 in a message box, and then the For clause increments `intNum` by 1, giving 13.
5. The For clause compares the `intNum` value (13) with the endValue (12) to determine whether the loop should end. 13 is greater than 12, so the loop ends. Processing will continue with the statement following the Next clause.

Figure 6-23   Processing tasks for Example 1 in Figure 6-22

A Different Version of the Projected Sales Application

Figure 6-24 shows the problem specification for a slightly different version of the Projected Sales application from earlier in this lesson. In this version, the Calculate Projected Sales button's Click event procedure will need to display the projected sales amount for each of four years, beginning with 2017. The figure also shows the procedure's pseudocode and flowchart.

Problem Specification

Create an application that displays the amount of a company's projected sales for each of four years, using a 3% growth rate per year and beginning with 2017.

Pseudocode for the Calculate Projected Sales button's Click event procedure
1. store current sales in sales variable
2. display Year and Sales column headings
3. repeat for year from 2017 to 2020 in increments of 1
      increase = sales * growth rate
      sales = sales + increase
      display year and sales
   end repeat for

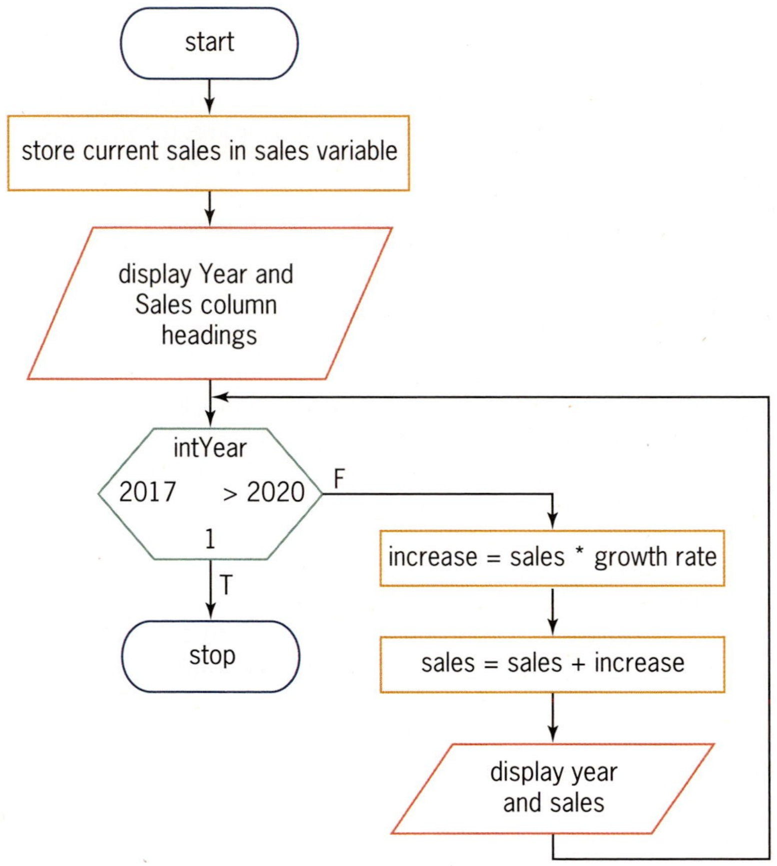

Figure 6-24   Problem specification, pseudocode, and flowchart for another version of the Projected Sales application

Many programmers use a hexagon (a six-sided figure) to represent the For clause in a flowchart, as shown in Figure 6-24. Within the hexagon, you record the four items contained in a For clause: *counterVariableName*, *startValue*, *endValue*, and *stepValue*. The counterVariableName and stepValue are placed at the top and bottom, respectively, of the hexagon. The startValue and endValue are placed on the left and right side, respectively. The hexagon in Figure 6-24 indicates that the counterVariableName is `intYear`, the startValue is 2017, the endValue is 2020, and the stepValue is 1. Notice that a greater than sign (>) precedes the endValue in the hexagon. The > sign indicates that the loop will end when the counter variable's value is greater than 2020.

To code and then test this version of the application:

1. Open the Sales Solution (Sales Solution.sln) file contained in the VB2015\Chap06\Sales Solution-For Next folder. Open the Code Editor window. Replace <your name> and <current date> in the comments with your name and the current date, respectively.

2. Locate the btnCalc_Click procedure. In the blank line above the End Sub clause, type the following For clause and then press **Enter**. (When you press Enter, the Code Editor will automatically enter a Next clause for you.)

   For intYear As Integer = 2017 To 2020

3. Change the Next clause to **Next intYear**, and then enter the loop body instructions indicated in Figure 6-25.

```
Private Sub btnCalc_Click(sender As Object, e As EventArgs
) Handles btnCalc.Click
    ' display the projected sales

    Const dblGROWTH_RATE As Double = 0.03
    Dim dblSales As Double
    Dim dblIncrease As Double

    Double.TryParse(txtCurrentSales.Text, dblSales)
    lblProjSales.Text = "Year     Sales" &
        ControlChars.NewLine

    For intYear As Integer = 2017 To 2020
        dblIncrease = dblSales * dblGROWTH_RATE
        dblSales = dblSales + dblIncrease
        lblProjSales.Text = lblProjSales.Text &
            intYear.ToString & "     " &
            dblSales.ToString("c0") &
            ControlChars.NewLine
    Next intYear
End Sub
```

enter these statements

Figure 6-25   Completed btnCalc_Click procedure

4. Save the solution and then start the application. Type **92000** in the Current sales box, and then click the **Calculate Projected Sales** button. See Figure 6-26.

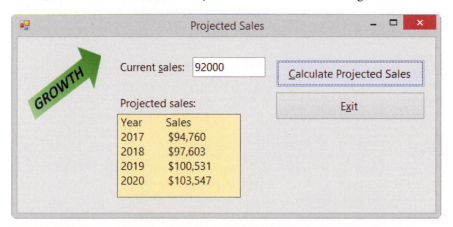

Figure 6-26   Interface showing the year and projected sales amounts

5. Click the **Exit** button. Close the Code Editor window and then close the solution.

Comparing the For...Next and Do...Loop Statements

As mentioned earlier, you can code a counter-controlled loop by using either the For...Next statement or the Do...Loop statement; however, the For...Next statement is more convenient to use. Figure 6-27 shows an example of using both loops to display the string "Hi" three times. Notice that when using the Do...Loop statement to code a counter-controlled loop, you must include a statement to declare and initialize the counter variable as well as a statement to update the counter variable. In addition, you must include the appropriate comparison in the Do clause. In a For...Next statement, the declaration, initialization, update, and comparison tasks are handled by the For clause.

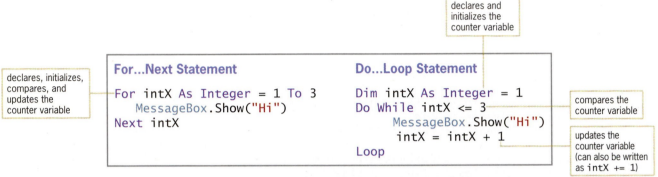

Figure 6-27   Comparison of the For...Next and Do...Loop statements

YOU DO IT 4!

Create an application named YouDoIt 4 and save it in the VB2015\Chap06 folder. Add two labels and a button to the form. The button's Click event procedure should display the number of integers from 14 to 23 in one of the labels and the sum of those integers in the other label. Code the procedure using the For...Next statement. Save the solution, and then start and test the application. Close the solution.

Lesson A Summary

- To have the computer repeatedly process one or more program instructions while the looping condition is true or until the loop exit condition has been met:

  Use a repetition structure (loop). You can code a repetition structure in Visual Basic by using one of the following statements: For...Next, Do...Loop, and For Each...Next. (The For Each... Next statement is covered in Chapter 9.)

- To use the Do...Loop statement to code a loop:

  Refer to Figure 6-8 for the two versions of the statement's syntax. The statement can be used to code both pretest and posttest loops. In a pretest loop, the loop condition appears in the Do clause; it appears in the Loop clause in a posttest loop. The loop condition must evaluate to a Boolean value.

- To represent the loop condition in a flowchart:

  Use the decision symbol, which is a diamond.

- To stop an endless (infinite) loop:

  Click Debug on the menu bar, and then click Stop Debugging. Or, click the Stop Debugging button (the red square) on the Standard toolbar.

- To use a counter:

  Initialize and update the counter. The initialization is done outside of the loop that uses the counter; the update is done within the loop. You update a counter by either incrementing or decrementing its value by a constant amount, which can be either positive or negative, integer or non-integer.

- To use an accumulator:

  Initialize and update the accumulator. The initialization is done outside of the loop that uses the accumulator; the update is done within the loop. In most cases, you update an accumulator by incrementing (rather than by decrementing) its value by an amount that varies. The amount can be either positive or negative, integer or non-integer.

- To abbreviate an assignment statement:

  Use the arithmetic assignment operators listed in Figure 6-21. The assignment statement you want to abbreviate must follow this format, in which *variableName* on both sides of the equal sign is the name of the same variable: *variableName = variableName arithmeticOperator value*.

- To use the For...Next statement to code a counter-controlled loop:

  Refer to Figure 6-22 for the statement's syntax. The statement can be used to code pretest loops only. In the syntax, counterVariableName is the name of a numeric variable that the computer will use to keep track of the number of times the loop body instructions are processed. The number of iterations is controlled by the For clause's startValue, endValue, and stepValue. The startValue, endValue, and stepValue must be numeric and can be positive or negative, integer or non-integer. If you omit the stepValue, a stepValue of positive 1 is used.

- To flowchart a For...Next loop:

  Many programmers use a hexagon to represent the For clause. Inside the hexagon, you record the counter variable's name and its startValue, stepValue, and endValue.

Lesson A Key Terms

Accumulator—a numeric variable used for accumulating (adding together) something

Arithmetic assignment operators—composed of an arithmetic operator followed by the assignment operator; used to abbreviate an assignment statement that has the following format, in which *variableName* on both sides of the equal sign is the name of the same variable: *variableName = variableName arithmeticOperator value*

Counter—a numeric variable used for counting something

Counter-controlled loop—a loop whose processing is controlled by a counter; the loop body will be processed a precise number of times

Decrementing—decreasing a value

Do...Loop statement—a Visual Basic statement that can be used to code both pretest loops and posttest loops

Endless loop—a loop whose instructions are processed indefinitely; also called an infinite loop

For...Next statement—a Visual Basic statement that is used to code a specific type of pretest loop, called a counter-controlled loop

Incrementing—increasing a value

Infinite loop—another name for an endless loop

Initializing—the process of assigning a beginning value to a memory location, such as a counter or accumulator variable

Loop—another name for the repetition structure

Loop body—the instructions within a loop

Loop exit condition—the requirement that must be met for the computer to *stop* processing the loop body instructions

Looping condition—the requirement that must be met for the computer to *continue* processing the loop body instructions

Multiline property—determines whether a text box can accept and display only one line of text or multiple lines of text

Overflow error—occurs when the value assigned to a memory location is too large for the location's data type

Posttest loop—a loop whose condition is evaluated *after* the instructions in its loop body are processed

Pretest loop—a loop whose condition is evaluated *before* the instructions in its loop body are processed

ReadOnly property—controls whether the user is allowed to change the contents of a text box during run time

Repetition structure—the control structure used to repeatedly process one or more program instructions; also called a loop

ScrollBars property—a property of a text box; specifies whether the text box has scroll bars

Updating—the process of either adding a number to or subtracting a number from the value stored in a counter or accumulator variable

Lesson A Review Questions

1. Which of the following clauses stops the loop when the value in the `intPopulation` variable is less than the number 5000?

    a. `Do While intPopulation >= 5000`
    b. `Do Until intPopulation < 5000`
    c. `Loop While intPopulation >= 5000`
    d. all of the above

2. Which of the following statements can be used to code a loop whose instructions you want processed 10 times?

    a. Do...Loop   c. either a or b
    b. For...Next

3. The instructions in a _____ loop might not be processed at all, whereas the instructions in a _____ loop are always processed at least once.

    a. posttest, pretest   b. pretest, posttest

4.   How many times will the MessageBox.Show method in the following code be processed?

```
Dim intCount As Integer
Do While intCount > 4
   MessageBox.Show("Hello")
   intCount += 1
Loop
```

a.   zero

b.   one

c.   four

d.   five

5.   How many times will the MessageBox.Show method in the following code be processed?

```
Dim intCount As Integer
Do
   MessageBox.Show("Hello")
   intCount += 1
Loop While intCount > 4
```

a.   zero

b.   one

c.   four

d.   five

6.   How many times will the MessageBox.Show method in the following code be processed?

```
For intCount As Integer = 6 To 13 Step 2
   MessageBox.Show("Hello")
Next intCount
```

a.   three

b.   four

c.   five

d.   eight

7.   The computer will stop processing the loop in Review Question 6 when the `intCount` variable contains the number _____ .

a.   11

b.   12

c.   13

d.   14

Refer to Figure 6-28 to answer Review Questions 8 through 11.

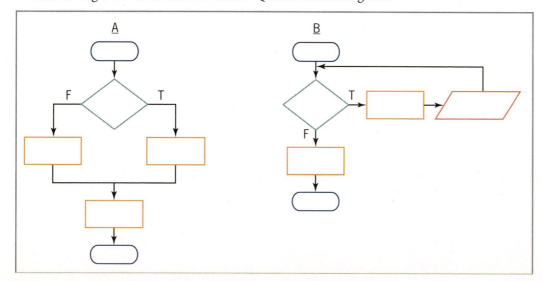

Figure 6-28   Flowcharts for Review Questions 8 through 11 *(continues)*

(continued)

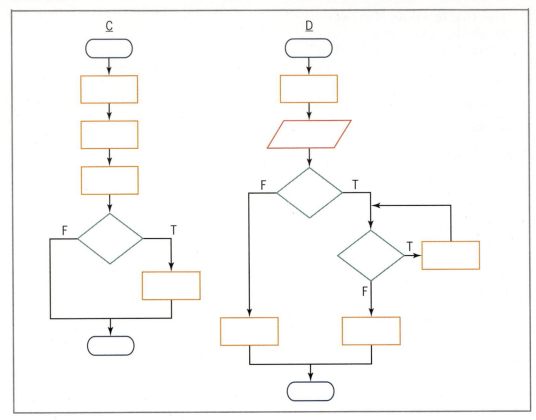

Figure 6-28   Flowcharts for Review Questions 8 through 11

8. Which of the following control structures are used in flowchart A in Figure 6-28? (Select all that apply.)

   a. sequence

   c. repetition

   b. selection

9. Which of the following control structures are used in flowchart B in Figure 6-28? (Select all that apply.)

   a. sequence

   c. repetition

   b. selection

10. Which of the following control structures are used in flowchart C in Figure 6-28? (Select all that apply.)

    a. sequence

    c. repetition

    b. selection

11. Which of the following control structures are used in flowchart D in Figure 6-28? (Select all that apply.)

    a. sequence

    c. repetition

    b. selection

12. Which of the following statements is equivalent to the statement
    `dblTotal = dblTotal + dblScore`?

    a. `dblTotal += dblScore`   c. `dblTotal =+ dblScore`

    b. `dblScore += dblTotal`   d. `dblScore =+ dblTotal`

13. Which of the following For clauses indicates that the loop instructions should be
    processed as long as the `intX` variable's value is less than 100?

    a. `For intX As Integer = 10 To 100`
    b. `For intX As Integer = 10 To 99`
    c. `For intX As Integer = 10 To 101`
    d. none of the above

14. The loop controlled by the correct For clause from Review Question 13 will end when
    the `intX` variable contains the number _____.

    a. 100   c. 101

    b. 111   d. 110

Lesson A Exercises

1. Write a Visual Basic Do clause that processes the loop instructions as long as the
    value in the `intNum` variable is less than or equal to the number 100. Use the `While`
    keyword. Then rewrite the Do clause using the `Until` keyword.
    INTRODUCTORY

2. Write a Visual Basic Do clause that stops the loop when the value in the `intOrdered`
    variable is greater than the value in the `intOnHand` variable. Use the `Until` keyword.
    Then rewrite the Do clause using the `While` keyword.
    INTRODUCTORY

3. Write a Visual Basic Loop clause that processes the loop instructions as long as the
    value in the `strContinue` variable is either Y or y. Use the `While` keyword. Then
    rewrite the Loop clause using the `Until` keyword.
    INTRODUCTORY

4. Write a Visual Basic Do clause that processes the loop instructions as long as the value
    in the `strName` variable is not "Done" (in any case). Use the `While` keyword. Then
    rewrite the Do clause using the `Until` keyword.
    INTRODUCTORY

5. What will the following code display in message boxes?
    INTRODUCTORY

    ```
    Dim intX As Integer = 1
    Do While intX < 5
       MessageBox.Show(intX.ToString)
       intX += 1
    Loop
    ```

6. What will the following code display in message boxes?
    INTRODUCTORY

    ```
    Dim intX As Integer = 1
    Do
       MessageBox.Show(intX.ToString)
       intX = intX + 1
    Loop Until intX > 5
    ```

7. Write a Visual Basic assignment statement that updates the `intTotal` counter variable by 3.

8. Write a Visual Basic assignment statement that updates the `decTotal` accumulator variable by the value stored in the `decSales` variable.

9. Figure 6-29 shows a problem specification, two illustrations, and two solutions containing loops.

   a. Will both loops work when Sherri is one or more steps away from the fountain, as shown in Illustration A? If not, why not?

   b. Will both loops work when Sherri is directly in front of the fountain, as shown in Illustration B? If not, why not?

Problem Specification

Sherri is standing an unknown number of steps away from the Burlington Fountain. Write the instructions that direct Sherri to walk from her current location to the fountain.

Illustration A

Illustration B

Solution 1 – pretest loop
repeat while you are not directly in front of the fountain
    walk forward
end repeat while

Solution 2 – posttest loop
repeat
    walk forward
end repeat while you are not directly in front of the fountain

---

Figure 6-29 Information for Exercise 9
Image by Diane Zak; created with Reallusion CrazyTalk Animator

10. Write a Visual Basic assignment statement that updates the `intTotal` counter variable by −3.

11. Write a Visual Basic assignment statement that subtracts the contents of the `decReturns` variable from the contents of the `decSales` accumulator variable.

12. Modify Solution 2 shown earlier in Figure 6-4. The solution should now keep track of the number of times Sahirah's laser beam missed the spider. After saying "You are safe now. The spider is dead.", Sahirah should say one of the following: "I got him immediately."; "I missed him one time."; or "I missed him *x* times." (where *x* is the value in the counter). — INTERMEDIATE

13. Write the Visual Basic code for a pretest loop that uses an Integer variable named **intEven** to display the even integers from 2 through 20 in the lblEven control. Use the For...Next statement. Display each number on a separate line in the control. Then create an application to test your code using the following names for the solution and project, respectively: Even Solution and Even Project. Save the application in the VB2015\ Chap06 folder. Add a button and a label to the interface. Enter your code in the button's Click event procedure, and then test the application appropriately. — INTERMEDIATE

14. Rewrite the pretest loop from Exercise 13 using the Do...Loop statement. Add another button to the interface created in Exercise 13. Enter your code from this exercise in the button's Click event procedure, and then test the application appropriately. — INTERMEDIATE

15. Rewrite the pretest loop from Exercise 14 as a posttest loop. Add another button to the interface used in Exercise 14. Enter your code from this exercise in the button's Click event procedure. Test the application appropriately. — INTERMEDIATE

16. Write the Visual Basic code that corresponds to the flowchart shown in Figure 6-30. Display the calculated results on separate lines in the lblCount control. — INTERMEDIATE

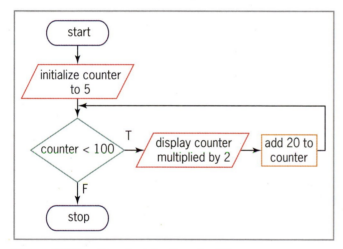

Figure 6-30   Flowchart for Exercise 16

17. Write a For...Next statement that displays the numbers from 6 through 60 in increments of 6 in the lblNums control. Display each number on a separate line in the control. — INTERMEDIATE

18. Write a For...Next statement that calculates and displays the squares of odd numbers from 3 through 15 (e.g., 9, 25, and so on). Display each number on a separate line in the lblNums control. — INTERMEDIATE

19. What will the following code display? — INTERMEDIATE

```
Dim intTotal As Integer
Do While intTotal <= 7
   MessageBox.Show(intTotal.ToString)
   intTotal += 3
Loop
```

INTERMEDIATE
20. What will the following code display?

```
Dim intTotal As Integer
Do
    MessageBox.Show(intTotal.ToString)
    intTotal = intTotal + 2
Loop Until intTotal >= 2
```

INTERMEDIATE
21. In this exercise, you modify one of the Projected Sales applications from this lesson. Use Windows to make a copy of the Sales Solution folder. Rename the copy Sales Solution-Intermediate. Open the Sales Solution (Sales Solution.sln) file contained in the Sales Solution-Intermediate folder. Rather than using $150,000 as the sales goal, the user should be able to enter any sales goal. Modify the interface and code as needed, and then test the application appropriately.

INTERMEDIATE
22. In this exercise, you modify the Addition application from this lesson. Use Windows to make a copy of the Addition Solution folder. Rename the copy Addition Solution-Intermediate. Open the Addition Solution (Addition Solution.sln) file contained in the Addition Solution-Intermediate folder. The application should now also display (in label controls) the number of integers entered and the average integer entered. Modify the interface and code as needed, and then test the application appropriately.

INTERMEDIATE
23. In this exercise, you modify one of the Projected Sales applications from this lesson. Use Windows to make a copy of the Sales Solution-For Next folder. Rename the copy Sales Solution-Do While. Open the Sales Solution (Sales Solution.sln) file contained in the Sales Solution-Do While folder. Change the For...Next statement in the btnCalc_Click procedure to a Do...Loop statement, and then test the application appropriately.

INTERMEDIATE
24. Open the VB2015\Chap06\Multiplication Solution (Multiplication Solution.sln) file. Code the application to display a multiplication table similar to the one shown in Figure 6-31. Use the For...Next statement in the btnForNext_Click procedure, and use the Do...Loop statement in the btnDoLoop_Click procedure. Test the application appropriately.

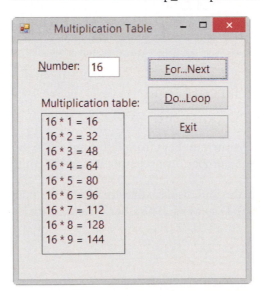

Figure 6-31   Sample multiplication table for Exercise 24

25. Create an application, using the following names for the solution and project, respectively: General Solution and General Project. Save the application in the VB2015\ Chap06 folder. The application's interface is shown in Figure 6-32. The interface allows the user to enter an item's price, which should be displayed in the Prices entered text box. The Prices entered text box should have its Multiline, ReadOnly, ScrollBars, and TextAlign properties set to True, True, Vertical, and Right, respectively. The Add to Total button's Click event procedure should accumulate the prices entered by the user, always displaying the accumulated value plus a 3% sales tax in the Total due box. In other words, if the user enters the number 5 as the item's price, the Total due box should display $5.15. If the user subsequently enters the number 10, the Total due box should display $15.45. The Next Order button should allow the user to start accumulating the values for the next order. Test the application appropriately.

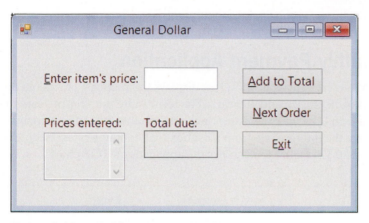

Figure 6-32   Interface for Exercise 25

INTERMEDIATE

26. Open the Debug Solution (Debug Solution.sln) file contained in the VB2015\Chap06\ Debug Solution-A26 folder. The code should display a 10% bonus for each sales amount that is entered, but it is not working correctly. Correct the code. (Hint: If you need to stop an endless loop, click the Stop Debugging button on the Standard toolbar.)

SWAT THE BUGS

27. Open the Debug Solution (Debug Solution.sln) file contained in the VB2015\Chap06\ Debug Solution-A27 folder. The code should display the numbers 1 through 4, but it is not working correctly. Correct the code. (Hint: If you need to stop an endless loop, click the Stop Debugging button on the Standard toolbar.)

SWAT THE BUGS

28. Open the Debug Solution (Debug Solution.sln) file contained in the VB2015\Chap06\ Debug Solution-A28 folder. The code should display the numbers 10 through 1, but it is not working correctly. Correct the code. (Hint: If you need to stop an endless loop, click the Stop Debugging button on the Standard toolbar.)

SWAT THE BUGS

29. Open the Debug Solution (Debug Solution.sln) file contained in the VB2015\Chap06\ Debug Solution-A29 folder. The code should display a 5% commission for each sales amount that is entered, but it is not working correctly. Correct the code.

SWAT THE BUGS

■ LESSON B

After studying Lesson B, you should be able to:

• Include a list box on a form

• Add items to a list box

• Clear the items from a list box

• Sort the items in a list box

• Select a list box item from code

• Determine the selected item in a list box

• Calculate a periodic payment using the Financial.Pmt method

Creating the Monthly Payment Application

Your task in this chapter is to create an application that displays the monthly payments on a mortgage loan, using terms of 15, 20, 25, and 30 years. The term is the number of years the borrower has to pay off the loan. The user will enter the loan amount, called the principal, in a text box. He or she will select the interest rate from a list box that contains rates ranging from 2.0% to 7.0% in increments of 0.5%. Figure 6-33 shows the application's TOE chart.

Task	Object	Event
End the application	btnExit	Click
1. Clear the contents of lblPay 2. Calculate the monthly payment 3. Display the monthly payment in lblPay	btnCalc	Click
1. Fill lstRates with values (2% to 7% in increments of 0.5%) 2. Select a default value in lstRates	frmMain	Load
Display the monthly payment (from btnCalc)	lblPay	None
Get and display the interest rate	lstRates	None
Get and display the principal	txtPrincipal	None
Clear the contents of lblPay	lstRates txtPrincipal	SelectedValueChanged TextChanged
Allow text box to accept only numbers and the Backspace key	txtPrincipal	KeyPress
Select the contents of the text box	txtPrincipal	Enter

Figure 6-33   TOE chart for the Monthly Payment application

INTRODUCTORY

To open the partially completed Monthly Payment application:

1. If necessary, start Visual Studio 2015. Open the VB2015\Chap06\Payment Solution\ Payment Solution (Payment Solution.sln) file. The interface contains four labels, two buttons, a picture box, and a text box. Missing from the interface is the list box for selecting the interest rate.

Including a List Box in an Interface

You add a list box to an interface using the ListBox tool in the toolbox. A **list box** displays a list of items from which the user can select zero items, one item, or multiple items. The number of items the user can select is controlled by the list box's **SelectionMode property**. The default value for the property, One, allows the user to select only one item at a time. (You can learn more about the property in Exercise 12 at the end of this lesson.)

Although you can make a list box any size you want, you should follow the Windows standard, which is to display a minimum of three items and a maximum of eight items at a time. If you have more items than can fit into the list box, the control automatically displays a scroll bar for viewing the complete list of items. You should use a label control to provide keyboard access to the list box. For the access key to work correctly, you must set the label's TabIndex property to a value that is one number less than the list box's TabIndex value.

INTRODUCTORY

To complete the user interface:

1. Click the ListBox tool in the toolbox, and then drag the mouse pointer to the form. Position the mouse pointer below the Rate label, and then release the mouse button.

2. Position and size the list box to match Figure 6-34.

Figure 6-34 Correct location and size of the list box

3. The three-character ID for list box names is lst. Change the list box's name to **lstRates**.

4. Lock the controls on the form, and then use the information shown in Figure 6-35 to set the TabIndex values.

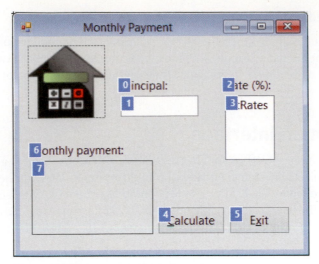

Figure 6-35   Correct TabIndex values

5.   Press **Esc** to remove the TabIndex boxes, and then save the solution.

Adding Items to a List Box

The items in a list box belong to a collection called the **Items collection**. A **collection** is a group of individual objects treated as one unit. The first item in the Items collection appears as the first item in the list box. The second item in the collection appears as the second item in the list box, and so on.

A unique number, called an index, identifies each item in the Items collection. The first item in the collection (which is also the first item in the list box) has an index of 0, the second item has an index of 1, and so on.

You specify each item to display in a list box using the Items collection's **Add method**. Figure 6-36 shows the method's syntax and includes examples and the results of using the method. In the syntax, *object* is the name of the list box control, and the *item* argument is the text you want added to the control's list. In most cases, you enter the Add methods in a form's Load event procedure because you typically want the list box to display its values when the form first appears on the screen.

Add Method (Items Collection)

Syntax
object.**Items.Add(***item***)**

Example 1
```
lstAnimal.Items.Add("Dog")
lstAnimal.Items.Add("Cat")
lstAnimal.Items.Add("Horse")
```
adds Dog, Cat, and Horse to the lstAnimal control

Example 2
```
For intCode As Integer = 100 To 105
    lstCode.Items.Add(intCode.ToString)
Next intCode
```
adds 100, 101, 102, 103, 104, and 105 to the lstCode control; you also can write the Add method
like this: `lstCode.Items.Add(Convert.ToString(intCode))`

Results

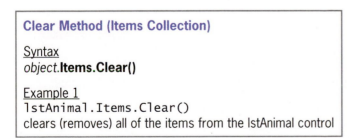

scroll box for
viewing the
other codes

Figure 6-36   Syntax, examples, and results of the Items collection's Add method

Clearing the Items from a List Box

To learn more
about list boxes,
complete
Exercises 12,
13, and 14 at
the end of this lesson.

You can use the Items collection's **Clear method** to clear (remove) the items from a list box. The
method's syntax and an example of using the method are shown in Figure 6-37.

Clear Method (Items Collection)

Syntax
object.**Items.Clear()**

Example 1
```
lstAnimal.Items.Clear()
```
clears (removes) all of the items from the lstAnimal control

Figure 6-37   Syntax and an example of the Items collection's Clear method

The Sorted Property

The position of an item in a list box depends on the value stored in the list box's **Sorted property**. When the property is set to False (the default value), the item is added at the end of the list. When it is set to True, the item is sorted along with the existing items and then placed in its proper position in the list.

Visual Basic sorts the list box items in dictionary order, which means that numbers are sorted before letters, and a lowercase letter is sorted before its uppercase equivalent. The items in a list box are sorted based on the leftmost characters in each item. As a result, the items "Personnel", "Inventory", and "Payroll" will appear in the following order when the lstDepartment control's Sorted property is set to True: Inventory, Payroll, Personnel. Likewise, the items 1, 2, 3, and 10 will appear in the following order when the lstNumber control's Sorted property is set to True: 1, 10, 2, 3. Both list boxes are shown in Figure 6-38.

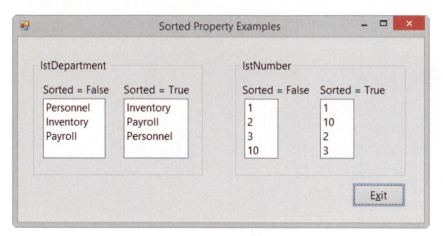

Figure 6-38 Examples of the list box's Sorted property

The requirements of the application you are creating determine whether you display the list box items in either sorted order or the order in which they are added to the list box. If several list items are selected much more frequently than other items, you typically leave the list box's Sorted property set to False and then add the frequently used items first to ensure that they appear at the beginning of the list. However, if the list box items are selected fairly equally, you typically set the list box's Sorted property to True because it is easier to locate items when they appear in a sorted order.

GUI DESIGN TIP List Box Standards

- Use a list box only when you need to offer the user at least three different choices.

- Don't overwhelm the user with a lot of choices at the same time; instead, display from three to eight items and let the user employ the scroll bar to view the remaining ones.

- Use a label control to provide keyboard access to the list box. Set the label's TabIndex property to a value that is one number less than the list box's TabIndex value.

- List box items are either arranged by use, with the most used entries appearing first in the list, or sorted in ascending order.

Coding the Monthly Payment Application

When the Monthly Payment interface appears on the screen, the lstRates control should display interest rates ranging from 2.0% to 7.0% in increments of 0.5%.

To specify the rates to display in the list box:

START HERE

1. Open the Code Editor window. Replace <your name> and <current date> in the comments with your name and the current date, respectively.

2. Locate the form's Load event procedure, and then enter the For...Next loop shown in Figure 6-39. Be sure to change the Next clause as shown in the figure.

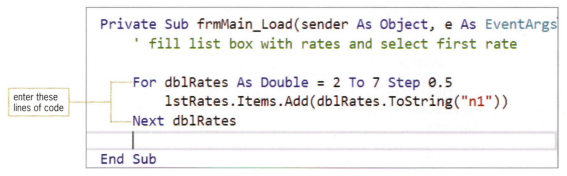

enter these lines of code

```
Private Sub frmMain_Load(sender As Object, e As EventArgs
    ' fill list box with rates and select first rate

    For dblRates As Double = 2 To 7 Step 0.5
        lstRates.Items.Add(dblRates.ToString("n1"))
    Next dblRates

End Sub
```

Figure 6-39   For...Next loop entered in the Load event procedure

3. Save the solution and then start the application. Scroll down the Rate list box to verify that it contains numbers ranging from 2.0 to 7.0 in increments of 0.5.

4. Scroll to the top of the list box, and then click **2.0** in the list. When you select an item in a list box, the item appears highlighted in the list, as shown in Figure 6-40. In addition, the item's value and index are stored in the list box's SelectedItem property and SelectedIndex property, respectively.

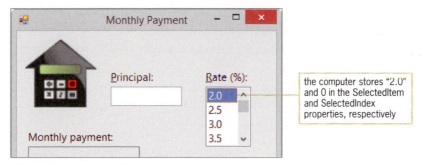

the computer stores "2.0" and 0 in the SelectedItem and SelectedIndex properties, respectively

Figure 6-40   First item selected in the list box

5. Click the **Exit** button.

The SelectedItem and SelectedIndex Properties

You can use either the **SelectedItem property** or the **SelectedIndex property** to determine whether an item is selected in a list box. When no item is selected, the SelectedItem property contains the empty string and the SelectedIndex property contains the number −1 (negative 1). Otherwise, the SelectedItem and SelectedIndex properties contain the value of the selected item and the item's index, respectively. Figure 6-41 shows examples of using the SelectedItem and SelectedIndex properties to determine the selected item in a list box.

Determining the Selected Item in a List Box

Example 1 (SelectedItem property)
```
strRate = Convert.ToString(lstRates.SelectedItem)
```
converts the selected item to String and then assigns the result to the `strRate` variable

Example 2 (SelectedItem property)
```
If Convert.ToDouble(lstRates.SelectedItem) = 3.5 Then
```
converts the selected item to Double and then compares the result to the Double number 3.5 (You also can convert the selected item to String and then compare the result with the string "3.5" as follows: `If Convert.ToString(lstRates.SelectedItem) = "3.5".`)

Example 3 (SelectedItem property)
```
If Convert.ToString(lstRates.SelectedItem) <> String.Empty Then
```
converts the selected item to String and then compares the result to the empty string
(You can replace the `Convert.ToString(lstRates.SelectedItem)` part of the If clause with lstRates.SelectedItem.ToString. However, keep in mind that the ToString method will result in a run time error if no item is selected in the list box.)

Example 4 (SelectedIndex property)
```
MessageBox.Show(Convert.ToString(lstRates.SelectedIndex))
```
converts the index of the selected item to String and then displays the result in a message box

Example 5 (SelectedIndex property)
```
If lstRates.SelectedIndex = 0 Then
```
compares the selected item's index with the number 0

Figure 6-41   Examples of determining the selected item in a list box

If a list box allows the user to make only one selection, it is customary in Windows applications to have one of the list box items already selected when the interface appears. The selected item, called the **default list box item**, should be either the item selected most frequently or the first item in the list. You can use either the SelectedItem property or the SelectedIndex property to select the default list box item from code, as shown in the examples in Figure 6-42. In most cases, you enter the appropriate code in the form's Load event procedure.

Selecting the Default Item in a List Box

Example 1 (SelectedItem property)
```
lstRates.SelectedItem = "3.5"
```
selects the 3.5 item in the lstRates control

Example 2 (SelectedIndex property)
```
lstRates.SelectedIndex = 0
```
selects the first item in the lstRates control

Figure 6-42 Examples of selecting the default item in a list box

START HERE

To select a default item in the lstRates control:

1. The insertion point should be positioned as shown earlier in Figure 6-39. Currently, the most popular mortgage rate is 3%. Type the following assignment statement and then press **Enter**:

   lstRates.SelectedItem = "3.0"

2. Save the solution and then start the application. See Figure 6-43.

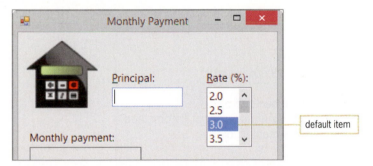

Figure 6-43 Default item selected in the list box

3. Click the **Exit** button.

GUI DESIGN TIP Default List Box Item

- If a list box allows the user to make only one selection, a default item is typically selected when the interface first appears. The default item should be either the item selected most frequently or the first item in the list. However, if a list box allows more than one selection at a time, you do not select a default item.

The SelectedValueChanged and SelectedIndexChanged Events

Each time either the user or a statement selects an item in a list box, the list box's **SelectedValueChanged event** and its **SelectedIndexChanged event** occur. You can use the procedures associated with these events to perform one or more tasks when the selected item has changed. In the Monthly Payment application, you will associate the list box's SelectedValueChanged procedure with the ClearPayment procedure, which currently clears the contents of the lblPay control when a change is made to the txtPrincipal control.

START HERE ▶

To associate the list box's SelectedValueChanged procedure with the ClearPayment procedure:

1. Locate the ClearPayment procedure, and then type the following at the end of the Handles clause (be sure to type the comma): **, lstRates.SelectedValueChanged**.

2. Save the solution.

Coding the Calculate Button's Click Event Procedure

Figure 6-44 shows the pseudocode for the btnCalc_Click procedure. It also includes a list of the variables the procedure will use.

```
btnCalc Click event procedure
1. store the principal and rate in variables
2. divide the rate by 100 to get its decimal equivalent
3. clear the contents of lblPay
4. repeat for term from 15 to 30 in increments of 5
        calculate the monthly payment using the Financial.Pmt method
        display the term and monthly payment in lblPay
   end repeat for
```

Variables	Data type
intPrincipal	Integer
dblRate	Double
dblPay	Double
intTerm	Integer (declare in a For clause)

Figure 6-44   Pseudocode and variables for the btnCalc_Click procedure

START HERE ▶

To begin coding the btnCalc_Click procedure:

1. Locate the btnCalc_Click procedure. Click the **blank line** above the End Sub clause, and then enter the following three Dim statements. Press **Enter** twice after typing the last Dim statement.

    Dim intPrincipal As Integer
    Dim dblRate As Double
    Dim dblPay As Double

2. The first step in the pseudocode is to store the principal and the rate in variables. The user enters the principal in the txtPrincipal control and selects the rate in the lstRates control. Enter the TryParse methods shown in Figure 6-45.

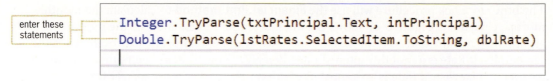

Figure 6-45   TryParse methods entered in the btnCalc_Click procedure

3. The second step in the pseudocode divides the rate by 100 to get its decimal equivalent. Type the following assignment statement (or type the statement **dblRate /= 100**) and then press **Enter** twice:

    dblRate = dblRate / 100

4. The next step in the pseudocode clears the previous monthly payments from the lblPay control. Type the following assigment statement and then press **Enter**:

    lblPay.Text = String.Empty

5. The last step in the pseudocode is a loop that repeats its instructions for terms from 15 years to 30 years in increments of 5 years. Enter the following For clause:

    For intTerm As Integer = 15 To 30 Step 5

6. Change the Next clause to **Next intTerm**, and then save the solution.

The first instruction in the loop calculates the monthly payment using the Financial.Pmt method.

The Financial.Pmt Method

Visual Basic's Financial class contains many methods that your applications can use to perform financial calculations. Figure 6-46 lists some of the more commonly used methods defined in the class. All of the methods return the result of their calculation as a Double number.

Method	Purpose
Financial.DDB	calculate the depreciation of an asset for a specific time period using the double-declining balance method
Financial.FV	calculate the future value of an annuity based on periodic, fixed payments and a fixed interest rate
Financial.IPmt	calculate the interest payment for a given period of an annuity based on periodic, fixed payments and a fixed interest rate
Financial.IRR	calculate the internal rate of return for a series of periodic cash flows (payments and receipts)
Financial.Pmt	calculate the payment for an annuity based on periodic, fixed payments and a fixed interest rate
Financial.PPmt	calculate the principal payment for a given period of an annuity based on periodic fixed payments and a fixed interest rate
Financial.PV	calculate the present value of an annuity based on periodic, fixed payments to be paid in the future and a fixed interest rate
Financial.SLN	calculate the straight-line depreciation of an asset for a single period
Financial.SYD	calculate the sum-of-the-years' digits depreciation of an asset for a specified period

Figure 6-46   Some of the methods defined in the Financial class

The btnCalc_Click procedure will use the **Financial.Pmt method** to calculate the monthly mortgage payment. Figure 6-47 shows the method's basic syntax and lists the meaning of each argument. The *Rate* and *NPer* (number of periods) arguments must be expressed using the same units. If Rate is a monthly interest rate, then NPer must specify the number of monthly payments. Likewise, if Rate is an annual interest rate, then NPer must specify the number of annual payments. The figure also includes examples of using the method.

You can use the PMT function in Microsoft Excel to verify that the payments shown in Figure 6-47 are correct.

Financial.Pmt Method

Syntax
Financial.Pmt(*Rate*, *NPer*, *PV***)**

Argument	Meaning
Rate	interest rate per period
NPer	total number of payment periods in the term
PV	present value of the loan (the principal)

Example 1
```
Financial.Pmt(0.05, 3, 9000)
```
Calculates the annual payment for a loan of $9,000 for 3 years with a 5% interest rate. *Rate* is 0.05, *NPer* is 3, and *PV* is 9000. The annual payment returned by the method (rounded to the nearest cent) is –3304.88.

Example 2
```
-Financial.Pmt(0.03 / 12, 15 * 12, 150000)
```
Calculates the monthly payment for a loan of $150,000 for 15 years with a 3% interest rate. *Rate* is 0.03 / 12, *NPer* is 15 * 12, and *PV* is 150000. The monthly payment returned by the method (rounded to the nearest cent and expressed as a positive number) is 1035.87.

Figure 6-47   Syntax and examples of the Financial.Pmt method

Example 1 calculates the annual payment for a loan of $9,000 for 3 years with a 5% interest rate. As the example indicates, the annual payment returned by the method (rounded to the nearest cent) is –3304.88. This means that if you borrow $9,000 for 3 years at 5% interest, you will need to make three annual payments of $3,304.88 to pay off the loan. Notice that the Financial.Pmt method returns a negative number. You can change the negative number to a positive number by preceding the method with the negation operator, like this: `-Financial.Pmt(.05, 3, 9000)`.

The Financial.Pmt method shown in Example 2 calculates the monthly payment for a loan of $150,000 for 15 years with a 3% interest rate. In this example, the Rate and NPer arguments are expressed in monthly terms rather than in annual terms. You change an annual rate to a monthly rate by dividing the annual rate by 12. You change the term from years to months by multiplying the number of years by 12. The monthly payment for the loan in Example 2, rounded to the nearest cent and expressed as a positive number, is 1035.87.

START HERE

To complete and then test the btnCalc_Click procedure:

1. Complete the btnCalc_Click procedure by entering the two assignment statements indicated in Figure 6-48. The assignment statements calculate and display the monthly payment.

```
For intTerm As Integer = 15 To 30 Step 5
    dblPay = -Financial.Pmt(dblRate / 12,
                            intTerm * 12, intPrincipal)
    lblPay.Text = lblPay.Text & intTerm.ToString &
        " years:   " & dblPay.ToString("c2") &
        ControlChars.NewLine
Next intTerm
```

enter these two assignment statements

Figure 6-48   Completed btnCalc_Click procedure

2. Save the solution and then start the application. Type **150000** in the Principal box and then click the **Calculate** button. See Figure 6-49.

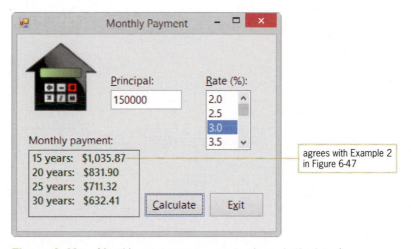

agrees with Example 2 in Figure 6-47

Figure 6-49   Monthly mortgage payments shown in the interface

3. Click **2.0** in the Rate list box. The list box's SelectedValueChanged procedure clears the contents of the Monthly payment box. Click the **Calculate** button to display the new monthly payments.

4. Change the Principal to **75000**. The text box's TextChanged procedure clears the contents of the Monthly payment box. Click the **Calculate** button to display the new monthly payments.

5. Click the **Exit** button. Close the Code Editor window and then close the solution. Figure 6-50 shows the Monthly Payment application's code.

```vb
1  ' Name:          Payment Project
2  ' Purpose:       Display the monthly mortgage payments
3  '                for terms of 15, 20, 25, and 30 years
4  ' Programmer:    <your name> on <current date>
5
6  Option Explicit On
7  Option Strict On
8  Option Infer Off
9
10 Public Class frmMain
11
12     Private Sub frmMain_Load(sender As Object, e As EventArgs
       ) Handles Me.Load
13         ' fill list box with rates and select first rate
14
15         For dblRates As Double = 2 To 7 Step 0.5
16             lstRates.Items.Add(dblRates.ToString("n1"))
17         Next dblRates
18         lstRates.SelectedItem = "3.0"
19
20     End Sub
21
22     Private Sub btnCalc_Click(sender As Object, e As EventArgs
       ) Handles btnCalc.Click
23         ' display the monthly mortgage payment
24
25         Dim intPrincipal As Integer
26         Dim dblRate As Double
27         Dim dblPay As Double
28
29         Integer.TryParse(txtPrincipal.Text, intPrincipal)
30         Double.TryParse(lstRates.SelectedItem.ToString, dblRate)
31         dblRate = dblRate / 100
32
33         lblPay.Text = String.Empty
34         For intTerm As Integer = 15 To 30 Step 5
35             dblPay = -Financial.Pmt(dblRate / 12,
36                                     intTerm * 12, intPrincipal)
37             lblPay.Text = lblPay.Text & intTerm.ToString &
38                 " years:   " & dblPay.ToString("c2") &
39                 ControlChars.NewLine
40         Next intTerm
41     End Sub
42
43     Private Sub btnExit_Click(sender As Object, e As EventArgs
       ) Handles btnExit.Click
44         Me.Close()
45     End Sub
46
47     Private Sub txtPrincipal_Enter(sender As Object,
       e As EventArgs) Handles txtPrincipal.Enter
48         txtPrincipal.SelectAll()
```

Figure 6-50 Monthly Payment application's code *(continues)*

(continued)

```
49      End Sub
50
51      Private Sub ClearPayment(sender As Object, e As EventArgs
        ) Handles txtPrincipal.TextChanged,
        lstRates.SelectedValueChanged
52          lblPay.Text = String.Empty
53      End Sub
54
55      Private Sub txtPrincipal_KeyPress(sender As Object,
        e As KeyPressEventArgs) Handles txtPrincipal.KeyPress
56          ' accept only numbers and the Backspace key
57
58          If (e.KeyChar < "0" OrElse e.KeyChar > "9") AndAlso
59                  e.KeyChar <> ControlChars.Back Then
60                  e.Handled = True
61          End If
62      End Sub
63 End Class
```

Figure 6-50   Monthly Payment application's code

Lesson B Summary

- To add a list box to a form:

  Use the ListBox tool in the toolbox.

- To specify whether the user can select zero items, one item, or multiple items in a list box:

  Set the list box's SelectionMode property.

- To add items to a list box:

  Use the Items collection's Add method. The method's syntax is *object*`.Items.Add(`*item*`)`. In the syntax, *object* is the name of the list box control and the *item* argument is the text you want added to the control's list.

- To clear (remove) the items from a list box:

  Use the Items collection's Clear method. The method's syntax is *object*`.Items.Clear()`.

- To automatically sort the items in a list box:

  Set the list box's Sorted property to True.

- To determine the item selected in a list box or to select a list box item from code:

  Use either the list box's SelectedItem property or its SelectedIndex property.

- To perform tasks when a different item is selected in a list box:

  Enter the code in either the list box's SelectedValueChanged procedure or its SelectedIndexChanged procedure.

- To calculate a periodic payment on either a loan or an investment:

  Use the Financial.Pmt method. The method's syntax is `Financial.Pmt(`*Rate*`,` *NPer*`,` *PV*`)`.

Lesson B Key Terms

Add method—the Items collection's method used to add items to a list box

Clear method—the Items collection's method used to clear (remove) items from a list box

Collection—a group of individual objects treated as one unit

Default list box item—the item automatically selected in a list box when the interface appears on the screen

Financial.Pmt method—used to calculate the periodic payment on either a loan or an investment

Items collection—the collection composed of the items in a list box

List box—a control used to display a list of items from which the user can select zero items, one item, or multiple items

SelectedIndex property—stores the index of the item selected in a list box

SelectedIndexChanged event—occurs when an item is selected in a list box

SelectedItem property—stores the value of the item selected in a list box

SelectedValueChanged event—occurs when an item is selected in a list box

SelectionMode property—determines the number of items that can be selected in a list box

Sorted property—specifies whether the list box items should appear in the order they are entered or in sorted order

Lesson B Review Questions

1. Which of the following methods is used to add items to a list box?

   a. Add

   b. AddList

   c. Item

   d. ItemAdd

2. The items in a list box belong to which collection?

   a. Items

   b. List

   c. ListItems

   d. Values

3. Which of the following properties stores the index of the item selected in a list box?

   a. Index

   b. SelectedIndex

   c. Selection

   d. SelectionIndex

4. Which of the following statements selects the fourth item in the lstNames control?

   a. `lstNames.SelectIndex = 3`

   b. `lstNames.SelectIndex = 4`

   c. `lstNames.SelectedIndex = 3`

   d. `lstNames.SelectedItem = 4`

5. Which event occurs when the user selects a different item in a list box?

   a. SelectionChanged

   b. SelectedItemChanged

   c. SelectedValueChanged

   d. none of the above

Lesson B Exercises

1. In this exercise, you modify the Monthly Payment application from this lesson. Use Windows to make a copy of the Payment Solution folder. Rename the copy Payment Solution-DoLoop. Open the Payment Solution (Payment Solution.sln) file contained in the Payment Solution-DoLoop folder. Change both For...Next statements in the application's code to Do...Loop statements. Test the application appropriately.   INTRODUCTORY

2. In this exercise, you create an application that displays the ZIP code (or codes) corresponding to the city name selected in a list box. The city names and ZIP codes are shown in Figure 6-51. Create the application, using the following names for the solution and project, respectively: Zip Solution and Zip Project. Save the application in the VB2015\Chap06 folder. The interface should include a list box whose Sorted property is set to True. The form's Load event procedure should add the city names to the list box and then select the first name in the list. The list box's SelectedValueChanged event procedure should assign the item selected in the list box to a variable. It then should use the Select Case statement to display the city's ZIP code(s) in a label control. Test the application appropriately.   INTRODUCTORY

City	ZIP Code(s)
Baxley	31513, 31515
Newton	39870
Adairsville	30103
Statesboro	30458, 30459, 30460, 30461
Canton	30114, 30115

Figure 6-51   Information for Exercise 2

3. In this exercise, you modify the application from Exercise 2. Use Windows to make a copy of the Zip Solution folder. Rename the copy Modified Zip Solution. Open the Zip Solution (Zip Solution.sln) file contained in the Modified Zip Solution folder. Modify the list box's SelectedValueChanged procedure so that it assigns the index of the item selected in the list box to a variable. Modify the Select Case statement so that it displays the ZIP code(s) corresponding to the index stored in the variable. Test the application appropriately.   INTRODUCTORY

4. Create an application, using the following names for the solution and project, respectively: President Solution and President Project. Save the application in the VB2015\Chap06 folder. Add the names of five U.S. presidents of your choosing to a list box. When the user clicks a name in the list box, the name of the corresponding vice president should appear in a label control. Test the application appropriately.   INTRODUCTORY

5. In this exercise, you create an application for Discount Warehouse. The interface should allow the user to enter an item's original price and its discount rate. The discount rates should range from 10% through 40% in increments of 5%. Use a text box for entering the original price, and use a list box for entering the discount rates. The application should display the amount of the discount and also the discounted price. Create the application, using the following names for the solution and project, respectively: Discount Solution and Discount Project. Save the application in the VB2015\Chap06 folder. Test the application appropriately.   INTERMEDIATE

INTERMEDIATE

6. In this exercise, you modify the Monthly Payment application from this lesson. Use Windows to make a copy of the Payment Solution folder. Rename the copy Modified Payment Solution. Open the Payment Solution (Payment Solution.sln) file contained in the Modified Payment Solution folder. Modify the interface to allow the user to select the term from a list box. The Calculate button should now display only the monthly payment corresponding to the term selected in the list box. Test the application appropriately.

INTERMEDIATE

7. Mills Skating Rink holds a weekly ice-skating competition. Competing skaters must perform a two-minute program in front of a panel of judges. The number of judges varies from week to week. At the end of a skater's program, each judge assigns a score of 0 through 10 to the skater. The manager of the ice rink wants you to create an application that allows him to enter each judge's score for a specific skater. The application should calculate and display the skater's average score. It also should display the skater's total score and the number of scores entered. Figure 6-52 shows a sample run of the application, assuming the manager entered two scores: 10 and 8. (Hint: You enter a score by selecting it from the list box and then clicking the Record Score button.) Create the application, using the following names for the solution and project, respectively: Mills Solution and Mills Project. Save the application in the VB2015\Chap06 folder. Test the application appropriately.

Figure 6-52   Interface for Exercise 7

INTERMEDIATE

8. In this exercise, you create an application that allows the user to enter the gender (either F or M) and GPA for any number of students. The application's interface is shown in Figure 6-53. The application should calculate the average GPA for all students, the average GPA for male students, and the average GPA for female students. The list box should list GPAs from 1.0 through 4.0 in increments of 0.1 (e.g., 1.0, 1.1, 1.2, 1.3, and so on). Create the application, using the following names for the solution and project, respectively: GPA Solution and GPA Project. Save the application in the VB2015\ Chap06 folder. Test the application appropriately.

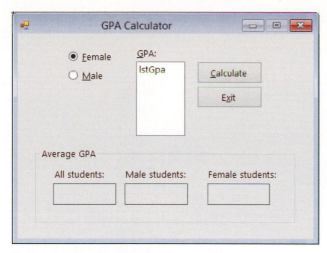

Figure 6-53   Interface for Exercise 8

9.   Open the VB2015\Chap06\Random Solution\Random Solution (Random Solution.sln)   ADVANCED
     file. The application should give the user 10 chances to guess a random number generated
     by the computer. The random number should be an integer from 1 through 50, inclusive.
     Each time the user makes an incorrect guess, the application should display a message
     that tells the user either to guess a higher number or to guess a lower number. When the
     user guesses the random number, the application should display a "Congratulations!"
     message. If the user is not able to guess the random number after 10 tries, the application
     should display the random number in a message. Test the application appropriately.

10. Open the VB2015\Chap06\Fibonacci Solution\Fibonacci Solution (Fibonacci Solution.sln)   ADVANCED
     file. The application should display the first 10 Fibonacci numbers: 1, 1, 2, 3, 5, 8, 13, 21, 34,
     and 55. Notice that beginning with the third number in the series, each Fibonacci number
     is the sum of the prior two numbers. In other words, 2 is the sum of 1 plus 1, 3 is the sum
     of 1 plus 2, 5 is the sum of 2 plus 3, and so on. Display the numbers in the lblNumbers
     control. Test the application appropriately.

11. The accountant at Canton Manufacturing Company wants you to create an application   ADVANCED
     that calculates an asset's annual depreciation using the double-declining balance and
     sum-of-the-years' digits methods. The accountant will enter the asset's cost, useful
     life (in years), and salvage value (which is the value of the asset at the end of its useful
     life). A sample run of the application is shown in Figure 6-54. The interface provides
     text boxes for entering the asset cost and salvage value. It also provides a list box
     for selecting the useful life, which ranges from 3 through 20 years. The depreciation
     amounts are displayed in list boxes. (Hint: You can use the DDB and SYD functions in
     Microsoft Excel to verify that the amounts shown in Figure 6-54 are correct.) Create
     the application, using the following names for the solution and project, respectively:
     Canton Solution and Canton Project. Save the application in the VB2015\Chap06
     folder. You can use Visual Basic's Financial.DDB method to calculate the double-
     declining balance depreciation, and use its Financial.SYD method to calculate
     the sum-of-the-years' digits depreciation. The Financial.DDB method's syntax is
     `Financial.DDB(`*cost, salvage, life, period*`)`. The Financial.SYD method's syntax
     is `Financial.SYD(`*cost, salvage, life, period*`)`. In both syntaxes, the *cost, salvage,*
     and *life* arguments are the asset's cost, salvage value, and useful life, respectively.

The *period* argument is the period for which you want the depreciation amount calculated. Both methods return the depreciation amount as a Double number. Test the application appropriately

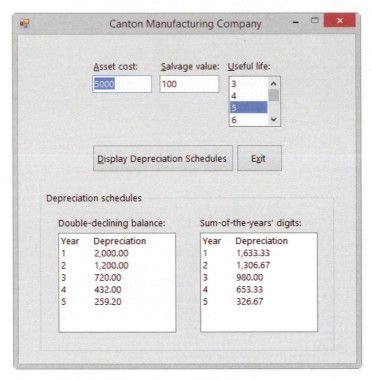

Figure 6-54   Sample run of the application for Exercise 11

12. In this exercise, you learn how to create a list box that allows the user to select more than one item at a time. Open the VB2015\Chap06\Multi Solution\Multi Solution (Multi Solution.sln) file. The interface contains a list box named lstNames. The list box's Sorted and SelectionMode properties are set to True and One, respectively.

a. Open the Code Editor window. The frmMain_Load procedure adds five names to the lstNames control. Code the btnSingle_Click procedure so that it displays, in the lblResult control, the item selected in the list box. For example, if the user clicks Debbie in the list box and then clicks the Single Selection button, the name Debbie should appear in the lblResult control. (Hint: Use the Convert.ToString method.)

b. Save the solution and then start the application. Click Debbie in the list box, then click Ahmad, and then click Bill. Notice that when the list box's SelectionMode property is set to One, you can select only one item at a time in the list.

c. Click the Single Selection button. The name Bill appears in the lblResult control. Click the Exit button.

d. Change the list box's SelectionMode property to MultiSimple. Save the solution and then start the application. Click Debbie in the list box, then click Ahmad, then click Bill, and then click Ahmad. Notice that when the list box's SelectionMode property is set to MultiSimple, you can select more than one item at a time in the list. Also notice that you click to both select and deselect an item. (Hint: You also can use Ctrl+click and Shift+click, as well as press the spacebar, to select and deselect items when the list box's SelectionMode property is set to MultiSimple.) Click the Exit button.

e. Change the list box's SelectionMode property to MultiExtended. Save the solution and then start the application. Click Debbie in the list, and then click Jim. Notice that in this case, clicking Jim deselects Debbie. When a list box's SelectionMode property is set to MultiExtended, you use Ctrl+click to select multiple items in the list. You also use Ctrl+click to deselect items in the list. Click Debbie in the list, then Ctrl+click Ahmad, and then Ctrl+click Debbie.

f. Next, click Bill in the list, and then Shift+click Jim. This selects all of the names from Bill through Jim. Click the Exit button.

g. As you know, when a list box's SelectionMode property is set to One, the item selected in the list box is stored in the SelectedItem property, and the item's index is stored in the SelectedIndex property. However, when a list box's SelectionMode property is set to either MultiSimple or MultiExtended, the items selected in the list box are stored in the SelectedItems property, and the indices of the items are stored in the SelectedIndices property. Code the btnMulti_Click procedure so that it first clears the contents of the lblResult control. The procedure should then display the selected names (which are stored in the SelectedItems property) on separate lines in the lblResult control.

h. Save the solution and then start the application. Click Ahmad in the list box, and then Shift+click Jim. Click the Multi-Selection button. The five names should appear on separate lines in the lblResult control. Click the Exit button.

13. In this exercise, you learn how to use the Items collection's Insert, Remove, RemoveAt, and Clear methods. You also learn how to use the Items collection's Count property. Open the VB2015\Chap06\Items Solution\Items Solution (Items Solution.sln) file.   ◄ DISCOVERY

a. The Items collection's Insert method allows you to add an item at a desired position in a list box during run time. The Insert method's syntax is *object*.`Items.Insert(`*position*`, `*item*`)`, where *position* is the index of the item. Code the btnInsert_Click procedure so it adds your name as the fourth item in the list box.

b. The Items collection's Remove method allows you to remove an item from a list box during run time. The Remove method's syntax is *object*.`Items.Remove(`*item*`)`, where *item* is the item's value. Code the btnRemove_Click procedure so it removes your name from the list box.

c. Like the Remove method, the Items collection's RemoveAt method also allows you to remove an item from a list box while an application is running. However, in the RemoveAt method, you specify the item's index rather than its value. The RemoveAt method's syntax is *object*.`Items.RemoveAt(`*index*`)`, where *index* is the item's index. Code the btnRemoveAt_Click procedure so it removes the second name from the list box.

d. You can use the Items collection's Clear method to remove all items from a list box during run time. As you learned in this lesson, the method's syntax is *object*.`Items.Clear()`. Code the btnClear_Click procedure so it clears the items from the list box.

e. The Items collection's Count property stores the number of items contained in a list box. Code the btnCount_Click procedure so it displays (in a message box) the number of items listed in the lstNames control.

f. Save the solution, and then start and test the application.

DISCOVERY

14. In this exercise, you learn how to use the String Collection Editor window to fill a list box with values. Open the VB2015\Chap06\ListBox Solution\ListBox Solution (ListBox Solution.sln) file. Open the Code Editor window. Remove the Add methods and the For...Next statement from the form's Load event procedure, and then close the Code Editor window. Click the lstAnimal control on the form. Click the Items property in the Properties list, and then click the ellipsis (...) button in the Settings box. The String Collection Editor window opens. Type Dog and then press Enter. Type Cat and then press Enter. Finally, type Horse and then press Enter. Click the OK button to close the dialog box. Use the String Collection Editor window to enter the following codes in the lstCode control: 100, 101, 102, 103, 104, and 105. Save the solution and then start the application.

SWAT THE BUGS

15. Open the Debug Solution (Debug Solution.sln) file contained in the VB2015\Chap06\ Debug Solution-B15 folder. Open the Code Editor window and review the existing code. Start and then test the application. Be sure to include non-integers in your test data. (Hint: If you need to stop an endless loop, click the Stop Debugging button on the Standard toolbar.) Correct any errors in the code. Save the solution, and then start and test the application again.

LESSON C

After studying Lesson C, you should be able to:

- Explain the purpose of the priming and update reads

- Nest repetition structures

- Refresh the screen

- Delay program execution

The Electric Bill Application

Figure 6-55 shows the problem specification for the Electric Bill application, which uses a loop, a counter, and an accumulator to calculate a customer's average electric bill. The figure also shows the pseudocode for the Calculate button's Click event procedure. In addition, it shows a sample run of the application. (You can view the procedure's flowchart in the VB2015\Chap06\ElectricFlowchart.pdf file.)

Problem Specification

Create an application that displays a customer's average electric bill, given the amount of his or her monthly electric bill for any number of months.

Calculate button's Click event procedure
1. initialize the intMonths counter to 0
2. initialize the dblTotal accumulator to 0
3. clear the lstMonthly and lblAvg controls
4. get a monthly amount from the user————————————— priming read
5. repeat while the user entered a monthly amount
      convert the monthly amount to a number
      if the monthly amount can be converted to a number
         display the monthly amount in the lstMonthly control
         add 1 to the intMonths counter
         add the monthly amount to the dblTotal accumulator
      else
         display an appropriate message
      end if
      get a monthly amount from the user——————————— update read
   end repeat while
6. if the value in the intMonths counter is greater than 0
      average bill = dblTotal accumulator / intMonths counter
      display average bill in lblAvg control
  else
      display "N/A" in lblAvg control
  end if

Figure 6-55 Problem specification, pseudocode, and a sample run for the Electric Bill application
(continues)

(continued)

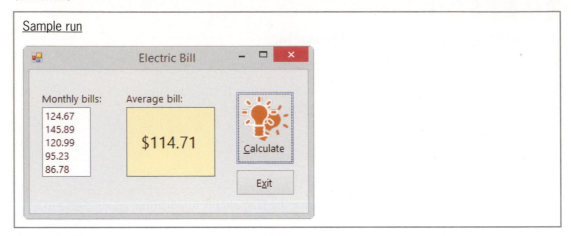

Sample run

Figure 6-55   Problem specification, pseudocode, and a sample run for the Electric Bill application

Notice that the Calculate button's pseudocode contains two "get a monthly amount from the user" instructions. One of the instructions appears above the loop, and the other appears as the last instruction in the loop body. The "get a monthly amount from the user" instruction above the loop is referred to as the **priming read** because it is used to prime (i.e., prepare or set up) the loop. The priming read initializes the loop condition by providing its first value—in this case, the first monthly amount. Because the loop is a pretest loop, this amount determines whether the instructions in the loop body are processed at all. If the loop body instructions *are* processed, the "get a monthly amount from the user" instruction in the loop body gets the remaining monthly amounts (if any). This instruction is referred to as the **update read** because it allows the user to update the value of the input item (in this case, the monthly amount) associated with the loop's condition. The update read is often an exact copy of the priming read.

The importance of the update read cannot be stressed enough. If you don't include the update read in the loop body, there will be no way to enter a value that will stop the loop after it has been processed the first time. This is because the priming read is processed only once and gets only the first amount from the user. Without the update read, the loop will have no way of stopping on its own. As you learned earlier, a loop that has no way to end is called an infinite (or endless) loop. Recall that you can stop an infinite loop by clicking Debug on the menu bar and then clicking Stop Debugging, or you can use the Stop Debugging button on the Standard toolbar.

START HERE

To open the Electric Bill application:

1. If necessary, start Visual Studio 2015. Open the VB2015\Chap06\Electric Solution\ Electric Solution (Electric Solution.sln) file. Open the Code Editor window. Replace <your name> and <current date> in the comments with your name and the current date, respectively.

2. Locate the btnCalc_Click procedure. The procedure declares the two named constants and six variables shown in Figure 6-56. The named constants and the `strMonthBill` variable will be used along with the InputBox function to get a monthly amount from the user. The `dblMonthBill` and `blnNumeric` variables will be used by the TryParse method when it attempts to convert the monthly amount to the Double data type. The `intMonths` variable will be the counter that keeps track of the number of amounts entered, and the `dblTotal` variable will accumulate the amounts. The `dblAvg` variable will store the average amount after it has been calculated.

```
Private Sub btnCalc_Click(sender As Object, e As EventAr
    ' calculate the average electric bill

    Const strPROMPT As String =
        "Enter electric bill. " &
        "Click Cancel or leave blank to end."
    Const strTITLE As String = "Monthly Bill"
    Dim strMonthBill As String
    Dim dblMonthBill As Double
    Dim blnNumeric As Boolean
    Dim intMonths As Integer      ' counter
    Dim dblTotal As Double        ' accumulator
    Dim dblAvg As Double
```

Figure 6-56   Named constants and variables declared in the btnCalc_Click procedure

The first two steps in the Calculate button's pseudocode initialize the counter and accumulator variables to 0. Because the Dim statement automatically assigns the number 0 to Integer and Double variables when the variables are created, you do not need to enter any additional code to initialize the `intMonths` and `dblTotal` variables. In cases where you need to initialize a counter or an accumulator to a value other than 0, you can do so either in the Dim statement that declares the variable or in an assignment statement. For example, to initialize the `intMonths` variable to the number 1, you could use either the declaration statement `Dim intMonths As Integer = 1` or the assignment statement `intMonths = 1` in your code. However, to use the assignment statement, the `intMonths` variable must be declared before the assignment statement is processed.

To code and then test the btnCalc_Click procedure:

START HERE

1. The next step in the pseudocode clears the contents of the lstMonthly and lblAvg controls. Click the **blank line** below the `' clear lstMonthly and lblAvg` comment, and then enter the following lines of code:

    lstMonthly.Items.Clear()
    lblAvg.Text = String.Empty

2. Next, you need to get the first monthly amount from the user. Enter the following assignment statement in the blank line below the `' get first amount` comment:

    strMonthBill = InputBox(strPROMPT, strTITLE, "0")

3. The next step in the pseudocode is a pretest loop whose condition determines whether the user entered an amount. If no amount was entered, the InputBox function returns the empty string. In this case, you want the loop body instructions processed only when the function returns a value other than the empty string. Click the **blank line** below the `' repeat as long as the user enters an amount` comment, and then enter the following Do While clause:

    Do While strMonthBill <> String.Empty

4. If the user entered an amount, the first instruction in the loop body will attempt to convert the amount to Double. Enter the following assignment statement:

blnNumeric = Double.TryParse(strMonthBill, dblMonthBill)

5. The second instruction in the loop body is a selection structure whose condition determines whether the TryParse method was successful. Enter the following If clause:

If blnNumeric Then

6. If the TryParse method was successful, the selection structure's true path should display the amount in the lstMonthly control and then update the counter and accumulator; otherwise, its false path should display an appropriate message. Enter the additional comments and code shown in Figure 6-57, and then position the insertion point as shown in the figure.

```
        If blnNumeric Then
                ' display the amount in the list box
                lstMonthly.Items.Add(dblMonthBill.ToString("N2"))

                ' update the counter and accumulator
                intMonths += 1
                dblTotal += dblMonthBill
        Else
                MessageBox.Show("Please enter a number.",
                                "Monthly Bill",
                                MessageBoxButtons.OK,
                                MessageBoxIcon.Information)
        End If

    Loop
```

enter these comments and lines of code

position the insertion point here

Figure 6-57   Loop entered in the btnCalc_Click procedure

7. The last instruction before the loop ends is the update read, which is identical to the priming read. Type the following assignment statement, and then click the **blank line** above the End Sub clause:

strMonthBill = InputBox(strPROMPT, strTITLE, "0")

8. When the user has finished entering monthly amounts, the loop ends and processing continues with Step 6 in the pseudocode. Step 6 is a selection structure whose condition verifies that the value stored in the intMonths counter variable is greater than the number 0. This verification is necessary because the first instruction in the selection structure's true path uses the variable as the divisor when calculating the average electric bill. Before using a variable as the divisor in an expression, you should always verify that the variable does not contain the number 0 because, as in mathematics, division by 0 is not possible. Dividing by 0 in a procedure will give you unexpected results, such as either causing the application to end abruptly with an error or displaying either the Visual Basic constant NaN (which stands for *Not a Number*) or the Visual Basic constant Infinity. In the blank line above the End Sub clause, enter the following If clause:

If intMonths > 0 Then

9. If the value in the `intMonths` variable is greater than 0, the selection structure's true path should calculate and display the average electric bill; otherwise, it should display the string "N/A" (which stands for *Not Available*). Complete the selection structure's true and false paths as indicated in Figure 6-58.

```vbnet
Private Sub btnCalc_Click(sender As Object, e As EventArgs
) Handles btnCalc.Click
    ' calculate the average electric bill

    Const strPROMPT As String =
        "Enter electric bill. " &
        "Click Cancel or leave blank to end."
    Const strTITLE As String = "Monthly Bill"
    Dim strMonthBill As String
    Dim dblMonthBill As Double
    Dim blnNumeric As Boolean
    Dim intMonths As Integer    ' counter
    Dim dblTotal As Double      ' accumulator
    Dim dblAvg As Double

    ' clear lstMonthly and lblAvg
    lstMonthly.Items.Clear()
    lblAvg.Text = String.Empty

    ' get first amount
    strMonthBill = InputBox(strPROMPT, strTITLE, "0")

    ' repeat as long as the user enters an amount
    Do While strMonthBill <> String.Empty
        blnNumeric = Double.TryParse(strMonthBill, dblMonthBill)
        If blnNumeric Then
            ' display the amount in the list box
            lstMonthly.Items.Add(dblMonthBill.ToString("N2"))

            ' update the counter and accumulator
            intMonths += 1
            dblTotal += dblMonthBill
        Else
            MessageBox.Show("Please enter a number.",
                            "Monthly Bill",
                            MessageBoxButtons.OK,
                            MessageBoxIcon.Information)
        End If
        strMonthBill = InputBox(strPROMPT, strTITLE, "0")
    Loop

    ' verify that the counter is greater than 0
    If intMonths > 0 Then
        dblAvg = dblTotal / intMonths
        lblAvg.Text = dblAvg.ToString("c2")
    Else
        lblAvg.Text = "N/A"
    End If
End Sub
```

enter these four lines of code

Figure 6-58   Completed btnCalc_Click procedure

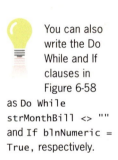

You can also write the Do While and If clauses in Figure 6-58 as `Do While strMonthBill <> ""` and `If blnNumeric = True`, respectively.

10. Save the solution and then start the application. Click the **Calculate** button. Use the Monthly Bill dialog box to enter the following six amounts, one at a time: **132.99**, **145.67**, **150.23**, **110.89**, **105.77**, and **74.98**.

11. Click the **Cancel** button in the dialog box. See Figure 6-59.

Figure 6-59 Monthly and average bill amounts shown in the interface

12. Click the **Exit** button. Close the Code Editor window and then close the solution.

YOU DO IT 5!

Create an application named YouDoIt 5 and save it in the VB2015\Chap06 folder. Add three labels and a button to the form. The button's Click event procedure should allow the user to enter one or more prices. It then should display (in the labels) the number of prices entered, the total of the prices entered, and the average price entered. If the user does not enter any numbers, the procedure should display the string "None" in the three labels. Code the button's Click event procedure using a pretest loop and the InputBox function. Save the solution, and then start and test the application. Close the solution.

Nested Repetition Structures

Like selection structures, repetition structures can be nested, which means you can place one loop (called the nested or inner loop) within another loop (called the outer loop). Both loops can be pretest loops, or both can be posttest loops. Or, one can be a pretest loop and the other a posttest loop.

A clock uses nested loops to keep track of the time. For simplicity, consider a clock's minute and second hands only. The second hand on a clock moves one position, clockwise, for every second that has elapsed. After the second hand moves 60 positions, the minute hand moves one position, also clockwise. The second hand then begins its journey around the clock again.

Figure 6-60 shows the logic used by a clock's minute and second hands. As the figure indicates, an outer loop controls the minute hand, while the inner (nested) loop controls the second hand. Notice that the entire nested loop is contained within the outer loop; this must be true for the loop to be nested and for it to work correctly. The next iteration of the outer loop (which controls the minute hand) occurs only after the nested loop (which controls the second hand) has finished processing.

```
repeat for minutes from 0 to 59
    repeat for seconds from 0 to 59
        move second hand 1 position, clockwise         nested loop
    end repeat for seconds
    move minute hand 1 position, clockwise
end repeat for minutes
```

Figure 6-60   Logic used by a clock's minute and second hands

To code and then test the Clock application: START HERE

1. Open the VB2015\Chap06\Clock Solution\Clock Solution (Clock Solution.sln) file. See Figure 6-61.

Figure 6-61   Clock application's interface

2. Open the Code Editor window. Replace <your name> and <current date> in the comments with your name and the current date, respectively.

3. Locate the btnStart_Click procedure. The procedure will use an outer loop to display the number of minutes and a nested loop to display the number of seconds. For simplicity in watching the minutes and seconds tick away, you will display minute values from 0 to 2 and second values from 0 to 5.

4. Click the **blank line** above the End Sub clause, and then enter the following nested loops:

```
For intMinutes As Integer = 0 To 2
    lblMinutes.Text = intMinutes.ToString
    For intSeconds As Integer = 0 To 5
        lblSeconds.Text = intSeconds.ToString
    Next intSeconds
Next intMinutes
```

5. Save the solution and then start the application. Click the **Start** button. The computer processes the code entered in the button's Click event procedure so quickly that you don't get a chance to see each of the values assigned to the labels. Instead, only the final values (2 and 5) appear in the interface. You can fix this problem by refreshing the interface and then delaying program execution each time the value in the lblSeconds control changes.

6. Click the **Exit** button.

The Refresh and Sleep Methods

You can refresh (or redraw) the interface using the form's Refresh method. The **Refresh method** ensures that the computer processes any previous lines of code that affect the interface's appearance. The Refresh method's syntax is Me.Refresh(), in which Me refers to the current form. You can delay program execution using the **Sleep method** in the following syntax: System.Threading.Thread.Sleep(*milliseconds*). The *milliseconds* argument is the number of milliseconds to suspend the program. A millisecond is 1/1000 of a second; in other words, there are 1000 milliseconds in a second. In the Clock application, you will delay program execution for half of a second, which is 500 milliseconds.

START HERE

To include the Refresh and Sleep methods in the procedure and then test the code:

1. Enter the additional comment and two lines of code indicated in Figure 6-62.

```vb
Private Sub btnStart_Click(sender As Object, e As EventArgs
    ' display minutes (from 0 through 2 only)
    ' and seconds (from 0 through 5 only)

    For intMinutes As Integer = 0 To 2
        lblMinutes.Text = intMinutes.ToString
        For intSeconds As Integer = 0 To 5
            lblSeconds.Text = intSeconds.ToString
            ' refresh interface and then pause execution
            Me.Refresh()
            System.Threading.Thread.Sleep(500)
        Next intSeconds
    Next intMinutes
End Sub
```

enter this comment and these two lines of code

Figure 6-62   Refresh and Sleep methods added to the procedure

2. Save the solution and then start the application. Click the **Start** button. The number 0 appears in the lblMinutes control, and the numbers 0 to 5 appear (one at a time) in the lblSeconds control. Notice that the number of minutes is increased by 1 when the number of seconds changes from 5 to 0. When the procedure ends, the lblMinutes and lblSeconds controls contain the numbers 2 and 5, respectively. (Hint: If you want to end the procedure before it has finished processing, click the Stop Debugging button on the Standard toolbar.)

3. Click the **Exit** button. Close the Code Editor window and then close the solution.

Trixie at the Diner

A programmer determines whether a problem's solution requires a nested loop by studying the problem specification. The first problem specification you will examine in this chapter involves a waitress named Trixie. The problem specification and an illustration of the problem are shown in Figure 6-63, along with an appropriate solution. The solution requires a loop because the instructions for telling each table about the daily specials must be repeated for every table that needs to be waited on. However, the solution does not require a nested loop. This is because the instructions within the loop should be followed only once per table.

Problem Specification

A waitress named Trixie works at a local diner. The diner just opened for the day, and customers are already sitting at several of the tables. Write the instructions that direct Trixie to go over to each table that needs to be waited on and tell the customers about the daily specials.

Solution
repeat for each table that needs to be waited on
    go to a table that needs to be waited on ⎯⎯⎯⎯⎯⎯⎯ follow these
      tell the customers at the table about the daily specials ⎯ instructions for each table
end repeat for

Figure 6-63 Problem specification and solution that requires a loop
Image by Diane Zak; created with Reallusion CrazyTalk Animator

Now we'll add some additional tasks for Trixie to perform. This time, after telling the customers at the table about the daily specials, Trixie should take each customer's order and then submit the order for the entire table to the cook. Figure 6-64 shows the modified problem specification along with the modified solution, which requires a nested loop. The outer loop begins with "repeat for each table that needs to be waited on", and it ends with the last "end repeat for". The nested loop begins with "repeat for each customer at the table", and it ends with the first "end repeat for". Here again, notice that the entire nested loop is contained within the outer loop. Recall that this is a requirement for the loop to be nested and work correctly.

Problem Specification

A waitress named Trixie works at a local diner. The diner just opened for the day, and customers are already sitting at several of the tables. Write the instructions that direct Trixie to go over to each table that needs to be waited on and tell the customers about the daily specials. While at each table, Trixie should take each customer's order. She then should submit the entire table's order to the cook.

Figure 6-64 Modified problem specification and solution that requires a nested loop *(continues)*

(continued)

Solution
repeat for each table that needs to be waited on
      go to a table that needs to be waited on
      tell the customers at the table about the daily specials
      repeat for each customer at the table
           ask the customer for his or her order
           record the order on the order slip for that table
      end repeat for
      go over to the cook at the counter
      tear the appropriate order slip from the order pad
      give the order slip to the cook
end repeat for

follow these instructions for each table

follow these instructions for each customer at the current table

Figure 6-64   Modified problem specification and solution that requires a nested loop

The Savings Account Application

Figure 6-65 shows the problem specification for the Savings Account application, which displays the balance in a savings account at the end of each of five years, using rates from 3% to 7%. It also shows the pseudocode for the Calculate button's Click event procedure. Notice that the procedure requires two loops, one nested within the other. The outer loop controls the rates, which range from 3% to 7% in increments of 1%. The inner loop controls the years, which range from 1 to 5 in increments of 1. The figure also shows a sample run of the application.

Problem Specification

Create an application that displays the balance in a savings account at the end of each of five years, given the amount of money deposited into the savings account at the beginning of the year and using annual interest rates of 3% to 7% in increments of 1%. The interest is compounded annually, and no withdrawals or additional deposits are made during any of the years.

Pseudocode for the Calculate button's Click event procedure
1. store deposit in a variable
2. display Rate, Year, and Balance column headings
3. repeat for rate from 3% to 7% in increments of 1%
      display rate
      repeat for year from 1 to 5 in increments of 1
           balance = deposit * (1 + rate) ^ year
           display year and balance
      end repeat for
    end repeat for

Figure 6-65   Problem specification, pseudocode, and sample run for the Savings Account application
(continues)

(continued)

<u>Sample run</u>

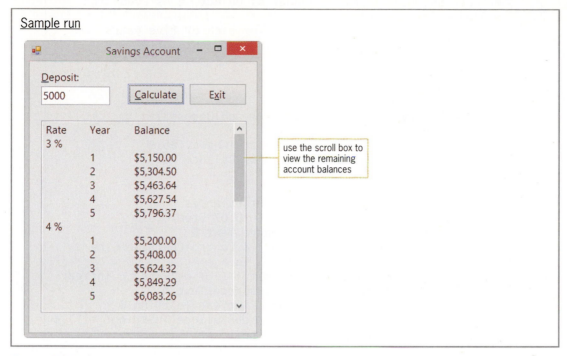

Figure 6-65 Problem specification, pseudocode, and sample run for the Savings Account application

To code and then test the btnCalc_Click procedure:

START HERE

1. Open the VB2015\Chap06\Savings Solution\Savings Solution (Savings Solution.sln) file. Open the Code Editor window. Replace <your name> and <current date> in the comments with your name and the current date, respectively.

2. Locate the btnCalc_Click procedure. The procedure contains the Dim statements that declare the `dblDeposit` and `dblBalance` variables. It also contains the TryParse method that converts the user's input (the deposit) to the Double data type. In addition, it contains an assignment statement that displays the appropriate column headings in the txtBalance control. The assignment statement uses the `ControlChars.Tab` and `ControlsChars.NewLine` constants, which represent the Tab and Enter keys, respectively.

3. First, you will enter the outer loop, which controls the rates. Click the **blank line** above the End Sub clause, and then enter the following For clause:

   For dblRate As Double = .03 To .07 Step .01

4. Change the Next clause to **Next dblRate**.

5. According to its pseudocode, the procedure should display the rate next. Click the **blank line** below the For clause, and then enter the following lines of code:

   txtBalance.Text = txtBalance.Text &
   dblRate.ToString("p0") & ControlChars.NewLine

6. Next, you will enter the nested loop, which controls the years. The loop instructions should calculate the account balance and then display the year number and account balance in the txtBalance control. Enter the nested loop shown in Figure 6-66.

```vb
Private Sub btnCalc_Click(sender As Object, e As EventArgs
) Handles btnCalc.Click
    ' calculate account balances for each of five years
    ' using rates from 3% to 7% in increments of 1%

    Dim dblDeposit As Double
    Dim dblBalance As Double

    Double.TryParse(txtDeposit.Text, dblDeposit)

    txtBalance.Text = "Rate" & ControlChars.Tab &
        "Year" & ControlChars.Tab & "Balance" &
        ControlChars.NewLine

    ' calculate and display account balances
    For dblRate As Double = 0.03 To 0.07 Step 0.01
        txtBalance.Text = txtBalance.Text &
            dblRate.ToString("p0") & ControlChars.NewLine
        For intYear As Integer = 1 To 5
            dblBalance = dblDeposit * (1 + dblRate) ^ intYear
            txtBalance.Text = txtBalance.Text &
                ControlChars.Tab & intYear.ToString &
                ControlChars.Tab & dblBalance.ToString("c2") &
                ControlChars.NewLine
        Next intYear
    Next dblRate
End Sub
```

enter this nested loop

Figure 6-66   Completed btnCalc_Click procedure

7. Save the solution and then start the application. Type **5000** in the Deposit box, and then click the **Calculate** button. The account balances appear in the txtBalance control, as shown earlier in Figure 6-65.

8. Use the control's scroll box to verify that the control contains the account balances for each of the five rates.

9. Click the **Exit** button. Close the Code Editor window and then close the solution.

A Caution About Real Numbers

Not all **real numbers**, which are numbers with a decimal place, can be stored precisely in the computer's internal memory. Many can be stored only as an approximation, which may lead to unexpected results when two real numbers are compared with each other. For example, sometimes a Double number that is the result of a calculation doesn't compare precisely with the same number stored as a literal constant. This is why it is so important to test your application's code thoroughly. In the next set of steps, you will observe how the comparison problem would affect the Savings Account application from the previous section.

START HERE

To modify the application from the previous section:

1. Use Windows to make a copy of the Savings Solution folder. Rename the copy Modified Savings Solution, and then open the Savings Solution (Savings Solution.sln) file contained in the Modified Savings Solution folder.

2. Open the Code Editor window. Change 7% in the fourth comment to 6%. Then, locate the btnCalc_Click procedure. Change 7% in the second comment to 6%. Let's assume that the user still wants to display the account balances for each of the five years, but for rates from 3% to 6% (rather than from 3% to 7%). In the outer For clause, change 0.07 to **0.06**.

3. Save the solution and then start the application. Click the **Calculate** button, and then scroll to the bottom of the txtBalance control. See Figure 6-67. Notice that the information associated with the 6% rate is missing from the control.

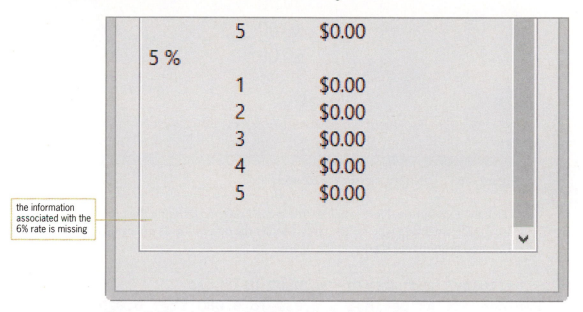

the information associated with the 6% rate is missing

Figure 6-67   Interface showing the 6% information missing

4. Click the **Exit** button.

Consider why the loop that controls the rates failed to display the 6% information. Recall that the For clause in that loop looks like this: `For dblRate As Double = 0.03 To 0.06 Step 0.01`. The clause tells the computer to stop processing the loop instructions when the value in the `dblRate` variable is greater than 0.06. This indicates that when the For clause updates the `dblRate` variable to 0.06 and then compares that value with the 0.06 literal constant, the value in the variable is viewed as *greater* than the literal constant, so the loop ends prematurely. To fix this problem, you can either increase the literal constant's value slightly (e.g., you can use 0.0600001) or use the Decimal data type for the loop that controls the rates. You will try both methods in the next set of steps.

To fix the comparison problem in the application:

START HERE

1. First, you'll increase the literal constant's value. Change 0.06 in the outer For clause to **0.0600001**. Save the solution and then start the application. Click the **Calculate** button, and then scroll to the bottom of the txtBalance control. The control now includes the information pertaining to the 6% rate. See Figure 6-68.

the text box now includes the information associated with the 6% rate

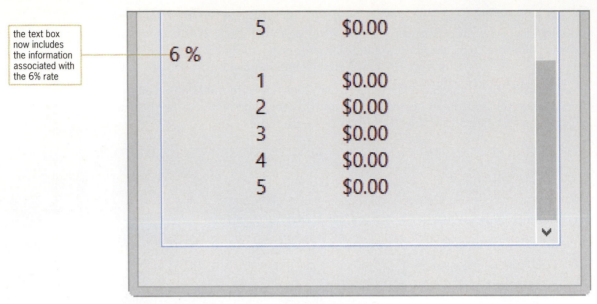

5	$0.00
6 %	
1	$0.00
2	$0.00
3	$0.00
4	$0.00
5	$0.00

Figure 6-68 Interface showing the 6% information

2. Click the **Exit** button. Next, you'll try the second method of fixing the problem, which is to use the Decimal data type for the rates. Modify the outer loop as indicated in Figure 6-69. The modifications are shaded in the figure.

make the shaded modifications

```
' calculate and display account balances
For decRate As Decimal = 0.03D To 0.06D Step 0.01D
    txtBalance.Text = txtBalance.Text &
        decRate.ToString("p0") & ControlChars.NewLine
    For intYear As Integer = 1 To 5
        dblBalance = dblDeposit * (1 + decRate) ^ intYear
        txtBalance.Text = txtBalance.Text &
            ControlChars.Tab & intYear.ToString &
            ControlChars.Tab & dblBalance.ToString("c2") &
            ControlChars.NewLine
    Next intYear
Next decRate
```

Figure 6-69 Modifications made to the nested loop that controls the interest rates

3. Save the solution and then start the application. Click the **Calculate** button, and then scroll to the bottom of the txtBalance control. The 6% rate information appears in the control, as shown earlier in Figure 6-68.

4. Click the **Exit** button. Close the Code Editor window and then close the solution.

Lesson C Summary

- To nest a repetition structure (loop):

  Place the entire inner loop within the outer loop.

- To refresh the interface:

  Use the Refresh method. The method's syntax is `Me.Refresh()`.

- To pause program execution:

  Use the Sleep method. The method's syntax is `System.Threading.Thread.Sleep` (*milliseconds*).

Lesson C Key Terms

Priming read—the input instruction that appears above the loop that it controls; used to get the first input item from the user

Real numbers—numbers with a decimal place

Refresh method—can be used to refresh (redraw) a form

Sleep method—can be used to delay program execution

Update read—the input instruction that appears within a loop and is associated with the priming read

Lesson C Review Questions

1. A procedure allows the user to enter one or more values. The first input instruction will get the first value only and is referred to as the _____ read.

   a. entering   c. priming

   b. initializer   d. starter

2. What will the following code display in the lblAsterisks control?

   ```
   For intX As Integer = 1 To 2
     For intY As Integer = 1 To 3
        lblAsterisks.Text = lblAsterisks.Text & "*"
     Next intY
     lblAsterisks.Text = lblAsterisks.Text &
        ControlChars.NewLine
   Next intX
   ```

   a. ***   c. **
      ***   **
                    **

   b. ***
      ***   d. ***
      ***   ***
                    ***
                    ***

3. What will the following code display in the lblSum control?

```
Dim intSum As Integer
Dim intY As Integer
Do While intY < 3
  For intX As Integer = 1 To 4
    intSum += intX
  Next intX
  intY += 1
Loop
lblSum.Text = intSum.ToString
```

a. 5

b. 8

c. 15

d. 30

4. Which of the following statements pauses program execution for one second?

a. `System.Threading.Thread.Pause(1000)`

c. `System.Threading.Thread.Sleep(1000)`

b. `System.Threading.Thread.Pause(1)`

d. `System.Threading.Thread.Sleep(100)`

Lesson C Exercises

INTRODUCTORY

1. In this exercise, you modify the Clock application from this lesson. Use Windows to make a copy of the Clock Solution folder. Rename the copy Clock Solution-Introductory. Open the Clock Solution (Clock Solution.sln) file contained in the Clock Solution-Introductory folder. Open the Code Editor window. Change the outer For...Next statement to a Do...Loop statement. Test the application appropriately.

INTRODUCTORY

2. In this exercise, you modify the Savings Account application from this lesson. Use Windows to make a copy of the Savings Solution folder. Rename the copy Savings Solution-Introductory. Open the Savings Solution (Savings Solution.sln) file contained in the Savings Solution-Introductory folder. In the btnCalc_Click procedure, change the For...Next statement that controls the years to a Do...Loop statement. Test the application appropriately.

INTERMEDIATE

3. In this exercise, you modify the Clock application from this lesson. Use Windows to make a copy of the Clock Solution folder. Rename the copy Clock Solution-Intermediate. Open the Clock Solution (Clock Solution.sln) file contained in the Clock Solution-Intermediate folder. In the btnStart_Click procedure, change both For...Next statements to Do...Loop statements. Test the application appropriately.

INTERMEDIATE

4. In this exercise, you modify the Savings Account application from this lesson. Use Windows to make a copy of the Savings Solution folder. Rename the copy Savings Solution-Intermediate. Open the Savings Solution (Savings Solution.sln) file contained in the Savings Solution-Intermediate folder. In the btnCalc_Click procedure, change both For...Next statements to Do...Loop statements. Test the application appropriately.

INTERMEDIATE

5. In this exercise, you modify the Modified Savings Account application from this lesson. Use Windows to make a copy of the Modified Savings Solution folder. Rename the copy Modified Savings Solution-Intermediate. Open the Savings Solution (Savings

Solution.sln) file contained in the Modified Savings Solution-Intermediate folder. The btnCalc_Click procedure should now display the amounts by rate within year (rather than by year within rate). Figure 6-70 shows a sample run of the application. Make the appropriate modifications to the code. Test the application appropriately.

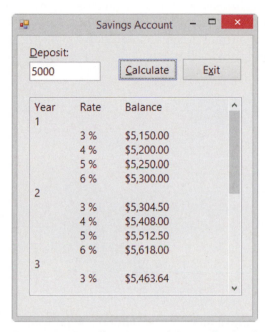

Figure 6-70   Sample run of the application for Exercise 5

6.   Open the VB2015\Chap06\Grade Solution\Grade Solution (Grade Solution.sln) file. Professor Mason wants you to create an application that allows her to assign a grade to any number of students. Each student's grade is based on four test scores, with each test worth 100 points. The application should total the test scores and then assign the appropriate grade using the information shown in Figure 6-71. Test the application appropriately.   **INTERMEDIATE**

Total points earned	Grade
at least 372	A
340–371	B
280–339	C
240–279	D
below 240	F

Figure 6-71   Grade information for Exercise 6

7.   Create an application, using the following names for the solution and project, respectively: Table Solution and Table Project. Save the application in the VB2015\ Chap06 folder. The application should display a table consisting of four rows and five columns. The first column should contain the numbers 1 through 4. The second and subsequent columns should contain the result of multiplying the number in the first column by the numbers 2 through 5. Create a suitable interface, and then code the application. Test the application appropriately.   **INTERMEDIATE**

INTERMEDIATE

8. Create an application, using the following names for the solution and project, respectively: Barclay Solution and Barclay Project. Save the application in the VB2015\ Chap06 folder. The application's interface is shown in Figure 6-72. The Calculate button's Click event procedure should use a loop and the InputBox function to get the prices of the candies purchased by the user. Each price should be displayed in the lstPrices control. The procedure should also accumulate the prices. When the user has finished entering the prices for the current order, the procedure should display the accumulated value plus a 5% sales tax in the Total due box. Test the application appropriately.

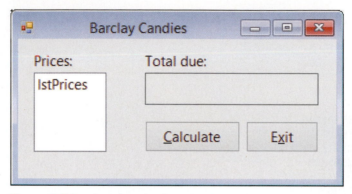

Figure 6-72   Interface for Exercise 8

INTERMEDIATE

9. Create an application, using the following names for the solution and project, respectively: New Salary Solution and New Salary Project. Save the application in the VB2015\Chap06 folder. Assume that at the beginning of every year, you receive a raise on your previous year's salary. Create a program that displays the amount of your annual raises and also your new salaries for the next five years, using raise rates of 1.5%, 2%, 2.5%, and 3%. Create a suitable interface, and then code the application and test it appropriately.

ADVANCED

10. Create an application, using the following names for the solution and project, respectively: Bar Chart Solution and Bar Chart Project. Save the application in the VB2015\Chap06 folder. The application should allow the user to enter the ratings for five different movies. Each rating should be a number from 1 through 10 only. The application should graph the ratings using a horizontal bar chart consisting of five rows, with one row for each movie. Each row should contain from one to 10 plus signs (+). The number of plus signs depends on the movie's rating. Create a suitable interface, and then code the application and test it appropriately.

ADVANCED

11. Open the VB2015\Chap06\Car Solution\Car Solution (Car Solution.sln) file. (The image is provided courtesy of OpenClipArt.org/Keistutis.) The btnClickMe_Click procedure should make the "I WANT THIS CAR!" message blink 10 times. In other words, the message should disappear and then reappear, disappear and then reappear, and so on, 10 times. Use the For...Next statement. Test the application appropriately.

CHAPTER 7

Sub and Function Procedures

Creating the Cerruti Company Application

In this chapter, you create an application for Lucy Malkin, the payroll manager at Cerruti Company. Currently, Ms. Malkin manually calculates each employee's weekly gross pay, federal withholding tax (FWT), Social Security and Medicare (FICA) tax, and net pay. The process of performing these calculations manually is both time-consuming and prone to mathematical errors. Ms. Malkin has asked you to create an application that she can use to perform the payroll calculations both efficiently and accurately.

Previewing the Cerruti Company Application

Before you start the first lesson in this chapter, you will preview the completed application contained in the VB2015\Chap07 folder.

START HERE

To preview the completed application:

1. Use Windows to locate and then open the VB2015\Chap07 folder. Right-click **Cerruti** (**Cerruti.exe**) and then click the **Open** button. Type **Joe Chang** in the Name box and then click the **Married** radio button.

2. Scroll down the Hours list box and then click **42.5** in the list. Scroll down the Rate list box and then click **13.50** in the list.

3. The interface contains a combo box that allows you to either type the number of withholding allowances or select the number from a list. Click the **list arrow** in the Allowances combo box and then click **2** in the list.

4. Click the **Calculate** button. The gross pay, taxes, and net pay appear in the interface. See Figure 7-1.

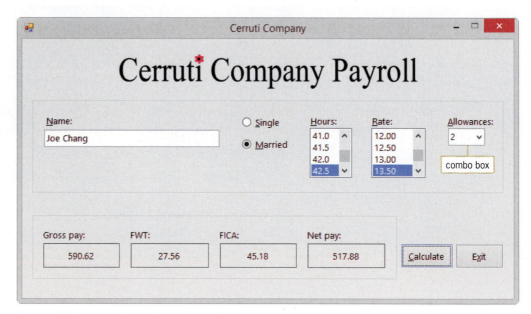

Figure 7-1　Interface showing the payroll calculations

5. Click the **Exit** button. The "Do you want to exit?" message appears in a message box. See Figure 7-2.

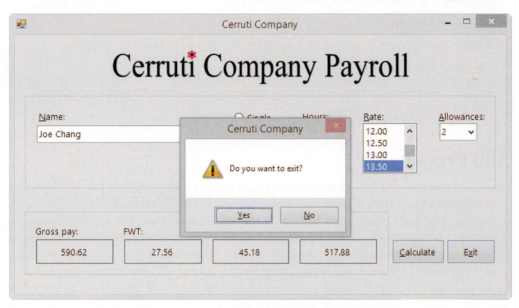

Figure 7-2   Message box containing a confirmation message

6. Click the **No** button. Notice that the form remains on the screen. In Lesson C, you will learn how to prevent the computer from closing a form.

7. Click the **Exit** button, and then click the **Yes** button in the message box. The application ends.

The Cerruti Company application uses a combo box and a Function procedure. You will learn about Function procedures, more simply referred to as functions, in Lesson A. Combo boxes are covered in Lesson B. You will code the Cerruti Company application in Lesson C. Be sure to complete each lesson in full and do all of the end-of-lesson questions and several exercises before continuing to the next lesson.

■ LESSON A

After studying Lesson A, you should be able to:

- Create and call an independent Sub procedure
- Explain the difference between a Sub procedure and a Function procedure
- Create a procedure that receives information passed to it
- Explain the difference between passing data *by value* and passing data *by reference*
- Create a Function procedure

Sub Procedures

There are two types of Sub procedures in Visual Basic: event procedures and independent Sub procedures. As you already know, an event procedure is a Sub procedure that is associated with a specific object and event, such as a button's Click event or a text box's TextChanged event. The computer automatically processes an event procedure's code when the event occurs. An **independent Sub procedure**, on the other hand, is a procedure that is independent of any object and event. An independent Sub procedure is processed only when called (invoked) from code. In Visual Basic, you invoke an independent Sub procedure using the **Call statement**.

Programmers use independent Sub procedures for several reasons, which are listed in Figure 7-3.

Reasons for using independent Sub procedures

1. They allow you to avoid duplicating code when different sections of a program need to perform the same task. Rather than entering the code in each of those sections, you can enter the code in a procedure and then have each section call the procedure to perform its task when needed.
2. If an event procedure must perform many tasks, you can prevent the procedure's code from getting unwieldy and difficult to understand by assigning some of the tasks to one or more independent Sub procedures. Doing this makes the event procedure easier to code because it allows you to concentrate on one small piece of the code at a time.
3. Independent Sub procedures are used extensively in large and complex programs, which typically are written by a team of programmers. The programming team will break up the program into small and manageable tasks, and then assign some of the tasks to different team members to be coded as independent Sub procedures. Doing this allows more than one programmer to work on the program at the same time, decreasing the time it takes to write the program.

Figure 7-3   Reasons programmers use independent Sub procedures

Using Pascal case, you capitalize the first letter in the procedure name and the first letter of each subsequent word in the name.

Figure 7-4 shows the syntax of both an independent Sub procedure and the Call statement in Visual Basic. Like event procedures, independent Sub procedures have a procedure header and a procedure footer. In most cases, the procedure header begins with the `Private` keyword, which indicates that the procedure can be used only within the current Code Editor window. Following the `Private` keyword is the `Sub` keyword, which identifies the procedure as a Sub procedure. After the `Sub` keyword comes the procedure name. The rules for naming an independent Sub procedure are the same as those for naming variables; however, procedure names are usually entered using Pascal case. The Sub procedure's name should indicate the task the procedure performs. It is a common practice to begin the name with a verb. For example, a good name for a Sub procedure that displays two random integers is DisplayRandomIntegers.

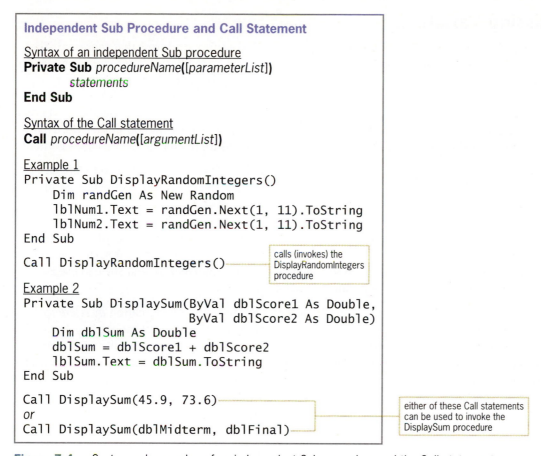

Independent Sub Procedure and Call Statement

Syntax of an independent Sub procedure
Private Sub *procedureName*(*[parameterList]*)
      statements
End Sub

Syntax of the Call statement
Call *procedureName*(*[argumentList]*)

Example 1
```
Private Sub DisplayRandomIntegers()
    Dim randGen As New Random
    lblNum1.Text = randGen.Next(1, 11).ToString
    lblNum2.Text = randGen.Next(1, 11).ToString
End Sub

Call DisplayRandomIntegers()
```
calls (invokes) the DisplayRandomIntegers procedure

Example 2
```
Private Sub DisplaySum(ByVal dblScore1 As Double,
                      ByVal dblScore2 As Double)
    Dim dblSum As Double
    dblSum = dblScore1 + dblScore2
    lblSum.Text = dblSum.ToString
End Sub

Call DisplaySum(45.9, 73.6)
  or
Call DisplaySum(dblMidterm, dblFinal)
```
either of these Call statements can be used to invoke the DisplaySum procedure

Figure 7-4 Syntax and examples of an independent Sub procedure and the Call statement

Following the procedure name in the procedure header is a set of parentheses that contains an optional *parameterList*, which lists the data type and name of one or more parameters. As you learned in Chapter 4, a parameter represents information that is passed to a procedure when the procedure is invoked. Each parameter in the parameterList has procedure scope and each stores an item of data, which is passed to the procedure through the Call statement's *argumentList*. The number of arguments should agree with the number of parameters. If the parameterList does not contain any parameters, as shown in Example 1 in Figure 7-4, then an empty set of parentheses follows the procedure name in the Call statement. However, if the parameterList contains one parameter, then the argumentList should have one argument. Similarly, a procedure that contains three parameters requires three arguments in the Call statement that invokes it. (Refer to the Tip on this page for an exception to this general rule.)

In addition to having the same number of arguments as parameters, the data type and order (or position) of each argument should agree with the data type and order (position) of its corresponding parameter. If the first parameter has a data type of String and the second has a data type of Double, then the first argument in the Call statement should have the String data type and the second should have the Double data type. This is because when the procedure is called, the computer stores the value of the first argument in the procedure's first parameter, the value of the second argument in its second parameter, and so on.

An argument can be a literal constant (as shown in the first Call statement in Example 2 in Figure 7-4), a named constant, a keyword, or a variable (as shown in the second Call statement in Example 2 in Figure 7-4). However, in most cases, the argument will be a variable.

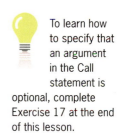
To learn how to specify that an argument in the Call statement is optional, complete Exercise 17 at the end of this lesson.

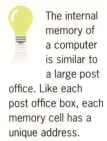

The internal memory of a computer is similar to a large post office. Like each post office box, each memory cell has a unique address.

Ch07A-Passing Variables

Passing Variables

Each variable declared in a program has both a value and a unique address that represents the location of the variable in the computer's internal memory. Visual Basic allows you to pass either a copy of the variable's value or its address to the receiving procedure. Passing a copy of a variable's value is referred to as **passing by value**, whereas passing its address is referred to as **passing by reference**. The method you choose—*by value* or *by reference*—depends on whether you want the receiving procedure to have access to the variable in memory. In other words, it depends on whether you want to allow the receiving procedure to change the variable's contents.

Although the idea of passing information *by value* and *by reference* may sound confusing at first, it is a concept with which you are already familiar. We'll use the illustrations shown in Figure 7-5 to demonstrate this fact. Assume you have a savings account at a local bank. (Think of the savings account as a variable.) During a conversation with your friend, Joan, you mention the amount of money you have in the account, as shown in Illustration A. Sharing this information with Joan is similar to passing a variable *by value*. Knowing the balance in your savings account does not give Joan access to the account. It merely provides information that she can use to compare with the amount of money she has saved.

Now we'll use the savings account example to demonstrate passing information *by reference*. (Here again, think of your savings account as a variable.) To either deposit money in your account or withdraw money from your account, you must provide the bank teller with your account number, as shown in Illustration B in Figure 7-5. Doing so is similar to passing a variable *by reference*. The account number represents the location of your account at the bank and allows the teller to change the contents of your bank account, similar to the way a variable's address allows the receiving procedure to change the contents of the variable.

Figure 7-5   Illustrations of passing *by value* and passing *by reference*
Image by Diane Zak; created with Reallusion CrazyTalk Animator

Passing Variables by Value

To pass a variable *by value*, you include the keyword `ByVal` before the name of its corresponding parameter in the receiving procedure's parameterList. When you pass a variable *by value*, the computer passes a copy of the variable's contents to the receiving procedure. When only a copy of the contents is passed, the receiving procedure is not given access to the variable in memory. Therefore, it cannot change the value stored inside the variable. It is appropriate to pass a variable *by value* when the receiving procedure needs to *know* the variable's contents but does not need to *change* the contents. In this section, you will finish coding the Favorites application, which passes two variables *by value* to an independent Sub procedure.

To open the Favorites application:

START HERE

1. If necessary, start Visual Studio 2015. Open the VB2015\Chap07\Favorites Solution\ Favorites Solution (Favorites Solution.sln) file. Open the Code Editor window. Replace <your name> and <current date> in the comments with your name and the current date, respectively.

2. Locate the btnGet_Click procedure, which is shown in Figure 7-6. Depending on which radio button is selected, the event procedure gets the name of the user's favorite actor, actress, movie, singer, or song.

```vb
Private Sub btnGet_Click(sender As Object, e As EventArgs
) Handles btnGet.Click
    ' gets the favorite and then calls
    ' a procedure to display the favorite

    Dim strCategory As String
    Dim strName As String

    Select Case True
        Case radActor.Checked
            strCategory = "actor"
        Case radActress.Checked
            strCategory = "actress"
        Case radMovie.Checked
            strCategory = "movie"
        Case radSinger.Checked
            strCategory = "singer"
        Case Else
            strCategory = "song"
    End Select
    strName = InputBox("Your favorite " &
            strCategory & "?", "Favorite")

End Sub
```

Figure 7-6   Partially completed btnGet_Click procedure

Before the event procedure ends, it will call an independent Sub procedure named DisplayMsg to display the message "Your favorite *category* is *name*." In the message, *category* is one of the following: actor, actress, movie, singer, or song. *Name* is the name of the user's favorite actor, actress, movie, singer, or song. The Call statement will need to pass the appropriate category and name to the independent Sub procedure. The category and name are stored in the `strCategory` and `strName` variables, respectively. You should pass both variables *by value* because the DisplayMsg procedure does not need to change their values.

Recall that it is a common practice to begin a procedure's name with a verb and to enter the name using Pascal case.

To begin coding the Favorites application:

START HERE

1. Enter the following Call statement in the blank line above the End Sub clause. (Hint: The jagged line that appears below DisplayMsg will disappear when you create the procedure in the next set of steps.)

Call DisplayMsg(strCategory, strName)

Next, you will create the DisplayMsg procedure. The procedure will store the two String values it receives from the Call statement in two parameters named `strType` and `strFavorite`. Some programmers enter independent Sub procedures above the first event procedure, while others enter them below the last event procedure. Still others enter them either immediately above or immediately below the procedure from which they are invoked. Whichever way is chosen, however, all independent Sub procedures must appear between the Public Class and End Class clauses and outside of any other procedure. In this book, the independent Sub procedures will be entered above the first event procedure in the Code Editor window.

START HERE

To finish coding the Favorites application and then test it:

1. If necessary, scroll to the top of the Code Editor window. Click the **blank line** below the `' independent Sub procedure` comment, and then enter the DisplayMsg procedure shown in Figure 7-7. Notice that when you press Enter after typing the procedure header, the Code Editor automatically enters the procedure footer (End Sub) for you.

enter the DisplayMsg procedure

```
' independent Sub procedure
Private Sub DisplayMsg(ByVal strType As String,
                        ByVal strFavorite As String)
    lblFavorite.Text = "Your favorite " & strType &
        " is " & strFavorite & "."
End Sub
```

Figure 7-7 DisplayMsg procedure

2. Save the solution and then start the application. Click the **Get Favorite** button. The InputBox function in the btnGet_Click procedure prompts you to enter the name of your favorite actor. Type **Johnny Depp** in the Favorite dialog box and then press **Enter**. The Call statement in the event procedure invokes the DisplayMsg procedure, passing it a copy of the value stored in the `strCategory` variable (actor) and a copy of the value stored in the `strName` variable (Johnny Depp). The DisplayMsg procedure header stores the values passed to it in its `strType` and `strFavorite` parameters. The assignment statement in the procedure then displays the appropriate message in the lblFavorite control. See Figure 7-8.

Figure 7-8 Message shown in the interface

3. Click the **Song** radio button and then click the **Get Favorite** button. Type the name of your favorite song in the Favorite dialog box and then press **Enter**. A message containing the name of your favorite song appears in the lblFavorite control.

4. On your own, verify that the application displays the names of your favorite actress, movie, and singer.

5. Click the **Exit** button. Close the Code Editor window and then close the solution.

Figure 7-9 shows the DisplayMsg procedure header and the Call statement that invokes the procedure. Notice that the number, data type, and order (position) of the arguments in the Call statement match the number, data type, and order (position) of the corresponding parameters in the DisplayMsg procedure header. Also notice that the names of the arguments do not need to be identical to the names of the corresponding parameters. In fact, to avoid confusion, you should use different names for an argument and its corresponding parameter. Finally, notice that the Call statement does not indicate whether a variable is being passed *by value* or *by reference*. To make that determination, you need to look at the receiving procedure's header.

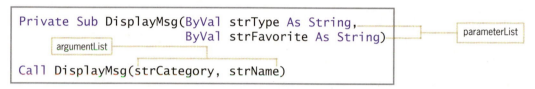

```
Private Sub DisplayMsg(ByVal strType As String,
                       ByVal strFavorite As String)
argumentList
Call DisplayMsg(strCategory, strName)
```
parameterList

Figure 7-9   DisplayMsg procedure header and Call statement

YOU DO IT 1!

Create an application named YouDoIt 1 and save it in the VB2015\Chap07 folder. Add a text box, a label, and a button to the form. The button's Click event procedure should assign the text box value to a Double variable and then pass a copy of the variable's value to an independent Sub procedure named ShowDouble. The ShowDouble procedure should multiply the variable's value by 2 and then display the result in the label control. Code the button's Click event procedure and the ShowDouble procedure. Save the solution, and then start and test the application. Close the solution.

Passing Variables by Reference

Instead of passing a copy of a variable's value to a procedure, you can pass its address. In other words, you can pass the variable's location in the computer's internal memory. As you learned earlier, passing a variable's address is referred to as passing *by reference*, and it gives the receiving procedure access to the variable being passed. You pass a variable *by reference* when you want the receiving procedure to change the contents of the variable.

To pass a variable *by reference* in Visual Basic, you include the keyword **ByRef** before the name of the corresponding parameter in the receiving procedure's header. The **ByRef** keyword tells the computer to pass the variable's address rather than a copy of its contents. In this section, you will finish coding the Concert Tickets application, which uses an independent Sub procedure named AssignDiscount. The Call statement that invokes the procedure will have three variables in its argumentList. The first two variables will be passed *by value*; the third will be passed *by reference*.

START HERE

To open the Concert Tickets application:

1. Open the Concert Solution (Concert Solution.sln) file contained in the VB2015\Chap07\Concert Solution-Sub folder. See Figure 7-10.

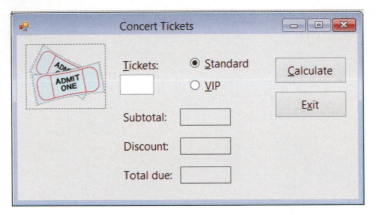

Figure 7-10   Interface for the Concert Tickets application

The interface provides a text box for entering the number of tickets purchased. It also provides radio buttons for specifying whether the tickets are Standard or VIP. The prices for Standard and VIP tickets are $62.50 and $102.75, respectively. However, the purchaser receives a 10% discount when the number of tickets purchased is at least 6, and a 2% discount when the number of tickets purchased is at least 4. The application will use an independent Sub procedure named AssignDiscount to determine the appropriate discount amount (which could be 0).

START HERE

To view the partially completed btnCalc_Click procedure:

1. Open the Code Editor window. Replace <your name> and <current date> in the comments with your name and the current date, respectively.

2. Locate the btnCalc_Click procedure. Most of the procedure's code has already been entered for you. Missing from the procedure is the statement that calls the independent AssignDiscount procedure. See Figure 7-11.

```
Private Sub btnCalc_Click(sender As Object, e As EventArgs
) Handles btnCalc.Click
    ' display subtotal, discount, and total due

    Const dblSTANDARD As Double = 62.5
    Const dblVIP As Double = 102.75
    Dim intTickets As Integer
    Dim dblSubtotal As Double
    Dim dblDiscount As Double
    Dim dblTotalDue As Double

    Integer.TryParse(txtTickets.Text, intTickets)

    ' calculate subtotal
    If radStandard.Checked Then
        dblSubtotal = intTickets * dblSTANDARD
    Else
        dblSubtotal = intTickets * dblVIP
    End If

    ' call a procedure to assign the discount                    the Call statement
                                                                  is missing
    ' calculate total due
    dblTotalDue = dblSubtotal - dblDiscount

    lblSubtotal.Text = dblSubtotal.ToString("n2")
    lblDiscount.Text = dblDiscount.ToString("n2")
    lblTotalDue.Text = dblTotalDue.ToString("n2")
End Sub
```

Figure 7-11   Partially completed btnCalc_Click procedure

The independent AssignDiscount procedure will determine the appropriate discount amount, which could be 10% of the subtotal, 2% of the subtotal, or 0. For the procedure to perform its task, it needs to know the number of tickets purchased and the subtotal; those values are stored in the `intTickets` and `dblSubtotal` variables, respectively. The procedure will not need to change the values stored in the variables, so you will pass the variables *by value*. The procedure also needs to know where to store the discount amount after it has been determined. To have the procedure store the amount in the `dblDiscount` variable, you will need to pass the variable's address to the procedure. In other words, you will need to pass the variable *by reference*.

To add the Call statement to the btnCalc_Click procedure:

START HERE

1. Click the **blank line** below the `' call a procedure to assign the discount` comment, and then enter the following Call statement:

   Call AssignDiscount(intTickets, dblSubtotal, dblDiscount)

2. Next, you will create the AssignDiscount procedure, which will receive a copy of the values stored in the `intTickets` and `dblSubtotal` variables as well as the address of the `dblDiscount` variable. The procedure will store the information it receives in its three parameters: `intNum`, `dblSub`, and `dblDisc`. If necessary, scroll to the top of the Code Editor window. Click the **blank line** below the `' independent Sub procedure` comment, and then enter the AssignDiscount procedure shown in Figure 7-12.

enter the AssignDiscount procedure

```
' independent Sub procedure
Private Sub AssignDiscount(ByVal intNum As Integer,
                           ByVal dblSub As Double,
                           ByRef dblDisc As Double)
    Select Case intNum
        Case Is >= 6
            dblDisc = dblSub * 0.1
        Case Is >= 4
            dblDisc = dblSub * 0.02
        Case Else
            dblDisc = 0
    End Select
End Sub
```

Figure 7-12 AssignDiscount Sub procedure

3. Save the solution and then start the application. Type **6** in the Tickets box and then click the **Calculate** button. See Figure 7-13.

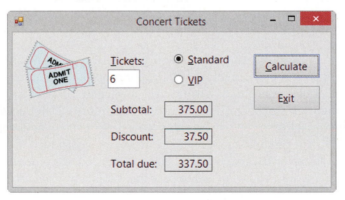

Figure 7-13 Calculated amounts shown in the interface

4. Change the number of tickets to **4**. Click the **VIP** radio button and then click the **Calculate** button. The subtotal, discount, and total due are 411.00, 8.22, and 402.78, respectively.

5. Change the number of tickets to **2** and then click the **Calculate** button. The subtotal, discount, and total due are 205.50, 0.00, and 205.50, respectively.

6. Click the **Exit** button. Close the Code Editor window and then close the solution.

Figure 7-14 shows the AssignDiscount and btnCalc_Click procedures. Notice that the number, data type, and order (position) of the arguments in the Call statement match the number, data type, and order (position) of the corresponding parameters in the AssignDiscount procedure header. ByVal in the parameterList indicates that the first two variables in the argumentList are passed *by value*, whereas ByRef indicates that the third variable is passed *by reference*. Notice that the Call statement does not indicate the way a variable is being passed; that information is found only in the receiving procedure's header. Also notice that the names of the arguments are not identical to the names of their corresponding parameters.

```vb
Private Sub AssignDiscount(ByVal intNum As Integer,
                          ByVal dblSub As Double,
                          ByRef dblDisc As Double)          ⟶ parameterList
    Select Case intNum
        Case Is >= 6
            dblDisc = dblSub * 0.1
        Case Is >= 4
            dblDisc = dblSub * 0.02
        Case Else
            dblDisc = 0
    End Select
End Sub

Private Sub btnCalc_Click(sender As Object, e As EventArgs
) Handles btnCalc.Click
    ' display subtotal, discount, and total due

    Const dblSTANDARD As Double = 62.5
    Const dblVIP As Double = 102.75
    Dim intTickets As Integer
    Dim dblSubtotal As Double
    Dim dblDiscount As Double
    Dim dblTotalDue As Double

    Integer.TryParse(txtTickets.Text, intTickets)

    ' calculate subtotal
    If radStandard.Checked Then
        dblSubtotal = intTickets * dblSTANDARD
    Else
        dblSubtotal = intTickets * dblVIP
    End If                                          argument
                                                    passed by
                                                    reference
    ' call a procedure to assign the discount
    Call AssignDiscount(intTickets, dblSubtotal, dblDiscount)
                                                         arguments
    ' calculate total due                                passed by
    dblTotalDue = dblSubtotal - dblDiscount              value

    lblSubtotal.Text = dblSubtotal.ToString("n2")
    lblDiscount.Text = dblDiscount.ToString("n2")
    lblTotalDue.Text = dblTotalDue.ToString("n2")
End Sub
```

Figure 7-14   AssignDiscount and btnCalc_Click procedures

Desk-checking the procedures shown in Figure 7-14 will help clarify the difference between passing *by value* and passing *by reference*. When the user clicks the Calculate button after typing 6 in the Tickets box, the Dim statements in the btnCalc_Click procedure create and initialize the two named constants and four variables. Next, the TryParse method stores the number of tickets in the `intTickets` variable. The selection structure then calculates the subtotal based on the selected radio button; in this case, the Standard radio button is selected. Figure 7-15 shows the contents of the named constants and variables before the Call statement is processed.

Ch07A-Sub Desk-Check

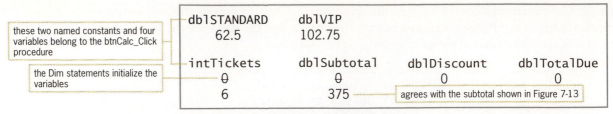

Figure 7-15   Desk-check table before the Call statement is processed

The Call statement invokes the AssignDiscount procedure, passing it three arguments. At this point, the computer temporarily leaves the btnCalc_Click procedure to process the code contained in the AssignDiscount procedure; the procedure header, which contains three parameters, is processed first. The `ByVal` keyword indicates that the first two parameters are receiving values from the Call statement—in this case, copies of the numbers stored in the `intTickets` and `dblSubtotal` variables. As a result, the computer creates the `intNum` and `dblSub` variables listed in the parameterList, and it stores the numbers 6 and 375, respectively, in the variables.

The `ByRef` keyword indicates that the third parameter is receiving the address of a variable. When you pass a variable's address to a procedure, the computer uses the address to locate the variable in its internal memory. It then assigns the parameter name to the memory location. In this case, the computer locates the `dblDiscount` variable in memory and assigns the name `dblDisc` to it. As indicated in the desk-check table shown in Figure 7-16, the memory location now has two names: one assigned by the btnCalc_Click procedure and the other assigned by the AssignDiscount procedure. Although both procedures can access the memory location, each procedure uses a different name to do so. The `dblDiscount` variable is recognized only within the btnCalc_Click procedure, and the `dblDisc` variable is recognized only within the AssignDiscount procedure.

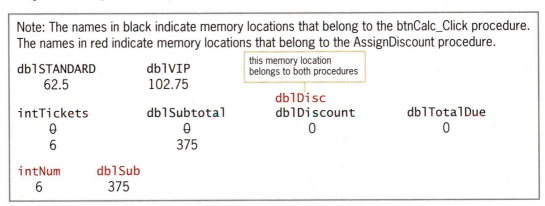

Figure 7-16   Desk-check table after the Call statement and AssignDiscount procedure header are processed

Next, the Select Case statement in the AssignDiscount procedure determines the appropriate discount based on the contents of the `intNum` variable. The variable contains the number 6, so the first Case clause multiplies the contents of the `dblSub` variable (375) by 0.1 and then assigns the result (37.5) to the `dblDisc` variable, as shown in Figure 7-17. Notice that changing the value in the `dblDisc` variable also changes the value in the `dblDiscount` variable. This is because both variable names refer to the same location in memory.

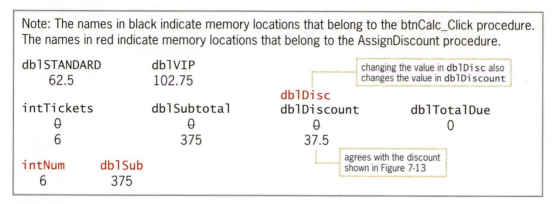

Figure 7-17 Desk-check table after assigning the discount

The AssignDiscount procedure's End Sub clause is processed next and ends the procedure. At this point, the computer removes the `intNum` and `dblSub` variables from memory. It also removes the `dblDisc` name from the appropriate location in memory, as indicated in Figure 7-18. Notice that the `dblDiscount` memory location now has only one name: the name assigned to it by the btnCalc_Click procedure.

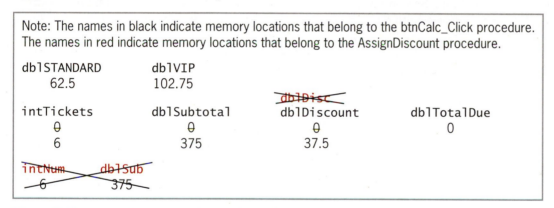

Figure 7-18 Desk-check table after the AssignDiscount procedure ends

After the AssignDiscount procedure ends, the computer returns to the btnCalc_Click procedure to finish processing the event procedure's code. More specifically, it returns to the assignment statement located below the Call statement. The assignment statement calculates the total due by subtracting the discount stored in the `dblDiscount` variable from the subtotal stored in the `dblSubtotal` variable, and then assigns the result to the `dblTotalDue` variable, as shown in Figure 7-19.

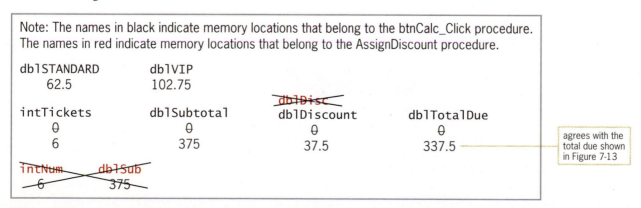

Figure 7-19 Desk-check table after assigning the total due

The last three assignment statements in the btnCalc_Click procedure display the subtotal, discount, and total due in their corresponding label controls. When the procedure ends, the computer removes the procedure's named constants and variables from memory.

YOU DO IT 2!

Create an application named YouDoIt 2 and save it in the VB2015\Chap07 folder. Add a text box, a label, and a button named btnCalc to the form. The btnCalc_Click procedure should assign the text box value to an Integer variable and then pass a copy of the variable's value, along with the address of a different Integer variable, to an independent Sub procedure named CalcDouble. The CalcDouble procedure should multiply the first Integer variable's value by 2 and then store the result in the second Integer variable. The btnCalc_Click procedure should display the contents of the second Integer variable in the label control. Code both procedures. Save the solution, and then start and test the application. Close the solution.

Function Procedures

In addition to creating Sub procedures in Visual Basic, you can also create Function procedures. The difference between both types of procedures is that a **Function procedure** returns a value after performing its assigned task, whereas a Sub procedure does not return a value. Function procedures are referred to more simply as **functions**. The problem specification and illustration shown in Figure 7-20 may help clarify the difference between Sub procedures and functions. Like a Sub procedure, Jacob will perform his task but won't need to return anything to Sarah after doing so. However, like a function, Sonja will perform her task and then return a value (the bottle of perfume) to Sarah for wrapping.

Problem Specification

Sarah and her two siblings are planning a surprise birthday party for their mother. Being the oldest of the three children, Sarah will handle most of the party plans herself. However, she does need to delegate some tasks to her brother and sister. She delegates the task of putting up the decorations (streamers, balloons, and so on) to Jacob, and she delegates the task of buying the birthday present (a bottle of perfume) to Sonja.

Figure 7-20   Problem specification along with an illustration of a Sub procedure and a function
Image by Diane Zak; created with Reallusion CrazyTalk Animator

Figure 7-21 provides another example of the difference between a Sub procedure and a function. In Illustration A, Helen is at the ticket counter in her local movie theater, requesting a ticket for the current movie. Helen gives the ticket agent a $5 bill and expects a ticket in return. The ticket agent is similar to a function in that he performs his task (fulfilling Helen's request for a ticket) and then returns a value (a ticket) to Helen. Compare that with Illustration B, where Helen and her granddaughter, Penelope, are at the Blast Off Games arcade. Helen wants Penelope to have fun, so she gives Penelope a $5 bill to play some games. But, unlike with the ticket agent, Helen expects nothing from Penelope in return. This is similar to the way a Sub procedure works. Penelope performs her task (having fun by playing games) but doesn't need to return any value to her grandmother.

Illustration A

Helen:
1. ask ticket agent for a senior ticket
2. give ticket agent $5
3. receive senior ticket from ticket agent

Ticket agent (function):
1. take $5 from Helen
2. give Helen a senior ticket

Illustration B

Helen:
1. tell Penelope to have fun playing games
2. give Penelope $5

Penelope (Sub procedure):
1. take $5 from Helen
2. buy game tickets with the $5
3. play games and have fun

Figure 7-21 Another example of the difference between a Sub procedure and a function
Image by Diane Zak; created with Reallusion CrazyTalk Animator

Figure 7-22 shows the syntax and examples of functions in Visual Basic. Unlike a Sub procedure, a function's header and footer contain the `Function` keyword rather than the `Sub` keyword. A function's header also includes the `As` *dataType* section, which specifies the data type of the value the function will return. The value is returned by the **Return statement**, which typically is the last statement within a function. The statement's syntax is `Return` *expression*, where *expression* represents the one and only value that will be returned to the statement that invoked the function. The data type of the *expression* must agree with the data type specified in the `As` *dataType* section of the header. Like a Sub procedure, a function can receive information either *by value* or *by reference*. The information it receives is listed in its parameterList.

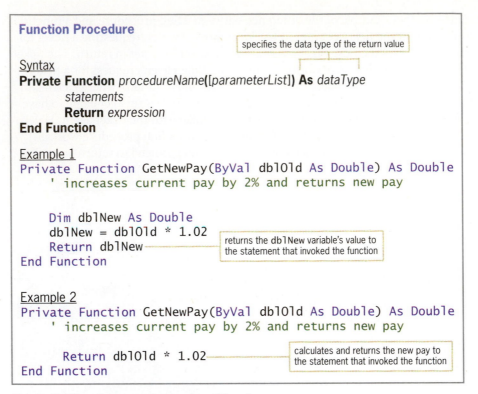

Figure 7-22 Syntax and examples of functions

As with Sub procedures, you can enter your functions anywhere in the Code Editor window as long as you enter them between the Public Class and End Class clauses and outside of any other procedure. In this book, the functions will be entered above the first event procedure in the Code Editor window. Like Sub procedure names, function names are entered using Pascal case and typically begin with a verb. The name should indicate the task the function performs. The GetNewPay name used in the examples in Figure 7-22 indicates that each function returns a new pay amount.

You can invoke a function from one or more places in an application's code. You invoke a function that you create in exactly the same way as you invoke one of Visual Basic's built-in functions, such as the InputBox function. You do this by including the function's name and arguments (if any) in a statement. The number, data type, and position of the arguments should agree with the number, data type, and position of the function's parameters. In most cases, the statement that invokes a function assigns the function's return value to a variable. However, it also may use the return value in a calculation or simply display the return value. Figure 7-23 shows examples of invoking the GetNewPay function from Figure 7-22. The GetNewPay(dblPay) entry in each example invokes the function, passing it the value stored in the dblPay variable.

Invoking a Function

Example 1 – assigns the return value to a variable
```
dblNewPay = GetNewPay(dblPay)
        or
dblPay = GetNewPay(dblPay)
```

Example 2 – uses the return value in a calculation
```
dblNewWeekly = GetNewPay(dblPay) * 40
```
the assignment statement multiplies the function's return value by the number 40 and then assigns the result to the **dblNewWeekly** variable

Example 3 – displays the return value
```
lblNewPay.Text = GetNewPay(dblPay).ToString("C2")
```

Figure 7-23 Examples of invoking the GetNewPay function

In the next set of steps, you will code the Concert Tickets application from the previous section using a function named GetDiscount (rather than a Sub procedure named AssignDiscount) to determine the appropriate discount amount.

To code the Concert Tickets application using a function:

START HERE

1. Open the Concert Solution (Concert Solution.sln) file contained in the VB2015\ Chap07\Concert Solution-Function folder. Open the Code Editor window. Replace <your name> and <current date> in the comments with your name and the current date, respectively.

2. Locate the btnCalc_Click procedure. Most of the procedure's code has already been entered for you. Missing from the procedure is the statement that invokes the GetDiscount function. For the function to perform its task, it needs to know the number of tickets purchased and the subtotal; those values are stored in the **intTickets** and **dblSubtotal** variables, respectively. The function will not need to change the values stored in the variables, so you will pass the variables *by value*. The btnCalc_Click procedure will assign the function's return value to the **dblDiscount** variable. Click the **blank line** below the ' use a function to get the discount comment and then enter the following assignment statement:

    dblDiscount = GetDiscount(intTickets, dblSubtotal)

3. Next, you will create the GetDiscount procedure, which will receive a copy of the values stored in the **intTickets** and **dblSubtotal** variables. The procedure will store the information it receives in its two parameters: **intNum** and **dblSub**. If necessary, scroll to the top of the Code Editor window. Click the **blank line** below the ' function comment, and then enter the GetDiscount procedure shown in Figure 7-24.

```
' function
Private Function GetDiscount(ByVal intNum As Integer,
                            ByVal dblSub As Double) As Double
    Dim dblDisc As Double

    Select Case intNum
        Case Is >= 6
            dblDisc = dblSub * 0.1
        Case Is >= 4
            dblDisc = dblSub * 0.02
        Case Else
            dblDisc = 0
    End Select

    Return dblDisc
End Function
```

enter the GetDiscount function

Figure 7-24   GetDiscount function

Notice that unlike the AssignDiscount Sub procedure, the GetDiscount function doesn't need the address of a variable in which to store the discount. This is because the function will return the discount to the statement that invoked it. In this case, it returns the value to the `dblDiscount = GetDiscount(intTickets, dblSubtotal)` assignment statement in the btnCalc_Click procedure. The assignment statement assigns the function's return value to the `dblDiscount` variable.

START HERE   **To test this version of the Concert Tickets application:**

1. Save the solution and then start the application. Type **6** in the Tickets box and then click the **Calculate** button. The calculated amounts appear in the interface, as shown earlier in Figure 7-13.

2. Click the **Exit** button. Close the Code Editor window and then close the solution.

Figure 7-25 shows the code entered in the GetDiscount function and the btnCalc_Click procedure. The lines of code that are different from those shown earlier in Figure 7-14 are shaded in the figure. (Figure 7-14 contains the code for the AssignDiscount and btnCalc_Click procedures.)

```vb
Private Function GetDiscount(ByVal intNum As Integer,
                            ByVal dblSub As Double) As Double
    Dim dblDisc As Double

    Select Case intNum
        Case Is >= 6
            dblDisc = dblSub * 0.1
        Case Is >= 4
            dblDisc = dblSub * 0.02
        Case Else
            dblDisc = 0
    End Select

    Return dblDisc
End Function

Private Sub btnCalc_Click(sender As Object, e As EventArgs
) Handles btnCalc.Click
    ' display subtotal, discount, and total due

    Const dblSTANDARD As Double = 62.5
    Const dblVIP As Double = 102.75
    Dim intTickets As Integer
    Dim dblSubtotal As Double
    Dim dblDiscount As Double
    Dim dblTotalDue As Double

    Integer.TryParse(txtTickets.Text, intTickets)

    ' calculate subtotal
    If radStandard.Checked Then
        dblSubtotal = intTickets * dblSTANDARD
    Else
        dblSubtotal = intTickets * dblVIP
    End If

    ' use a function to get the discount
    dblDiscount = GetDiscount(intTickets, dblSubtotal)        ⟵ invokes the function and
                                                                 assigns the return value
                                                                 to the dblDiscount
                                                                 variable
    ' calculate total due
    dblTotalDue = dblSubtotal - dblDiscount

    lblSubtotal.Text = dblSubtotal.ToString("n2")
    lblDiscount.Text = dblDiscount.ToString("n2")
    lblTotalDue.Text = dblTotalDue.ToString("n2")
End Sub
```

Figure 7-25   GetDiscount function and btnCalc_Click procedure

Now we'll desk-check the code shown in Figure 7-25. When the user clicks the Calculate button after typing 6 in the Tickets box, the Dim statements in the btnCalc_Click procedure create and initialize the two named constants and four variables. Next, the TryParse method stores the number of tickets in the intTickets variable. The selection structure then calculates the subtotal based on the selected radio button; in this case, the Standard radio button is selected. Figure 7-26 shows the contents of the named constants and variables before the GetDiscount function is invoked.

Ch07A-Function
Desk-Check

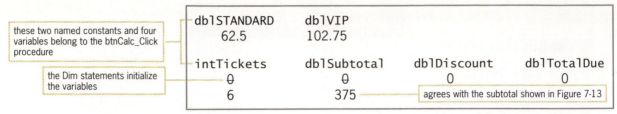

these two named constants and four variables belong to the btnCalc_Click procedure

the Dim statements initialize the variables

dblSTANDARD	dblVIP		
62.5	102.75		
intTickets	dblSubtotal	dblDiscount	dblTotalDue
0̶	0̶	0	0
6	375		

agrees with the subtotal shown in Figure 7-13

Figure 7-26   Desk-check table before the GetDiscount function is invoked

The dblDiscount = GetDiscount(intTickets, dblSubtotal) statement invokes the GetDiscount function, passing it two arguments. At this point, the computer temporarily leaves the btnCalc_Click procedure to process the code contained in the function, beginning with the function header. The ByVal keyword indicates that the two parameters are receiving values from the statement that invoked the function—in this case, copies of the numbers stored in the intTickets and dblSubtotal variables. As a result, the computer creates the intNum and dblSub variables listed in the parameterList, and it stores the numbers 6 and 375, respectively, in the variables. The Dim statement in the function creates and initializes a Double variable named dblDisc. The Select Case statement then determines the appropriate discount based on the contents of the intNum variable. The variable contains the number 6, so the first Case clause multiplies the contents of the dblSub variable (375) by 0.1 and then assigns the result (37.5) to the dblDisc variable. Figure 7-27 shows the desk-check table before the next statement, Return dblDisc, is processed.

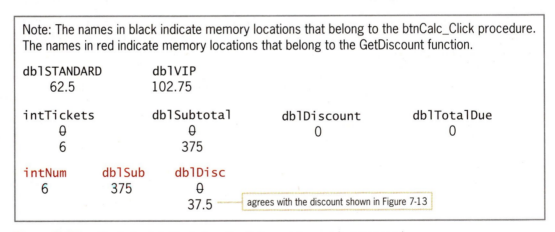

Note: The names in black indicate memory locations that belong to the btnCalc_Click procedure. The names in red indicate memory locations that belong to the GetDiscount function.

dblSTANDARD	dblVIP		
62.5	102.75		
intTickets	dblSubtotal	dblDiscount	dblTotalDue
0̶	0̶	0	0
6	375		
intNum	dblSub	dblDisc	
6	375	0̶	
		37.5	

agrees with the discount shown in Figure 7-13

Figure 7-27   Desk-check table before the Return statement is processed

The Return dblDisc statement returns the contents of the dblDisc variable to the statement that invoked the function: the dblDiscount = GetDiscount(intTickets, dblSubtotal) assignment statement in the btnCalc_Click procedure. The assignment statement assigns the function's return value to the dblDiscount variable. The End Function clause is processed next and ends the GetDiscount function. At this point, the computer removes the function's variables from its internal memory. Figure 7-28 shows the desk-check table after the GetDiscount function ends. Notice that the dblDiscount variable now contains the discount amount.

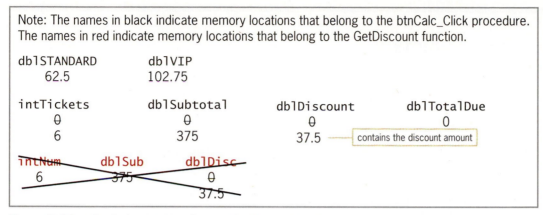

Figure 7-28   Desk-check table after the GetDiscount function ends

After the GetDiscount function ends, the computer returns to the btnCalc_Click procedure. The assignment statement that calculates the total due is processed next. That statement subtracts the discount stored in the `dblDiscount` variable from the subtotal stored in the `dblSubtotal` variable and then assigns the result to the `dblTotalDue` variable, as shown in Figure 7-29.

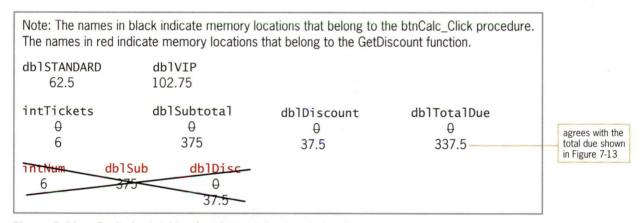

Figure 7-29   Desk-check table after the total due is calculated

The last three assignment statements in the btnCalc_Click procedure display the subtotal, discount, and total due in their corresponding label controls. When the procedure ends, the computer removes the procedure's named constants and variables from memory.

YOU DO IT 3!

Create an application named YouDoIt 3 and save it in the VB2015\Chap07 folder. Add a text box, a label, and a button named btnCalc to the form. The btnCalc_Click procedure should assign the text box value to an Integer variable and then pass a copy of the variable's value to a function named GetBonus. The GetBonus function should multiply the integer it receives by 10% and then return the result. The btnCalc_Click procedure should display the function's return value in the label control. Code the GetBonus function and the btnCalc_Click procedure. Save the solution, and then start and test the application. Close the solution.

Lesson A Summary

- To create an independent Sub procedure:

  Refer to the syntax shown in Figure 7-4.

- To call an independent Sub procedure:

  Use the Call statement, whose syntax is `Call` *procedureName* `([`*argumentList*`])`.

- To pass information to a Sub or Function procedure:

  Include the information in the procedure's argumentList. In the parameterList in the procedure header, include the names of variables that will store the information. The number, data type, and order (position) of the arguments in the argumentList should agree with the number, data type, and order (position) of the parameters in the parameterList.

- To pass a variable *by value* to a procedure:

  Include the `ByVal` keyword before the parameter name in the receiving procedure's parameterList. Because only a copy of the variable's value is passed, the receiving procedure cannot access the variable.

- To pass a variable *by reference*:

  Include the `ByRef` keyword before the parameter name in the receiving procedure's parameterList. Because the variable's address is passed, the receiving procedure can change the contents of the variable.

- To create a Function procedure:

  Refer to the syntax shown in Figure 7-22.

Lesson A Key Terms

Call statement—the Visual Basic statement used to invoke (call) an independent Sub procedure

Function procedure—a procedure that returns a value after performing its assigned task

Functions—another name for Function procedures

Independent Sub procedure—a procedure that is independent of any object and event; the procedure is processed only when called (invoked) from code

Passing by reference—refers to the process of passing a variable's address to a procedure so that the value in the variable can be changed

Passing by value—refers to the process of passing a copy of a variable's value to a procedure

Return statement—the Visual Basic statement that returns a function's value to the statement that invoked the function

Lesson A Review Questions

1. Which of the following is false?

   a. A function can return only one value to the statement that invoked it.
   b. A Sub procedure can accept only one item of data passed to it.
   c. The parameterList in a procedure header is optional.
   d. At times, a variable inside the computer's internal memory may have more than one name.

2. The items listed in the Call statement are referred to as _____.

   a. arguments   c. passers
   b. parameters   d. none of the above

3. Each memory location listed in the parameterList in the procedure header is referred to as _____.

   a. an address   c. a parameter
   b. a constraint   d. a value

4. To determine whether a variable is being passed to a procedure *by value* or *by reference*, you will need to examine _____.

   a. the Call statement
   b. the procedure header
   c. the statements entered in the procedure
   d. either a or b

5. Which of the following statements invokes the GetArea Sub procedure, passing it two variables *by value*?

   a. `Call GetArea(dblLength, dblWidth)`
   b. `Call GetArea(ByVal dblLength, ByVal dblWidth)`
   c. `Invoke GetArea(dblLength, dblWidth)`
   d. `GetArea(dblLength, dblWidth) As Double`

6. Which of the following is a valid header for a procedure that receives a copy of the value stored in a String variable?

   a. `Private Sub DisplayName(ByContents strName As String)`
   b. `Private Sub DisplayName(ByValue strName As String)`
   c. `Private Sub DisplayName ByVal(strName As String)`
   d. none of the above

7. Which of the following is a valid header for a procedure that receives an integer followed by a number with a decimal place?

   a. `Private Sub GetFee(intBase As Value, decRate As Value)`
   b. `Private Sub GetFee(ByRef intBase As Integer, ByRef decRate As Decimal)`
   c. `Private Sub GetFee(ByVal intBase As Integer, ByVal decRate As Decimal)`
   d. none of the above

8. Which of the following is false?

   a. The order of the arguments listed in the Call statement should agree with the order of the parameters listed in the receiving procedure's header.

   b. The data type of each argument in the Call statement should match the data type of its corresponding parameter in the procedure header.

   c. The name of each argument in the Call statement should be identical to the name of its corresponding parameter in the procedure header.

   d. When you pass information to a procedure *by value*, the procedure stores the value of each item it receives in a separate memory location.

9. Which of the following instructs a function to return the contents of the `dblBonus` variable?

   a. `Return dblBonus`   c. `Send dblBonus`

   b. `Return ByVal dblBonus`   d. `SendBack dblBonus`

10. Which of the following is a valid header for a procedure that receives the address of a Decimal variable followed by an integer?

   a. `Private Sub GetFee(ByVal decX As Decimal, ByAdd intY As Integer)`

   b. `Private Sub GetFee(decX As Decimal, intY As Integer)`

   c. `Private Sub GetFee(ByRef decX As Decimal, ByRef intY As Integer)`

   d. none of the above

11. Which of the following is a valid header for a procedure that is passed the number 15?

   a. `Private Function GetTax(ByVal intRate As Integer) As Decimal`

   b. `Private Function GetTax(ByAdd intRate As Integer) As Decimal`

   c. `Private Sub CalcTax(ByVal intRate As Integer)`

   d. both a and c

12. If the statement `Call CalcNet(decNetPay)` passes the variable's address, the variable is said to be passed _____.

   a. *by address*   c. *by reference*

   b. *by content*   d. *by value*

13. Which of the following is false?

   a. When you pass a variable *by reference*, the receiving procedure can change its contents.

   b. To pass a variable *by reference* in Visual Basic, you include the `ByRef` keyword before the variable's name in the Call statement.

   c. When you pass a variable *by value*, the receiving procedure creates a procedure-level variable that it uses to store the value passed to it.

   d. When you pass a variable *by value*, the receiving procedure cannot change its contents.

14. A Sub procedure named GetEndingInventory is passed four Integer variables named `intBegin`, `intSales`, `intPurchases`, and `intEnding`. The procedure should calculate the ending inventory using the beginning inventory, sales, and purchase amounts passed to the procedure. The result should be stored in the `intEnding` variable. Which of the following procedure headers is correct?

    a. ```
Private Sub GetEndingInventory(ByVal intB As Integer, ByVal
intS As Integer, ByVal intP As Integer, ByRef intFinal As
Integer)
```
    b. ```
Private Sub GetEndingInventory(ByVal intB As Integer, ByVal
intS As Integer, ByVal intP As Integer, ByVal intFinal As
Integer)
```
    c. ```
Private Sub GetEndingInventory(ByRef intB As Integer, ByRef
intS As Integer, ByRef intP As Integer, ByVal intFinal As
Integer)
```
    d. ```
Private Sub GetEndingInventory(ByRef intB As Integer, ByRef
intS As Integer, ByRef intP As Integer, ByRef intFinal As
Integer)
```

15. Which of the following statements should you use to call the GetEndingInventory procedure described in Review Question 14?

    a. ```
Call GetEndingInventory(intBegin, intSales, intPurchases,
intEnding)
```
    b. ```
Call GetEndingInventory(ByVal intBegin, ByVal intSales,
ByVal intPurchases, ByRef intEnding)
```
    c. ```
Call GetEndingInventory(ByRef intBegin, ByRef intSales,
ByRef intPurchases, ByRef intEnding)
```
    d. ```
Call GetEndingInventory(ByVal intBegin, ByVal intSales,
ByVal intPurchases, ByVal intEnding)
```

16. The memory locations listed in the parameterList in a procedure header have procedure scope and are removed from the computer's internal memory when the procedure ends.

    a. True
    b. False

17. Which of the following statements invokes the GetDiscount function, passing it the contents of two Decimal variables named **decSales** and **decRate**? The statement should assign the function's return value to the **decDiscount** variable.

    a. `decDiscount = Call GetDiscount(decSales, decRate)`
    b. `Call GetDiscount(decSales, decRate, decDiscount)`
    c. `decDiscount = GetDiscount(decSales, decRate)`
    d. none of the above

18. Explain the difference between a Sub procedure and a Function procedure.

19. Explain the difference between passing a variable *by value* and passing it *by reference*.

20. Explain the difference between invoking a Sub procedure and invoking a function.

Lesson A Exercises

INTRODUCTORY

1. Write the code for a Sub procedure that receives a Double number passed to it. The procedure should multiply the number by 1.5 and then display the result in the lblAnswer control. Name the procedure IncreaseNum. Then write a statement to invoke the procedure, passing it the number 75.5.

INTRODUCTORY

2. Write the code for a Sub procedure named GetState. The procedure should prompt the user to enter the name of a U.S. state, storing the user's response in its `strState` parameter. Then write a statement to invoke the procedure, passing it the `strName` variable.

INTRODUCTORY

3. Write the code for a function named GetState. The function should prompt the user to enter the name of a U.S. state and then return the user's response. Then write a statement to invoke the GetState function. Display the function's return value in a message box.

INTRODUCTORY

4. Write the code for a Sub procedure that receives three Integer variables: the first two *by value* and the last one *by reference*. The procedure should multiply the first variable by the second variable and then store the result in the third variable. Name the procedure CalcProduct.

INTRODUCTORY

5. Write the code for a function that receives a copy of the value stored in an Integer variable. The function should divide the value by 2 and then return the result, which may contain a decimal place. Name the function GetQuotient. Then write an appropriate statement to invoke the function, passing it the `intNumber` variable. Assign the function's return value to the `dblAnswer` variable.

INTRODUCTORY

6. In this exercise, you experiment with passing variables *by value* and *by reference*. Open the VB2015\Chap07\Passing Solution\Passing Solution (Passing Solution.sln) file.

    a. Open the Code Editor window and review the existing code. Notice that the `strMyName` variable is passed *by value* to the GetName procedure. Start the application. Click the Display Name button. When prompted to enter a name, type your name and press Enter. Explain why the btnDisplay_Click procedure does not display your name in the lblName control. Stop the application.

    b. Modify the btnDisplay_Click procedure so that it passes the `strMyName` variable *by reference* to the GetName procedure. Save the solution and then start the application. Click the Display Name button. When prompted to enter a name, type your name and press Enter. This time, your name appears in the lblName control. Explain why the btnDisplay_Click procedure now works correctly.

INTRODUCTORY

7. In this exercise, you modify the Favorites application from this lesson. Use Windows to make a copy of the Favorites Solution folder. Rename the copy Modified Favorites Solution. Open the Favorites Solution (Favorites Solution.sln) file contained in the Modified Favorites Solution folder. Modify the interface and code to allow the user to also enter the name of his or her favorite book. Save the solution, and then start and test the application. Close the Code Editor window and then close the solution.

INTRODUCTORY

8. In this exercise, you modify one of the Concert Tickets applications from this lesson. Use Windows to make a copy of the Concert Solution-Sub folder. Rename the copy Modified Concert Solution-Sub. Open the Concert Solution (Concert Solution.sln) file contained in the Modified Concert Solution-Sub folder. Add another Sub procedure to the application's code. The Sub procedure should calculate the total due. Test the application appropriately.

9. In this exercise, you modify one of the Concert Tickets applications from this lesson. Use Windows to make a copy of the Concert Solution-Function folder. Rename the copy Modified Concert Solution-Function. Open the Concert Solution (Concert Solution.sln) file contained in the Modified Concert Solution-Function folder. Add another function to the application's code. The function should calculate and return the total due. Test the application appropriately.

INTRODUCTORY

10. Create an application, using the following names for the solution and project, respectively: Gross Solution-Sub and Gross Project. The application's interface is shown in Figure 7-30. The lstHours control should display the number of hours worked from 1 to 60 in increments of 1. The lstRates control should display pay rates from 10.00 to 30.00 in increments of 0.5. The default selections in the lstHours and lstRates controls should be 40 and 10.00, respectively. The application should use a Sub procedure to calculate an employee's gross pay, which is based on the number of hours worked and the pay rate selected in the list boxes. However, employees receive double-time for hours worked over 40. Test the application appropriately.

(right margin) **INTERMEDIATE**

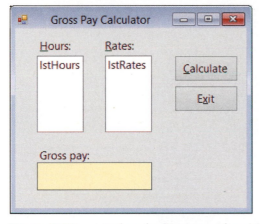

Figure 7-30 Interface for Exercises 10 and 11

11. Create an application, using the following names for the solution and project, respectively: Gross Solution-Function and Gross Project. The application's interface is shown in Figure 7-30. The lstHours control should display the number of hours worked from 1 to 60 in increments of 1. The lstRates control should display pay rates from 10.00 to 30.00 in increments of 0.5. The default selections in the lstHours and lstRates controls should be 37 and 10.00, respectively. The application should use a function to calculate and return an employee's gross pay, which is based on the number of hours worked and the pay rate selected in the list boxes. Employees are paid their regular pay rate for hours worked from 1 through 37. They are paid time and a half for the hours worked from 38 through 50, and they are paid double-time for hours worked over 50. Test the application appropriately. (Hint: If an employee earns $10 per hour and works 37 hours, the gross pay is $370.00. If he or she works 38 hours, the gross pay is $385.00. If he or she works 51 hours, the gross pay is $585.00.)

(right margin) **INTERMEDIATE**

12. Open the VB2015\Chap07\Average Solution\Average Solution (Average Solution.sln) file. Open the Code Editor window and review the existing code. The btnAvg_Click procedure should use a function to calculate and return the average score. Complete the application's code, and then test it appropriately.

(right margin) **INTERMEDIATE**

INTERMEDIATE 13. Create an application, using the following names for the solution and project, respectively: Savings Solution-Function and Savings Project. The application's interface is shown in Figure 7-31. The interface provides a text box for the user to enter a one-time deposit into a savings account. If no additional deposits or withdrawals are made, how much money will be in the account at the end of one through five years using annual interest rates of 2%, 3%, and 4%? You can calculate the savings account balances using the following formula: $b = p * (1 + r)^n$. In the formula, p is the principal (the amount of the initial deposit), r is the annual interest rate, n is the number of years, and b is the balance in the savings account at the end of the nth year. Use a function to calculate each balance. Display the account balances by year for each rate. In other words, display the balances at the end of each of the five years using the 2% rate, then display the five balances using the 3% rate, and so on. Test the application appropriately.

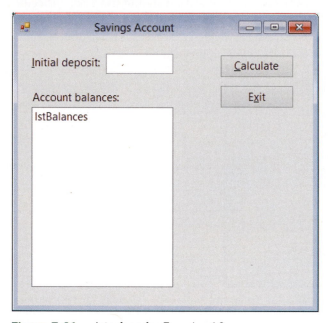

Figure 7-31 Interface for Exercise 13

INTERMEDIATE 14. In this exercise, you modify the Savings Account application from Exercise 13. Use Windows to make a copy of the Savings Solution-Function folder. Rename the copy Savings Solution-Sub. Also change the solution file's name to Savings Solution.sln. Open the Savings Solution (Savings Solution.sln) file contained in the Savings Solution-Sub folder. Change the function that calculates the account balances to an independent Sub procedure. Test the application appropriately.

INTERMEDIATE 15. Open the Conversion Solution (Conversion Solution.sln) file contained in the VB2015\Chap07\Conversion Solution-Sub folder. Code the application so that it uses two independent Sub procedures: one to convert a measurement from inches to centimeters, and one to convert a measurement from centimeters to inches. Display the result with two decimal places. Test the application appropriately.

INTERMEDIATE 16. Open the Conversion Solution (Conversion Solution.sln) file contained in the VB2015\Chap07\Conversion Solution-Function folder. Code the application so that it uses two functions: one to convert a measurement from inches to centimeters, and one to convert a measurement from centimeters to inches. Display the result with two decimal places. Test the application appropriately.

DISCOVERY

17. In this exercise, you learn how to specify that one or more arguments are optional in a Call statement. Open the VB2015\Chap07\Optional Solution\Optional Solution (Optional Solution.sln) file.

   a. Open the Code Editor window and review the existing code. The btnCalc_Click procedure contains two Call statements. The first Call statement passes three variables to the CalcBonus procedure. The second Call statement, however, passes only two variables to the procedure. (Hint: Do not be concerned about the jagged line that appears below the second Call statement.) Notice that the `dblRate` variable is omitted from the second Call statement. You indicate that a variable is optional in the Call statement by including the keyword `Optional` before the variable's corresponding parameter in the procedure header. You enter the `Optional` keyword before the `ByVal` keyword. You also assign a default value that the procedure will use for the missing parameter when the procedure is called. You assign the default value by entering the assignment operator and the default value after the parameter. In this case, you will assign the number 0.1 as the default value for the `dblRate` variable. (Hint: Optional parameters must be listed at the end of the procedure header.) Make the appropriate changes to the `ByVal dblBonusRate As Double` statement in the procedure header.

   b. Save the solution and then start the application. Enter the letter a and the number 1000 in the Code and Sales boxes, respectively. Click the Calculate button, and then type .05 and press Enter. The `Call CalcBonus(dblSales, dblBonus, dblRate)` statement calls the CalcBonus procedure, passing it the number 1000, the address of the `dblBonus` variable, and the number .05. The CalcBonus procedure stores the number 1000 in the `dblTotalSales` variable. It also assigns the name `dblBonusAmount` to the `dblBonus` variable and stores the number .05 in the `dblBonusRate` variable. The procedure then multiplies the contents of the `dblTotalSales` variable (1000) by the contents of the `dblBonusRate` variable (.05), assigning the result (50) to the `dblBonusAmount` variable. The `lblBonus.Text = dblBonus.ToString("C2")` statement then displays $50.00 in the lblBonus control.

   c. Next, enter the letter b and the number 2000 in the Code and Sales boxes, respectively. Click the Calculate button. The `Call CalcBonus(dblSales, dblBonus)` statement calls the CalcBonus procedure, passing it the number 2000 and the address of the `dblBonus` variable. The CalcBonus procedure stores the number 2000 in the `dblTotalSales` variable and assigns the name `dblBonusAmount` to the `dblBonus` variable. Because the Call statement did not supply a value for the `dblBonusRate` parameter, the default value (0.1) is assigned to the variable. The procedure then multiplies the contents of the `dblTotalSales` variable (2000) by the contents of the `dblBonusRate` variable (0.1), assigning the result (200) to the `dblBonusAmount` variable. The `lblBonus.Text = dblBonus.ToString("C2")` statement then displays $200.00 in the lblBonus control. Stop the application. Close the Code Editor window and then close the solution.

SWAT THE BUGS

18. Open the Debug Solution (Debug Solution.sln) file contained in the VB2015\Chap07\ Debug Solution-Lesson A folder. Open the Code Editor window and review the existing code. Start the application. Enter 100, 200.55, and .04 in the Store 1 sales, Store 2 sales, and Commission rate boxes, respectively. Click the Calculate Commission button. Notice that the application is not working properly. Correct the application's code, and then test it appropriately.

LESSON B

After studying Lesson B, you should be able to:

- Include a combo box in an interface
- Add items to a combo box
- Select a combo box item from code
- Determine the number of items in the list portion of a combo box
- Sort the items in the list portion of a combo box
- Determine the item either selected or entered in a combo box
- Code a combo box's TextChanged event procedure

Including a Combo Box in an Interface

In many interfaces, combo boxes are used in place of list boxes. You add a combo box to an interface using the ComboBox tool in the toolbox. A **combo box** is similar to a list box in that it offers the user a list of choices from which to select. However, unlike a list box, the full list of choices in a combo box can be hidden, allowing you to save space on the form. Also unlike a list box, a combo box contains a text field, which may or may not be editable by the user.

Three styles of combo boxes are available in Visual Basic. The style is controlled by the combo box's **DropDownStyle property**, which can be set to Simple, DropDown (the default), or DropDownList. Each style of combo box contains a text portion and a list portion. When the DropDownStyle property is set to either Simple or DropDown, the text portion of the combo box is editable. However, in a Simple combo box, the list portion is always displayed, while in a DropDown combo box, the list portion appears only when the user clicks the combo box's list arrow. When the DropDownStyle property is set to the third style, DropDownList, the text portion of the combo box is not editable and the user must click the combo box's list arrow to display the list of choices.

 To experiment with the combo boxes shown in Figure 7-32, open the application contained in the Combo Box Styles Solution folder.

Figure 7-32 shows an example of each combo box style. You should use a label control to provide keyboard access to the combo box, as shown in the figure. For the access key to work correctly, you must set the label's TabIndex property to a value that is one number less than the combo box's TabIndex value. Like the items in a list box, the items in the list portion of a combo box are either arranged by use, with the most used entries listed first, or sorted in ascending order. To sort the items in the list portion of a combo box, you set the combo box's Sorted property to True.

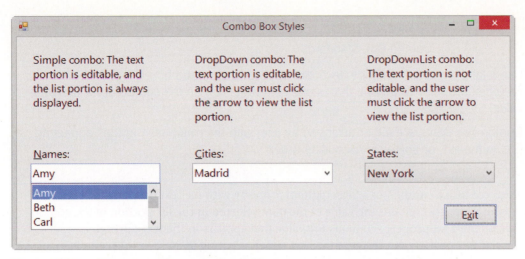

Figure 7-32   Examples of the combo box styles

Figure 7-33 shows the code used to fill the combo boxes in Figure 7-32 with values. As you do with a list box, you use the Items collection's Add method to add an item to a combo box. Like the first item in a list box, the first item in a combo box has an index of 0. You can use any of the following properties to select a default item, which will appear in the text portion of the combo box: SelectedIndex, SelectedItem, or Text. If no item is selected, the SelectedItem and Text properties contain the empty string, and the SelectedIndex property contains −1 (negative one). If you need to determine the number of items in the list portion of a combo box, you can use the Items collection's Count property. The property's syntax is *object*`.Items.Count`, in which *object* is the name of the combo box.

```
Private Sub frmMain_Load(sender As Object,
e As EventArgs) Handles Me.Load
    ' fills the combo boxes with values

    cboName.Items.Add("Amy")
    cboName.Items.Add("Beth")
    cboName.Items.Add("Carl")
    cboName.Items.Add("Dan")
    cboName.Items.Add("Jan")
    cboName.SelectedIndex = 0

    cboCity.Items.Add("London")
    cboCity.Items.Add("Madrid")
    cboCity.Items.Add("Paris")
    cboCity.SelectedItem = "Madrid"

    cboState.Items.Add("Alabama")
    cboState.Items.Add("Maine")
    cboState.Items.Add("New York")
    cboState.Items.Add("South Dakota")
    cboState.Text = "New York"
End Sub
```

you can use any of these three properties to select the default item in a combo box

Figure 7-33   Code associated with the combo boxes in Figure 7-32

GUI DESIGN TIP Combo Box Standards

- Use a label control to provide keyboard access to a combo box. Set the label's TabIndex property to a value that is one number less than the combo box's TabIndex value.

- Combo box items are either arranged by use, with the most used entries appearing first in the list, or sorted in ascending order.

It is easy to confuse a combo box's SelectedItem property with its Text property. The SelectedItem property contains the value of the item selected in the list portion of the combo box, whereas the Text property contains the value that appears in the text portion. A value can appear in the text portion as a result of the user either selecting an item in the list portion of the control or typing an entry in the text portion itself. It can also appear in the text portion as a result of a statement that assigns a value to the control's SelectedIndex, SelectedItem, or Text property.

If the combo box is a DropDownList style, where the text portion is not editable, you can use the SelectedItem and Text properties interchangeably. However, if the combo box is either a Simple or DropDown style, where the user can type an entry in the text portion, you should use the Text property because it contains the value either selected or entered by the user. When the value in the text portion of a combo box changes, the combo box's TextChanged event occurs. In the next set of steps, you will replace the list box in Chapter 6's Monthly Payment application with a combo box.

START HERE ▶

To modify the Monthly Payment application:

1. If necessary, start Visual Studio 2015. Open the VB2015\Chap07\Payment Solution\ Payment Solution (Payment Solution.sln) file.

2. Unlock the controls on the form. Click the **lstRates** control and then press **Delete**. Click the **ComboBox** tool in the toolbox, and then drag the mouse pointer to the form. Position the mouse pointer below the Rate label, and then release the mouse button. Size and position the combo box to match Figure 7-34.

Figure 7-34 Correct location and size of the combo box

3. Change the combo box's DropDownStyle property to **DropDownList**.

4. The three-character ID for combo box names is cbo. Change the combo box's name to **cboRates**.

5. Lock the controls on the form, and then use the information shown in Figure 7-35 to set the TabIndex values.

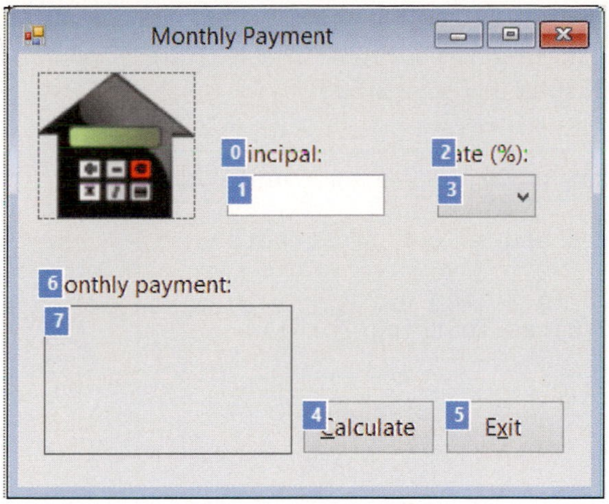

Figure 7-35 Correct TabIndex values

6. Press **Esc** to remove the TabIndex boxes from the form.

7. Open the Code Editor window. Replace <your name> and <current date> with your name and the current date, respectively.

8. Locate the frmMain_Load procedure. Change `list` in the first comment to **combo**. Then change both occurrences of lstRates to **cboRates**.

9. Locate the btnCalc_Click procedure. Replace `lstRates.SelectedItem.ToString` in the second TryParse method with **cboRates.Text**.

10. Locate the ClearPayment procedure. Type **, cboRates.TextChanged** at the end of the Handles clause. (Be sure to type the comma.)

11. Save the solution and then start the application. Type **125000** in the Principal box. Click the **list arrow** in the combo box and then click **2.5** in the list. Click the **Calculate** button. See Figure 7-36.

![Monthly Payment window showing Principal: 125000, Rate (%): 2.5, and Monthly payment list: 15 years: $833.49, 20 years: $662.38, 25 years: $560.77, 30 years: $493.90, with Calculate and Exit buttons]

Figure 7-36 Monthly payments shown in the interface

12. Click the **Exit** button. Close the Code Editor window and then close the solution.

Figure 7-37 shows the code entered in the frmMain_Load, btnCalc_Click, and ClearPayment procedures. The modifications made to the original code from Chapter 6 are shaded in the figure. (The original code is shown in Chapter 6's Figure 6-50.)

```vb
Private Sub frmMain_Load(sender As Object, e As EventArgs
) Handles Me.Load
    ' fill combo box with rates and select first rate

    For dblRates As Double = 2 To 7 Step 0.5
        cboRates.Items.Add(dblRates.ToString("n1"))
    Next dblRates
    cboRates.SelectedItem = "3.0"

End Sub

Private Sub btnCalc_Click(sender As Object, e As EventArgs
) Handles btnCalc.Click
    ' display the monthly mortgage payment

    Dim intPrincipal As Integer
    Dim dblRate As Double
    Dim dblPay As Double

    Integer.TryParse(txtPrincipal.Text, intPrincipal)
    Double.TryParse(cboRates.Text, dblRate)
    dblRate = dblRate / 100

    lblPay.Text = String.Empty
    For intTerm As Integer = 15 To 30 Step 5
        dblPay = -Financial.Pmt(dblRate / 12,
                    intTerm * 12, intPrincipal)
        lblPay.Text = lblPay.Text & intTerm.ToString &
            " years:    " & dblPay.ToString("c2") &
            ControlChars.NewLine
    Next intTerm
End Sub

Private Sub ClearPayment(sender As Object, e As EventArgs
) Handles txtPrincipal.TextChanged, cboRates.TextChanged
    lblPay.Text = String.Empty
End Sub
```

Figure 7-37   Modified code for the Monthly Payment application

Lesson B Summary

- To add a combo box to a form:

  Use the ComboBox tool in the toolbox.

- To specify the style of a combo box:

  Set the combo box's DropDownStyle property.

- To add items to a combo box:

Use the Items collection's Add method. The method's syntax is *object*.`Items.Add(`*item*`)`. In the syntax, *object* is the name of the combo box and *item* is the text you want added to the list portion of the control.

- To automatically sort the items in the list portion of a combo box:

Set the combo box's Sorted property to True.

- To determine the number of items in the list portion of a combo box:

Use the Items collection's Count property. Its syntax is *object*.`Items.Count`, in which *object* is the name of the combo box.

- To select a combo box item from code:

Use any of the following properties: SelectedIndex, SelectedItem, or Text.

- To determine the item either selected in the list portion of a combo box or entered in the text portion:

Use the combo box's Text property. However, if the combo box is a DropDownList style, you can also use the SelectedIndex or SelectedItem property.

- To process code when the value in a combo box's Text property changes:

Enter the code in the combo box's TextChanged event procedure.

Lesson B Key Terms

Combo box—a control that offers the user a list of choices and also has a text field that may or may not be editable

DropDownStyle property—determines the style of a combo box

Lesson B Review Questions

1. Which property is used to specify a combo box's style?

    a. ComboBoxStyle   c. DropStyle

    b. DropDownStyle   d. Style

2. The items in a combo box belong to which collection?

    a. Items   c. ListBox

    b. List   d. Values

3. Which of the following selects the Cat item, which appears third in the cboAnimal control?

    a. `cboAnimal.SelectedIndex = 2`
    b. `cboAnimal.SelectedItem = "Cat"`
    c. `cboAnimal.Text = "Cat"`
    d. all of the above

4. The item that appears in the text portion of a combo box is stored in which property?

    a. SelectedText   c. Text

    b. SelectedValue   d. TextItem

5. Which event occurs when the user either types a value in the text portion of a combo box or selects a different item in the list portion?

a. ChangedItem

c. SelectedItemChanged

b. ChangedValue

d. TextChanged

Lesson B Exercises

INTRODUCTORY

1. In this exercise, you create an application that displays the name of the artist corresponding to the song title selected in a combo box. Create the application, using the following names for the solution and project, respectively: Song Solution and Song Project. Save the application in the VB2015\Chap07 folder. Add the names of any five songs to a combo box whose DropDownStyle property is set to DropDownList. When the user clicks an entry in the combo box, the name of the artist should appear in a label control. (For example, if the user clicks the song title "Moves Like Jagger," the application should display "Maroon 5" in the label.) Create a suitable interface, and then code and test the application.

INTRODUCTORY

2. In this exercise, you create an application that displays the capital of the state whose name is selected in a combo box. Create an application, using the following names for the solution and project, respectively: Capital Solution and Capital Project. Save the application in the VB2015\Chap07 folder. Add the names of any five states to a combo box whose DropDownStyle property is set to DropDownList. When the user clicks an entry in the combo box, the name of the state's capital should appear in a label control. Create a suitable interface, and then code and test the application.

INTERMEDIATE

3. In this exercise, you modify the Favorites application from Lesson A. Use Windows to make a copy of the Favorites Solution folder. Rename the copy Favorites Solution-Intermediate. Open the Favorites Solution (Favorites Solution.sln) file contained in the Favorites Solution-Intermediate folder. Replace the radio buttons with a combo box, and then modify the application's code. Test the application appropriately.

INTERMEDIATE

4. Create an application, using the following names for the solution and project, respectively: Planets Solution and Planets Project. Save the application in the VB2015\Chap07 folder. Create the interface shown in Figure 7-38. The combo box should have the DropDownList style and contain the following planet names: Mercury, Venus, Mars, Jupiter, Saturn, Uranus, Neptune, and Pluto. When the user clicks a planet name, the application should convert the earth weight to the weight on that planet and then display the converted weight in the label control. Use the Internet to research the formula for making the conversions. Test the application appropriately.

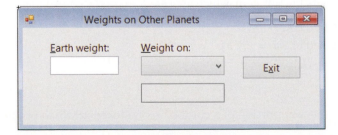

Figure 7-38   Interface for Exercise 4

5. In this exercise, you modify the application from Exercise 4. Use Windows to make a copy of the Planets Solution folder. Rename the copy Planets Solution-Sub. Open the Planets Solution (Planets Solution.sln) file contained in the Planets Solution-Sub folder. Modify the code to use an independent Sub procedure to calculate the weight on another planet. Test the application appropriately.

6. In this exercise, you modify the application from Exercise 4. Use Windows to make a copy of the Planets Solution folder. Rename the copy Planets Solution-Function. Open the Planets Solution (Planets Solution.sln) file contained in the Planets Solution-Function folder. Modify the code to use a function to calculate and return the weight on another planet. Test the application appropriately.

7. In this exercise, you modify one of the Concert Tickets applications from Lesson A. Use Windows to make a copy of the Concert Solution-Function folder. Rename the copy Concert Solution-Intermediate. Open the Concert Solution (Concert Solution.sln) file contained in the Concert Solution-Intermediate folder. Replace the text box with a combo box that displays integers from 1 through 25, and then modify the application's code. Test the application appropriately.

■ LESSON C

After studying Lesson C, you should be able to:

- Prevent a form from closing
- Round a number

Creating the Cerruti Company Application

Your task in this chapter is to create an application that calculates an employee's weekly gross pay, federal withholding tax (FWT), Social Security and Medicare (FICA) tax, and net pay. The application's TOE chart is shown in Figure 7-39.

Task	Object	Event
End the application	btnExit	Click
1. Calculate gross pay, FWT, FICA, and net pay 2. Display calculated amounts in appropriate labels	btnCalc	Click
Display calculated amounts (from btnCalc)	lblGross, lblFwt, lblFica, lblNet	None
Clear lblGross, lblFwt, lblFica, and lblNet	txtName, cboAllowances	TextChanged
	lstHours, lstRates	SelectedValueChanged
	radMarried, radSingle	CheckedChanged
Select the existing text	txtName	Enter
Allow only numbers and the Backspace key	cboAllowances	KeyPress
Get and display the name, hours worked, pay rate, marital status, and withholding allowances	txtName, lstHours, lstRates, radMarried, radSingle, cboAllowances	None
Fill lstHours, lstRates, and cboAllowances with values, and then select a default item	frmMain	Load
Verify that the user wants to close the application, and then take the appropriate action based on the user's response		FormClosing

Figure 7-39　TOE chart for the Cerruti Company application

To open the Cerruti Company application:

1. If necessary, start Visual Studio 2015. Open the VB2015\Chap07\Cerruti Solution\ Cerruti Solution (Cerruti Solution.sln) file. See Figure 7-40.

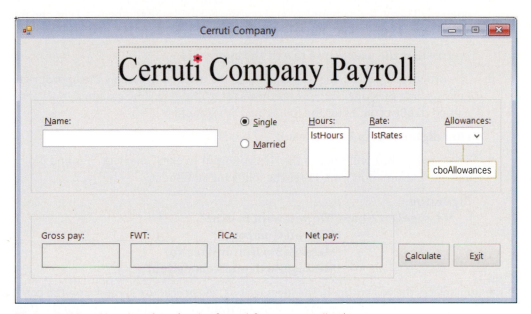

Figure 7-40   User interface for the Cerruti Company application

The application's interface provides a text box for entering the employee's name, and radio buttons for entering his or her marital status. It also provides list boxes for specifying the hours worked and rate of pay. The combo box in the interface allows the user to either select the number of withholding allowances from the list portion of the control or type a number in the text portion. To complete the Cerruti Company application, you will need to code the btnCalc_Click and frmMain_FormClosing procedures.

Coding the FormClosing Event Procedure

A form's **FormClosing event** occurs when a form is about to be closed. In most cases, this happens when the computer processes the `Me.Close()` statement in the application's code. However, it also occurs when the user clicks the Close button on the form's title bar. According to the application's TOE chart, the FormClosing event procedure is responsible for verifying that the user wants to close the application and then taking the appropriate action based on the user's response. Figure 7-41 shows the procedure's pseudocode.

```
frmMain FormClosing event procedure
1. use a message box to ask the user whether he or she wants to exit the application
2. if the user does not want to exit the application
        prevent the form from closing
   end if
```

Figure 7-41   Pseudocode for the FormClosing event procedure

START HERE **To begin coding the frmMain_FormClosing procedure:**

1. Open the Code Editor window. Replace <your name> and <current date> in the comments with your name and the current date, respectively.

2. Open the code template for the frmMain_FormClosing event procedure. (Be sure to open the FormClosing template and not the FormClosed template.) Type the following comment and then press **Enter** twice:

   ' verify that the user wants to exit the application

3. The procedure will use the MessageBox.Show method to display the appropriate message in a message box. The method's return value will be assigned to a variable named dlgButton. Enter the following Dim statement:

   Dim dlgButton As DialogResult

4. The message box will contain the "Do you want to exit?" message, Yes and No buttons, and the Exclamation icon. Enter the following statement:

   dlgButton =
   MessageBox.Show("Do you want to exit?",
   "Cerruti Company",
   MessageBoxButtons.YesNo,
   MessageBoxIcon.Exclamation)

If the user selects the No button in the message box, the procedure should stop the computer from closing the form. You prevent the computer from closing a form by setting the **Cancel property** of the FormClosing event procedure's **e** parameter to True.

START HERE **To complete the frmMain_FormClosing procedure and then test it:**

1. Enter the following comment and selection structure:

   ' if the No button was selected, don't close the form
   If dlgButton = DialogResult.No Then
   **   e.Cancel = True**
   End If

2. Save the solution and then start the application. Click the **Close** button on the form's title bar. See Figure 7-42.

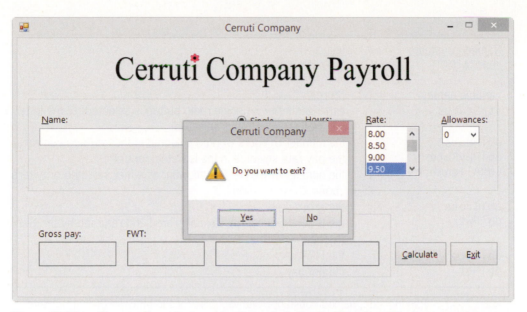

Figure 7-42 Message box displayed by the code in the frmMain_FormClosing procedure

3. Click the **No** button in the message box. Notice that the form remains on the screen.

4. Click the **Exit** button. This time, click the **Yes** button in the message box. The application ends.

Coding the btnCalc_Click Procedure

According to the application's TOE chart, the btnCalc_Click procedure is responsible for calculating and displaying the gross pay, FWT (federal withholding tax), FICA tax, and net pay. The procedure's pseudocode and a listing of its named constants and variables are shown in Figure 7-43.

---

btnCalc Click event procedure
1. store user input (hours, pay rate, and allowances) in variables
2. if the Single radio button is selected
      assign "S" as the marital status
   else
      assign "M" as the marital status
   end if
3. if the number of hours is less than or equal to 40
      calculate the gross pay = hours * pay rate
   else
      calculate the gross pay = 40 * pay rate + (hours – 40) * pay rate * 1.5
   end if
4. use a function named GetFwt to calculate and return the FWT
5. calculate the FICA tax = gross pay * the FICA rate of 7.65%
6. round the gross pay, FWT, and FICA tax to two decimal places
7. calculate the net pay = gross pay – FWT – FICA tax
8. display the gross pay, FWT, FICA tax, and net pay in the appropriate labels

---

Figure 7-43 Pseudocode, named constants, and variables for the btnCalc_Click procedure *(continues)*

(continued)

Named constants	Value
dblFICA_RATE	0.0765

Variable names	Stores
strStatus	either the letter S (Single radio button is selected) or the letter M (Married radio button is selected)
dblHours	the number of hours worked selected in the lstHours control
dblPayRate	the pay rate selected in the lstRates control
intAllowances	the number of withholding allowances either selected or entered in the cboAllowances control
dblGross	the gross pay
dblFwt	the federal withholding tax calculated and returned by the GetFwt function
dblFica	the FICA tax
dblNet	the net pay

Figure 7-43   Pseudocode, named constants, and variables for the btnCalc_Click procedure

START HERE

To begin coding the btnCalc_Click procedure:

1. Open the code template for the btnCalc_Click procedure. Type the following comment and then press **Enter** twice:

   ' displays gross pay, taxes, and net pay

2. Enter the following nine declaration statements. Press **Enter** twice after typing the last declaration statement.

   Const dblFICA_RATE As Double = 0.0765
   Dim strStatus As String
   Dim dblHours As Double
   Dim dblPayRate As Double
   Dim intAllowances As Integer
   Dim dblGross As Double
   Dim dblFwt As Double
   Dim dblFica As Double
   Dim dblNet As Double

3. The first step in the procedure's pseudocode is to store the user input in variables. Enter the following statements. Press **Enter** twice after typing the last statement.

   Double.TryParse(lstHours.SelectedItem.ToString, dblHours)
   Double.TryParse(lstRates.SelectedItem.ToString, dblPayRate)
   Integer.TryParse(cboAllowances.Text, intAllowances)

4. The second step in the pseudocode is a selection structure whose condition determines the employee's marital status. Type the following selection structure:

   If radSingle.Checked Then
     strStatus = "S"
   Else
     strStatus = "M"
   End If

5. The third step in the pseudocode is a selection structure whose condition compares the number of hours worked with the number 40. If the number of hours worked is less than or equal to 40, the selection structure's true path should calculate the gross pay by multiplying the number of hours worked by the pay rate. Insert two blank lines below the End If clause, and then enter the following comment and lines of code:

   ' calculate gross pay
   If dblHours <= 40 Then
       dblGross = dblHours * dblPayRate

6. If the number of hours worked is greater than 40, the employee is entitled to his or her regular pay rate for the hours worked up to and including 40, and then the employee is paid time and a half for the hours worked over 40. Enter the Else clause and assignment statement shown in Figure 7-44, and then save the solution.

```
        ' calculate gross pay
        If dblHours <= 40 Then
            dblGross = dblHours * dblPayRate
        Else
            dblGross = 40 * dblPayRate +
                (dblHours - 40) * dblPayRate * 1.5
        End If
    End Sub
```

enter the Else clause and the assignment statement

Figure 7-44   Second selection structure entered in the procedure

The fourth step in the procedure's pseudocode uses a function named GetFwt to calculate and return the FWT. Before entering the appropriate instruction, you will create the function.

Creating the GetFwt Function

The amount of FWT to deduct from an employee's weekly gross pay is based on his or her weekly taxable wages and filing status, which is either single (including head of household) or married. You calculate the weekly taxable wages by first multiplying the number of withholding allowances by $76 (the value of a withholding allowance in 2014) and then subtracting the result from the weekly gross pay. For example, if your weekly gross pay is $400 and you have two withholding allowances, your weekly taxable wages are $248. The $248 is calculated by multiplying 76 by 2 and then subtracting the result (152) from 400. You use the weekly taxable wages, along with the filing status and the appropriate weekly Federal Withholding Tax table, to determine the amount of FWT to withhold. The weekly tax tables for 2014 are shown in Figure 7-45.

FWT Tables – Weekly Payroll Period

Single person (including head of household)
If the taxable
wages are: The amount of income tax to withhold is:

Over	But not over	Base amount	Percentage	Of excess over
	$ 43	0		
$ 43	$ 218	0	10%	$ 43
$ 218	$ 753	$ 17.50 plus	15%	$ 218
$ 753	$1,762	$ 97.75 plus	25%	$ 753
$1,762	$3,627	$ 350.00 plus	28%	$1,762
$3,627	$7,834	$ 872.20 plus	33%	$3,627
$7,834	$7,865	$2,260.51 plus	35%	$7,834
$7,865		$2,271.36 plus	39.6%	$7,865

Married person
If the taxable
wages are: The amount of income tax to withhold is:

Over	But not over	Base amount	Percentage	Of excess over
	$ 163	0		
$ 163	$ 512	0	10%	$ 163
$ 512	$1,582	$ 34.90 plus	15%	$ 512
$1,582	$3,025	$ 195.40 plus	25%	$1,582
$3,025	$4,525	$ 556.15 plus	28%	$3,025
$4,525	$7,953	$ 976.15 plus	33%	$4,525
$7,953	$8,963	$2,107.39 plus	35%	$7,953
$8,963		$2,460.89 plus	39.6%	$8,963

Figure 7-45   Weekly FWT tables for the year 2014

Each table in Figure 7-45 contains five columns of information. The first two columns list various ranges, also called brackets, of taxable wage amounts. The first column (Over) lists the amount that a taxable wage in that bracket must be over, and the second column (But not over) lists the maximum amount included in the bracket. The remaining three columns (Base amount, Percentage, and Of excess over) tell you how to calculate the tax for each range. For example, assume that you are single and your weekly taxable wages are $248. Before you can calculate the amount of your tax, you need to locate your taxable wages in the first two columns of the Single table. Taxable wages of $248 fall within the $218 through $753 bracket. After locating the bracket that contains your taxable wages, you then use the remaining three columns in the table to calculate your tax. In this case, you calculate the tax by first subtracting 218 (the amount shown in the Of excess over column) from your taxable wages of 248, giving 30. You then multiply 30 by 15% (the amount shown in the Percentage column), giving 4.50. You then add that amount to the amount shown in the Base amount column (in this case, 17.50), giving $22 as your tax. The calculations are shown in Figure 7-46, along with the calculations for a married taxpayer whose weekly taxable wages are $1,659.50.

Single with weekly taxable wages of $248.00		Married with weekly taxable wages of $1,659.50	
Taxable wages	$ 248.00	Taxable wages	$ 1,659.50
Of excess over	– 218.00	Of excess over	– 1,582.00
	30.00		77.50
Percentage	* 0.15	Percentage	* 0.25
	4.50		19.38
Base amount	+ 17.50	Base amount	+ 195.40
Tax	$ 22.00	Tax	$ 214.78

Figure 7-46 Examples of FWT calculations

To calculate the federal withholding tax, the GetFwt function needs to know the employee's gross pay amount, number of withholding allowances, and marital status. The gross pay amount and number of withholding allowances are necessary to calculate the taxable wages, and the marital status indicates the appropriate FWT table to use when calculating the tax. The function will receive the necessary information from the btnCalc_Click procedure, which will pass the information when it invokes the function. Recall that the information is stored in the btnCalc_Click procedure's `dblGross`, `intAllowances`, and `strStatus` variables. Figure 7-47 shows the function's pseudocode.

```
GetFwt function
1. calculate the taxable wages = gross pay – number of withholding allowances * 76
2. if the marital status is Single
        calculate the FWT using the Single FWT table
   else
        calculate the FWT using the Married FWT table
   end if
3. return the FWT
```

Figure 7-47 Pseudocode for the GetFwt function

To create the GetFwt function:

START HERE

1. Scroll to the top of the Code Editor window, and then click the **blank line** below the `'GetFwt function` comment.

2. When it invokes the GetFwt function, the btnCalc_Click procedure will pass the values stored in its `dblGross`, `intAllowances`, and `strStatus` variables. You do not want the GetFwt function to change the contents of the variables, so you will pass a copy of each variable's value (rather than the variable's address). You will store the values passed to the function in three parameters named `dblWeekPay`, `intNumAllow`, and `strMarital`. The GetFwt function will use the information it receives to calculate and return the FWT as a Double number. Type the function header and comment shown in Figure 7-48, and then position the insertion point as indicated in the figure. (The Code Editor automatically enters the End Function clause for you.)

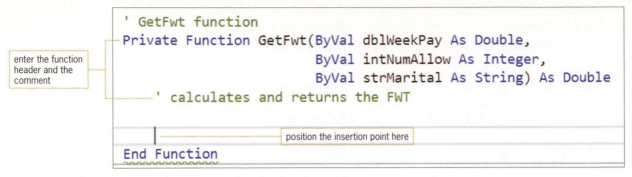

Figure 7-48   GetFwt function header and footer

3. The function will use a named constant for the withholding allowance amount ($76). It will also use two additional variables: one to store the taxable wages, and one to store the FWT. Enter the following declaration statements. Press **Enter** twice after typing the last declaration statement.

Const dblONE_ALLOW As Double = 76
Dim dblTaxWages As Double
Dim dblTax As Double

4. The first step in the function's pseudocode calculates the taxable wages. Enter the following comment and assignment statement. Press **Enter** twice after typing the assignment statement.

' calculate taxable wages
dblTaxWages =
    dblWeekPay – intNumAllow * dblONE_ALLOW

5. The second step in the pseudocode is a selection structure whose condition determines the marital status. Enter the following comment and If clause:

' determine marital status and then calculate FWT
If strMarital = "S" Then

6. If the `strMarital` variable contains the letter S, the selection structure's true path should calculate the federal withholding tax using the information from the Single tax table. For your convenience, you will find the appropriate code in the Single.txt file. Click **File** on the menu bar, point to **Open**, and then click **File**. If necessary, open the Cerruti Project folder. Click **Single.txt** in the list of filenames and then click the **Open** button. The Single.txt file appears in a separate window in the IDE. Click **Edit** on the menu bar and then click **Select All**. Press **Ctrl+c** to copy the selected text to the Windows Clipboard, and then close the Single.txt window.

7. The insertion point should be in the blank line below the If clause. Press **Ctrl+v** to paste the copied text into the selection structure's true path.

8. Type **Else** and then press **Tab** twice. Type **' strMarital = "M"** and then press **Enter**.

9. If the `strMarital` variable does not contain the letter S, the selection structure's false path should calculate the federal withholding tax using the information from the Married tax table. You will find the appropriate code in the Married.txt file. Click **File**, point to Open, and then click **File**. Click **Married.txt** in the list of filenames, and then click the **Open** button. Click **Edit** and then click **Select All**. Press **Ctrl+c** to copy the selected text to the Windows Clipboard, and then close the Married.txt window.

10. The insertion point should be in the blank line below the Else clause. Press **Ctrl+v** to paste the copied text into the selection structure's false path.

11. The last step in the function's pseudocode returns the federal withholding tax amount, which is stored in the db1Tax variable, to the statement that invoked the function. Click **after the letter f** in the End If clause, and then press **Enter** twice. Type **Return dblTax** and then click the **blank line** above the Return statement. Save the solution. (You can look ahead to Figure 7-53 to view the function's code.)

Completing the btnCalc_Click Procedure

Now that you have created the GetFwt function, you can invoke the function from the btnCalc_Click procedure. Invoking the GetFwt function is the fourth step listed in the procedure's pseudocode (shown earlier in Figure 7-43).

To continue coding the btnCalc_Click procedure:

START HERE

1. Locate the btnCalc_Click procedure. Click **after the letter f** in the second End If clause, and then press **Enter** twice.

2. Recall that the procedure needs to send the GetFwt function a copy of the values stored in the db1Gross, intAllowances, and strStatus variables. The procedure will assign the function's return value to the db1Fwt variable. Enter the following comment and assignment statement:

' get the FWT
dblFwt = GetFwt(dblGross, intAllowances, strStatus)

3. The next step in the procedure's pseudocode calculates the FICA tax by multiplying the gross pay amount by the FICA rate. Enter the following comment and assignment statement:

' calculate FICA tax
dblFica = dblGross * dblFICA_RATE

4. Save the solution.

Rounding Numbers

The sixth step in the procedure's pseudocode rounds the gross pay, FWT, and FICA tax amounts to two decimal places. Rounding these amounts before making the net pay calculation will prevent the "penny off" error from occurring. (You can observe the "penny off" error by completing Exercise 1 at the end of this lesson.) You can use the **Math.Round function** to return a number rounded to a specific number of decimal places. The function's syntax and examples are shown in Figure 7-49. In the syntax, *value* is a numeric expression and *digits* (which is optional) is an integer indicating how many places to the right of the decimal point are included in the rounding. If the *digits* argument is omitted, the Math.Round function returns an integer.

Math.Round Function

Syntax
Math.Round(value[, digits]**)**

Examples	Result
Math.Round(3.235, 2)	3.24
Math.Round(6.517, 1)	6.5
Math.Round(8.99)	9

Figure 7-49   Syntax and examples of the Math.Round function

START HERE

To complete the btnCalc_Click procedure:

1. Enter the following comment and assignment statements:

   ' round gross pay, FWT, and FICA tax
   dblGross = Math.Round(dblGross, 2)
   dblFwt = Math.Round(dblFwt, 2)
   dblFica = Math.Round(dblFica, 2)

2. Next, the procedure should calculate the net pay by subtracting the two tax amounts from the gross pay amount. Enter the following comment and assignment statement. Press **Enter** twice after typing the assignment statement.

   ' calculate net pay
   dblNet = dblGross – dblFwt – dblFica

3. The last step in the procedure's pseudocode displays the calculated amounts in the appropriate label controls. Enter the following comment and assignment statements:

   ' display calculated amounts
   lblGross.Text = dblGross.ToString("n2")
   lblFwt.Text = dblFwt.ToString("n2")
   lblFica.Text = dblFica.ToString("n2")
   lblNet.Text = dblNet.ToString("n2")

4. Save the solution.

You will test the application twice using the data shown in Figure 7-50. The figure also shows the correct amounts for the gross pay, taxes, and net pay.

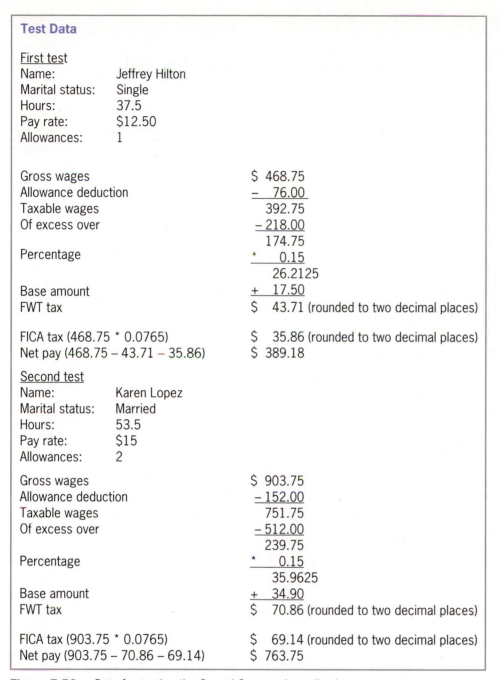

Test Data

First test
Name: Jeffrey Hilton
Marital status: Single
Hours: 37.5
Pay rate: $12.50
Allowances: 1

Gross wages	$ 468.75
Allowance deduction	− 76.00
Taxable wages	392.75
Of excess over	− 218.00
	174.75
Percentage	* 0.15
	26.2125
Base amount	+ 17.50
FWT tax	$ 43.71 (rounded to two decimal places)
FICA tax (468.75 * 0.0765)	$ 35.86 (rounded to two decimal places)
Net pay (468.75 − 43.71 − 35.86)	$ 389.18

Second test
Name: Karen Lopez
Marital status: Married
Hours: 53.5
Pay rate: $15
Allowances: 2

Gross wages	$ 903.75
Allowance deduction	− 152.00
Taxable wages	751.75
Of excess over	− 512.00
	239.75
Percentage	* 0.15
	35.9625
Base amount	+ 34.90
FWT tax	$ 70.86 (rounded to two decimal places)
FICA tax (903.75 * 0.0765)	$ 69.14 (rounded to two decimal places)
Net pay (903.75 − 70.86 − 69.14)	$ 763.75

Figure 7-50   Data for testing the Cerruti Company's application

To test the Cerruti Company application:

START HERE

1. Start the application. Type **Jeffrey Hilton** in the Name box. Click **37.5** in the Hours list box, **12.50** in the Rate list box, and **1** in the Allowances combo box. Click the **Calculate** button. See Figure 7-51. The gross pay, taxes, and net pay agree with the manual calculations from Figure 7-50.

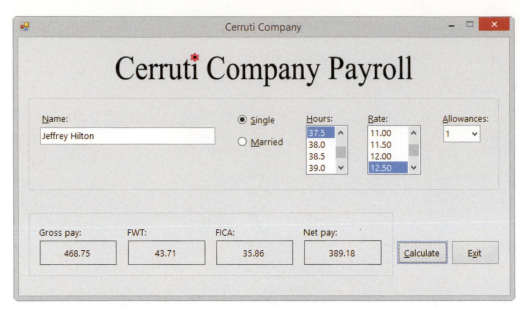

Figure 7-51 Payroll calculations using the first set of test data

2. Change the name entered in the Name box to **Karen Lopez** and then click the **Married** radio button. Click **53.5** in the Hours list box and **15.00** in the Rate list box. Press **Tab** to move the focus to the Allowances combo box. In addition to selecting the number of allowances in the list portion of the combo box, the user can also type the number in the text portion. Type **2** and then click the **Calculate** button. See Figure 7-52. The gross pay, taxes, and net pay agree with the manual calculations from Figure 7-50.

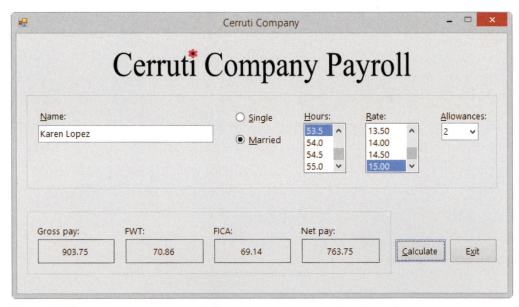

Figure 7-52 Payroll calculations using the second set of test data

3. Click the **Exit** button and then click the **Yes** button. Close the Code Editor window and then close the solution. Figure 7-53 shows the Cerruti Company application's code.

```
 1 ' Name:         Cerruti Project
 2 ' Purpose:      Displays gross pay, taxes, and net pay
 3 ' Programmer:   <your name> on <current date>
 4
 5 Option Explicit On
 6 Option Strict On
 7 Option Infer Off
 8
 9 Public Class frmMain
10
11    ' GetFwt function
12    Private Function GetFwt(ByVal dblWeekPay As Double,
13                    ByVal intNumAllow As Integer,
14                    ByVal strMarital As String) As Double
15        ' calculates and returns the FWT
16
17        Const dblONE_ALLOW As Double = 76
18        Dim dblTaxWages As Double
19        Dim dblTax As Double
20
21        ' calculate taxable wages
22        dblTaxWages =
23            dblWeekPay - intNumAllow * dblONE_ALLOW
24
25        ' determine marital status and then calculate FWT
26        If strMarital = "S" Then
27            Select Case dblTaxWages
28                Case Is <= 43
29                    dblTax = 0
30                Case Is <= 218
31                    dblTax = 0.1 * (dblTaxWages - 43)
32                Case Is <= 753
33                    dblTax = 17.5 + 0.15 * (dblTaxWages - 218)
34                Case Is <= 1762
35                    dblTax = 97.75 + 0.25 * (dblTaxWages - 753)
36                Case Is <= 3627
37                    dblTax = 350 + 0.28 * (dblTaxWages - 1762)
38                Case Is <= 7834
39                    dblTax = 872.2 + 0.33 * (dblTaxWages - 3627)
40                Case Is <= 7865
41                    dblTax = 2260.51 + 0.35 * (dblTaxWages - 7834)
42                Case Else
43                    dblTax = 2271.36 + 0.396 * (dblTaxWages - 7865)
44            End Select
45        Else          ' strMarital = "M"
46            Select Case dblTaxWages
47                Case Is <= 163
48                    dblTax = 0
49                Case Is <= 512
50                    dblTax = 0.1 * (dblTaxWages - 163)
51                Case Is <= 1582
52                    dblTax = 34.9 + 0.15 * (dblTaxWages - 512)
53                Case Is <= 3025
54                    dblTax = 195.4 + 0.25 * (dblTaxWages - 1582)
55                Case Is <= 4525
56                    dblTax = 556.15 + 0.28 * (dblTaxWages - 3025)
```

Figure 7-53   Cerruti Company application's code (continues)

(continued)

```
57              Case Is <= 7953
58                  dblTax = 976.15 + 0.33 * (dblTaxWages - 4525)
59              Case Is <= 8963
60                  dblTax = 2107.39 + 0.35 * (dblTaxWages - 7953)
61              Case Else
62                  dblTax = 2460.89 + 0.396 * (dblTaxWages - 8963)
63          End Select
64      End If
65
66      Return dblTax
67  End Function
68
69  Private Sub btnExit_Click(sender As Object, e As EventArgs
    ) Handles btnExit.Click
70      Me.Close()
71  End Sub
72
73  Private Sub txtName_Enter(sender As Object, e As EventArgs
    ) Handles txtName.Enter
74      ' select the existing text
75
76      txtName.SelectAll()
77  End Sub
78
79  Private Sub cboAllowances_KeyPress(sender As Object,
    e As KeyPressEventArgs) Handles cboAllowances.KeyPress
80      ' allow only numbers and the Backspace key
81
82      If (e.KeyChar < "0" OrElse e.KeyChar > "9") AndAlso
        e.KeyChar <> ControlChars.Back Then
83          e.Handled = True
84      End If
85  End Sub
86
87  Private Sub ClearLabels(sender As Object, e As EventArgs
    ) Handles lstHours.SelectedValueChanged,
88  lstRates.SelectedValueChanged, radSingle.CheckedChanged,
    radMarried.CheckedChanged,
89  txtName.TextChanged, cboAllowances.TextChanged
90
91      lblGross.Text = String.Empty
92      lblFwt.Text = String.Empty
93      lblFica.Text = String.Empty
94      lblNet.Text = String.Empty
95  End Sub
96
97  Private Sub frmMain_Load(sender As Object, e As EventArgs
    ) Handles Me.Load
98      ' fill list boxes and combo box with values
99      ' then select a default value in each
100
101     For dblHours As Double = 0 To 55 Step 0.5
102         lstHours.Items.Add(dblHours.ToString("N1"))
103     Next dblHours
104
```

Figure 7-53   Cerruti Company application's code *(continues)*

(continued)

```
105         For dblRates As Double = 7.5 To 15.5 Step 0.5
106             lstRates.Items.Add(dblRates.ToString("N2"))
107         Next dblRates
108
109         For intAllow As Integer = 0 To 10
110             cboAllowances.Items.Add(intAllow.ToString)
111         Next intAllow
112
113         lstHours.SelectedItem = "40.0"
114         lstRates.SelectedItem = "9.50"
115         cboAllowances.SelectedIndex = 0
116     End Sub
117
118     Private Sub frmMain_FormClosing(sender As Object,
        e As FormClosingEventArgs) Handles Me.FormClosing
119         ' verify that the user wants to exit the application
120
121         Dim dlgButton As DialogResult
122         dlgButton =
123             MessageBox.Show("Do you want to exit?",
124                             "Cerruti Company",
125                             MessageBoxButtons.YesNo,
126                             MessageBoxIcon.Exclamation)
127         ' if the No button was selected, don't close the form
128         If dlgButton = DialogResult.No Then
129             e.Cancel = True
130         End If
131     End Sub
132
133     Private Sub btnCalc_Click(sender As Object, e As EventArgs
        ) Handles btnCalc.Click
134         ' displays gross pay, taxes, and net pay
135
136         Const dblFICA_RATE As Double = 0.0765
137         Dim strStatus As String
138         Dim dblHours As Double
139         Dim dblPayRate As Double
140         Dim intAllowances As Integer
141         Dim dblGross As Double
142         Dim dblFwt As Double
143         Dim dblFica As Double
144         Dim dblNet As Double
145
146         Double.TryParse(lstHours.SelectedItem.ToString, dblHours)
147         Double.TryParse(lstRates.SelectedItem.ToString, dblPayRate)
148         Integer.TryParse(cboAllowances.Text, intAllowances)
149
150         If radSingle.Checked Then
151             strStatus = "S"
152         Else
153             strStatus = "M"
154         End If
155
```

Figure 7-53   Cerruti Company application's code *(continues)*

(continued)

```
156        ' calculate gross pay
157        If dblHours <= 40 Then
158            dblGross = dblHours * dblPayRate
159        Else
160            dblGross = 40 * dblPayRate +
161                (dblHours - 40) * dblPayRate * 1.5
162        End If
163
164        ' get the FWT
165        dblFwt = GetFwt(dblGross, intAllowances, strStatus)
166        ' calculate FICA tax
167        dblFica = dblGross * dblFICA_RATE
168        ' round gross pay, FWT, and FICA tax
169        dblGross = Math.Round(dblGross, 2)
170        dblFwt = Math.Round(dblFwt, 2)
171        dblFica = Math.Round(dblFica, 2)
172        ' calculate net pay
173        dblNet = dblGross - dblFwt - dblFica
174
175        ' display calculated amounts
176        lblGross.Text = dblGross.ToString("n2")
177        lblFwt.Text = dblFwt.ToString("n2")
178        lblFica.Text = dblFica.ToString("n2")
179        lblNet.Text = dblNet.ToString("n2")
180
181    End Sub
182 End Class
```

Figure 7-53   Cerruti Company application's code

Lesson C Summary

- To process code when a form is about to be closed:

  Enter the code in the form's FormClosing event procedure. The FormClosing event occurs when the user clicks the Close button on a form's title bar or when the computer processes the `Me.Close()` statement.

- To prevent a form from being closed:

  Set the Cancel property of the FormClosing event procedure's **e** parameter to True, like this: `e.Cancel = True`.

- To round a number to a specific number of decimal places:

  Use the Math.Round function. The function's syntax is `Math.Round(value[, digits])`, where *value* is a numeric expression and *digits* (which is optional) is an integer indicating how many places to the right of the decimal point are included in the rounding. If the *digits* argument is omitted, the Math.Round function returns an integer.

Lesson C Key Terms

Cancel property—a property of the **e** parameter in the form's FormClosing event procedure; when set to True, it prevents the form from closing

FormClosing event—occurs when a form is about to be closed, which can happen as a result of the computer processing the `Me.Close()` statement or the user clicking the Close button on the form's title bar

Math.Round function—rounds a number to a specific number of decimal places

Lesson C Review Questions

1. Which of a form's events is triggered when you click the Close button on its title bar?

    a. Close
    b. CloseForm

    c. FormClose
    d. FormClosing

2. Which of the following rounds the contents of the **dblNum** variable to two decimal places?

    a. `Math.Round(dblNum, 2)`
    b. `Math.Round(2, dblNum)`

    c. `Round.Math(dblNum, 2)`
    d. `Round.Math(2, dblNum)`

3. Which event is triggered when the computer processes the `Me.Close()` statement entered in the btnExit_Click procedure?

    a. the form's Closing event
    b. the form's FormClosing event
    c. the btnExit control's Closing event
    d. the btnExit control's FormClosing event

4. Which of the following statements prevents a form from being closed?

    a. `e.Cancel = False`
    b. `e.Cancel = True`

    c. `e.Close = False`
    d. `sender.Close = False`

Lesson C Exercises

1. In this exercise, you will remove the Math.Round function from the payroll application created in the lesson; doing this will allow you to observe the "penny off" error. Use Windows to make a copy of the Cerruti Solution folder. Rename the copy No Rounding Cerruti Solution. Open the Cerruti Solution (Cerruti Solution.sln) file contained in the No Rounding Cerruti Solution folder. Open the Code Editor window. The Math.Round function appears in three statements in the btnCalc_Click procedure. Type an apostrophe at the beginning of each of the three statements, making them into comments. Save the solution and then start the application. Test the application by clicking 38.5 in the Hours list box and 10.50 in the Rate list box. Click the Calculate button. What is wrong with the net pay amount? Stop the application and close the solution.

INTRODUCTORY

2. In this exercise, you modify the Monthly Payment application from Lesson B. Use Windows to make a copy of the Payment Solution folder. Rename the copy Payment Solution-FormClosing. Open the Payment Solution (Payment Solution.sln) file contained in the Payment Solution-FormClosing folder. The frmMain_FormClosing procedure should ask the user whether he or she wants to exit the application, and then take the appropriate action based on the user's response. Modify the code to implement these changes. Test the application appropriately.

3. In this exercise, you modify the Cerruti Company application from this lesson. Use Windows to make a copy of the Cerruti Solution folder. Rename the copy Cerruti Solution-Sub. Open the Cerruti Solution (Cerruti Solution.sln) file contained in the Cerruti Solution-Sub folder. Change the GetFwt function to an independent Sub procedure, and then modify the statement that calls the procedure. Also use an independent Sub procedure to round the gross pay and taxes. Test the application appropriately.

4. In this exercise, you modify the Cerruti Company application from this lesson. Use Windows to make a copy of the Cerruti Solution folder. Rename the copy Modified Cerruti Solution. Open the Cerruti Solution (Cerruti Solution.sln) file contained in the Modified Cerruti Solution folder. Modify the code so that the GetFwt function (rather than btnCalc_Click procedure) determines the selected radio button. Test the application appropriately.

5. Open the Translator Solution (Translator Solution.sln) file contained in the VB2015\Chap07\Translator Solution-Sub folder. The application should use three independent Sub procedures to translate the English words into French, German, or Spanish. Code the application. (Hint: Depending on the way you code this application, the Code Editor might indicate that a String variable is being either passed or used before it has been assigned a value. If this is the case, assign the `String.Empty` constant to the variable in the Dim statement.) Test the application appropriately.

6. Open the Translator Solution (Translator Solution.sln) file contained in the VB2015\Chap07\Translator Solution-Function folder. The application should use three functions to translate the English words into French, German, or Spanish. Code the application. (Hint: Depending on the way you code this application, the Code Editor might indicate that a String variable is being either passed or used before it has been assigned a value. If this is the case, assign the `String.Empty` constant to the variable in the Dim statement.) Test the application appropriately.

7. The Donut Shoppe sells four varieties of doughnuts: Glazed ($.75), Sugar ($.75), Chocolate ($.75), and Filled ($.95). It also sells regular coffee ($1.50) and cappuccino ($2.75). The store manager wants you to create an application that displays a customer's subtotal, 4.5% sales tax, and total due. Create the application, using the following names for the solution and project, respectively: Donut Solution and Donut Project. Save the application in the VB2015\Chap07 folder. Create the interface shown in Figure 7-54. The image for the picture box is stored in the VB2015\Chap07\DonutCoffee.png file. When coding the application, use one function to calculate and return the cost of the doughnut, and use another function to calculate and return the cost of the coffee. Use a third function to calculate and return the sales tax. Test the application appropriately.

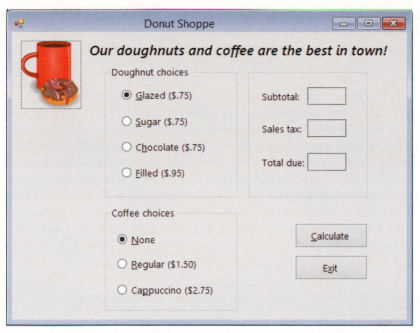

Figure 7-54   User interface for Exercise 7

8. In this exercise, you modify the Donut Shoppe application from Exercise 7. Use   INTERMEDIATE
    Windows to make a copy of the Donut Solution folder. Rename the copy Modified
    Donut Solution. Open the Donut Solution (Donut Solution.sln) file contained in the
    Modified Donut Solution folder. Change the three functions to independent Sub
    procedures. Test the application appropriately.

9. Create an application, using the following names for the solution and project,   INTERMEDIATE
    respectively: Mats Solution and Mats Project. Save the application in the VB2015\
    Chap07 folder. Mats-R-Us sells three different type of mats: Standard ($99), Deluxe
    ($129), and Premium ($179). All of the mats are available in blue, red ($10 extra), and
    pink ($15 extra). There is also an extra $25 charge if the customer wants the mat to be
    foldable. The application's interface is shown in Figure 7-55. Use a function to calculate
    the total additional charge (if any). Test the application appropriately.

Figure 7-55   User interface for Exercise 9

INTERMEDIATE

10. In this exercise, you modify the Mats-R-Us application from Exercise 9. Use Windows to make a copy of the Mats Solution folder. Rename the copy Modified Mats Solution. Open the Mats Solution (Mats Solution.sln) file contained in the Modified Mats Solution folder. Change the function to an independent Sub procedure. Test the application appropriately.

ADVANCED

11. Create an application, using the following names for the solution and project, respectively: Cable Direct Solution and Cable Direct Project. Save the application in the VB2015\Chap07 folder. Create the interface shown in Figure 7-56. The list boxes are named lstPremium and lstConnections. Display numbers from 0 through 20 in the lstPremium control. Display numbers from 0 through 100 in the lstConnections control. The Calculate Total Due button's Click event procedure should calculate and display a customer's cable bill. The cable rates are included in Figure 7-56. Business customers must have at least one connection. Use two functions: one to calculate and return the total due for business customers, and one to calculate and return the total due for residential customers. The form's FormClosing event procedure should verify that the user wants to close the application. Test the application appropriately.

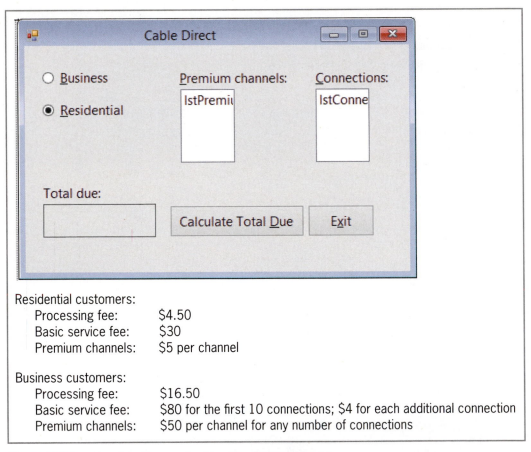

Figure 7-56   User interface and cable rates for Exercise 11

SWAT THE BUGS

12. The purpose of this exercise is to demonstrate a common error made when using functions. Open the Debug Solution (Debug Solution.sln) file contained in the VB2015\ Chap07\Debug Solution-Lesson C folder. Start the application. Click 20 in the Length list box, and then click 30 in the Width list box. Click the Calculate Area button, which should display the area of a rectangle having a length of 20 feet and a width of 30 feet. Notice that the application is not working properly. Stop the application. Correct the application's code and then test it appropriately.

CHAPTER 8

String Manipulation

Creating the Pizza Application

In this chapter, you create the Pizza Game application. The game requires two people to play. Player 1 provides a six-letter word that Player 2 must guess, letter by letter. If Player 2's letter is not contained in the word, the application removes one of the seven pizza slices from the interface. The game is over when Player 2 either guesses all of the letters in the word or makes seven incorrect guesses, whichever comes first.

Previewing the Pizza Game Application

Before you start the first lesson in this chapter, you will preview the completed application contained in the VB2015\Chap08 folder.

START HERE

To preview the completed application:

1. Use Windows to locate and then open the VB2015\Chap08 folder. Right-click **Pizza** (**Pizza.exe**) and then click the **Open** button. The interface contains a File menu, as shown in Figure 8-1. Menus are covered in Lesson B. Notice that the pizza tray contains seven slices of pizza.

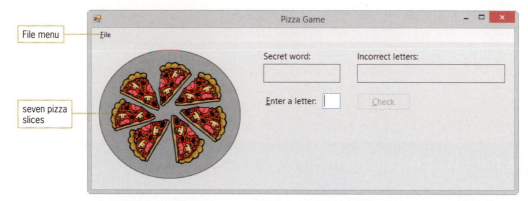

File menu

seven pizza
slices

Figure 8-1 Interface for the Pizza Game application

2. Click **File** on the menu bar and then click **New Game**. An input dialog box opens and prompts you to enter a word that contains six letters.

3. Type **summer** and then press **Enter**. Six dashes (hyphens) appear in the Secret word box. Each dash represents a letter in the word *summer*.

4. Type **r** in the Enter a letter text box. The lowercase letter r is changed to its uppercase equivalent because the text box's CharacterCasing property is set to Upper. Press **Enter** to select the Check button, which is the default button on the form. The last dash in the Secret word box is replaced with the uppercase letter R, indicating that R is the last letter in the secret word.

5. Type **b** in the text box and then press **Enter**. The word *summer* does not contain the letter b, so the application displays B in the Incorrect letters box and also removes a slice of pizza from the tray.

6. Type **a** in the text box and then press **Enter**. The application displays A in the Incorrect letters box and also removes another slice of pizza from the tray.

7. Type **o** in the text box and then press **Enter**. The application displays O in the Incorrect letters box and also removes another slice of pizza from the tray.

8. Type **m** in the text box and then press **Enter**. The application replaces the third and fourth dashes in the Secret word box with the letter M.

9. Next, type the following three letters, one at a time, pressing **Enter** after typing each one: **e**, **s**, and **u**. The application replaces the fifth, first, and second dashes in the Secret word box with the letters E, S, and U, respectively. It also displays the "Great guessing!" message in a message box. Drag the Game Over message box to the location shown in Figure 8-2.

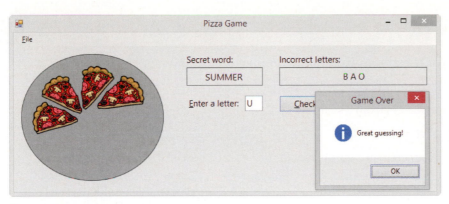

Figure 8-2   Interface after guessing the secret word

10. Close the message box. Click **File** and then click **New Game**. Type **fall** in the input dialog box, and then press **Enter**. The message "6 letters are required" appears in a message box. Close the message box.

11. Press **Ctrl+n** to open the input dialog box. Type **spring** and then press **Enter**. Type **s** in the text box and then press **Enter**. The application replaces the first dash in the Secret word box with the letter S.

12. Next, type the following seven letters, one at a time, pressing **Enter** after typing each one: **e**, **a**, **d**, **x**, **y**, **z**, and **t**. The letters you entered do not appear in the word *spring*, so the application displays the letters in the Incorrect letters box. It also removes the pizza slices from the tray, replacing them with the "All gone!" message. In addition, the application displays the message "Sorry, the word is SPRING." in a message box. Drag the Game Over message box to the location shown in Figure 8-3.

Figure 8-3   Interface after not guessing the secret word

13. Close the message box. Click **File** and then click **Exit** to end the application.

Before you can begin coding the Pizza Game application, you need to learn how to both manipulate strings and create menus. String manipulation is covered in Lesson A; menus are covered in Lesson B. You will code the application in Lessons B and C. Be sure to complete each lesson in full and do all of the end-of-lesson questions and several exercises before continuing to the next lesson.

▌ LESSON A

After studying Lesson A, you should be able to:

- Determine the number of characters in a string
- Remove characters from a string
- Insert characters in a string
- Align the characters in a string
- Search a string
- Access characters in a string
- Compare strings using pattern matching

Working with Strings

In many cases, an application's code will need to manipulate (process) string data in some way. For example, it may need to look at the first character in an inventory part number to determine the part's location in the warehouse. Or, it may need to search an address to determine the street name. Or, it may need to verify that the input entered by the user is in the expected format. In this lesson, you will learn several ways of manipulating strings in Visual Basic. You will begin by learning how to determine the number of characters in a string.

Determining the Number of Characters in a String

If an application expects the user to enter a seven-digit phone number or a five-digit ZIP code, you should verify that the user's input contains the required number of characters. The number of characters contained in a string is stored as an integer in the string's **Length property**. Figure 8-4 shows the property's syntax and includes examples of using the property. In the syntax, *string* can be a String variable, a String named constant, or the Text property of a control.

Determining the Number of Characters in a String

Syntax
string.**Length**

Example 1
```
strCountry = "Canada"
intNumChars = strCountry.Length
```
assigns the number 6 to the `intNumChars` variable

Example 2
```
intChars = txtName.Text.Length
```
assigns the number of characters in the txtName control's Text property to the `intChars` variable

Example 3
```
Do
     strZip = InputBox("5-digit ZIP code", "ZIP")
Loop Until strZip.Length = 5
```
continues prompting the user for a ZIP code until the user enters exactly five characters

---

Figure 8-4 Syntax and examples of the Length property

Removing Characters from a String

Visual Basic provides two methods for removing characters from a string. The **Trim method** removes (trims) any space characters from both the beginning and the end of a string. The **Remove method**, on the other hand, removes a specified number of characters located anywhere in a string. Figure 8-5 shows the syntax of both methods and includes examples of using the methods. In each syntax, *string* can be a String variable, a String named constant, or the Text property of a control. When processing either method, the computer first makes a temporary copy of the *string* in memory. It then performs the specified removal on the copy only. In other words, neither method removes any characters from the original *string*. Both methods return a string with the appropriate characters removed.

The *startIndex* argument in the Remove method is the index of the first character you want removed from the copy of the *string*. A character's index is an integer that indicates the character's position in the string. The first character in a string has an index of 0; the second character has an index of 1, and so on. The optional *numCharsToRemove* argument is the number of characters you want removed. To remove only the first character from a string, you use 0 as the startIndex and 1 as the numCharsToRemove. To remove the fourth through eighth characters, you use 3 as the startIndex and 5 as the numCharsToRemove. If the numCharsToRemove argument is omitted, the Remove method removes all of the characters from the startIndex position through the end of the string, as shown in Example 3 in Figure 8-5.

To learn more about the Trim method, as well as its companion TrimStart and TrimEnd methods, complete Exercises 17 and 18 at the end of this lesson.

Removing Characters from a String

Syntax
string.**Trim**
string.**Remove(**startIndex[, numCharsToRemove]**)**

Example 1
```
strCountry = txtCountry.Text.Trim
```
assigns the contents of the txtCountry control's Text property, excluding any leading and trailing spaces, to the strCountry variable

Example 2
```
strCityState = "Nashville, TN"
txtState.Text = strCityState.Remove(0, 11)
```
assigns the string "TN" to the txtState control's Text property

Example 3
```
strCityState = "Nashville, TN"
txtCity.Text = strCityState.Remove(9)
```
assigns the string "Nashville" to the txtCity control's Text property; you can also write the assignment statement as txtCity.Text = strCityState.Remove(9, 4)

Example 4
```
strFirst = "John"
strFirst = strFirst.Remove(2, 1)
```
assigns the string "Jon" to the strFirst variable

Figure 8-5 Syntax and examples of the Trim and Remove methods

The Product ID Application

You will use the Length property and the Trim method in the Product ID application, which displays a listing of the product IDs entered by the user. Each product ID must contain exactly five characters.

START HERE

To code and then test the Product ID application:

1. If necessary, start Visual Studio 2015. Open the VB2015\Chap08\Product Solution\ Product Solution (Product Solution.sln) file. Open the Code Editor window. Replace \<your name> and \<current date> in the comments with your name and the current date, respectively.

2. Locate the btnAdd_Click procedure. First, the procedure will remove any leading and trailing spaces from the ID. It then will determine whether the ID contains exactly five characters. Make the shaded modifications shown in Figure 8-6.

```
Private Sub btnAdd_Click(sender As Object, e As EventArgs
) Handles btnAdd.Click
    ' adds a product ID to a list

    Dim strId As String

    ' remove any leading and trailing spaces
    strId = txtId.Text.Trim
    ' verify length
    If strId.Length = 5 Then
        lstId.Items.Add(strId.ToUpper)
    Else
        MessageBox.Show("The ID must contain 5 characters.",
                        "Product ID", MessageBoxButtons.OK,
                        MessageBoxIcon.Information)
    End If
    txtId.Focus()
End Sub
```

Figure 8-6   btnAdd_Click procedure

3. Save the solution and then start the application. First, you will enter an ID that contains four characters. Type **abcd** as the product ID, and then click the **Add to List** button. A message box opens and displays the message "The ID must contain 5 characters." Close the message box.

4. Next, you will include two leading spaces in the ID. Click **immediately before the letter a** in the text box. Press the **Spacebar** twice, and then type the number **2**. The text box now contains two space characters followed by 2abcd. Click the **Add to List** button. 2ABCD appears in the listing of product IDs. See Figure 8-7.

Figure 8-7 Sample run of the Product ID application

5. On your own, test the application using an ID that contains nine characters. Also test it using an ID that contains both leading and trailing spaces. When you are finished testing the application, click the **Exit** button. Close the Code Editor window and then close the solution.

YOU DO IT 1!

Create an application named YouDoIt 1 and save it in the VB2015\Chap08 folder. Add a text box, a label, and a button to the form. The button's Click event procedure should remove any leading or trailing spaces from the text entered in the text box. If the remaining text contains more than four characters, the button's Click event procedure should display only the first four characters in the label; otherwise, it should display the remaining text in the label. Code the procedure. Save the solution, and then start and test the application. Close the solution.

Inserting Characters in a String

Visual Basic's **Insert method** allows you to insert characters anywhere in a string. The method's syntax is shown in Figure 8-8 along with examples of using the method. In the syntax, *string* can be a String variable, a String named constant, or the Text property of a control. When processing the Insert method, the computer first makes a temporary copy of the *string* in memory. It then performs the specified insertion on the copy only. The Insert method does not affect the original *string*. The *startIndex* argument in the Insert method is an integer that specifies where in the string's copy you want the *value* inserted. The integer represents the character's index— in other words, its position in the string. To insert the value at the beginning of a string, you use a startIndex of 0, as shown in Example 1 in Figure 8-8. To insert the value beginning with the eighth character in the string, you use a startIndex of 7, as shown in Example 2. The Insert method returns a string with the appropriate characters inserted.

Inserting Characters in a String

Syntax
string.**Insert**(*startIndex*, *value*)

Example 1
```
strPhone = "111-2222"
txtPhone.Text = strPhone.Insert(0, "(877) ")
```
assigns the string "(877) 111-2222" to the txtPhone control's Text property

Example 2
```
strName = "Lebron Jefferson"
strName = strName.Insert(7, "K. ")
```
assigns the string "Lebron K. Jefferson" to the strName variable

---

Figure 8-8   Syntax and examples of the Insert method

Aligning the Characters in a String

You can use Visual Basic's PadLeft and PadRight methods to align the characters in a string. The methods do this by inserting (padding) the string with zero or more characters until the string is a specified length; each method then returns the padded string. The **PadLeft method** pads the string on the left, which means it inserts the padded characters at the beginning of the string, thereby right-aligning the characters within the string. The **PadRight method**, on the other hand, pads the string on the right, which means it inserts the padded characters at the end of the string and left-aligns the characters within the string.

Figure 8-9 shows the syntax of both methods and includes examples of using them. In each syntax, *string* can be a String variable, a String named constant, or the Text property of a control. When processing the PadLeft and PadRight methods, the computer first makes a temporary copy of the *string* in memory; it then pads the copy only. The *totalChars* argument in each syntax is an integer that represents the total number of characters you want the string's copy to contain. The optional *padCharacter* argument is the character that each method uses to pad the string until the desired number of characters is reached. If the padCharacter argument is omitted, the default padding character is the space character.

Aligning the Characters in a String

Syntax
string.**PadLeft**(*totalChars*[, *padCharacter*])
string.**PadRight**(*totalChars*[, *padCharacter*])

Example 1
```
strNumber = "300.99"
txtNum.Text = strNumber.PadLeft(9)
```
assigns the string "   300.99" to the txtNum control's Text property

three space characters

Example 2
```
strFirst = "Charles"
strFirst = strFirst.PadRight(15)
```
assigns the string "Charles   " to the strFirst variable

eight space characters

Figure 8-9   Syntax and examples of the PadLeft and PadRight methods *(continues)*

(continued)

> Example 3
> ```
> dblNet = 633.75
> strFormattedNet =
>     dblNet.ToString("C2").PadLeft(10, "*"c)
> ```
> assigns the string "***$633.75" to the `strFormattedNet` variable (Many companies use this type of formatting on their employee paychecks because it makes it more difficult for someone to change the amount.)

Figure 8-9 Syntax and examples of the PadLeft and PadRight methods

Notice that the expression in Example 3 contains the ToString and PadLeft methods. When an expression contains more than one method, the computer processes the methods from left to right. In this case, the computer will process the ToString method before processing the PadLeft method. Also notice the letter c that appears at the end of the *padCharacter* argument in Example 3. The letter c is one of the literal type characters in Visual Basic. As you learned in Chapter 3, a literal type character forces a literal constant to assume a data type other than the one its form indicates. In this case, the letter c forces the "*" string in the padCharacter argument to assume the Char (character) data type.

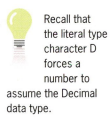

Recall that the literal type character D forces a number to assume the Decimal data type.

The Net Pay Application

The Net Pay application will use the Insert and PadLeft methods to display an employee's net pay with a leading dollar sign, asterisks, and two decimal places.

To code and then test the Net Pay application:

START HERE

1. Open the VB2015\Chap08\Net Pay Solution\Net Pay Solution (Net Pay Solution.sln) file. Open the Code Editor window. Replace <your name> and <current date> in the comments with your name and the current date, respectively.

2. Locate the btnFormat_Click procedure. First, the procedure will format the net pay to include two decimal places. It then will pad the net pay with asterisks until it contains 10 characters. Finally, it will insert a dollar sign at the beginning of the formatted net pay. Make the shaded modifications shown in Figure 8-10.

```vb
Private Sub btnFormat_Click(sender As Object, e As EventArgs
) Handles btnFormat.Click
    ' format the net pay with two decimal places, then
    ' pad with asterisks and insert a dollar sign as the
    ' first character

    Dim decNet As Decimal
    Dim strFormatted As String

    Decimal.TryParse(txtNetPay.Text, decNet)
    ' format the net pay with two decimal places
    strFormatted = decNet.ToString("n2")
    ' pad the net pay with asterisks until its length is 10
    strFormatted = strFormatted.PadLeft(10, "*"c)
    ' insert a dollar sign as the first character
    strFormatted = strFormatted.Insert(0, "$")
```

Figure 8-10 btnFormat_Click procedure *(continues)*

(continued)

```
        ' display the net pay, then set the focus
        lblFormatted.Text = strFormatted
        txtNetPay.Focus()
End Sub
```

Figure 8-10   btnFormat_Click procedure

3. Save the solution and then start the application. Type **1056** as the net pay and then click the **Format** button. The button's Click event procedure displays $**1,056.00 in the interface, as shown in Figure 8-11. Click the **Exit** button. Close the Code Editor window and then close the solution.

Figure 8-11   Interface showing the formatted net pay

YOU DO IT 2!

Create an application named YouDoIt 2 and save it in the VB2015\Chap08 folder. Add a text box, a label, and a button to the form. Set the text box's MaxLength property to 5. The button's Click event procedure should assign the contents of the text box to a String variable. It then should remove any leading or trailing spaces from the string stored in the variable. If the variable contains more than three characters, the procedure should insert a number sign (#) as the second character and then pad the variable's value with asterisks until the variable contains 10 characters. Insert the asterisks at the end of the string stored in the variable. Finally, the procedure should display the variable's contents in the label. Code the procedure. Save the solution, and then start and test the application. Close the solution.

Searching a String

You can use either the Contains method or the IndexOf method to determine whether a string contains a specific sequence of characters. Figure 8-12 shows the syntax of both methods. In each syntax, *string* can be a String variable, a String named constant, or the Text property of a control. The *subString* argument in each syntax represents the sequence of characters for which you are searching. Both methods perform a case-sensitive search, which means the case of the subString must match the case of the string in order for both to be considered equal.

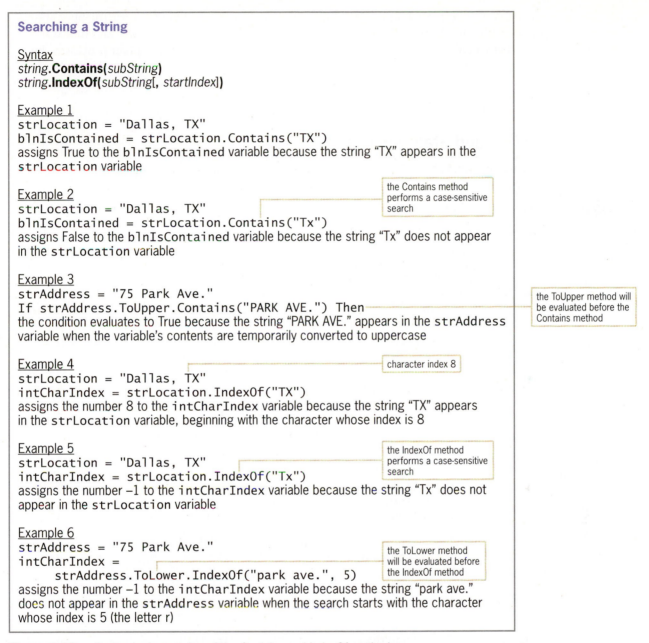

Searching a String

Syntax
string.**Contains**(*subString*)
string.**IndexOf**(*subString*[, *startIndex*])

Example 1
```
strLocation = "Dallas, TX"
blnIsContained = strLocation.Contains("TX")
```
assigns True to the blnIsContained variable because the string "TX" appears in the strLocation variable

Example 2
```
strLocation = "Dallas, TX"
blnIsContained = strLocation.Contains("Tx")
```
assigns False to the blnIsContained variable because the string "Tx" does not appear in the strLocation variable

> the Contains method performs a case-sensitive search

Example 3
```
strAddress = "75 Park Ave."
If strAddress.ToUpper.Contains("PARK AVE.") Then
```
the condition evaluates to True because the string "PARK AVE." appears in the strAddress variable when the variable's contents are temporarily converted to uppercase

> the ToUpper method will be evaluated before the Contains method

Example 4
```
strLocation = "Dallas, TX"
intCharIndex = strLocation.IndexOf("TX")
```
assigns the number 8 to the intCharIndex variable because the string "TX" appears in the strLocation variable, beginning with the character whose index is 8

> character index 8

Example 5
```
strLocation = "Dallas, TX"
intCharIndex = strLocation.IndexOf("Tx")
```
assigns the number −1 to the intCharIndex variable because the string "Tx" does not appear in the strLocation variable

> the IndexOf method performs a case-sensitive search

Example 6
```
strAddress = "75 Park Ave."
intCharIndex =
    strAddress.ToLower.IndexOf("park ave.", 5)
```
assigns the number −1 to the intCharIndex variable because the string "park ave." does not appear in the strAddress variable when the search starts with the character whose index is 5 (the letter r)

> the ToLower method will be evaluated before the IndexOf method

Figure 8-12   Syntax and examples of the Contains and IndexOf methods

The **Contains method**, which appears in Examples 1 through 3 in Figure 8-12, returns the Boolean value True when the subString is contained anywhere in the string; otherwise, it returns the Boolean value False. The Contains method always begins the search with the first character in the string.

The **IndexOf method**, which appears in Examples 4 through 6, returns an integer: either −1 or a number that is greater than or equal to 0. The −1 indicates that the subString is not contained in the string. A number other than −1 is the character index of the subString's starting position in the string. Unless you specify otherwise, the IndexOf method starts the search with the first character in the string. To specify a different starting location, you use the optional *startIndex* argument.

Notice that the expression in Example 3 in Figure 8-12 contains two methods: ToUpper and Contains. Two methods also appear in the expression in Example 6: ToLower and IndexOf. Recall that when an expression contains more than one method, the computer processes the methods from left to right. In this case, the computer will process the ToUpper method before the Contains method in Example 3, and it will process the ToLower method before the IndexOf method in Example 6.

The City and State Application

The City and State application will use the IndexOf method to locate the comma contained in a string.

START HERE

To code and then test the City and State application:

1. Open the VB2015\Chap08\City State Solution\City State Solution (City State Solution.sln) file. Open the Code Editor window. Replace <your name> and <current date> in the comments with your name and the current date, respectively.

2. Locate the btnLocate_Click procedure. To begin the search with the first character in the string, you can use either `strCityState.IndexOf(",", 0)` or `strCityState.IndexOf(",")`. You will assign the IndexOf method's return value to the `intCommaIndex` variable. Enter the assignment statement shaded in Figure 8-13.

```
Private Sub btnLocate_Click(sender As Object, e As EventArgs
) Handles btnLocate.Click
    ' displays the index of the comma in a string

    Dim strCityState As String
    Dim intCommaIndex As Integer

    strCityState = txtCityState.Text
    ' determine the comma's index
    intCommaIndex = strCityState.IndexOf(",")

    lblCommaIndex.Text = intCommaIndex.ToString
    txtCityState.Focus()
End Sub
```

Figure 8-13　btnLocate_Click procedure

3. Save the solution and then start the application. Type **Dallas, TX** in the text box, and then click the **Locate the Comma** button. As Figure 8-14 shows, the comma's index is 6.

Figure 8-14　Interface showing the comma's index

4. Next, type **New York** in the text box, and then click the **Locate the Comma** button. The −1 that appears in the label indicates that the text box does not contain a comma. Click the **Exit** button. Close the Code Editor window and then close the solution.

YOU DO IT 3!

Create an application named YouDoIt 3 and save it in the VB2015\Chap08 folder. Add a text box, a label, and a button to the form. The button's Click event procedure should determine whether a 9 appears anywhere in the text box and then display the result (either True or False) in the label. Code the procedure. Save the solution, and then start and test the application. Close the solution.

Accessing the Characters in a String

Visual Basic provides the **Substring method** for accessing any number of characters in a string. Figure 8-15 shows the method's syntax and includes examples of using the method. In the syntax, *string* can be a String variable, a String named constant, or the Text property of a control. The *startIndex* argument in the syntax is the index of the first character you want to access. As you already know, the first character in a string has an index of 0. The optional *numCharsToAccess* argument specifies the number of characters you want to access. The Substring method returns a string that contains the number of characters specified in the numCharsToAccess argument, beginning with the character whose index is startIndex. If you omit the numCharsToAccess argument, the Substring method returns all characters from the startIndex position through the end of the string.

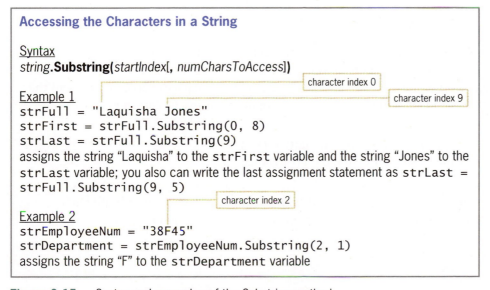

Accessing the Characters in a String

Syntax
string.**Substring**(*startIndex*[, *numCharsToAccess*])

character index 0

character index 9

Example 1
```
strFull = "Laquisha Jones"
strFirst = strFull.Substring(0, 8)
strLast = strFull.Substring(9)
```
assigns the string "Laquisha" to the strFirst variable and the string "Jones" to the strLast variable; you also can write the last assignment statement as strLast = strFull.Substring(9, 5)

character index 2

Example 2
```
strEmployeeNum = "38F45"
strDepartment = strEmployeeNum.Substring(2, 1)
```
assigns the string "F" to the strDepartment variable

Figure 8-15   Syntax and examples of the Substring method

The Rearrange Name Application

ChO8A

You will use the Substring method in the Rearrange Name application. The application's interface provides a text box for entering a person's first name followed by a space and the person's last name. The application rearranges the name so that the last name comes first, followed by a comma, a space, and the first name.

START HERE

To code and then test the Rearrange Name application:

1. Open the VB2015\Chap08\Rearrange Name Solution\Rearrange Name Solution (Rearrange Name Solution.sln) file. Open the Code Editor window. Replace <your name> and <current date> in the comments with your name and the current date, respectively.

2. Locate the btnRearrange_Click procedure. The procedure assigns the name entered by the user, excluding any leading or trailing spaces, to the `strName` variable.

3. Before you can rearrange the name stored in the `strName` variable, you need to separate the first name from the last name. To do this, you first search for the space character that appears between the names. Click the **blank line** below the `' search for the space in the name` comment, and then enter the following assignment statement, being sure to include a space character between the quotation marks:

    intIndex = strName.IndexOf(" ")

4. If the value in the `intIndex` variable is not −1, it means that the IndexOf method found a space character in the `strName` variable. In that case, the selection structure's true path should continue rearranging the name; otherwise, its false path should display the "Invalid name format" message. Notice that the statement to display the message is already entered in the selection structure's false path. Change the If clause in the procedure to the following:

    If intIndex <> −1 Then

5. Now you can use the value stored in the `intIndex` variable to separate the first name from the last name. Click the **blank line** below the `' separate the first and last names` comment. All of the characters to the left of the space character represent the first name, and all of the characters to the right of the space character represent the last name. Enter the following assignment statements:

    strFirstName = strName.Substring(0, intIndex)
    strLastName = strName.Substring(intIndex + 1)

6. Finally, you will display the rearranged name in the interface. Click the **blank line** above the Else clause. Enter the additional assignment statement indicated in Figure 8-16. Be sure to include a space character after the comma.

```
Private Sub btnRearrange_Click(sender As Object, e As
EventArgs
) Handles btnRearrange.Click
    ' rearranges and then displays a name

    Dim strName As String
    Dim strFirstName As String
    Dim strLastName As String
    Dim intIndex As Integer

    strName = txtName.Text.Trim
    ' search for the space in the name
    intIndex = strName.IndexOf(" ")

    ' if the input contains a space
    If intIndex <> -1 Then
        ' separate the first and last names
        strFirstName = strName.Substring(0, intIndex)
        strLastName = strName.Substring(intIndex + 1)

        ' display last name, comma, space, and first name
        lblRearrangedName.Text =
            strLastName & ", " & strFirstName

    Else    ' the name does not contain a space
        MessageBox.Show("Invalid name format",
                        "Rearrange Name",
                        MessageBoxButtons.OK,
                        MessageBoxIcon.Information)

    End If
End Sub
```

enter this assignment statement

Figure 8-16   btnRearrange_Click procedure

7. Save the solution and then start the application. Type **Sophia Waterson** as the name and then click the **Rearrange Name** button. The rearranged name appears in the interface, as shown in Figure 8-17.

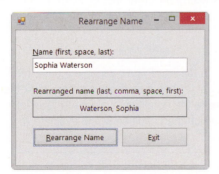

Figure 8-17   Interface showing the rearranged name

8. Change the name to **Cher** and then click the **Rearrange Name** button. The "Invalid name format" message appears in a message box. Click the **OK** button.

9. Click the **Exit** button. Close the Code Editor window and then close the solution.

YOU DO IT 4!

Create an application named YouDoIt 4 and save it in the VB2015\Chap08 folder. Add a label and a button to the form. The button's Click event procedure should declare a String variable named `strMessage` and initialize it to the 26 uppercase letters of the alphabet. It then should use the Substring method to display only the letters K, L, M, N, and O in the label. Code the procedure. Save the solution, and then start and test the application. Close the solution.

Using Pattern Matching to Compare Strings

The **Like operator** allows you to use pattern-matching characters to determine whether one string is equal to another string. Figure 8-18 shows the operator's syntax and examples of using the operator. In the syntax, *string* can be a String variable, a String named constant, or the Text property of a control. *Pattern* is a String expression containing one or more of the pattern-matching characters listed in the figure.

Using Pattern Matching to Compare Strings

<u>Syntax</u>
string **Like** *pattern*

<u>Pattern-matching characters</u>	<u>Matches in *string*</u>
?	any single character
*	zero or more characters
#	any single digit (0 through 9)
[*characterList*]	any single character in the *characterList* (for example, "[A5T]" matches A, 5, or T, whereas "[a-z]" matches any lowercase letter)
[!*characterList*]	any single character *not* in the *characterList* (for example, "[!A5T]" matches any character other than A, 5, or T, whereas "[!a-z]" matches any character that is not a lowercase letter)

<u>Example 1</u>
```
If strFirst.ToUpper Like "B?LL" Then
```
The condition evaluates to True when the string stored in the `strFirst` variable (converted to uppercase) begins with the letter B followed by one character and then the two letters LL; otherwise, it evaluates to False. Examples of strings that would make the condition evaluate to True include "Bill", "Ball", "bell", and "bull". Examples of strings for which the condition would evaluate to False include "BPL", "BLL", and "billy".

Figure 8-18 Syntax and examples of the Like operator *(continues)*

(continued)

Example 2
```
If txtState.Text Like "K*" Then
```
The condition evaluates to True when the value in the txtState control's Text property begins with the letter K followed by zero or more characters; otherwise, it evaluates to False. Examples of strings that would make the condition evaluate to True include "KANSAS", "Ky", and "Kentucky". Examples of strings for which the condition would evaluate to False include "kansas" and "ky".

Example 3
```
Do While strId Like "###*"
```
The condition evaluates to True when the string stored in the strId variable begins with three digits followed by zero or more characters; otherwise, it evaluates to False. Examples of strings that would make the condition evaluate to True include "178" and "983Ab". Examples of strings for which the condition would evaluate to False include "X34" and "34Z5".

Example 4
```
If strFirst.ToUpper Like "T[OI]M" Then
```
The condition evaluates to True when the string stored in the strFirst variable (converted to uppercase) is either "TOM" or "TIM". When the variable does not contain "TOM" or "TIM"—for example, when it contains "Tam" or "Tommy"—the condition evaluates to False.

Example 5
```
If strLetter Like "[a-z]" Then
```
The condition evaluates to True when the string stored in the strLetter variable is one lowercase letter; otherwise, it evaluates to False.

Example 6
```
For intIndex As Integer = 0 To strInput.Length - 1
    strChar = strInput.Substring(intIndex, 1)
    If strChar Like "[!a-zA-Z]" Then
        intNonLetter += 1
    End If
Next intIndex
```
Compares each character contained in the strInput variable with the lowercase and uppercase letters of the alphabet, and counts the number of characters that are not letters.

Example 7
```
If strInput Like "*.*" Then
```
The condition evaluates to True when a period appears anywhere in the strInput variable; otherwise, it evaluates to False.

Example 8
```
If strInput.ToUpper Like "[A-Z][A-Z]##" Then
```
The condition evaluates to True when the value in the strInput variable (converted to uppercase) is two letters followed by two numbers; otherwise, it evaluates to False.

Figure 8-18   Syntax and examples of the Like operator

As Figure 8-18 indicates, the question mark (?) character in a pattern represents one character only, whereas the asterisk (*) character represents zero or more characters. To represent a single digit in a pattern, you use the number sign (#) character. The last two pattern-matching characters listed in the figure contain a *characterList*, which is simply a listing of characters. "[A9M]" is a characterList that contains three characters: A, 9, and M. You can also include a range of values in a characterList. You do this using a hyphen to separate the lowest value in the range from the highest value in the range. For example, to include all lowercase letters in a characterList, you use "[a-z]". To include both lowercase and uppercase letters in a characterList, you use "[a-zA-Z]".

The Like operator performs a case-sensitive comparison of the string to the pattern. If the string matches the pattern, the Like operator returns the Boolean value True; otherwise, it returns the Boolean value False.

Modifying the Product ID Application

In the following set of steps, you will modify the Product ID application from earlier in this lesson. The modified application will ensure that the five characters entered by the user consist of three letters followed by two numbers.

START HERE

To modify and then test the Product ID application:

1. Open the Product Solution (Product Solution.sln) file contained in the VB2015\Chap08\Modified Product Solution folder.

2. Open the Code Editor window and locate the btnAdd_Click procedure. First, you will change the user's entry to uppercase. Change the strId = txtId.Text.Trim statement to the following:

   strId = txtId.Text.Trim.ToUpper

3. Now you can use the Like operator to verify that the user's entry contains three letters followed by two numbers. Change the If clause to the following:

   If strId Like "[A-Z][A-Z][A-Z]##" Then

4. In the statement below the If clause, change strId.ToUpper to **strId**. Finally, change the message in the MessageBox.Show method to **"Invalid product ID"**. Figure 8-19 shows the modified procedure. The modifications you made are shaded in the figure.

```vb
Private Sub btnAdd_Click(sender As Object, e As EventArgs
) Handles btnAdd.Click
    ' adds a product ID to a list

    Dim strId As String

    ' remove any leading and trailing spaces
    ' and then convert to uppercase
    strId = txtId.Text.Trim.ToUpper
    ' verify that the ID contains 3 letters followed by 2 numbers
    If strId Like "[A-Z][A-Z][A-Z]##" Then
        lstId.Items.Add(strId)
    Else
        MessageBox.Show("Invalid product ID",
                        "Product ID", MessageBoxButtons.OK,
                        MessageBoxIcon.Information)
    End If
    txtId.Focus()
End Sub
```

Figure 8-19 Modified Click event procedure for the btnAdd control

5. Save the solution and then start the application. First, test the application using an invalid ID. Type **abc2f** as the product ID and then click the **Add to List** button. The "Invalid product ID" message appears in a message box. Close the message box.

6. Next, enter a valid ID. Change the product ID to **abc23** and then click the **Add to List** button. ABC23 appears in the list of product IDs, as shown in Figure 8-20.

Figure 8-20   Product ID added to the list box

7. On your own, test the application using different valid and invalid IDs. When you are finished testing the application, click the **Exit** button. Close the Code Editor window and then close the solution.

YOU DO IT 5!

Create an application named YouDoIt 5 and save it in the VB2015\Chap08 folder. Add a text box, a label, and a button to the form. The button's Click event procedure should display the message "OK" when the text box contains two numbers followed by zero or more characters; otherwise, it should display the message "Not OK". Display the message in the label control. Code the procedure. Save the solution, and then start and test the application. Close the solution.

Lesson A Summary

- To manipulate strings in Visual Basic:

  Use one of the string manipulation techniques listed in Figure 8-21.

Technique	Syntax	Purpose
Length property	*string*.**Length**	stores an integer that represents the number of characters contained in a string
Trim method	*string*.**Trim**	removes any spaces from both the beginning and the end of a string
Remove method	*string*.**Remove(***startIndex* [, *numCharsToRemove*]**)**	removes characters from a string
Insert method	*string*.**Insert(***startIndex*, *value***)**	inserts characters in a string
Contains method	*string*.**Contains(***subString***)**	determines whether a string contains a specific sequence of characters; returns a Boolean value
IndexOf method	*string*.**IndexOf(***subString*[, *startIndex*]**)**	determines whether a string contains a specific sequence of characters; returns either –1 or an integer that indicates the starting position of the characters in the string
Substring method	*string*.**Substring(***startIndex* [, *numCharsToAccess*]**)**	accesses one or more characters in a string
PadLeft method	*string*.**PadLeft(***totalChars*[, *padCharacter*]**)**	pads the beginning of a string with a character until the string has the specified number of characters; right-aligns the string

Figure 8-21 String manipulation techniques *(continues)*

(continued)

PadRight method	*string*.**PadRight**(*totalChars*[, *padCharacter*])	pads the end of a string with a character until the string has the specified number of characters; left-aligns the string
Like operator	*string* **Like** *pattern*	uses pattern matching to compare strings

Important note: The following additional techniques are covered in the Discovery Exercises at the end of this lesson: the StartsWith and EndsWith methods, the Replace method, the full syntax of the Trim method, the TrimStart and TrimEnd methods, and the Mid statement.

Figure 8-21 String manipulation techniques

Lesson A Key Terms

Contains method—determines whether a string contains a specific sequence of characters; returns a Boolean value

IndexOf method—determines whether a string contains a specific sequence of characters; returns either −1 (if the string does not contain the sequence of characters) or an integer that represents the starting position of the sequence of characters

Insert method—inserts characters anywhere in a string

Length property—stores an integer that represents the number of characters contained in a string

Like operator—uses pattern-matching characters to determine whether one string is equal to another string

PadLeft method—right-aligns a string by inserting characters at the beginning of the string

PadRight method—left-aligns a string by inserting characters at the end of the string

Remove method—removes a specified number of characters located anywhere in a string

Substring method—used to access any number of characters contained in a string

Trim method—removes spaces from both the beginning and end of a string

Lesson A Review Questions

1. The txtState control contains the word *Alaska* followed by one space. Which of the following statements removes the space from the control's contents?

   a. `txtState.Text = txtState.Text.Trim`
   b. `txtState.Text = Trim(txtState.Text)`
   c. `txtState.Text = txtState.Trim`
   d. `txtState.Text.Trim`

2. Which of the following statements assigns the first four characters in the strItem variable to the strWarehouse variable?

   a. `strWarehouse = strItem.Assign(0, 4)`
   b. `strWarehouse = strItem.Assign(1, 4)`
   c. `strWarehouse = strItem.Substring(0, 4)`
   d. `strWarehouse = strItem.Substring(1, 4)`

3. The strName variable contains the string "Carlson". Which of the following statements changes the contents of the variable to the string "Carl"?

   a. `strName = strName.Remove(0, 4)`
   b. `strName = strName.Remove(4, 3)`
   c. `strName = strName.Remove(5, 3)`
   d. `strName = strName.Remove(5)`

4. Which of the following statements changes the contents of the strZip variable from 60521 to 60561?

   a. `strZip = strZip.Insert(3, "6")`
     `strZip = strZip.Remove(4, 1)`
   b. `strZip = strZip.Insert(4, "6")`
     `strZip = strZip.Remove(3, 1)`
   c. `strZip = strZip.Remove(3, 1)`
     `strZip = strZip.Insert(3, "6")`
   d. all of the above

5. Which of the following methods can be used to determine whether the strAmount variable contains the dollar sign?

   a. `blnResult = strAmount.Contains("$")`
   b. `intResult = strAmount.IndexOf("$")`
   c. `intResult = strAmount.IndexOf("$", 0)`
   d. all of the above

6. Which of the following statements changes the contents of the strWord variable from "sting" to "string"?

   a. `strWord = strWord.AddTo(2, "r")`
   b. `strWord = strWord.Insert(2, "r")`
   c. `strWord = strWord.Insert(3, "r")`
   d. `strWord = strWord.Insert(3, "r"c)`

7. If the strPresident variable contains the string "Abraham Lincoln", what value will the `strPresident.IndexOf("Lincoln")` method return?

   a. −1   c. 9
   b. 8   d. True

8. If the `strWord` variable contains the string "chimes", which of the following statements assigns the letter m to the `strLetter` variable?

   a. `strLetter = strWord.Substring(3)`
   b. `strLetter = strWord.Substring(3, 1)`
   c. `strLetter = strWord.Substring(4, 1)`
   d. none of the above

9. Which of the following expressions evaluates to True when the `strItem` variable contains the string "1234Y5"?

   a. `strItem Like "####[A-Z]#"`
   b. `strItem Like "9999[A-Z]9"`
   c. `strItem Like "######"`
   d. none of the above

10. The `strName` variable contains the string "Jones John". Which of the following changes the variable's contents to the string "Jones, John"?

    a. `strName = strName.Insert(5, ",")`
    b. `strName = strName.Insert(6, ",")`
    c. `strName = strName.Insert(6, 1, ",")`
    d. none of the above

11. If the `strMsg` variable contains the string "The party is Saturday.", which of the following assigns the number 13 to the `intNum` variable?

    a. `intNum = strMsg.Substring(0, "S")`
    b. `intNum = strMsg.Contains("S")`
    c. `intNum = strMsg.IndexOf("S")`
    d. `intNum = strMsg.IndexOf(0, "S")`

12. If the `strName` variable contains the string "Sam Harris", which of the following changes the contents of the variable to the string "Sam H. Harris"?

    a. `strName = strName.Insert(3, " H.")`
    b. `strName = strName.Insert(4, "H.")`
    c. `strName = strName.Insert(5, "H. ")`
    d. none of the above

13. The `strAmount` variable contains the string "245.69". Which of the following statements changes the contents of the variable to the string "245.69!!"?

    a. `strAmount = strAmount.PadLeft(8, "!"c)`
    b. `strAmount = strAmount.PadRight(8, "!"c)`
    c. `strAmount = strAmount.PadRight(2, "!"c)`
    d. none of the above

14. If the `strLocation` variable contains the string "75 Oak Avenue", what will the `strAddress.IndexOf("Oak")` method return?

    a. −1   c. 4
    b. 3   d. True

15. If the `strAddress` variable contains the string "2345 Hawthorne Blvd", what will the `strAddress.IndexOf("Hawthorne", 5)` method return?

    a. −1

    b. 5

    c. 6

    d. False

Lesson A Exercises

INTRODUCTORY 1. Write a Visual Basic statement that removes the leading and trailing spaces from the txtAddress control.

INTRODUCTORY 2. Write a Visual Basic statement that uses the Insert method to change the contents of the `strState` variable from "Il" to "Illinois".

INTRODUCTORY 3. Using the Insert and Remove methods, write the Visual Basic statements to change the contents of the `strWord` variable from "late" to "crate".

INTRODUCTORY 4. The `strItem` variable contains the string "YMBlueX". Write a Visual Basic statement that assigns the string "Blue" from the `strItem` variable to the `strColor` variable.

INTRODUCTORY 5. Write the Visual Basic statements to accomplish the following tasks:

    a. In the lblSize control, display the number of characters contained in the `strMsg` variable.

    b. Remove the leading and trailing spaces from the `strState` variable.

    c. Use the Insert and Remove methods to change the contents of the `strWord` variable from "cater" to "critter".

    d. Use the Insert method to change the contents of the `strWord` variable from "day" to "Monday".

    e. Change the contents of the `strPay` variable from "765.44" to "****765.44".

INTRODUCTORY 6. The `strAmount` variable contains the string "3,123,560". Write the Visual Basic statements to change the contents of the variable to "3123560"; use the Remove method.

INTRODUCTORY 7. Write the Visual Basic statement that uses the Contains method to determine whether the `strAddress` variable contains the string "Jefferson Street" (entered in uppercase, lowercase, or a combination of uppercase and lowercase). Assign the method's return value to a Boolean variable named `blnIsContained`.

INTRODUCTORY 8. The `strAmount` variable contains the string "3123560". Write the Visual Basic statements to change the variable's contents to "$3,123,560".

INTRODUCTORY 9. Open the VB2015\Chap08\State Solution\State Solution (State Solution.sln) file. The interface provides an editable combo box for entering the name of a state. Code the btnAdd_Click procedure so that it removes any leading and/or trailing spaces from the state name. If the name contains at least one character, add the name to the combo box. The procedure should also send the focus to the combo box. Test the application by entering spaces before and after the following names: South Carolina and Alaska. Also enter only spaces in the text portion of the combo box.

INTRODUCTORY 10. Open the VB2015\Chap08\Prices Solution\Prices Solution (Prices Solution.sln) file. Modify the frmMain_Load procedure so that it right-aligns the prices listed in the cboRight control and then selects the first price. Save the solution and then start the application. (The prices listed in the cboLeft control should still be left-aligned.)

11. Open the VB2015\Chap08\Date Solution\Date Solution (Date Solution.sln) file. The interface provides a text box for entering a date. The btnChange_Click procedure should verify that the date was entered in the correct format, which is two numbers followed by a slash, two numbers, a slash, and two numbers. If the date was not entered correctly, the procedure should display an appropriate message. However, if the date was entered correctly, the procedure should change the year number from *yy* to 20*yy* before displaying the date in the lblDate control. Test the application appropriately. INTERMEDIATE

12. Open the VB2015\Chap08\Tax Solution\Tax Solution (Tax Solution.sln) file. The interface provides a text box and a combo box for entering a sales amount and a tax rate, respectively. The btnCalc_Click procedure should remove the percent sign and the space that precedes it from the tax rate before using the rate to calculate the sales tax. Test the application appropriately. INTERMEDIATE

13. Open the VB2015\Chap08\Zip Solution\Zip Solution (Zip Solution.sln) file. The btnDisplay_Click procedure should display the correct shipping charge based on the ZIP code entered by the user. To be valid, the ZIP code must contain exactly five digits, and the first three digits must be either "605" or "606". The shipping charge for "605" ZIP codes is $25. The shipping charge for "606" ZIP codes is $30. Display an appropriate message if the ZIP code is invalid. Test the application using the following ZIP codes: 60677, 60511, 60344, and 7130. INTERMEDIATE

14. Open the Social Security Solution (Social Security Solution.sln) file contained in the VB2015\Chap08\Social Security Solution-Remove folder. The interface provides a text box for entering a Social Security number. The btnRemove_Click procedure should verify that the Social Security number contains three numbers followed by a hyphen, two numbers, a hyphen, and four numbers. If the Social Security number is in the correct format, the procedure should remove the dashes from the number before displaying the number in the lblNumber control; otherwise, it should display an error message to the user. Test the application appropriately. INTERMEDIATE

15. Visual Basic provides the StartsWith and EndsWith methods for determining whether a specific sequence of characters occurs at the beginning or end, respectively, of a string. The StartsWith method's syntax is *string*.**StartsWith**(*subString*), and the EndsWith method's syntax is *string*.**EndsWith**(*subString*). Open the VB2015\Chap08\City Solution\City Solution (City Solution.sln) file. The interface provides a text box for the user to enter the name of a city. The btnAdd_Click procedure should add the city name to the list box, but only if the city name begins with either the letter L or the letters Ch. The letters can be entered in uppercase, lowercase, or a combination of uppercase and lowercase. Test the application appropriately. DISCOVERY

16. Visual Basic provides the Replace method for replacing a sequence of characters in a string with another sequence of characters. The method's syntax is *string*.**Replace**(*oldValue*, *newValue*). When processing the Replace method, the computer makes a temporary copy of the *string* in memory; it then replaces the characters in the copy only. The Replace method returns a string with all occurrences of *oldValue* replaced with *newValue*. Open the Social Security Solution (Social Security Solution.sln) file contained in the VB2015\Chap08\Social Security Solution-Replace DISCOVERY

folder. The interface provides a text box for the user to enter a Social Security number. The btnRemove_Click procedure should verify that the Social Security number is in the correct format. If it is, the procedure should remove the dashes from the number before displaying the number in the lblNumber control. Test the application appropriately.

DISCOVERY

17. In this lesson, you learned how to use the Trim method to remove space characters from both the beginning and end of a string. You can also use the Trim method to remove other characters. The syntax for doing this is *string*.**Trim**[(*trimChars*)]. The optional *trimChars* argument is a comma-separated list of characters that you want removed (trimmed). For example, if the txtInput control contains the string "#$456#", you can remove the number signs and dollar sign from the control's Text property using the statement `txtInput.Text = txtInput.Text.Trim("#"c, "$"c)`. When processing the Trim method, the computer makes a temporary copy of the *string* in memory; it then removes the characters in the copy only. Open the VB2015\Chap08\ Trim Method Solution\Trim Method Solution (Trim Method Solution.sln) file. The btnTrim_Click procedure should remove any leading or trailing dollar signs, spaces, or percent signs. Test the application appropriately.

DISCOVERY

18. Visual Basic provides the TrimStart and TrimEnd methods for removing one or more characters from the beginning or end, respectively, of a string. The TrimStart method's syntax is *string*.**TrimStart**[(*trimChars*)], and the TrimEnd method's syntax is *string*.**TrimEnd**[(*trimChars*)]. The optional *trimChars* argument is a comma-separated list of characters that you want removed (trimmed). For example, if the txtSales control contains the string "$56.80", you can remove the dollar sign from the control's Text property using the statement `txtSales.Text = txtSales.Text.TrimStart("$"c)`. The default value for the *trimChars* argument is the space character (" "c). When processing the TrimStart and TrimEnd methods, the computer makes a temporary copy of the *string* in memory; it then removes the characters from the copy only. Open the VB2015\Chap08\Tax Calculator Solution\Tax Calculator Solution (Tax Calculator Solution.sln) file. The btnCalc_Click procedure should calculate and display the sales tax using the amount entered in the text box and the rate selected in the list box. Be sure to remove any leading dollar signs from the sales amount. Also remove the trailing percent sign from the rate. Test the application appropriately.

DISCOVERY

19. Visual Basic provides the Mid statement for replacing a specified number of characters in a string with another string. The statement's syntax is **Mid(***targetString***,** *start* [**,** *count*]) = *replacementString*. In the syntax, the *targetString* argument is the string in which you want characters replaced, and *replacementString* contains the replacement characters. The *start* argument is the position of the first character you want replaced in the targetString. The first character in the targetString is in position 1; the second is in position 2, and so on. The optional *count* argument specifies the number of characters to replace in the targetString. If the count argument is omitted, the Mid statement replaces the lesser of either the number of characters in the replacementString or the number of characters in the targetString from position *start* through the end of the targetString. Open the VB2015\Chap08\Area Code Solution\Area Code Solution (Area Code Solution.sln) file. The interface provides a text box for the user to enter a phone number, including the area code. The btnChange_Click procedure should verify that the phone number is in the proper format. If the format is valid, the procedure should use the Mid statement to change the area code to 800 before displaying the phone number in the lblNew control. Test the application appropriately.

LESSON B

After studying Lesson B, you should be able to:

- Include a MenuStrip control on a form
- Add elements to a menu
- Assign access keys to menu elements
- Enable and disable a control
- Assign shortcut keys to commonly used menu items
- Code a menu item's Click event procedure
- Include the Like operator in a procedure

Adding a Menu to a Form

The Menus and Toolbars section of the toolbox contains a MenuStrip tool for instantiating a menu strip control. You use a **menu strip control** to include one or more menus on a Windows form. Each menu contains a menu title, which appears on the menu bar at the top of the form. When you click a menu title, its corresponding menu opens and displays a list of options, called menu items. The menu items can be commands (such as Open or Exit), separator bars, or submenu titles. As in all Windows applications, clicking a command on a menu executes the command, and clicking a submenu title opens an additional menu of options. Each of the options on a submenu is referred to as a submenu item. You can use a separator bar to visually group together related items on a menu or submenu. Figure 8-22 identifies the location of these menu elements. Although you can create many levels of submenus, it is best to use only one level in your application because including too many layers of submenus can confuse the user.

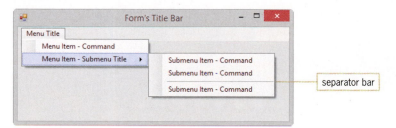

Figure 8-22   Location of menu elements

Each menu element is considered an object and has a set of properties associated with it. The most commonly used properties for a menu element are the Name and Text properties. The programmer uses the Name property to refer to the menu element in code. The Text property stores the menu element's caption, which is the text that the user sees when he or she is working with the menu. The caption indicates the purpose of the menu element. Examples of familiar captions for menu elements include Edit, Save As, Copy, and Exit.

Menu title captions should be one word, with only the first letter capitalized. Each menu title should have a unique access key. The access key allows the user to open the menu by pressing the Alt key in combination with the access key. Unlike the captions for menu titles, the captions for menu items typically consist of one to three words and are entered using book title capitalization. Each menu item should have an access key that is unique within its menu. The access key allows the user to select the item by pressing the access key when the menu is open. If a menu item requires additional information from the user, the Windows standard is to place an ellipsis (...) at the end of the caption. The ellipsis alerts the user that the menu item requires more information before it can perform its task.

The menus included in your application should follow the standard Windows conventions. For example, if your application uses a File menu, it should be the first menu on the menu bar. File menus typically contain commands for opening, saving, and printing files, as well as exiting the application. If your application requires Cut, Copy, and Paste commands, the commands should be placed on an Edit menu, which is usually the second menu on the menu bar.

ChO8B

In the next set of steps, you will add a File menu to the Pizza Game application's interface. The menu will contain three menu items: a New Game command, a separator bar, and an Exit command.

START HERE

To complete the Pizza Game application's interface:

1. If necessary, start Visual Studio 2015. Open the VB2015\Chap08\Pizza Solution\ Pizza Solution (Pizza Solution.sln) file. If necessary, open the designer, Toolbox, and Properties windows. The interface contains five labels, nine picture boxes, one text box, and one button.

2. Click the **MenuStrip** tool, which is located in the Menus & Toolbars section of the toolbox. Drag the mouse pointer to the form, and then release the mouse button. A MenuStrip control named MenuStrip1 appears in the component tray, and the words "Type Here" appear in a box below the form's title bar. See Figure 8-23.

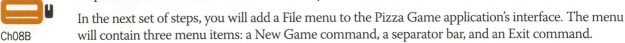
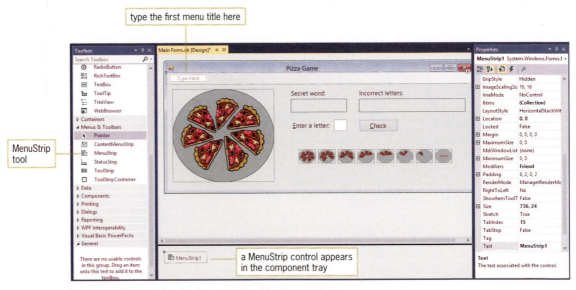

Figure 8-23   MenuStrip control added to the form

3. Auto-hide the toolbox. Click the **Type Here** box on the menu bar, and then type **&File**. See Figure 8-24. You use the Type Here box that appears below the menu title to add a menu item to the File menu. You use the Type Here box that appears to the right of the menu title to add another menu title to the menu bar.

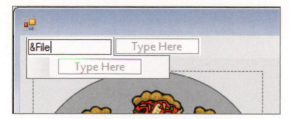

Figure 8-24   Menu title included on the form

4. Press **Enter** and then click the **File** menu title. Scroll the Properties window until you see the Text property, which contains &File. Next, scroll to the top of the Properties window and then click **(Name)**. Type **mnuFile** and then press **Enter**.

5. Click the **Type Here** box that appears below the File menu title. Type **&New Game** and then press **Enter**. Click the **New Game** menu item, and then change its name to **mnuFileNew**.

6. Next, you will add a separator bar to the menu. Place your mouse pointer on the Type Here box that appears below the New Game menu item, but don't click the box. Instead, click the **list arrow** that appears inside the box. See Figure 8-25.

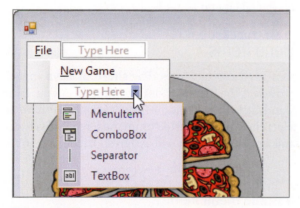

Figure 8-25   Drop-down list

7. Click **Separator** in the list. A horizontal line, called a separator bar, appears below the New Game menu item.

8. Click the **Type Here** box that appears below the separator bar. Type **E&xit** and then press **Enter**. Click the **Exit** menu item, and then change its name to **mnuFileExit**.

9. Save the solution and then start the application. Click **File** on the menu bar. The menu opens and offers two options separated by a separator bar. See Figure 8-26.

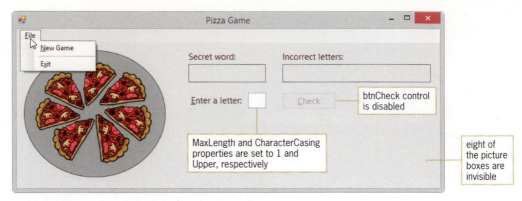

Figure 8-26   File menu opened during run time

10. Click the **Close** button on the form's title bar.

As indicated in Figure 8-26, the text box's MaxLength and CharacterCasing properties are set to 1 and Upper, respectively, and eight of the picture boxes are invisible. Also, the btnCheck control is disabled, which means it is not currently available to the user. You disable a control by setting its **Enabled property** to False either in the Properties window or in code; you enable it by setting the property to True (the default value). When a control is disabled, it appears dimmed (grayed out) during run time, as shown in the figure. The btnCheck control will remain disabled until the user selects the New Game option on the File menu.

Assigning Shortcut Keys to Menu Items

> A menu item's access key can be used only when the menu is open. A menu item's shortcut keys can be used only when the menu is closed.

Commonly used menu items should be assigned shortcut keys. The **shortcut keys** appear to the right of a menu item and allow the user to select the item without opening the menu. Examples of familiar shortcut keys include Ctrl+X and Ctrl+V. In Windows applications that have an Edit menu, Ctrl+X and Ctrl+V are used to select the Cut and Paste commands, respectively, when the Edit menu is closed. In the Pizza Game application, you will assign shortcut keys to the New Game option on the File menu.

START HERE

To assign shortcut keys to the New Game menu item:

1. Click the **New Game** menu item on the File menu. Click **ShortcutKeys** in the Properties window, and then click the **list arrow** in the Settings box. A box opens and allows you to specify a modifier and a key. In this case, the modifier and key will be Ctrl and N, respectively. Click the **Ctrl** check box to select it, and then click the **list arrow** that appears in the Key combo box. An alphabetical list of keys appears. Scroll the list until you see the letter N, and then click **N** in the list. See Figure 8-27.

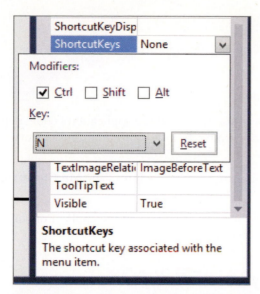

Figure 8-27   Shortcut keys specified in the ShortcutKeys box

2. Press **Enter**. Ctrl+N appears in the ShortcutKeys property in the Properties list. It also appears to the right of the New Game menu item.

3. Auto-hide the Properties window. Save the solution and then start the application. Click **File** on the menu bar. See Figure 8-28.

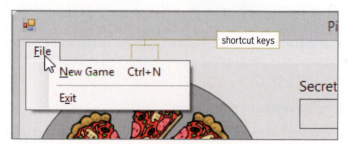

Figure 8-28   Location of the shortcut keys on the menu

4. Click the **Close** button on the form's title bar.

GUI DESIGN TIP Menu Standards

- Menu title captions should be one word, with only the first letter capitalized. Each menu title should have a unique access key.

- Menu item captions can be from one to three words. Use book title capitalization, and assign a unique access key to each menu item on the same menu.

- Assign unique shortcut keys to commonly used menu items.

- If a menu item requires additional information from the user, place an ellipsis (...) at the end of the item's caption, which is entered in the item's Text property.

- Follow the Windows standards for the placement of menu titles and items.

- Use a separator bar to separate groups of related menu items.

Coding the Exit Menu Item

When the user clicks the Exit option on the File menu, the option's Click event procedure should end the application.

START HERE

To code and then test the Exit menu item:

1. Open the Code Editor window, which contains most of the application's code. Replace <your name> and <current date> in the comments with your name and the current date, respectively.

2. Open the code template for the mnuFileExit_Click procedure. Type **Me.Close()** and press **Enter**.

3. Save the solution and then start the application. Click **File** on the application's menu bar and then click **Exit** to end the application.

Coding the txtLetter Control's KeyPress Event

As indicated earlier in Figure 8-26, the text box's MaxLength and CharacterCasing properties are set to 1 and Upper, respectively. As a result, the text box will accept one character only. If the character is a letter of the alphabet, it will be converted to uppercase. In the next set of steps, you will prevent the text box from accepting a character that is not either a letter of the alphabet or the Backspace key. You can do this by using an If...Then...Else statement with the following condition: `e.KeyChar Like "[!A-Za-z]" AndAlso e.KeyChar <> ControlChars.Back`. The subcondition on the left side of the AndAlso operator will evaluate to True if the user's entry is not one of the uppercase or lowercase letters of the alphabet. The subcondition on the right side of the AndAlso operator will evaluate to True if the user's entry is not the Backspace key. If both subconditions evaluate to True, the compound condition will evaluate to True and the text box should not accept the user's entry.

START HERE

To code and then test the KeyPress event procedure:

1. Locate the txtLetter_KeyPress procedure, and then enter the selection structure shown in Figure 8-29.

```
Private Sub txtLetter_KeyPress(sender As Object, e
    ' allows only letters and the Backspace key

    If e.KeyChar Like "[!A-Za-z]" AndAlso
            e.KeyChar <> ControlChars.Back Then
        e.Handled = True
    End If
End Sub
```

enter this selection structure

Figure 8-29   txtLetter_KeyPress procedure

2. Save the solution and then start the application. Type **a** in the text box. Notice that the letter is changed to its uppercase equivalent, A. Press the **Backspace** key to delete the letter A.

3. Next, try to enter a character other than a letter of the alphabet or the Backspace key; you won't be able to do so. Also try to enter more than one letter; here, too, you won't be able to do so.

4. Click **File** on the application's menu bar and then click **Exit**. Close the Code Editor window and then close the solution.

Lesson B Summary

- To add a MenuStrip control to a form:

  Use the MenuStrip tool, which is located in the Menus & Toolbars section of the toolbox.

- To create a menu:

  Replace the words "Type Here" with the menu element's caption. Assign a meaningful name and a unique access key to each menu element, with the exception of separator bars.

- To include a separator bar on a menu:

  Place your mouse pointer on a Type Here box, and then click the list arrow that appears inside the box. Click Separator on the list.

- To enable/disable a control during run time:

  Set its Enabled property to True (enable) or False (disable) either in the Properties window or in code.

- To assign shortcut keys to a menu item:

  Set the menu item's ShortcutKeys property.

Lesson B Key Terms

Enabled property—used to enable (True) or disable (False) a control during run time

Menu strip control—used to include one or more menus on a form

Shortcut keys—appear to the right of a menu item and allow the user to select the item without opening the menu

Lesson B Review Questions

1. The horizontal line in a menu is called _____.

   a. a menu bar   c. an item separator

   b. a separator bar   d. none of the above

2. The underlined letter in a menu element's caption is called _____.

   a. an access key   c. a shortcut key

   b. a menu key   d. none of the above

3. Which of the following allows the user to access a menu item without opening the menu?

    a. an access key   c. shortcut keys

    b. a menu key   d. none of the above

4. Which of the following is false?

    a. Menu titles should be one word only.

    b. Each menu title should have a unique access key.

    c. You should assign shortcut keys to commonly used menu titles.

    d. Menu items should be entered using book title capitalization.

5. Which property determines whether a control is available to the user during run time?

    a. Available   c. Unavailable

    b. Enabled   d. Disabled

6. Explain the difference between a menu item's access key and its shortcut keys.

Lesson B Exercises

INTRODUCTORY

1. Use Windows to make a copy of the Net Pay Solution folder from Lesson A. Rename the copy Net Pay Solution-Menu. Open the Net Pay Solution (Net Pay Solution.sln) file contained in the Net Pay Solution-Menu folder. Remove the Exit button and its associated code. Add a File menu that contains an Exit menu item. The menu item should end the application. Save the solution and then start the application. Use the Exit menu item to end the application.

INTRODUCTORY

2. Open the VB2015\Chap08\Commission Solution\Commission Solution (Commission Solution.sln) file. Add a File menu that contains an Exit menu item. The menu item should end the application. Save the solution and then start the application. Use the Exit menu item to end the application.

INTERMEDIATE

3. Open the VB2015\Chap08\Bonus Solution\Bonus Solution (Bonus Solution.sln) file. Add a File menu and a Calculate menu to the form. Include an Exit menu item on the File menu. Include two menu items on the Calculate menu: 10% Bonus and 15% Bonus. Assign shortcut keys to the Calculate menu's items. The Exit menu item should end the application. The menu items on the Calculate menu should display the appropriate bonus: either 10% of the sales or 15% of the sales. Use a program-defined function to calculate and return the bonus. Test the application appropriately.

LESSON C

After studying Lesson C, you should be able to:

- Include the Length property in a procedure
- Include the Substring method in a procedure
- Include the Like operator in a procedure
- Include the Remove method in a procedure
- Include the Insert method in a procedure
- Include the Contains method in a procedure

Completing the Pizza Game Application

Figure 8-30 shows the Pizza Game application's TOE chart. You coded the mnuFileExit_Click and txtLetter_KeyPress procedures in Lesson B. In this lesson, you will complete the application by coding the mnuFileNew_Click and btnCheck_Click procedures.

Task	Object	Event
1. Clear lblWord, lblIncorrect, and txtLetter 2. Set incorrect guesses counter to 0 3. Get a 6-letter word from player 1, trim spaces, and convert to uppercase 4. Determine whether the word contains 6 letters 5. If the word contains 6 letters, display the full pizza image in picPizzaStatus, display 6 dashes in lblWord, enable btnCheck, and send the focus to txtLetter 6. If the word doesn't contain 6 letters, display "6 letters are required" in a message box and disable btnCheck	mnuFileNew	Click
1. Search the word for the letter entered by player 2 2. If the letter is contained in the word, replace the appropriate dashes in lblWord; if there aren't any other dashes in the word, the game is over because player 2 guessed the word, so display "Great guessing!" in a message box, and disable btnCheck 3. If the letter is not contained in the word, display the letter in lblIncorrect, add 1 to the incorrect guesses counter, and assign the appropriate image to picPizzaStatus; if player 2 made 7 incorrect guesses, the game is over, so display "Sorry, the word is *word*." in a message box, and disable btnCheck 4. Clear txtLetter and send focus to it	btnCheck	Click

Figure 8-30   TOE chart for the Pizza Game application *(continues)*

(continued)

End the application	mnuFileExit	Click
Display the pizza images	picFullPizza, pic6Slices, pic5Slices, pic4Slices, pic3Slices, pic2Slices, pic1Slice, picTray, picPizzaStatus	None
Allow only letters and the Backspace key	txtLetter	KeyPress
Display dashes and letters (from mnuFileNew and btnCheck)	lblWord	None
Display the incorrect letters (from mnuFileNew and btnCheck)	lblIncorrect	None

Figure 8-30 TOE chart for the Pizza Game application

START HERE

To open the Pizza Game application from Lesson B:

1. If necessary, start Visual Studio 2015. Open the Pizza Solution (Pizza Solution.sln) file from Lesson B.

2. Open the Code Editor window. The form's Declarations section declares two class-level variables, as shown in Figure 8-31. The `strWord` variable will store the word entered by player 1, and the `intIncorrect` variable will keep track of the number of incorrect letters entered by player 2.

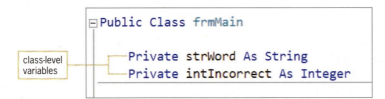

Figure 8-31 Declaration statements for the class-level variables

Coding the File Menu's New Game Option

The mnuFileNew_Click procedure is invoked when the user either clicks the New Game option on the File menu or presses Ctrl+N (the option's shortcut keys). The procedure's pseudocode is shown in Figure 8-32.

```
mnuFileNew Click event procedure
1. clear secret word from lblWord, incorrect letters from lblIncorrect, and letter from txtLetter
2. assign 0 to the counter variable that keeps track of the number of incorrect letters
3. get a 6-letter word from player 1, trim leading and trailing spaces, and convert to uppercase
4. if the word contains 6 letters
        display the full pizza image in picPizzaStatus
        display 6 dashes in lblWord
        enable btnCheck
        send the focus to txtLetter
   else
        display the "6 letters are required" message in a message box
        disable btnCheck
   end if
```

Figure 8-32   Pseudocode for the mnuFileNew_Click procedure

To begin coding the mnuFileNew_Click procedure:

START HERE

1. Open the code template for the mnuFileNew_Click procedure. Type the following comment and then press **Enter** twice:

   ' start a new game

2. According to its pseudocode, the procedure should begin by clearing the contents of the lblWord, lblIncorrect, and txtLetter controls. Enter the following three assignment statements:

   lblWord.Text = String.Empty
   lblIncorrect.Text = String.Empty
   txtLetter.Text = String.Empty

3. Next, the procedure should reset the variable that keeps track of the number of incorrect letters—in this case, the class-level `intIncorrect` variable—to 0. Type the following assignment statement and then press **Enter** twice:

   intIncorrect = 0

4. The third step in the pseudocode gets a word that contains six letters from player 1. The procedure should trim any leading and trailing spaces from the word and also convert the word to uppercase. Enter the following comment and lines of code. Press **Enter** twice after typing the last line.

   ' get a 6-letter word from player 1
   ' trim and convert to uppercase
   strWord = InputBox("Enter a 6-letter word:",
   **   "Pizza Game").Trim.ToUpper**

Next, the procedure should verify that player 1's word contains exactly six letters. Figure 8-33 shows two ways of accomplishing this task. Example 1 uses the Length property and the Substring method; both are shaded in the figure. Example 2 uses the Like operator, which also is shaded in the figure. Although the code in both examples produces the same result, Example 2's code is much more concise and easier to understand.

```
Example 1
Dim blnValidWord As Boolean

' determine whether the word contains 6 letters
blnValidWord = True   ' assume word is valid
If strWord.Length <> 6 Then
    blnValidWord = False
Else
    Dim intIndex As Integer
    Do While intIndex < 6 AndAlso blnValidWord = True
        If strWord.Substring(intIndex, 1) Like "[!A-Z]" Then
            blnValidWord = False
        End If
        intIndex += 1
    Loop
End If

If blnValidWord = True Then
    instructions to be processed when the word is valid
Else
    instructions to be processed when the word is not valid
End If

Example 2
If strWord Like "[A-Z][A-Z][A-Z][A-Z][A-Z][A-Z]" Then
    instructions to be processed when the word is valid
Else
    instructions to be processed when the word is not valid
End If
```

Figure 8-33   Two ways of determining whether the word contains six letters

START HERE ▶   **To complete and then test the mnuFileNew_Click procedure:**

1. Enter the following comment and If clause:

    ' determine whether the word contains 6 letters
    If strWord Like "[A-Z][A-Z][A-Z][A-Z][A-Z]][A-Z]" Then

2. If player 1's word contains six letters, the selection structure's true path should display the image of the full pizza in the picPizzaStatus control. Enter the following comment and assignment statement:

    ' display the full pizza image
    picPizzaStatus.Image = picFullPizza.Image

3. Next, the true path should display six dashes (one for each letter in the word) in the lblWord control. Enter the following comment and assignment statement:

    ' display 6 dashes
    lblWord.Text = "------"

4. The final two tasks in the selection structure's true path enable the btnCheck control and send the focus to the txtLetter control. Enter the following comment and statements:

    ' enable button and set focus
    btnCheck.Enabled = True
    txtLetter.Focus()

5. Next, you need to code the selection structure's false path. According to the pseudocode, the false path should display a message and disable the btnCheck control when player 1's word does not contain six letters. Enter the additional code indicated in Figure 8-34.

enter these four lines of code

```
            txtLetter.Focus()
        Else
            MessageBox.Show("6 letters are required", "Pizza Game",
                            MessageBoxButtons.OK, MessageBoxIcon.Information)
            btnCheck.Enabled = False
        End If
    End Sub
```

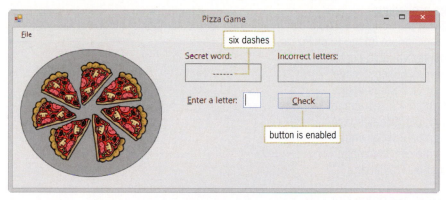

Figure 8-34 Selection structure's false path

6. Save the solution and then run the application. Click **File** and then click **New Game**. The Pizza Game dialog box opens and prompts you to enter a word that contains six letters. Type **leaves** in the dialog box and then press **Enter**. Six dashes appear in the Secret word box. In addition, the Check button is enabled for the user. See Figure 8-35.

Figure 8-35 Result of entering a valid word

7. Next, you will enter a word that contains fewer than six letters. Press **Ctrl+n**, which are the shortcut keys for the New Game option. Type **fall** in the dialog box and then press **Enter**. The message "6 letters are required" appears in a message box. Close the message box. Notice that the Check button is now disabled.

8. On your own, test the procedure using a word that has more than six letters. Also test it using a word that contains five characters followed by a number. In both cases, the message "6 letters are required" appears in a message box. When you are finished testing the procedure, use the **Exit** option on the game's File menu to end the application.

Completing the Check Button's Click Event Procedure

Figure 8-36 shows the pseudocode for the btnCheck_Click procedure. It also shows the pseudocode for two independent Sub procedures used by the btnCheck_Click procedure: AssignImage and DetermineGameOver.

btnCheck Click event procedure
1. repeat for each letter in player 1's word
        if the current letter is the same as the letter entered by player 2
                replace the corresponding dash in lblWord
                assign True to the blnDashReplaced variable
        end if
    end repeat
2. if the blnDashReplaced variable contains True
        call the DetermineGameOver procedure to determine whether player 2 guessed the
        word; pass the blnDashReplaced variable
    else
        display player 2's letter in lblIncorrect
        add 1 to the counter variable that keeps track of the number of incorrect letters
        call the AssignImage procedure to display the appropriate image in picPizzaStatus

        call the DetermineGameOver procedure to determine whether player 2 made 7
        incorrect guesses; pass the blnDashReplaced variable
    end if
3. clear txtLetter and send focus to it

AssignImage procedure
use the value in the counter variable that keeps track of the number of incorrect letters to
assign the appropriate image to picPizzaStatus
    if the counter variable contains:
    1   assign pic6Slices image
    2   assign pic5Slices image
    3   assign pic4Slices image
    4   assign pic3Slices image
    5   assign pic2Slices image
    6   assign pic1Slice image
    7   assign picTray image

DetermineGameOver procedure
if a dash was replaced in player 1's word
    if there aren't any other dashes in the word
        display "Great guessing!" in a message box
        disable btnCheck
    end if
else
    if the user entered 7 incorrect letters
        display "Sorry, the word is word." in a message box
        disable btnCheck
    end if
end if

Figure 8-36   Pseudocode for the btnCheck_Click, AssignImage, and DetermineGameOver
procedures

The AssignImage and DetermineGameOver procedures have already been coded for you.
The Code Editor window also contains most of the btnCheck_Click procedure's code. You will
complete the procedure in the next set of steps.

To complete the btnCheck_Click procedure:

START HERE

1. Locate the btnCheck_Click procedure. The first step in the procedure's pseudocode is a loop that performs its instructions for each letter in player 1's word. The word, which is stored in the class-level `strWord` variable, contains six letters whose indexes are 0, 1, 2, 3, 4, and 5. Click the **blank line** below the `' look at each letter in the word` comment, and then enter the following For clause:

   For intIndex As Integer = 0 To 5

2. Change the Next clause to **Next intIndex** and then click the **blank line** below the For clause.

3. According to the pseudocode, the first instruction in the loop is a selection structure that compares the current letter in the `strWord` variable with the letter entered by player 2. Recall from Lesson A that you can use the Substring method to access an individual character in a string. The method's *startIndex* argument is the index of the first character you want to access, and its optional *numCharsToAccess* argument specifies the number of characters you want to access. Enter the following If clause:

   If strWord.Substring(intIndex, 1) = strLetter Then

4. If the current letter in the `strWord` variable matches player 2's letter, the selection structure's true path should replace the corresponding dash in the lblWord control with player 2's letter. You can use the Remove and Insert methods to make the replacement. Enter the following comments and assignment statements:

   ' if the letter appears in the word, replace
   ' the corresponding dash with the letter
   lblWord.Text =
       lblWord.Text.Remove(intIndex, 1)
   lblWord.Text =
       lblWord.Text.Insert(intIndex, strLetter)

5. Finally, the selection structure's true path should assign the Boolean value True to the `blnDashReplaced` variable to indicate that a replacement was made. Type **blnDashReplaced = True** and then click the **blank line** below the Next clause.

6. Save the solution.

Before testing the btnCheck_Click procedure, review the code contained in the AssignImage and DetermineGameOver procedures. Notice that the DetermineGameOver procedure uses the Contains method to determine whether there are any dashes in the lblWord control.

To test the btnCheck_Click procedure:

START HERE

1. Start the application. Click **File** and then click **New Game**. Type **summer** in the input dialog box, and then press **Enter**. The picPizzaStatus control shows seven slices of pizza.

2. Type **m** in the Enter a letter text box, and then press **Enter**. The letter M replaces two of the dashes in the Secret word box.

3. Type **x** in the text box and then press **Enter**. The letter X appears in the Incorrect letters box, and the picPizzaStatus control now shows only six slices of pizza.

4. Type the following letters in the text box, pressing **Enter** after typing each one: **a**, **e**, **s**, **r**, **i**, and **u**. Each time you make an incorrect guess, another slice of pizza is removed from the picPizzaStatus control.

5. When the Game Over message box opens, drag it to the location shown in Figure 8-37.

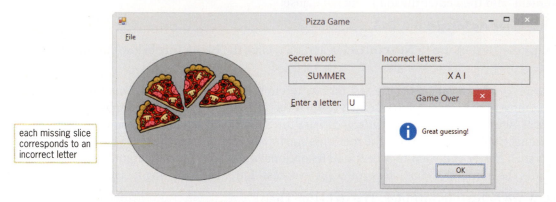

each missing slice corresponds to an incorrect letter

Figure 8-37 Result of guessing the secret word

6. Close the message box and then press **Ctrl+n**. Type **window** in the input dialog box and then press **Enter**.

7. Next, type the following letters in the text box, pressing **Enter** after typing each one: **c**, **w**, **t**, **e**, **a**, **n**, **p**, **x**, and **z**.

8. When the Game Over message box opens, drag it to the location shown in Figure 8-38.

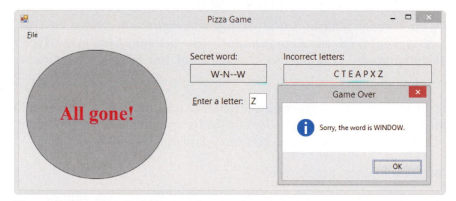

Figure 8-38 Result of not guessing the secret word

9. Close the message box. Click **File** on the application's menu bar, and then click **Exit**. Close the Code Editor window and then close the solution. Figure 8-39 shows the application's code.

```
 1 ' Name:          Pizza Project
 2 ' Purpose:       A game that allows the user to guess a
 3 '                word letter-by-letter
 4 ' Programmer:    <your name> on <current date>
 5
 6 Option Explicit On
 7 Option Strict On
 8 Option Infer Off
 9
10 Public Class frmMain
11
12     Private strWord As String
13     Private intIncorrect As Integer
14
15     Private Sub AssignImage()
16         ' assign appropriate image
17
18         Select Case intIncorrect
19             Case 1
20                 picPizzaStatus.Image = pic6Slices.Image
21             Case 2
22                 picPizzaStatus.Image = pic5Slices.Image
23             Case 3
24                 picPizzaStatus.Image = pic4Slices.Image
25             Case 4
26                 picPizzaStatus.Image = pic3Slices.Image
27             Case 5
28                 picPizzaStatus.Image = pic2Slices.Image
29             Case 6
30                 picPizzaStatus.Image = pic1Slice.Image
31             Case Else
32                 picPizzaStatus.Image = picTray.Image
33         End Select
34     End Sub
35
36     Private Sub DetermineGameOver(ByVal
    blnADashWasReplaced As Boolean)
37         ' determine whether the game is over and
38         ' take the appropriate action
39
40         If blnADashWasReplaced Then
41             ' if the word does not contain any dashes, the game
42             ' is over because player 2 guessed the word
43             If lblWord.Text.Contains("-") = False Then
44                 MessageBox.Show("Great guessing!", "Game Over",
45                                 MessageBoxButtons.OK,
46                                 MessageBoxIcon.Information)
47                 btnCheck.Enabled = False
48             End If
49         Else
50             ' if 7 incorrect guesses, the game is over
51             If intIncorrect = 7 Then
52                 MessageBox.Show("Sorry, the word is " &
53                                 strWord & ".", "Game Over",
```

Figure 8-39   Pizza Game application's code (continues)

(continued)

```
54                                    MessageBoxButtons.OK,
55                                    MessageBoxIcon.Information)
56                btnCheck.Enabled = False
57            End If
58        End If
59    End Sub
60
61    Private Sub btnCheck_Click(sender As Object, e As EventArgs
      ) Handles btnCheck.Click
62        ' check if the letter appears in the word
63
64        Dim strLetter As String
65        Dim blnDashReplaced As Boolean
66
67        strLetter = txtLetter.Text
68
69        ' look at each letter in the word
70        For intIndex As Integer = 0 To 5
71            If strWord.Substring(intIndex, 1) = strLetter Then
72                ' if the letter appears in the word, replace
73                ' the corresponding dash with the letter
74                lblWord.Text =
75                    lblWord.Text.Remove(intIndex, 1)
76                lblWord.Text =
77                    lblWord.Text.Insert(intIndex, strLetter)
78                blnDashReplaced = True
79            End If
80        Next intIndex
81
82        If blnDashReplaced Then
83            Call DetermineGameOver(blnDashReplaced)
84        Else  ' no dash was replaced
85            lblIncorrect.Text =
86                lblIncorrect.Text & " " & strLetter
87            intIncorrect += 1
88            Call AssignImage()
89            Call DetermineGameOver(blnDashReplaced)
90        End If
91
92        ' clear text box and set focus
93        txtLetter.Text = String.Empty
94        txtLetter.Focus()
95    End Sub
96
97    Private Sub txtLetter_KeyPress(sender As Object,
      e As KeyPressEventArgs) Handles txtLetter.KeyPress
98        ' allows only letters and the Backspace key
99
100       If e.KeyChar Like "[!A-Za-z]" AndAlso
101           e.KeyChar <> ControlChars.Back Then
102           e.Handled = True
103       End If
104   End Sub
105
```

Figure 8-39   Pizza Game application's code (continues)

(continued)

```
106     Private Sub mnuFileExit_Click(sender As Object, e As EventArgs
        ) Handles mnuFileExit.Click
107        Me.Close()
108
109     End Sub
110
111     Private Sub mnuFileNew_Click(sender As Object, e As EventArgs
        ) Handles mnuFileNew.Click
112        ' start a new game
113
114        lblWord.Text = String.Empty
115        lblIncorrect.Text = String.Empty
116        txtLetter.Text = String.Empty
117        intIncorrect = 0
118
119        ' get a 6-letter word from player 1
120        ' trim and convert to uppercase
121        strWord = InputBox("Enter a 6-letter word:",
122                           "Pizza Game").Trim.ToUpper
123
124        ' determine whether the word contains 6 letters
125        If strWord Like "[A-Z][A-Z][A-Z][A-Z][A-Z][A-Z]" Then
126            ' display the full pizza image
127            picPizzaStatus.Image = picFullPizza.Image
128            ' display 6 dashes
129            lblWord.Text = "------"
130            ' enable button and set focus
131            btnCheck.Enabled = True
132            txtLetter.Focus()
133        Else
134            MessageBox.Show("6 letters are required", "Pizza Game",
135                    MessageBoxButtons.OK,
                        MessageBoxIcon.Information)
136            btnCheck.Enabled = False
137        End If
138    End Sub
139 End Class
```

Figure 8-39 Pizza Game application's code

Lesson C Summary

- To determine the length of a string:

  Use the string's Length property.

- To access one or more characters in a string:

  Use the Substring method.

- To use pattern matching to compare two strings:

  Use the Like operator.

- To remove a specified number of characters located anywhere in a string:

  Use the Remove method.

- To insert characters anywhere in a string:

  Use the Insert method.

- To determine whether a specific character is contained in a string:

  Use the Contains method.

Lesson C Key Terms

There are no key terms in Lesson C.

Lesson C Review Questions

1. The `strItem` variable contains 25 characters. Which of the following For clauses will access each character contained in the variable, character by character?

   a. `For intIndex As Integer = 0 To 25`
   b. `For intIndex As Integer = 1 To 25`
   c. `For intIndex As Integer = 0 To strItem.Length - 1`
   d. `For intIndex As Integer = 1 To strItem.Length - 1`

2. Which of the following changes the contents of the `strName` variable from Will to William?

   a. `strName = strName.Append(5, "iam")`
   b. `strName = strName.Append(4, "iam")`
   c. `strName = strName.Insert(5, "iam")`
   d. `strName = strName.Insert(4, "iam")`

3. If the `strWord` variable contains the string "Irene Turner", what value will the `strWord.Contains("e")` method return?

   a. True   c. 2
   b. False   d. 3

4. The `strItem` variable contains uppercase letters only. Which of the following determines whether the variable contains either the word "SHIRT" or the word "SKIRT"?

   a. `If strItem Like "S[H-K]IRT" Then`
   b. `If strItem Like "S[HK]IRT" Then`
   c. `If strItem = "S[HK]IRT" Then`
   d. `If strItem = "SHIRT" AndAlso strItem = "SKIRT" Then`

5. Which of the following returns the Boolean value True when the `strPetName` variable contains the string "Felix"?

   a. `strPetName.Contains("x")`
   b. `strPetName Like "F*"`
   c. `strPetName.Substring(1, 2) = "el"`
   d. all of the above

Lesson C Exercises

1. Open the VB2015\Chap08\Item Solution\Item Solution (Item Solution.sln) file. The btnVerify_Click procedure should determine whether the item number was entered in the required format: two digits, a letter, a hyphen, a letter, a hyphen, and a digit. The procedure should display a message indicating whether the format is correct or incorrect. Test the application appropriately. **INTRODUCTORY**

2. Open the VB2015\Chap08\Color Solution\Color Solution (Color Solution.sln) file. The btnDisplay_Click procedure should display the color of the item whose item number is entered by the user. All item numbers contain exactly five characters. All items are available in four colors: blue, green, red, and white. The third character in the item number indicates the item's color, as follows: a B or b indicates Blue, a G or g indicates Green, an R or r indicates Red, and a W or w indicates White. The procedure should display an appropriate error message if the item number does not contain exactly five characters, or if the third character is not one of the valid color characters. Test the application appropriately. **INTRODUCTORY**

3. In this exercise, you modify the Pizza Game application completed in this lesson. Use Windows to make a copy of the Pizza Solution folder. Rename the copy Modified Pizza Solution. Open the Pizza Solution (Pizza Solution.sln) file contained in the Modified Pizza Solution folder. Modify the code to allow Player 1 to enter a word that contains any number of letters, up to a maximum of 10 letters. Test the application appropriately. **INTERMEDIATE**

4. Open the VB2015\Chap08\Reverse Solution\Reverse Solution (Reverse Solution.sln) file. The interface provides a text box for the user to enter one or more words. The btnReverse_Click procedure should display the letters in reverse order. In other words, if the user enters the words "Have a great day", the procedure should display "yad taerg a evaH". Test the application appropriately. **INTERMEDIATE**

5. Open the VB2015\Chap08\Proper Solution\Proper Solution (Proper Solution.sln) file. The interface provides a text box for entering a person's first and last names. The btnProper_Click procedure should display the first and last names in the proper case. In other words, the first and last names should begin with an uppercase letter and the remaining letters should be lowercase. If the user enters only one name, display the name in proper case. Test the application appropriately. **INTERMEDIATE**

6. Open the VB2015\Chap08\Shipping Solution\Shipping Solution (Shipping Solution.sln) file. The interface provides a text box for entering a shipping code, which should consist of two numbers followed by either one or two letters. The letter(s) represent the delivery method, as follows: MS represents Mail – Standard, MP represents Mail – Priority, FS represents FedEx – Standard, FO represents FedEx – Overnight, and U represents UPS. The btnDelivery_Click procedure should use the Like operator to determine the delivery method to select in the list box. For example, if the shipping code is 73mp, the procedure should select the Mail – Priority item in the list box. The procedure should display an **INTERMEDIATE**

error message when the shipping code does not contain two numbers followed by one or two letters, or when the letters do not represent a valid delivery method. Test the application using the following data: 73mp, 34fs, 12u, 78h, 9FO, 88FO, and 34ms.

INTERMEDIATE   7.   Before completing this exercise, you should complete Lesson A's Discovery Exercise 16. Open the VB2015\Chap08\Jacobson Solution\Jacobson Solution (Jacobson Solution.sln) file. The interface provides a text box for entering a password. The password can contain five, six, or seven characters; however, none of the characters can be a space. The btnDisplay_Click procedure should create and display a new password using the following four rules. First, replace all numbers with the letter B. Second, replace the vowels A, E, and O with the letter X. Third, replace the vowels I and U with the number 6. Fourth, reverse the characters in the password. Test the application appropriately.

ADVANCED   8.   Each salesperson at Rembrandt Auto-Mart is assigned an ID number that consists of five characters. The first three characters are numbers. The fourth character is a letter: either the letter N if the salesperson sells new cars or the letter U if the salesperson sells used cars. The fifth character is also a letter: either the letter F if the salesperson is a full-time employee or the letter P if the salesperson is a part-time employee. Create an application, using the following names for the solution and project, respectively: Rembrandt Solution and Rembrandt Project. Save the application in the VB2015\ Chap08 folder. Create the interface shown in Figure 8-40. Make the Calculate button the default button. The application should allow the sales manager to enter the ID and the number of cars sold for as many salespeople as needed. The btnCalc_Click procedure should display the total number of cars sold by each of the following four categories of employees: full-time employees, part-time employees, employees selling new cars, and employees selling used cars. Test the application appropriately.

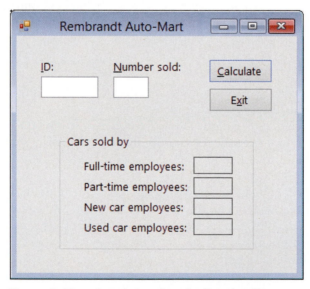

Figure 8-40   Sample interface for Exercise 8

ADVANCED   9.   Credit card companies typically assign a special digit, called a check digit, to the end of each customer's credit card number. The check digit allows companies to verify that the credit card number was entered accurately. Many methods for creating the check digit have been developed, including the one you will use in this exercise. Create an application, using the following names for the solution and project, respectively: Merryweather Solution and Merryweather Project. Save the application in the VB2015\Chap08 folder. Create the interface shown in Figure 8-41. Make the Verify button the default button. The interface provides a text box for entering a five-digit credit card number, with the fifth digit being the check digit. The btnVerify_Click procedure should use the method shown and illustrated in Figure 8-42 to verify the credit card number. It should then display a message indicating whether the credit card number is valid or invalid. For example, if the user enters 18531 as the credit card number, the application should indicate that the credit card number is valid. However, if the user enters 1853 followed by either the number 0 or any number from 2 through 9, the application should indicate that the credit card number is not valid. Test the application appropriately.

Figure 8-41   Sample interface for Exercise 9

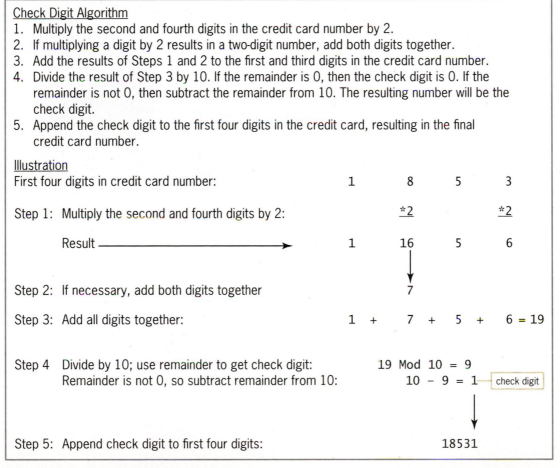

Check Digit Algorithm
1. Multiply the second and fourth digits in the credit card number by 2.
2. If multiplying a digit by 2 results in a two-digit number, add both digits together.
3. Add the results of Steps 1 and 2 to the first and third digits in the credit card number.
4. Divide the result of Step 3 by 10. If the remainder is 0, then the check digit is 0. If the remainder is not 0, then subtract the remainder from 10. The resulting number will be the check digit.
5. Append the check digit to the first four digits in the credit card, resulting in the final credit card number.

Illustration
First four digits in credit card number: 1   8   5   3

Step 1: Multiply the second and fourth digits by 2:   *2   *2

         Result ──────────────────────────→   1   16   5   6

                                                                    ↓
Step 2: If necessary, add both digits together   7

Step 3: Add all digits together: 1   +   7   +   5   +   6 = 19

Step 4   Divide by 10; use remainder to get check digit: 19 Mod 10 = 9
         Remainder is not 0, so subtract remainder from 10:   10 − 9 = 1── check digit
                                                                                        ↓
Step 5: Append check digit to first four digits: 18531

Figure 8-42   Check digit algorithm and illustration

ADVANCED   10. Open the VB2015\Chap08\Count Solution\Count Solution (Count Solution.sln) file. The interface provides a text box for the user to enter a string. The btnSearch_Click procedure should prompt the user to enter the sequence of characters for which he or she wants to search. The procedure should determine the number of times the sequence of characters appears in the string. Use the IndexOf method to search the string for the sequence of characters. Save the solution and then start the application. Enter the string "The weather is beautiful!" (without the quotes), and then click the Search button. Search for the two characters "ea" (without the quotes). The two characters appear twice in the string. On your own, test the application using other data.

SWAT THE BUGS   11. Open the Debug Solution (Debug Solution.sln) file contained in the VB2015\Chap08\ Debug Solution 1 folder. Open the Code Editor window and review the existing code. Start and then test the application. Notice that the application is not working correctly. Correct the application's code, and then test it appropriately.

SWAT THE BUGS   12. Open the Debug Solution (Debug Solution.sln) file contained in the VB2015\Chap08\ Debug Solution 2 folder. Open the Code Editor window and review the existing code. Start and then test the application. Notice that the application is not working correctly. Correct the application's code, and then test it appropriately.

SWAT THE BUGS   13. Open the Debug Solution (Debug Solution.sln) file contained in the VB2015\Chap08\ Debug Solution 3 folder. Open the Code Editor window and review the existing code. Start and then test the application. Notice that the application is not working correctly. Correct the application's code, and then test it appropriately.

CHAPTER 9

Arrays

Coding the Die Tracker Application

In this chapter, you will code an application that simulates the rolling of a die. The application will display the number of times each of the six die faces appears.

Previewing the Die Tracker Application

Before you start the first lesson in this chapter, you will preview the completed application contained in the VB2015\Chap09 folder.

START HERE

To preview the completed application:

1. Use Windows to locate and then open the VB2015\Chap09 folder. Right-click **Die Tracker** (**Die Tracker.exe**) and then click the **Open** button. Click the **Roll** button. A die face appears in the picRandDie control, and its associated counter label contains the number 1. See Figure 9-1. Because the Roll button's Click event procedure uses random numbers, your die face and counter label might be different from those shown in the figure.

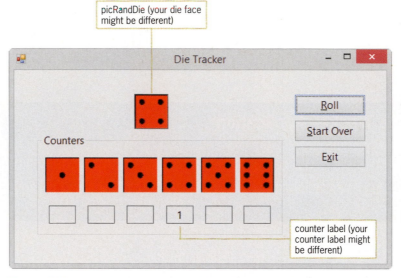

Figure 9-1   Result of clicking the Roll button the first time

2. Click the **Roll** button several more times. Each time you click the button, a die face appears in the picRandDie control and its associated counter label is updated by 1.

3. Next, click the **Start Over** button. The contents of the counter labels and the picRandDie control are cleared. Click the **Roll** button. A die face appears in the picRandDie control, and its associated counter label contains the number 1.

4. Click the **Exit** button.

Before you can begin coding the Die Tracker application, you need to learn about arrays. One-dimensional arrays are covered in Lessons A and B. Lesson C covers two-dimensional arrays. You will code the Die Tracker application in Lesson B. Be sure to complete each lesson in full and do all of the end-of-lesson questions and several exercises before continuing to the next lesson.

LESSON A

After studying Lesson A, you should be able to:

- Declare and initialize a one-dimensional array
- Store data in a one-dimensional array
- Determine the number of array elements and the highest subscript
- Traverse a one-dimensional array
- Code a loop using the For Each...Next statement
- Compute the total and average of a one-dimensional array's contents
- Find the highest value in a one-dimensional array
- Sort a one-dimensional array

Arrays

All of the variables you have used so far have been simple variables. A **simple variable**, also called a **scalar variable**, is one that is unrelated to any other variable in memory. At times, however, you will encounter situations in which some of the variables *are* related to each other. In those cases, it is easier and more efficient to treat the related variables as a group.

You already are familiar with the concept of grouping. The clothes in your closet are probably separated into groups, such as coats, sweaters, shirts, and so on. Grouping your clothes in this manner allows you to easily locate your favorite sweater because you only need to look through the sweater group rather than through the entire closet. You may also have the songs on your MP3 player grouped by either music type or artist. If the songs are grouped by artist, it will take only a few seconds to find all of your Katy Perry songs and, depending on the number of Katy Perry songs you own, only a short time after that to locate a particular song.

When you group together related variables, the group is referred to as an array of variables or, more simply, an **array**. You might use an array of 50 variables to store the population of each U.S. state. Or, you might use an array of eight variables to store the sales made in each of your company's eight sales regions. Storing data in an array increases the efficiency of a program because data can be both stored in and retrieved from the computer's internal memory much faster than it can be written to and read from a file on a disk. In addition, after the data is entered into an array, which typically is done at the beginning of a program, the program can use the data as many times as necessary without having to enter the data again. Your company's sales program, for example, can use the sales amounts stored in an array to calculate the total company sales and the percentage that each region contributed to the total sales. It can also use the sales amounts in the array either to calculate the average sales amount or to simply display the sales made in a specific region. As you will learn in this lesson, the variables in an array can be used just like any other variables. You can assign values to them, use them in calculations, display their contents, and so on.

The most commonly used arrays in business applications are one-dimensional and two-dimensional. You will learn about one-dimensional arrays in this lesson and in Lesson B. Two-dimensional arrays are covered in Lesson C. Arrays having more than two dimensions are beyond the scope of this book.

At this point, it is important to point out that arrays are one of the more challenging topics for beginning programmers. Therefore, it is important for you to read and study each section in each lesson thoroughly before moving on to the next section. If you still feel overwhelmed at the end of a lesson, try reading the lesson again, paying particular attention to the examples and procedures shown in the figures.

One-Dimensional Arrays

A subscript is also called an index.

The variables in an array are stored in consecutive locations in the computer's internal memory. Each variable in an array has the same name and data type. You distinguish one variable in a **one-dimensional array** from another variable in the same array using a unique number. The unique number, which is always an integer, is called a subscript. The **subscript** indicates the variable's position in the array and is assigned by the computer when the array is created in internal memory. The first variable in a one-dimensional array is assigned a subscript of 0, the second a subscript of 1, and so on.

You refer to each variable in an array by the array's name and the variable's subscript, which is specified in a set of parentheses immediately following the array name. Figure 9-2 illustrates a one-dimensional array named `strScientists` that contains three variables. You use `strScientists(0)`—read "`strScientists` sub zero"—to refer to the first variable in the array. You use `strScientists(1)` to refer to the second variable in the array, and you use `strScientists(2)` to refer to the third (and last) variable in the array. The last subscript in an array is always one number less than the total number of variables in the array; this is because array subscripts in Visual Basic (and in many other programming languages) start at 0.

strScientists(0)	strScientists(1)	strScientists(2)
Marie Curie	Charles Darwin	Albert Einstein

Figure 9-2   Illustration of the one-dimensional `strScientists` array
Image by Diane Zak; created with Reallusion CrazyTalk Animator

Declaring a One-Dimensional Array

Before you can use an array in a program, you must declare (create) it using one of the two syntax versions shown in Figure 9-3. The {Dim | Private | Static} portion in each version indicates that you can select only one of the keywords appearing within the braces. The appropriate keyword depends on whether you are creating a procedure-level array or a class-level array. *ArrayName* is the name of the array, and *dataType* is the type of data the array variables, referred to as **elements**, will store. In syntax Version 1, *highestSubscript* is an integer that specifies the highest subscript in the array. Because the first element in a one-dimensional array has a subscript of 0, the array will contain one element more than the number specified in the highestSubscript argument. In other words, an array whose highest subscript is 2 will contain three elements. In syntax Version 2, *initialValues* is a comma-separated list of values you want assigned to the array elements. Also included in Figure 9-3 are examples of using both versions of the syntax.

Declaring a One-Dimensional Array

Syntax – Version 1
{**Dim** | **Private** | **Static**} *arrayName*(*highestSubscript*) **As** *dataType*

Syntax – Version 2
{**Dim** | **Private** | **Static**} *arrayName*() **As** *dataType* = {*initialValues*}

Example 1
```
Dim strWarehouse(2) As String
```
declares a three-element procedure-level array named `strWarehouse`; each element is automatically initialized using the keyword `Nothing`

Example 2
```
Static intNumbers(4) As Integer
```
declares a static, five-element procedure-level array named `intNumbers`; each element is automatically initialized to 0

Example 3
```
Dim strBond() As String = {"Goldfinger", "Moonraker",
                          "Skyfall", "For Your Eyes Only"}
```
declares and initializes a four-element procedure-level array named `strBond`

Example 4
```
Private dblRates() As Double = {2.5, 3.25, 4.5, 9.75, 5.5}
```
declares and initializes a five-element class-level array named `dblRates`

Figure 9-3 Syntax versions and examples of declaring a one-dimensional array

Like class-level variables, class-level arrays are declared in the form's Declarations section.

When you use syntax Version 1, the computer automatically initializes each array element when the array is created. If the array's data type is String, each element is initialized using the keyword `Nothing`. As you learned in Chapter 3, variables initialized to `Nothing` do not actually contain the word *Nothing*; rather, they contain no data at all. Elements in a numeric array are initialized to the number 0, and elements in a Boolean array are initialized using the Boolean keyword `False`. Date array elements are initialized to 12:00 AM January 1, 0001.

Rather than having the computer use a default value to initialize each array element, you can use syntax Version 2 to specify each element's initial value when the array is declared. Assigning initial values to an array is often referred to as **populating the array**. You list the initial values in the initialValues section of the syntax, using commas to separate the values, and you enclose the list of values in braces ({}).

Notice that syntax Version 2 does not include the highestSubscript argument; instead, an empty set of parentheses follows the array name. The computer automatically calculates the highest subscript based on the number of values listed in the initialValues section. Because the first subscript in a one-dimensional array is the number 0, the highest subscript is always one number less than the number of values listed in the initialValues section. The Dim statement in Example 3 in Figure 9-3, for instance, creates a four-element array with subscripts of 0, 1, 2, and 3. Similarly, the Private statement in Example 4 creates a five-element array with subscripts of 0, 1, 2, 3, and 4. The arrays are initialized as shown in Figure 9-4.

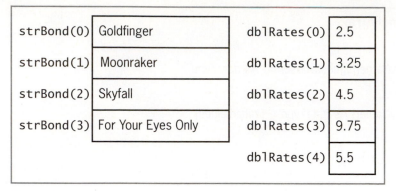

Figure 9-4 Illustration of the `strBond` and `dblRates` arrays

Storing Data in a One-Dimensional Array

After an array is declared, you can use another statement to store a different value in an array element. Examples of such statements include assignment statements and statements that contain the TryParse method. Figure 9-5 shows examples of both types of statements.

Storing Data in a One-Dimensional Array

Example 1
```
strWarehouse(0) = "Nashville"
```
assigns the string "Nashville" to the first element in the `strWarehouse` array

Example 2
```
For intX As Integer = 1 To 5
    intNumbers(intX - 1) = intX ^ 2
Next intX
```
assigns the squares of the numbers from 1 through 5 to the `intNumbers` array

Example 3
```
Dim intSub As Integer
Do While intSub < 5
    intNumbers(intSub) = 100
    intSub += 1
Loop
```
assigns the number 100 to each element in the `intNumbers` array

Example 4
```
dblRates(1) = dblRates(1) * 1.25
```
multiplies the contents of the second element in the `dblRates` array by 1.25 and then assigns the result to the element; you also can write this statement as `dblRates(1) *= 1.25`

Example 5
```
Double.TryParse(txtRate.Text, dblRates(2))
```
assigns either the value entered in the txtRate control (converted to Double) or the number 0 to the third element in the `dblRates` array

---

Figure 9-5 Examples of statements used to store data in a one-dimensional array

Determining the Number of Elements in a One-Dimensional Array

The number of elements in a one-dimensional array is stored as an integer in the array's **Length property**. Figure 9-6 shows the property's syntax and includes an example of using the property. The Length function is highlighted in the example.

Using a One-Dimensional Array's Length Property

Syntax
arrayName.**Length**

Example
```
Dim strNames(3) As String
Dim intNumElements As Integer
intNumElements = strNames.Length
```
assigns the number 4 to the `intNumElements` variable

Figure 9-6   Syntax and an example of a one-dimensional array's Length property

Determining the Highest Subscript in a One-Dimensional Array

As you learned earlier, the highest subscript in a one-dimensional array is always one number less than the number of array elements. Therefore, one way to determine the highest subscript is by subtracting the number 1 from the array's Length property. However, you also can use the array's GetUpperBound method, as shown in Figure 9-7. The **GetUpperBound method** returns an integer that represents the highest subscript in the specified dimension in the array. When used with a one-dimensional array, the specified dimension, which appears between the parentheses after the method's name, is always 0. (The GetUpperBound method is highlighted in the example.)

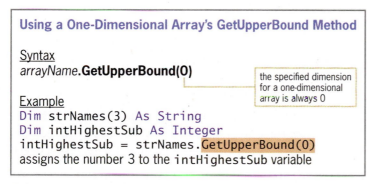

Using a One-Dimensional Array's GetUpperBound Method

Syntax
arrayName.**GetUpperBound(0)**

> the specified dimension for a one-dimensional array is always 0

Example
```
Dim strNames(3) As String
Dim intHighestSub As Integer
intHighestSub = strNames.GetUpperBound(0)
```
assigns the number 3 to the `intHighestSub` variable

Figure 9-7   Syntax and an example of a one-dimensional array's GetUpperBound method

YOU DO IT 1!

Create an application named YouDoIt 1 and save it in the VB2015\Chap09 folder. Add two labels and a button to the form. The button's Click event procedure should declare and initialize an Integer array named `intNums`. Use the following numbers to initialize the array: 2, 4, 6, 8, 10, and 12. The procedure should display the number of array elements in the label controls. Use the Length property for one of the labels, and use the GetUpperBound method for the other label. Code the procedure. Save the solution, and then start and test the application. Close the solution.

Traversing a One-Dimensional Array

At times, you may need to traverse an array, which means to look at each array element, one by one, beginning with the first element and ending with the last element. You traverse an array using a loop. Figure 9-8 shows two examples of loops that traverse the `strBond` array, displaying each element's value in the lstBondMovies control.

Traversing a One-Dimensional Array

Example 1—For...Next
```
Dim intHighSub As Integer = strBond.GetUpperBound(0)
For intSub As Integer = 0 To intHighSub
    lstBondMovies.Items.Add(strBond(intSub))
Next intSub
```

Example 2—Do...Loop
```
Dim intHighSub As Integer = strBond.Length - 1
Dim intSub As Integer
Do While intSub <= intHighSub
    lstBondMovies.Items.Add(strBond(intSub))
    intSub += 1
Loop
```

Figure 9-8   Examples of loops used to traverse a one-dimensional array

START HERE

To code and then test the Bond Movies application:

1. If necessary, start Visual Studio 2015. Open the VB2015\Chap09\Bond Solution\Bond Solution (Bond Solution.sln) file. Open the Code Editor window. Replace <your name> and <current date> in the comments with your name and the current date, respectively.

2. Locate the code template for the frmMain_Load procedure. Click the **blank line** above the End Sub clause. Type the following array declaration statement and then press **Enter** twice:

   **Dim strBond() As String = {"Goldfinger", "Moonraker",
                                "Skyfall", "For Your Eyes Only"}**

3. The procedure will use the array to fill the list box with values. Enter the lines of code shown in either Example 1 or Example 2 in Figure 9-8.

4. Finally, the procedure will select the first item in the list box. Insert a blank line above the End Sub clause, and then enter the following assignment statement:

lstBondMovies.SelectedIndex = 0

5. Save the solution and then start the application. The frmMain_Load procedure creates and initializes the strBond array. The first time the procedure's loop is processed, the intSub variable contains the number 0. Therefore, the Add method in the loop adds the contents of the strBond(0) element (Goldfinger) to the list box. The loop then increases the intSub variable's value by 1, giving 1. When the loop is processed the second time, the Add method in the loop adds the contents of the strBond(1) element (Moonraker) to the list box, and so on. The loop instructions will be repeated for each element in the strBond array. The loop stops when the intSub variable contains the number 4, which is one number more than the highest subscript in the array. The statement you entered in Step 4 invokes the list box's SelectedValueChanged event procedure, which displays the selected item in the You selected box, as shown in Figure 9-9.

Figure 9-9   Sample run of the Bond Movies application

6. Click **Skyfall** in the list box. Skyfall appears in the You selected box.

7. Click the **Exit** button. Close the Code Editor window and then close the solution.

The For Each...Next Statement

In addition to coding loops using the Do...Loop and For...Next statements, which you learned about in Chapter 6, you also can use the For Each...Next statement. The **For Each...Next statement** provides a convenient way of coding a loop whose instructions you want processed for each element in a group, such as for each variable in an array. An advantage of using the For Each...Next statement to process an array is that your code does not need to keep track of the array subscripts or even know the number of array elements. However, unlike the loop instructions in a Do...Loop or For...Next statement, the instructions in a For Each...Next statement can only read the array values; they cannot permanently modify the values.

Figure 9-10 shows the For Each...Next statement's syntax. The *elementVariableName* that appears in the For Each and Next clauses is the name of a variable that the computer can use to keep track of each element in the *group*. The variable's data type is specified in the **As** *dataType* portion of the For Each clause and must be the same as the group's data type. A variable declared in the For Each clause has block scope (which you learned about in Chapter 4) and is recognized only by the instructions within the For Each...Next loop. The example in Figure 9-10 shows how to write the loops from Figure 9-8 using the For Each...Next statement.

Although you do not need to specify the *elementVariableName* in the Next clause, doing so is highly recommended because it makes your code clearer and easier to understand.

For Each...Next Statement

Syntax
For Each *elementVariableName* **As** *dataType* **In** *group*
    loop body instructions
Next *elementVariableName*

Example
```
For Each strElement As String In strBond
    lstBondMovies.Items.Add(strElement)
Next strElement
```

Figure 9-10   Syntax and an example of the For Each...Next statement

---

START HERE   **To use the For Each...Next statement in the Bond Movies application:**

1. Open the Bond Solution (Bond Solution.sln) file contained in the VB2015\Chap09\Bond Solution-ForEachNext folder. Open the Code Editor window. Replace <your name> and <current date> in the comments with your name and the current date, respectively.

2. Locate the frmMain_Load procedure. Click the **blank line** above the assignment statement, and then enter the lines of code shown in the example in Figure 9-10.

3. Save the solution and then start the application. The four array values appear in the list box, as shown earlier in Figure 9-9. Click **each movie title**, one at a time, to verify that the application works correctly.

4. Click the **Exit** button. Close the Code Editor window and then close the solution.

YOU DO IT 2!

Create an application named YouDoIt 2 and save it in the VB2015\Chap09 folder. Add a button and three list boxes to the form. The button's Click event procedure should declare and initialize a one-dimensional String array. Use any four names to initialize the array. The procedure should display the contents of the array three times: first using the For Each...Next statement, then using the Do...Loop statement, and then using the For...Next statement. Display the array contents in the list boxes. Code the procedure. Save the solution, and then start and test the application. Close the solution.

Calculating the Average Stock Price

Figure 9-11 shows the problem specification for the Waterson Company application, which displays the average price of the company's stock.

Problem Specification

Create an application that displays the average price of the Waterson Company stock. The stock prices for the last 10 days were $91.80, $91.60, $92.00, $90.00, $90.50, $90.05, $90.12, $90.70, $90.80, and $90.83. The application should store the daily stock prices in a one-dimensional array and also display the prices in a list box. The average stock price is calculated by first accumulating the prices stored in the array and then dividing the sum by the number of array elements.

Figure 9-11 Problem specification for the Waterson Company application

To begin coding the Waterson Company application:

START HERE

1. Open the Stock Solution (Stock Solution.sln) file contained in the VB2015\Chap09\ Stock Solution-Avg folder. Open the Code Editor window. Replace <your name> and <current date> in the comments with your name and the current date, respectively.

2. The application will store the daily stock prices in a class-level array named `dblPrices`. A class-level array is appropriate in this case because more than one procedure (namely, the frmMain_Load and btnCalc_Click procedures) will need access to the array. Click the **blank line** below the `' class-level array` comment, and then enter the following Private statement:

    Private dblPrices() As Double = {91.8, 91.6, 92,
    90, 90.5, 90.05, 90.12, 90.7, 90.8, 90.83}

3. Locate the frmMain_Load procedure. The procedure will use the For Each...Next statement to fill the list box with the prices stored in the array. Enter the loop shown in Figure 9-12.

```
Private Sub frmMain_Load(sender As Object, e As EventArg
    ' fill list box with prices

    For Each dblElement As Double In dblPrices
        lstPrices.Items.Add(dblElement.ToString("n2"))      enter this loop
    Next dblElement
End Sub
```

Figure 9-12 frmMain_Load procedure

4. Locate the btnCalc_Click procedure. The procedure declares two variables named `dblTotal` and `dblAvg`. The `dblTotal` variable will be used to accumulate the prices stored in the array. The `dblAvg` variable will store the average price.

Figure 9-13 shows three examples of code you could use to accumulate the values stored in the array. In each example, a loop is used to add each array element's value to the `dblTotal` variable. Notice that you need to specify the highest array subscript in the Do...Loop and For...Next statements, but not in the For Each...Next statement. The Do...Loop and For...Next statements must also keep track of the array subscripts; this task is not necessary in the For Each...Next statement. When each loop has finished processing, the `dblTotal` variable contains the sum of the daily prices stored in the array.

Ch09A

```
Example 1—Do...Loop statement
Dim intHighSub As Integer = dblPrices.GetUpperBound(0)
Dim intSub As Integer

' accumulate stock prices
Do While intSub <= intHighSub
    dblTotal += dblPrices(intSub)
    intSub += 1
Loop

Example 2—For...Next statement
Dim intHighSub As Integer = dblPrices.GetUpperBound(0)

' accumulate stock prices
For intSub As Integer = 0 To intHighSub
    dblTotal += dblPrices(intSub)
Next intSub

Example 3—For Each...Next statement
' accumulate stock prices
For Each dblDay As Double In dblPrices
    dblTotal += dblDay
Next dblDay
```

Figure 9-13   Examples of accumulating the array values

START HERE

To finish coding the Waterson Company application:

1. In the btnCalc_Click procedure, enter the comment and code shown in any of the three examples from Figure 9-13.

2. Next, the procedure will calculate the average price by dividing the value stored in the dblTotal variable by the number of array elements. It then will display the average price. Click the **blank line** above the End Sub clause, and then enter the following comment and assignment statements:

   ' calculate and display average
   dblAvg = dblTotal / dblPrices.Length
   lblAvg.Text = dblAvg.ToString("c2")

3. Save the solution and then start the application. Click the **Calculate** button. See Figure 9-14.

Figure 9-14   Average stock price shown in the interface

4. Click the **Exit** button. Close the Code Editor window and then close the solution.

YOU DO IT 3!

Create an application named YouDoIt 3 and save it in the VB2015\Chap09 folder. Add three labels and a button to the form. The button's Click event procedure should declare and initialize a one-dimensional Integer array. Use any five integers to initialize the array. The procedure should total the five integers and then display the result in the labels. Use the Do...Loop statement to calculate the total to display in the first label. Use the For Each...Next statement to calculate the total to display in the second label. Use the For...Next statement to calculate the total to display in the third label. Code the procedure. Save the solution, and then start and test the application. Close the solution.

Finding the Highest Value

Figure 9-15 shows the problem specification for a different Waterson Company application. Rather than displaying the average stock price, this application displays the highest stock price and the number of days the stock closed at that price.

Problem Specification

Create an application that displays the highest price for the Waterson Company stock and the number of days the stock closed at that price. The application should store the daily stock prices in a one-dimensional array and also display the prices in a list box. The application will need to examine each element in the array, looking for the highest price. A counter variable will be used to keep track of the number of array elements containing that price.

Figure 9-15   Problem specification for a different Waterson Company application

To open this version of the Waterson Company application:

START HERE

1. Open the Stock Solution (Stock Solution.sln) file contained in the VB2015\Chap09\ Stock Solution-Highest folder. Open the Code Editor window. Replace <your name> and <current date> in the comments with your name and the current date, respectively.

2. Notice that the Code Editor window already contains the declaration statement for the class-level `dblPrices` array. It also contains the completed frmMain_Load procedure.

3. Locate the btnCalc_Click procedure. The procedure declares the `intLastSub` variable and initializes it to the highest subscript in the `dblPrices` array. The procedure also contains the statements to display the two output items.

Figure 9-16 shows the pseudocode and flowchart for the btnCalc_Click procedure, which is responsible for determining the highest price stored in the array and the number of elements containing that price. You will use the For...Next statement to code the procedure's loop; however, you could also use either the For Each...Next statement or the Do...Loop statement.

---

1. assign the first array element's price as the highest price
2. set the number of days counter to 1
3. repeat for each element in the array
      if the price stored in the current element is equal to the highest price
          add 1 to the number of days counter

Figure 9-16   Pseudocode and flowchart for the btnCalc_Click procedure *(continues)*

(continued)

else
      if the price stored in the current element is greater than the highest price
         assign the current element's price as the highest price
         set the number of days counter to 1
      end if
    end if
  end repeat
4. display the highest price and the number of days the stock closed at that price

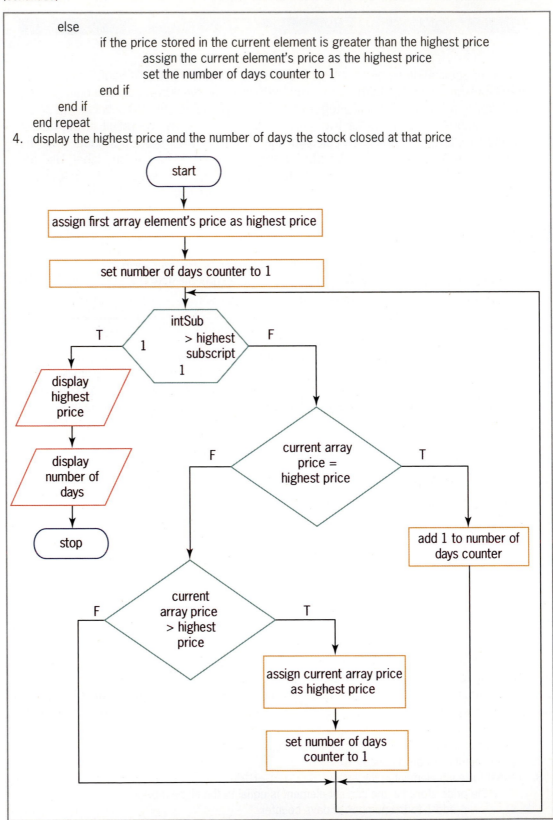

Figure 9-16   Pseudocode and flowchart for the btnCalc_Click procedure

To code and then test the btnCalc_Click procedure:

1. The procedure will use a variable named `dblHighest` to keep track of the highest price in the array. When searching an array for the highest (or lowest) value, it's a common programming practice to initialize the variable to the value stored in the first array element. Click the **blank line** below the existing Dim statement, and then enter the following Dim statement:

   Dim dblHighest As Double = dblPrices(0)

2. Next, the procedure will declare and initialize a counter variable to keep track of the number of elements (days) whose stock price matches the value stored in the `dblHighest` variable. The procedure will initialize the variable to 1 because, at this point, only one element (the first one) contains the price currently stored in the `dblHighest` variable. Type the following Dim statement and then press **Enter** twice:

   Dim intDays As Integer = 1

3. Next, the procedure will use the For...Next statement to traverse the second through the last elements in the array. Each element's value will be compared, one at a time, to the value stored in the `dblHighest` variable. You don't need to look at the first element because its value is already contained in the `dblHighest` variable. Enter the following For clause:

   For intSub As Integer = 1 To intLastSub

4. Change the `Next` clause to **Next intSub**, and then click the **blank line** below the For clause.

5. The first instruction in the loop will determine whether the price stored in the current array element is equal to the price stored in the `dblHighest` variable. Enter the following If clause:

   If dblPrices(intSub) = dblHighest Then

6. If both prices are equal, the selection structure's true path will add 1 to the `intDays` counter variable. Enter the following assignment statement:

   intDays += 1

7. If both prices are not equal, the selection structure's false path will determine whether the price stored in the current array element is greater than the price stored in the `dblHighest` variable. Enter the following Else and If clauses:

   Else
       If dblPrices(intSub) > dblHighest Then

8. If the price in the current array element is greater than the price in the `dblHighest` variable, the nested selection structure's true path should assign the higher value to the `dblHighest` variable. It also should reset the number of days counter to 1 because, at this point, only one element (the current one) contains that price. Enter the additional two assignment statements shaded in Figure 9-17.

```
Private Sub btnCalc_Click(sender As Object, e As EventArgs
) Handles btnCalc.Click
    ' displays the highest stock price and number of
    ' days the stock closed at that price

    Dim intLastSub As Integer = dblPrices.GetUpperBound(0)
    Dim dblHighest As Double = dblPrices(0)
    Dim intDays As Integer = 1

    For intSub As Integer = 1 To intLastSub
        If dblPrices(intSub) = dblHighest Then
            intDays += 1
        Else
            If dblPrices(intSub) > dblHighest Then
                dblHighest = dblPrices(intSub)
                intDays = 1
            End If
        End If
    Next intSub

    lblHighest.Text = dblHighest.ToString("c2")
    lblDays.Text = intDays.ToString
End Sub
```

assigns the first element's value and the number 1 to the appropriate variables

searches the second through the last array elements

Figure 9-17   btnCalc_Click procedure

9. Save the solution and then start the application. Click the **Calculate** button. See Figure 9-18.

Figure 9-18   Highest price and number of days shown in the interface

10. Click the **Exit** button. Close the Code Editor window and then close the solution.

YOU DO IT 4!

Create an application named YouDoIt 4 and save it in the VB2015\Chap09 folder. Add a label and a button to the form. The button's Click event procedure should declare and initialize a one-dimensional Double array. Use any six numbers to initialize the array. The procedure should display (in the label) the lowest value stored in the array. Code the procedure using the For...Next statement. Save the solution, and then start and test the application. Close the solution.

Sorting a One-Dimensional Array

In some applications, you might need to arrange the contents of an array in either ascending or descending order. Arranging data in a specific order is called **sorting**. When an array is sorted in ascending order, the first element in the array contains the smallest value and the last element contains the largest value. When an array is sorted in descending order, on the other hand, the first element contains the largest value and the last element contains the smallest value.

You can use the **Array.Sort method** to sort the values in a one-dimensional array in ascending order. To sort the values in descending order, you first use the Array.Sort method to sort the values in ascending order, and then you use the **Array.Reverse method** to reverse the values. Figure 9-19 shows the syntax of both methods. In each syntax, *arrayName* is the name of a one-dimensional array.

Array.Sort and Array.Reverse Methods

<u>Syntax</u>
Array.Sort(arrayName**)**
Array.Reverse(arrayName**)**

<u>Example 1</u>
```
Dim intScores() As Integer = {78, 90, 75, 83}
Array.Sort(intScores)
```
sorts the contents of the array in ascending order, as follows: 75, 78, 83, and 90

<u>Example 2</u>
```
Dim intScores() As Integer = {78, 90, 75, 83}
Array.Reverse(intScores)
```
reverses the contents of the array, placing the values in the following order: 83, 75, 90, and 78

<u>Example 3</u>
```
Dim intScores() As Integer = {78, 90, 75, 83}
Array.Sort(intScores)
Array.Reverse(intScores)
```
sorts the contents of the array in ascending order and then reverses the contents, placing the values in descending order as follows: 90, 83, 78, and 75

Figure 9-19 Syntax and examples of the Array.Sort and Array.Reverse methods

You will use the Array.Sort and Array.Reverse methods in the Continent application, which you finish coding in the next set of steps. The application stores the names of the seven continents in a one-dimensional array named `strContinents`. It then allows the user to display the names in a list box, in either ascending or descending order.

To complete and then test the Continent application: START HERE

1. Open the VB2015\Chap09\Continent Solution\Continent Solution (Continent Solution.sln) file. Open the Code Editor window. Replace <your name> and <current date> in the comments with your name and the current date, respectively.

2. Notice that the Code Editor already contains the declaration statement for the class-level `strContinents` array. It also contains the declaration statement for the class-level `intLastSub` variable, which is initialized to the highest subscript in the array. The array and variable were declared as class-level memory locations because both need to be accessed by more than one procedure.

3. Locate the btnAscending_Click and btnDescending_Click procedures. Both procedures contain the `lstContinents.Items.Clear()` statement, which clears the contents of the list box. Both procedures also contain a loop to display the array contents in the list box. Enter the three statements shaded in Figure 9-20.

declared in the form's
Declarations section

```
' class-level array and variable
Private strContinents() As String = {"North America", "Africa",
    "South America", "Antarctica", "Australia", "Asia", "Europe"}
Private intLastSub As Integer = strContinents.GetUpperBound(0)

Private Sub btnAscending_Click(sender As Object, e As EventArgs
) Handles btnAscending.Click
    ' sorts the array values in ascending order

    lstContinents.Items.Clear()
    Array.Sort(strContinents)
    For intSub As Integer = 0 To intLastSub
        lstContinents.Items.Add(strContinents(intSub))
    Next intSub
End Sub

Private Sub btnDescending_Click(sender As Object, e As EventArgs
) Handles btnDescending.Click
    ' sorts the array values in descending order

    lstContinents.Items.Clear()
    Array.Sort(strContinents)
    Array.Reverse(strContinents)
    For intSub As Integer = 0 To intLastSub
        lstContinents.Items.Add(strContinents(intSub))
    Next intSub
End Sub
```

Figure 9-20   Most of the Continent application's code

4. Save the solution and then start the application. Click the **Ascending Order** button to display the names in ascending order. See Figure 9-21.

Figure 9-21   Continent names displayed in ascending order

5. Click the **Descending Order** button to display the names in descending order.

6. Click the **Exit** button. Close the Code Editor window and then close the solution.

Lesson A Summary

- To refer to an element in a one-dimensional array:

  Use the array's name followed by the element's subscript. The subscript is specified in a set of parentheses immediately following the array name.

- To declare a one-dimensional array:

  Use either of the syntax versions shown below. The *highestSubscript* argument in Version 1 is an integer that specifies the highest subscript in the array. Using Version 1's syntax, the computer automatically initializes the array elements. The *initialValues* section in Version 2 is a list of values separated by commas and enclosed in braces. The values are used to initialize each element in the array.

  Version 1: {**Dim** | **Private** | **Static**} *arrayName*(*highestSubscript*) **As** *dataType*

  Version 2: {**Dim** | **Private** | **Static**} *arrayName*() **As** *dataType* = {*initialValues*}

- To determine the number of elements in a one-dimensional array:

  Use the array's Length property as follows: *arrayName*.**Length**. Alternatively, you can add the number 1 to the value returned by the array's GetUpperBound method.

- To determine the highest subscript in a one-dimensional array:

  Use the array's GetUpperBound method as follows: *arrayName*.**GetUpperBound(0)**. Alternatively, you can subtract the number 1 from the value stored in the array's Length property.

- To traverse (or look at) each element in a one-dimensional array:

  Use a loop coded with one of the following statements: Do...Loop, For...Next, or For Each...Next.

- To process instructions for each element in a group:

  Use the For Each...Next statement. The statement's syntax is shown in Figure 9-10.

- To sort the values stored in a one-dimensional array in ascending order:

  Use the Array.Sort method. The method's syntax is **Array.Sort(***arrayName***)**.

- To reverse the order of the values stored in a one-dimensional array:

  Use the Array.Reverse method. The method's syntax is **Array.Reverse(***arrayName***)**.

Lesson A Key Terms

Array—a group of related variables that have the same name and data type and are stored in consecutive locations in the computer's internal memory

Array.Reverse method—reverses the order of the values stored in a one-dimensional array

Array.Sort method—sorts the values stored in a one-dimensional array in ascending order

Elements—the variables in an array

For Each...Next statement—used to code a loop whose instructions should be processed for each element in a group

GetUpperBound method—returns an integer that represents the highest subscript in a specified dimension of an array; when used with a one-dimensional array, the dimension is 0

Length property—one of the properties of an array; stores an integer that represents the number of array elements

One-dimensional array—an array whose elements are identified by a unique subscript

Populating the array—refers to the process of initializing the elements in an array

Scalar variable—another name for a simple variable

Simple variable—a variable that is unrelated to any other variable in the computer's internal memory; also called a scalar variable

Sorting—the process of arranging data in a specific order

Subscript—a unique integer that identifies the position of an element in an array

Lesson A Review Questions

1. Which of the following declares a five-element one-dimensional array?

   a. `Dim intSold(4) As Integer`
   b. `Dim intSold(5) As Integer = {4, 78, 65, 23, 2}`
   c. `Dim intSold() As Integer = {4, 78, 65, 23, 2}`
   d. both a and c

2. The `strItems` array is declared as follows: `Dim strItems(20) As String`. The `intSub` variable keeps track of the array subscripts and is initialized to 0. Which of the following Do clauses will process the loop instructions for each element in the array?

   a. `Do While intSub > 20`
   b. `Do While intSub < 20`
   c. `Do While intSub >= 20`
   d. `Do While intSub <= 20`

3. The `intSales` array is declared as follows: `Dim intSales() As Integer = {10000, 12000, 900, 500, 20000}`. The statement `intSales(2) += 10` will _____.

   a. replace the 900 amount with 10
   b. replace the 900 amount with 910
   c. replace the 12000 amount with 10
   d. replace the 12000 amount with 12010

4. The `intSales` array is declared as follows: `Dim intSales() As Integer =` `{10000, 12000, 900, 500, 20000}`. Which of the following loops will correctly multiply each element by 2? The `intSub` variable contains the number 0 before the loop is processed.

   a. ```
   Do While intSub <= 4
       intSub *= 2
   Loop
   ```
   b. ```
   Do While intSub <= 4
       intSales *= 2
   Loop
   ```
   c. ```
   Do While intSub < 5
       intSales(intSub) *= 2
   Loop
   ```
   d. none of the above

5. The `intNums` array is declared as follows: `Dim intNums() As Integer =` `{10, 5, 7, 2}`. Which of the following blocks of code correctly calculates the average value stored in the array? The `intTotal`, `intSub`, and `dblAvg` variables contain the number 0 before the loop is processed.

   a. ```
   Do While intSub < 4
       intNums(intSub) = intTotal + intTotal
       intSub += 1
   Loop
   dblAvg = intTotal / intSub
   ```
   b. ```
   Do While intSub < 4
       intTotal += intNums(intSub)
       intSub = intSub + 1
   Loop
   dblAvg = intTotal / intSub
   ```
   c. ```
   Do While intSub < 4
       intTotal += intNums(intSub)
       intSub += 1
   Loop
   dblAvg = intTotal / intSub - 1
   ```
   d. ```
   Do While intSub < 4
       intTotal = intTotal + intNums(intSub)
       intSub = intSub + 1
   Loop
   dblAvg = intTotal / (intSub - 1)
   ```

6. What will the code in Review Question 5's answer a assign to the **dblAvg** variable?

   a. 0        c. 6
   b. 5        d. 8

7. What will the code in Review Question 5's answer b assign to the **dblAvg** variable?

   a. 0        c. 6
   b. 5        d. 8
   ```

8. What will the code in Review Question 5's answer c assign to the **dblAvg** variable?

   a. 0   c. 6

   b. 5   d. 8

9. What will the code in Review Question 5's answer d assign to the **dblAvg** variable?

   a. 0   c. 6

   b. 5   d. 8

10. Which of the following statements sorts the **intQuantities** array in ascending order?

    a. `Array.Sort(intQuantities)`
    b. `intQuantities.Sort`
    c. `Sort(intQuantities)`
    d. `SortArray(intQuantities)`

11. If the **intNums** array contains six elements, which of the following statements assigns the number 6 to the **intElements** variable?

    a. `intElements = Len(intNums)`
    b. `intElements = Length(intNums)`
    c. `intElements = intNums.Len`
    d. `intElements = intNums.Length`

12. Which of the following assigns the string "Rover" to the fifth element in a one-dimensional array named **strPetNames**?

    a. `strPetNames(4) = "Rover"`
    b. `strPetNames[4] = "Rover"`
    c. `strPetNames(5) = "Rover"`
    d. `strPetNames.Items.Add(5) = "Rover"`

13. The **intCounters** array contains five elements. Which of the following assigns the number 1 to each element?

    a.
```
For intSub As Integer = 0 To 4
    intCounters(intSub) = 1
Next intSub
```
    b.
```
Dim intSub As Integer
Do While intSub < 5
    intCounters(intSub) = 1
    intSub += 1
Loop
```
    c.
```
For intSub As Integer = 1 To 5
    intCounters(intSub - 1) = 1
Next intSub
```
    d. all of the above

14. The `intNums` array is declared as follows: `Dim intNums() As Integer = {10, 5, 7, 2}`. Which of the following blocks of code correctly calculates the average value stored in the array? The `intTotal`, `intSub`, and `dblAvg` variables contain the number 0 before the loop is processed.

   a.
```
For Each intX As Integer In intNums
    intTotal += intX
Next intX
dblAvg = intTotal / intNums.Length
```
   b.
```
For Each intX As Integer In intNums
    intTotal += intNums(intX)
Next intX
dblAvg = intTotal / intX
```
   c.
```
For Each intX As Integer In intNums
    intTotal += intNums(intX)
    intX += 1
Next intX
dblAvg = intTotal / intX
```
   d. none of the above

15. The `strNames` array contains 100 elements. Which of the following statements assigns the number 99 to the `intLastSub` variable?

   a. `intLastSub = strNames.Length`
   b. `intLastSub = strNames.GetUpperBound(0) + 1`
   c. `intLastSub = strNames.GetUpperBound(0)`
   d. both a and b

Lesson A Exercises

1. Write the statement to declare a procedure-level one-dimensional array named `intOrders`. The array should be able to store 20 integers. Then write the statement to store the number 25 in the third element.

   INTRODUCTORY

2. Write the statement to declare a class-level one-dimensional array named `strStates`. The array should be able to store 50 strings. Then write the statement to store the string "North Dakota" in the first element.

   INTRODUCTORY

3. Write the statement to declare and initialize a procedure-level one-dimensional array named `dblTaxRates`. Use the following numbers to initialize the array: 5.5, 7.25, and 3.4.

   INTRODUCTORY

4. The `intNumbers` array is a one-dimensional array. Write the statement to multiply the number stored in the first array element by 3, storing the result in the `intResult` variable.

   INTRODUCTORY

5. The `intNumbers` array is a one-dimensional array. Write the statement to add together the numbers stored in the first and second array elements, displaying the sum in the lblSum control.

   INTRODUCTORY

INTRODUCTORY

6. In this exercise, you modify one of the Waterson Company applications from this lesson. Use Windows to make a copy of the Stock Solution-Highest folder. Rename the copy Stock Solution-Highest-DoLoop. Open the Stock Solution (Stock Solution.sln) file contained in the Stock Solution-Highest-DoLoop folder. Change the For...Next statement in the btnCalc_Click procedure to the Do...Loop statement. Test the application appropriately.

INTRODUCTORY

7. In this exercise, you modify one of the Waterson Company applications from this lesson. Use Windows to make a copy of the Stock Solution-Highest folder. Rename the copy Stock Solution-Highest-ForEachNext. Open the Stock Solution (Stock Solution.sln) file contained in the Stock Solution-Highest-ForEachNext folder. Change the For...Next statement in the btnCalc_Click procedure to the For Each...Next statement. Test the application appropriately.

INTRODUCTORY

8. Open the VB2015\Chap09\Tea Solution\Tea Solution (Tea Solution.sln) file. Open the Code Editor window. Enter the statement to declare and initialize a class-level one-dimensional array named **dblPounds**. Use the following numbers to initialize the array: 35.6, 15, 67.9, 78.8, 12.5, and 27.5. The btnForNext_Click procedure should use the For...Next statement to display the contents of the **dblPounds** array, in ascending order, in the lstPounds control. The btnForEachNext_Click procedure should use the For Each...Next statement to display the contents of the **dblPounds** array, in descending order, in the lstPounds control. Test the application appropriately.

INTERMEDIATE

9. Open the VB2015\Chap09\Sold Solution\Sold Solution (Sold Solution.sln) file. The For...Next, For Each...Next, and Do...Loop buttons should display the average number sold. Open the Code Editor window. Enter the statement to declare and initialize a class-level one-dimensional array named **intSold**. Use the following numbers to initialize the array: 250, 225, 193, and 260. Use the For...Next statement to complete the btnForNext_Click procedure. Use the For Each...Next statement to complete the btnForEachNext_Click procedure. Use the Do...Loop statement to complete the btnDoLoop_Click procedure. Test the application appropriately.

INTRODUCTORY

10. In this exercise, you modify one of the Waterson Company applications from this lesson. Use Windows to make a copy of the Stock Solution-Highest folder. Rename the copy Stock Solution-Highest-Lowest. Open the Stock Solution (Stock Solution.sln) file contained in the Stock Solution-Highest-Lowest folder. In addition to displaying the highest price and the number of days the stock closed at that price, the btnCalc_Click procedure should display the lowest price and the number of days the stock closed at that price. Make the appropriate modifications to the interface and code, and then test the application appropriately.

INTERMEDIATE

11. Open the VB2015\Chap09\Projected Solution\Projected Solution (Projected Solution.sln) file. The btnIncrease_Click procedure should increase each element in the **intSales** array by 10%, displaying the results in the lstProjected control. Test the application appropriately.

INTERMEDIATE

12. Open the VB2015\Chap09\Inventory Solution\Inventory Solution (Inventory Solution.sln) file. The interface provides a text box for entering an amount that represents the preferred quantity on hand. The application should display the number of array elements containing at least that amount. Finish coding the application, and then test it appropriately.

13. Open the VB2015\Chap09\Retail Solution\Retail Solution (Retail Solution.sln) file. Open the Code Editor window. Notice that the code declares and initializes a class-level array named dblWholesale. The btnRetail_Click procedure should ask the user for a percentage amount and then use that amount to increase each price stored in the array. The increased prices should be displayed (right-aligned with two decimal places) in the lstRetail control. Test the application appropriately.

14. In this exercise, you modify the application from Exercise 13. The modified application allows the user to update a specific price. Use Windows to make a copy of the Retail Solution folder. Rename the folder Modified Retail Solution. Open the Retail Solution (Retail Solution.sln) file contained in the Modified Retail Solution folder. Modify the btnRetail_Click procedure so it also asks the user to enter a number from 1 through 10. If the user enters the number 1, the procedure should update the first price in the array. If the user enters the number 2, the procedure should update the second price in the array, and so on. Save the solution and then start the application. Increase the second price by 10%. Then, increase the tenth price by 5%. (Hint: The second price in the list box should still reflect the 10% increase.)

15. Open the VB2015\Chap09\Commission Solution\Commission Solution (Commission Solution.sln) file. The btnDisplay_Click procedure should declare a 20-element, one-dimensional Integer array named intCommission. Assign the following 20 numbers to the array: 300, 500, 200, 150, 600, 750, 900, 150, 100, 200, 250, 650, 300, 750, 800, 350, 250, 150, 100, 300. The procedure should prompt the user to enter a commission amount from 0 through 1000. It then should display (in a message box) the number of salespeople who earned that commission. Use the application to answer the following questions:

How many salespeople earned a commission of 100?

How many salespeople earned a commission of 300?

How many salespeople earned a commission of 50?

How many salespeople earned a commission of 900?

16. In this exercise, you modify the application from Exercise 15. The modified application allows the user to display the number of salespeople earning a commission within a specific range. Use Windows to make a copy of the Commission Solution folder. Rename the folder Modified Commission Solution. Open the Commission Solution (Commission Solution.sln) file contained in the Modified Commission Solution folder. Modify the btnDisplay_Click procedure to prompt the user to enter both a minimum commission amount and a maximum commission amount. The procedure then should display (in a message box) the number of salespeople who earned a commission within that range. Use the application to answer the following questions:

How many salespeople earned a commission from 100 through 300?

How many salespeople earned a commission from 700 through 800?

How many salespeople earned a commission from 0 through 200?

ADVANCED

17. In this exercise, you code an application that generates and displays six unique random numbers for a lottery game. Each lottery number can range from 1 through 54 only. Open the VB2015\Chap09\Lottery Solution\Lottery Solution (Lottery Solution.sln) file. (The image in the picture box is provided courtesy of OpenClipArt.org/ivak.) The btnDisplay_Click procedure should display six unique random numbers in the interface. (Hint: Store the numbers in a one-dimensional array.) Code the application, and then test it appropriately.

DISCOVERY

18. Research the Visual Basic ReDim statement. What is the purpose of the statement? What is the purpose of the **Preserve** keyword?

   a. Open the VB2015\Chap09\ReDim Solution\ReDim Solution (ReDim Solution.sln) file. Open the Code Editor window and locate the btnDisplay_Click procedure. Study the existing code, and then modify the procedure so that it stores any number of sales amounts in the `intSales` array. (Hint: Declare the array using empty sets of parentheses and braces. Use the ReDim statement to add an element to the array.)

   b. Save the solution and then start the application. Click the Display Sales button and then enter the following sales amounts, one at a time: 700, 550, and 800. Click the Cancel button in the input box. The three sales amounts should appear in the list box.

   c. Click the Display Sales button again and then enter the following sales amounts, one at a time: 5, 9, 45, 67, 8, and 0. Click the Cancel button in the input box. This time, six sales amounts should appear in the list box. Close the Code Editor window and then close the solution.

LESSON B

After studying Lesson B, you should be able to:

- Associate a list box with a one-dimensional array
- Use a one-dimensional array as an accumulator or a counter
- Explain the relationship between the elements in parallel one-dimensional arrays
- Create parallel one-dimensional arrays
- Locate information in two parallel one-dimensional arrays

Arrays and Collections

It is not uncommon for programmers to associate the items in a list box with the values stored in an array. This is because the items in a list box belong to a collection (namely, the Items collection), and collections and arrays have several things in common. First, each is a group of individual objects treated as one unit. Second, each individual object in the group is identified by a unique number, which is called an index when referring to a collection, but a subscript when referring to an array. Third, both the first index in a collection and the first subscript in an array are 0. These commonalities allow you to associate the list box items and array elements by their positions within their respective groups. In other words, you can associate the first item in a list box with the first element in an array, the second item with the second element, and so on.

To associate a list box with an array, you first add the appropriate items to the list box. You then store each item's related value in its corresponding position in the array. Figure 9-22 shows the problem specification for the Presidents - Vice Presidents application, which uses a list box named lstPresidents and a one-dimensional array named strVicePres. The figure also illustrates the relationship between the list box items and the array elements.

Problem Specification

Create an application that displays the names of five U.S. presidents in a list box. The application should store the names of the corresponding vice presidents in a one-dimensional array, and then use the index of the selected list box item to access the appropriate vice president's name from the array. Display the vice president's name in a label control.

Presidents (lstPresidents items)		Vice Presidents (strVicePres array elements)	
George Washington		John Adams	
Dwight Eisenhower		Richard Nixon	
John F. Kennedy	the indexes are 0, 1, 2, 3, and 4	Lyndon Johnson	the subscripts are 0, 1, 2, 3, and 4
Ronald Reagan		George H.W. Bush	
Barack Obama		Joe Biden	

Figure 9-22 Problem specification and illustration of list box and array relationship

To finish coding the Presidents - Vice Presidents application:

START HERE

1. If necessary, start Visual Studio 2015. Open the VB2015\Chap09\Presidents Solution\ Presidents Solution (Presidents Solution.sln) file. Open the Code Editor window. Replace <your name> and <current date> in the comments with your name and the current date, respectively. The code to declare and initialize the strVicePres array is already entered for you. The code to fill the list box with the names of the presidents and then select the first name in the list is entered as well. See Figure 9-23. The array

declaration statement initializes the first element to John Adams, which is the name of the vice president associated with the first item in the list box (George Washington). The remaining array elements are initialized to the names of the vice presidents corresponding to their list box items.

```
' class-level array
Private strVicePres() As String = {"John Adams",          vice president's name stored
                                   "Richard Nixon",        in the first array element
                                   "Lyndon Johnson",
                                   "George H.W. Bush",
                                   "Joe Biden"}

Private Sub frmMain_Load(sender As Object, e As EventArgs) Handles Me.Load
    ' fill list boxes with names of presidents

    lstPresidents.Items.Add("George Washington")          president's name listed
    lstPresidents.Items.Add("Dwight Eisenhower")          first in the list box
    lstPresidents.Items.Add("John F. Kennedy")
    lstPresidents.Items.Add("Ronald Reagan")
    lstPresidents.Items.Add("Barack Obama")
    lstPresidents.SelectedIndex = 0
End Sub
```

Figure 9-23   Array declaration and frmMain_Load procedure

2. When the user clicks the name of a president in the list box, the list box's SelectedIndexChanged procedure should display the appropriate vice president's name in the Vice President box. Locate the lstPresidents_SelectedIndexChanged procedure. The procedure will use the index of the selected list box item to access the appropriate name from the `strVicePres` array. Click the **blank line** above the End Sub clause, and then enter the following Dim statement:

Dim intSub As Integer = lstPresidents.SelectedIndex

3. If the first item is selected in the list box, the Dim statement you entered in Step 2 will initialize the `intSub` variable to 0. If the second item is selected, it will initialize the variable to 1, and so on. As a result, you can use the `intSub` variable to access the appropriate name from the array. Enter the following assignment statement:

lblVicePres.Text = strVicePres(intSub)

4. Save the solution and then start the application. The first item in the list box (George Washington) is already selected, and the name of his vice president (John Adams) appears in the Vice President box. See Figure 9-24.

Figure 9-24   Name of the associated vice president displayed in the interface

5. On your own, verify that the application displays the appropriate vice president's name for the remaining list box items.

6. Click the **Exit** button.

If a new item is added to the lstPresidents control, the programmer will need to enter the corresponding vice president's name in the `strVicePres` array. If the programmer neglects to do so, a run time error will occur when the user selects the new item in the list. This is because the lstPresidents_SelectedIndexChanged procedure will try to access a memory location that is outside the bounds of the array. Before closing the Presidents - Vice Presidents application, you will observe this run time error.

To modify and then test the application's code:

START HERE

1. Locate the frmMain_Load procedure. Insert a blank line above the assignment statement, and then enter the following statement:

   lstPresidents.Items.Add("Abraham Lincoln")

2. Save the solution and then start the application. Click **Abraham Lincoln** in the list box. A run time error occurs because this list box item does not have a corresponding entry in the `strVicePres` array. An arrow points to the statement where the error was encountered, and the statement is highlighted. In addition, the Error Correction window opens and provides information pertaining to the error. In this case, the information indicates that the statement is trying to access an element that is outside the bounds of the array.

3. Place your mouse pointer on `intSub` in the highlighted statement, as shown in Figure 9-25. The variable contains the number 5, which is not a valid subscript for the array; the valid subscripts are 0, 1, 2, 3, and 4.

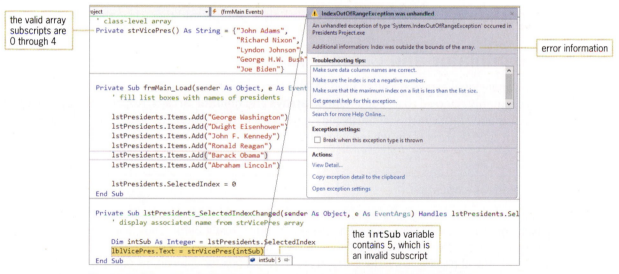

Figure 9-25 Result of the run time error caused by an invalid subscript

4. Click **Debug** on the menu bar and then click **Stop Debugging**.

Before accessing an individual array element, you should verify that the subscript you are using is within the acceptable range for the array. The acceptable range would be a number that is greater than or equal to 0 but less than or equal to the highest subscript in the array.

To continue modifying and testing the application's code:

1. Add the selection structure shown in Figure 9-26 to the lstPresidents_SelectedIndexChanged procedure. Be sure to move the assignment statement into the selection structure's true path.

```
Private Sub lstPresidents_SelectedIndexChanged(sender As Object, e As E
    ' display associated name from strVicePres array

    Dim intSub As Integer = lstPresidents.SelectedIndex
    If intSub >= 0 AndAlso intSub <= strVicePres.GetUpperBound(0) Then
        lblVicePres.Text = strVicePres(intSub)
    Else
        lblVicePres.Text = "N/A"
    End If

End Sub
```

enter this selection structure

Figure 9-26   Modified lstPresidents_SelectedIndexChanged procedure

2. Save the solution and then start the application. Click **Abraham Lincoln** in the list box. This time, N/A appears in the Vice President box. Click the **Exit** button.

3. Delete the `lstPresidents.Items.Add("Abraham Lincoln")` statement from the form's Load event procedure.

4. Save the solution, and then start and test the application to verify that it is still working correctly.

5. Click the **Exit** button. Close the Code Editor window and then close the solution.

Accumulator and Counter Arrays

One-dimensional arrays are often used to either accumulate or count related values; such arrays are commonly referred to as **accumulator arrays** and **counter arrays**, respectively. The Warren School application, which you finish coding next, uses an accumulator array. The application's problem specification is shown in Figure 9-27.

Problem Specification

Warren School is having its annual Chocolate Fund Raiser event. Students sell the following five types of candy: Choco Bar, Choco Bar-Peanuts, Kit Kat, Peanut Butter Cups, and Take 5 Bar. Create an application that allows the user to enter the amount of each candy type sold by each student. The application's interface should provide a list box for entering the candy type and a text box for entering the amount sold. Use a five-element one-dimensional array to accumulate the amounts sold. Display the total number sold for each candy type in label controls in the interface.

Figure 9-27   Problem specification for the Warren School application

START HERE

To open the Warren School application:

1. Open the VB2015\Chap09\Warren Solution\Warren Solution (Warren Solution.sln) file. Open the Code Editor window. Replace <your name> and <current date> in the comments with your name and the current date, respectively. The frmMain_Load procedure fills the list box with the five candy types and then selects the first item in the list. See Figure 9-28.

```
Private Sub frmMain_Load(sender As Object, e As E
    ' fill the list box with values

    lstCandy.Items.Add("Choco Bar")
    lstCandy.Items.Add("Choco Bar-Peanuts")
    lstCandy.Items.Add("Kit Kat")
    lstCandy.Items.Add("Peanut Butter Cups")
    lstCandy.Items.Add("Take 5 Bar")
    lstCandy.SelectedIndex = 0
End Sub
```

Figure 9-28   frmMain_Load procedure

In the next set of steps, you will finish coding the btnAdd_Click procedure, which should accumulate the amounts sold by candy type. The procedure will accomplish its task using a one-dimensional accumulator array named `intCandies`. The array will have five elements, with each corresponding to an item listed in the list box. The first array element will correspond to the Choco Bar item, the second array element to the Choco Bar-Peanuts item, and so on. Each array element will be used to accumulate the sales of its corresponding list box item.

START HERE

To complete the btnAdd_Click procedure:

1. Locate the btnAdd_Click procedure. Click the **blank line** below the `' declare array and variables` comment.

2. The `intCandies` array will need to retain its values until the application ends. You can accomplish this by declaring the array in either the form's Declarations section (using the `Private` keyword to make it a class-level array) or the btnAdd_Click procedure (using the `Static` keyword to make it a static procedure-level array); you will use the latter approach. Like static variables, which you learned about in Chapter 3, static arrays remain in memory and retain their values until the application ends. Enter the following declaration statement:

   Static intCandies(4) As Integer

3. In addition to the array, the procedure will use two Integer variables: one to store the amount sold and one to store the index of the item selected in the list box. Enter the following Dim statements. Press **Enter** twice after typing the last Dim statement.

   Dim intSold As Integer
   Dim intSub As Integer

4. The procedure will convert the contents of the txtSold control to Integer, storing the result in the `intSold` variable. Enter the following TryParse method:

   Integer.TryParse(txtSold.Text, intSold)

5. Next, the procedure will assign the index of the selected list box item to the `intSub` variable. Enter the following assignment statement:

intSub = lstCandy.SelectedIndex

6. The procedure will use the number stored in the `intSub` variable to update the appropriate array element, but only if the number is within the acceptable range for the array. The acceptable range is from 0 through the highest array subscript. Click the **blank line** below the `' update array value` comment, and then enter the following If clause and assignment statement:

If intSub >= 0 AndAlso intSub <= intCandies.GetUpperBound(0) Then
    intCandies(intSub) += intSold

7. If the `intSub` variable's value is not within the acceptable range, the procedure will display an appropriate message. Enter the following lines of code:

Else
    MessageBox.Show("Can't update this candy's sales.",
                "Warren School", MessageBoxButtons.OK,
                MessageBoxIcon.Information)

8. If necessary, delete the blank line above the End If clause.

9. Finally, the procedure will display the array values in the interface. Click the **blank line** below the `' display array values` comment, and then enter the five assignment statements indicated in Figure 9-29.

```
Private Sub btnAdd_Click(sender As Object, e As EventArgs
) Handles btnAdd.Click
    ' add amount sold to the appropriate total

    ' declare array and variables
    Static intCandies(4) As Integer          ← static procedure-level array
    Dim intSold As Integer
    Dim intSub As Integer

    Integer.TryParse(txtSold.Text, intSold)
    intSub = lstCandy.SelectedIndex

    ' update array value
    If intSub >= 0 AndAlso intSub <= intCandies.GetUpperBound(0) Then
        intCandies(intSub) += intSold         ← uses the selected item's index as the array subscript
    Else
        MessageBox.Show("Can't update this candy's sales.",
                        "Warren School", MessageBoxButtons.OK,
                        MessageBoxIcon.Information)
    End If

    ' display array values
    lblChocoBar.Text = intCandies(0).ToString
    lblChocoBarPeanuts.Text = intCandies(1).ToString     ← enter these assignment statements
    lblKitKat.Text = intCandies(2).ToString
    lblPeanutButCups.Text = intCandies(3).ToString
    lblTake5Bar.Text = intCandies(4).ToString

    txtSold.Focus()
End Sub
```

Figure 9-29 btnAdd_Click procedure

To test the application:

START HERE

1. Save the solution and then start the application. Type **100** in the Sold box and then click the **Add to Total** button. The number 100 appears in the Choco Bar box.

2. Click **Kit Kat** in the Candy list box. Change the 100 in the Sold box to **45** and then click the **Add to Total** button.

3. Next, change the 45 in the Sold box to **–6** (a negative number 6) and then click the **Add to Total** button.

4. Next, change the –6 in the Sold box to **36** and then click the **Add to Total** button.

5. Click **Peanut Butter Cups** and then press **Enter** to select the Add to Total button.

6. On your own, record the following two candy sales: **10** of the **Take 5 Bar** and **2** of the **Choco Bar-Peanuts**. See Figure 9-30.

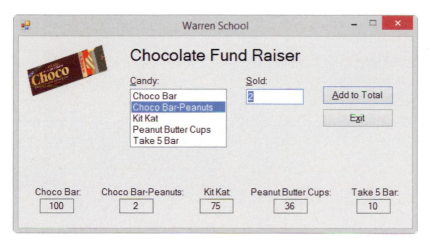

Figure 9-30   Accumulator array values displayed in the interface

7. On your own, test the application using different candy types and sales amounts.

8. Click the **Exit** button. Close the Code Editor window and then close the solution.

YOU DO IT 5!

Create an application named YouDoIt 5 and save it in the VB2015\Chap09 folder. Add two list boxes and a button to the form. The button's Click event procedure should declare and initialize a one-dimensional Integer array. Use any 10 numbers to initialize the array. The procedure should use the For Each...Next statement to display the contents of the array in the first list box. The procedure should then use the For...Next statement to increase each array element's value by 2. Finally, it should use the Do...Loop statement to display the updated results in the second list box. Code the procedure. Save the solution, and then start and test the application. Close the solution.

Parallel One-Dimensional Arrays

Figure 9-31 shows the problem specification for the Paper Warehouse, which displays the price of an item corresponding to an ID entered by the user.

Problem Specification

Create an application that displays the price of an item corresponding to an ID entered by the user. The IDs and corresponding prices are shown here. However, employees are entitled to a 10% discount. The application should store the price list in an array.

Item ID	Price
A45G	8.99
J63Y	12.99
M93K	5.99
C20P	13.50
F77T	7.25

Figure 9-31   Problem specification for the Paper Warehouse

As you learned in Lesson A, all of the variables in an array have the same data type. So how can you store a price list composed of a string (the ID) and a number (the price) in an array? One solution is to use two one-dimensional arrays: a String array to store the IDs and a Double array to store the prices. Both arrays are illustrated in Figure 9-32.

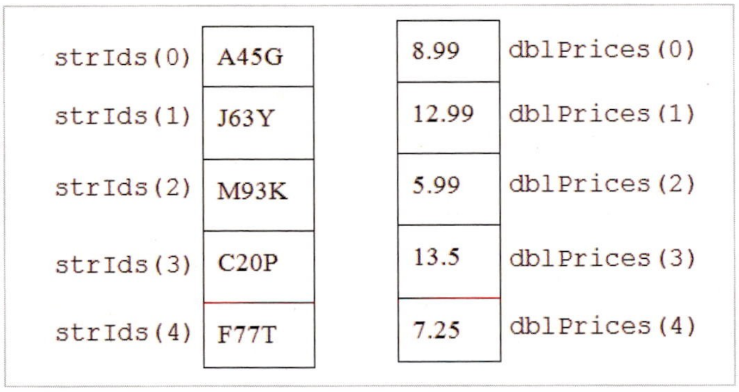

strIds(0)	A45G		8.99	dblPrices(0)
strIds(1)	J63Y		12.99	dblPrices(1)
strIds(2)	M93K		5.99	dblPrices(2)
strIds(3)	C20P		13.5	dblPrices(3)
strIds(4)	F77T		7.25	dblPrices(4)

Figure 9-32   Illustration of two parallel one-dimensional arrays

The arrays in Figure 9-32 are referred to as **parallel arrays**, which are two or more arrays whose elements are related by their positions in the arrays; in other words, they are related by their subscripts. The arrays are parallel because each element in the strIds array corresponds to the element located in the same position in the dblPrices array. For example, the price of item A45G [strIds(0)] is $8.99 [dblPrices(0)]. Likewise, the price of item J63Y [strIds(1)] is $12.99 [dblPrices(1)]. The same relationship is true for the remaining elements in both arrays. To determine an item's price, you locate the item's ID in the strIds array and then view its corresponding element in the dblPrices array.

START HERE

To open the Paper Warehouse application:

1. Open the Paper Solution (Paper Solution.sln) file contained in the VB2015\Chap09\ Paper Solution-Parallel folder. See Figure 9-33.

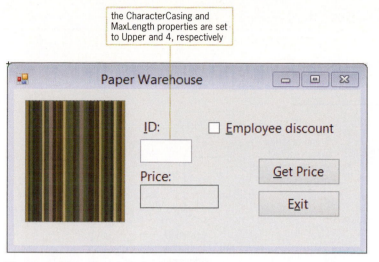

the CharacterCasing and
MaxLength properties are set
to Upper and 4, respectively

Figure 9-33   User interface for the Paper Warehouse application

2. Open the Code Editor window. Replace <your name> and <current date> in the comments with your name and the current date, respectively.

3. Notice that the code to declare the parallel arrays is already entered in the form's Declarations section. See Figure 9-34.

```
' declare parallel arrays
Private strIds() As String =
    {"A45G", "J63Y", "M93K", "C20P", "F77T"}
Private dblPrices() As Double = {8.99, 12.99, 5.99, 13.5, 7.25}
```

Figure 9-34   Array declaration statements

Figure 9-35 shows the pseudocode and flowchart for the btnGet_Click procedure.

1. assign search ID to a variable
2. repeat until either the end of the strIds array is reached or the search ID is located in the array
         add 1 to the array subscript to search the next element in the array
     end repeat
3. if the search ID was located in the strIds array
         assign the price contained in the same location in the dblPrices array to a variable
         if the Employee discount check box is selected
             price = price * .9
         end if
         display price in lblPrice
     else
         display "Invalid ID" message in a message box
     end if

Figure 9-35   Pseudocode and flowchart for the btnGet_Click procedure *(continues)*

(continued)

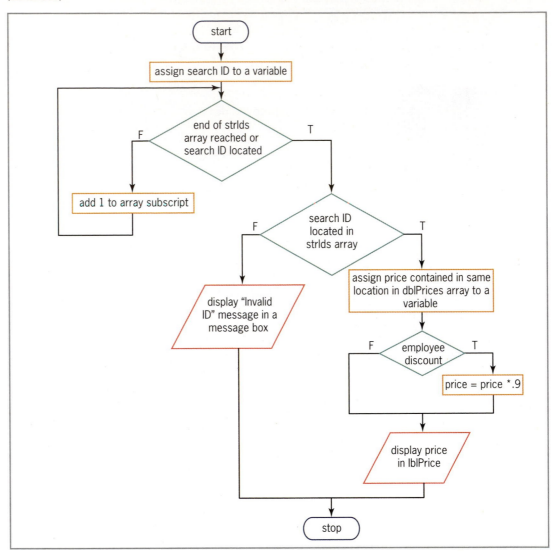

Figure 9-35   Pseudocode and flowchart for the btnGet_Click procedure

START HERE

To finish coding the application and then test it:

1. Locate the btnGet_Click procedure. The procedure declares three variables named `strSearchId`, `intSub`, and `dblItemPrice`. It then assigns the contents of the txtId control to the `strSearchId` variable.

2. The procedure will use a loop to search each element in the `strIds` array, stopping either when the end of the array is reached or when the ID is located in the array. Click the **blank line** above the End Sub clause, and then enter the following code:

   Do Until intSub = strIds.Length OrElse
       strIds(intSub) = strSearchId
       intSub += 1
   Loop

3. Next, the procedure will use a selection structure to determine why the loop ended. You can make this determination by looking at the value in the `intSub` variable. If the loop ended because it reached the end of the `strIds` array without locating the ID, the

`intSub` variable's value will be equal to the array's length. On the other hand, if the loop ended because it located the ID in the `strIds` array, the `intSub` variable's value will be less than the array's length. Insert two blank lines above the End Sub clause. In the blank line immediately above the End Sub clause, enter the following If clause:

If intSub < strIds.Length Then

4. If the selection structure's condition evaluates to True, it means that the ID was located in the `strIds` array. In that case, the structure's true path should assign the price located in the same position in the `dblPrices` array to a variable. Enter the following assignment statement:

dblItemPrice = dblPrices(intSub)

5. The selection structure's true path then needs to determine whether the Employee discount check box is selected. If it is, the price should be reduced by 10%. Enter the following nested selection structure:

If chkDisc.Checked Then
    dblItemPrice *= 0.9
End If

6. Finally, the selection structure's true path should display the item's price in the lblPrice control. Insert a blank line below the nested End If clause, and then enter the following assignment statement:

lblPrice.Text = dblItemPrice.ToString("c2")

7. If the outer selection structure's condition evaluates to False, on the other hand, it means that the ID was not located in the `strIds` array. In that case, the structure's false path should display the "Invalid ID" message in a message box. Enter the additional lines of code shaded in Figure 9-36.

```
' declare parallel arrays
Private strIds() As String =                              ┐ parallel one-
    {"A45G", "J63Y", "M93K", "C20P", "F77T"}              │ dimensional arrays
Private dblPrices() As Double = {8.99, 12.99, 5.99, 13.5, 7.25} │ declared in the
                                                          ┘ form's Declarations
                                                            section
Private Sub btnGet_Click(sender As Object, e As EventArgs
) Handles btnGet.Click
    ' display an item's price

    Dim strSearchId As String
    Dim intSub As Integer
    Dim dblItemPrice As Double

    strSearchId = txtId.Text

    ' search the strIds array until the
    ' end of the array or the ID is found
    Do Until intSub = strIds.Length OrElse          ┐
        strIds(intSub) = strSearchId                 │ searches for
        intSub += 1                                  │ the ID in the
    Loop                                             ┘ strIds array
```

Figure 9-36   Most of the code for the Paper Warehouse application using parallel arrays *(continues)*

(continued)

```
    If intSub < strIds.Length Then
        dblItemPrice = dblPrices(intSub) ──── assigns the corresponding
        If chkDisc.Checked Then                price from the dblPrices
            dblItemPrice *= 0.9                 array to a variable
        End If
        lblPrice.Text = dblItemPrice.ToString("c2")
    Else
        MessageBox.Show("Invalid ID", "Paper Warehouse",
                        MessageBoxButtons.OK,
                        MessageBoxIcon.Information)
    End If
End Sub
```

Figure 9-36   Most of the code for the Paper Warehouse application using parallel arrays

8. Save the solution and then start the application. Type **m93k** in the ID box and then click the **Get Price** button. $5.99 appears in the Price box. See Figure 9-37.

Figure 9-37   Interface showing the price for item M93K

9. Click the **Employee discount** check box and then click the **Get Price** button. $5.39 appears in the Price box.

10. Type **a45h** in the ID box and then click the **Get Price** button. The "Invalid ID" message appears in a message box. Close the message box.

11. On your own, test the application using other valid and invalid IDs. When you are finished testing the application, click the **Exit** button. Close the Code Editor window and then close the solution.

The Die Tracker Application

Your task in this chapter is to create the Die Tracker application. The application simulates the roll of a die and keeps track of the number of times each die face appears.

START HERE ▶

To open the Die Tracker application:

1. Open the VB2015\Chap09\Die Solution\Die Solution (Die Solution.sln) file. See Figure 9-38.

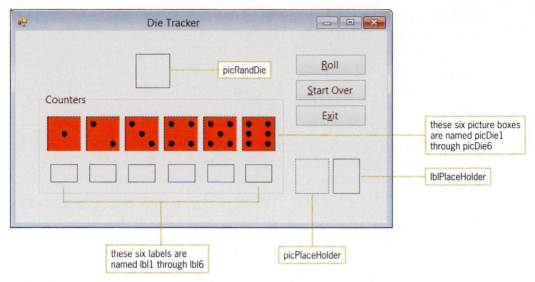

Figure 9-38 User interface for the Die Tracker application

2. Open the Code Editor window. Replace <your name> and <current date> in the comments with your name and the current date, respectively.

The Die Tracker application will use three parallel arrays: a PictureBox array named `picDice`, a Label array named `lblCounters`, and an Integer array named `intCounters`. The arrays are illustrated in Figure 9-39.

Subscripts	picDice array	lblCounters array	intCounters array
0	picPlaceHolder	lblPlaceHolder	0
1	picDie1	lbl1	0
2	picDie2	lbl2	0
3	picDie3	lbl3	0
4	picDie4	lbl4	0
5	picDie5	lbl5	0
6	picDie6	lbl6	0

Figure 9-39 Illustration of the three parallel arrays

Notice that even though there are only six faces on a die, the arrays contain seven elements rather than six elements. This is because the application's code will be much easier to understand if the number of dots on each die corresponds to the location of the die's information in the arrays. In other words, the information pertaining to the one-dot die will be contained in the array elements whose subscript is 1, the two-dot die's information will be contained in the array elements whose subscript is 2, and so on. When coding the application, the first element in each array will be ignored. (Recall that the first element in an array has a subscript of 0.)

To code the Die Tracker application:

START HERE

1. First, declare the three parallel arrays. Click the **blank line** below the `' declare arrays` comment in the form's Declarations section, and then enter the following declaration statements:

    Private picDice(6) As PictureBox
    Private lblCounters(6) as Label
    Private intCounters(6) As Integer

2. Locate the frmMain_Load procedure, which will fill the picture box and label arrays with the appropriate controls. Click the **blank line** above the procedure's End Sub clause, and then enter the following assignment statements:

picDice = {picPlaceHolder, picDie1, picDie2,
picDie3, picDie4, picDie5, picDie6}
lblCounters = {lblPlaceHolder, lbl1, lbl2,
lbl3, lbl4, lbl5, lbl6}

3. Locate the btnRoll_Click procedure. The procedure will use a random number to select one of the six picture boxes from the picDice array. Click the **blank line** above the procedure's End Sub clause, and then enter the following declaration statements. Press **Enter** twice after typing the second statement.

Dim randGen As New Random
Dim intRand As Integer

4. The procedure should generate a random number from 1 through 6. Enter the following comment and assignment statement:

' generate a random number from 1 - 6
intRand = randGen.Next(1, 7)

5. The procedure will use the random number to display the appropriate die face in the picRandDie control. Enter the following comment and assignment statement:

' display current roll of the die
picRandDie.Image = picDice(intRand).Image

6. The random number will also be used to update the associated counter in the intCounters array. Enter the following comment and assignment statement:

' update associated counter
intCounters(intRand) += 1

7. Finally, the procedure will use the random number to display the updated counter's value in its associated label control in the lblCounters array. Enter the following comment and assignment statement:

' display updated counter
lblCounters(intRand).Text = intCounters(intRand).ToString

8. Locate the btnStartOver_Click procedure. The procedure will use a loop to reset the counters in the intCounters array to 0 and also clear the contents of the label controls contained in the lblCounters array. The loop will access the second through the seventh element in each array. It's not necessary to access the first element because that element's value will never change from its initial value in either array. Click the **blank line** above the procedure's End Sub clause, and then enter the following loop:

For intSub As Integer = 1 To 6
intCounters(intSub) = 0
lblCounters(intSub).Text = String.Empty
Next intSub

9. Finally, the procedure will clear the contents of the picRandDie control. Insert a blank line below the Next intSub clause, and then enter the following assignment statement:

picRandDie.Image = Nothing

Figure 9-40 shows most of the application's code.

```
' declare arrays
Private picDice(6) As PictureBox
Private lblCounters(6) As Label
Private intCounters(6) As Integer

Private Sub frmMain_Load(sender As Object, e As EventArgs
) Handles Me.Load
    ' fill picture box and label arrays

    picDice = {picPlaceHolder, picDie1, picDie2,
            picDie3, picDie4, picDie5, picDie6}
    lblCounters = {lblPlaceHolder, lbl1, lbl2,
            lbl3, lbl4, lbl5, lbl6}

End Sub

Private Sub btnRoll_Click(sender As Object, e As EventArgs
) Handles btnRoll.Click
    ' calculates and displays the number
    ' of times each die face appears

    Dim randGen As New Random
    Dim intRand As Integer

    ' generate a random number from 1 - 6
    intRand = randGen.Next(1, 7)
    ' display current roll of the die
    picRandDie.Image = picDice(intRand).Image
    ' update associated counter
    intCounters(intRand) += 1
    ' display updated counter
    lblCounters(intRand).Text = intCounters(intRand).ToString

End Sub

Private Sub btnStartOver_Click(sender As Object, e As EventArgs
) Handles btnStartOver.Click
    ' reset the counters and clear the counter labels

    For intSub As Integer = 1 To 6
        intCounters(intSub) = 0
        lblCounters(intSub).Text = String.Empty
    Next intSub
    picRandDie.Image = Nothing

End Sub
```

Figure 9-40   Most of the code for the Die Tracker application

To test the Die Tracker application:

START HERE

1. Save the solution and then start the application. Click the **Roll** button. A die face appears in the picRandDie control, and its associated counter label contains the number 1. See Figure 9-41. Because the btnRoll_Click procedure uses random numbers, your die face and counter label might be different from those shown in the figure.

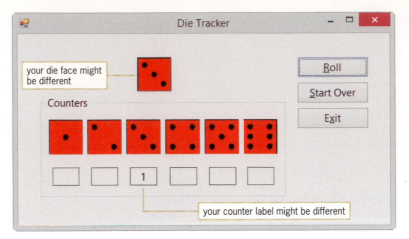

Figure 9-41 Sample run of the Die Tracker application

2. Click the **Roll** button several more times. Each time you click the button, a die face appears in the picRandDie control and its associated counter label is updated by 1.

3. Click the **Start Over** button. The btnStartOver_Click procedure resets the counters in the `intCounters` array to 0. It also clears the contents of the labels in the `lblCounters` array as well as the contents of the picRandDie control.

4. Click the **Roll** button. A die face appears in the picRandDie control, and its associated counter label contains the number 1.

5. Click the **Exit** button. Close the Code Editor window and then close the solution.

Lesson B Summary

- To associate the items in a list box with the elements in an array:

  Use each list box item's index and each array element's subscript.

- To create parallel one-dimensional arrays:

  Create two or more one-dimensional arrays. When assigning values to the arrays, be sure that the value stored in each element in the first array corresponds to the values stored in the same elements in the other arrays.

Lesson B Key Terms

Accumulator arrays—arrays whose elements are used to accumulate (add together) values

Counter arrays—arrays whose elements are used for counting something

Parallel arrays—two or more arrays whose elements are related by their subscripts (positions) in the arrays

Lesson B Review Questions

1. The `intSales` array is declared as follows: `Dim intSales() As Integer = {10000, 12000, 900, 500, 20000}`. Which of the following If clauses determines whether the `intSub` variable contains a valid subscript for the array?

   a. `If intSub >= 0 AndAlso intSub <= 4 Then`

   b. `If intSub >= 0 AndAlso intSub < 4 Then`

   c. `If intSub >= 0 AndAlso intSub <= 5 Then`

   d. `If intSub > 0 AndAlso intSub < 5 Then`

2. If the elements in two arrays are related by their subscripts, the arrays are called _____ arrays.

   a. associated   c. matching

   b. coupled   d. parallel

3. The `strStates` and `strCapitals` arrays are parallel arrays. If Illinois is stored in the second element in the `strStates` array, where is its capital (Springfield) stored?

   a. `strCapitals(1)`

   b. `strCapitals(2)`

4. The `dblNums` array is a six-element Double array. Which of the following If clauses determines whether the entire array has been searched?

   a. `If intSub = dblNums.Length Then`

   b. `If intSub <= dblNums.Length Then`

   c. `If intSub > dblNums.GetUpperBound(0) Then`

   d. both a and c

Lesson B Exercises

1. Open the VB2015\Chap09\Days Solution\Days Solution (Days Solution.sln) file. The frmMain_Load procedure should declare a one-dimensional String array, using the names of the seven days of the week to initialize the array. The procedure should use the For Each...Next statement to display the contents of the array in the list box. The lstDays_SelectedValueChanged procedure should display the name of the selected day in the label control. Test the application appropriately.

   INTRODUCTORY

2. Open the VB2015\Chap09\Pay Solution\Pay Solution (Pay Solution.sln) file. The application should allow the user to select a pay code from the list box. The btnCalc_Click procedure should display the gross pay, using the number of hours worked and the pay rate corresponding to the selected code. The pay codes and rates are listed in Figure 9-42. Code the application, using a class-level array to store the pay rates. Test the application appropriately.

   INTRODUCTORY

Pay code	Pay rate
A07	8.50
A10	8.75
B03	9.25
B24	9.90
C23	10.50

Figure 9-42 Pay codes and rates for Exercise 2

INTRODUCTORY

3. Open the VB2015\Chap09\City Solution\City Solution (City Solution.sln) file. Open the Code Editor window. The form's Declarations section declares and initializes two parallel one-dimensional arrays named **strCities** and **strStates**. Locate the btnDisplay_Click procedure. The procedure should display the contents of the arrays in the list box, using the following format: the city name followed by a comma, a space, and the state name. Test the application appropriately.

INTERMEDIATE

4. In this exercise, you modify the Die Tracker application completed in this lesson. Use Windows to make a copy of the Die Solution folder. Rename the copy Modified Die Solution. Open the Die Solution (Die Solution.sln) file contained in the Modified Die Solution folder. Code the application without using the picPlaceHolder and lblPlaceHolder controls. Remove both controls from the interface. Be sure to change the *highestSubscript* argument in the three array declaration statements to 5. Test the application appropriately.

INTERMEDIATE

5. Open the VB2015\Chap09\Computer Solution\Computer Solution (Computer Solution.sln) file. The interface allows the user to enter the number of either new or refurbished computers sold. The Add to Total button should use an array to accumulate the numbers sold by type. It also should display (in the labels) the total number sold for each type. Test the application appropriately.

INTERMEDIATE

6. In this exercise, you code an application that displays a grade based on the number of points entered by the user. The grading scale is shown in Figure 9-43. Open the VB2015\Chap09\Chang Solution\Chang Solution (Chang Solution.sln) file. Store the minimum points and grades in two parallel one-dimensional arrays named **intMins** and **strGrades**. The btnDisplay_Click procedure should search the **intMins** array for the number of points entered by the user. It then should display the corresponding grade from the **strGrades** array. Test the application appropriately.

Minimum points	Maximum points	Grade
0	299	F
300	349	D
350	414	C
415	464	B
465	500	A

Figure 9-43 Grading scale for Exercise 6

INTERMEDIATE

7. In this exercise, you code an application that displays a grade based on the number of points entered by the user. The grading scale is shown in Figure 9-44. Open the VB2015\Chap09\Perez Solution\Perez Solution (Perez Solution.sln) file. The user will enter the total possible points in the Possible points box. The btnCreate_Click procedure should store the minimum number of points and the grades in two parallel one-dimensional arrays. The btnDisplay_Click procedure should display the grade corresponding to the number of

points entered in the Earned points box. Save the solution and then start the application. Enter 300 in the Possible points box, and then click the Create Grading Scale button. Enter 185 in the Earned points box, and then click the Display Grade button. The letter D should appear in the Grade box. Next, enter 275 in the Earned points box, and then click the Display Grade button. The letter B should appear in the Grade box. Enter 500 in the Possible points box, and then click the Create Grading Scale button. Enter 400 in the Earned points box, and then click the Display Grade button. The letter C should appear in the Grade box. Test the application using different values for the possible and earned points.

Minimum points	Grade
92% of the total possible points	A
82% of the total possible points	B
75% of the total possible points	C
60% of the total possible points	D
0	F

Figure 9-44   Grading scale for Exercise 7

8. Open the Shipping Solution (Shipping Solution.sln) file contained in the VB2015\Chap09\Shipping Solution-Parallel folder. The btnDisplay_Click procedure should display a shipping charge that is based on the number of items a customer orders. The order amounts and shipping charges are listed in Figure 9-45. Store the minimum order amounts and shipping charges in parallel arrays. Display the appropriate shipping charge with a dollar sign and two decimal places. Test the application appropriately.

INTERMEDIATE

Minimum order	Maximum order	Shipping charge
1	5	10.99
6	10	7.99
11	20	3.99
21	No maximum	0

Figure 9-45   Order amounts and shipping charges for Exercise 8

9. In this exercise, you code a modified version of the Die Tracker application completed in this lesson. Open the Dice Solution (Dice Solution.sln) file contained in the VB2015\Chap09\Dice Solution-Advanced folder. The application should simulate the roll of two dice (rather than one die). It also should display the total amount rolled. For example, if one die shows two dots and the other shows four dots, the number 6 should appear in the Total box. The application should keep track of the number of times each total (from 2 through 12) is rolled. Test the application appropriately.

ADVANCED

10. Create an application, using the following names for the solution and project, respectively: Stock Market Solution and Stock Market Project. Save the application in the VB2015\Chap09 folder. The application should declare a Double array that contains 30 elements. Each element will store the price of a stock. Initialize the first 10 elements using the following values: 2.25, 2.4, 1.97, 1.97, 1.99, 1.97, 2.25, 2.87, 2.5, and 2.4. Use your own values to initialize the remaining 20 elements. The application should display the following items: the average price of the stock, the number of days the stock price increased from the previous day, the number of days the stock price decreased from the previous day, and the number of days the stock price stayed the same as the previous day. Create a suitable interface and then code the application. Display the average price with a dollar sign and two decimal places. Test the application appropriately.

ADVANCED

■ LESSON C

After studying Lesson C, you should be able to:

- Declare and initialize a two-dimensional array
- Store data in a two-dimensional array
- Sum the values in a two-dimensional array
- Search a two-dimensional array

Two-Dimensional Arrays

As you learned in Lesson A, the most commonly used arrays in business applications are one-dimensional and two-dimensional. You can visualize a one-dimensional array as a column of variables in memory. A **two-dimensional array**, on the other hand, resembles a table in that the variables (elements) are in rows and columns. You can determine the number of elements in a two-dimensional array by multiplying the number of its rows by the number of its columns. An array that has four rows and three columns, for example, contains 12 elements.

Each element in a two-dimensional array is identified by a unique combination of two subscripts that the computer assigns to the element when the array is created. The subscripts specify the element's row and column positions in the array. Elements located in the first row in a two-dimensional array are assigned a row subscript of 0, elements in the second row are assigned a row subscript of 1, and so on. Similarly, elements located in the first column in a two-dimensional array are assigned a column subscript of 0, elements in the second column are assigned a column subscript of 1, and so on.

You refer to each element in a two-dimensional array by the array's name and the element's row and column subscripts, with the row subscript listed first and the column subscript listed second. The subscripts are separated by a comma and specified in a set of parentheses immediately following the array name. For example, to refer to the element located in the first row, first column in a two-dimensional array named strSongs, you use strSongs(0, 0)— read "strSongs sub zero comma zero." Similarly, to refer to the element located in the second row, fourth column, you use strSongs(1, 3). Notice that the subscripts are one number less than the row and column in which the element is located. This is because the row and column subscripts start at 0 rather than at 1. You will find that the last row subscript in a two-dimensional array is always one number less than the number of rows in the array. Likewise, the last column subscript is always one number less than the number of columns in the array. Figure 9-46 illustrates the elements contained in the two-dimensional strSongs array.

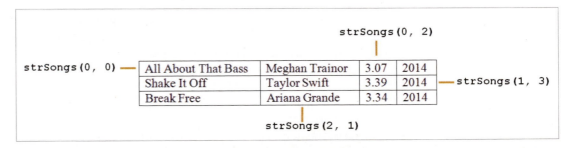

Figure 9-46   Names of some of the elements in the strSongs array

Figure 9-47 shows two versions of the syntax for declaring a two-dimensional array in Visual Basic. The figure also includes examples of using both syntax versions. In each version, *dataType* is the type of data the array variables will store.

Declaring a Two-Dimensional Array

Syntax – Version 1
{**Dim** | **Private** | **Static**} *arrayName*(*highestRowSubscript*, *highestColumnSubscript*) **As** *dataType*

Syntax – Version 2
{**Dim** | **Private** | **Static**} *arrayName*(**,**) **As** *dataType* = {{*initialValues*},…{*initialValues*}}

Example 1
```
Dim strStateCapitals(49, 1) As String
```
declares a 50-row, two-column procedure-level array named `strStateCapitals`; each element is automatically initialized using the keyword `Nothing`

Example 2
```
Static intNumSold(5, 4) As Integer
```
declares a static, six-row, five-column procedure-level array named `intNumSold`; each element is automatically initialized to 0

Example 3
```
Private strSongs(,) As String =
      {{"All About That Bass", "Meghan Trainor", "3.07", "2014"},
       {"Shake It Off", "Taylor Swift", "3.39", "2014"},
       {"Break Free", "Ariana Grande", "3.34", "2014"}}
```
declares and initializes a three-row, four-column class-level array named `strSongs` (the array is illustrated in Figure 9-46)

Example 4
```
Private dblSales(,) As Double = {{75.33, 9.65},
                                 {23.55, 6.89},
                                 {4.5, 89.3},
                                 {100.67, 38.92}}
```
declares and initializes a four-row, two-column class-level array named `dblPrices`

Figure 9-47   Syntax versions and examples of declaring a two-dimensional array

In Version 1's syntax, *highestRowSubscript* and *highestColumnSubscript* are integers that specify the highest row and column subscripts, respectively, in the array. When the array is created, it will contain one row more than the number specified in the highestRowSubscript argument and one column more than the number specified in the highestColumnSubscript argument. This is because the first row and column subscripts in a two-dimensional array are 0. When you declare a two-dimensional array using Version 1's syntax, the computer automatically initializes each element in the array when the array is created.

You would use Version 2's syntax when you want to specify each variable's initial value. You do this by including a separate *initialValues* section, enclosed in braces, for each row in the array. If the array has two rows, then the statement that declares and initializes the array should have two initialValues sections. If the array has five rows, then the declaration statement should have five initialValues sections. Within the individual initialValues sections, you enter one or more values separated by commas. The number of values to enter corresponds to the number of columns in the array. If the array contains 10 columns, then each individual initialValues section should contain 10 values. In addition to the set of braces enclosing each individual initialValues section, Version 2's syntax also requires all of the initialValues sections to be enclosed in a set of braces.

When using Version 2's syntax, be sure to include a comma within the parentheses that follow the array's name. The comma indicates that the array is a two-dimensional array. (Recall that a comma is used to separate the row subscript from the column subscript in a two-dimensional array.)

After an array is declared, you can use another statement to store a different value in an array element. Examples of such statements include assignment statements and statements that contain the TryParse method. Figure 9-48 shows examples of both types of statements, using three of the arrays declared in Figure 9-47.

Storing Data in a Two-Dimensional Array

Example 1
```
strStateCapitals(0, 0) = "AL"
strStateCapitals(0, 1) = "Montgomery"
```
assigns the strings "AL" and "Montgomery" to the elements located in the first row in the strStateCapitals array; "AL" is assigned to the first column, and "Montgomery" is assigned to the second column

Example 2
```
For intRow As Integer = 0 To 5
    For intColumn As Integer = 0 To 4
        intNumSold(intRow, intColumn) += 1
    Next intColumn
Next intRow
```
adds the number 1 to the contents of each element in the intNumSold array

Example 3
```
Dim intRow As Integer
Dim intCol As Integer
Do While intRow <= 3
    intCol = 0
    Do While intCol <= 1
        dblSales(intRow, intCol) *= 1.1
        intCol += 1
    Loop
    intRow += 1
Loop
```
multiplies each element in the dblSales array by 1.1

Example 4
```
dblSales(2, 1) *= 0.07
```
multiplies the value contained in the third row, second column in the dblSales array by 0.07 and then assigns the result to the element; you can also write this statement as dblSales(2, 1) = dblSales(2, 1) * 0.07

Example 5
```
Double.TryParse(txtSales.Text, dblSales(0, 0))
```
assigns either the value entered in the txtSales control (converted to Double) or the number 0 to the element located in the first row, first column in the dblSales array

---

Figure 9-48   Examples of statements used to store data in a two-dimensional array

In Lesson A, you learned how to use the GetUpperBound method to determine the highest subscript in a one-dimensional array. You can also use the GetUpperBound method to determine the highest row and column subscripts in a two-dimensional array, as shown in Figure 9-49.

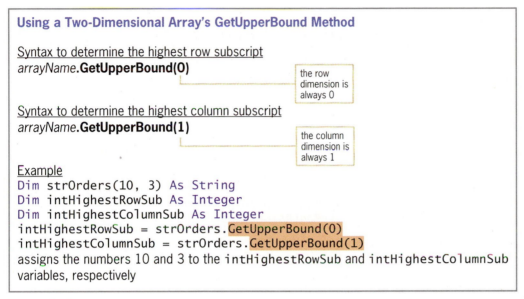

Using a Two-Dimensional Array's GetUpperBound Method

Syntax to determine the highest row subscript
arrayName.**GetUpperBound(0)**

the row dimension is always 0

Syntax to determine the highest column subscript
arrayName.**GetUpperBound(1)**

the column dimension is always 1

Example
```
Dim strOrders(10, 3) As String
Dim intHighestRowSub As Integer
Dim intHighestColumnSub As Integer
intHighestRowSub = strOrders.GetUpperBound(0)
intHighestColumnSub = strOrders.GetUpperBound(1)
```
assigns the numbers 10 and 3 to the intHighestRowSub and intHighestColumnSub variables, respectively

Figure 9-49   Syntax and an example of a two-dimensional array's GetUpperBound method

Traversing a Two-Dimensional Array

Recall that you use a loop to traverse a one-dimensional array. To traverse a two-dimensional array, you typically use two loops: an outer loop and a nested loop. One of the loops keeps track of the row subscript, and the other keeps track of the column subscript. You can code the loops using either the For...Next statement or the Do...Loop statement. Rather than using two loops to traverse a two-dimensional array, you can also use one For Each...Next loop. However, recall that the instructions in a For Each...Next loop can only read the array values; they cannot permanently modify the values.

Figure 9-50 shows examples of loops that traverse the strMonths array, displaying each element's value in the lstMonths control. Both loops in Example 1 are coded using the For... Next statement. However, either one of the loops could be coded using the Do...Loop statement instead. Or, both loops could be coded using the Do...Loop statement, as shown in Example 2. The loop in Example 3 is coded using the For Each...Next statement.

Traversing a Two-Dimensional Array

```
Private strMonths(,) As String = {{"Jan", "31"},
                                  {"Feb", "28"},
                                  {"Mar", "31"},
                                  {"Apr", "30"}}
```

Example 1
```
Dim intHighRow As Integer = strMonths.GetUpperBound(0)
Dim intHighCol As Integer = strMonths.GetUpperBound(1)
For intR As Integer = 0 To intHighRow
    For intC As Integer = 0 To intHighCol
        lstMonths.Items.Add(strMonths(intR, intC))
    Next intC
Next intR
```
displays the contents of the strMonths array in the lstMonths control; the array values are
displayed row by row, as follows: Jan, 31, Feb, 28, Mar, 31, Apr, and 30

Example 2
```
Dim intHighRow As Integer = strMonths.GetUpperBound(0)
Dim intHighCol As Integer = strMonths.GetUpperBound(1)
Dim intR As Integer
Dim intC As Integer
Do While intC <= intHighCol
    intR = 0
    Do While intR <= intHighRow
        lstMonths.Items.Add(strMonths(intR, intC))
        intR += 1
    Loop
    intC += 1
Loop
```
displays the contents of the strMonths array in the lstMonths control; the array values are
displayed column by column, as follows: Jan, Feb, Mar, Apr, 31, 28, 31, and 30

Example 3
```
For Each strElement As String In strMonths
    lstMonths.Items.Add(strElement)
Next strElement
```
displays the contents of the strMonths array in the lstMonths control; the array values are
displayed as follows: Jan, 31, Feb, 28, Mar, 31, Apr, and 30

Figure 9-50   Examples of loops used to traverse a two-dimensional array

Totaling the Values Stored in a Two-Dimensional Array

Figure 9-51 shows the problem specification for the Jenko Booksellers application, which
displays the total of the sales stored in a two-dimensional array.

Problem Specification

Jenko Booksellers sells paperback and hardcover books in each of its three stores. The sales amounts for the month of July (rounded to the nearest dollar) are shown here. Create an application that displays the total monthly sales. Store the sales amounts in a two-dimensional array that has three rows and two columns. Each row should contain the data pertaining to one of the three stores. Store the sales amounts for paperback books in the first column, and store the sales amounts for hardcover books in the second column.

	Paperback sales ($)	Hardcover sales ($)
Store 1	1500	2535
Store 2	2300	3678
Store 3	1850	2473

Figure 9-51   Problem specification for the Jenko Booksellers application

To code and then test the Jenko Booksellers application:

START HERE

1. If necessary, start Visual Studio 2015. Open the VB2015\Chap09\Jenko Solution\Jenko Solution (Jenko Solution.sln) file. Open the Code Editor window. Replace <your name> and <current date> in the comments with your name and the current date, respectively.

2. Locate the btnCalc_Click procedure. First, the procedure will declare and initialize a two-dimensional array to store the sales amounts. The array will contain three rows (one for each store) and two columns. The first column will contain the paperback book sales, and the second column will contain the hardcover book sales. Click the **blank line** above the End Sub clause, and then enter the following array declaration statement:

    Dim intSales(,) As Integer = {{1500, 2535},
    {2300, 3678},
    {1850, 2473}}

3. The procedure will also declare a variable that it can use to accumulate the sales amounts stored in the array. Type the following declaration statement, and then press **Enter** twice:

    Dim intTotal As Integer

4. The procedure will use a loop to total the values stored in the array. Enter the following lines of code:

    For Each intElement As Integer In intSales
    **   intTotal += intElement**
    Next intElement

5. Finally, the procedure will display the total sales. Insert a blank line below the `Next intElement` clause, and then enter the additional assignment statement indicated in Figure 9-52.

```
Private Sub btnCalc_Click(sender As Object, e As E
      ' displays the total sales

      Dim intSales(,) As Integer = {{1500, 2535},
                                    {2300, 3678},
                                    {1850, 2473}}
      Dim intTotal As Integer

      For Each intElement As Integer In intSales
          intTotal += intElement
      Next intElement
      lblTotal.Text = intTotal.ToString("c0")


End Sub
```

enter this additional assignment statement

Figure 9-52   btnCalc_Click procedure

6. Save the solution and then start the application. Click the **Calculate** button. The Total sales box indicates that the total monthly sales amount is $14,336. See Figure 9-53.

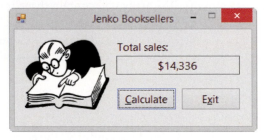

Figure 9-53   Total sales displayed in the interface

7. Click the **Exit** button. Close the Code Editor window and then close the solution.

Searching a Two-Dimensional Array

In Lesson B, you used two parallel one-dimensional arrays to code the Paper Warehouse application: a String array for the item IDs and a Double array for the corresponding prices. Instead of storing the price list in two parallel one-dimensional arrays, you can store it in a two-dimensional array. To do this, you store the IDs in the first column of the array, and you store the corresponding prices in the second column. However, you will need to treat the prices as strings because all of the data in a two-dimensional array must have the same data type.

START HERE

To use a two-dimensional array to code the Paper Warehouse application:

1. Open the Paper Solution (Paper Solution.sln) file contained in the VB2015\Chap09\ Paper Solution-Two-Dimensional folder. The text box's CharacterCasing and MaxLength properties are set to Upper and 4, respectively.

2. Open the Code Editor window. Replace <your name> and <current date> in the comments with your name and the current date, respectively.

3. Notice that the code to declare the two-dimensional array is already entered in the form's Declarations section. See Figure 9-54.

```
' declare two-dimensional array
Private strItems(,) As String = {{"A45G", "8.99"},
                                 {"J63Y", "12.99"},
                                 {"M93K", "5.99"},
                                 {"C20P", "13.5"},
                                 {"F77T", "7.25"}}
```

Figure 9-54   Array declaration statement

4. Locate the btnGet_Click procedure. The procedure declares three variables named strSearchId, intRow, and dblItemPrice. It then assigns the contents of the txtId control to the strSearchId variable.

5. The procedure will use a loop to search each element in the first column in the strItems array, stopping either when the end of the first column is reached or when the ID is located in the first column. Click the **blank line** above the End Sub clause, and then enter the following code:

```
Do Until intRow > strItems.GetUpperBound(0) OrElse
        strItems(intRow, 0) = strSearchId
        intRow += 1
Loop
```

6. Next, the procedure will use a selection structure to determine why the loop ended. You can make this determination by looking at the value in the intRow variable. If the loop ended because it reached the end of the array's first column without locating the ID, the intRow variable's value will be greater than the highest row subscript. On the other hand, if the loop ended because it located the ID in the first column, the intRow variable's value will be less than or equal to the highest row subscript. Insert two blank lines above the End Sub clause. In the blank line immediately above the End Sub clause, enter the following If clause:

```
If intRow <= strItems.GetUpperBound(0) Then
```

7. If the selection structure's condition evaluates to True, it means that the ID was located in the first column of the array. In that case, the structure's true path should assign the price contained in the same row as the ID, but in the second column in the array. Because the price is stored as a string, the procedure will need to convert it to a number before storing it in the dblItemPrice variable. Enter the following TryParse method:

```
Double.TryParse(strItems(intRow, 1), dblItemPrice)
```

8. The selection structure's true path then needs to determine whether the Employee discount check box is selected. If it is, the price should be reduced by 10%. Enter the following nested selection structure:

```
If chkDisc.Checked Then
    dblItemPrice *= 0.9
End If
```

9. Finally, the selection structure's true path should display the item's price in the lblPrice control. Insert a blank line below the nested End If clause, and then enter the following assignment statement:

lblPrice.Text = dblItemPrice.ToString("c2")

10. If the outer selection structure's condition evaluates to False, on the other hand, it means that the ID was not located in the first column of the array. In that case, the structure's false path should display the "Invalid ID" message in a message box. Enter the additional lines of code shaded in Figure 9-55.

```
' declare two-dimensional array
Private strItems(,) As String = {{"A45G", "8.99"},
                                 {"J63Y", "12.99"},
                                 {"M93K", "5.99"},
                                 {"C20P", "13.5"},
                                 {"F77T", "7.25"}}

Private Sub btnGet_Click(sender As Object, e As EventArgs
) Handles btnGet.Click
    ' display an item's price

    Dim strSearchId As String
    Dim intRow As Integer
    Dim dblItemPrice As Double

    strSearchId = txtId.Text

    ' search the first column for the ID
    ' continue searching until the end of the
    ' first column or the ID is found
    Do Until intRow > strItems.GetUpperBound(0) OrElse
        strItems(intRow, 0) = strSearchId
        intRow += 1
    Loop

    If intRow <= strItems.GetUpperBound(0) Then
        Double.TryParse(strItems(intRow, 1), dblItemPrice)
        If chkDisc.Checked Then
            dblItemPrice *= 0.9
        End If
        lblPrice.Text = dblItemPrice.ToString("c2")
    Else
        MessageBox.Show("Invalid ID", "Paper Warehouse",
                        MessageBoxButtons.OK,
                        MessageBoxIcon.Information)
    End If
End Sub
```

two-dimensional array declared in the form's Declarations section

searches for the ID in the array's first column

stores the corresponding price from the array's second column in a variable

Figure 9-55 Most of the code for the Paper Warehouse application using a two-dimensional array

START HERE **To test the Paper Warehouse application:**

1. Save the solution and then start the application. Type **m93k** in the ID box. Click the **Employee discount** check box to select it, and then click the **Get Price** button. $5.39 appears in the Price box. See Figure 9-56.

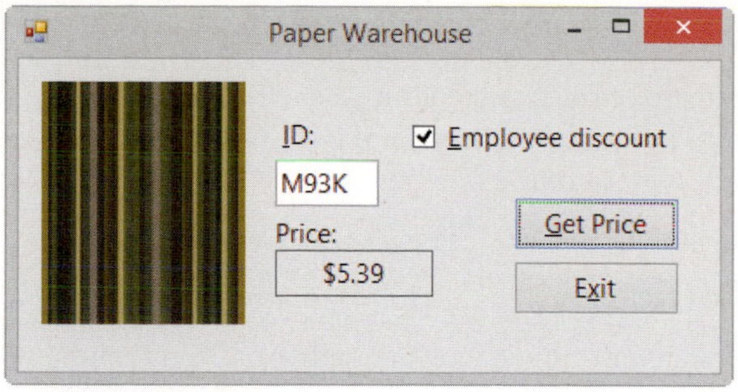

Figure 9-56 Interface showing the employee price for item M93K

2. Click the **Employee discount** check box to deselect it, and then click the **Get Price** button. $5.99 appears in the Price box.

3. Type **a45h** in the ID box, and then click the **Get Price** button. The "Invalid ID" message appears in a message box. Close the message box.

4. On your own, test the application using other valid and invalid IDs. When you are finished testing the application, click the **Exit** button. Close the Code Editor window and then close the solution.

Lesson C Summary

- To declare a two-dimensional array:

  Use either of the syntax versions shown below. In Version 1, the *highestRowSubscript* and *highestColumnSubscript* arguments are integers that specify the highest row and column subscripts, respectively, in the array. Using Version 1's syntax, the computer automatically initializes the array elements. In Version 2, the *initialValues* section is a list of values separated by commas and enclosed in braces. You include a separate initialValues section for each row in the array. Each initialValues section should contain the same number of values as there are columns in the array.

  Version 1: {**Dim** | **Private** | **Static**} *arrayName*(*highestRowSubscript*, *highestColumnSubscript*) **As** *dataType*

  Version 2: {**Dim** | **Private** | **Static**} *arrayName*(,) **As** *dataType* = {{*initialValues*},...{*initialValues*}}

- To refer to an element in a two-dimensional array:

  Use the syntax *arrayName*(*rowSubscript*, *columnSubscript*).

- To determine the highest row subscript in a two-dimensional array:

  Use the GetUpperBound method as follows: *arrayName*.**GetUpperBound(0)**.

- To determine the highest column subscript in a two-dimensional array:

  Use the GetUpperBound method as follows: *arrayName*.**GetUpperBound(1)**.

Lesson C Key Term

Two-dimensional array—an array made up of rows and columns; each element has the same name and data type and is identified by a unique combination of two subscripts: a row subscript and a column subscript

Lesson C Review Questions

1. Which of the following declares a two-dimensional array that has four rows and three columns?

   a. `Dim decNums(2, 3) As Decimal`
   b. `Dim decNums(3, 4) As Decimal`
   c. `Dim decNums(3, 2) As Decimal`
   d. `Dim decNums(4, 3) As Decimal`

2. The `intNum` array is declared as follows: `Dim intNum(,) As Integer = {{6, 12, 9, 5, 2}, {35, 60, 17, 8, 10}}`. The `intNum(1, 4) = intNum(1, 2) - 5` statement will _____.

   a. replace the 10 amount with 12   c. replace the 2 amount with 4
   b. replace the 5 amount with 7   d. none of the above

3. The `intNum` array is declared as follows: `Dim intNum(,) As Integer = {{6, 12, 9, 5, 2}, {35, 60, 17, 8, 10}}`. Which of the following If clauses determines whether the `intRow` and `intCol` variables contain valid row and column subscripts, respectively, for the array?

   a. `If intNum(intRow, intCol) >= 0 AndAlso`
      `    intNum(intRow, intCol) < 5 Then`
   b. `If intNum(intRow, intCol) >= 0 AndAlso`
      `    intNum(intRow, intCol) <= 5 Then`
   c. `If intRow >= 0 AndAlso intRow < 3 AndAlso`
      `    intCol >= 0 AndAlso intCol < 6 Then`
   d. `If intRow >= 0 AndAlso intRow < 2 AndAlso`
      `    intCol >= 0 AndAlso intCol < 5 Then`

4. Which of the following statements assigns the string "California" to the element located in the fourth column, sixth row in the two-dimensional `strStates` array?

   a. `strStates(3, 5) = "California"`
   b. `strStates(5, 3) = "California"`
   c. `strStates(6, 3) = "California"`
   d. `strStates(3, 6) = "California"`

5. Which of the following assigns the number 0 to each element in a two-row, four-column Integer array named `intSums`?

   a. `For intRow As Integer = 0 To 1`
      `    For intCol As Integer = 0 To 3`
      `        intSums(intRow, intCol) = 0`
      `    Next intCol`
      `Next intRow`

b.
```
Dim intRow As Integer
Dim intCol As Integer
Do While intRow < 2
   intCol = 0
   Do While intCol < 4
      intSums(intRow, intCol) = 0
      intCol += 1
   Loop
   intRow += 1
Loop
```

c.
```
For intX As Integer = 1 To 2
   For intY As Integer = 1 To 4
      intSums(intX - 1, intY - 1) = 0
   Next intY
Next intX
```

d. all of the above

6. Which of the following returns the highest column subscript in a two-dimensional array named `decPays`?

   a. `decPays.GetUpperBound(1)`
   b. `decPays.GetUpperBound(0)`
   c. `decPays.GetUpperSubscript(0)`
   d. `decPays.GetHighestColumn(0)`

Lesson C Exercises

1. Write the statement to declare a procedure-level array named `intBalances`. The array should have seven rows and three columns. Then write the statement to store the number 100 in the element located in the third row, second column.   INTRODUCTORY

2. Write a loop to store the number 0 in each element in the `intBalances` array from Exercise 1. Use the For...Next statement.   INTRODUCTORY

3. Rewrite the code from Exercise 2 using a Do...Loop statement.   INTRODUCTORY

4. Write the statement to assign the Boolean value True to the variable located in the second row, third column of a two-dimensional Boolean array named `blnAnswers`.   INTRODUCTORY

5. Write the Private statement to declare an Integer array named `intOrders` that has three rows and two columns. Use the following values to initialize the array: 1, 2, 10, 20, 100, 200.   INTRODUCTORY

6. Write the statements that determine the highest row and highest column subscripts in the `strTypes` array. The statements should assign the subscripts to the `intHighRow` and `intHighCol` variables, respectively.   INTRODUCTORY

7. Write the statement that determines the number of elements in a two-dimensional array named `strTypes`. The statement should assign the number to the `intNumTypes` variable.   INTRODUCTORY

8. Open the VB2015\Chap09\Westin Solution\Westin Solution (Westin Solution.sln) file. The btnForEach_Click procedure should use the For Each...Next statement to display the contents of the **strParts** array in the lstForEachParts control. The btnFor_Click procedure should use the For...Next statement to display the contents of the **strParts** array in the lstForParts control, column by column. Test the application appropriately.

9. Open the VB2015\Chp09\Bonus Solution\Bonus Solution (Bonus Solution.sln) file. The btnCalc_Click procedure should display the sum of the numbers stored in the following three array elements: the second row, second column; the first row, fourth column; and the third row, first column. Test the application appropriately.

10. Open the VB2015\Chap09\Sales Solution\Sales Solution (Sales Solution.sln) file. The btnCalc_Click procedure should increase the value stored in each array element by 25% and then display the results in the list box. Use two For...Next statements. Test the application appropriately.

11. Open the Shipping Solution (Shipping Solution.sln) file contained in the VB2015\ Chap09\Shipping Solution-Two-Dimensional folder. The btnDisplay_Click procedure should display a shipping charge that is based on the number of items a customer orders. The order amounts and shipping charges are listed in Figure 9-57. Store the minimum order amounts and shipping charges in a two-dimensional array. Display the appropriate shipping charge with a dollar sign and two decimal places. Test the application appropriately.

Minimum order	Maximum order	Shipping charge
1	5	10.99
6	10	7.99
11	20	3.99
21	No maximum	0

Figure 9-57   Order amounts and shipping charges for Exercise 11

12. In this exercise, you code an application that displays a grade based on the number of points entered by the user. Open the VB2015\Chap09\Kranton Solution\Kranton Solution (Kranton Solution.sln) file. The grading scale is shown in Figure 9-58. Store the minimum points and grades in a two-dimensional array. Test the application appropriately.

Minimum points	Maximum points	Grade
0	299	F
300	349	D
350	414	C
415	464	B
465	500	A

Figure 9-58   Grading scale for Exercise 12

13. Open the VB2015\Chap09\Gross Solution\Gross Solution (Gross Solution.sln) file. The application should store the pay codes and rates listed in Figure 9-59 in a two-dimensional array. It should also display the pay codes from the array in a list box. The btnCalc_Click procedure should display the gross pay, using the number of hours worked and the pay rate corresponding to the selected code. Test the application appropriately.

Pay code	Pay rate
A07	8.50
A10	8.75
B03	9.25
B24	9.90
C23	10.50

Figure 9-59   Pay codes and rates for Exercise 13

14. The sales manager at Lorenzo Markets wants you to create an application that displays the total sales made in each of three regions: the U.S., Canada, and Mexico. The application should also display the total company sales as well as the percentage that each region contributed to the total sales. The sales amounts for six months are shown in Figure 9-60. Create an application, using the following names for the solution and project, respectively: Lorenzo Solution and Lorenzo Project. Save the application in the VB2015\Chap09 folder. Create a suitable interface and then code the application. Store the sales amounts in a two-dimensional array. Test the application appropriately.

ADVANCED

Month	U.S. sales ($)	Canada sales ($)	Mexico sales ($)
1	120,000	90,000	65,000
2	190,000	85,000	64,000
3	175,000	80,000	71,000
4	188,000	83,000	67,000
5	125,000	87,000	65,000
6	163,000	80,000	64,000

Figure 9-60   Sales amounts for Exercise 14

15. Open the VB2015\Chap09\Harrison Solution\Harrison Solution (Harrison Solution.sln) file. The btnDisplay_Click procedure should display the largest number stored in the first column of the array. Code the procedure using the For...Next statement. Test the application appropriately.

ADVANCED

16. Open the VB2015\Chap09\Count Solution\Count Solution (Count Solution.sln) file. The btnDisplay_Click procedure should display the number of times each of the numbers from 1 through 9 appears in the `intNumbers` array. (Hint: Store the counts in a one-dimensional array.) Test the application appropriately.

ADVANCED

17. Create an application, using the following names for the solution and project, respectively: Bindy Solution and Bindy Project. Save the application in the VB2015\Chap09 folder. Bindy Enterprises sells the 10 items listed in Figure 9-61. Code the application in a way that allows the user to perform the tasks listed in the figure. (For Tasks 1 and 2, you can use either a text box or a list box to get the ID and/or color information from the user.) Test the application appropriately.

ADVANCED

ID	Color	Price
101	Blue	4.99
102	Red	4.99
103	Blue	10.49
104	Red	10.49
105	White	6.79
106	Red	6.79
107	Blue	6.79
108	Black	21.99
109	White	21.99
110	Blue	21.99

Tasks

1)   When the user either enters the ID in a text box or selects the ID from a list box, the application should display the ID's color and price.

2)   When the user either enters the color in a text box or selects the color from a list box, the application should display the IDs and prices of all items available in that color.

3)   When the user enters a price in a text box, the application should display the IDs, colors, and prices of items selling at or below that price.

Figure 9-61   Information for Exercise 17

SWAT THE BUGS

18. Open the VB2015\Chap09\Debug Solution\Debug Solution (Debug Solution.sln) file. Open the Code Editor window and review the existing code. The first column in the **strNames** array contains first names, and the second column contains last names. The btnDisplay_Click procedure should display the first and last names in the lstFirst and lstLast controls, respectively. Correct the code to remove the jagged lines. Save the solution and then start the application. Click the Display button. Notice that the application is not working correctly. Correct the errors in the application's code, and then test the application appropriately.

Structures and Sequential Access Files

Creating the eBook Collection Application

In this chapter, you will create an application that keeps track of a person's collection of eBooks. The application will save, in a sequential access file named Ebooks.txt, three items of information for each eBook: the title, the author's name, and the price. When the application is started, it will display the contents of the file in a list box. The user can then add information to the list box and file, as well as remove information from the list box and file.

Previewing the eBook Collection Application

Before you start the first lesson in this chapter, you will preview the completed application contained in the VB2015\Chap10 folder.

START HERE

To preview the completed application:

1. Use Windows to locate and then open the VB2015\Chap10 folder. Right-click **Ebook** (**Ebook.exe**) in the list of filenames and then click **Open**. The application's user interface appears on the screen, with the contents of the Ebooks.txt file displayed in three columns in the list box. You will learn how to align columns of information in Lesson C.

2. First, you will add John Grisham's Gray Mountain eBook to the list box. The eBook is priced at $9.99. Click the **Add an eBook** button. Type **Gray Mountain** and press **Enter**. Type **John Grisham** and press **Enter**. Type **9.99** and press **Enter**. The list box's Sorted property is set to True, so the information you entered appears as the fourth item in the list box. See Figure 10-1.

the eBook information you entered

Figure 10-1   eBook information added to the list box

3. Click the **Exit** button. The `Me.Close()` instruction in the btnExit_Click procedure invokes the form's FormClosing event, which you learned about in Chapter 7. The frmMain_FormClosing procedure saves the contents of the list box in the Ebooks.txt sequential access file. You will learn about sequential access files in Lesson B.

4. Use Windows to open the VB2015\Chap10 folder. Right-click **Ebooks.txt** in the list of filenames. Point to **Open with** and then click **Notepad** to view the contents of the Ebooks.txt file. See Figure 10-2.

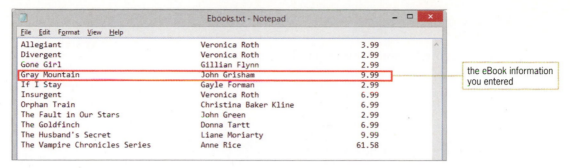

Figure 10-2 Contents of the Ebooks.txt file

5. Close Notepad. Start the application again. The list box displays the current contents of the Ebooks.txt file, which includes the eBook information added in Step 2.

6. Now you will remove the Gray Mountain eBook from the list box. Click **Gray Mountain** in the list box, and then click the **Remove an eBook** button.

7. Click the **Exit** button. Open the Ebooks.txt file in Notepad. Notice that the Gray Mountain eBook, which you removed in the previous step, no longer appears in the file. Close Notepad.

In Lesson A, you will learn how to create a structure in Visual Basic. Lesson B covers sequential access files. You will code the eBook Collection application in Lesson C. Be sure to complete each lesson in full and do all of the end-of-lesson questions and several exercises before continuing to the next lesson.

▌ LESSON A

After studying Lesson A, you should be able to:

- Create a structure
- Declare and use a structure variable
- Pass a structure variable to a procedure
- Create an array of structure variables

Structures

The data types used in previous chapters, such as Integer and Double, are built into the Visual Basic language. You can also create your own data types using the **Structure statement**, whose syntax is shown in Figure 10-3. Data types created by the Structure statement are referred to as **user-defined data types** or **structures**.

Structure Statement

Syntax
Structure *structureName*
      Public *memberVariableName1* **As** *dataType*
      [**Public** *memberVariableNameN* **As** *dataType*]
End Structure

Example
```
Structure Employee
    Public strId As String
    Public strFirst As String
    Public strLast As String
    Public dblPay As Double
End Structure
```

Figure 10-3   Syntax and an example of the Structure statement

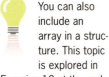

Most programmers use the Class statement (rather than the Structure statement) to create data types that contain procedures. You will learn about the Class statement in Chapter 11.

You can also include an array in a structure. This topic is explored in Exercise 12 at the end of this lesson.

The structures you create are composed of members, which are defined between the Structure and End Structure clauses. The members can be variables, constants, or procedures. However, in most cases, the members will be variables; such variables are referred to as **member variables**. The *dataType* in the member variable definition identifies the type of data the member variable will store, and it can be any of the standard data types available in Visual Basic; it can also be another structure (user-defined data type). The Structure statement is typically entered in the form's Declarations section, which begins with the Public Class clause and ends with the End Class clause. The structure's name is usually entered using Pascal case, whereas the member variable names are entered using camel case.

The Structure statement allows the programmer to group related items into one unit: a structure. However, keep in mind that the Structure statement merely defines the structure members. It does not reserve any memory locations inside the computer. You reserve memory locations by declaring a structure variable.

Declaring and Using a Structure Variable

After entering the Structure statement in the Code Editor window, you then can use the structure to declare a variable. Variables declared using a structure are often referred to as **structure variables**. The syntax for creating a structure variable is shown in Figure 10-4. The figure also includes examples of declaring structure variables using the Employee structure from Figure 10-3.

Declaring a Structure Variable

Syntax
{**Dim** | **Private**} *structureVariableName* **As** *structureName*

Example 1
Dim hourly As Employee
declares a procedure-level Employee structure variable named hourly

Example 2
Private salaried As Employee
declares a class-level Employee structure variable named salaried

---

Figure 10-4   Syntax and examples of declaring a structure variable

Similar to the way the Dim intAge As Integer instruction declares an Integer variable named intAge, the Dim hourly As Employee instruction in Example 1 declares an Employee variable named hourly. However, unlike the intAge variable, the hourly variable contains four member variables. In code, you refer to the entire structure variable by its name—in this case, hourly. You refer to a member variable by preceding its name with the name of the structure variable in which it is defined. You use the dot member access operator (a period) to separate the structure variable's name from the member variable's name, like this: hourly.strId, hourly.strFirst, hourly.strLast, and hourly.dblPay. The dot member access operator indicates that strId, strFirst, strLast, and dblPay are members of the hourly structure variable.

The Private salaried As Employee instruction in Example 2 in Figure 10-4 declares a class-level Employee variable named salaried. The names of the member variables within the salaried variable are salaried.strId, salaried.strFirst, salaried.strLast, and salaried.dblPay.

The member variables in a structure variable can be used just like any other variables. You can assign values to them, use them in calculations, display their contents, and so on. Figure 10-5 shows various ways of using the member variables created by the statements shown in Figure 10-4.

Using a Member Variable

Example 1
```
hourly.strFirst = "Caroline"
```
assigns the string "Caroline" to the `hourly.strFirst` member variable

Example 2
```
hourly.dblPay *= 1.05
```
multiplies the contents of the `hourly.dblPay` member variable by 1.05 and then assigns the result to the member variable; you can also write the statement as `hourly.dblPay = hourly.dblPay * 1.05`

Example 3
```
lblSalary.Text = salaried.dblPay.ToString("C2")
```
formats the value contained in the `salaried.dblPay` member variable and then displays the result in the lblSalary control

---

Figure 10-5   Examples of using a member variable

Programmers use structure variables when they need to pass a group of related items to a procedure for further processing. This is because it's easier to pass one structure variable rather than many individual variables. Programmers also use structure variables to store related items in an array, even when the members have different data types. In the next two sections, you will learn how to pass a structure variable to a procedure and also how to store a structure variable in an array.

Passing a Structure Variable to a Procedure

The sales manager at Norbert Pool & Spa Depot wants you to create an application that determines the amount of water required to fill a rectangular pool. To perform this task, the application will need to calculate the volume of the pool. You calculate the volume by first multiplying the pool's length by its width and then multiplying the result by the pool's depth. Assuming the length, width, and depth are measured in feet, this gives you the volume in cubic feet. To determine the number of gallons of water, you multiply the number of cubic feet by 7.48 because there are 7.48 gallons in one cubic foot.

START HERE

To open and then test the Norbert application:

1. If necessary, start Visual Studio 2015. Open the VB2015\Chap10\Norbert Solution\ Norbert Solution (Norbert Solution.sln) file. Start the application. Type **100** in the Length box, type **30** in the Width box, and type **4** in the Depth box. Click the **Calculate** button. The required number of gallons appears in the interface. See Figure 10-6.

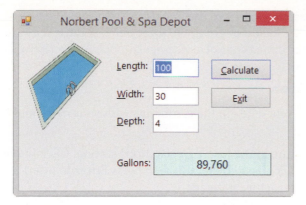

Figure 10-6 Interface showing the required number of gallons

2. Click the **Exit** button to end the application, and then open the Code Editor window.

Figure 10-7 shows the GetGallons function and the btnCalc_Click procedure. The procedure calls the function, passing it three variables *by value*. The function uses the values to calculate the number of gallons required to fill the pool. The function returns the number of gallons as a Double number to the procedure, which assigns the value to the dblGallons variable.

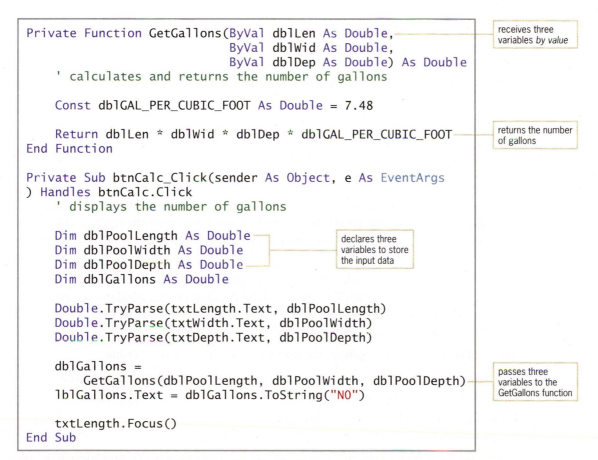

```vb
Private Function GetGallons(ByVal dblLen As Double,          receives three
                            ByVal dblWid As Double,          variables by value
                            ByVal dblDep As Double) As Double
    ' calculates and returns the number of gallons

    Const dblGAL_PER_CUBIC_FOOT As Double = 7.48

    Return dblLen * dblWid * dblDep * dblGAL_PER_CUBIC_FOOT   returns the number
End Function                                                 of gallons

Private Sub btnCalc_Click(sender As Object, e As EventArgs
) Handles btnCalc.Click
    ' displays the number of gallons

    Dim dblPoolLength As Double       declares three
    Dim dblPoolWidth As Double        variables to store
    Dim dblPoolDepth As Double        the input data
    Dim dblGallons As Double

    Double.TryParse(txtLength.Text, dblPoolLength)
    Double.TryParse(txtWidth.Text, dblPoolWidth)
    Double.TryParse(txtDepth.Text, dblPoolDepth)

    dblGallons =
        GetGallons(dblPoolLength, dblPoolWidth, dblPoolDepth)   passes three
    lblGallons.Text = dblGallons.ToString("N0")                variables to the
                                                               GetGallons function
    txtLength.Focus()
End Sub
```

Figure 10-7 Code for the Norbert Pool & Spa Depot application (without a structure)

A more convenient way of coding the application is to use a structure to group together the input items: length, width, and depth. It's logical to group the three items because they are related; each represents one of the three dimensions of a rectangular pool. A descriptive name for the structure would be Dimensions.

START HERE

To use a structure in the application:

1. Replace <your name> and <current date> in the comments with your name and the current date, respectively.

2. First, you will declare the structure in the form's Declarations section. Click the **blank line** immediately below the Public Class clause, and then press **Enter** to insert another blank line. Enter the following Structure statement:

   Structure Dimensions
       Public dblLength As Double
       Public dblWidth As Double
       Public dblDepth As Double
   End Structure

3. Locate the btnCalc_Click procedure. The procedure will use a structure variable (rather than three separate variables) to store the input items. Replace the first three Dim statements with the following Dim statement:

   Dim poolSize As Dimensions

4. Next, you will store each input item in its corresponding member in the structure variable. In the three TryParse methods, change `dblPoolLength`, `dblPoolWidth`, and `dblPoolDepth` to **poolSize.dblLength**, **poolSize.dblWidth**, and **poolSize.dblDepth**, respectively.

5. Instead of sending three separate variables to the GetGallons function, the procedure now needs to send only one variable: the structure variable. When you pass a structure variable to a procedure, all of its members are passed automatically. Although passing one structure variable rather than three separate variables may not seem like a huge advantage, consider the convenience of passing one structure variable rather than 10 separate variables! Change the statement that invokes the GetGallons function to **dblGallons = GetGallons(poolSize)**. Don't be concerned about the squiggle (jagged line) that appears below `GetGallons(poolSize)` in the statement. It will disappear when you modify the GetGallons function in the next step.

6. Locate the GetGallons function. The function will now receive a Dimensions structure variable rather than three Double variables. Like the Double variables, the structure variable will be passed *by value* because the function does not need to change any member's value. Change the function's header to the following:

   Private Function GetGallons(ByVal pool As Dimensions) As Double

7. The function will now use the members of the structure variable to calculate the number of gallons. Change the Return statement as follows:

   Return pool.dblLength * pool.dblWidth *
       pool.dblDepth * dblGAL_PER_CUBIC_FOOT

Figure 10-8 shows the Structure statement, the GetGallons function, and the btnCalc_Click procedure. The procedure calls the function, passing it a structure variable *by value*. The function uses the values contained in the structure variable to calculate the number of gallons required to fill the pool. The function returns the number of gallons as a Double number to the procedure, which assigns the value to the `dblGallons` variable.

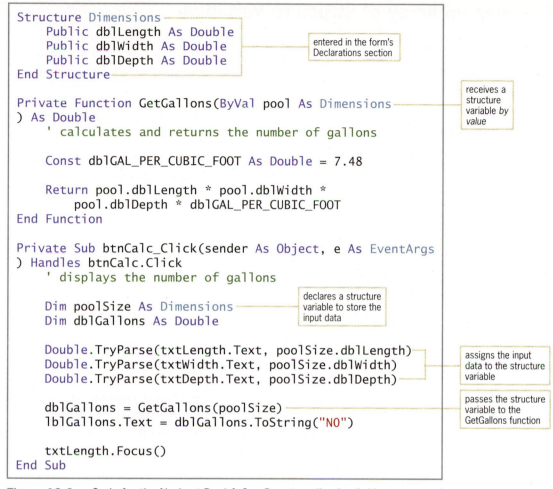

```
Structure Dimensions
    Public dblLength As Double
    Public dblWidth As Double
    Public dblDepth As Double
End Structure

Private Function GetGallons(ByVal pool As Dimensions
) As Double
    ' calculates and returns the number of gallons

    Const dblGAL_PER_CUBIC_FOOT As Double = 7.48

    Return pool.dblLength * pool.dblWidth *
        pool.dblDepth * dblGAL_PER_CUBIC_FOOT
End Function

Private Sub btnCalc_Click(sender As Object, e As EventArgs
) Handles btnCalc.Click
    ' displays the number of gallons

    Dim poolSize As Dimensions
    Dim dblGallons As Double

    Double.TryParse(txtLength.Text, poolSize.dblLength)
    Double.TryParse(txtWidth.Text, poolSize.dblWidth)
    Double.TryParse(txtDepth.Text, poolSize.dblDepth)

    dblGallons = GetGallons(poolSize)
    lblGallons.Text = dblGallons.ToString("N0")

    txtLength.Focus()
End Sub
```

Callouts:
- entered in the form's Declarations section
- receives a structure variable *by value*
- declares a structure variable to store the input data
- assigns the input data to the structure variable
- passes the structure variable to the GetGallons function

Figure 10-8 Code for the Norbert Pool & Spa Depot application (with a structure)

To test the modified code:

START HERE

1. Save the solution and then start the application. Type **100**, **30**, and **4** in the Length, Width, and Depth boxes, respectively. Press **Enter** to select the Calculate button. The required number of gallons (89,760) appears in the interface, as shown earlier in Figure 10-6.

2. Click the **Exit** button. Close the Code Editor window and then close the solution.

YOU DO IT 1!

Create an application named YouDoIt 1 and save it in the VB2015\Chap10 folder. Add two text boxes, a label, and a button to the form. Open the Code Editor window. Create a structure named Rectangle. The structure should have two members: one for the rectangle's length and one for its width. The button's Click event procedure should declare a Rectangle variable named myRectangle. It then should assign the text box values to the variable's members. Next, the procedure should pass the myRectangle variable to a function that calculates and returns the area of the rectangle. Finally, the procedure should display the function's return value in the label. Code the procedure. Save the solution, and then start and test the application. Close the solution.

Creating an Array of Structure Variables

As mentioned earlier, another advantage of using a structure is that a structure variable can be stored in an array, even when its members have different data types. The Paper Warehouse application from Chapter 9 can be used to illustrate this concept. The problem specification is shown in Figure 10-9.

Problem Specification

Create an application that displays the price of an item corresponding to an ID entered by the user. The IDs and corresponding prices are shown here. However, employees are entitled to a 10% discount. The application should store the price list in an array.

Item ID	Price
A45G	8.99
J63Y	12.99
M93K	5.99
C20P	13.50
F77T	7.25

Figure 10-9 Problem specification for the Paper Warehouse application

In Chapter 9's Lesson B, you coded the application using two parallel one-dimensional arrays: one having the String data type and the other having the Double data type. Then, in Lesson C, you coded it using a two-dimensional String array. In this lesson, you will code the application using a one-dimensional array of structure variables. (Notice that there are many different ways of solving the same problem.) Each structure variable will contain two member variables: a String variable for the ID and a Double variable for the price.

START HERE

To open the Paper Warehouse application:

1. Open the Paper Solution (Paper Solution.sln) file contained in the VB2015\Chap10\ Paper Solution-Structure folder. See Figure 10-10.

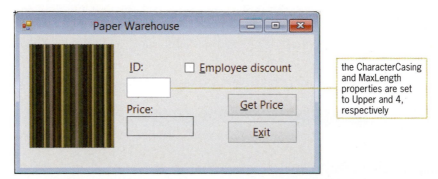

the CharacterCasing and MaxLength properties are set to Upper and 4, respectively

Figure 10-10 Interface for the Paper Warehouse application

2. Open the Code Editor window. Replace <your name> and <current date> in the comments with your name and the current date, respectively.

Figure 10-11 shows the code entered in both the form's Declarations section and the btnGet_Click procedure. The code, which comes from Chapter 9's Lesson B, uses two parallel one-dimensional arrays. In the remainder of this lesson, you will modify the code to use a structure.

```
' declare parallel arrays
Private strIds() As String =
    {"A45G", "J63Y", "M93K", "C20P", "F77T"}
Private dblPrices() As Double = {8.99, 12.99, 5.99, 13.5, 7.25}

Private Sub btnGet_Click(sender As Object, e As EventArgs
) Handles btnGet.Click
    ' display an item's price

    Dim strSearchId As String
    Dim intSub As Integer
    Dim dblItemPrice As Double

    strSearchId = txtId.Text

    ' search the strIds array until the
    ' end of the array or the ID is found
    Do Until intSub = strIds.Length OrElse
        strIds(intSub) = strSearchId
        intSub += 1
    Loop

    If intSub < strIds.Length Then
        dblItemPrice = dblPrices(intSub)
        If chkDisc.Checked Then
            dblItemPrice *= 0.9
        End If
        lblPrice.Text = dblItemPrice.ToString("c2")
    Else
        MessageBox.Show("Invalid ID", "Paper Warehouse",
                MessageBoxButtons.OK,
                MessageBoxIcon.Information)
    End If
End Sub
```

form's Declarations section

btnGet_Click procedure

Figure 10-11   Code for the Paper Warehouse application (without a structure)

To begin modifying the code to use a structure:

START HERE

1. First, you will declare the ProductInfo structure, which will contain two members: one for the item ID and one for the price. Click the **blank line** immediately below the Public Class clause, and then press **Enter** to insert another blank line. Enter the following Structure statement:

   Structure ProductInfo
   **   Public strId As String**
   **   Public dblPrice As Double**
   End Structure

2. If necessary, insert a blank line below the End Structure clause.

3. Rather than using two parallel one-dimensional arrays to store the price list, the procedure will use a one-dimensional array of ProductInfo structure variables. Change the ' declare parallel arrays comment to '**declare array of structure variables**.

4. Replace the two array declaration statements with the following statement:

Private priceList(4) As ProductInfo

The frmMain_Load procedure will be responsible for storing the five IDs and prices in the priceList array. Keep in mind that each element in the array is a structure variable, and each structure variable contains two member variables: strId and dblPrice. You refer to a member variable in an array element using the syntax shown in Figure 10-12. The figure also indicates how you would refer to some of the member variables contained in the priceList array. For example, to refer to the strId member contained in the first array element, you use priceList(0).strId. Similarly, you use priceList(4).dblPrice to refer to the dblPrice member contained in the last array element.

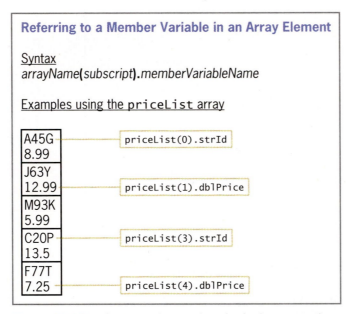

Figure 10-12   Syntax and examples of referring to member variables in an array

START HERE

To continue modifying the code:

1. Open the form's Load event procedure. Type the following comment and then press **Enter** twice:

' **fill array with IDs and prices**

2. Enter the following assignment statements:

priceList(0).strId = "A45G"
priceList(0).dblPrice = 8.99
priceList(1).strId = "J63Y"
priceList(1).dblPrice = 12.99
priceList(2).strId = "M93K"
priceList(2).dblPrice = 5.99
priceList(3).strId = "C20P"
priceList(3).dblPrice = 13.5
priceList(4).strId = "F77T"
priceList(4).dblPrice = 7.25

3. Locate the btnGet_Click procedure. The loop now needs to search the `priceList` array (rather than the `strIds` array). Change `strIds` in the `' search the strIds array until the` comment to **priceList**.

4. The loop should search each element in the array, comparing the value contained in the current element's `strId` member with the value stored in the `strSearchId` variable. The loop should stop searching either when the end of the array is reached or when the ID is found. Change the Do clause to the following:

    Do Until intSub = priceList.Length OrElse
        priceList(intSub).strId = strSearchId

5. The selection structure in the procedure determines why the loop ended and then takes the appropriate action. Currently, the statement's condition compares the value contained in the `intSub` variable with the value stored in the `strIds` array's Length property. Recall that a one-dimensional array's Length property stores an integer that represents the number of elements in the array. You will need to modify the condition so that it compares the `intSub` variable's value with the value stored in the `priceList` array's Length property. Change `strIds.Length` in the If clause to **priceList.Length**.

6. If the value contained in the `intSub` variable is less than the number of array elements, the loop ended because the ID was located in the array. In that case, the selection structure's true path should assign the corresponding price to the `dblItemPrice` variable. In the assignment statement below the If clause, change `dblPrices(intSub)` to **priceList(intSub).dblPrice**.

Figure 10-13 shows the form's Declarations section, the btnGet_Click procedure, and the frmMain_Load procedure. The code pertaining to the structure is shaded in the figure.

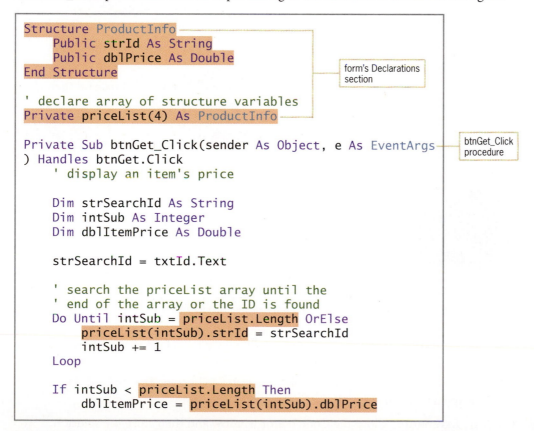

You can also write the first expression in the Do loop's condition as `intSub > priceList.GetUpperBound(0)`.

Figure 10-13 Code for the Paper Warehouse application (with a structure) *(continues)*

(continued)

```
        If chkDisc.Checked Then
            dblItemPrice *= 0.9
        End If
        lblPrice.Text = dblItemPrice.ToString("c2")
    Else
        MessageBox.Show("Invalid ID", "Paper Warehouse",
                        MessageBoxButtons.OK,
                        MessageBoxIcon.Information)
    End If
End Sub

Private Sub frmMain_Load(sender As Object, e As EventArgs──── frmMain_Load
) Handles Me.Load                                             procedure
    ' fill array with IDs and prices

    priceList(0).strId = "A45G"
    priceList(0).dblPrice = 8.99
    priceList(1).strId = "J63Y"
    priceList(1).dblPrice = 12.99
    priceList(2).strId = "M93K"
    priceList(2).dblPrice = 5.99
    priceList(3).strId = "C20P"
    priceList(3).dblPrice = 13.5
    priceList(4).strId = "F77T"
    priceList(4).dblPrice = 7.25

End Sub
```

Figure 10-13   Code for the Paper Warehouse application (with a structure)

START HERE **To test the application's code:**

1. Save the solution and then start the application. Type **f77t** in the ID box, and then click the **Get Price** button. $7.25 appears in the Price box. See Figure 10-14.

Figure 10-14   Interface showing the price for product ID F77T

2. Click the **Employee discount** check box, and then click the **Get Price** button. $6.53 appears in the Price box.

3. Type **a45h** in the ID box, and then click the **Get Price** button. The "Invalid ID" message appears in a message box. Close the message box.

4. Click the **Exit** button. Close the Code Editor window and then close the solution.

Lesson A Summary

- To create a structure (user-defined data type):

  Use the Structure statement, whose syntax is shown in Figure 10-3. In most applications, the Structure statement is entered in the form's Declarations section.

- To declare a structure variable:

  Use the following syntax: {`Dim` | `Private`} *structureVariableName* `As` *structureName*.

- To refer to a member within a structure variable:

  Use the syntax *structureVariableName.memberVariableName*.

- To create an array of structure variables:

  Declare the array using the structure as the data type.

- To refer to a member within a structure variable stored in an array:

  Use the syntax *arrayName(subscript).memberVariableName*.

Lesson A Key Terms

Member variables—the variables contained in a structure

Structure statement—used to create user-defined data types, called structures

Structure variables—variables declared using a structure as the data type

Structures—data types created by the Structure statement; allow the programmer to group related items into one unit; also called user-defined data types

User-defined data types—data types created by the Structure statement; also called structures

Lesson A Review Questions

1. Which statement is used to create a user-defined data type?

    a. Declare
    b. Define
    c. Structure
    d. UserType

2. The `course` structure variable contains a member variable named `strGrade`. Which of the following statements assigns the string "B" to the member variable?

    a. `course.strGrade(0) = "B"`
    b. `course.strGrade = "B"`
    c. `strGrade.course = "B"`
    d. none of the above

3. An array is declared using the statement `Dim cities(10) As CityInfo`. Which of the following statements assigns the number 4500 to the `intPopulation` member variable contained in the last array element?

    a. `cities.intPopulation(10) = 4500`
    b. `CityInfo.cities.intPopulation = 4500`
    c. `cities(9).intPopulation = 4500`
    d. `cities(10).intPopulation = 4500`

4. An application uses a structure named `Employee`. Which of the following statements declares a five-element array of Employee structure variables?

    a. `Dim workers(4) As Employee`
    b. `Dim workers(5) As Employee`
    c. `Dim workers As Employee(4)`
    d. `Dim workers As Employee(5)`

5. Where is the Structure statement typically entered?

    a. the form's Declarations section
    b. the Definition section in the Code Editor window
    c. the form's Load event procedure
    d. the User-defined section in the Code Editor window

Lesson A Exercises

INTRODUCTORY

1. Write a Structure statement that defines a structure named Book. The structure contains three member variables named `strTitle`, `strAuthor`, and `decPrice`. Then write a Dim statement that declares a Book variable named `fiction`.

INTRODUCTORY

2. Write a Structure statement that defines a structure named SongInfo. The structure contains three member variables named `strName`, `strArtist`, and `strSongLength`. Then write a Private statement that declares a SongInfo variable named `mySongs`.

INTRODUCTORY

3. An application contains the Structure statement shown here. Write a Dim statement that declares a Computer variable named `homeUse`. Then write an assignment statement that assigns the string "KRZ45" to the `strModel` member. Finally, write an assignment statement that assigns the number 149.99 to the `dblCost` member.

```
Structure Computer
    Public strModel As String
    Public dblCost As Double
End Structure
```

INTRODUCTORY

4. An application contains the Structure statement shown here. Write a Dim statement that declares a MyFriend variable named `school`. Then write assignment statements that assign the value in the txtFirst control to the `strFirst` member and assign the value in the txtLast control to the `strLast` member. Finally, write assignment statements that assign the value in the `strLast` member to the lblLast control and assign the value in the `strFirst` member to the lblFirst control.

```
Structure MyFriend
   Public strLast As String
   Public strFirst As String
End Structure
```

5. An application contains the Structure statement shown here. Write a Private statement that declares a 10-element one-dimensional array of Computer variables. Name the array **business**. Then write an assignment statement that assigns the string "AR456" to the **strModel** member contained in the first array element. Finally, write an assignment statement that assigns the number 699.99 to the **decCost** member contained in the first array element.

    INTRODUCTORY

```
Structure Computer
   Public strModel As String
   Public decCost As Decimal
End Structure
```

6. An application contains the Structure statement shown here. Write a Dim statement that declares a five-element one-dimensional array of MyFriend variables. Name the array **home**. Then write an assignment statement that assigns the value in the txtName control to the **strName** member contained in the last array element. Finally, write an assignment statement that assigns the value in the txtBirthday control to the **strBirthday** member contained in the last array element.

    INTRODUCTORY

```
Structure MyFriend
   Public strName As String
   Public strBirthday As String
End Structure
```

7. Open the VB2015\Chap10\City Solution\City Solution (City Solution.sln) file. Open the Code Editor window and review the existing code. Locate the btnDisplay_Click procedure. The procedure should display the contents of the array of structure variables in the list box, using the following format: the city name followed by a comma, a space, and the state name. Test the application appropriately.

    INTRODUCTORY

8. In this exercise, you modify the Paper Warehouse application completed in this lesson. Use Windows to make a copy of the Paper Solution-Structure folder. Rename the folder Modified Paper Solution-Structure. Open the Paper Solution (Paper Solution.sln) file contained in the Modified Paper Solution-Structure folder. The modified application should display both the name and the price corresponding to the ID entered by the user. The names of the items are shown in Figure 10-15. Make the appropriate modifications to the interface and the code (including the Structure statement). Test the application appropriately.

    INTERMEDIATE

ID	Name
A45G	Stripes
J63Y	Dotted Swiss
M93K	Checkered
C20P	Chevron
F77T	Circles

Figure 10-15   Product information for Exercise 8

INTERMEDIATE

9. In this exercise, you code an application that displays a grade based on the number of points entered by the user. The grading scale is shown in Figure 10-16. Open the VB2015\Chap10\Chang Solution\Chang Solution (Chang Solution.sln) file. Create a structure that contains two members: an Integer variable for the minimum points and a String variable for the grades. Use the structure to declare a class-level one-dimensional array that has five elements. In the form's Load event procedure, store the minimum points and grades in the array. The application should search the array for the number of points entered by the user and then display the appropriate grade from the array. Test the application appropriately.

Minimum points	Maximum points	Grade
0	299	F
300	349	D
350	414	C
415	464	B
465	500	A

Figure 10-16   Grading scale for Exercise 9

ADVANCED

10. Create an application, using the following names for the solution and project, respectively: Car Solution and Car Project. Save the application in the VB2015\Chap10 folder. Create the interface shown in Figure 10-17. Fill the list boxes in the frmMain_Load procedure. Create a structure that groups together a salesperson's name, the number of new cars he or she sold, and the number of used cars he or she sold. Use an array of four structure variables to keep track of the information for the four salespeople. The Add to Total button should add the number sold to the appropriate array element. For example, if the user selects Sam Jeeter in the Salesperson list box, selects New in the Car type list box, and then types 5 in the Sold box, the button should add the number 5 to the number of new cars Sam sold. The Display button should display the number of new cars sold, the number of used cars sold, and the total number of cars sold by the salesperson whose name is selected in the Salesperson list box. Test the application appropriately.

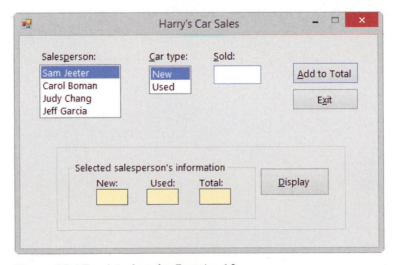

Figure 10-17   Interface for Exercise 10

11. In this exercise, you modify the Die Tracker application from Chapter 9. Copy the Die Solution folder from the VB2015\Chap09 folder to the VB2015\Chap10 folder, and then open the Die Solution (Die Solution.sln) file. Rather than using three parallel arrays, the application should use an array of structure variables. Each structure variable should contain three members. Modify the application's code and then test it appropriately. ADVANCED

12. Open the VB2015\Chap10\Average Solution\Average Solution (Average Solution.sln) file. The application should display a student's name and the average of five test scores entered by the user. DISCOVERY

    a. Create a structure named StudentInfo. The structure should contain two members: a String variable for the student's name and a Double array for the test scores. An array contained in a structure cannot be assigned an initial size, so you will need to include an empty set of parentheses after the array name, like this: `Public dblScores() As Double`.

    b. Open the code template for the btnCalc_Click procedure. First, use the StudentInfo structure to declare a structure variable. Next, research the Visual Basic ReDim statement. Use the ReDim statement to declare the array's size. The array should have five elements.

    c. The btnCalc_Click procedure should use the InputBox function to get the student's name. It should also use a repetition structure and the InputBox function to get the five test scores from the user, storing each in the array. The procedure should display the student's name and his or her average test score in the lblAverage control. Test the appliation appropriately.

13. In this exercise, you modify the application from Exercise 12. Use Windows to make a copy of the Average Solution folder. Rename the folder Modified Average Solution. Open the Average Solution (Average Solution.sln) file contained in the Modified Average Solution folder. Change the font used in the lblAverage control to Courier New. Change the control's TextAlign property to TopLeft, and then resize the control to display four lines of text. Open the Code Editor window. Modify the application to calculate the average of five test scores for each of four students. (Hint: Use an array of structure variables.) Display each student's name and average test score in the lblAverage control. Test the application appropriately. DISCOVERY

LESSON B

After studying Lesson B, you should be able to:

- Open and close a sequential access file

- Write data to a sequential access file

- Read data from a sequential access file

- Determine whether a sequential access file exists

- Test for the end of a sequential access file

Ch10B

Sequential Access Files

In addition to getting data from the keyboard and sending data to the computer screen, an application can also read data from and write data to a file on a disk. Files to which data is written are called **output files** because the files store the output produced by an application. Files that are read by the computer are called **input files** because an application uses the data in these files as input.

Most input and output files are composed of lines of text that are both read and written in consecutive order, one line at a time, beginning with the first line in the file and ending with the last line in the file. Such files are referred to as **sequential access files** because of the manner in which the lines of text are accessed. They are also called **text files** because they are composed of lines of text. Examples of text stored in sequential access files include an employee list, a memo, and a sales report.

Writing Data to a Sequential Access File

An item of data—such as the string "Robert"—is viewed differently by a human being and by a computer. To a human being, the string represents a person's name; to a computer, it is merely a sequence of characters. Programmers refer to a sequence of characters as a **stream of characters**.

In Visual Basic, you use a **StreamWriter object** to write a stream of characters to a sequential access file. Before you create the object, you first declare a variable to store the object in the computer's internal memory. Figure 10-18 shows the syntax and an example of declaring a StreamWriter variable. The IO in the syntax stands for Input/Output.

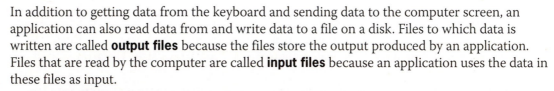

Declaring a StreamWriter Variable

<u>Syntax</u>
{**Dim** | **Private**} *streamWriterVariableName* **As IO.StreamWriter**

<u>Example</u>
Dim outFile As IO.StreamWriter
declares a StreamWriter variable named outFile

Figure 10-18   Syntax and an example of declaring a StreamWriter variable

You will use a StreamWriter variable in the Game Show Contestants application. The application writes the names of contestants to a sequential access file and then reads the names and displays them in a list box.

To begin coding the application:

START HERE

1. If necessary, start Visual Studio 2015. Open the Game Show Solution (Game Show Solution.sln) file contained in the VB2015\Chap10\Game Show Solution folder. See Figure 10-19.

Figure 10-19   Interface for the Game Show Contestants application

2. Open the Code Editor window. Replace <your name> and <current date> in the comments with your name and the current date, respectively.

3. Locate the **btnWrite_Click** procedure. Click the **blank line** below the `' declare a StreamWriter variable` comment, and then enter the following declaration statement:

Dim outFile As IO.StreamWriter

After declaring a StreamWriter variable, you can use the syntax shown in Figure 10-20 to create a StreamWriter object. As the figure indicates, creating a StreamWriter object involves opening a sequential access file using either the CreateText method or the AppendText method. You use the **CreateText method** to open a sequential access file for output. When you open a file for output, the computer creates a new, empty file to which data can be written. If the file already exists, the computer erases the contents of the file before writing any data to it. You use the **AppendText method** to open a sequential access file for append. When a file is opened for append, new data is written after any existing data in the file. If the file does not exist, the computer creates the file for you. In addition to opening the file, both methods automatically create a StreamWriter object to represent the file in the application. You assign the StreamWriter object to a StreamWriter variable, which you use to refer to the file in code.

CreateText and AppendText Methods

Syntax
IO.File.*method*(*fileName*)

method	Description
CreateText	opens a sequential access file for output
AppendText	opens a sequential access file for append

Example 1
```
outFile = IO.File.CreateText("employee.txt")
```
opens the employee.txt file for output; creates a StreamWriter object and assigns
it to the outFile variable

Example 2
```
outFile = IO.File.AppendText("F:\Chap10\report.txt")
```
opens the report.txt file for append; creates a StreamWriter object and assigns
it to the outFile variable

Figure 10-20   Syntax and examples of the CreateText and AppendText methods

When processing the statement in Example 1, the computer searches for the employee.txt
file in the default folder, which is the current project's bin\Debug folder. If the file exists, its
contents are erased and the file is opened for output; otherwise, a new, empty file is created
and opened for output. The statement then creates a StreamWriter object and assigns it to the
outFile variable.

Unlike the *fileName* argument in Example 1, the *fileName* argument in Example 2 contains
a folder path. When processing the statement in Example 2, the computer searches for the
report.txt file in the Chap10 folder on the F drive. If the computer locates the file, it opens the
file for append. If it does not find the file, it creates a new, empty file and then opens the file for
append. Like the statement in Example 1, the statement in Example 2 creates a StreamWriter
object and assigns it to the outFile variable. When deciding whether to include the folder
path in the *fileName* argument, keep in mind that a USB drive may have a different letter
designation on another computer. Therefore, you should specify the folder path only when you
are sure that it will not change.

When the user clicks the Write to File button in the Game Show Contestants interface, the
name entered in the Name box should be added to the end of the existing names in the file.
Therefore, you will need to open the sequential access file for append. A descriptive name for
a file that stores the names of contestants is contestants.txt. Although it is not a requirement,
the "txt" (short for "text") filename extension is commonly used when naming sequential access
files; this is because the files contain text.

START HERE ▶ **To continue coding the btnWrite_Click procedure:**

1. Click the **blank line** below the ' open the file for append comment, and then
   enter the following statement:

   outFile = IO.File.AppendText("contestants.txt")

After opening a file for either output or append, you can begin writing data to it using either
the **Write method** or the **WriteLine method**. The difference between these methods is that the
WriteLine method writes a newline character after the data. Figure 10-21 shows the syntax and
an example of both methods. As the figure indicates, when using the Write method, the next
character written to the file will appear immediately after the letter o in the string "Hello". When

using the WriteLine method, however, the next character written to the file will appear on the line immediately below the string. You do not need to include the file's name in either method's syntax because the data will be written to the file associated with the StreamWriter variable.

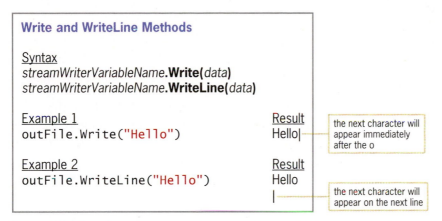

Write and WriteLine Methods

Syntax
streamWriterVariableName.**Write**(*data*)
streamWriterVariableName.**WriteLine**(*data*)

Example 1   Result
```
outFile.Write("Hello")
```
Hello| the next character will appear immediately after the o

Example 2   Result
```
outFile.WriteLine("Hello")
```
Hello
| the next character will appear on the next line

Figure 10-21   Syntax and examples of the Write and WriteLine methods

Each contestant's name should appear on a separate line in the file, so you will use the WriteLine method to write each name to the file.

To continue coding the btnWrite_Click procedure: START HERE

1. Click the **blank line** below the ' write the name on a separate line in the file comment, and then enter the following statement:

    outFile.WriteLine(txtName.Text)

Closing an Output Sequential Access File

You should use the **Close method** to close an output sequential access file as soon as you are finished using it. This ensures that the data is saved, and it makes the file available for use elsewhere in the application. The syntax to close an output sequential access file is shown in Figure 10-22 along with an example of using the method. Here, again, notice that you use the StreamWriter variable to refer to the file you want to close.

Close Method (Output Sequential Access File)

Syntax
streamWriterVariableName.**Close()**

Example
```
outFile.Close()
```
closes the file associated with the outFile variable

Figure 10-22   Syntax and an example of closing an output sequential access file

A run time error will occur if a program statement attempts to open a file that is already open.

To finish coding and then test the btnWrite_Click procedure: START HERE

1. Click the **blank line** below the ' close the file comment, and then enter the following statement:

    outFile.Close()

2. Save the solution and then start the application. Type **Sunita Patel** in the Name box and then click the **Write to File** button. Use the application to write the following four names to the file:

Thomas Widder
Sonja Shepperd
Phillip Perez
Chris Chang

3. Click the **Exit** button.

4. Next, you will open the contestants.txt file to verify its contents. Click **File** on the menu bar, point to **Open**, and then click **File**. Open the project's bin\Debug folder. Click **contestants.txt** in the list of filenames and then click the **Open** button. The contestants.txt window opens and shows the five names contained in the file. See Figure 10-23.

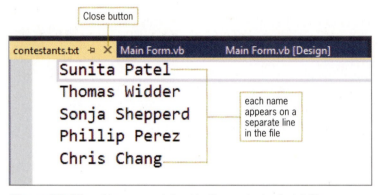

Figure 10-23   Names contained in the contestants.txt file

5. Close the contestants.txt window by clicking its **Close** button.

Reading Data from a Sequential Access File

In Visual Basic, you use a **StreamReader object** to read data from a sequential access file. Before creating the object, you first declare a variable to store the object in the computer's internal memory. Figure 10-24 shows the syntax and an example of declaring a StreamReader variable. As mentioned earlier, the IO in the syntax stands for Input/Output.

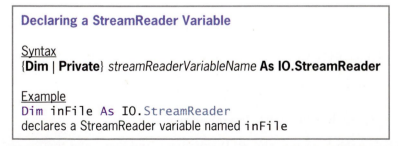

Figure 10-24   Syntax and an example of declaring a StreamReader variable

To begin coding the btnRead_Click procedure:

1. Locate the btnRead_Click procedure. Click the **blank line** below the `' declare variables` comment, and then enter the following declaration statement:

   Dim inFile As IO.StreamReader

After declaring a StreamReader variable, you can use the **OpenText method** to open a sequential access file for input, which will automatically create a StreamReader object. When a file is opened for input, the computer can read the lines of text stored in the file. Figure 10-25 shows the OpenText method's syntax along with an example of using the method. The *fileName* argument in the example does not include a folder path, so the computer will search for the employee.txt file in the default folder, which is the current project's bin\Debug folder. If the computer finds the file, it opens the file for input. If the computer does not find the file, a run time error occurs. You assign the StreamReader object created by the OpenText method to a StreamReader variable, which you use to refer to the file in code.

OpenText Method

Syntax
IO.File.OpenText(*fileName***)**

Example
```
inFile = IO.File.OpenText("employee.txt")
```
opens the employee.txt file for input; creates a StreamReader object and assigns it to the `inFile` variable

---

Figure 10-25   Syntax and an example of the OpenText method

The run time error that occurs when the computer cannot locate the file you want opened for input will cause the application to end abruptly. You can use the Exists method to avoid this run time error. Figure 10-26 shows the method's syntax and includes an example of using the method. If the *fileName* argument does not include a folder path, the computer searches for the file in the current project's bin\Debug folder. The **Exists method** returns the Boolean value True if the file exists; otherwise, it returns the Boolean value False.

Exists Method

Syntax
IO.File.Exists(*fileName***)**

Example
```
If IO.File.Exists("employee.txt") Then
```
determines whether the employee.txt file exists in the current project's bin\Debug folder; you can also write the If clause as `If IO.File.Exists("employee.txt") = True Then`

Figure 10-26   Syntax and an example of the Exists method

START HERE

To continue coding the btnRead_Click procedure:

1. Click the **blank line** below the ' determine whether the file exists comment, and then enter the following If clause:

   If IO.File.Exists("contestants.txt") Then

2. If the file exists, the selection structure's true path will use the OpenText method to open the file. Enter the following comment and assignment statement. Press **Enter** twice after typing the assignment statement.

   ' open the file for input
   inFile = IO.File.OpenText("contestants.txt")

3. If the file does not exist, the selection structure's false path will display an appropriate message. Enter the additional lines of code shown in Figure 10-27.

```
' determine whether the file exists
If IO.File.Exists("contestants.txt") Then
     ' open the file for input
     inFile = IO.File.OpenText("contestants.txt")

Else
     MessageBox.Show("Can't find the file",
                "Game Show Contestants",
                MessageBoxButtons.OK,
                MessageBoxIcon.Information)
End If
```

enter these five lines of code

Figure 10-27   False path entered in the procedure

After opening a file for input, you can use the **ReadLine method** to read the file's contents, one line at a time. A **line** is defined as a sequence (stream) of characters followed by the newline character. The ReadLine method returns a string that contains only the sequence of characters in the current line. The returned string does not include the newline character at the end of the line. In most cases, you assign the string returned by the ReadLine method to a String variable. Figure 10-28 shows the ReadLine method's syntax and includes an example of using the method. The ReadLine method does not require you to provide the file's name because it uses the file associated with the StreamReader variable.

ReadLine Method

Syntax
streamReaderVariableName.**ReadLine**

Example
```
Dim strMessage As String
strMessage = inFile.ReadLine
```
reads a line of text from the sequential access file associated with the inFile variable and assigns the line, excluding the newline character, to the strMessage variable

---

Figure 10-28   Syntax and an example of the ReadLine method

In most cases, an application will need to read each line of text contained in a sequential access file, one line at a time. You can do this using a loop along with the **Peek method**, which "peeks" into the file to determine whether the file contains another character to read. If the file contains another character, the Peek method returns the character; otherwise, it returns the number −1 (a negative 1). The Peek method's syntax is shown in Figure 10-29 along with an example of using the method. The Do clause in the example tells the computer to process the loop instructions until the Peek method returns the number −1, which indicates that there are no more characters to read. In other words, the Do clause tells the computer to process the loop instructions until the end of the file is reached.

Peek Method

Syntax
streamReaderVariableName.**Peek**

Example
```
Dim strLineOfText As String
Do Until inFile.Peek = -1
    strLineOfText = inFile.ReadLine
    MessageBox.Show(strLineOfText)
Loop
```
reads each line of text from the sequential access file associated with the `inFile` variable, line by line; each line (excluding the newline character) is assigned to the `strLineOfText` variable and is then displayed in a message box

---

Figure 10-29 Syntax and an example of the Peek method

To continue coding the btnRead_Click procedure:

START HERE

1. The procedure needs a variable in which it can store the string returned by the ReadLine method. Each line in the contestants.txt file represents a name, so you will call the variable `strName`. Click the **blank line** below the Dim statement, and then enter the following declaration statement:

   Dim strName As String

2. The Do clause is next. Click the **blank line** below the statement that opens the contestants.txt file. Enter the following comment and Do clause, being sure to type the minus sign before the number 1:

   ' process loop instructions until end of file
   Do Until inFile.Peek = −1

3. The first instruction in the loop should read a line of text and assign it (excluding the newline character) to the `strName` variable. Enter the following comment and assignment statement:

   ' read a name
   strName = inFile.ReadLine

4. Next, the procedure will add the name to the Contestants list box. Enter the following comment and statement:

   ' add name to list box
   lstContestants.Items.Add(strName)

5. If necessary, delete the blank line above the Loop clause.

Closing an Input Sequential Access File

Just as you do with an output sequential access file, you should use the Close method to close an input sequential access file as soon as you are finished using it. Doing this makes the file available for use elsewhere in the application. The syntax to close an input sequential access file is shown in Figure 10-30 along with an example of using the method. Notice that you use the StreamReader variable to refer to the file you want to close.

 A run time error will occur if a program statement attempts to open a file that is already open.

Close Method (Input Sequential Access File)

Syntax
streamReaderVariableName.**Close()**

Example
`inFile.Close()`
closes the file associated with the `inFile` variable

Figure 10-30   Syntax and an example of closing an input sequential access file

START HERE

To finish coding the btnRead_Click procedure:

1. Insert a blank line below the Loop clause, and then enter the following comment and statement:

   ' close the file
   inFile.Close()

Figure 10-31 shows the code entered in the btnWrite_Click and btnRead_Click procedures.

```
Private Sub btnWrite_Click(sender As Object, e As EventArgs
) Handles btnWrite.Click
    ' writes a name to a sequential access file

    ' declare a StreamWriter variable
    Dim outFile As IO.StreamWriter

    ' open the file for append
    outFile = IO.File.AppendText("contestants.txt")

    ' write the name on a separate line in the file
    outFile.WriteLine(txtName.Text)

    ' close the file
    outFile.Close()

    ' clear the list box and then set the focus
    lstContestants.Items.Clear()
    txtName.Focus()
End Sub

Private Sub btnRead_Click(sender As Object, e As EventArgs
) Handles btnRead.Click
    ' reads names from a sequential access file
    ' and displays them in the interface

    ' declare variables
```

Figure 10-31   btnWrite_Click and btnRead_Click procedures *(continues)*

(continued)

```vb
    Dim inFile As IO.StreamReader
    Dim strName As String

    ' clear previous names from the list box
    lstContestants.Items.Clear()

    ' determine whether the file exists
    If IO.File.Exists("contestants.txt") Then
        ' open the file for input
        inFile = IO.File.OpenText("contestants.txt")
        ' process loop instructions until end of file
        Do Until inFile.Peek = -1
            ' read a name
            strName = inFile.ReadLine
            ' add name to list box
            lstContestants.Items.Add(strName)
        Loop
        ' close the file
        inFile.Close()

    Else
        MessageBox.Show("Can't find the file",
                        "Game Show Contestants",
                        MessageBoxButtons.OK,
                        MessageBoxIcon.Information)
    End If
End Sub
```

Figure 10-31   btnWrite_Click and btnRead_Click procedures

To test the application's code:

START HERE

1. Save the solution and then start the application. Click the **Read from File** button. The five names contained in the contestants.txt file appear in the Contestants box, as shown in Figure 10-32.

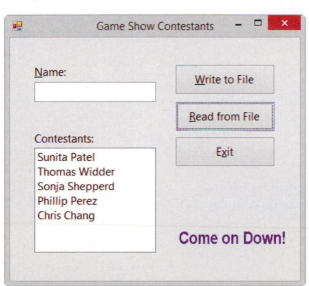

Figure 10-32   Five contestant names listed in the Contestants box

2. Add the following four names to the file:

Carla Cartwright
William Smith
Inez Hampton
Dustin Malewski

3. Click the **Read from File** button to display the nine names in the list box. See Figure 10-33.

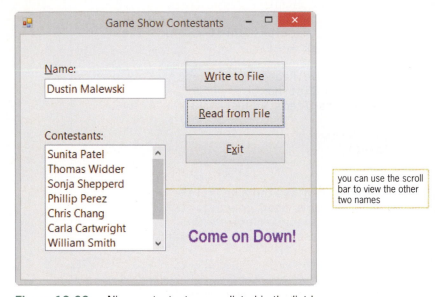

Figure 10-33 Nine contestant names listed in the list box

4. Click the **Exit** button.

Next, you will modify the If clause in the btnRead_Click procedure. More specifically, you will change the filename in the If clause from contestants.txt to contestant.txt. Doing this will allow you to test the code entered in the selection structure's false path.

START HERE

To test the selection structure's false path:

1. In the If clause, change contestants.txt to **contestant.txt**.

2. Save the solution and then start the application. Click the **Read from File** button. Because the contestant.txt file does not exist, the Exists method in the If clause returns the Boolean value False. As a result, the instruction in the selection structure's false path displays the "Can't find the file" message in a message box. Close the message box and then click the **Exit** button.

3. In the If clause, change contestant.txt to **contestants.txt**. Save the solution and then start the application. Click the **Read from File** button, which displays the nine names in the list box.

4. Click the **Exit** button. Close the Code Editor window and then close the solution.

YOU DO IT 2!

Create an application named YouDoIt 2 and save it in the VB2015\Chap10 folder. Add a label and two buttons to the form. The first button's Click event procedure should use the InputBox function to get one or more numbers from the user. Each number should be saved on a separate line in a sequential access file. The second button's Click event procedure should total the numbers contained in the sequential access file and then display the total in the label control. Code the procedures. Save the solution, and then start and test the application. Close the solution.

Lesson B Summary

- To write data to a sequential access file:

  Declare a StreamWriter variable, and then use either the CreateText method or the AppendText method to open a sequential access file. Assign the method's return value to the StreamWriter variable. Use either the Write method or the WriteLine method to write the data to the file. Close the file using the Close method.

- To read data from a sequential access file:

  Declare a StreamReader variable. Use the Exists method to determine whether the sequential access file exists. If the file exists, use the OpenText method to open the file. Assign the method's return value to the StreamReader variable. Use the ReadLine and Peek methods to read the data from the file. Close the file using the Close method.

- To determine whether a sequential access file exists:

  Use the Exists method. The method's syntax is `IO.File.Exists(`*fileName*`)`. The method returns the Boolean value True if the file exists; otherwise, it returns the Boolean value False.

- To determine whether the end of a sequential access file has been reached:

  Use the Peek method. The method's syntax is *streamReaderVariableName*`.Peek`. The method returns the number –1 when the end of the file has been reached; otherwise, it returns the next character in the file.

Lesson B Key Terms

AppendText method—used with a StreamWriter variable to open a sequential access file for append

Close method—used with either a StreamWriter variable or a StreamReader variable to close a sequential access file

CreateText method—used with a StreamWriter variable to open a sequential access file for output

Exists method—used to determine whether a file exists

Input files—files from which an application reads data

Line—a sequence (stream) of characters followed by the newline character

OpenText method—used with a StreamReader variable to open a sequential access file for input

Output files—files to which an application writes data

Peek method—used with a StreamReader variable to determine whether a file contains another character to read

ReadLine method—used with a StreamReader variable to read a line of text from a sequential access file

Sequential access files—files composed of lines of text that are both read and written sequentially; also called text files

Stream of characters—a sequence of characters

StreamReader object—used to read a sequence (stream) of characters from a sequential access file

StreamWriter object—used to write a sequence (stream) of characters to a sequential access file

Text files—another name for sequential access files

Write method—used with a StreamWriter variable to write data to a sequential access file; differs from the WriteLine method in that it does not write a newline character after the data

WriteLine method—used with a StreamWriter variable to write data to a sequential access file; differs from the Write method in that it writes a newline character after the data

Lesson B Review Questions

1. Which of the following opens the employ.txt file and allows the computer to write new data to the end of the file's existing data?

    a. `outFile = IO.File.AddText("employ.txt")`

    b. `outFile = IO.File.AppendText("employ.txt")`

    c. `outFile = IO.File.InsertText("employ.txt")`

    d. `outFile = IO.File.WriteText("employ.txt")`

2. If the file to be opened exists, the _____ method erases the file's contents.

    a. AppendText   c. InsertText

    b. CreateText   d. OpenText

3. Which of the following reads a line of text from a sequential access file and assigns the line (excluding the newline character) to the `strText` variable?

    a. `inFile.Read(strText)`

    b. `inFile.ReadLine(strText)`

    c. `strText = inFile.ReadLine`

    d. `strText = inFile.Read(line)`

4. What does the Peek method return when the end of the file is reached?

    a. −1   c. the last character in the file

    b. 0   d. the newline character

5. Which of the following can be used to determine whether the employ.txt file exists?

   a. `If IO.File.Exists("employ.txt") Then`

   b. `If IO.File("employ.txt").Exists Then`

   c. `If IO.Exists("employ.txt") = True Then`

   d. `If IO.Exists.File("employ.txt") = True Then`

6. What type of object is created by the OpenText method?

   a. File

   b. SequenceReader

   c. StreamWriter

   d. none of the above

7. What type of object is created by the AppendText method?

   a. File

   b. SequenceReader

   c. StreamWriter

   d. none of the above

Lesson B Exercises

1. Write the code to declare a variable named `outFile` that can be used to write data to a sequential access file. Then write the statement to open a sequential access file named inventory.txt for output.   *INTRODUCTORY*

2. Write the code to declare a variable named `inFile` that can be used to read data from a sequential access file. Then write the statement to open a sequential access file named inventory.txt for input.   *INTRODUCTORY*

3. Write the code to close the sequential access file associated with a StreamWriter variable named `outFile`.   *INTRODUCTORY*

4. Write an If clause that determines whether the inventory.txt sequential access file exists.   *INTRODUCTORY*

5. Write a Do clause that determines whether the end of a sequential access file has been reached. The file is associated with a StreamReader variable named `inFile`.   *INTRODUCTORY*

6. Open the VB2015\Chap10\Bonus Solution\Bonus Solution (Bonus Solution.sln) file. The Save button should write the bonus amounts entered by the user to a sequential access file named bonus.txt. Save the file in the project's bin\Debug folder. The Display button should read the bonus amounts from the bonus.txt file and display each (right-aligned and formatted with a dollar sign and two decimal places) in the list box. Test the application using the following 10 bonus amounts: 465.50, 1050, 567.75, 325.89, 2000, 567, 321.50, 540, 1600, and 345.75.   *INTRODUCTORY*

7. Open the VB2015\Chap10\States Solution\States Solution (States Solution.sln) file. Open the Code Editor window, and then open the states.txt file contained in the project's bin\Debug folder. The sequential access file contains the names of five U.S. states. Close the states.txt window. The btnDisplay_Click procedure should read the five names contained in the states.txt file, storing each in a five-element one-dimensional array. The procedure should sort the array in descending order and then display the contents of the array in the list box. Test the application appropriately. (Hint: If you need to recreate the states.txt file, open the file in a window in the IDE. Delete the contents of the file, and then type the following five names, pressing Enter after typing each name: Florida, California, Illinois, Delaware, and Alaska.)   *INTERMEDIATE*

INTERMEDIATE

8. Open the VB2015\Chap10\Pay Solution\Pay Solution (Pay Solution.sln) file. Open the Code Editor window. The application stores six hourly pay rates in a one-dimensional array named **dblRates**. Each rate corresponds to a pay code from 1 through 6. Code 1's rate is stored in the **dblRates(0)** element in the array, code 2's rate is stored in the **dblRates(1)** element, and so on. The btnDisplay_Click procedure prompts the user to enter a pay code. It then displays the amount associated with the code. Currently, the Private statement assigns the six hourly pay rates to the array. Modify the code so that the form's Load event procedure reads the rates from the payrates.txt file and stores each in the array. The file is contained in the project's bin\Debug folder. Test the application appropriately.

INTERMEDIATE

9. Open the Test Scores Solution (Test Scores Solution.sln) file contained in the VB2015\ Chap10\Test Scores Solution folder. The btnSave_Click procedure should allow the user to enter an unknown number of test scores, saving each score in a sequential access file. The btnDisplay_Click procedure should display the number of scores stored in the file and the average score. Test the application appropriately.

INTERMEDIATE

10. Open the VB2015\Chap10\Sales Solution\Sales Solution (Sales Solution.sln) file. The frmMain_Load procedure should read the five sales amounts contained in the sales.txt file, storing the amounts in a one-dimensional array and also displaying the amounts in the lstOriginal control. The sales.txt file is contained in the project's bin\Debug folder. The btnProjected_Click procedure should calculate the projected sales amounts by increasing each value in the array by 25%. The procedure should display each projected sales amount in the lstProjected control and also save the projected amounts in an empty sales.txt file. Test the application appropriately. Be sure to verify that the sales.txt file contains the projected amounts listed in the lstProjected control. (Hint: If you need to recreate the sales.txt file, open the file in a window in the IDE. Delete the contents of the file, and then type the following sales amounts: 1000, 3000, 2500, 989.95, and 1243.89.)

ADVANCED

11. Create an application, using the following names for the solution and project, respectively: PAO Solution and PAO Project. Save the application in the VB2015\ Chap10 folder. Create the interface shown in Figure 10-34. The Party list box should contain three items: Democratic, Republican, and Independent. The Age text box should accept only numbers and the Backspace key. The minimum age for a respondent is 18. The Write to File button should save each respondent's information (political party and age) to a sequential access file. Using the information stored in the file, the Display Totals button should display the number of Democrats, Republicans, and Independents by age group and in total. Test the application appropriately.

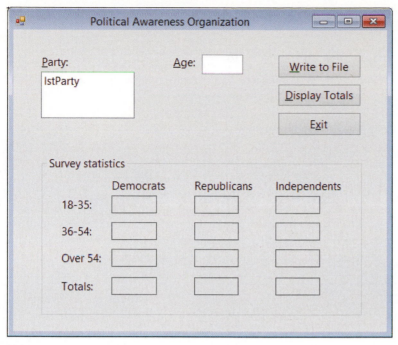

Figure 10-34   Interface for Exercise 11

12. In this exercise, you modify the application from Exercise 11. Use Windows to make a copy of the PAO Solution folder. Rename the folder Modified PAO Solution. Open the PAO Solution (PAO Solution.sln) file contained in the Modified PAO Solution folder. Modify the code to use a structure in the Display Totals button's Click event procedure. Test the application appropriately.

ADVANCED

13. Open the VB2015\Chap10\Debug Solution\Debug Solution (Debug Solution.sln) file. Open the Code Editor window and study the existing code. Start the application. Test the application by entering Sue and 1000, and then by entering Pete and 5000. A run time error occurs. Read the error message. Click Debug on the menu bar and then click Stop Debugging. Open the bonus.txt file contained in the project's bin\Debug folder. Notice that the file is empty. Close the bonus.txt window. Locate and correct the error in the code. Save the solution, and then start and test the application again. Verify that the bonus.txt file contains the two names and bonus amounts.

SWAT THE BUGS

LESSON C

After studying Lesson C, you should be able to:

- Add an item to a list box while an application is running

- Align columns of information

- Remove an item from a list box while an application is running

- Save list box items in a sequential access file

Coding the eBook Collection Application

Your task in this chapter is to create an application that uses a sequential access file to keep track of a person's collection of eBooks. The application's TOE chart and user interface are shown in Figure 10-35.

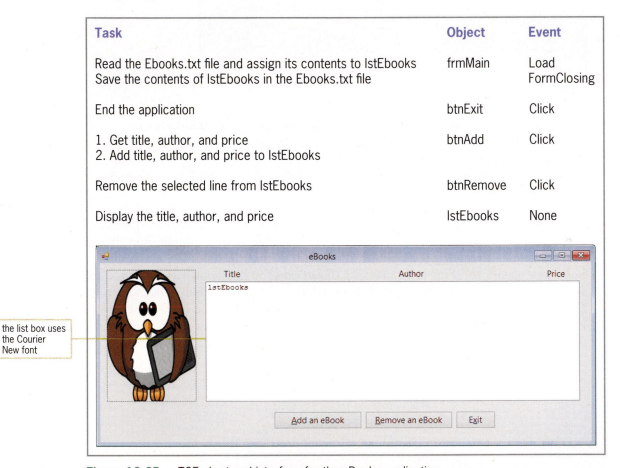

Task	Object	Event
Read the Ebooks.txt file and assign its contents to lstEbooks Save the contents of lstEbooks in the Ebooks.txt file	frmMain	Load FormClosing
End the application	btnExit	Click
1. Get title, author, and price 2. Add title, author, and price to lstEbooks	btnAdd	Click
Remove the selected line from lstEbooks	btnRemove	Click
Display the title, author, and price	lstEbooks	None

the list box uses the Courier New font

eBooks — Title | Author | Price

lstEbooks

Add an eBook   Remove an eBook   Exit

Figure 10-35 TOE chart and interface for the eBooks application

START HERE

To open the application and then view the Ebooks.txt file:

1. If necessary, start Visual Studio 2015. Open the VB2015\Chap10\Ebook Solution\ Ebook Solution (Ebook Solution.sln) file.

2. Click **File** on the menu bar, point to **Open**, and then click **File**. Open the project's bin\
Debug folder. Click **Ebooks.txt** in the list of filenames and then click the **Open** button.
See Figure 10-36. The eBook titles are listed in the first column, the author names in the
second column, and the prices in the third column.

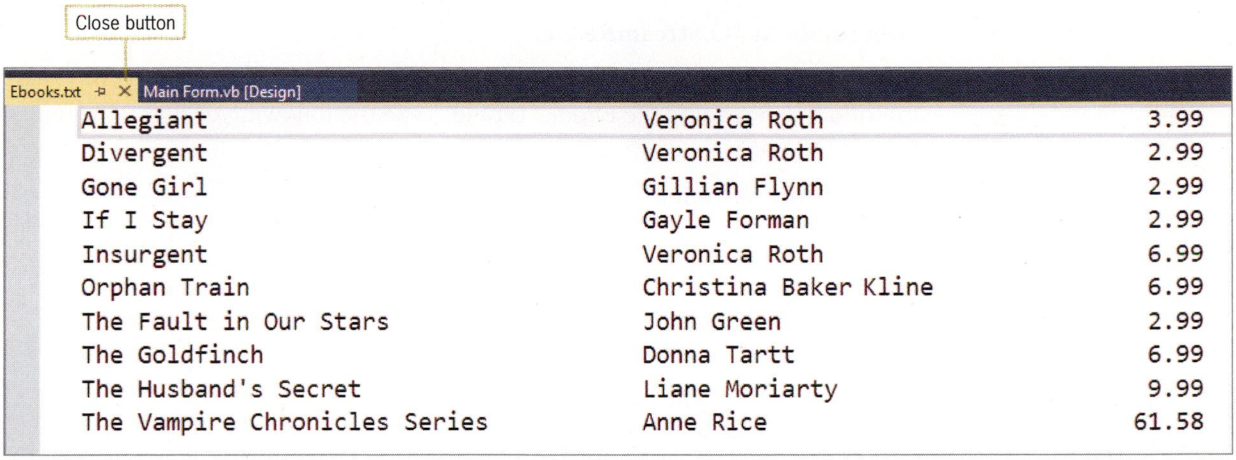

Close button

Ebooks.txt ⏸ ✕ Main Form.vb [Design]		
Allegiant	Veronica Roth	3.99
Divergent	Veronica Roth	2.99
Gone Girl	Gillian Flynn	2.99
If I Stay	Gayle Forman	2.99
Insurgent	Veronica Roth	6.99
Orphan Train	Christina Baker Kline	6.99
The Fault in Our Stars	John Green	2.99
The Goldfinch	Donna Tartt	6.99
The Husband's Secret	Liane Moriarty	9.99
The Vampire Chronicles Series	Anne Rice	61.58

Figure 10-36   Ebooks.txt window

3. Close the Ebooks.txt window by clicking its **Close** button.

Coding the frmMain_Load Procedure

According to the application's TOE chart, the frmMain_Load procedure is responsible for
displaying the contents of the Ebooks.txt file in the list box. The procedure's pseudocode is
shown in Figure 10-37.

```
frmMain Load event procedure
if the Ebooks.txt sequential access file exists
    open the file for input
    repeat until the end of the file
        read a line from the file
        add the line to the lstEbooks control
    end repeat
    close the file
    select the first line in the lstEbooks control
else
    display the "Can't find the Ebooks.txt file" message
end if
```

Figure 10-37   Pseudocode for the frmMain_Load procedure

To code and then test the frmMain_Load procedure:

START HERE

1. Open the Code Editor window. Replace <your name> and <current date> in the
comments with your name and the current date, respectively.

2. Locate the frmMain_Load procedure. As you learned in Lesson B, you use a StreamReader object to read data from a sequential access file. Before creating the StreamReader object, you first declare a StreamReader variable to store the object in the computer's internal memory. Click the **blank line** above the End Sub clause, and then enter the following declaration statement:

   Dim inFile As IO.StreamReader

3. The procedure will also need a variable to store the string returned by the ReadLine method when reading the Ebooks.txt file. Type the following declaration statement and then press **Enter** twice:

   Dim strInfo As String

4. According to its pseudocode, the procedure should display an appropriate message if the Ebooks.txt file does not exist. Enter the comment and selection structure shown in Figure 10-38, and then position the insertion point as shown in the figure.

```
Dim inFile As IO.StreamReader
Dim strInfo As String

' verify that the file exists
If IO.File.Exists("Ebooks.txt") Then
                                              position the insertion
                                              point here
Else
    MessageBox.Show("Can't find the Ebooks.txt file",
                    "eBooks", MessageBoxButtons.OK,
                    MessageBoxIcon.Information)
End If
End Sub
```

enter this comment and selection structure

Figure 10-38   Additional comment and code entered in the frmMain_Load procedure

5. If the file exists, the procedure should open the file for input. Enter the following comment and assignment statement:

   ' open the file for input
   inFile = IO.File.OpenText("Ebooks.txt")

6. Next, the procedure should use a loop to read each line from the file, adding each to the list box. Enter the following comment and lines of code:

   ' process loop instructions until end of file
   Do Until inFile.Peek = −1
   **   strInfo = inFile.ReadLine**
   **   lstEbooks.Items.Add(strInfo)**
   Loop

7. After the loop ends, the procedure should close the file. Insert a blank line below the loop clause. Type **inFile.Close()** and then press **Enter**.

8. The last task in the selection structure's true path selects the first line in the list box. Enter the following comment and line of code:

' select the first line in the list box
lstEbooks.SelectedIndex = 0

9. Save the solution and then start the application. The information contained in the Ebooks.txt file appears in the list box, as shown in Figure 10-39. The list box's Sorted property is set to True, so the information appears in alphabetical order by the eBook title.

Figure 10-39   Contents of the Ebooks.txt file shown in the list box

10. Click the **Exit** button.

Coding the btnAdd_Click Procedure

According to the application's TOE chart, the btnAdd_Click procedure should get an eBook's title, author, and price from the user, and then display that information in the list box. Figure 10-40 shows the procedure's pseudocode.

btnAdd Click event procedure
1. use the InputBox function to get the eBook's title, author, and price
2. concatenate the title, author, and price, and then add the concatenated string to the lstEbooks control

Figure 10-40   Pseudocode for the btnAdd_Click procedure

To begin coding the btnAdd_Click procedure:

START HERE

1. Locate the btnAdd_Click procedure, and then click the **blank line** below the ' declare variables comment. The procedure will use four String variables: three to store the input items and one to store the concatenated string. It will also use a Double variable to store the numeric equivalent of the eBook's price. Enter the following five declaration statements:

Dim strTitle As String
Dim strAuthor As String
Dim strPrice As String
Dim strConcatenatedInfo As String
Dim dblPrice As Double

2. The procedure will use the InputBox function to get the eBook information from the user. Click the **blank line** below the ' get the eBook information comment, and then enter the following assignment statements:

strTitle = InputBox("Title:", "eBooks")
strAuthor = InputBox("Author:", "eBooks")
strPrice = InputBox("Price:", "eBooks")

Step 2 in the procedure's pseudocode concatenates the three input items and then adds the concatenated string to the list box. Notice that each input item appears in a separate column in the list box shown earlier in Figure 10-39. The titles and author names in the first two columns are left-aligned within their respective column. The prices in the third column, however, are right-aligned within the column.

Aligning Columns of Information

In Chapter 8, you learned how to use the PadLeft and PadRight methods to pad a string with a character until the string is a specified length. Each method's syntax is shown in Figure 10-41. Recall that when processing the methods, the computer first makes a temporary copy of the *string* in memory; it then pads the copy only. The *totalChars* argument in each syntax is an integer that represents the total number of characters you want the string's copy to contain. The optional *padCharacter* argument is the character that each method uses to pad the string until it reaches the desired number of characters. If the padCharacter argument is omitted, the default padding character is the space character. You can use the PadLeft and PadRight methods to align columns of information, as shown in the examples in Figure 10-41.

Aligning Columns of Information

Syntax
string.**PadLeft**(*totalChars*[, *padCharacter*])
string.**PadRight**(*totalChars*[, *padCharacter*])

Example 1
```
Dim strPrice As String
For dblPrice As Double = 9 To 11 Step 0.5
    strPrice = dblPrice.ToString("N2").PadLeft(5)
    lstPrices.Items.Add(strPrice)
Next dblPrice
```

Result
```
 9.00
 9.50
10.00
10.50
11.00
```

Example 2
```
Dim outFile As IO.StreamWriter
Dim strHeading As String =
    "Name" & Strings.Space(11) & "City"
Dim strName As String
Dim strCity As String
```
contains the Strings.Space method

Figure 10-41   Examples of aligning columns of information *(continues)*

(continued)

```
outFile = IO.File.CreateText("Example2.txt")
outFile.WriteLine(strHeading)

strName = InputBox("Enter name:", "Name")
Do While strName <> String.Empty
    strCity = InputBox("Enter city:", "City")
    outFile.WriteLine(strName.PadRight(15) & strCity)
    strName = InputBox("Enter name:", "Name")
Loop
outFile.Close()

Result (when the user enters the following: Janice, Paris, Sue, Rome)
Name            City
Janice          Paris
Sue             Rome
```

Figure 10-41   Examples of aligning columns of information

Example 1's code aligns a column of numbers, which are displayed in the lstPrices control, by the decimal point. Notice that you first format each number in the column to ensure that each has the same number of digits to the right of the decimal point. You then use the PadLeft method to insert spaces at the beginning of the number (if necessary); this right-aligns the number within the column. Because each number has the same number of digits to the right of the decimal point, aligning each number on the right will align each by its decimal point. You also need to set the lstPrices control's Font property to a fixed-spaced font, such as Courier New. A fixed-space font uses the same amount of space to display each character.

Example 2's code shows how you can align the second column of information when the first column contains strings with varying lengths. First, you use either the PadRight or PadLeft method to ensure that each string in the first column contains the same number of characters. You then concatenate the padded string to the information in the second column. Example 2's code, for instance, uses the PadRight method to ensure that each name in the first column contains exactly 15 characters. It then concatenates the 15 characters with the string stored in the `strCity` variable before writing the concatenated string to a sequential access file. Because each name has 15 characters, each city entry will automatically appear beginning in character position 16 in the file. Example 2 also shows how you can use the **Strings.Space method** to include a specific number of space characters in a string. The method's syntax is `Strings.Space(number)`, in which *number* is an integer representing the number of spaces to include.

To complete and then test the btnAdd_Click procedure:

START HERE

1. Click the blank line below the `' characters for the price` comment. First, the procedure will format the price to ensure that it contains two decimal places. Enter the following lines of code:

    Double.TryParse(strPrice, dblPrice)
    strPrice = dblPrice.ToString("n2")

2. Next, the procedure will concatenate the three input items, reserving 40 characters for the title, 35 characters for the author's name, and 5 characters for the price. The procedure will left-align the first two columns but right-align the last column. Enter the following assignment statement:

    strConcatenatedInfo = strTitle.PadRight(40) &
    strAuthor.PadRight(35) & strPrice.PadLeft(5)

3. Next, the procedure will add the concatenated string to the list box. Click the **blank line** above the End Sub clause, and then enter the following line of code:

lstEbooks.Items.Add(strConcatenatedInfo)

4. Save the solution and then start the application. Click the **Add an eBook** button. Type **Gray Mountain** as the title, and then press **Enter**. Type **John Grisham** as the author, and then press **Enter**. Type **9.99** as the price, and then press **Enter**. The btnAdd_Click procedure adds the eBook information to the list box. The list box's Sorted property is set to True, so the information you entered appears in the fourth line of the list box. See Figure 10-42.

Figure 10-42   eBook information added to the list box

5. Click the **Exit** button.

Coding the btnRemove_Click Procedure

According to the application's TOE chart, the btnRemove_Click procedure should remove the selected line from the lstEbooks control. The procedure's pseudocode is shown in Figure 10-43.

```
btnRemove Click event procedure
if a line is selected in the lstEbooks control
    remove the line from the control
end if
```

Figure 10-43   Pseudocode for the btnRemove_Click procedure

You remove an item from a list box by using either the Items collection's Remove method or its RemoveAt method. Figure 10-44 shows each method's syntax and includes an example of using each method. In each syntax, *object* is the name of the list box control. The **Remove method** removes the item whose value is specified in its *item* argument. The **RemoveAt method** removes the item whose index is specified in its *index* argument.

Remove and RemoveAt Methods (Items Collection)

Syntax
object.**Items.Remove**(*item*)
object.**Items.RemoveAt**(*index*)

Example 1 – Remove
`lstAnimal.Items.Remove("Cat")`
removes the Cat item from the lstAnimal control

Example 2 – RemoveAt
`lstAnimal.Items.RemoveAt(0)`
removes the first item from the lstAnimal control

Figure 10-44   Syntax and examples of the Items collection's Remove and RemoveAt methods

To code and then test the btnRemove_Click procedure:

START HERE

1. Locate the btnRemove_Click procedure. If a line is selected in the list box, the list box's SelectedIndex property will contain the line's index; otherwise, it will contain −1. Therefore, if the SelectedIndex property does not contain the number −1, the procedure should remove the selected line from the list box. Click the **blank line** above the End Sub clause, and then enter the following selection structure:

   If lstEbooks.SelectedIndex <> −1 Then
       lstEbooks.Items.RemoveAt(lstEbooks.SelectedIndex)
   End If

2. Save the solution and then start the application. Click **Gone Girl** in the list box, and then click the **Remove an eBook** button. The btnRemove_Click procedure removes the Gone Girl eBook from the list box.

3. Click the **Exit** button.

Coding the frmMain_FormClosing Procedure

According to the application's TOE chart, the frmMain_FormClosing procedure is responsible for saving the contents of the lstEbooks control in the Ebooks.txt file. Figure 10-45 shows the procedure's pseudocode.

---

frmMain FormClosing event procedure
1. open the Ebooks.txt file for output
2. repeat for each line in the list box
      write the line to the file
   end repeat
3. close the file

Figure 10-45   Pseudocode for the frmMain_FormClosing procedure

START HERE **To code and then test the frmMain_FormClosing procedure:**

1. Locate the frmMain_FormClosing procedure. As you learned in Lesson B, you use a StreamWriter object to write data to a sequential access file. Before creating the StreamWriter object, you first declare a variable to store the object in the computer's internal memory. Click the **blank line** below the ' declare a StreamWriter variable comment, and then enter the following declaration statement:

   Dim outFile As IO.StreamWriter

2. Step 1 in the pseudocode opens the Ebooks.txt file for output. Click the **blank line** below the ' open the file for output comment, and then enter the following line of code:

   outFile = IO.File.CreateText("Ebooks.txt")

3. The next step in the pseudocode is a loop that will write each line from the list box to the file. Click the **blank line** below the ' write each line in the list box comment, and then enter the following loop:

   For intIndex As Integer = 0 To lstEbooks.Items.Count – 1
       outFile.WriteLine(lstEbooks.Items(intIndex))
   Next intIndex

4. The last step in the pseudocode closes the file. Click the **blank line** below the ' close the file comment. Type **outFile.Close()** and then press **Enter**.

5. Save the solution and then start the application. Click the **Add an eBook** button. Use the input boxes to enter the following title, author, and price: **Gray Mountain**, **John Grisham**, and **9.99**. The btnAdd_Click procedure adds the eBook information to the list box.

6. Click the **Exit** button. The computer processes the Me.Close() statement in the btnExit_Click procedure; doing this invokes the form's FormClosing event. The FormClosing event procedure saves the contents of the list box to the Ebooks.txt file.

7. Next, you will verify that the eBook information you entered was saved to the Ebooks.txt file. Click **File** on the menu bar, point to **Open**, and then click **File**. Open the Ebooks.txt file contained in the project's bin\Debug folder. The eBook information you entered appears in the fourth line in the file, as shown in Figure 10-46.

Ebooks.txt → ✕ Main Form.vb Main Form.vb [Design]		
Allegiant	Veronica Roth	3.99
Divergent	Veronica Roth	2.99
Gone Girl	Gillian Flynn	2.99
Gray Mountain	John Grisham	9.99
If I Stay	Gayle Forman	2.99
Insurgent	Veronica Roth	6.99
Orphan Train	Christina Baker Kline	6.99
The Fault in Our Stars	John Green	2.99
The Goldfinch	Donna Tartt	6.99
The Husband's Secret	Liane Moriarty	9.99
The Vampire Chronicles Series	Anne Rice	61.58

the information you entered

Figure 10-46 eBook information saved in the Ebooks.txt file

8. Close the Ebooks.txt window, and then start the application again. Click **Gray Mountain** in the list box, and then click the **Remove an eBook** button. The btnRemove_Click procedure removes that eBook's information from the list box.

9. Click the **Exit** button, and then open the Ebooks.txt file. See Figure 10-47. Notice that the Gray Mountain information does not appear in the file.

```
Ebooks.txt ⇆ ✕ Main Form.vb      Main Form.vb [Design]
Allegiant                        Veronica Roth           3.99
Divergent                        Veronica Roth           2.99
Gone Girl                        Gillian Flynn           2.99
If I Stay                        Gayle Forman            2.99
Insurgent                        Veronica Roth           6.99
Orphan Train                     Christina Baker Kline   6.99
The Fault in Our Stars           John Green              2.99
The Goldfinch                    Donna Tartt             6.99
The Husband's Secret             Liane Moriarty          9.99
The Vampire Chronicles Series    Anne Rice              61.58
```

the Gray Mountain information doesn't appear in the file

Figure 10-47   Current contents of the Ebooks.txt file

10. Close the Ebooks.txt and Code Editor windows, and then close the solution. Figure 10-48 shows the application's code.

```vb
1 ' Name:          Ebook Project
2 ' Purpose:       Adds and deletes list box entries
3 '                Reads information from a sequential access file
4 '                Writes information to a sequential access file
5 ' Programmer:    <your name> on <current date>
6
7 Option Explicit On
8 Option Strict On
9 Option Infer Off
10
11 Public Class frmMain
12
13     Private Sub frmMain_Load(sender As Object, e As EventArgs
       ) Handles Me.Load
14         ' fills the list box with data from
15         ' a sequential access file
16
17         Dim inFile As IO.StreamReader
18         Dim strInfo As String
19
20         ' verify that the file exists
21         If IO.File.Exists("Ebooks.txt") Then
22             ' open the file for input
23             inFile = IO.File.OpenText("Ebooks.txt")
24             ' process loop instructions until end of file
25             Do Until inFile.Peek = -1
26                 strInfo = inFile.ReadLine
27                 lstEbooks.Items.Add(strInfo)
28             Loop
29             inFile.Close()
30             'select the first line in the list box
31             lstEbooks.SelectedIndex = 0
32
33         Else
34             MessageBox.Show("Can't find the Ebooks.txt file",
35                             "eBooks", MessageBoxButtons.OK,
36                             MessageBoxIcon.Information)
```

Figure 10-48   Code for the eBooks application *(continues)*

(continued)

```
37          End If
38      End Sub
39
40      Private Sub btnAdd_Click(sender As Object, e As EventArgs
        ) Handles btnAdd.Click
41          ' adds eBook information to the list box
42
43          ' declare variables
44          Dim strTitle As String
45          Dim strAuthor As String
46          Dim strPrice As String
47          Dim strConcatenatedInfo As String
48          Dim dblPrice As Double
49
50          ' get the eBook information
51          strTitle = InputBox("Title:", "eBooks")
52          strAuthor = InputBox("Author:", "eBooks")
53          strPrice = InputBox("Price:", "eBooks")
54
55          ' format the price, then concatenate the input
56          ' items, using 40 characters for the title,
57          ' 35 characters for the author, and 5
58          ' characters for the price
59          Double.TryParse(strPrice, dblPrice)
60          strPrice = dblPrice.ToString("n2")
61          strConcatenatedInfo = strTitle.PadRight(40) &
62              strAuthor.PadRight(35) & strPrice.PadLeft(5)
63
64          ' add the information to the list box
65          lstEbooks.Items.Add(strConcatenatedInfo)
66
67      End Sub
68
69      Private Sub btnRemove_Click(sender As Object, e As EventArgs
        ) Handles btnRemove.Click
70          ' removes the selected line from the list box
71
72          ' if a line is selected, remove the line
73          If lstEbooks.SelectedIndex <> -1 Then
74              lstEbooks.Items.RemoveAt(lstEbooks.SelectedIndex)
75          End If
76      End Sub
77
78      Private Sub frmMain_FormClosing(sender As Object,
        e As FormClosingEventArgs) Handles Me.FormClosing
79          ' save the list box information
80
81          ' declare a StreamWriter variable
82          Dim outFile As IO.StreamWriter
83
84          ' open the file for output
85          outFile = IO.File.CreateText("Ebooks.txt")
86
87          ' write each line in the list box
88          For intIndex As Integer = 0 To lstEbooks.Items.Count - 1
```

Figure 10-48 Code for the eBooks application *(continues)*

(continued)

```
 89              outFile.WriteLine(lstEbooks.Items(intIndex))
 90          Next intIndex
 91
 92          ' close the file
 93          outFile.Close()
 94
 95      End Sub
 96
 97      Private Sub btnExit_Click(sender As Object, e As EventArgs
            ) Handles btnExit.Click
 98          Me.Close()
 99      End Sub
100  End Class
```

Figure 10-48   Code for the eBooks application

Lesson C Summary

- To align columns of information:

  Use the PadLeft and PadRight methods.

- To align a column of numbers by the decimal point:

  Format each number in the column to ensure that each has the same number of digits to the right of the decimal point, and then use the PadLeft method to right-align the numbers.

- To include a specific number of spaces in a string:

  Use the Strings.Space method. The method's syntax is **Strings.Space**(*number*), in which *number* is an integer that represents the number of spaces to include.

- To remove an item from a list box:

  Use either the Items collection's Remove method or its RemoveAt method. The Remove method's syntax is *object*.**Items.Remove**(*item*), where *item* is the value of the item you want to remove. The RemoveAt method's syntax is *object*.**Items.RemoveAt**(*index*), where *index* is the index of the item you want removed.

Lesson C Key Terms

Remove method—used to specify the value of the item to remove from a list box

RemoveAt method—used to specify the index of the item to remove from a list box

Strings.Space method—used to include a specific number of spaces in a string

Lesson C Review Questions

1. Which of the following opens a sequential access file named MyFriends.txt for input?

   a. `inFile = IO.File.Input("MyFriends.txt")`
   b. `inFile = IO.InputFile("MyFriends.txt")`
   c. `inFile = IO.File.InputText("MyFriends.txt")`
   d. `inFile = IO.File.OpenText("MyFriends.txt")`

2. Which of the following right-aligns the contents of the `strNumbers` variable?

   a. `strNumbers = strNumbers.PadLeft(10)`
   b. `strNumbers = strNumbers.PadRight(10)`
   c. `strNumbers = strNumbers.AlignLeft(10)`
   d. `strNumbers = strNumbers.RightAlign(10)`

3. Which of the following removes the fourth item from the lstFriends control?

   a. `lstFriends.Items.Remove(4)`
   b. `lstFriends.Items.RemoveAt(4)`
   c. `lstFriends.Items.RemoveIndex(3)`
   d. none of the above

4. Which of the following determines whether an item is selected in the lstFriends control?

   a. `If lstFriends.SelectedIndex >= 0 Then`
   b. `If lstFriends.SelectedItem <> –1 Then`
   c. `If lstFriends.IndexSelected = –1 Then`
   d. none of the above

5. The lstFriends control contains five items. Which of the following writes the last item to the file associated with the `outFile` variable?

   a. `outFile.WriteLine(lstFriends.Items(5))`
   b. `outFile.WriteLine(lstFriends.Items(4))`
   c. `outFile.WriteLine(lstFriends.Index(4))`
   d. none of the above

Lesson C Exercises

INTRODUCTORY

1. In this exercise, you modify the eBook Collection application from this lesson. Use Windows to make a copy of the Ebook Solution folder. Rename the copy Ebook Solution-Verify Save. Open the Ebook Solution (Ebook Solution.sln) file contained in the Ebook Solution-Verify Save folder. The frmMain_FormClosing procedure should verify that the user wants to save the changes made to the list box. It then should take the necessary action based on the user's response. Test the application appropriately.

INTERMEDIATE

2. In this exercise, you modify the eBook Collection application from this lesson. Use Windows to make a copy of the Ebook Solution folder. Rename the copy Ebook Solution-Verify Remove. Open the Ebook Solution (Ebook Solution.sln) file contained in the Ebook Solution-Verify Remove folder. The btnRemove_Click procedure should verify that the user wants to remove the selected eBook from the list box. Use the

message "Do you want to remove the *x* eBook?", where *x* is the eBook's title. The procedure should take the appropriate action based on the user's response. Test the application by entering appropriate information.

3. Open the VB2015\Chap10\Movies Solution\Movies Solution (Movies Solution.sln) file. The btnAdd_Click procedure should add the movie title entered in the text portion of the combo box to the list portion, but only if the title is not already in the list. The btnRemove_Click procedure should remove (from the list portion of the combo box) the title either entered in the text portion or selected in the list portion. The frmMain_FormClosing procedure should save the combo box items in a sequential access file named Movies.txt. The frmMain_Load procedure should read the names from the Movies.txt file and add each to the combo box. Test the application appropriately.   INTERMEDIATE

4. In this exercise, you modify the eBook Collection application from this lesson. Use Windows to make a copy of the Ebook Solution folder. Rename the copy Ebook Solution-No Duplicate. Open the Ebook Solution (Ebook Solution.sln) file contained in the Ebook Solution-No Duplicate folder. Before getting the author's name and the price, the btnAdd_Click procedure should determine whether the eBook's title is already included in the list box. If the list box contains the title, the procedure should display an appropriate message, and it should not add the eBook to the list. Save the solution, and then start and test the application. Close the Code Editor window and then close the solution.   INTERMEDIATE

5. In this exercise, you modify the eBook Collection application from this lesson. Use Windows to make a copy of the Ebook Solution folder. Rename the copy Ebook Solution-Undo. Open the Ebook Solution (Ebook Solution.sln) file contained in the Ebook Solution-Undo folder. Add an Undo Remove button to the form. The button's Click event procedure should restore the last line removed by the Remove an eBook button. Test the application appropriately.   INTERMEDIATE

6. In this exercise, you modify the eBook Collection application from this lesson. Use Windows to make a copy of the Ebook Solution folder. Rename the copy Ebook Solution-Structure. Open the Ebook Solution (Ebook Solution.sln) file contained in the Ebook Solution-Structure folder. Create a structure for the input information, and then use the structure in the btnAdd_Click procedure. Test the application appropriately.   INTERMEDIATE

7. Zander Inc. stores employee IDs and salaries in a sequential access file named Employees.txt. Open the VB2015\Chap10\Zander Solution\Zander Solution (Zander Solution.sln) file. Open the Employees.txt file, which is contained in the project's bin\Debug folder. The ID and salary information appear on separate lines in the file. Close the Employees.txt window.   INTERMEDIATE

   a. Define a structure named Employee. The structure should contain two member variables: a String variable to store the ID and a Double variable to store the salary.

   b. Declare a class-level array that contains five Employee structure variables.

   c. The frmMain_Load procedure should read the IDs and salaries from the Employees.txt file and store them in the class-level array. It should also add the IDs to the list box.

   d. When the user selects an employee ID in the list box, the employee's salary should appear in the lblSalary control.

   e. Test the application appropriately.

ADVANCED

8. Create an application, using the following names for the solution and project, respectively: Commercial Solution and Commercial Project. Save the application in the VB2015\Chap10 folder. Each year, KJPR-Radio polls its audience to determine the best Super Bowl commercial. Create the interface shown in Figure 10-49. The list box should display the following choices: Cheerios, Doritos, T-Mobile, and RadioShack. The Save Vote button should save each caller's choice in a sequential access file. The Display Votes button should display the number of votes for each commercial as well as the percentage of the total contributed by each choice. Test the application appropriately.

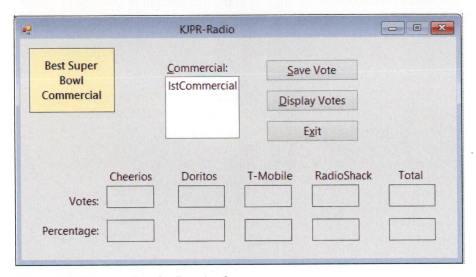

Figure 10-49   Interface for Exercise 8

ADVANCED

9. Preston Enterprises stores employee IDs and salaries in a sequential access file named Employees.txt. Open the VB2015\Chap10\Preston Solution\Preston Solution (Preston Solution.sln) file. Open the Employees.txt file, which is contained in the project's bin\ Debug folder. Each line contains an employee's ID followed by a comma and a salary amount. Close the Employees.txt window.

   a. Define a structure named Employee. The structure should contain two member variables: a String variable to store the ID and a Double variable to store the salary.

   b. Declare a class-level array that contains five Employee structure variables.

   c. The frmMain_Load procedure should read the IDs and salaries from the Employees. txt file and store them in the class-level array. It should also add the IDs to the list box.

   d. When the user selects an employee ID in the list box, the employee's salary should appear in the lblSalary control.

   e. Test the application appropriately.

Classes and Objects

Creating the Woods Manufacturing Application

In this chapter, you will create an application that calculates and displays the gross pay for salaried and hourly employees. Salaried employees are paid twice per month. Therefore, each salaried employee's gross pay is calculated by dividing his or her annual salary by 24. Hourly employees are paid weekly. The gross pay for an hourly employee is calculated by multiplying the number of hours the employee worked during the week by his or her hourly pay rate. The application will also display a report showing each employee's number, name, and gross pay.

Previewing the Woods Manufacturing Application

Before you start the first lesson in this chapter, you will preview the completed application contained in the VB2015\Chap11 folder.

START HERE

To preview the completed application:

1. Use Windows to locate and then open the VB2015\Chap11 folder. Right-click **Woods** (**Woods.exe**) in the list of filenames and then click **Open**.

2. First, you will calculate the gross pay for Cameron Ramos, whose employee number is 4536. Cameron worked 38.5 hours and earns $9.50 per hour. Type **4536** and **Cameron Ramos** in the Number and Name boxes, respectively. Click **38.5** and **9.50** in the Hours and Rate list boxes, respectively. Click the **Calculate** button. $365.75 appears in the Gross pay box, and Cameron's information appears in the Report box. See Figure 11-1.

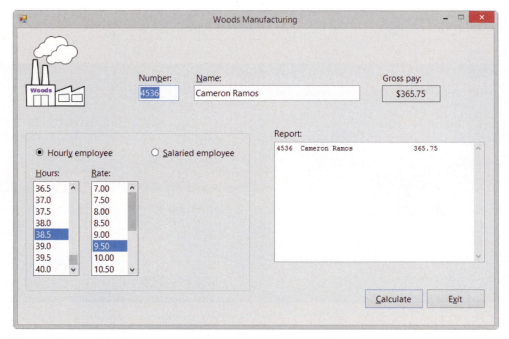

Figure 11-1   Interface showing Cameron's gross pay and information

3. Next, you will calculate the gross pay for a salaried employee earning $34,000 per year. Type **9999** and **Sydney James** in the Number and Name boxes, respectively. Click the **Salaried employee** radio button. Scroll the Annual salary list box and then click **34000** in the list. Click the **Calculate** button. $1,416.67 appears in the Gross pay box, and Sydney's information appears below Cameron's information in the Report box. See Figure 11-2.

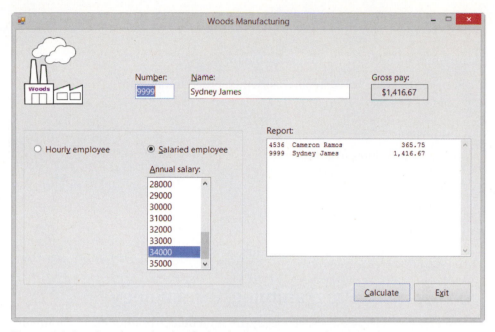

Figure 11-2 Interface showing Sydney's gross pay and information

4. Click the **Exit** button to end the application.

In Lesson A, you will learn about object-oriented programming (OOP). More specifically, you will learn how to define a class and how to use the class to instantiate an object that can be used in an application. Lesson B will teach you how to include ReadOnly and auto-implemented properties in a class. You will also learn how to overload a class method. You will code the Woods Manufacturing application in Lesson B. Lesson C covers an advanced OOP topic: inheritance. Be sure to complete each lesson in full and do all of the end-of-lesson questions and several exercises before continuing to the next lesson.

LESSON A

After studying Lesson A, you should be able to:

- Explain the terminology used in object-oriented programming
- Create a class
- Instantiate an object
- Add Property procedures to a class
- Include data validation in a class
- Create a default constructor
- Create a parameterized constructor
- Include methods other than constructors in a class

Object-Oriented Programming Terminology

Ch11A

As you learned in the Overview, Visual Basic 2015 is an **object-oriented programming language**, which is a language that allows the programmer to use objects to accomplish a program's goal. An **object** is anything that can be seen, touched, or used. In other words, an object is nearly any *thing*. The objects used in an object-oriented program can take on many different forms. The text boxes, list boxes, and buttons included in most Windows applications are objects, and so are the application's named constants and variables. An object can also represent something found in real life, such as a wristwatch or a car.

Every object in an object-oriented program is created from a **class**, which is a pattern that the computer uses to create the object. The class contains the instructions that tell the computer how the object should look and behave. Using object-oriented programming (**OOP**) terminology, objects are **instantiated** (created) from a class, and each object is referred to as an **instance** of the class. A button control, for example, is an instance of the Button class. The button is instantiated when you drag the Button tool from the toolbox to the form. A String variable, on the other hand, is an instance of the String class and is instantiated the first time you refer to the variable in code. Keep in mind that the class itself is not an object. Only an instance of a class is an object.

Every object has **attributes**, which are the characteristics that describe the object. Attributes are also called properties. Included in the attributes of buttons and text boxes are the Name and Text properties. List boxes have a Name property as well as a Sorted property.

In addition to attributes, every object also has behaviors. An object's **behaviors** include methods and events. **Methods** are the operations (actions) that the object is capable of performing. For example, a button can use its Focus method to send the focus to itself. Similarly, a String variable can use its ToUpper method to temporarily convert its contents to uppercase. **Events**, on the other hand, are the actions to which an object can respond. A button's Click event, for instance, allows the button to respond to a mouse click.

A class contains—or, in OOP terms, it **encapsulates**—all of the attributes and behaviors of the object it instantiates. The term *encapsulate* means to enclose in a capsule. In the context of OOP, the "capsule" is a class.

Creating a Class

In previous chapters, you instantiated objects using classes that are built into Visual Basic, such as the TextBox and Label classes. You used the instantiated objects in a variety of ways in many different applications. In some applications, you used a text box to enter a name; in other applications, you used it to enter a sales tax rate. Similarly, you used label controls to identify text boxes and also to display the result of calculations. The ability to use an object for more than one purpose saves programming time and money—an advantage that contributes to the popularity of object-oriented programming.

You can also define your own classes in Visual Basic and then create instances (objects) from those classes. You define a class using the **Class statement**, which you enter in a class file. Figure 11-3 shows the statement's syntax and lists the steps for adding a class file to an open project.

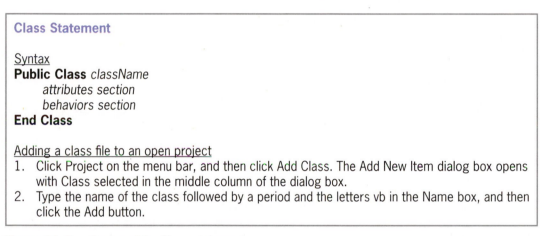

Class Statement

Syntax
Public Class *className*
    attributes section
    behaviors section
End Class

Adding a class file to an open project
1. Click Project on the menu bar, and then click Add Class. The Add New Item dialog box opens with Class selected in the middle column of the dialog box.
2. Type the name of the class followed by a period and the letters vb in the Name box, and then click the Add button.

Figure 11-3 Syntax of the Class statement

Although it is not a requirement, the convention is to use Pascal case for the class name. The names of Visual Basic classes (for example, Integer and TextBox) also follow this naming convention. Within the Class statement, you define the attributes and behaviors of the objects the class will create. In most cases, the attributes are represented by Private variables and Public properties. The behaviors are represented by methods, which are usually Sub or Function procedures. (You can also include Event procedures in a Class statement. However, that topic is beyond the scope of this book.)

Figure 11-4 shows an example of the Class statement entered in a class file. The three Option statements included in the figure have the same meaning in a class file as they have in a form file.

 The creation of a good class, which is one whose objects can be used in a variety of ways by many different applications, requires a lot of planning.

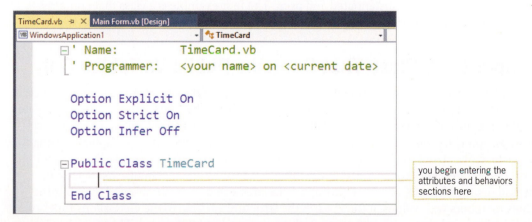

Figure 11-4 Class statement entered in the TimeCard.vb class file

After you define a class, you can use either of the syntax versions in Figure 11-5 to instantiate one or more objects. In both versions, *variableName* is the name of a variable that will represent the object. The difference between the versions relates to when the object is actually created. The computer creates the object only when it processes the statement containing the New keyword, which you will learn more about later in this lesson. Also included in Figure 11-5 is an example of using each version of the syntax.

Instantiating an Object from a Class

Syntax – Version 1
{**Dim | Private**} *variableName* **As** *className*
variableName = **New** *className*

Syntax – Version 2
{**Dim | Private**} *variableName* **As New** *className*

Example 1 (using Syntax Version 1)
`Private hoursInfo As TimeCard`
`hoursInfo = New TimeCard`
The Private instruction creates a TimeCard variable named `hoursInfo`; the assignment statement instantiates a TimeCard object and assigns it to the `hoursInfo` variable.

Example 2 (using Syntax Version 2)
`Dim hoursInfo As New TimeCard`
The Dim instruction creates a TimeCard variable named `hoursInfo` and also instantiates a TimeCard object, which it assigns to the `hoursInfo` variable.

Figure 11-5   Syntax and examples of instantiating an object

In Example 1, the `Private hoursInfo As TimeCard` instruction creates a class-level variable that can represent a TimeCard object; however, it does not create the object. The object isn't created until the computer processes the `hoursInfo = New TimeCard` statement, which uses the TimeCard class to instantiate a TimeCard object. The statement assigns the object to the `hoursInfo` variable. In Example 2, the `Dim hoursInfo As New TimeCard` instruction creates a procedure-level variable named `hoursInfo`. It also instantiates a TimeCard object and assigns it to the variable.

In the remainder of this lesson, you will view examples of class definitions and also examples of code in which objects are instantiated and used. The first example is a class that contains attributes only, with each attribute represented by a Public variable.

Example 1—A Class That Contains Public Variables Only

In its simplest form, the Class statement can be used in place of the Structure statement, which you learned about in Chapter 10. Like the Structure statement, the Class statement groups related items into one unit. However, the unit is called a class rather than a structure. In the following set of steps, you will modify the Norbert Pool & Spa Depot application from Chapter 10 using a class instead of a structure. The application's code from Chapter 10 is shown in Figure 11-6. The Structure statement groups together the three dimensions of a rectangular pool: length, width, and depth. The btnCalc_Click procedure declares a structure variable and then fills the variable's members with values. It then passes the structure variable to the GetGallons function, which calculates and returns the number of gallons required to fill the pool. The btnCalc_Click procedure then displays the returned value in the lblGallons control.

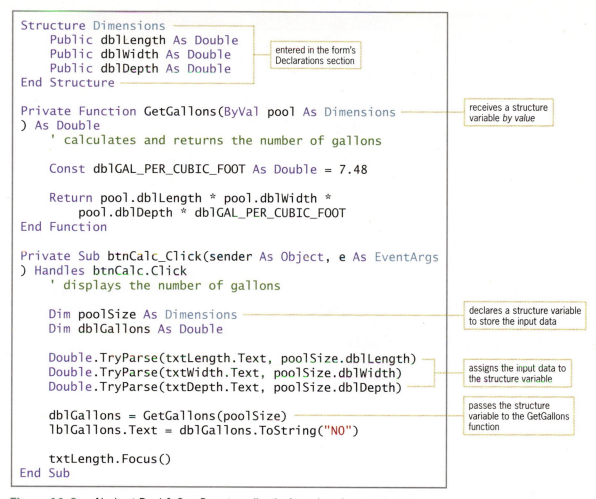

```
Structure Dimensions ─────┐
    Public dblLength As Double    ┌─── entered in the form's
    Public dblWidth As Double     │    Declarations section
    Public dblDepth As Double     │
End Structure ────────────────────┘

Private Function GetGallons(ByVal pool As Dimensions ─────── receives a structure
) As Double                                                  variable by value
    ' calculates and returns the number of gallons

    Const dblGAL_PER_CUBIC_FOOT As Double = 7.48

    Return pool.dblLength * pool.dblWidth *
        pool.dblDepth * dblGAL_PER_CUBIC_FOOT
End Function

Private Sub btnCalc_Click(sender As Object, e As EventArgs
) Handles btnCalc.Click
    ' displays the number of gallons

    Dim poolSize As Dimensions ──────────── declares a structure variable
    Dim dblGallons As Double                to store the input data

    Double.TryParse(txtLength.Text, poolSize.dblLength)
    Double.TryParse(txtWidth.Text, poolSize.dblWidth) ─── assigns the input data to
    Double.TryParse(txtDepth.Text, poolSize.dblDepth)     the structure variable

    dblGallons = GetGallons(poolSize) ──── passes the structure
    lblGallons.Text = dblGallons.ToString("N0")   variable to the GetGallons
                                                   function
    txtLength.Focus()
End Sub
```

Figure 11-6   Norbert Pool & Spa Depot application's code using a structure

To begin modifying the application:

START HERE

1. If necessary, start Visual Studio 2015. Open the VB2015\Chap11\Norbert Solution\ Norbert Solution (Norbert Solution.sln) file. Open the Code Editor window.

2. First, you will add a class file to the project. Click **Project** on the menu bar and then click **Add Class**. The Add New Item dialog box opens with Class selected in the middle column of the dialog box. Type **RectangularPool.vb** in the Name box. As you learned in Chapter 1, the .vb in a filename indicates that the file contains Visual Basic code.

3. Click the **Add** button. The computer adds the RectangularPool.vb file to the project. It also opens the file, which contains the Class statement, in a separate window. Temporarily display the Solution Explorer window, if necessary, to verify that the class file's name appears in the window.

4. Insert a blank line above the Class statement, and then enter the comments and Option statements shown in Figure 11-7. Replace <your name> and <current date> in the comments with your name and the current date, respectively. Also, position the insertion point as shown in the figure.

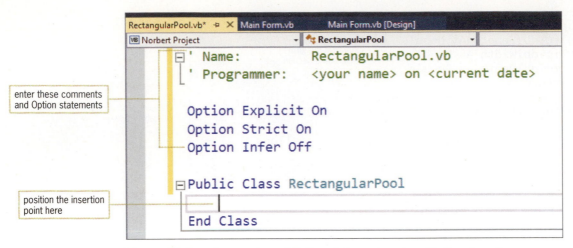

enter these comments
and Option statements

position the insertion
point here

Figure 11-7   Comments and Option statements entered in the class file

A RectangularPool object has three attributes: length, width, and depth. In the Class statement, each attribute will be represented by a Public variable. When a variable in a class is declared using the `Public` keyword, it can be accessed by any application that contains an instance of the class. The convention is to use Pascal case for the names of the Public variables in a class and to omit the three-character ID that indicates the variable's data type. This is because Public variables represent properties that will be seen by anyone using an object created from the class. The properties of Visual Basic objects, such as the Text and StartPosition properties, also follow this naming convention.

START HERE ▶

To enter the Public variables in the class definition:

1. Enter the following three Public statements:

   Public Length As Double
   Public Width As Double
   Public Depth As Double

2. Delete the blank line above the End Class clause, if necessary, and then save the solution.

Next, you will modify the application's code to use the RectangularPool class rather than the Dimensions structure.

START HERE ▶

To modify the code to use the RectangularPool class:

1. Click the **Main Form.vb** tab to return to the form's Code Editor window. Replace <your name> and <current date> in the comments with your name and the current date, respectively.

2. First, delete the Structure statement from the form's Declarations section.

3. Next, locate the btnCalc_Click procedure. Instead of declaring a Dimensions structure variable, the procedure will instantiate a RectangularPool object. Replace the `Dim poolSize As Dimensions` instruction with the following instruction:

   Dim customerPool As New RectangularPool

4. Rather than using the three members of the `poolSize` structure variable, the TryParse methods will now use the RectangularPool object's three Public variables. Highlight (select) `poolSize.dblLength` in the first TryParse method. Type **customerPool.** (be sure to type the period). The Public variables appear in the IntelliSense list, as shown in Figure 11-8.

```
Double.TryParse(txtLength.Text, customerPool.|)
Double.TryParse(txtWidth (field) RectangularPool.Depth As Double ● | Depth
Double.TryParse(txtDepth.Text, poolSize.dblDe          ● Equals
                                                       ● GetHashCode
                                                       ● GetType
dblGallons = GetGallons(poolSize)                      ● Length
lblGallons.Text = dblGallons.ToString("N0")            ● ToString
                                                       ● Width
```

IntelliSense list

Figure 11-8   Public variables included in the IntelliSense list

5. Click **Length** and then press **Tab**. Change `poolSize.dblWidth` and `poolSize.dblDepth` in the remaining TryParse methods to **customerPool.Width** and **customerPool.Depth**, respectively.

6. Instead of passing the `poolSize` structure variable to the GetGallons function, the procedure needs to pass the RectangularPool object. Change `poolSize` in the `dblGallons = GetGallons(poolSize)` statement to **customerPool**.

7. Locate the GetGallons function. The function will need to receive a RectangularPool object rather than a Dimensions structure variable. Change `Dimensions` in the function header to **RectangularPool**.

8. Finally, change `dblLength`, `dblWidth`, and `dblDepth` in the Return statement to **Length**, **Width**, and **Depth**, respectively. Recall that Length, Width, and Depth are the names of the RectangularPool object's properties.

Figure 11-9 shows the Class statement, the GetGallons function, and the btnCalc_Click procedure. The changes made to the original function and procedure (both of which were shown earlier in Figure 11-6) are shaded in the figure.

```
Class statement entered in the RectangularPool.vb file
Public Class RectangularPool
    Public Length As Double
    Public Width As Double
    Public Depth As Double
End Class

GetGallons function and btnCalc_Click procedure entered in the Main Form.vb file
Private Function GetGallons(ByVal pool As RectangularPool) As Double
    ' calculates and returns the number of gallons

    Const dblGAL_PER_CUBIC_FOOT As Double = 7.48

    Return pool.Length * pool.Width *
        pool.Depth * dblGAL_PER_CUBIC_FOOT
End Function
```

receives a RectangularPool object *by value*

Figure 11-9   Class definition, GetGallons function, and btnCalc_Click procedure *(continues)*

(continued)

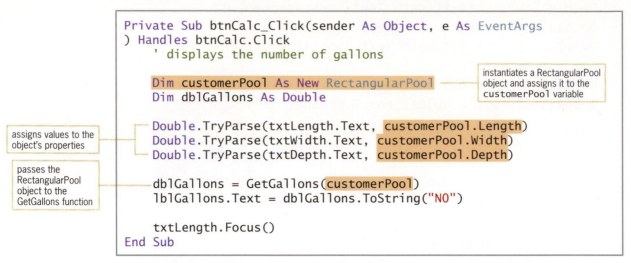

```
Private Sub btnCalc_Click(sender As Object, e As EventArgs
) Handles btnCalc.Click
    ' displays the number of gallons

    Dim customerPool As New RectangularPool
    Dim dblGallons As Double

    Double.TryParse(txtLength.Text, customerPool.Length)
    Double.TryParse(txtWidth.Text, customerPool.Width)
    Double.TryParse(txtDepth.Text, customerPool.Depth)

    dblGallons = GetGallons(customerPool)
    lblGallons.Text = dblGallons.ToString("N0")

    txtLength.Focus()
End Sub
```

instantiates a RectangularPool object and assigns it to the customerPool variable

assigns values to the object's properties

passes the RectangularPool object to the GetGallons function

Figure 11-9 Class definition, GetGallons function, and btnCalc_Click procedure

START HERE

To test the modified code:

1. Save the solution and then start the application. Use the application to display the number of gallons of water required to fill a pool that is 100 feet long, 30 feet wide, and 4 feet deep. See Figure 11-10.

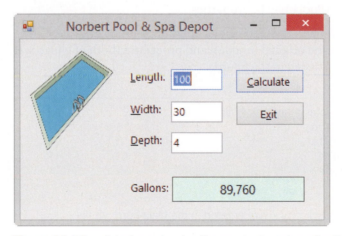

Figure 11-10 Interface showing the required number of gallons

2. Click the **Exit** button. Close the Main Form.vb and RectangularPool.vb windows, and then close the solution.

Example 2—A Class That Contains Private Variables, Public Properties, and Methods

Although you can define a class that contains only attributes represented by Public variables—like the RectangularPool class shown in Figure 11-9—that is rarely done. The disadvantage of using Public variables in a class is that a class cannot control the values assigned to its Public variables. As a result, the class cannot validate the values to ensure they are appropriate for the variables. Furthermore, most classes contain not only attributes, but behaviors as well. This is because the purpose of a class in OOP is to encapsulate the properties that describe an object, the methods that allow the object to perform tasks, and the events that allow the object to respond to actions.

In this section, you will create a class that contains data validation code and methods. (Including events in a class is beyond the scope of this book.) The class will be used in the Sunnyside Decks application, which displays the number of square feet of building material required for a rectangular deck. It also displays the cost of the deck.

To add a class file to the application:

START HERE

1. Open the VB2015\Chap11\Sunnyside Solution\Sunnyside Solution (Sunnyside Solution.sln) file. The interface provides list boxes for the user to enter the length and width of the deck as well as the price of a square foot of material. See Figure 11-11.

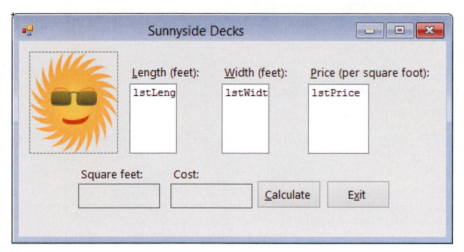

Figure 11-11   Interface for the Sunnyside Decks application

2. Use the Project menu to add a new class file to the project. Name the class file **Rectangle.vb**.

3. Insert a blank line above the Class statement, and then enter the comments and Option statements shown in Figure 11-12. Replace <your name> and <current date> in the comments with your name and the current date, respectively. Also, position the insertion point as shown in the figure.

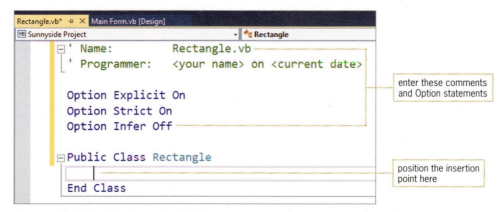

Figure 11-12   Comments and Option statements entered in the class file

A rectangular deck has two attributes: length and width. Rather than using Public variables to represent both attributes, the Rectangle class will use Private variables and Public Property procedures.

Private Variables and Public Property Procedures

Unlike a class's Public variables, its Private variables are not visible to applications that contain an instance of the class. Because of this, the names of the Private variables will not appear in the IntelliSense list as you are coding, nor will they be recognized within the application's code. A class's Private variables can be used only by instructions within the class itself. When naming a class's Private variables, many programmers use the underscore as the first character in the name and then camel case for the remainder of the name, like this: `_intLength` and `_intWidth`.

START HERE
To include Private variables in the Rectangle class:

1. Enter the following two Private statements. Press **Enter** twice after typing the last statement.

   Private _intLength As Integer
   Private _intWidth As Integer

2. Save the solution.

When an application instantiates an object, only the Public members of the object's class are visible to the application. Using OOP terminology, the Public members are "exposed" to the application, whereas the Private members are "hidden" from the application. For an application to assign data to or retrieve data from a Private variable, it must use a Public property. In other words, an application cannot directly refer to a Private variable in a class. Rather, it must refer to the variable indirectly, through the use of a Public property.

You create a Public property using a **Property procedure**, whose syntax is shown in Figure 11-13. A Public Property procedure creates a property that is visible to any application that contains an instance of the class. In most cases, a Property procedure header begins with the keywords `Public Property`. However, as the syntax indicates, the header can also include one of the following keywords: `ReadOnly` or `WriteOnly`. The **ReadOnly keyword** indicates that the property's value can be retrieved (read) by an application, but the application cannot set (write to) the property. The property would get its value from the class itself rather than from the application. The **WriteOnly keyword** indicates that an application can set the property's value, but it cannot retrieve the value. In this case, the value would be set by the application for use within the class.

As Figure 11-13 shows, the name of the property follows the `Property` keyword in the header. You should use nouns and adjectives to name a property and enter the name using Pascal case, as in Side, Bonus, and AnnualSales. Following the property name is an optional *parameterList* enclosed in parentheses, the keyword `As`, and the property's *dataType*. The dataType must match the data type of the Private variable associated with the Property procedure.

Property Procedure

<u>Syntax</u>
Public [ReadOnly | WriteOnly] Property *propertyName*[(*parameterList*)] **As** *dataType*
   Get
      [*instructions*]
      Return *privateVariable*
   End Get
   Set(value As *dataType***)**
      [*instructions*]
      privateVariable = {**value** | *defaultValue*}
   End Set
End Property

<u>Example 1 – an application can both retrieve and set the Side property's value</u>
```
Private _intSide As Integer

Public Property Side As Integer
    Get
        Return _intSide
    End Get
    Set(value As Integer)
        If value > 0 Then
            _intSide = value
        Else
            _intSide = 0
        End If
    End Set
End Property
```

<u>Example 2 – an application can retrieve, but not set, the Bonus property's value</u>
```
Private _dblBonus As Double

Public ReadOnly Property Bonus As Double
    Get
        Return _dblBonus
    End Get
End Property
```

<u>Example 3 – an application can set, but not retrieve, the AnnualSales property's value</u>
```
Private _decAnnualSales As Decimal

Public WriteOnly Property AnnualSales As Decimal
    Set(value As Decimal)
        _decAnnualSales = value
    End Set
End Property
```

Figure 11-13   Syntax and examples of a Property procedure

Between a Property procedure's header and footer, you include a Get block of code, a Set block of code, or both Get and Set blocks of code. The appropriate block or blocks of code to include depends on the keywords contained in the procedure header. If the header contains the `ReadOnly` keyword, you include only a Get block of code in the Property procedure. The code contained in the **Get block** allows an application to retrieve the contents of the Private variable associated with the property. In the Property procedure shown in Example 2 in Figure 11-13, the

The Length property of a one-dimensional array is an example of a ReadOnly property.

ReadOnly keyword indicates that an application can retrieve the contents of the Bonus property, but it cannot set the property's value. The value can be set only by a procedure within the class.

If the header contains the WriteOnly keyword, on the other hand, you include only a Set block of code in the procedure. The code in the **Set block** allows an application to assign a value to the Private variable associated with the property. In the Property procedure shown in Example 3 in Figure 11-13, the WriteOnly keyword indicates that an application can assign a value to the AnnualSales property, but it cannot retrieve the property's contents. Only a procedure within the class can retrieve the value.

If the Property procedure header does not contain the ReadOnly or WriteOnly keywords, you include both a Get block of code and a Set block of code in the procedure, as shown in Example 1 in Figure 11-13. In this case, an application can both retrieve and set the Side property's value.

The Get block in a Property procedure contains the **Get statement**, which begins with the Get clause and ends with the End Get clause. Most times, you will enter only the Return *privateVariable* instruction within the Get statement. The instruction returns the contents of the Private variable associated with the property. In Example 1 in Figure 11-13, the Return _intSide statement returns the contents of the _intSide variable, which is the Private variable associated with the Side property. Similarly, the Return _dblBonus statement in Example 2 returns the contents of the _dblBonus variable, which is the Private variable associated with the Bonus property. Example 3 does not contain a Get statement because the AnnualSales property is designated as a WriteOnly property.

The Set block contains the **Set statement**, which begins with the Set clause and ends with the End Set clause. The Set clause's value parameter temporarily stores the value that is passed to the property by the application. The value parameter's *dataType* must match the data type of the Private variable associated with the Property procedure. You can enter one or more instructions between the Set and End Set clauses. One of the instructions should assign the contents of the value parameter to the Private variable associated with the property. In Example 3 in Figure 11-13, the _decAnnualSales = value statement assigns the contents of the property's value parameter to the Private _decAnnualSales variable.

In the Set statement, you often will include instructions to validate the value received from the application before assigning it to the Private variable. The Set statement in Example 1 in Figure 11-13 includes a selection structure that determines whether the side measurement received from the application is greater than 0. If it is, the _intSide = value instruction assigns the integer stored in the value parameter to the Private _intSide variable. Otherwise, the _intSide = 0 instruction assigns a default value (in this case, 0) to the variable. The Property procedure in Example 2 in Figure 11-13 does not contain a Set statement because the Bonus property is designated as a ReadOnly property.

START HERE ▶   **To enter a Property procedure for each Private variable in the Rectangle class:**

1. The insertion point should be positioned in the blank line above the End Class clause. Enter the following Property procedure header and Get clause. When you press Enter after typing the Get clause, the Code Editor automatically enters the End Get clause, the Set statement, and the End Property clause.

    Public Property Length As Integer
    Get

2. Recall that in most cases, the Get statement simply returns the contents of the Private variable associated with the Property procedure. Type the following statement, but don't press Enter:

    Return _intLength

3. The Set statement should assign either the contents of its `value` parameter or a default value to the Private variable associated with the Property procedure. In this case, you will assign the integer stored in the `value` parameter only when it is greater than 0; otherwise, you will assign the number 0. Enter the additional code shaded in Figure 11-14.

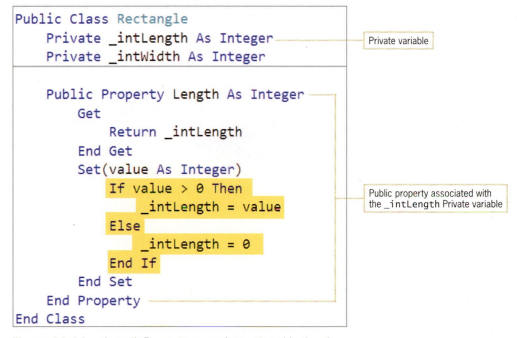

```
Public Class Rectangle
     Private _intLength As Integer          ──── Private variable
     Private _intWidth As Integer

     Public Property Length As Integer
          Get
               Return _intLength
          End Get
          Set(value As Integer)
               If value > 0 Then
                    _intLength = value         Public property associated with
               Else                            the _intLength Private variable
                    _intLength = 0
               End If
          End Set
     End Property
End Class
```

Figure 11-14   Length Property procedure entered in the class

4. Insert two blank lines below the End Property clause. On your own, enter a similar Property procedure for the `_intWidth` variable. Use **Width** as the property's name. (If you need help, you can look ahead to Figure 11-20.)

5. Save the solution.

You have finished entering the class's Private variables and Public Property procedures. The class's methods are next. The first method you will learn about is a constructor.

Constructors

Most classes contain at least one constructor. A **constructor** is a class method, always named New, whose sole purpose is to initialize the class's Private variables. Constructors never return a value, so they are always Sub procedures rather than Function procedures. The syntax for creating a constructor is shown in Figure 11-15. Notice that a constructor's *parameterList* is optional. A constructor that has no parameters, like the constructor in Example 1, is called the **default constructor**. A class can have only one default constructor. A constructor that contains one or more parameters, like the constructor in Example 2, is called a **parameterized constructor**. A class can have as many parameterized constructors as needed. However, the parameterList in each parameterized constructor must be unique within the class. The method name (in this case, New) combined with its optional parameterList is called the method's **signature**.

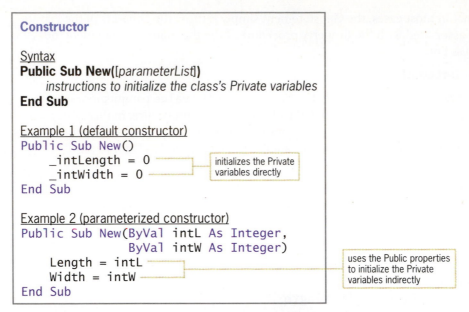

Figure 11-15   Syntax and examples of a constructor

The Dim randGen As New Random statement from Chapter 5 instantiates a Random object and invokes the class's default constructor.

When an object is instantiated, the computer uses one of the class's constructors to initialize the class's Private variables. If a class contains more than one constructor, the computer determines the appropriate constructor by matching the number, data type, and position of the arguments in the statement that instantiates the object with the number, data type, and position of the parameters listed in each constructor's parameterList. The statements in Examples 1 and 2 in Figure 11-16 will invoke the default constructor because neither statement contains any arguments. The statements in Examples 3 and 4 will invoke the parameterized constructor because both statements contain two arguments whose data type is Integer.

Example 1 – invokes the default constructor
```
Dim deck As New Rectangle
```

Example 2 – invokes the default constructor
```
deck = New Rectangle
```

Example 3 – invokes the parameterized constructor
```
Dim deck As New Rectangle(16, 14)
```

Example 4 – invokes the parameterized constructor
```
deck = New Rectangle(intDeckLen, intDeckWid)
```

Figure 11-16   Statements that invoke the constructors shown in Figure 11-15

A default constructor is allowed to initialize the class's Private variables directly, as indicated earlier in Example 1 in Figure 11-15. Parameterized constructors, on the other hand, should use the class's Public properties to access the Private variables indirectly. This is because the values passed to a parameterized constructor come from the application rather than from the class itself. Using a Public property to access a Private variable ensures that the Property procedure's Set block, which typically contains validation code, is processed. The parameterized constructor shown earlier in Example 2 in Figure 11-15 uses the class's Public properties to initialize its Private variables, thereby invoking each property's validation code.

To include a default constructor in the Rectangle class:

START HERE

1. Insert two blank lines below the Width property's End Property clause, and then enter the following default constructor:

```
Public Sub New()
    _intLength = 0
    _intWidth = 0
End Sub
```

Methods Other than Constructors

Except for constructors, which must be Sub procedures, the other methods in a class can be either Sub procedures or Function procedures. Recall from Chapter 7 that the difference between these two types of procedures is that a Function procedure returns a value after performing its assigned task, whereas a Sub procedure does not return a value.

Figure 11-17 shows the syntax for a method that is not a constructor. Like property names, method names should be entered using Pascal case. However, unlike property names, the first word in a method name should be a verb, and any subsequent words should be nouns and adjectives. (Visual Basic's SelectAll and TryParse methods follow this naming convention.) Figure 11-17 also includes two examples of a method that allows a Rectangle object to calculate its area. Notice that you can write the method as either a Function procedure or a Sub procedure. You will use the GetArea method in the Sunnyside Decks application to calculate the area of the deck the customer wants to build. Calculating the area will give you the number of square feet of material required for the deck.

Method That Is Not a Constructor

Syntax
Public {Sub | Function} *methodName*(*[parameterList]*) **[As** *dataType*]
    instructions
End {Sub | Function}

Example 1 – Function procedure
```
Public Function GetArea() As Integer
    Return _intLength * _intWidth
End Function
```

Example 2 – Sub procedure
```
Public Sub GetArea(ByRef intA As Integer)
    intA = _intLength * _intWidth
End Sub
```

Figure 11-17   Syntax and examples of a method that is not a constructor

To enter the GetArea method from Example 1:

START HERE

1. Insert two blank lines below the default constructor's End Sub clause.

2. Enter the GetArea method shown in Example 1 in Figure 11-17, and then save the solution.

Coding the Sunnyside Decks Application

The Calculate button's Click event procedure is the only procedure you need to code in the Sunnyside Decks application. Figure 11-18 shows the procedure's pseudocode.

---

btnCalc Click event procedure
1. instantiate a Rectangle object to represent the deck
2. declare variables to store the price per square foot of material, the required number of square feet of material, and the cost of the deck
3. assign the input data to the appropriate properties and variable
4. calculate the required number of square feet of material by finding the deck's area; use the object's GetArea method
5. calculate the cost of the deck by multiplying the required number of square feet of material by the price per square foot of material
6. display the required number of square feet of material and the cost of the deck

---

Figure 11-18   Pseudocode for the btnCalc_Click procedure

START HERE ▶

To code the btnCalc_Click procedure:

1. Click the **designer window's tab**, and then open the form's Code Editor window. Replace <your name> and <current date> in the comments with your name and the current date, respectively.

2. Locate the btnCalc_Click procedure. The first step in the pseudocode is to instantiate a Rectangle object to represent the deck. Enter the following Dim statement in the blank line below the ' instantiate a Rectangle object comment:

   Dim deck As New Rectangle

3. Next, the procedure will declare variables to store the price of a square foot of material, the number of square feet needed, and the cost of the deck. Click the **blank line** below the ' declare variables comment, and then enter the following three Dim statements:

   Dim dblPriceSqFt As Double
   Dim intSqFt As Integer
   Dim dblCost As Double

4. Now the procedure will assign the length and width entries to the Rectangle object's Length and Width properties, respectively. It will also assign the price entry to the dblPriceSqFt variable. Click the **blank line** below the ' assign values to the object's Public properties comment, and then enter the three TryParse methods shown in Figure 11-19. Notice that when you press the period after typing **deck** in the first two TryParse methods, the **deck** object's Length and Width properties appear in the IntelliSense list.

```
' assign values to the object's Public properties
Integer.TryParse(lstLength.SelectedItem.ToString, deck.Length)
Integer.TryParse(lstWidth.SelectedItem.ToString, deck.Width)
Double.TryParse(lstPrice.SelectedItem.ToString, dblPriceSqFt)
```

Figure 11-19   TryParse methods entered in the procedure

5. The fourth step in the pseudocode calculates the required number of square feet of material; it does this using the object's GetArea method. Click the **blank line** below the ' calculate the square feet comment, and then enter the following assignment statement. Here, again, notice that when you press the period after typing deck, the deck object's GetArea method appears in the IntelliSense list.

intSqFt = deck.GetArea

6. The next step in the pseudocode calculates the cost of the deck by multiplying the number of square feet by the price per square foot. Enter the following assignment statement in the blank line below the ' calculate the deck cost comment:

dblCost = intSqFt * dblPriceSqFt

7. The last step in the pseudocode displays the required number of square feet and the cost of the deck. Click the **blank line** below the ' display output comment, and then enter the following assignment statements:

lblSquareFeet.Text = intSqFt.ToString
lblCost.Text = dblCost.ToString("c2")

Figure 11-20 shows the Rectangle class definition contained in the Rectangle.vb file. It also shows the btnCalc_Click procedure contained in the Main Form.vb file.

```
Class statement entered in the Rectangle.vb file
Public Class Rectangle
    Private _intLength As Integer
    Private _intWidth As Integer

    Public Property Length As Integer
        Get
            Return _intLength
        End Get
        Set(value As Integer)
            If value > 0 Then
                _intLength = value
            Else
                _intLength = 0
            End If
        End Set
    End Property

    Public Property Width As Integer
        Get
            Return _intWidth
        End Get
        Set(value As Integer)
            If value > 0 Then
                _intWidth = value
            Else
                _intWidth = 0
            End If
        End Set
    End Property
```

Figure 11-20   Rectangle class definition and btnCalc_Click procedure *(continues)*

(continued)

```vb
    Public Sub New()
        _intLength = 0
        _intWidth = 0
    End Sub

    Public Function GetArea() As Integer
        Return _intLength * _intWidth
    End Function
End Class
```

btnCalc_Click procedure entered in the Main Form.vb file

```vb
Private Sub btnCalc_Click(sender As Object, e As EventArgs) Handles
btnCalc.Click
    ' displays square feet and deck cost

    ' instantiate a Rectangle object
    Dim deck As New Rectangle                          ─── instantiates a
                                                            Rectangle object

    ' declare variables
    Dim dblPriceSqFt As Double
    Dim intSqFt As Integer
    Dim dblCost As Double

    ' assign values to the object's Public properties
    Integer.TryParse(lstLength.SelectedItem.ToString, deck.Length)
    Integer.TryParse(lstWidth.SelectedItem.ToString, deck.Width)
    Double.TryParse(lstPrice.SelectedItem.ToString, dblPriceSqFt)

    ' calculate the square feet
    intSqFt = deck.GetArea             ─── invokes the object's
                                            GetArea method
    ' calculate the deck cost
    dblCost = intSqFt * dblPriceSqFt

    ' display output
    lblSquareFeet.Text = intSqFt.ToString
    lblCost.Text = dblCost.ToString("c2")

End Sub
```

assigns values to the object's Public properties

Figure 11-20   Rectangle class definition and btnCalc_Click procedure

START HERE

To test the application:

1. Save the solution and then start the application. Click **16** and **14** in the Length and Width list boxes, respectively. Click **9.50** in the Price list box and then click the **Calculate** button. The `Dim deck As New Rectangle` instruction in the btnCalc_Click procedure instantiates a Rectangle object, using the class's default constructor to initialize the object's Private variables to the number 0. The next three Dim statements in the procedure create and initialize two Double variables and one Integer variable. The first two TryParse methods use the Rectangle object's Public properties to assign the appropriate values to the object's Private variables. The third TryParse method assigns the selected price per square foot to the `dblPriceSqFt` variable. Next, the procedure uses the Rectangle object's GetArea method to calculate and return the

deck's area, which represents the required number of square feet of building material. Finally, the procedure calculates the cost of the deck, and then it displays both the required number of square feet and the cost. See Figure 11-21.

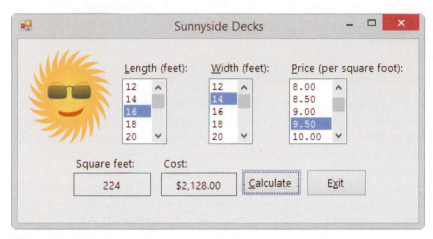

Figure 11-21 Square feet and cost displayed in the interface

2. On your own, test the application using different lengths, widths, and prices. When you are finished, click the **Exit** button. Close the Main Form.vb and Rectangle.vb windows, and then close the solution.

YOU DO IT 1!

Create an application named YouDoIt 1 and save it in the VB2015\Chap11 folder. Add a text box, a label, and a button to the form. Add a class file named Circle.vb to the project. Define a class named Circle that contains one attribute: the circle's radius. It should also contain a default constructor and a method that calculates and returns the circle's area. Use the following formula to calculate the area: $3.141592 * radius^2$. Open the form's Code Editor window. Code the button's Click event procedure so that it displays the circle's area, using the radius entered by the user. Test the application appropriately, and then close the solution.

Example 3—A Class That Contains a Parameterized Constructor

In this example, you will add a parameterized constructor to the Rectangle class created in Example 2 and then use the parameterized constructor in the Sunnyside Decks application. Recall that a parameterized constructor is simply a constructor that has parameters.

To add a parameterized constructor to the Rectangle.vb file:

START HERE

1. Use Windows to make a copy of the Sunnyside Solution folder from Example 2. Rename the copy **Modified Sunnyside Solution**. Open the Sunnyside Solution (Sunnyside Solution.sln) file contained in the Modified Sunnyside Solution folder.

2. Right-click **Rectangle.vb** in the Solution Explorer window, and then click **View Code**.

3. Locate the default constructor. Click the **blank line** below the default constructor's End Sub clause, and then press **Enter** twice to insert two blank lines. Press the **up arrow** key on your keyboard, and then enter the following parameterized constructor:

Public Sub New(ByVal intL As Integer, ByVal intW As Integer)
  Length = intL
  Width = intW
End Sub

4. Save the solution and then close the Rectangle.vb window.

Figure 11-22 shows the Rectangle class's default and parameterized constructors. Unlike the default constructor, which automatically initializes the Private variables to 0 when a Rectangle object is created, a parameterized constructor allows an application to specify the object's initial values. In this case, the initial values must have the Integer data type because the constructor's parameterList contains two Integer variables. You include the initial values, enclosed in a set of parentheses, in the statement that instantiates the object. In other words, you include them in the statement that contains the New keyword, such as the Dim deck As New Rectangle(16, 14) statement or the deck = New Rectangle(intDeckLen, intDeckWid) statement.

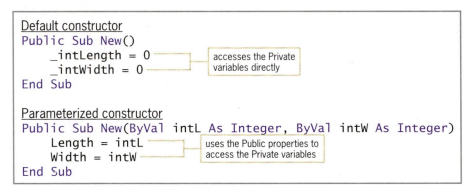

```
Default constructor
Public Sub New()
     _intLength = 0 ─────┐
     _intWidth = 0 ──────┤ accesses the Private
End Sub                    variables directly


Parameterized constructor
Public Sub New(ByVal intL As Integer, ByVal intW As Integer)
     Length = intL ──────┐
     Width = intW ───────┤ uses the Public properties to
End Sub                    access the Private variables
```

Figure 11-22   Default and parameterized constructors

START HERE

To use the parameterized constructor in the btnCalc_Click procedure:

1. Open the form's Code Editor window. Locate the btnCalc_Click procedure. Change the second comment in the procedure to '**declare a variable for a Rectangle object**.

2. Delete the New keyword from the first Dim statement. The statement should now say Dim deck As Rectangle.

3. Click the **blank line** below the last Dim statement, and then enter the following two declaration statements:

Dim intDeckLen As Integer
Dim intDeckWid As Integer

4. In the first TryParse method, replace deck.Length with **intDeckLen**. Then, in the second TryParse method, replace deck.Width with **intDeckWid**.

5. Click the **blank line** below the last TryParse method and then press **Enter**. Enter the following comment and assignment statement:

'**instantiate and initialize a Rectangle object**
deck = New Rectangle(intDeckLen, intDeckWid)

The modifications made to the original code, shown earlier in Figure 11-20, are shaded in Figure 11-23.

Modified Class statement entered in the Rectangle.vb file

```vb
Public Class Rectangle
    Private _intLength As Integer
    Private _intWidth As Integer

    Public Property Length As Integer
        Get
            Return _intLength
        End Get
        Set(value As Integer)
            If value > 0 Then
                _intLength = value
            Else
                _intLength = 0
            End If
        End Set
    End Property

    Public Property Width As Integer
        Get
            Return _intWidth
        End Get
        Set(value As Integer)
            If value > 0 Then
                _intWidth = value
            Else
                _intWidth = 0
            End If
        End Set
    End Property

    Public Sub New()
        _intLength = 0
        _intWidth = 0
    End Sub

    Public Sub New(ByVal intL As Integer, ByVal intW As Integer)       ─┐
        Length = intL                                                   │ parameterized constructor
        Width = intW                                                    │
    End Sub  ────────────────────────────────────────────────────────┘

    Public Function GetArea() As Integer
        Return _intLength * _intWidth
    End Function
End Class
```

Modified btnCalc_Click procedure entered in the Main Form.vb file

```vb
Private Sub btnCalc_Click(sender As Object, e As EventArgs
) Handles btnCalc.Click
    ' displays square feet and deck cost
```

Figure 11-23   Modified Rectangle class definition and btnCalc_Click procedure *(continues)*

(continued)

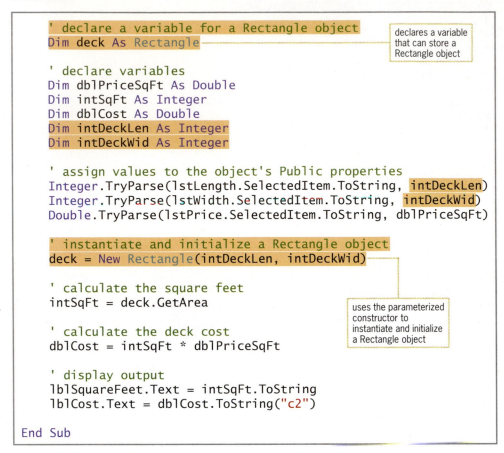

```
' declare a variable for a Rectangle object
Dim deck As Rectangle ──────────────────     declares a variable
                                              that can store a
                                              Rectangle object
' declare variables
Dim dblPriceSqFt As Double
Dim intSqFt As Integer
Dim dblCost As Double
Dim intDeckLen As Integer
Dim intDeckWid As Integer

' assign values to the object's Public properties
Integer.TryParse(lstLength.SelectedItem.ToString, intDeckLen)
Integer.TryParse(lstWidth.SelectedItem.ToString, intDeckWid)
Double.TryParse(lstPrice.SelectedItem.ToString, dblPriceSqFt)

' instantiate and initialize a Rectangle object
deck = New Rectangle(intDeckLen, intDeckWid)

' calculate the square feet
intSqFt = deck.GetArea                        uses the parameterized
                                              constructor to
                                              instantiate and initialize
' calculate the deck cost                     a Rectangle object
dblCost = intSqFt * dblPriceSqFt

' display output
lblSquareFeet.Text = intSqFt.ToString
lblCost.Text = dblCost.ToString("c2")

End Sub
```

Figure 11-23 Modified Rectangle class definition and btnCalc_Click procedure

When the user clicks the Calculate button, the `Dim deck As Rectangle` instruction in the btnCalc_Click procedure creates a variable that can store a Rectangle object; but it does not create the object. The remaining Dim statements create and initialize five variables. The TryParse methods assign the input values to the `intDeckLen`, `intDeckWid`, and `dblPriceSqFt` variables.

The next statement in the procedure, `deck = New Rectangle(intDeckLen, intDeckWid)`, instantiates a Rectangle object. The two Integer arguments in the statement tell the computer to use the parameterized constructor to initialize the Rectangle object's Private variables. The computer passes the two arguments (*by value*) to the constructor, which stores them in its `intL` and `intW` parameters. The assignment statements in the constructor then assign the parameter values to the Rectangle object's Public Length and Width properties.

When you assign a value to a property, the computer passes the value to the property's Set statement, where it is stored in the Set statement's `value` parameter. In this case, the selection structure in the Length property's Set statement compares the value stored in the `value` parameter with the number 0. If the value is greater than 0, the selection structure's true path assigns the value to the Private `_intLength` variable; otherwise, its false path assigns the number 0 to the variable. The selection structure in the Width property's Set statement works the same way, except it assigns the appropriate number to the Private `_intWidth` variable.

Notice that a parameterized constructor uses the class's Public properties to access the Private variables indirectly. This is because the values passed to a parameterized constructor come

Example 4—Reusing a Class **LESSON A**

633

from the application rather than from the class itself. As mentioned earlier, values that originate outside of the class should always be assigned to the Private variables indirectly through the Public properties. Doing this ensures that the Property procedure's Set block, which typically contains validation code, is processed.

After the Rectangle object is instantiated and its Private variables are initialized, the btnCalc_Click procedure uses the object's GetArea method to calculate and return the area of the deck. The area represents the required number of square feet of building material. Finally, the procedure calculates the cost of the deck and then displays both the required number of square feet and the cost.

To test the modified application:

START HERE

1. Save the solution and then start the application. Click the **Calculate** button. See Figure 11-24.

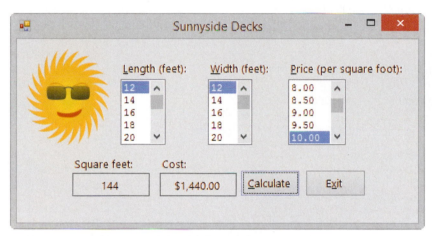

Figure 11-24   Interface showing the square feet and cost

2. On your own, test the application using different lengths, widths, and prices. When you are finished, click the **Exit** button. Close the Main Form.vb window and then close the solution.

Example 4—Reusing a Class

In Examples 2 and 3, you used the Rectangle class to create an object that represented a deck. In this example, you will use the Rectangle class to create an object that represents a square pizza. A square is simply a rectangle that has four equal sides. As mentioned earlier, the ability to use an object—in this case, a Rectangle object—for more than one purpose saves programming time and money, which contributes to the popularity of object-oriented programming.

To add the Rectangle.vb file to the Pete's Pizzeria application:

START HERE

1. Open the VB2015\Chap11\Pizzeria Solution\Pizzeria Solution (Pizzeria Solution.sln) file. The interface provides text boxes for entering the side measurements of both the entire pizza and a pizza slice. The application will use both measurements to calculate the number of pizza slices that can be cut from the entire pizza.

2. Use Windows to copy the Rectangle.vb file from the VB2015\Chap11\Modified Sunnyside Solution\Sunnyside Project folder to the Pizzeria Solution\Pizzeria Project folder. (If you did not complete the modified Sunnyside Decks application, you can copy the Rectangle.vb file contained in the VB2015\Chap11 folder.)

3. Click **Project** on the menu bar and then click **Add Existing Item**. Open the Pizzeria Project folder (if necessary), and then click **Rectangle.vb** in the list of filenames. Click the **Add** button. Temporarily display the Solution Explorer window (if necessary) to verify that the Rectangle.vb file was added to the project.

Figure 11-25 shows the pseudocode for the Calculate button's Click event procedure.

btnCalc Click event procedure
1. instantiate a Rectangle object to represent the entire square pizza
2. instantiate a Rectangle object to represent a square pizza slice
3. declare variables to store the area of the entire pizza, the area of a pizza slice, and the number of slices
4. assign the input data to the properties of the appropriate Rectangle object
5. calculate the area of the entire pizza
6. calculate the area of a pizza slice
7. if the area of a pizza slice is greater than 0
        calculate the number of pizza slices by dividing the area of the entire pizza by
        the area of a pizza slice
   else
        assign 0 as the number of pizza slices
   end if
8. display the number of pizza slices

Figure 11-25   Pseudocode for the btnCalc_Click procedure

START HERE ▶

To code the btnCalc_Click procedure:

1. Open the form's Code Editor window. Replace <your name> and <current date> in the comments with your name and the current date, respectively.

2. Locate the btnCalc_Click procedure. The first two steps in the pseudocode are to instantiate two Rectangle objects to represent the entire pizza and a pizza slice. Click the **blank line** above the End Sub clause, and then enter the following Dim statements:

   Dim entirePizza As New Rectangle
   Dim pizzaSlice As New Rectangle

3. The third step in the pseudocode is to declare variables to store the area of the entire pizza, the area of a pizza slice, and the number of slices. You won't need variables to store the side measurements entered by the user because the procedure will assign those values to each Rectangle object's Length and Width properties. Enter the following three Dim statements, pressing **Enter** twice after typing the last Dim statement:

   Dim intEntireArea As Integer
   Dim intSliceArea As Integer
   Dim dblSlices As Double

4. The fourth step in the pseudocode assigns the side measurements to the properties of the appropriate Rectangle object. Enter the following four lines of code. Notice that when you press the period after typing either `entirePizza` or `pizzaSlice`, the object's Length and Width properties appear in the IntelliSense list. Press **Enter** twice after typing the last line.

   Integer.TryParse(txtEntirePizza.Text, entirePizza.Length)
   Integer.TryParse(txtEntirePizza.Text, entirePizza.Width)
   Integer.TryParse(txtPizzaSlice.Text, pizzaSlice.Length)
   Integer.TryParse(txtPizzaSlice.Text, pizzaSlice.Width)

5. The fifth and sixth steps in the pseudocode calculate the areas of both the entire pizza and a pizza slice, respectively. You can accomplish both tasks using the Rectangle

object's GetArea method. Because the class already contains the code needed to calculate the area of a rectangle, you do not need to waste time planning and then reentering and retesting it. Enter the following comment and assignment statements:

' calculate areas
intEntireArea = entirePizza.GetArea
intSliceArea = pizzaSlice.GetArea

6. The seventh step in the pseudocode is a selection structure that determines whether the area of the pizza slice is greater than 0. You need to make this determination because the area is used as the divisor when calculating the number of pizza slices. If the area is greater than 0, the selection structure's true path should calculate the number of pizza slices; otherwise, its false path should assign 0 as the number of pizza slices. Enter the following comment and selection structure:

' calculate number of slices
If intSliceArea > 0 Then
**   dblSlices = intEntireArea / intSliceArea**
Else
**   dblSlices = 0**
End If

7. The last step in the pseudocode displays the number of pizza slices. Insert a blank line below the End If clause, and then enter the following comment and assignment statement:

' display number of slices
lblSlices.Text = dblSlices.ToString("n1")

The btnCalc_Click procedure is shown in Figure 11-26.

```vb
Private Sub btnCalc_Click(sender As Object, e As EventArgs
) Handles btnCalc.Click
    ' displays the number of square pizza slices

    Dim entirePizza As New Rectangle          ──── instantiates two
    Dim pizzaSlice As New Rectangle           ──── Rectangle objects
    Dim intEntireArea As Integer
    Dim intSliceArea As Integer
    Dim dblSlices As Double

    Integer.TryParse(txtEntirePizza.Text, entirePizza.Length)
    Integer.TryParse(txtEntirePizza.Text, entirePizza.Width)     assigns values to each
    Integer.TryParse(txtPizzaSlice.Text, pizzaSlice.Length)      object's Public properties
    Integer.TryParse(txtPizzaSlice.Text, pizzaSlice.Width)

    ' calculate areas
    intEntireArea = entirePizza.GetArea       ──── invokes each object's
    intSliceArea = pizzaSlice.GetArea         ──── GetArea method
    ' calculate number of slices
    If intSliceArea > 0 Then
        dblSlices = intEntireArea / intSliceArea
    Else
        dblSlices = 0
    End If
    ' display number of slices
    lblSlices.Text = dblSlices.ToString("n1")
End Sub
```

Figure 11-26   btnCalc_Click procedure

START HERE

To test the application's code:

1. Save the solution and then start the application. First, determine the number of 4-inch slices that can be cut from a 12-inch pizza. Type **12** in the Entire square pizza box, and then type **4** in the Square pizza slice box. Click the **Calculate** button. As Figure 11-27 indicates, the pizza can be cut into nine slices.

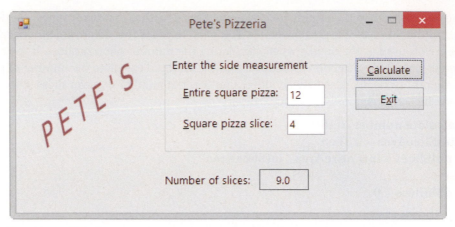

Figure 11-27   Number of pizza slices shown in the interface

2. On your own, test the application using different side measurements. When you are finished, click the **Exit** button. Close the Code Editor window and then close the solution.

Lesson A Summary

-   To define a class:

    Use the Class statement. The statement's syntax is shown in Figure 11-3.

-   To add a class file to a project:

    Click Project on the menu bar and then click Add Class. In the Name box, type the name of the class followed by a period and the letters vb, and then click the Add button.

-   To instantiate (create) an object from a class:

    Use either of the syntax versions shown in Figure 11-5.

-   To create a Property procedure:

    Use the syntax shown in Figure 11-13. The Get block allows an application to retrieve the contents of the Private variable associated with the Property procedure. The Set block allows an application to assign a value to the Private variable associated with the Property procedure.

-   To create a constructor:

    Use the syntax shown in Figure 11-15. A constructor that has no parameters is called the default constructor. A class can have only one default constructor. A constructor that has one or more parameters is called a parameterized constructor. A class can have as many parameterized constructors as needed. All constructors are Sub procedures that are named New. Each constructor must have a unique parameterList (if any) within the class.

* To create a method other than a constructor:

Use the syntax shown in Figure 11-17.

Lesson A Key Terms

Attributes—the characteristics that describe an object

Behaviors—an object's methods and events

Class—a pattern that the computer follows when instantiating (creating) an object

Class statement—the statement used to define a class in Visual Basic

Constructor—a method whose instructions are automatically processed each time the class is used to instantiate an object; used to initialize the class's Private variables; always a Sub procedure named New

Default constructor—a constructor that has no parameters; a class can have only one default constructor

Encapsulates—an OOP term that means "contains"

Events—the actions to which an object can respond

Get block—the section of a Property procedure that contains the Get statement

Get statement—appears in a Get block in a Property procedure; contains the code that allows an application to retrieve the contents of the Private variable associated with the property

Instance—an object created from a class

Instantiated—the process of creating an object from a class

Methods—the actions that an object is capable of performing

Object—anything that can be seen, touched, or used

Object-oriented programming language—a programming language that allows the use of objects to accomplish a program's goal

OOP—the acronym for object-oriented programming

Parameterized constructor—a constructor that contains one or more parameters

Property procedure—creates a Public property that an application can use to access a Private variable in a class

ReadOnly keyword—used when defining a Property procedure; indicates that the property's value can only be retrieved (read) by an application

Set block—the section of a Property procedure that contains the Set statement

Set statement—appears in a Set block in a Property procedure; contains the code that allows an application to assign a value to the Private variable associated with the property; may also contain validation code

Signature—a method's name combined with its optional parameterList

WriteOnly keyword—used when defining a Property procedure; indicates that an application can only set the property's value

Lesson A Review Questions

1. The name of a class file ends with _____.

   a. .cla

   b. .cls

   c. .vb

   d. none of the above

2. A constructor is _____.

   a. a Function procedure

   b. a Property procedure

   c. a Sub procedure

   d. either a Function procedure or a Sub procedure

3. The Inventory class contains a Private variable named `_strId`. The variable is associated with the Public ItemId property. An application instantiates an Inventory object and assigns it to a variable named `onHand`. Which of the following can be used by the application to assign the string "XG45" to the `_strId` variable?

   a. `onHand.ItemId = "XG45"`

   b. `ItemId._strId = "XG45"`

   c. `onHand._strId = "XG45"`

   d. `ItemId.strId = "XG45"`

4. The Item class contains a Public method named GetDiscount. The method is a Function procedure. An application instantiates an Item object and assigns it to a variable named `cellPhone`. Which of the following can be used by the application to invoke the GetDiscount method?

   a. `dblDiscount = Call cellPhone.GetDiscount`

   b. `dblDiscount = cellPhone.GetDiscount`

   c. `dblDiscount = GetDiscount.cellPhone`

   d. `Call cellPhone.GetDiscount`

5. Which of the following statements is false?

   a. A class can contain only one constructor.

   b. An example of a behavior is the SetTime method in a Time class.

   c. An object created from a class is referred to as an instance of the class.

   d. An instance of a class is considered an object.

6. A Private variable in a class can be accessed directly by a Public method in the same class.

   a. True

   b. False

7. An application can access the Private variables in a class _____.

   a. directly

   b. using properties created by Public Property procedures

   c. through Private procedures contained in the class

   d. none of the above

8. To hide a variable or method contained in a class, you declare the variable or method using the _____ keyword.

   a. `Hide`

   b. `Invisible`

   c. `Private`

   d. `ReadOnly`

9. Which of the following is the name of the Inventory class's default constructor?

    a. Inventory
    b. InventoryConstructor
    c. Default
    d. New

10. Which of the following instantiates an Inventory object and assigns it to the `chair` variable?

    a. `Dim chair As Inventory`
    b. `Dim chair As New Inventory`
    c. `Dim chair = New Inventory`
    d. `Dim New chair As Inventory`

11. If you need to validate a value before assigning it to a Private variable, you enter the validation code in the _____ block in a Property procedure.

    a. Assign
    b. Get
    c. Set
    d. Validate

12. The Return statement is entered in the _____ statement in a Property procedure.

    a. Get
    b. Set

13. A class contains a Private variable named `_strState`. The variable is associated with a Public property named State. Which of the following is the best way for a parameterized constructor to assign the value stored in its `strName` parameter to the variable?

    a. `_strState = strName`
    b. `State = _strName`
    c. `_strState = State.strName`
    d. `State = strName`

Lesson A Exercises

1. Explain how the computer determines the appropriate constructor to use when instantiating an object using a class that contains more than one constructor.　　　**INTRODUCTORY**

2. Write a Class statement that defines a class named Book. The class contains three Public variables: Title, Author, and Price. The Title and Author variables are String variables. The Price variable is a Decimal variable. Then use the syntax shown in Version 1 in Figure 11-5 to declare a variable that can store a Book object; name the variable `fiction`. Also write a statement that instantiates the Book object and assigns it to the `fiction` variable.　　　**INTRODUCTORY**

3. Rewrite the Class statement from Exercise 2 so that it uses Private variables rather than Public variables. Be sure to include the Property procedures and default constructor.　　　**INTRODUCTORY**

4. Write a Class statement that defines a class named SongInfo. The class contains three Private String variables named `_strName`, `_strArtist`, and `_strSongLength`. Name the corresponding properties SongName, Artist, and SongLength. Then, use the syntax shown in Version 2 in Figure 11-5 to create a Song object, assigning it to a variable named `hipHop`.　　　**INTRODUCTORY**

INTRODUCTORY

5. The Car class definition is shown in Figure 11-28. Write a Dim statement that uses the default constructor to instantiate a Car object in an application. The Dim statement should assign the object to a variable named `nissan`. Next, write assignment statements that the application can use to assign the string "370Z" and the number 30614.75 to the Model and Price properties, respectively. Finally, write an assignment statement that the application can use to invoke the GetNewPrice function. Assign the function's return value to a variable named `dblNewPrice`.

```
Public Class Car
    Private _strModel As String
    Private _dblPrice As Double

    Public Property Model As String
        Get
            Return _strModel
        End Get
        Set(value As String)
            _strModel = value
        End Set
    End Property

    Public Property Price As Double
        Get
            Return _dblPrice
        End Get
        Set(value As Double)
            _dblPrice = value
        End Set
    End Property

    Public Sub New()
        _strModel = String.Empty
        _dblPrice = 0
    End Sub

    Public Sub New(ByVal strM As String, ByVal dblP As Double)
        Model = strM
        Price = dblP
    End Sub

    Public Function GetNewPrice() As Double
        Return _dblPrice * 1.15
    End Function
End Class
```

Figure 11-28   Car class definition

INTRODUCTORY

6. Using the Car class from Figure 11-28, write a Dim statement that uses the parameterized constructor to instantiate a Car object. Pass the string "Fusion" and the number 22560.99 to the parameterized constructor. The Dim statement should assign the object to a variable named `rentalCar`.

INTRODUCTORY

7. An application contains the statement `Dim myCar As Car`. Using the Car class from Figure 11-28, write an assignment statement that instantiates a Car object and initializes it using the `strType` and `dblPrice` variables. The statement should assign the object to the `myCar` variable.

8. In this exercise, you modify the Pete's Pizzeria application from this lesson. Use Windows to make a copy of the Pizzeria Solution folder. Rename the copy Pizzeria Solution-Parameterized. Open the Pizzeria Solution (Pizzeria Solution.sln) file contained in the Pizzeria Solution-Parameterized folder. Modify the btnCalc_Click procedure to use the Rectangle class's parameterized constructor. Test the application appropriately.

9. In this exercise, you modify the Norbert Pool & Spa Depot application from this lesson. Use Windows to make a copy of the Norbert Solution folder. Rename the copy Norbert Solution-Introductory. Open the Norbert Solution (Norbert Solution.sln) file contained in the Norbert Solution-Introductory folder. Modify the RectangularPool class so that it uses Private variables and Public Property procedures rather than Public variables. Include both a default constructor and a parameterized constructor in the class. Test the application appropriately.

10. Open the VB2015\Chap11\Palace Solution\Palace Solution (Palace Solution.sln) file. Create a Rectangle class similar to the one shown earlier in Figure 11-23; however, use Double variables rather than Integer variables. The application should calculate and display the number of square yards of carpeting needed to carpet a rectangular floor. Code and then test the application appropriately.

11. In this exercise, you modify the Norbert Pool & Spa Depot application from Exercise 9. Use Windows to make a copy of the Norbert Solution-Introductory folder. Rename the copy Norbert Solution-Intermediate. Open the Norbert Solution (Norbert Solution.sln) file contained in the Norbert Solution-Intermediate folder.

   a. Add two labels to the form. Position one of the labels below the Gallons: label, and then change its Text property to Cost:. Position the other label below the lblGallons control, and then change its Name, TextAlign, AutoSize, and BorderStyle properties to lblCost, MiddleCenter, False, and FixedSingle, respectively. Remove the contents of its Text property, and then size the control appropriately. Also, change the control's Font and BackColor properties to match the lblGallons control.

   b. Add a method named GetVolume to the RectangularPool class. The method should calculate and return the volume of a RectangularPool object. The formula for calculating the volume is *length * width * depth*.

   c. Add a method named GetGallons to the RectangularPool class. The method should receive a Double number that represents a RectangularPool object's volume. It should use the information it receives to calculate and return the number of gallons of water.

   d. Remove the GetGallons function from the form's Code Editor window, and then modify the btnCalc_Click procedure to use the customerPool object's GetVolume and GetGallons methods. The procedure should also calculate and display the cost of filling the pool with water. The charge for water is $1.75 per 1,000 gallons (or $0.00175 per gallon). Test the application appropriately.

12. In this exercise, you create an application that can be used to estimate the cost of laying sod on a rectangular piece of property. Create the application, using the following names for the solution and project, respectively: Harston Solution and Harston Project. Save the application in the VB2015\Chap11 folder. Use Windows to copy the Rectangle.vb file from the VB2015\Chap11 folder to the VB2015\Chap11\Harston Solution\Harston Project

folder. Use the Project menu to add the Rectangle.vb class file to the project. Create the interface shown in Figure 11-29. The image for the picture box is stored in the VB2015\Chap11\Landscape.png file. Code the application, and then test it appropriately. (The length and width should be integers.)

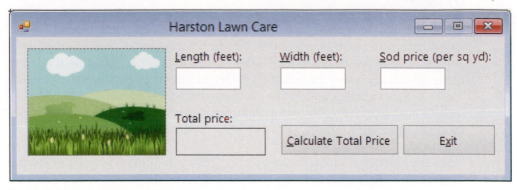

Figure 11-29   Interface for Exercise 12

13. In this exercise, you create an application that can be used to calculate the cost of installing a fence around a rectangular area. Create the application, using the following names for the solution and project, respectively: Fence Solution and Fence Project. Save the application in the VB2015\Chap11 folder. Use Windows to copy the Rectangle.vb file from the VB2015\Chap11 folder to the Fence Solution\Fence Project folder. Use the Project menu to add the Rectangle.vb class file to the project. Modify the class to use Double (rather than Integer) variables and properties. Add a method named GetPerimeter to the Rectangle class. The method should calculate and return the perimeter of a rectangle. To calculate the perimeter, the method will need to add together the length and width measurements, and then multiply the sum by 2. Create the interface shown in Figure 11-30. The image for the picture box is stored in the VB2015\Chap11\Fence.png file. Code the application and then test it appropriately. (Hint: Using 120 feet as the length, 75 feet as the width, and 10 as the cost per linear foot of fencing, the installation cost is $3,900.00.)

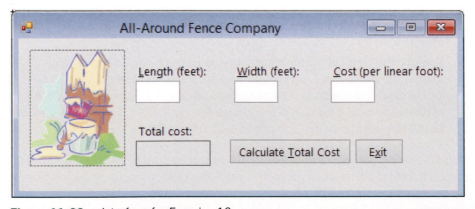

Figure 11-30   Interface for Exercise 13

14. Create an application, using the following names for the solution and project, respectively: Playground Solution and Playground Project. Save the application in the VB2015\Chap11 folder. The application should display the area of a triangular playground in square feet. It should also display the cost of covering the playground with artificial grass.

    a. Create a suitable interface. Provide list boxes for the user to enter the playground's base and height dimensions in yards. Both list boxes should display numbers from 20 to 50 in increments of 0.5. Also, provide a list box for entering the price per square foot. This list box should display numbers from 1 to 6 in increments of 0.5.

    b. Create a class named Triangle. The Triangle class should verify that the base and height dimensions are greater than 0 before assigning the values to the Private variables. (Although the dimensions come from list boxes in this application, the Triangle class might subsequently be used in an application whose dimensions come from text boxes.) The class should also include a default constructor, a parameterized constructor, and a method to calculate the area of a triangle.

    c. Code the application and then test it appropriately.

15. Create an application, using the following names for the solution and project, respectively: Fire Solution and Fire Project. Save the application in the VB2015\Chap11 folder. The application should display the capacity (volume) of a water tank on a fire engine in both cubic feet and gallons, given the tank's length, width and height measurements. Create a suitable interface. Code the application by using a class to instantiate a water tank object, and then test it appropriately. (Hint: There are 7.48 gallons in one cubic foot.)

16. Create an application, using the following names for the solution and project, respectively: Parking Solution and Parking Project. Save the application in the VB2015\Chap11 folder. The application should display the total cost of paving the parking lot shown in Figure 11-31. Create a suitable interface. Code the application by using a class to instantiate a parking lot object, and then test it appropriately.

Figure 11-31   Parking lot for Exercise 16

ADVANCED

ADVANCED

ADVANCED

LESSON B

After studying Lesson B, you should be able to:

- Include a ReadOnly property in a class

- Create an auto-implemented property

- Overload a method in a class

Example 5—A Class That Contains a ReadOnly Property

In Lesson A, you learned that the `ReadOnly` keyword in a Property procedure's header indicates that the property's value can only be retrieved (read) by an application; the application cannot set (write to) the property. A ReadOnly property gets its value from the class itself rather than from the application. In the next set of steps, you will add a ReadOnly property to a class named CourseGrade. You will also add the default constructor and a method that will assign the appropriate grade to the Private variable associated with the ReadOnly property.

START HERE

To modify the CourseGrade class:

1. If necessary, start Visual Studio 2015. Open the VB2015\Chap11\Grade Solution\Grade Solution (Grade Solution.sln) file. The interface provides list boxes for entering two test scores that can range from 0 to 100 points each. See Figure 11-32.

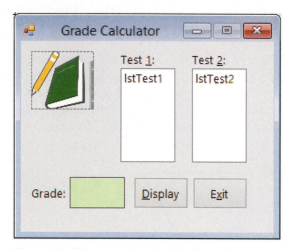

Figure 11-32   Interface for the Grade Calculator application

2. Right-click **CourseGrade.vb** in the Solution Explorer window, and then click **View Code**. Replace <your name> and <current date> in the comments with your name and the current date, respectively.

3. The CourseGrade class should contain three attributes: two test scores and a letter grade. The Private variable for the letter grade is missing from the code. Click the **blank line** below the `Private _intScore2 As Integer` statement, and then enter the following Private statement:

Private _strGrade As String

4. Next, you will create a Public property for the Private `_strGrade` variable. You will make the property ReadOnly so that the class (rather than the Grade Calculator application) determines the appropriate grade. By making the property ReadOnly,

the application will only be able to retrieve the grade; it will not be able to change the grade. Click the **blank line** immediately above the End Class clause, and then enter the following Property procedure header and Get clause. When you press Enter after typing the Get clause, the Code Editor automatically includes the End Get and End Property clauses in the procedure. It does not enter the Set block of code because the header contains the ReadOnly keyword.

Public ReadOnly Property Grade As String
Get

5. Type the following Return statement in the blank line below the Get clause, but don't press Enter:

Return _strGrade

6. Next, you will enter the default constructor in the class. The default constructor will initialize the Private variables when a CourseGrade object is instantiated. Insert two blank lines above the End Class clause, and then enter the following default constructor:

Public Sub New()
   _intScore1 = 0
   _intScore2 = 0
   _strGrade = String.Empty
End Sub

7. Finally, you will enter the DetermineGrade method, which will assign the appropriate letter grade to the _strGrade variable. The method will be a Sub procedure because it will not need to return a value to the application that calls it. Insert two blank lines above the End Class clause, and then enter the code shown in Figure 11-33.

```
Public Sub DetermineGrade()
    Select Case _intScore1 + _intScore2
        Case Is >= 180
            _strGrade = "A"
        Case Is >= 160
            _strGrade = "B"
        Case Is >= 140
            _strGrade = "C"
        Case Is >= 120
            _strGrade = "D"
        Case Else
            _strGrade = "F"
    End Select
End Sub
```

Figure 11-33   DetermineGrade method

8. Save the solution.

Now that you have finished defining the class, you can use the class to instantiate a CourseGrade object in the Grade Calculator application, which displays a grade based on two test scores entered by the user.

START HERE

To complete the Grade Calculator application:

1. Click the **designer window's tab**, and then open the form's Code Editor window. Replace <your name> and <current date> in the comments with your name and the current date, respectively.

2. Locate the btnDisplay_Click procedure. First, the procedure will instantiate a CourseGrade object. Click the **blank line** above the second comment, and then enter the following Dim statement:

   Dim studentGrade As New CourseGrade

3. Now the procedure will assign the test scores selected in the list boxes to the object's properties. Click the **blank line** below the second comment, and then enter the following TryParse methods:

   Integer.TryParse(lstTest1.SelectedItem.ToString, studentGrade.Score1)
   Integer.TryParse(lstTest2.SelectedItem.ToString, studentGrade.Score2)

4. Next, the procedure will use the object's DetermineGrade method to determine the appropriate grade. Click the **blank line** below the ' object's DetermineGrade method comment, and then enter the following Call statement:

   Call studentGrade.DetermineGrade()

5. Finally, the procedure will display the grade stored in the object's ReadOnly Grade property. Click the **blank line** above the End Sub clause. Type the following code (including the second period), but don't press Enter:

   lblGrade.Text = studentGrade.

6. Click **Grade** in the IntelliSense list. See Figure 11-34. The message that appears next to the IntelliSense list indicates that the Grade property is ReadOnly.

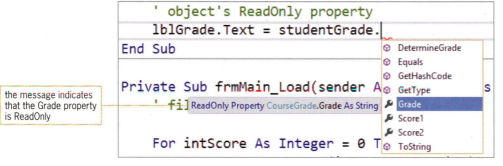

the message indicates that the Grade property is ReadOnly

Figure 11-34   ReadOnly property message

7. Press **Tab** to include the Grade property in the assignment statement. Figure 11-35 shows the CourseGrade class definition and the btnDisplay_Click procedure.

Class statement entered in the CourseGrade.vb file

```vb
Public Class CourseGrade
    Private _intScore1 As Integer
    Private _intScore2 As Integer
    Private _strGrade As String

    Public Property Score1 As Integer
        Get
            Return _intScore1
        End Get
        Set(value As Integer)
            _intScore1 = value
        End Set
    End Property

    Public Property Score2 As Integer
        Get
            Return _intScore2
        End Get
        Set(value As Integer)
            _intScore2 = value
        End Set
    End Property

    Public ReadOnly Property Grade As String
        Get
            Return _strGrade
        End Get
    End Property

    Public Sub New()
        _intScore1 = 0
        _intScore2 = 0
        _strGrade = String.Empty
    End Sub

    Public Sub DetermineGrade()
        Select Case _intScore1 + _intScore2
            Case Is >= 180
                _strGrade = "A"
            Case Is >= 160
                _strGrade = "B"
            Case Is >= 140
                _strGrade = "C"
            Case Is >= 120
                _strGrade = "D"
            Case Else
                _strGrade = "F"
        End Select
    End Sub
End Class
```

Figure 11-35   CourseGrade class definition and btnDisplay_Click procedure *(continues)*

(continued)

```
btnDisplay_Click procedure entered in the Main Form.vb file
Private Sub btnDisplay_Click(sender As Object, e As EventArgs
) Handles btnDisplay.Click
    ' calculates and displays a letter grade

    Dim studentGrade As New CourseGrade

    ' assign test scores to object's properties
    Integer.TryParse(lstTest1.SelectedItem.ToString, studentGrade.Score1)
    Integer.TryParse(lstTest2.SelectedItem.ToString, studentGrade.Score2)

    ' calculate the grade using the
    ' object's DetermineGrade method          calls the object's
    Call studentGrade.DetermineGrade()         DetermineGrade
                                               method

    ' display the grade stored in the
    ' object's ReadOnly property               refers to the object's
    lblGrade.Text = studentGrade.Grade         ReadOnly Grade property
End Sub
```

Figure 11-35 CourseGrade class definition and btnDisplay_Click procedure

START HERE

To test the Grade Calculator application:

1. Save the solution and then start the application. Click **72** and **88** in the Test 1 and Test 2 list boxes, respectively, and then click the **Display** button. The letter B appears in the Grade box, as shown in Figure 11-36.

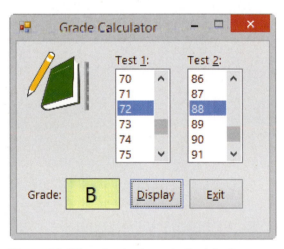

Figure 11-36 Grade shown in the interface

2. On your own, test the application using different test scores. When you are finished, click the **Exit** button. Close the Main Form.vb and CourseGrade.vb windows, and then close the solution.

Example 6—A Class That Contains Auto-Implemented Properties

The **auto-implemented properties** feature in Visual Basic enables you to specify the property of a class in one line of code, as shown in Figure 11-37. When you enter the line of code in the Code Editor window, Visual Basic automatically creates a hidden Private variable that it associates with the property. It also automatically creates hidden Get and Set blocks. The Private variable's name will be the same as the property's name, but it will be preceded by an underscore. For example, if you create an auto-implemented property named City, Visual Basic will create a hidden Private variable named _City. Although the auto-implemented properties feature provides a shorter syntax for you to use when creating a class, keep in mind that you will need to use the standard syntax if you want to add validation code to the Set block, or if you want the property to be either ReadOnly or WriteOnly.

Auto-Implemented Property

Syntax
Public Property propertyName **As** dataType

Example 1
```
Public Property City As Integer
```
creates a Public property named City, a hidden Private variable named _City, and hidden Get and Set blocks

Example 2
```
Public Property Sales As Integer
```
creates a Public property named Sales, a hidden Private variable named _Sales, and hidden Get and Set blocks

---

Figure 11-37   Syntax and examples of creating an auto-implemented property

You can use the auto-implemented properties feature to create the Score1 and Score2 properties in the CourseGrade class from Example 5. This is because neither of those properties is either ReadOnly or WriteOnly, and neither contains any validation code in its Set block. You cannot use the auto-implemented properties feature for the class's Grade property because that property is ReadOnly.

To use the auto-implemented properties feature in the CourseGrade class:

START HERE

1. Use Windows to make a copy of the Grade Solution folder from Example 5. Rename the copy Modified Grade Solution. Open the Grade Solution (Grade Solution.sln) file contained in the Modified Grade Solution folder.

2. Open the CourseGrade.vb file's Code Editor window. First, replace the two Private declaration statements with the following statements:

   Public Property Score1 As Integer
   Public Property Score2 As Integer

3. Next, delete the Score1 and Score2 Property procedures, but don't delete the Grade property procedure.

4. Recall that the name of the Private variable associated with an auto-implemented property is the property's name preceded by an underscore. In both the default constructor and the DetermineGrade method, change _intScore1 and _intScore2 to **_Score1** and **_Score2**, respectively.

Figure 11-38 shows the modified class definition. The code pertaining to the two auto-implemented properties (Score1 and Score2) is shaded in the figure.

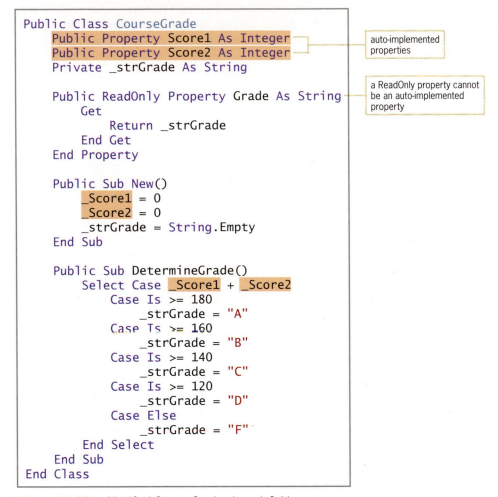

```
Public Class CourseGrade
    Public Property Score1 As Integer          ──┐ auto-implemented
    Public Property Score2 As Integer          ──┘ properties
    Private _strGrade As String

    Public ReadOnly Property Grade As String   ── a ReadOnly property cannot
        Get                                        be an auto-implemented
            Return _strGrade                       property
        End Get
    End Property

    Public Sub New()
        _Score1 = 0
        _Score2 = 0
        _strGrade = String.Empty
    End Sub

    Public Sub DetermineGrade()
        Select Case _Score1 + _Score2
            Case Is >= 180
                _strGrade = "A"
            Case Is >= 160
                _strGrade = "B"
            Case Is >= 140
                _strGrade = "C"
            Case Is >= 120
                _strGrade = "D"
            Case Else
                _strGrade = "F"
        End Select
    End Sub
End Class
```

Figure 11-38   Modified CourseGrade class definition

START HERE ▶

To test the modified Grade Calculator application:

1. Save the solution and then start the application. Click **95** and **88** in the Test 1 and Test 2 list boxes, respectively, and then click the **Display** button. The letter A appears in the Grade box.

2. On your own, test the application using different test scores. When you are finished, click the **Exit** button. Close the CourseGrade.vb window and then close the solution.

Example 7—A Class That Contains Overloaded Methods **LESSON B**

651

YOU DO IT 2!

Create an application named YouDoIt 2 and save it in the VB2015\Chap11 folder. Add a text box, a label, and a button to the form. Add a class file named Square.vb to the project. Define a class named Square. The class should contain an auto-implemented property that will store the side measurement of a square. It should also contain a default constructor and a method that calculates and returns the square's perimeter. Use the following formula to calculate the perimeter: 4 * *side*. Open the form's Code Editor window. Code the button's Click event procedure so that it displays the square's perimeter, using the side measurement entered by the user. Test the application appropriately, and then close the solution.

Example 7—A Class That Contains Overloaded Methods

In this example, you will use a class named Employee to instantiate an object. Employee objects have the attributes and behaviors listed in Figure 11-39.

Attributes of an Employee object
employee number
employee name

Behaviors of an Employee object
1. An employee object can initialize its attributes using values provided by the class.
2. An employee object can initialize its attributes using values provided by the application in which it is instantiated.
3. An employee object can calculate and return the gross pay for salaried employees, who are paid twice per month. The gross pay is calculated by dividing the salaried employee's annual salary by 24.
4. An employee object can calculate and return the gross pay for hourly employees, who are paid weekly. The gross pay is calculated by multiplying the number of hours the employee worked during the week by his or her pay rate.

Figure 11-39 Attributes and behaviors of an Employee object

Figure 11-40 shows the Employee class defined in the Employee.vb file. The class contains two auto-implemented properties and four methods. The two New methods are the class's default and parameterized constructors. Notice that the default constructor initializes the class's Private variables directly, while the parameterized constructor uses the class's Public properties to initialize the Private variables indirectly. As you learned in Lesson A, using a Public property in this manner ensures that the computer processes any validation code associated with the property. Even though the Number and EmpName properties in Figure 11-40 do not have any validation code, you should use the properties in the parameterized constructor in case validation code is added to the class in the future.

```vb
Public Class Employee
    Public Property Number As String ────┐ auto-implemented
    Public Property EmpName As String ───┘ properties

 ┌─ Public Sub New()
 │      _Number = String.Empty ──────┐ initializes the Private
 │      _EmpName = String.Empty ─────┘ variables directly
 │  End Sub
 │
 │  Public Sub New(ByVal strNum As String, ByVal strName As String)
 │      Number = strNum ──────┐ uses the Public properties to
 │      EmpName = strName ────┘ initialize the Private variables
 └─ End Sub

 ┌─ Public Function GetGross(ByVal dblSalary As Double) As Double
 │      ' calculates the gross pay for salaried
 │      ' employees, who are paid twice per month
 │
 │      Return dblSalary / 24
 │  End Function
 │
 │  Public Function GetGross(ByVal dblHours As Double,
 │                           ByVal dblRate As Double) As Double
 │      ' calculates the weekly gross pay for hourly employees
 │
 │      Return dblHours * dblRate
 └─ End Function
End Class
```

overloaded constructors

overloaded GetGross methods

Figure 11-40   Employee class definition

When two or more methods have the same name but different parameters, the methods are referred to as **overloaded methods**. The two constructors in Figure 11-40 are considered overloaded methods because each is named New and each has a different parameterList. You can overload any of the methods contained in a class, not just constructors. The two GetGross methods in the figure are also overloaded methods because they have the same name but a different parameterList.

In previous chapters, you used several of the overloaded methods built into Visual Basic, such as the ToString, TryParse, Convert.ToDecimal, and MessageBox.Show methods. When you enter an overloaded method in the Code Editor window, the Code Editor's IntelliSense feature displays a box that allows you to view a method's signatures, one signature at a time. Recall that a method's signature includes its name and an optional parameterList. The box shown in Figure 11-41 displays the first of the MessageBox.Show method's 21 signatures. You use the up and down arrows in the box to display the other signatures. If a class you create contains overloaded methods, the signatures of those methods will also be displayed in the IntelliSense box.

Figure 11-41   First of the MessageBox.Show method's signatures

Overloading is useful when two or more methods require different parameters to perform essentially the same task. Both overloaded constructors in the Employee class, for example, initialize the class's Private variables. However, the default constructor does not need to be passed any information to perform the task, whereas the parameterized constructor requires two items of information (the employee number and name). Similarly, both GetGross methods in the Employee class calculate and return a gross pay amount. However, the first GetGross method performs its task for salaried employees and requires an application to pass it one item of information: the employee's annual salary. The second GetGross method performs its task for hourly employees and requires two items of information: the number of hours the employee worked and his or her rate of pay. Rather than using two overloaded GetGross methods, you could have used two methods having different names, such as GetSalariedGross and GetHourlyGross. An advantage of overloading the GetGross method is that you need to remember the name of only one method.

You will use the Employee class when coding the Woods Manufacturing application, which displays the gross pay for salaried and hourly employees. Salaried employees are paid twice per month. Therefore, each salaried employee's gross pay is calculated by dividing his or her annual salary by 24. Hourly employees are paid weekly. The gross pay for an hourly employee is calculated by multiplying the number of hours the employee worked during the week by his or her hourly pay rate. The application also displays a report showing each employee's number, name, and gross pay.

To view the class file contained in the Woods Manufacturing application:

START HERE

1. Open the VB2015\Chap11\Woods Solution\Woods Solution (Woods Solution.sln) file. See Figure 11-42.

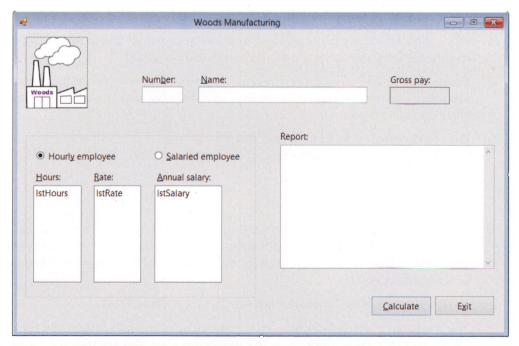

Figure 11-42 Interface for the Woods Manufacturing application

2. Open the Employee.vb file in the Code Editor window. The class definition from Figure 11-40 appears in the window.

3. Replace <your name> and <current date> in the comments with your name and the current date, respectively. Save the solution and then close the Employee.vb window.

You need to code only the Calculate button's Click event procedure. The procedure's pseudocode is shown in Figure 11-43.

btnCalc Click event procedure
1. declare variables to store an Employee object, the annual salary, hours worked, hourly pay rate, and gross pay
2. instantiate an Employee object to represent an employee; initialize the object's variables using the number and name entered in the text boxes
3. if the Hourly employee radio button is selected
      assign the hours worked and the hourly pay rate to the appropriate variables
      use the Employee object's GetGross method to calculate the gross pay for an hourly employee
  else
      assign the annual salary to the appropriate variable
      use the Employee object's GetGross method to calculate the gross pay for a salaried employee
  end if
4. display the gross pay and the report
5. send the focus to the txtNum control

Figure 11-43 Pseudocode for the btnCalc_Click procedure

START HERE ▶

To code the btnCalc_Click procedure:

1. Open the form's Code Editor window. Replace <your name> and <current date> in the comments with your name and the current date, respectively.

2. Locate the btnCalc_Click procedure. First, the procedure will declare the necessary variables. Click the **blank line** below the ' declare variables comment, and then enter the following five Dim statements:

   Dim ourEmployee As Employee
   Dim dblAnnualSalary As Double
   Dim dblHours As Double
   Dim dblHourRate As Double
   Dim dblGross As Double

3. Next, the procedure will instantiate an Employee object, using the text box values to initialize the object's variables. Click the **blank line** below the ' instantiate and initialize an Employee object comment, and then enter the following assignment statement:

   ourEmployee = New Employee(txtNum.Text, txtName.Text)

4. The third step in the pseudocode determines the selected radio button and then takes the appropriate action. Click the **blank line** below the ' determine the selected radio button comment, and then enter the following If clause:

   If radHourly.Checked Then

5. If the Hourly employee radio button is selected, the selection structure's true path should use the Employee object's GetGross method to calculate the gross pay for an hourly employee. Otherwise, its false path should use the method to calculate the gross pay for a salaried employee. Enter the comments and code indicated in Figure 11-44.

```
If radHourly.Checked Then
    ' calculate the gross pay for an hourly employee
    Double.TryParse(lstHours.SelectedItem.ToString, dblHours)
    Double.TryParse(lstRate.SelectedItem.ToString, dblHourRate)
    dblGross = ourEmployee.GetGross(dblHours, dblHourRate)
Else
    ' calculate the gross pay for a salaried employee
    Double.TryParse(lstSalary.SelectedItem.ToString,
                    dblAnnualSalary)
    dblGross = ourEmployee.GetGross(dblAnnualSalary)
End If
```

enter these comments and lines of code

Figure 11-44 Selection structure's true and false paths entered in the procedure

6. Next, the procedure needs to display the gross pay and the report. Click the **blank line** below the last comment in the procedure, and then enter the following lines of code:

lblGross.Text = dblGross.ToString("c2")
txtReport.Text = txtReport.Text &
   ourEmployee.Number.PadRight(6) &
   ourEmployee.EmpName.PadRight(25) &
   dblGross.ToString("n2").PadLeft(9) & ControlChars.NewLine

7. The last step in the pseudocode is to set the focus. The code for this step has already been entered in the Code Editor window.

Figure 11-45 shows the btnCalc_Click procedure.

```
Private Sub btnCalc_Click(sender As Object, e As EventArgs
) Handles btnCalc.Click
    ' displays the gross pay and a report

    ' declare variables
    Dim ourEmployee As Employee
    Dim dblAnnualSalary As Double
    Dim dblHours As Double
    Dim dblHourRate As Double
    Dim dblGross As Double

    ' instantiate and initialize an Employee object
    ourEmployee = New Employee(txtNum.Text, txtName.Text)
```

declares a variable to store an Employee object

instantiates and initializes an Employee object

Figure 11-45 btnCalc_Click procedure *(continues)*

(continued)

```
      ' determine the selected radio button
      If radHourly.Checked Then
          ' calculate the gross pay for an hourly employee
          Double.TryParse(lstHours.SelectedItem.ToString, dblHours)
          Double.TryParse(lstRate.SelectedItem.ToString, dblHourRate)
          dblGross = ourEmployee.GetGross(dblHours, dblHourRate)
      Else
          ' calculate the gross pay for a salaried employee
          Double.TryParse(lstSalary.SelectedItem.ToString,
                          dblAnnualSalary)
          dblGross = ourEmployee.GetGross(dblAnnualSalary)
      End If

      ' display the gross pay and report
      lblGross.Text = dblGross.ToString("c2")
      txtReport.Text = txtReport.Text &
          ourEmployee.Number.PadRight(6) &
          ourEmployee.EmpName.PadRight(25) &
          dblGross.ToString("n2").PadLeft(9) & ControlChars.NewLine

      txtNum.Focus()
  End Sub
```

calculates the gross pay for an hourly employee

calculates the gross pay for a salaried employee

Figure 11-45 btnCalc_Click procedure

START HERE

To test the application:

1. Save the solution and then start the application. Type **1156** and **Sharon Pawliki** in the Number and Name boxes, respectively. Click **10.50** in the Rate list box and then click the **Calculate** button. $420.00 appears in the Gross pay box, and Sharon's information appears in the Report box. See Figure 11-46.

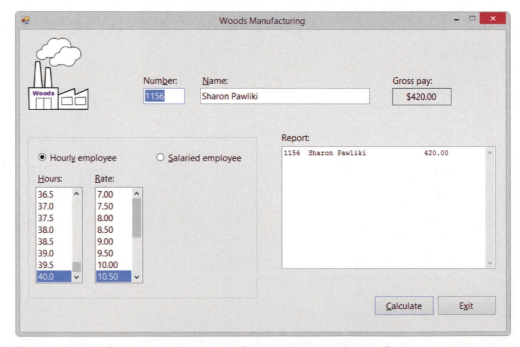

Figure 11-46 Sharon's gross pay and information shown in the interface

2. Type **1160** and **Carl Kraton** in the Number and Name boxes, respectively. Click the **Salaried employee** radio button. Scroll the Annual salary list box and then click **29000** in the list. Click the **Calculate** button. $1,208.33 appears in the Gross pay box, and Carl's information appears in the Report box. See Figure 11-47.

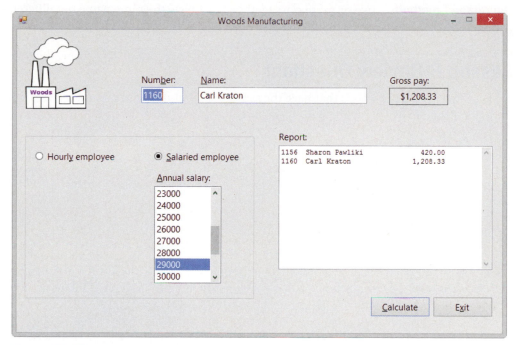

Figure 11-47   Carl's gross pay and information shown in the interface

3. Click the **Exit** button. Close the Code Editor window and then close the solution.

Lesson B Summary

- To create a property whose value an application can only retrieve:

  Include the **ReadOnly** keyword in the Property procedure's header.

- To specify the property of a class in one line:

  Create an auto-implemented property using the following syntax: **Public Property** *propertyName* **As** *dataType*.

- To include a parameterized method in a class:

  Enter the parameters between the parentheses that follow the method's name.

- To create two or more methods that perform the same task but require different parameters:

  Overload the methods by giving them the same name but different parameterLists.

Lesson B Key Terms

Auto-implemented properties—the feature that enables you to specify the property of a class in one line

Overloaded methods—two or more class methods that have the same name but different parameterLists

Lesson B Review Questions

1. Two or more methods that have the same name but different parameterLists are referred to as _____ methods.

   a. loaded
   b. overloaded
   c. parallel
   d. signature

2. The method name combined with the method's optional parameterList is called the method's _____.

   a. autograph
   b. inscription
   c. signature
   d. statement

3. A class contains an auto-implemented property named Title. Which of the following is the correct way for the default constructor to assign the string "Unknown" to the variable associated with the property?

   a. `_Title = "Unknown"`
   b. `_Title.strTitle = "Unknown"`
   c. `Title = "Unknown"`
   d. none of the above

4. A WriteOnly property can be an auto-implemented property.

   a. True
   b. False

5. The Purchase class contains a ReadOnly property named Tax. The property is associated with the Private `_dblTax` variable. A button's Click event procedure instantiates a Purchase object and assigns it to the `currentSale` variable. Which of the following is valid in the Click event procedure?

   a. `lblTax.Text = currentSale.Tax.ToString("C2")`
   b. `currentSale.Tax = 15`
   c. `currentSale.Tax = dblPrice * 0.05`
   d. all of the above

Lesson B Exercises

INTRODUCTORY

1. What are overloaded methods and why are they used?

INTRODUCTORY

2. Write the Property procedure for a ReadOnly property named `Sales`, which is associated with the `_dblSales` variable.

INTRODUCTORY

3. Write the code for an auto-implemented property named Commission. The property's data type is Decimal.

4. Write the class definition for a class named Worker. The class should include Private variables and Property procedures for a Worker object's name and salary. The salary may contain a decimal place. The class also should contain two constructors: the default constructor and a parameterized constructor.

    INTRODUCTORY

5. Rewrite the code from Exercise 4 using auto-implemented properties.

    INTRODUCTORY

6. Add a method named GetNewSalary to the Worker class from Exercise 5. The method should calculate a Worker object's new salary, which is based on a raise percentage provided by the application using the object. Before calculating the new salary, the method should verify that the raise percentage is greater than or equal to 0. If the raise percentage is less than 0, the method should assign 0 as the new salary.

    INTRODUCTORY

7. In this exercise, you modify the Norbert Pool & Spa Depot application from Lesson A. Use Windows to make a copy of the Norbert Solution folder. Rename the copy Norbert Solution-Auto. Open the Norbert Solution (Norbert Solution.sln) file contained in the Norbert Solution-Auto folder. Modify the RectangularPool class so that it uses Public auto-implemented properties rather than Public variables. Include a default constructor in the class. Test the application appropriately.

    INTRODUCTORY

8. Open the Hire Date Solution (Hire Date Solution.sln) file contained in the VB2015\ Chap11\Hire Date Solution folder. First, add a default constructor and a parameterized constructor to the FormattedDate class. Also, add a method that returns the month and day numbers separated by a slash (/). Next, code the btnDefault_Click and btnParameterized_Click procedures. Both procedures should display the hire date in the following format: *month/day*. For example, if the numbers 3 and 2 are selected in the Month and Day list boxes, respectively, the Click event procedures should display 3/2 in the Hire date box. Code the btnDefault_Click procedure using the FormattedDate class's default constructor. Code the btnParameterized_Click procedure using the class's parameterized constructor. Test the application appropriately.

    INTRODUCTORY

9. Open the VB2015\Chap11\Salary Solution\Salary Solution (Salary Solution.sln) file. Open the Worker.vb class file, and then enter the Worker class definition from Exercises 5 and 6. Save the solution and then close the Worker.vb window. Open the form's Code Editor window. Use the comments in the btnCalc_Click procedure to enter the missing instructions. Save the solution and then start the application. Test the application by entering your name, a current salary amount of 54000, and a raise percentage of 10 (for 10%). The new salary should be $59,400.00. Close the Code Editor window and then close the solution.

    INTERMEDIATE

10. In this exercise, you modify the Grade Calculator application from this lesson. Use Windows to make a copy of the Grade Solution folder. Rename the copy Grade Solution-Intermediate. Open the Grade Solution (Grade Solution.sln) file contained in the Grade Solution-Intermediate folder.

    INTERMEDIATE

    a. Open the CourseGrade.vb file. Modify the DetermineGrade method so that it accepts the maximum number of points that can be earned on both tests. (Hint: Currently, the maximum number of points is 200: 100 points per test.) For an A grade, the student must earn at least 90% of the total number of points. For a B, C, and D grade, the student must earn at least 80%, 70%, and 60%, respectively. If the student earns less than 60% of the total points, the grade is F. Make the appropriate modifications to the class, and then save the solution.

b. Add a label control and a text box to the form. Change the label control's Text property to "&Maximum points" (without the quotation marks). Change the text box's name to txtMax.

c. Open the form's Code Editor window. The text box should accept only numbers and the Backspace key. The maximum number allowed in the text box should be 400. Each list box should display numbers from 0 through 200. Make the necessary modifications to the code, and then test the application appropriately.

ADVANCED 11. Create an application, using the following names for the solution and project, respectively: Glasgow Solution and Glasgow Project. Save the application in the VB2015\Chap11 folder. Create the interface shown in Figure 11-48. Each member of Glasgow Health Club must pay monthly dues that consist of a basic fee and one or more optional charges. The basic monthly fee for a single membership is $50; for a family membership, it is $90. If the member has a single membership, the additional monthly charges are $30 for tennis, $25 for golf, and $20 for racquetball. If the member has a family membership, the additional monthly charges are $50 for tennis, $35 for golf, and $30 for racquetball. The application should display the member's basic fee, additional charges, and monthly dues. Code the application by using a class, and then test the application appropriately.

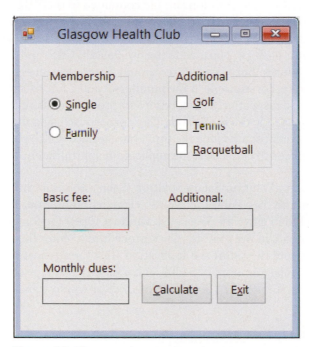

Figure 11-48 Interface for Exercise 11

12. Create an application, using the following names for the solution and project, respectively: Serenity Solution and Serenity Project. Save the application in the VB2015\Chap11 folder. Create the interface shown in Figure 11-49. The image for the picture box is stored in the VB2015\Chap11\Flower.png file. Karen Miller, the manager of the Accounts Payable department at Serenity Photos, wants you to create an application that keeps track of the checks written by her department. More specifically, she wants to record (in a sequential access file) the check number, date, payee, and amount of each check. Code the application by using a class, and then test the application appropriately.

ADVANCED

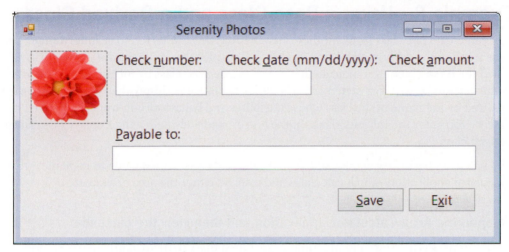

Figure 11-49   Interface for Exercise 12

■ LESSON C

After studying Lesson C, you should be able to:

- Create a derived class
- Refer to the base class using the `MyBase` keyword
- Override a method in the base class

Example 8—Using a Base Class and a Derived Class

You can create one class from another class; in OOP, this is referred to as **inheritance**. The new class is called the **derived class** and it inherits the attributes and behaviors of the original class, called the **base class**. You indicate that a class is a derived class by including the Inherits clause in the derived class's Class statement. The **Inherits clause** is simply the keyword `Inherits` followed by the name of the class whose attributes and behaviors you want the derived class to inherit. You enter the Inherits clause in the line immediately below the Public Class clause in the derived class.

You will use a base class named Square and a derived class named Cube to code the Area Calculator application, which calculates and displays either the area of a square or the surface area of a cube.

START HERE ▶ **To open the Area Calculator application and then view the class file:**

1. If necessary, start Visual Studio 2015. Open the VB2015\Chap11\Area Solution\Area Solution (Area Solution.sln) file. The interface provides a text box for entering the side measurement. See Figure 11-50.

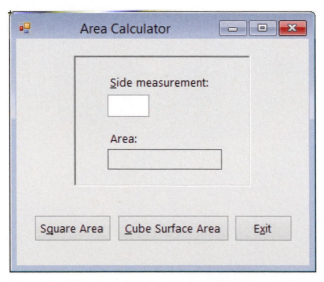

Figure 11-50   Interface for the Area Calculator application

2. Right-click **Shapes.vb** in the Solution Explorer window and then click **View Code**. Replace <your name> and <current date> in the comments with your name and the current date, respectively. The Shapes.vb file contains the Square class definition shown in Figure 11-51.

```
' Name:          Shapes.vb
' Programmer:    <your name> on <current date>

Option Explicit On
Option Strict On
Option Infer Off

' base class
Public Class Square
    Public Property Side As Double

    Public Sub New()
        _Side = 0
    End Sub

    Public Sub New(ByVal dblS As Double)
        Side = dblS
    End Sub

    Public Function GetArea() As Double
        ' returns the area of a square
        Return _Side ^ 2
    End Function
End Class

' derived class
```

Square class definition

Figure 11-51   Contents of the Shapes.vb file

The Square class contains a Public property named Side, two constructors, and a method named GetArea. The Side property represents an attribute of a Square object: its side measurement. Each time a Square object is instantiated, the computer will use one of the two constructors to initialize the object. The class's GetArea method can be used by an application to calculate and return the area of a Square object.

In this section, you will create a derived class from the Square class. The derived class will inherit only the base class's Side attribute and GetArea method. It will not inherit the two constructors because constructors are never inherited. You will name the derived class Cube.

To create a derived class named Cube:

START HERE

1. Click the **blank line** below the ' derived class comment, and then enter the following two lines of code. Press **Enter** twice after typing the Inherits clause.

   Public Class Cube
       Inherits Square

2. As already mentioned, the Cube class will not inherit the Square class's constructors. Therefore, it will need its own constructors. Enter the following procedure header for the default constructor:

   Public Sub New()

3. Insert two blank lines above the Cube class's End Class clause. In the blank line immediately above the End Class clause, enter the following procedure header for the parameterized constructor:

   Public Sub New(ByVal dblS As Double)

Recall that when a Square object is instantiated, the computer uses one of the Square class's constructors to initialize the object. When a Cube object is instantiated, its constructors will call upon the base class's constructors to initialize the object. You refer to the base class using the **MyBase** keyword. For example, the `MyBase.New()` statement tells the computer to process the code contained in the base class's default constructor. Similarly, the `MyBase.New(dblS)` statement tells the computer to process the code contained in the base class's parameterized constructor.

START HERE ▶

To finish coding the Cube class's constructors:

1. Click the **blank line** below the default constructor's procedure header and then type the following statement, but don't press Enter:

    MyBase.New()

2. Click the **blank line** below the parameterized constructor's procedure header and then type the following statement, but don't press Enter:

    MyBase.New(dblS)

3. Save the solution.

Recall that the Square (base) class contains a method named GetArea that calculates and returns the area of a Square object. You will also include a GetArea method in the Cube (derived) class. However, the Cube class's GetArea method will calculate and return the surface area of a Cube object. The formula for calculating the surface area is $sideMeasurement^2 * 6$. The GetArea method in the Cube class will use the Square class's GetArea method to calculate and return the first part of the formula: $sideMeasurement^2$. It then will simply multiply the return value by 6 to get the surface area of a Cube object.

In order to use the same method name—in this case, GetArea—in both a base class and a derived class, the method's procedure header in the base class will need to contain the `Overridable` keyword, and the method's procedure header in the derived class will need to contain the `Overrides` keyword. The **Overridable** keyword in the base class indicates that the method can be overridden by any class that is derived from the base class. In other words, classes derived from the Square (base) class will provide their own GetArea method. The **Overrides** keyword in the derived class indicates that the method overrides (replaces) the same method contained in the base class. In this case, for example, the GetArea method in the Cube class replaces the GetArea method in the Square class.

START HERE ▶

To finish coding the Cube class:

1. Locate the GetArea method in the Square class. Change the procedure header to the following:

    Public Overridable Function GetArea() As Double

2. Insert two blank lines above the Cube class's End Class clause. (Be sure to insert the lines in the Cube class rather than in the Square class.) Beginning in the blank line above the End Class clause, type **Public Overrides Function** and press the **Spacebar**. Click **GetArea()** in the list, and then press **Tab**. The Code Editor automatically enters `As Double` at the end of the procedure header. It also automatically enters the `Return MyBase.GetArea()` statement in the procedure.

3. Position the insertion point at the end of the Return statement (if necessary). Press the **Spacebar** and then type * **6**.

4. Save the solution.

Figure 11-52 shows the Square and Cube class definitions contained in the Shapes.vb file.

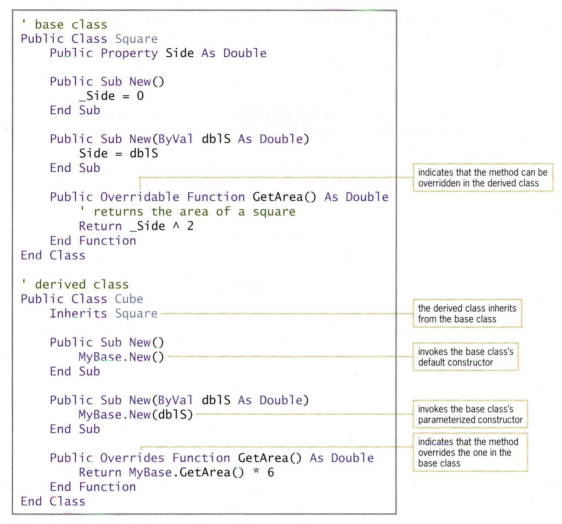

```
' base class
Public Class Square
    Public Property Side As Double

    Public Sub New()
        _Side = 0
    End Sub

    Public Sub New(ByVal dblS As Double)
        Side = dblS
    End Sub

    Public Overridable Function GetArea() As Double
        ' returns the area of a square
        Return _Side ^ 2
    End Function
End Class

' derived class
Public Class Cube
    Inherits Square

    Public Sub New()
        MyBase.New()
    End Sub

    Public Sub New(ByVal dblS As Double)
        MyBase.New(dblS)
    End Sub

    Public Overrides Function GetArea() As Double
        Return MyBase.GetArea() * 6
    End Function
End Class
```

indicates that the method can be overridden in the derived class

the derived class inherits from the base class

invokes the base class's default constructor

invokes the base class's parameterized constructor

indicates that the method overrides the one in the base class

Figure 11-52   Modified Square and Cube class definitions

To complete the application, you need to code the btnSquare_Click and btnCube_Click procedures.

To code and then test the btnSquare_Click procedure:

START HERE

1. Open the form's Code Editor window and locate the btnSquare_Click procedure. First, the procedure will instantiate a Square object. Click the **blank line** immediately above the End Sub clause, and then enter the following Dim statement:

   Dim mySquare As New Square

2. Next, the procedure will declare a variable to store the mySquare object's area. Type the following Dim statement and then press **Enter** twice:

   Dim dblArea As Double

3. Now, assign the side measurement to the mySquare object's Side property. Type the following TryParse method and then press **Enter** twice:

   Double.TryParse(txtSide.Text, mySquare.Side)

4. Next, the procedure will use the mySquare object's GetArea method to calculate the area. It will assign the method's return value to the `dblArea` variable. Enter the following comment and assignment statement:

' calculate the area
dblArea = mySquare.GetArea

5. Finally, the procedure will display the area in the lblArea control. Enter the following comment and assignment statement:

' display the area
lblArea.Text = "Square: " & dblArea.ToString("n1")

6. If necessary, delete the blank line above the End Sub clause.

7. Save the solution and then start the application. Type **10** in the Side measurement box and then click the **Square Area** button. The message "Square: 100.0" appears in the Area box, as shown in Figure 11-53.

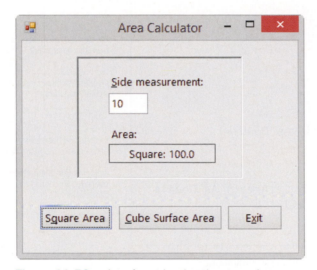

Figure 11-53   Interface showing the square's area

8. Click the **Exit** button.

Finally, you will code the btnCube_Click procedure.

START HERE

To code and then test the btnCube_Click procedure:

1. Locate the btnCube_Click procedure. First, the procedure will instantiate a Cube object. Click the **blank line** immediately above the End Sub clause, and then enter the following Dim statement:

Dim myCube As New Cube

2. Next, the procedure will declare a variable to store the myCube object's area. Type the following Dim statement and then press **Enter** twice:

Dim dblArea As Double

3. Now, assign the side measurement to the myCube object's Side property. Type the following TryParse method and then press **Enter** twice:

Double.TryParse(txtSide.Text, myCube.Side)

4. Next, the procedure will use the myCube object's GetArea method to calculate the area. It will assign the method's return value to the **dblArea** variable. Enter the following comment and assignment statement:

   ' calculate the area
   dblArea = myCube.GetArea

5. Finally, the procedure will display the area in the lblArea control. Enter the following comment and assignment statement:

   ' display the area
   lblArea.Text = "Cube: " & dblArea.ToString("n1")

6. If necessary, delete the blank line above the End Sub clause.

7. Save the solution and then start the application. Type **10** in the Side measurement box, and then click the **Cube Surface Area** button. The message "Cube: 600.0" appears in the Area box.

8. Click the **Exit** button. Close the form's Code Editor window and the Shapes.vb window, and then close the solution.

Figure 11-54 shows the btnSquare_Click and btnCube_Click procedures.

```vb
Private Sub btnSquare_Click(sender As Object, e As EventArgs
) Handles btnSquare.Click
    ' displays the area of a square

    Dim mySquare As New Square
    Dim dblArea As Double

    Double.TryParse(txtSide.Text, mySquare.Side)

    ' calculate the area
    dblArea = mySquare.GetArea
    ' display the area
    lblArea.Text = "Square: " & dblArea.ToString("n1")
End Sub

Private Sub btnCube_Click(sender As Object, e As EventArgs
) Handles btnCube.Click
    ' displays the surface area of a cube

    Dim myCube As New Cube
    Dim dblArea As Double

    Double.TryParse(txtSide.Text, myCube.Side)

    ' calculate the area
    dblArea = myCube.GetArea
    ' display the area
    lblArea.Text = "Cube: " & dblArea.ToString("n1")
End Sub
```

Figure 11-54   btnSquare_Click and btnCube_Click procedures

Lesson C Summary

- To allow a derived class to inherit the attributes and behaviors of a base class:

  Enter the Inherits clause in the line immediately below the Public Class clause in the derived class. The Inherits clause is the keyword `Inherits` followed by the name of the base class.

- To refer to the base class:

  Use the `MyBase` keyword.

- To indicate that a method in the base class can be overridden (replaced) in the derived class:

  Use the `Overridable` keyword in the method's header in the base class.

- To indicate that a method in the derived class overrides (replaces) a method in the base class:

  Use the `Overrides` keyword in the method's header in the derived class.

Lesson C Key Terms

Base class—the original class from which another class is derived

Derived class—a class that inherits the attributes and behaviors of a base class

Inheritance—the ability to create one class from another class

Inherits clause—entered in the line immediately below the Public Class clause in a derived class; specifies the name of the base class associated with the derived class

MyBase—the keyword used in a derived class to refer to the base class

Overridable—a keyword that can appear in a method's header in a base class; indicates that the method can be overridden by any class that is derived from the base class

Overrides—a keyword that can appear in a method's header in a derived class; indicates that the method overrides the method with the same name in the base class

Lesson C Review Questions

1. Which of the following clauses allows a derived class named Cat to have the same attributes and behaviors as its base class, which is named Animal?

   a. `Inherited Animal`   c. `Inherited Cat`
   b. `Inherits Animal`   d. `Inherits Cat`

2. A base class contains a method named GetTax. Which of the following procedure headers can be used in the base class to indicate that a derived class can provide its own code for the method?

   a. `Public Inherits Sub GetTax()`
   b. `Public Overridable Sub GetTax()`
   c. `Public Overrides Sub GetTax()`
   d. `Public Overriding Sub GetTax()`

3. A base class contains a method named GetTax. Which of the following procedure headers can be used in the derived class to indicate that it is providing its own code for the method?

    a. `Public Inherits Sub GetTax()`
    b. `Public Overridable Sub GetTax()`
    c. `Public Overrides Sub GetTax()`
    d. `Public Overriding Sub GetTax()`

4. The Salaried class is derived from a base class named Employee. Which of the following statements can be used by the Salaried class to invoke the Employee class's default constructor?

    a. `MyBase.New()`   c. `Call Employee.New`
    b. `MyEmployee.New()`   d. none of the above

Lesson C Exercises

INTRODUCTORY

1. Open the VB2015\Chap11\Formula Solution\Formula Solution (Formula Solution.sln) file. Open the Areas.vb file, which contains the Parallelogram class definition. The class contains two Public properties and two constructors. It also contains a GetArea method that calculates the area of a parallelogram.

    a. Create a derived class named Triangle. The derived class should inherit the properties and GetArea method from the Parallelogram class. However, the Triangle class's GetArea method should calculate the area of a triangle. The formula for calculating the area of a triangle is *base * height* / 2. Be sure to include a default constructor and a parameterized constructor in the derived class.
    b. The btnCalc_Click procedure should display either the area of a parallelogram or the area of a triangle. The appropriate area to display depends on the radio button selected in the interface. Code the button's Click event procedure, and then test the application appropriately.

INTERMEDIATE

2. Open the Kerry Sales Solution (Kerry Sales Solution.sln) file contained in the VB2015\Chap11\Kerry Sales Solution folder.

    a. Open the Payroll.vb file. Create a base class named Bonus. The class should contain two Public properties: a String property named SalesId and a Double property named Sales. Include a default constructor and a parameterized constructor in the class. Also include a GetBonus method (function) that calculates a salesperson's bonus using the following formula: *sales * 0.05*.
    b. Create a derived class named PremiumBonus. The derived class's GetBonus method should calculate the bonus as follows: *sales * 0.05 + (sales − 2500) * 0.01*. Be sure to include a default constructor and a parameterized constructor in the derived class.
    c. Complete the btnCalc_Click procedure, using the comments as a guide, and then test the application appropriately.

SWAT THE BUGS

3. Open the VB2015\Chap11\Debug Solution\Debug Solution (Debug Solution.sln) file. Open the Code Editor windows for the form and the class file. Review the existing code. Correct the code to remove the jagged lines in the Shape and Circle class definitions. Save the solution, and then start and test the application. Notice that the application is not working correctly. Locate and correct the errors in the code, and then test the application appropriately.

Web Applications

Creating the Satellite Radio Web Application

In this chapter, you will create a Web application for the Satellite Radio company. The company offers its customers a choice of three different satellite radio packages: Select, Gold, and Platinum. Each package includes a different number of radio stations, with the Select package having the least and the Platinum package having the most. Subscriptions to each package are available for either a 6-month term or a 12-month term only. The company also offers 6-month and 12-month subscriptions to its Internet listening service, which allows a customer to listen to the radio stations on his or her computer. New customers receive a 10% discount on the package subscription price only. The application will display the total cost of a 6-month subscription and the total cost of a 12-month subscription. (The company's offerings and pricing information are shown in Figure 12-48 in Lesson C.)

Previewing the Satellite Radio Web Application

Before you start the first lesson in this chapter, you will preview the completed application contained in the VB2015\Chap12 folder.

START HERE

To preview the completed application:

1. If necessary, start Visual Studio 2015. Click **File** on the menu bar and then click **Open Web Site**. The Open Web Site dialog box appears. If necessary, click the **File System** button. Click the **Radio-Preview** folder contained in the VB2015\Chap12 folder, and then click the **Open** button.

2. If the Default.aspx Web page does not appear in the Document window, right-click **Default.aspx** in the Solution Explorer window and then click **View Designer**.

3. Press **Ctrl+F5** to start the application. The Web page appears in a browser window.

4. Click the **Gold** radio button and the **Internet listening** check box. Click the **Calculate** button. As Figure 12-1 indicates, the cost for a 6-month subscription to the Gold package with Internet listening is $120.49, and the cost for a 12-month subscription is $212.49. (Your Web page will look slightly different if you are using a different browser, such as Google Chrome or Mozilla Firefox.)

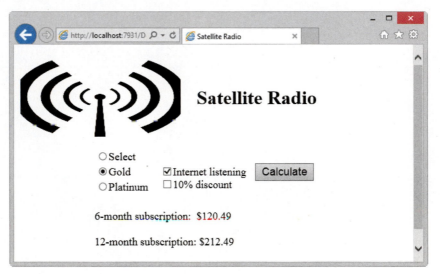

Figure 12-1   Subscription costs displayed on the Web page in Internet Explorer

5. Click the **10% discount** check box. Notice that the costs for both subscriptions are removed from the Web page. Click the **Calculate** button. The costs for the 6-month and 12-month subscriptions are now $110.89 and $195.79, respectively.

6. Close the browser window. Click **File** on the menu bar and then click **Close Solution**. If you are asked whether you want to save the changes to the Radio-Preview.sln file, click the **No** button.

In Lesson A, you will learn how to create static Web pages. Dynamic Web pages are covered in Lessons B and C. You will code the Satellite Radio application in Lesson C. Be sure to complete each lesson in full and do all of the end-of-lesson questions and several exercises before continuing to the next lesson.

LESSON A

After studying Lesson A, you should be able to:

- Define basic Web terminology
- Create a Web Site application
- Add Web pages to an application
- Customize a Web page
- Add static text to a Web page
- Format a Web page's static text
- Add a hyperlink and an image to a Web page
- Start a Web application
- Close and open a Web application
- Reposition a control on a Web page

Web Applications

The Internet is the world's largest computer network, connecting millions of computers located all around the world. One of the most popular features of the Internet is the World Wide Web, often referred to simply as the Web. The Web consists of documents called **Web pages** that are stored on Web servers. A **Web server** is a computer that contains special software that "serves up" Web pages in response to requests from client computers. A **client computer** is a computer that requests information from a Web server. The information is requested and subsequently viewed through the use of a program called a Web browser or, more simply, a **browser**. Currently, the most popular browsers are Google Chrome, Mozilla Firefox, and Microsoft Internet Explorer.

Many Web pages are static. A **static Web page** is a document whose purpose is merely to display information to the viewer. Static Web pages are not interactive. The only interaction that can occur between static Web pages and the user is through links that allow the user to "jump" from one Web page to another.

Figures 12-2 and 12-3 show examples of static Web pages created for The Fishbowl Emporium. The Web page in Figure 12-2 shows the store's name, address, and telephone number, and also provides a link to the Web page shown in Figure 12-3. That page shows the store's business hours and provides a link for returning to the first Web page. You will create both Web pages in this lesson.

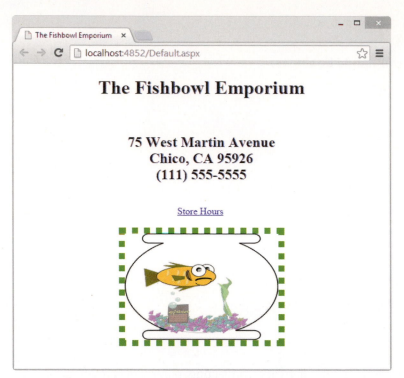

Figure 12-2   Example of a static Web page displayed using Google Chrome

Figure 12-3   Another example of a static Web page displayed using Google Chrome

Although static Web pages provide a means for a store to list its location and hours, a company wanting to do business on the Web must be able to do more than just list information: It must be able to interact with customers through its Web site. The Web site should allow customers to submit inquiries, select items for purchase, and submit payment information. It also should allow the company to track customer inquiries and process customer orders. Tasks such as these can be accomplished using dynamic Web pages.

Unlike a static Web page, a **dynamic Web page** is interactive in that it can accept information from the user and also retrieve information for the user. Examples of dynamic Web pages include forms for purchasing merchandise online and for submitting online résumés. Figure 12-4 shows an example of a dynamic Web page that calculates the number of gallons of water a rectangular aquarium holds. To use the Web page, you enter the length, width, and height of the aquarium and then click the Submit button. The button's Click event procedure displays the corresponding number of gallons on the Web page.

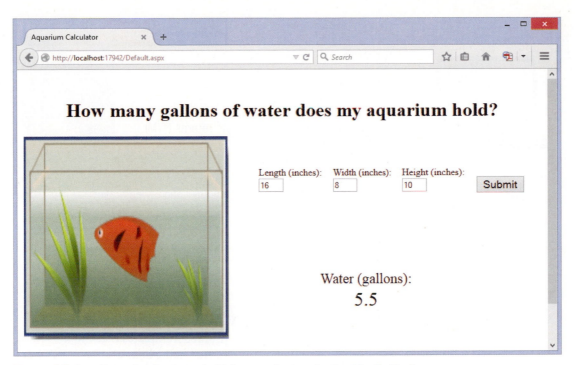

Figure 12-4   Example of a dynamic Web page displayed using Mozilla Firefox

The Web applications created in this chapter use a technology called ASP.NET 5. **ASP** stands for "active server page" and refers to the type of Web page created by the ASP technology. All ASP pages contain HTML (Hypertext Markup Language) tags that tell the client's browser how to render the page on the computer screen. For example, the instruction <h1>Hello</h1> uses the opening <h1> tag and its closing </h1> tag to display the word "Hello" as a heading on the Web page. Many ASP pages also contain ASP tags that specify the controls to include on the Web page. In addition to the HTML and ASP tags, dynamic ASP pages contain code that tells the objects on the Web page how to respond to the user's actions. In this chapter, you will write the appropriate code using the Visual Basic programming language.

When a client computer's browser sends a request for an ASP page, the Web server locates the page and then sends the appropriate HTML instructions to the client. The client's browser uses the instructions to render the Web page on the computer screen. If the Web page is a dynamic one, like the Web page shown in Figure 12-4, the user can interact with the page by entering data. In most cases, the user then clicks a button on the Web page to submit the page and data to the server for processing. Using Web terminology, the information is "posted back" to the server for processing; this event is referred to as a **postback**. When the server receives the information, it executes the Visual Basic code associated with the Web page. It then sends back the appropriate HTML, which now includes the result of processing the code and data, to the client for rendering in the browser window. Notice that the Web page's HTML is interpreted and executed by the client computer, whereas the program code is executed by the Web server. Figure 12-5 illustrates the relationship between the client computer and the Web server.

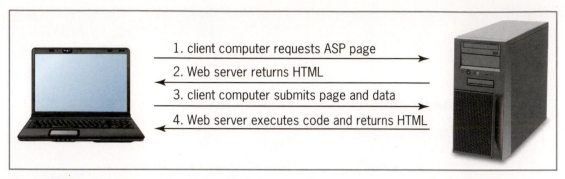

Figure 12-5 Illustration of the relationship between a client computer and a Web server

This lesson covers static Web pages. Dynamic Web pages are covered in Lessons B and C.

START HERE

To begin creating the static Fishbowl Emporium Web Site application:

1. If necessary, start Visual Studio 2015. Open the Solution Explorer and Properties windows, and auto-hide the Toolbox window.

2. Click **File** on the menu bar, and then click **New Web Site** to open the New Web Site dialog box. If necessary, click **Visual Basic** in the Installed Templates list. Click **ASP.NET Empty Web Site** in the middle column of the dialog box.

3. If necessary, change the entry in the Web location box to **File System**. The File System selection allows you to store your Web application in any folder on either your computer or a network drive.

4. In this chapter, you will be instructed to store your Web applications in the VB2015\Chap12 folder on the E drive; however, you should use the letter for the drive where your data is stored, which might not be the E drive. In the box that appears next to the Web location box, replace the existing text with **E:\VB2015\Chap12\Fishbowl**. See Figure 12-6.

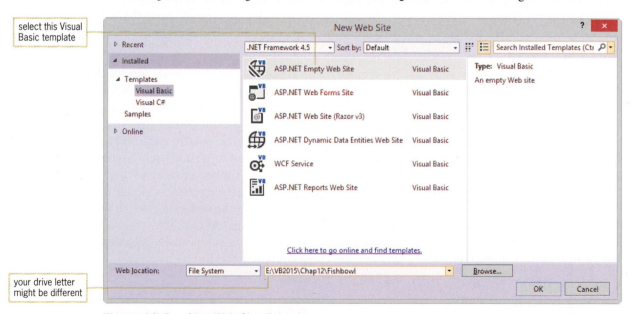

Figure 12-6 New Web Site dialog box

5. Click the **OK** button to close the dialog box. The computer creates an empty Web application named Fishbowl.

Adding the Default.aspx Web Page to the Application

After creating an empty Web application, you need to add a Web page to it. The first Web page added to an application is usually named Default.aspx.

To add the Default.aspx Web page to the application:

START HERE

1. Click **Website** on the menu bar, and then click **Add New Item** to open the Add New Item dialog box. (If Website does not appear on the menu bar, click the Web application's name—in this case, Fishbowl—in the Solution Explorer window.)

2. If necessary, click **Visual Basic** in the Installed list and then click **Web Form** in the middle column of the dialog box. Verify that the Place code in separate file check box is selected and that the Select master page check box is not selected. As indicated in Figure 12-7, the Web page will be named Default.aspx.

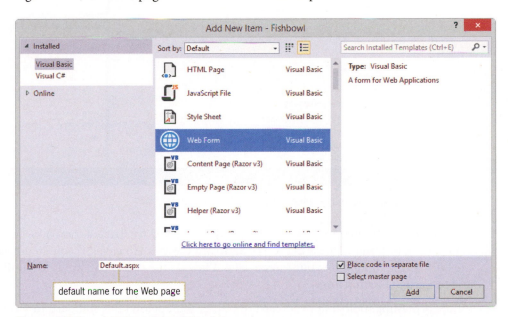

Figure 12-7   Add New Item dialog box

3. Click the **Add** button to display the Default.aspx page in the Document window. If necessary, click the **Design** tab that appears at the bottom of the IDE. When the Design tab is selected, the Web page appears in Design view in the Document window, as shown in Figure 12-8. You can use Design view to add text and controls to the Web page. If the div tag does not appear in the Document window, click the **<div>** button at the bottom of the IDE.

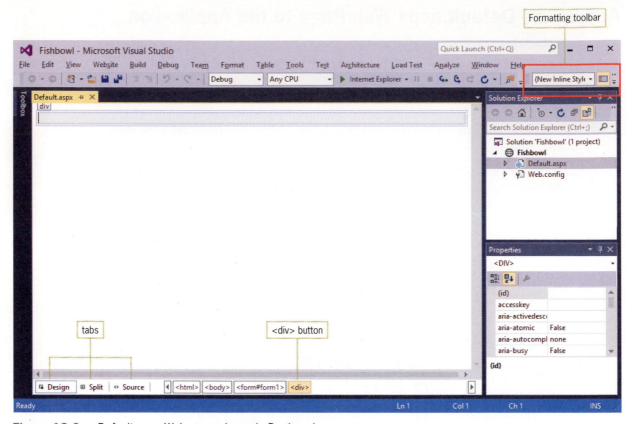

Figure 12-8 Default.aspx Web page shown in Design view

4. The Formatting toolbar may appear next to the Standard toolbar, as shown in Figure 12-8, or it may appear below the Standard toolbar. However, if you do not see the Formatting toolbar on your screen, click **View** on the menu bar, point to **Toolbars**, and then click **Formatting**.

5. If the Formatting toolbar appears next to (rather than below) the Standard toolbar, position your mouse pointer on the beginning of the Formatting toolbar until it turns into a move pointer, as shown in Figure 12-9.

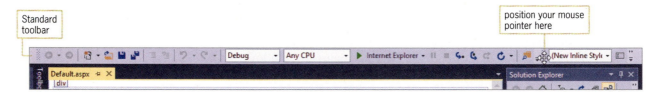

Figure 12-9 Move pointer on beginning of Formatting toolbar

6. Hold down the left mouse button as you drag the Formatting toolbar below the Standard toolbar, and then release the mouse button. See Figure 12-10.

Figure 12-10 Formatting toolbar positioned below Standard toolbar

7. Click the **Source** tab to display the Web page in Source view. This view shows the HTML and ASP tags that tell a browser how to render the Web page. The tags are automatically generated for you as you are creating the Web page in Design view. Currently, the Web page contains only HTML tags.

8. Click the **Split** tab to split the Document window into two parts. The upper half displays the Web page in Source view, and the lower half displays it in Design view.

9. Click the **Design** tab to return to Design view, and then auto-hide the Solution Explorer window.

Including a Title on a Web Page

You can use the Properties window to include a title on a Web page. The properties appear in the Properties window when you select DOCUMENT in the window's Object box.

To include a title on the Web page:

START HERE

1. Click the **down arrow** button in the Properties window's Object box, and then click **DOCUMENT** in the list. (If DOCUMENT does not appear in the Object box, click the Design tab.) The DOCUMENT object represents the Web page.

2. If necessary, click the **Alphabetical** button in the Properties window to display the properties in alphabetical order. Click **Title** in the Properties list. Type **The Fishbowl Emporium** in the Settings box, and then press **Enter**.

3. Auto-hide the Properties window. Save the application either by clicking the **Save All** button on the Standard toolbar or by clicking the **Save All** option on the File menu.

Adding Static Text to a Web Page

All Web pages contain some text that the user is not allowed to edit, such as a company name or the caption that identifies a text box. Text that cannot be changed by the user is referred to as **static text**. You can add static text to a Web page by simply typing the text on the page itself, or you can use a label control that you dragged to the Web page from the Toolbox window. In this lesson, you will type the static text on the Web page.

To add static text to the Web page:

START HERE

1. If necessary, click **inside the rectangle** that appears below the div tag at the top of the Document window. The div tag defines a division in a Web page. (If the div tag does not appear in the Document window, click the <div> button at the bottom of the IDE.)

2. Enter the following four lines of text. Press **Enter** twice after typing the last line.

   The Fishbowl Emporium
   75 West Martin Avenue
   Chico, CA 95926
   (111) 555-5555

3. Save the application.

You can use either the Format menu or the Formatting toolbar to format the static text on a Web page. Figure 12-11 indicates some of the tools available on the Formatting toolbar.

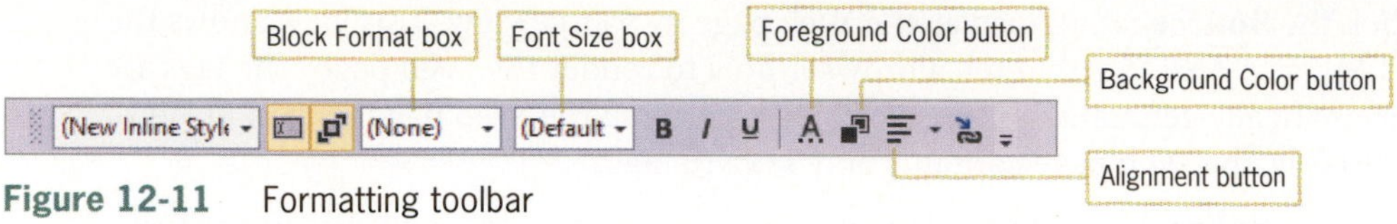

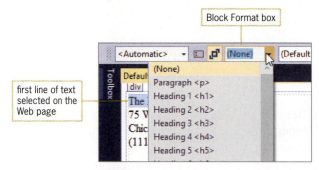

Figure 12-11   Formatting toolbar

START HERE

To use the Formatting toolbar to format the static text:

1. Select (highlight) the first line of text on the Web page. Click the **down arrow** in the Block Format box on the Formatting toolbar. See Figure 12-12.

Figure 12-12   Result of clicking the arrow in the Block Format box

2. Click **Heading 1 <h1>**.

3. Select the address and phone number text on the Web page. Click the **down arrow** in the Block Format box and then click **Heading 2 <h2>**.

4. Next, you will use the Formatting toolbar's Alignment button to center the static text. Select all of the static text on the Web page, and then click the **down arrow** on the Alignment button. See Figure 12-13.

Figure 12-13   Result of clicking the Alignment button

5. Click **Justify Center**. The selected text appears centered horizontally on the Web page. Click **anywhere below the phone number** to deselect the text, and then save the application.

Adding Another Web Page to the Application

In the next set of steps, you will add a second Web page to the application. The Web page will display the store's hours of operation.

To add another Web page to the application: START HERE

1. Click **Website** on the menu bar and then click **Add New Item**. (If Website does not appear on the menu bar, click Fishbowl in the Solution Explorer window.)

2. If necessary, click **Visual Basic** in the Installed list, and then click **Web Form** in the middle column of the dialog box. Change the filename in the Name box to **Hours** and then click the **Add** button. The computer appends the .aspx extension to the filename and then displays the Hours.aspx Web page in the Document window.

3. Temporarily display the Solution Explorer window. Notice that the window now contains the Hours.aspx filename.

4. Click the **Hours.aspx** tab, and then temporarily display the Properties window. Click the **down arrow** button in the Properties window's Object box, and then click **DOCUMENT** in the list. Change the Web page's Title property to **The Fishbowl Emporium**.

5. Click the **Hours.aspx** tab. The blinking insertion point should be inside the rectangle that appears below the div tag. (If the div tag does not appear in the Document window, click the <div> button at the bottom of the IDE.) Type **Please stop in and see us during these hours:** and press **Enter** twice.

6. Enter the following three lines of text. Press **Enter** twice after typing the last line.

    Monday – Friday 8am – 8pm
    Saturday 9am – 5pm
    Closed Sunday

7. Select the first line of text on the Web page. Click the **down arrow** in the Font Size box on the Formatting toolbar, and then click **x-large (24 pt)**. Also click the *I* (Italic) button on the toolbar.

8. Select the three lines of text that contain the store hours. Click the **down arrow** in the Font Size box and then click **large (18 pt)**. Also click the **B** (Bold) button.

9. Next, you will change the color of the selected text. Click the **Foreground Color** button on the Formatting toolbar to open the More Colors dialog box. Click **any red hexagon**, and then click the **OK** button.

10. Select all of the static text on the Web page. Click the **down arrow** on the Alignment button and then click **Justify Center**.

11. Click the **second blank line** below the store hours to deselect the text, and then save the application.

Adding a Hyperlink Control to a Web Page

The Toolbox window provides tools for adding controls to a Web page. In the next set of steps, you will add a **hyperlink control** to both Web pages. The hyperlink control on the Default.aspx page will display the Hours.aspx page. The hyperlink control on the Hours.aspx page will return the user to the Default.aspx Web page.

START HERE

To add a hyperlink control to both Web pages:

1. First, you will add a hyperlink control to the Hours.aspx page. Permanently display the Toolbox window. Expand the Standard node, if necessary, and then click the **HyperLink** tool. Drag your mouse pointer to the location shown in Figure 12-14, and then release the mouse button.

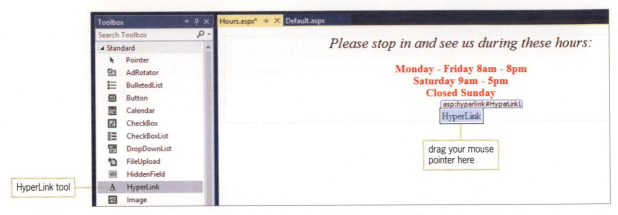

Figure 12-14 Hyperlink control added to the Hours.aspx Web page

2. Temporarily display the Properties window. Change the control's Text property to **Home Page**. Click **NavigateUrl** in the Properties list, and then click the **...** (ellipsis) button to open the Select URL dialog box. Click **Default.aspx** in the Contents of folder list. See Figure 12-15.

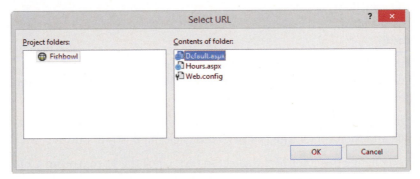

Figure 12-15 Select URL dialog box

3. Click the **OK** button to close the dialog box, and then click the **Hours.aspx** tab.

4. Next, you will add a hyperlink control to the Default.aspx page. Click the **Default.aspx** tab. Click the **HyperLink** tool. Drag your mouse pointer to the location shown in Figure 12-16, and then release the mouse button.

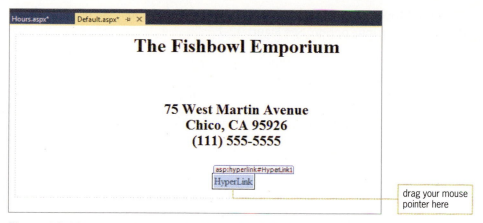

Figure 12-16   Hyperlink control added to the Default.aspx Web page

5. Temporarily display the Properties window. Change the control's Text property to **Store Hours** and then change its NavigateUrl property to **Hours.aspx**.

6. Click the **OK** button to close the Select URL dialog box, and then click the **Default.aspx** tab. Save the application.

Starting a Web Application

Typically, you start a Web application either by pressing Ctrl+F5 or by clicking the Start Without Debugging option on the Debug menu. The method you use—the shortcut keys or the menu option—is a matter of personal preference. If you prefer to use a menu option, you might need to add the Start Without Debugging option to the Debug menu because the option is not automatically included on the menu. You can add the option to the menu by performing the next set of steps. If you prefer to use the Ctrl+F5 shortcut keys, you can skip the next set of steps.

To add the Start Without Debugging option to the Debug menu:

START HERE

1. First, you will determine whether your Debug menu already contains the Start Without Debugging option. Click **Debug** on the menu bar. If the menu contains the Start Without Debugging option, close the menu by clicking **Debug** again, and then skip the remaining steps in this set of steps.

2. If the Debug menu does *not* contain the Start Without Debugging option, close the menu by clicking **Debug** again. Click **Tools** on the menu bar, and then click **Customize** to open the Customize dialog box.

3. Click the **Commands** tab. The Menu bar radio button should be selected. Click the **down arrow** in the Menu bar list box. Scroll down the list until you see Debug, and then click **Debug**.

4. Click the **Add Command** button to open the Add Command dialog box, and then click **Debug** in the Categories list. Scroll down the Commands list until you see Start Without Debugging, and then click **Start Without Debugging**. Click the **OK** button to close the Add Command dialog box.

5. Click the **Move Down** button until the Start Without Debugging option appears below the Start / Continue option. See Figure 12-17.

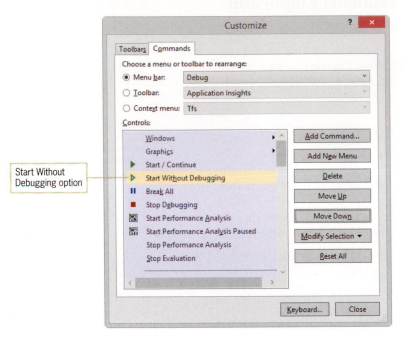

Start Without Debugging option

Figure 12-17 Customize dialog box

6. Click the **Close** button to close the Customize dialog box.

When you start a Web application, the computer creates a temporary Web server (on your local machine) that allows you to view your Web page in a browser. Keep in mind, however, that your Web page will need to be placed on an actual Web server for others to view it.

START HERE

To start the Web application:

Ch12A-Changing Browsers

1. Start the Web application either by pressing **Ctrl+F5** or by clicking the **Start Without Debugging** option on the Debug menu. (If the message "Intranet settings are turned off by default." appears, click the Don't show this message again button.) Your browser requests the Default.aspx page from the Web server. The server locates the page and then sends the appropriate HTML instructions to your default browser for rendering on the screen. Notice that the value in the page's Title property appears on the page's tab in the browser window. See Figure 12-18.

Figure 12-18   Default.aspx Web page displayed in a Google Chrome browser window

2. Click the **Store Hours** hyperlink to display the Hours.aspx page. See Figure 12-19.

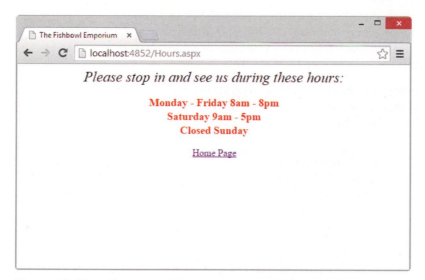

Figure 12-19   Hours.aspx Web page displayed in a Google Chrome browser window

3. Click the **Home Page** hyperlink to display the Default.aspx page, and then close the browser window.

Adding an Image to a Web Page

In the next set of steps, you will add an image to the Default.aspx page. The image is stored in the VB2015\Chap12\FishInBowl.png file.

To add an image to the Web page:

START HERE

1. First, you need to add the image file to the application. Click **Website** on the menu bar and then click **Add Existing Item**. Open the VB2015\Chap12 folder. Click the **down arrow** in the box that controls the file types, and then click **All Files (*.*)** in the list. Click **FishInBowl.png** in the list of filenames, and then click the **Add** button.

2. Click the **blank line** below the Store Hours hyperlink control. (If necessary, insert a blank line below the control.) Press **Enter** to insert another blank line. Click the **Image** tool in the toolbox. Drag your mouse pointer to the location shown in Figure 12-20, and then release the mouse button.

Figure 12-20   Image control added to the Default.aspx Web page

3. Temporarily display the Properties window. Click **ImageUrl** in the Properties list, if necessary, and then click the **...** (ellipsis) button to open the Select Image dialog box. Click **FishInBowl.png** in the Contents of folder section, and then click the **OK** button.

4. Place your mouse pointer on the lower-right corner of the image control, and then drag the control to make it smaller. See Figure 12-21. (The width and height measurements of the image in the figure are approximately 255px and 175px, respectively.)

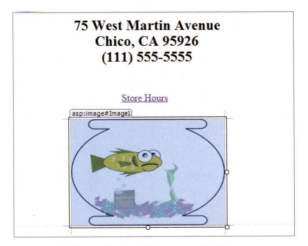

Figure 12-21   Resized image control

5. Next, you will put a border around the image control and also change the border's width to 10 pixels. Change the image control's BorderStyle property to **Dotted**, and then change its BorderWidth property to **10**. Press **Enter** after typing the number 10.

6. Now, you will change the color of the image's border to green. Click **BorderColor** in the Properties list and then click the **...** (ellipsis) button. When the More Colors dialog box opens, click **any green hexagon**. Click the **OK** button to close the dialog box, and then click the **Default.aspx** tab.

7. Auto-hide the toolbox. Save and then start the application. See Figure 12-22.

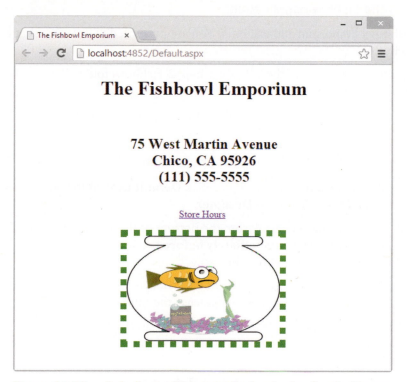

Figure 12-22   Default.aspx Web page displayed using Google Chrome

8. Verify that the browser window is not maximized. Place your mouse pointer on the window's right border, and then drag the border to the left to make the window narrower. Notice that the text and image remain centered in the visible portion of the window. Now, drag the right border to the right to make the window wider. Here, again, the text and image remain centered in the visible portion of the window.

9. Close the browser window.

Closing and Opening an Existing Web Application

You can use the File menu to close and also to open an existing Web application.

To close and then open the Web application: START HERE

1. Click **File** on the menu bar, and then click **Close Solution** to close the application.

2. Next, you will open the application. Click **File** on the menu bar, and then click **Open Web Site** to open the Open Web Site dialog box. If necessary, click the **File System** button. Locate the VB2015\Chap12\Fishbowl folder. Click the folder and then click the **Open** button.

3. Temporarily display the Solution Explorer window to verify that the application is open. If the Default.aspx Web page is not open in the Document window, right-click **Default.aspx** in the Solution Explorer window and then click **View Designer**.

Repositioning a Control on a Web Page

At times, you may want to reposition a control on a Web page. In this section, you will move the image and hyperlink controls to different locations on the Default.aspx Web page. First, however, you will create a copy of the Fishbowl application.

START HERE

To create a copy of the Fishbowl application:

1. Close the Fishbowl Emporium application. If you are prompted to save the .sln file, click the **No** button.

2. Use Windows to make a copy of the VB2015\Chap12\Fishbowl folder. Rename the folder **Modified Fishbowl**.

Now, you will open the Modified Fishbowl application and move the two controls to different locations on the Default.aspx Web page.

START HERE

To move the controls in the Modified Fishbowl application:

1. Open the Modified Fishbowl Web site. Right-click **Default.aspx** in the Solution Explorer window and then click **View Designer**.

2. First, you will move the image control from the bottom of the Web page to the top of the Web page. If necessary, click **immediately before the letter T** in the store's name. Press **Enter** to insert a blank line above the name.

3. Click the **image control** on the Web page. Drag the image control to the blank line immediately above the store name, and then release the mouse button.

4. Next, you will move the hyperlink control to the empty area below the store's name. Click the **hyperlink control**. Drag the control to the empty area below the store's name, and then release the mouse button.

5. Click **File** on the menu bar and then click **Save Default.aspx**.

6. Start the application. See Figure 12-23.

Figure 12-23 Modified Default.aspx Web page

7. Close the browser window and then close the application.

YOU DO IT 1!

Create an empty Web Site application named YouDoIt 1 and save it in the VB2015\ Chap12 folder. Add two Web pages to the application: one named Default.aspx and one named Address.aspx. The Default.aspx page should contain your name and a hyperlink control. Change the hyperlink control's Text property to Address. The control should display the Address.aspx page. The Address.aspx page should contain your address and a hyperlink control. Change this hyperlink control's Text property to Name. The control should display the Default.aspx page. Save the application and then start and test it. Close the browser window and then close the application.

Lesson A Summary

- To create an empty Web Site application:

  Click File on the menu bar, and then click New Web Site to open the New Web Site dialog box. If necessary, click Visual Basic in the Installed Templates list. Click ASP.NET Empty Web Site in the middle column of the dialog box. If necessary, change the entry in the Web location box to File System. In the box that appears next to the Web location box, enter the location where you want the Web application saved. Also enter the application's name. Click the OK button to close the New Web Site dialog box.

- To add a Web page to a Web application:

  Open the Web application. Click Website on the menu bar, and then click Add New Item to open the Add New Item dialog box. (If Website does not appear on the menu bar, click the Web application's name in the Solution Explorer window.) If necessary, click Visual Basic in the Installed list, and then click Web Form in the middle column of the dialog box. Verify that the Place code in separate file check box is selected and that the Select master page check box is not selected. Enter an appropriate name in the Name box. Click the Add button to display the Web page in the Document window. If necessary, click the Design tab that appears at the bottom of the IDE.

- To add a title to a Web page:

  Set the DOCUMENT's Title property.

- To add static text to a Web page:

  Either type the text on the Web page or use a label control that you dragged to the Web page from the Toolbox window.

- To format the static text on a Web page:

  Use either the Format menu or the Formatting toolbar.

- To add a hyperlink control to a Web page:

  Use the HyperLink tool in the toolbox to drag a hyperlink control to the Web page, and then set the control's Text and NavigateUrl properties.

- To display a Web page in a browser window:

  Start the Web application either by pressing Ctrl+F5 or by clicking the Start Without Debugging option on the Debug menu.

- To add an image file to an application:

  Click Website on the menu bar and then click Add Existing Item. Open the appropriate folder and then click the image filename. Click the Add button.

- To add an image control to a Web page:

  Use the Image tool in the toolbox to drag an image control to the Web page, and then set the image control's ImageUrl property.

- To close a Web application:

  Click File on the menu bar and then click Close Solution.

- To open an existing Web application:

  Click File on the menu bar and then click Open Web Site. If necessary, click the File System button in the Open Web Site dialog box. Click the name of the Web site and then click the Open button. If necessary, right-click the Web page's name in the Solution Explorer window, and then click View Designer.

- To reposition a control on a Web page:

  Drag the control to the new location.

Lesson A Key Terms

ASP—stands for "active server page"

Browser—a program that allows a client computer to request and view Web pages

Client computer—a computer that requests information from a Web server

Dynamic Web page—an interactive document that can accept information from the user and also retrieve information for the user

Hyperlink control—allows the user to "jump" from one Web page to another

Postback—occurs when the information on a dynamic Web page is sent (posted) back to a server for processing

Static text—text that the user is not allowed to edit

Static Web page—a non-interactive document whose purpose is merely to display information to the viewer

Web pages—the documents stored on Web servers

Web server—a computer that contains special software that "serves up" Web pages in response to requests from client computers

Lesson A Review Questions

1. A computer that requests an ASP page from a Web server is called a
   _____ computer.

   a. browser
   b. client

   c. requesting
   d. none of the above

2. A _____ is a program that uses HTML to render a Web page on the computer screen.

   a. browser
   b. client

   c. server
   d. none of the above

3. An online form used to purchase a product is an example of a _____ Web page.

   a. dynamic
   b. static

4. The first Web page in an empty Web application is automatically assigned the name
   _____.

   a. Default.aps
   b. Default1.vb

   c. Default.aspx
   d. WebFormDefault.aspx

5. The HTML instructions in a Web page are processed by the _____.

   a. client computer
   b. Web server

6. The text that appears on the application's tab in the browser window is determined by the _____ property.

    a. Application object's Name

    b. Application object's Title

    c. DOCUMENT object's Tab Name

    d. DOCUMENT object's Title

7. A _____ occurs when a user clicks a Submit button on a Web page.

    a. clientpost

    b. postback

    c. sendback

    d. serverpost

Lesson A Exercises

INTRODUCTORY

1. Create an empty Web Site application named Spa and save it in the VB2015\Chap12 folder. Add a new Web page named Default.aspx to the application. Change the DOCUMENT object's Title property to Spa Monique. Create a Web page similar to the one shown in Figure 12-24. The Spa Monique image is contained in the VB2015\Chap12\Spa.png file. Save and then start the application. Close the browser window and then close the application.

Figure 12-24 Default.aspx Web page for Spa Monique

INTRODUCTORY

2. Create an empty Web Site application named Carnival and save it in the VB2015\Chap12 folder. Add a new Web page named Default.aspx to the application. Change the DOCUMENT object's Title property to Brookfield. Create a Web page similar to the one shown in Figure 12-25. The image on the Web page is stored in the VB2015\Chap12\Carnival.png file. (Hint: To position the image as shown in the figure, click the image, click Format on the menu bar, click Position, and then click the Left button in the Wrapping style section of the Position dialog box.) Save and then start the application. Close the browser window and then close the application.

Brookfield Carnival

Come join us on July 4th for our annual carnival. Buy a $10 ticket and get unlimited rides and a chance to win a grand prize of $500. There will be games and great food. At 9pm, the fireworks show will begin. Don't miss it!

Sam Jenkins
Brookfield City Manager

Figure 12-25   Default.aspx Web page for the Brookfield Carnival

3. Create an empty Web Site application named Market and save it in the VB2015\Chap12 folder. Add three new Web pages named Default.aspx, Apples.aspx, and Oranges.aspx to the application. Change each DOCUMENT object's Title property to Corner Market. Create Web pages similar to the ones shown in Figures 12-26 through 12-28. The images are stored in the Apple.png and Orange.png files contained in the VB2015\Chap12 folder. Save and then start the application. Close the browser window and then close the application.

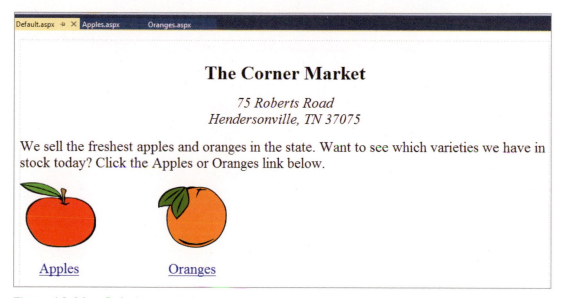

Figure 12-26   Default.aspx Web page for The Corner Market

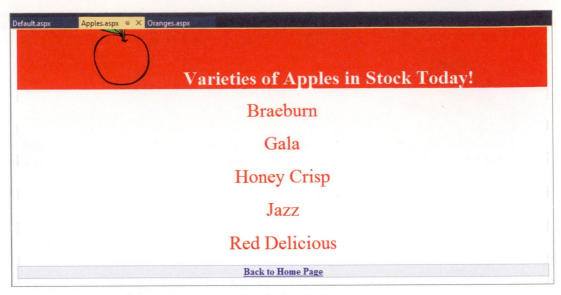

Figure 12-27   Apples.aspx Web page for The Corner Market

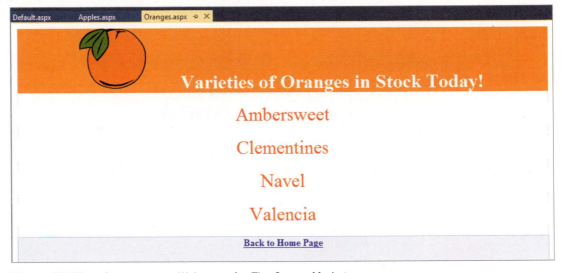

Figure 12-28   Oranges.aspx Web page for The Corner Market

LESSON B

After studying Lesson B, you should be able to:

- Add a table to a Web page
- Add a text box, a label, and a button to a Web page
- Code a control on a Web page
- Use a RequiredFieldValidator control

Dynamic Web Pages

A dynamic Web page contains controls with which the user can interact. It also contains code that tells the controls how to respond to the user's actions. In this lesson, you will create a dynamic Web page that displays the number of gallons of water a rectangular aquarium holds. The user will need to enter the aquarium's length, width, and height measurements in inches.

Before you add any text or controls to a Web page, you should plan the page's layout. Figure 12-29 shows a sketch of the Default.aspx Web page for the Aquarium application. The Web page will contain static text, a table, and the following controls: an image, three text boxes, a label, and a button.

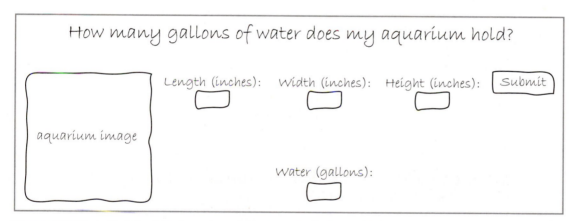

Figure 12-29   Sketch of the Aquarium application's Default.aspx Web page

To open the partially completed Web page:

START HERE

1. If necessary, start Visual Studio 2015. Open the Solution Explorer, Properties, and Toolbox windows.

2. Click **File** on the menu bar, and then click **Open Web Site**. If necessary, click the **File System** button in the Open Web Site dialog box. Click the **Aquarium** folder contained in the VB2015\Chap12 folder, and then click the **Open** button.

3. If the Default.aspx Web page is not open in the Document window, right-click **Default.aspx** in the Solution Explorer window, and then click **View Designer**.

In the next set of steps, you will complete the Web page's interface by adding a table, static text, and six controls to it.

START HERE **To complete the Web page's interface:**

1. Position the blinking insertion point as shown in Figure 12-30.

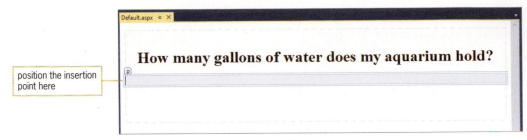

position the insertion point here

Figure 12-30 Default.aspx Web page

2. Click **Table** on the menu bar, and then click **Insert Table** to open the Insert Table dialog box. In the Size section of the dialog box, change the number of columns to **5**. In the Layout section, click the **In pixels** radio button, and then change the width to **850**. See Figure 12-31.

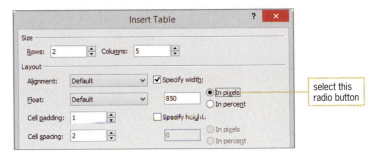

select this radio button

Figure 12-31 Insert Table dialog box

3. Click the **OK** button to close the dialog box. Select the two cells contained in the first column of the table. See Figure 12-32.

select these two cells

Figure 12-32 Two cells selected in the first column of the table

4. Click **Table** on the menu bar, point to **Modify**, and then click **Merge Cells**. The first column of the table now contains one large cell.

5. Click **Image** in the toolbox. Drag an image control into the first column of the table, and then set its ImageUrl property to **Aquarium.png**. Also set its Height and Width properties to **335px** and **340px**, respectively.

6. Position the insertion point in the top cell in the second column, as shown in Figure 12-33.

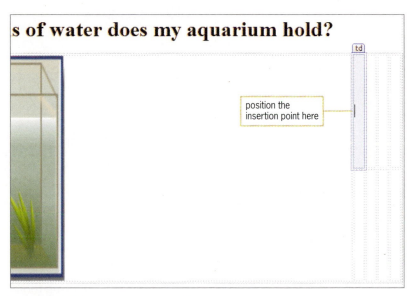

Figure 12-33   Insertion point positioned in the top cell in the second column

7. Type **Length (inches):** and press **Enter**. Click **TextBox** in the toolbox. Drag a text box control to the top cell in the second column, positioning it immediately below the Length (inches): text. Set the text box's Width property to **35px**. Unlike Windows controls, Web controls have an ID property rather than a Name property. Set the text box's ID property (which appears at the top of the Properties window) to **txtLength**.

8. Position the insertion point in the top cell in the third column. Type **Width (inches):** and press **Enter**. Drag a text box control immediately below the Width (inches): text, and then set its ID and Width properties to **txtWidth** and **35px**, respectively.

9. Position the insertion point in the top cell in the fourth column. Type **Height (inches):** and press **Enter**. Drag a text box control immediately below the Height (inches): text, and then set its ID and Width properties to **txtHeight** and **35px**, respectively.

10. Next, you will add a Button control to the table. Position the insertion point in the top cell in the fifth (last) column. Click **Button** in the toolbox, and then drag your mouse pointer into the cell. Release the mouse button. Set the button's ID and Text properties to **btnSubmit** and **Submit**, respectively. Expand the **Font** node in the Properties window, click the **Size** arrow, and then click **Large**.

11. Select the bottom cells in the second through fourth columns. See Figure 12-34.

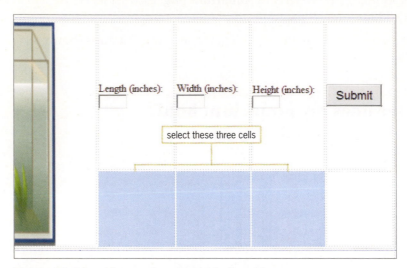

Figure 12-34 Three cells selected in the table

12. Click **Table** on the menu bar, point to **Modify**, and then click **Merge Cells**. The three selected cells become one large cell. Click the **large cell**, type **Water (gallons):**, and then press **Enter**.

13. Select the **Water (gallons):** text. Use the Font Size box on the Formatting toolbar to change the text's size to **x-large (24 pt)**. Then use the Alignment button on the Formatting toolbar to center the text.

14. Click **Label** in the toolbox. Drag a label control immediately below the Water (gallons): text. Set the control's ID, Font/Size, Height, and Width properties to **lblGals**, **XX-Large**, **35px**, **105px**, respectively.

15. Remove the contents of the label's Text property. When you clear the Text property, the control's ID appears in brackets. Auto-hide the Toolbox, Solution Explorer, and Properties windows. Click **File** on the menu bar and then click **Save Default.aspx**. The completed interface is shown in Figure 12-35.

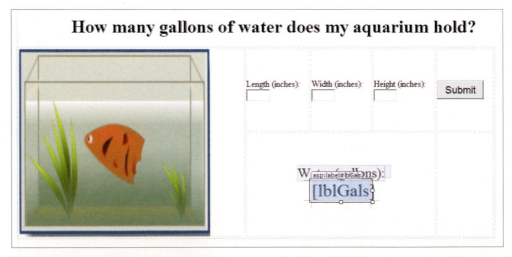

Figure 12-35 Completed interface

Coding the Submit Button's Click Event Procedure

When the user clicks a button on a Web page, a postback automatically occurs and the button's Click event procedure is automatically sent to the server for processing. In the following set of steps, you will code the Submit button's Click event procedure to calculate and display the number of gallons of water. The procedure's pseudocode is shown in Figure 12-36 along with a list of the variables the procedure will use.

---

btnSubmit Click event procedure
1. store user input (length, width, and height) in variables
2. calculate the volume in cubic inches by multiplying the length by the width and then multiplying the result by the height
3. calculate the number of gallons by dividing the volume in cubic inches by 231 (There are 231 cubic inches in a gallon.)
4. display the number of gallons in lblGals

Variable names	Stores
dblLength	the aquarium's length in inches
dblWidth	the aquarium's width in inches
dblHeight	the aquarium's height in inches
dblVolume	the volume in cubic inches
dblGals	the number of gallons of water

Figure 12-36   Pseudocode and variables for the btnSubmit_Click procedure

To code and then test the btnSubmit_Click procedure:

START HERE

1. Right-click the **Web page** and then click **View Code** on the context menu. The Default.aspx.vb window opens. Recall that the .vb extension on a filename indicates that the file contains Visual Basic code. In this case, the file is referred to as the code-behind file because it contains code that supports the Web page. Temporarily display the Solution Explorer window. See Figure 12-37.

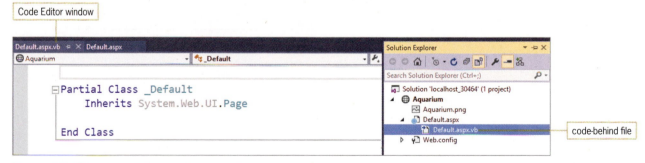

Figure 12-37   Code Editor and Solution Explorer windows

2. Click the **first blank line** in the Code Editor window. Enter the following comments, replacing <your name> and <current date> with your name and the current date, respectively. Press **Enter** twice after typing the last comment.

```
' Name:        Aquarium
' Purpose:     Display number of gallons of water
' Programmer:  <your name> on <current date>
```

3. Enter the following Option statements:

    Option Explicit On
    Option Strict On
    Option Infer Off

4. Open the btnSubmit_Click procedure. Type the following comment and then press **Enter** twice.

    ' displays number of gallons of water

5. Enter the following Dim statements. Press **Enter** twice after typing the last Dim statement.

    Dim dblLength As Double
    Dim dblWidth As Double
    Dim dblHeight As Double
    Dim dblVolume As Double
    Dim dblGals As Double

6. The first step in the procedure's pseudocode is to store the input items in variables. Enter the following three TryParse methods. Press **Enter** twice after typing the last TryParse method.

    Double.TryParse(txtLength.Text, dblLength)
    Double.TryParse(txtWidth.Text, dblWidth)
    Double.TryParse(txtHeight.Text, dblHeight)

7. The second step in the pseudocode calculates the volume of the rectangular aquarium in cubic inches. Enter the following assignment statement:

    dblVolume = dblLength * dblWidth * dblHeight

8. The third step in the pseudocode calculates the number of gallons of water in the rectangular aquarium. Enter the following assignment statement:

    dblGals = dblVolume / 231

9. The last step in the pseudocode displays the number of gallons of water. Enter the additional assignment statement indicated in Figure 12-38.

```
Private Sub btnSubmit_Click(sender As Object, e As EventArgs
) Handles btnSubmit.Click
    ' displays number of gallons of water

    Dim dblLength As Double
    Dim dblWidth As Double
    Dim dblHeight As Double
    Dim dblVolume As Double
    Dim dblGals As Double

    Double.TryParse(txtLength.Text, dblLength)
    Double.TryParse(txtWidth.Text, dblWidth)
    Double.TryParse(txtHeight.Text, dblHeight)

    dblVolume = dblLength * dblWidth * dblHeight
    dblGals = dblVolume / 231
    lblGals.Text = dblGals.ToString("n1")
End Sub
```

enter this statement ───── lblGals.Text = dblGals.ToString("n1")

Figure 12-38   btnSubmit_Click procedure

10. Click **File** on the menu bar and then click **Save Default.aspx.vb**. Start the application by pressing **Ctrl+F5**. Your browser requests the Default.aspx page from the server. The server locates the page and then sends the appropriate HTML instructions to your browser for rendering on the screen.

11. Type **20.5**, **10.5**, and **12.5** in the Length, Width, and Height boxes, respectively. Click the **Submit** button, which submits your entry to the server along with a request for additional services. At this point, a postback has occurred. The server processes the code contained in the button's Click event procedure and then sends the appropriate HTML to the browser for rendering on the screen. As Figure 12-39 indicates, the aquarium holds 11.6 gallons of water.

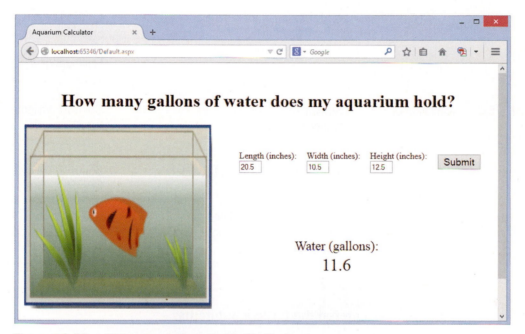

Figure 12-39 Web page displayed in Mozilla Firefox

12. Close the browser window and then close the Code Editor window.

Validating User Input

The Validation section of the toolbox provides several **validator tools** for validating user input. The name, purpose, and important properties of each validator tool are listed in Figure 12-40. In the Aquarium application, you will use RequiredFieldValidator controls to verify that the user entered the three input items.

Name	Purpose	Properties
CompareValidator	compare an entry with a constant value or the property stored in a control	ControlToCompare ControlToValidate ErrorMessage Operator Type ValueToCompare
CustomValidator	verify that an entry passes the specified validation logic	ClientValidationFunction ControlToValidate ErrorMessage
RangeValidator	verify that an entry is within the specified minimum and maximum values	ControlToValidate ErrorMessage MaximumValue MinimumValue Type
RegularExpressionValidator	verify that an entry matches a specific pattern	ControlToValidate ErrorMessage ValidationExpression
RequiredFieldValidator	verify that a control contains data	ControlToValidate ErrorMessage
ValidationSummary	display all of the validation error messages in a single location on a Web page	DisplayMode HeaderText

Figure 12-40 Validator tools

START HERE ▶ **To verify that the user entered the three input items:**

1. Click **to the immediate right of the txtLength control** and then press **Enter**.

2. Permanently display the Toolbox window. If necessary, expand the Validation section. Click the **RequiredFieldValidator** tool and then drag your mouse pointer to the Web page, positioning it immediately below the txtLength control. Release the mouse button. The RequiredFieldValidator1 control appears on the Web page.

3. Temporarily display the Properties window. Set the RequiredFieldValidator1 control's ControlToValidate and ErrorMessage properties to **txtLength** and **Required**, respectively. Click **ForeColor** in the Properties window, click the ... (ellipsis) button, click a **red hexagon**, and then click the **OK** button to close the More Colors dialog box.

4. Click **to the immediate right of the txtWidth control** and then press **Enter**. Drag a required field validator control below the txtWidth control. Set the RequiredFieldValidator2 control's ControlToValidate and ErrorMessage properties to **txtWidth** and **Required**, respectively. Also set its ForeColor property using the same red hexagon used in Step 3. Click the **OK** button to close the More Colors dialog box.

5. Click **to the immediate right of the txtHeight control** and then press **Enter**. Drag a required field validator control below the txtHeight control. Set the RequiredFieldValidator3 control's ControlToValidate and ErrorMessage properties to **txtHeight** and **Required**, respectively. Also set its ForeColor property using the same red hexagon used in Step 3. Click the **OK** button to close the More Colors dialog box.

6. Click the **Default.aspx** tab, and then auto-hide the Toolbox window. Click **File** on the menu bar and then click **Save Default.aspx**.

7. Start the application by pressing **Ctrl+F5**. If the error message shown in Figure 12-41 appears, close the browser window; otherwise, skip to Step 10.

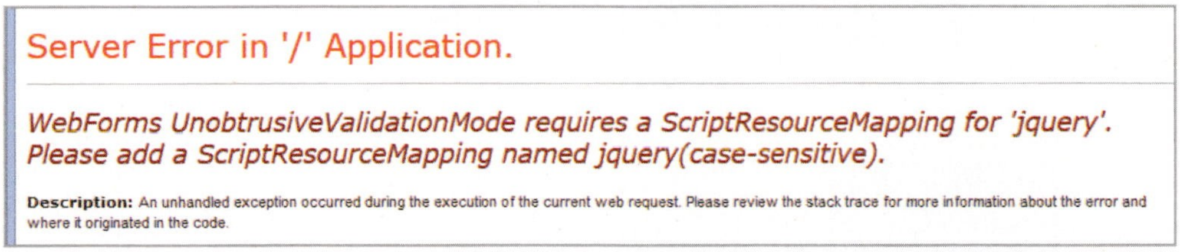

Server Error in '/' Application.

WebForms UnobtrusiveValidationMode requires a ScriptResourceMapping for 'jquery'. Please add a ScriptResourceMapping named jquery(case-sensitive).

Description: An unhandled exception occurred during the execution of the current web request. Please review the stack trace for more information about the error and where it originated in the code.

Figure 12-41   Error message that might appear

8. If you received the error message shown in Figure 12-41, right-click **Web.config** in the Solution Explorer window and then click **Open**. Now use one of the two solutions shown in Figure 12-42.

Solution A
Change the string in both targetFramework entries to **"4.0"**.

Solution B
Insert a blank line below the <configuration> tag, and then enter the following three lines:

```
<appSettings>
    <add key="ValidationSettings:UnobtrusiveValidationMode" value="None" />
</appSettings>
```

Figure 12-42   Solutions to the error message shown in Figure 12-41

9. Click **File** on the menu bar and then click **Save Web.config**. Close the Web.config window and then press **Ctrl+F5**.

10. Click the **Submit** button without entering any values. Each RequiredFieldValidator control displays the "Required" message, as shown in Figure 12-43. (The Web page in the figure is displayed in Mozilla Firefox.)

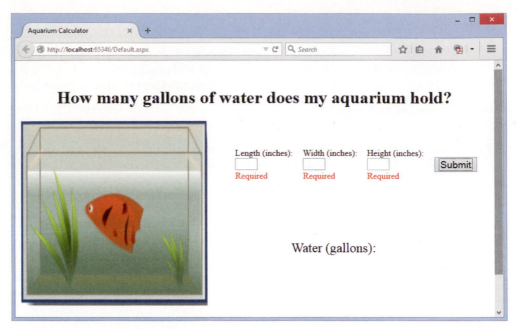

Figure 12-43 Result of clicking the Submit button when the text boxes are empty

11. Type **16** in the Length box, and then press **Tab** to move the insertion point into the Width box. Notice that the "Required" message below the Length box disappears.

12. Type **8** and **10** in the Width and Height boxes, respectively. Click the **Submit** button. The Web page indicates that the aquarium holds 5.5 gallons of water.

13. Close the browser window and then close the application. If you are asked whether you want to save the .sln file, click the **No** button.

YOU DO IT 2!

Create an empty Web Site application named YouDoIt 2 and save it in the VB2015\Chap12 folder. Add a Web page named Default.aspx to the application. The Web page should contain a text box, a label, and a button. When the user clicks the button, the application should multiply the number entered in the text box by 2 and then display the result in the label. Include a RequiredFieldValidator control on the Web page. Save the application, and then start and test it. Close the application.

Lesson B Summary

- To code a control on a Web page:

  Enter the code in the Code Editor window.

- To validate user input on a Web page:

  Use one or more of the validator tools contained in the Validation section of the toolbox. The controls are summarized in Figure 12-40.

Lesson B Key Term

Validator tools—the tools contained in the Validation section of the toolbox; used to validate user input on a Web page

Lesson B Review Questions

1. In code, you refer to a control on a Web page using the control's _____ property.

    a. Caption   c. Name

    b. ID   d. Text

2. The Visual Basic code in a Web page is processed by the _____.

    a. client computer

    b. Web server

3. You can use a _____ control to verify that a control on a Web page contains data.

    a. RequiredFieldValidator   c. RequiredValidator

    b. RequiredField   d. none of the above

4. You can use a _____ control to verify that an entry on a Web page is within minimum and maximum values.

    a. MinMaxValidation   c. EntryValidator

    b. MaxMinValidation   d. RangeValidator

Lesson B Exercises

1. Create an empty Web Site application named Circle and save it in the VB2015\Chap12 folder. Add a new Web page named Default.aspx to the application. Change the DOCUMENT object's Title property to Circle Area.

    INTRODUCTORY

    a. Use Figure 12-44 as a guide when designing the Web page. The circle image is contained in the VB2015\Chap12\Circle.png file. Set the RequiredFieldValidator control's ControlToValidate property to txtRadius. Also sets its ErrorMessage and ForeColor properties as appropriate.

    b. Open the Code Editor window. Use comments to document the application's name and purpose as well as your name and the current date. Also enter the appropriate Option statements. Code the Calculate Area button's Click event procedure. Use 3.14 as the value for Pi. Display the area with one decimal place.

    c. Save and then start the application. If you receive the error message shown earlier in Figure 12-41, right-click Web.config in the Solution Explorer window and then click Open. Then use one of the two solutions shown earlier in Figure 12-42. Click File on the menu bar and then click Save Web.config. Close the Web.config window and start the application again.

    d. Test the application appropriately and then close the browser window. Close the Code Editor window and the application.

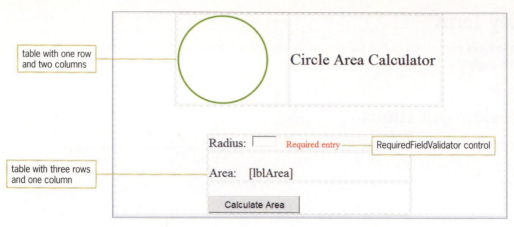

Figure 12-44 Web page for Exercise 1

2. Create an empty Web Site application named Tips and save it in the VB2015\
    Chap12 folder. Add a new Web page named Default.aspx to the application. Change
    the DOCUMENT object's Title property to Tip Calculator. Use Figure 12-45 as a
    guide when designing the Web page. In the Code Editor window, enter comments to
    document the application's name and purpose as well as your name and the current
    date. Also enter the appropriate Option statements. Code the Calculate Tip button's
    Click event procedure. Display the tips with a dollar sign and two decimal places. Save
    the application, and then start and test it. Close the browser window. Close the Code
    Editor window and then close the application.

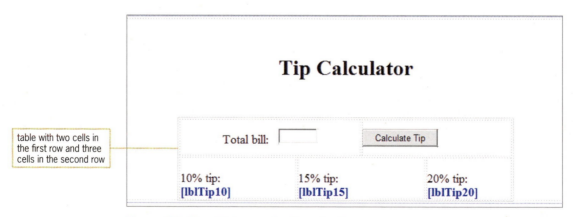

Figure 12-45 Web page for Exercise 2

3. Create an empty Web Site application named Bakery and save it in the VB2015\
    Chap12 folder. Add a new Web page named Default.aspx to the application. Change
    the DOCUMENT object's Title property to Meyer's. Use Figure 12-46 as a guide when
    designing the Web page. The image is contained in the VB2015\Chap12\Chef.png file.
    In the Code Editor window, enter comments to document the application's name
    and purpose as well as your name and the current date. Also enter the appropriate

Option statements. Code the Calculate button's Click event procedure to display the total number of items ordered and the total sales amount, including a 5% sales tax. A doughnut costs $0.50; a muffin costs $0.75. Save the application, and then start and test it. Close the browser window. Close the Code Editor window and then close the application.

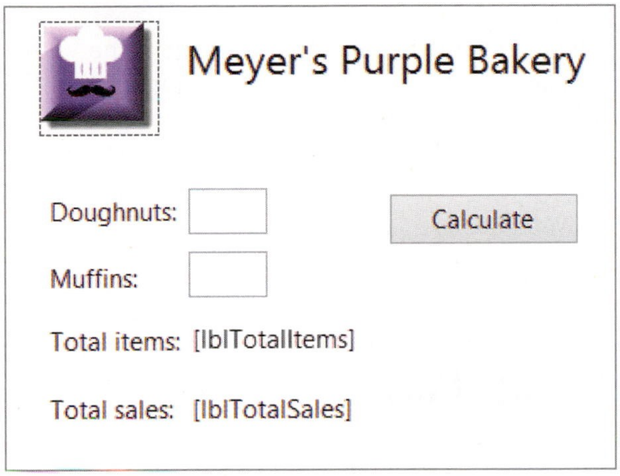

Figure 12-46   Web page for Exercise 3

4. The annual property tax in Richardson County is $1.50 for each $100 of a property's assessed value. The county clerk wants you to create a Web application that displays the property tax after he enters the property's assessed value. Create an empty Web Site application named Tax and save it in the VB2015\Chap12 folder. Add a new Web page named Default.aspx to the application. Change the DOCUMENT object's Title property to Richardson County. Design and create the Web page. Use a RequiredFieldValidator control to verify that the user entered the assessed value. Save the application, and then start and test it.

    INTERMEDIATE

5. Cranston Berries sells three types of berries: strawberries, blueberries, and raspberries. Sales have been booming this year and are expected to increase next year. The sales manager wants you to create an application that allows her to enter the projected increase (expressed as a decimal number) in berry sales for the following year. She will also enter the current year's sales for each type of berry. The application should display the projected sales for each berry type. As an example, if the projected increase in berry sales is 0.05 (the decimal equivalent of 5%) and the current sales amount for strawberries is $25,000, the projected sales total of strawberries for the following year is $26,250. Create an empty Web Site application named Berries and save it in the VB2015\Chap12 folder. Add a new Web page named Default.aspx to the application. Change the DOCUMENT object's Title property to Cranston Berries. Save the application, and then start and test it. Close the browser window. Close the Code Editor window and then close the application.

    INTERMEDIATE

INTERMEDIATE

6. In this exercise, you create a Web application that displays how much a person would weigh on the following planets, given his or her weight on Earth: Venus, Mars, and Jupiter. Create an empty Web Site application named Weight and save it in the VB2015\Chap12 folder. Add a new Web page named Default.aspx to the application. Change the DOCUMENT object's Title property to Weights. Design and create the Web page. Save the application, and then start and test it. Close the browser window. Close the Code Editor window and then close the application.

ADVANCED

7. Create an empty Web Site application named ZipCode and save it in the VB2015\Chap12 folder. Add a new Web page named Default.aspx to the application. Change the DOCUMENT object's Title property to Zip Code Verifier. Use Figure 12-47 as a guide when designing the Web page. Use a RequiredFieldValidator control to verify that the text box is not empty when the user presses the Enter key. Use a RegularExpressionValidator control to verify that the ZIP code is in the appropriate format. Save the application, and then start and test it. Close the browser window. Close the Code Editor window and then close the application.

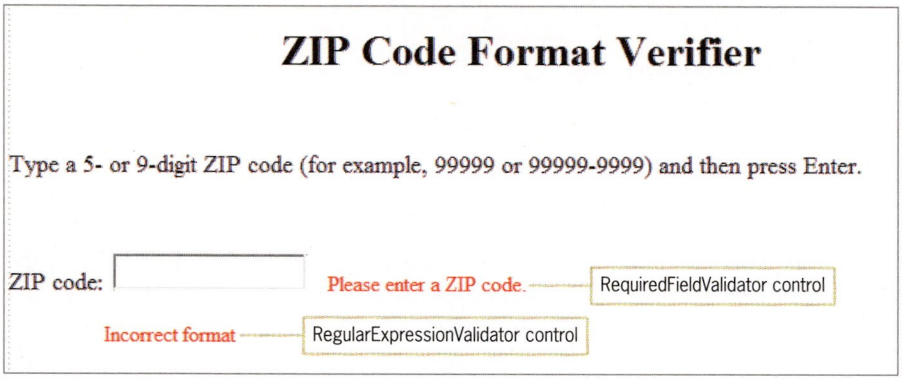

Figure 12-47   Web page for Exercise 7

■ LESSON C

After studying Lesson C, you should be able to:

- Utilize a radio button list control on a Web page

- Add a check box to a Web page

- Code a radio button list control's SelectedIndexChanged event procedure

- Code a check box's CheckedChanged event procedure

- Utilize a control's AutoPostBack property

Creating the Satellite Radio Application

Your task in this chapter is to create a Web Site application for the Satellite Radio company. The company's offerings and pricing information are shown in Figure 12-48. The application should display the cost of a 6-month subscription and the cost of a 12-month subscription.

Satellite Radio Pricing Sheet

Packages:

    Select

        6-month subscription $77.99

        12-month subscription $150.99

    Gold

        6-month subscription $95.99

        12-month subscription $166.99

    Platinum

        6-month subscription $119.99

        12-month subscription $200.99

Internet listening:

        6-month subscription $24.50

        12-month subscription $45.50

Discount for new customers:

    10% off the package subscription price only; does not apply to Internet listening subscription

Figure 12-48   Satellite Radio company's offerings and pricing information

To open the partially completed Satellite Radio application:

START HERE

1. If necessary, start Visual Studio 2015. Click **File** on the menu bar, and then click **Open Web Site**. If necessary, click the **File System** button in the Open Web Site dialog box. Click the **Radio** folder contained in the VB2015\Chap12 folder, and then click the **Open** button.

2. If the Default.aspx Web page is not open in the Document window, right-click **Default.aspx** in the Solution Explorer window and then click **View Designer**. See Figure 12-49. Notice that the Web page contains a two-row table. The first row has three cells; the second row has one cell.

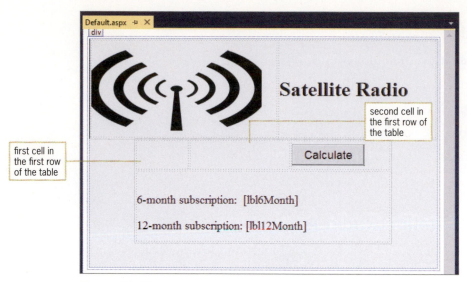

Figure 12-49   Partially completed Satellite Radio application

Using the RadioButtonList Tool

Unlike the toolbox for a Windows form, the toolbox for a Web form does not have a GroupBox tool that you can use to group together related radio buttons. Instead, the Web form toolbox provides the **RadioButtonList tool** for this purpose. The tool creates a **radio button list control** that contains related radio buttons.

START HERE

To add a radio button list control to the Web page:

1. Permanently display the Toolbox and Properties windows, and auto-hide the Solution Explorer window.

2. Click **RadioButtonList** in the Standard section of the toolbox, and then drag a radio button list control into the first cell in the first column of the table. See Figure 12-50.

Figure 12-50   Radio button list control added to the Web page

3. Change the radio button list control's ID property to **rblPkgs**.

4. Click the control's **task box** (>) to open its task list. Click **Edit Items** to open the ListItem Collection Editor dialog box, and then click the **Add** button. Change the first list item's Selected and Text properties to **True** and **Select**, respectively.

5. Click the **Add** button again. Change the second list item's Text property to **Gold**.

6. Click the **Add** button once again. Type **Platinum** in the third list item's Text property, and then press **Enter**. See Figure 12-51.

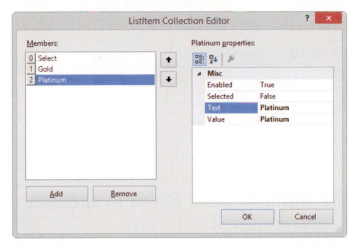

Figure 12-51   Completed ListItem Collection Editor dialog box

7. Click the **OK** button to close the dialog box.

8. Click an **empty area** of the Web page. If the word "Platinum" appears below its corresponding radio button, position your mouse pointer on the first cell's right border until the mouse pointer becomes a horizontal line with arrowheads on each end. Drag the border to the right until the word "Platinum" appears on the same line as its corresponding radio button, and then click an **empty area** of the Web page. See Figure 12-52.

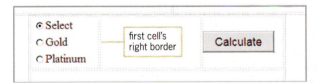

Figure 12-52   List items displayed in the radio button list control

Using the CheckBox Tool

The Web page's interface will provide check boxes for the Internet listening and 10% discount options. You instantiate a **check box** on a Web page using the **CheckBox tool** in the toolbox. A Web page can have one or more check boxes, and any number of check boxes can be selected at the same time.

To add two check boxes to the Web page:

START HERE

1. Click the **CheckBox** tool in the Standard section of the toolbox. Drag a check box control to the second cell in the first row of the table. Change the check box's ID and Text properties to **chkInternet** and **Internet listening**, respectively.

2. Click **immediately after the chkInternet control** and then press **Enter**. Drag another check box control to the cell, positioning it immediately below the chkInternet control. Change this check box's ID and Text properties to **chkDiscount** and **10% discount**, respectively. Click an **empty area** of the Web page. See Figure 12-53.

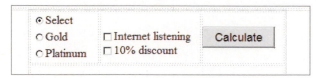

Figure 12-53   Check boxes added to the table

3. Auto-hide the toolbox and Properties windows. Click **File** on the menu bar and then click **Save Default.aspx**.

Coding the Calculate Button's Click Event Procedure

Figure 12-54 shows the pseudocode for the btnCalc_Click procedure.

btnCalc Click event procedure
1. use the radio button list control's SelectedIndex property to determine the appropriate package subscription cost
    if the property contains:
        0   assign the 6-month Select package rate as the 6-month subscription cost
                 assign the 12-month Select package rate as the 12-month subscription cost
        1   assign the 6-month Gold package rate as the 6-month subscription cost
                 assign the 12-month Gold package rate as the 12-month subscription cost
        2   assign the 6-month Premium package rate as the 6-month subscription cost
                 assign the 12-month Premium package rate as the 12-month subscription cost
2. if the 10% discount check box is selected
    subtract the discount rate from the number 1 and then multiply the difference by the 6-month subscription cost
    subtract the discount rate from the number 1 and then multiply the difference by the 12-month subscription cost
    end if
3. if the Internet listening check box is selected
    add 24.50 to the 6-month subscription cost
    add 45.50 to the 12-month subscription cost
    end if
4. display the 6-month and 12-month subscription costs

Figure 12-54   Pseudocode for the btnCalc_Click procedure

START HERE

To code and then test the btnCalc_Click procedure:

1. Right-click the **Web page** and then click **View Code**. Replace <your name> and <current date> in the comments with your name and the current date, respectively.

2. Locate the btnCalc_Click procedure, which contains the declaration statements for nine named constants and two variables.

3. The first step in the procedure's pseudocode uses the radio button list control's SelectedIndex property to determine the appropriate package subscription cost. Click the **blank line** above the End Sub clause. Enter the Select Case statement shown in Figure 12-55, and then position the insertion point as shown in the figure.

```
Select Case rblPkgs.SelectedIndex
    Case 0
        dblCost6Mths = dblSELECT6
        dblCost12Mths = dblSELECT12
    Case 1
        dblCost6Mths = dblGOLD6
        dblCost12Mths = dblGOLD12
    Case 2
        dblCost6Mths = dblPLATINUM6
        dblCost12Mths = dblPLATINUM12
    End Select


End Sub
```

enter the Select Case statement

position the insertion point here

Figure 12-55   Select Case statement entered in the btnCalc_Click procedure

4. The second step in the pseudocode determines whether the 10% discount check box is selected. If it is selected, the customer is entitled to a 10% discount on the package price. In other words, the package price should be 90% of its original price. Enter the following selection structure:

If chkDiscount.Checked Then
    dblCost6Mths *= (1 – dblDISCOUNT)
    dblCost12Mths *= (1 – dblDISCOUNT)
End If

5. Insert two blank lines below the End If clause.

6. The third step in the pseudocode determines whether the Internet listening check box is selected. If it is selected, appropriate amounts are added to the 6-month and 12-month costs. Beginning in the blank line above the End Sub clause, enter the following selection structure:

If chkInternet.Checked Then
    dblCost6Mths += dblINTERNET6
    dblCost12Mths += dblINTERNET12
End If

7. Insert two blank lines below the second End If clause.

8. The last step in the pseudocode displays the 6-month and 12-month subscription costs. Enter the additional assignment statements indicated in Figure 12-56.

```vb
Private Sub btnCalc_Click(sender As Object, e As EventArgs
) Handles btnCalc.Click
    ' display 6-month and 12-month subscription costs

    Const dblSELECT6 As Double = 77.99
    Const dblSELECT12 As Double = 150.99
    Const dblGOLD6 As Double = 95.99
    Const dblGOLD12 As Double = 166.99
    Const dblPLATINUM6 As Double = 119.99
    Const dblPLATINUM12 As Double = 200.99
    Const dblINTERNET6 As Double = 24.5
    Const dblINTERNET12 As Double = 45.5
    Const dblDISCOUNT As Double = 0.1
    Dim dblCost6Mths As Double
    Dim dblCost12Mths As Double

    Select Case rblPkgs.SelectedIndex
        Case 0
         dblCost6Mths = dblSELECT6
         dblCost12Mths = dblSELECT12
        Case 1
         dblCost6Mths = dblGOLD6
         dblCost12Mths = dblGOLD12
        Case 2
         dblCost6Mths = dblPLATINUM6
         dblCost12Mths = dblPLATINUM12
    End Select

    If chkDiscount.Checked Then
        dblCost6Mths *= (1 - dblDISCOUNT)
        dblCost12Mths *= (1 - dblDISCOUNT)
    End If

    If chkInternet.Checked Then
        dblCost6Mths += dblINTERNET6
        dblCost12Mths += dblINTERNET12
    End If

    lbl6Month.Text = dblCost6Mths.ToString("c2")
    lbl12Month.Text = dblCost12Mths.ToString("c2")
End Sub
```

enter these assignment statements

Figure 12-56 Completed btnCalc_Click procedure

9. Click **File** on the menu bar, and then click **Save Default.aspx.vb**. Press **Ctrl+F5** to start the application. Click the **Calculate** button. The 6-month and 12-month subscriptions will cost $77.99 and $150.99, respectively. See Figure 12-57.

Figure 12-57   Web page displayed in Internet Explorer

10. Click the **Gold** radio button. Notice that the previous subscription costs still appear on the screen, even though a different package was selected. The amounts could be misleading to a customer, who may not realize that he or she needs to click the Calculate button to recalculate the costs. You will fix this problem in the next section. Click the **Calculate** button, which changes the subscription costs to $95.99 and $166.99.

11. Click the **Platinum** radio button and then click the **Calculate** button. The subscription costs are now $119.99 and $200.99.

12. Click **both check boxes** to select them. Here, too, notice that the previous subscription costs still appear on the screen, which could be misleading to a customer. Click the **Calculate** button, which changes the subscription costs to $132.49 and $226.39.

13. Close the browser window.

Clearing the Previous Subscription Costs

Each time the customer selects a different radio button, the application should clear the contents of the labels that display the subscription costs. The contents of the labels should also be cleared when the customer either selects or deselects a check box. You will accomplish these tasks by creating a procedure named ClearCosts. The procedure will be associated with the following three events: rblPkgs_SelectedIndexChanged, chkDiscount_CheckedChanged, and chkInternet_CheckedChanged.

To create the ClearCosts procedure:

START HERE

1. Open the code template for the rblPkgs_SelectedIndexChanged event procedure. Change rblPkgs_SelectedIndexChanged in the procedure header to **ClearCosts**.

2. Click immediately before the **)** in the procedure header, and then press **Enter**. Make the modifications shaded in Figure 12-58.

```
Private Sub ClearCosts(sender As Object, e As EventArgs
                       ) Handles rblPkgs.SelectedIndexChanged,
                       chkDiscount.CheckedChanged,
                       chkInternet.CheckedChanged

    lbl6Month.Text = String.Empty
    lbl12Month.Text = String.Empty
End Sub
```

Figure 12-58   ClearCosts procedure

3. Click **File** on the menu bar and then click **Save Default.aspx.vb**. Press **Ctrl+F5** to start the application, and then click the **Calculate** button. Click the **Gold** radio button. Notice that the ClearCosts procedure did not clear the subscription costs from the labels. Close the browser window.

A button on a Web page—like the Calculate button used in this lesson or the Submit button used in Lesson B—automatically triggers a postback when it is clicked, sending the page's information and the button's Click event procedure to the server for processing. Radio button list controls and check boxes, however, do not trigger an automatic postback. As a result, the code contained in a radio button list control's SelectedIndexChanged procedure, as well as the code contained in a check box's CheckedChanged procedure, is not automatically processed by the server. To have these controls trigger an automatic postback, you simply need to change their **AutoPostBack property** from its default value of False to True.

START HERE

To change the AutoPostBack property for three of the controls:

1. Close the Code Editor window. Click the **rblPkgs** control, and then Ctrl+click the **chkInternet** and **chkDiscount** controls; the three controls are now selected. Use the Properties window to set the controls' AutoPostBack property to **True**.

2. Click an **empty area** of the Web page to deselect the controls. Click **File** on the menu bar and then click **Save Default.aspx.vb**. Press **Ctrl+F5** to start the application. Click the **Calculate** button. A postback occurs, and the code in the btnCalc_Click procedure is sent to the server for processing. The server returns $77.99 and $150.99 as the costs for a 6-month and 12-month subscription, respectively.

3. Click the **Gold** radio button. A postback occurs, and the code in the ClearCosts procedure, which is associated with the rblPkgs_SelectedIndexChanged event, is sent to the server for processing. The code clears the contents of the labels that display the subscription costs. See Figure 12-59.

Figure 12-59   Result of clicking a different radio button

4. Click the **Calculate** button. A postback occurs, and the server returns $95.99 and $166.99 as the costs of a 6-month and 12-month subscription, respectively.

5. Click the **Internet listening** check box. A postback occurs, and the code in the ClearCosts procedure, which is associated with the chkInternet_CheckedChanged event, is sent to the server for processing. The code clears the contents of the labels that display the subscription costs.

6. Click the **Calculate** button. A postback occurs, and the server returns $120.49 and $212.49 as the costs of a 6-month and 12-month subscription, respectively.

7. On your own, verify that the Platinum radio button and the 10% discount check box work correctly. When you are finished testing the Web page, close the browser window and then close the application.

Lesson C Summary

- To group together related radio buttons on a Web page:

  Use the RadioButtonList tool in the Standard section of the toolbox to instantiate a radio button list control. Use the Edit Items option on the task list to add radio button items to the control. Set each item's Text property. Set the Selected property of one of the items to True.

- To include a check box on a Web page:

  Use the CheckBox tool in the Standard section of the toolbox to instantiate a check box control. Set the check box's ID and Text properties.

- To determine which radio button is selected in a radio button list control:

  Use the control's SelectedIndex property. The index of the first radio button is 0.

- To determine whether a check box is selected or unselected:

  Use the check box's Checked property, which will contain either the Boolean value True (selected) or the Boolean value False (unselected).

- To perform one or more tasks when a different radio button is selected in a radio button list control:

  Enter the appropriate code in the control's SelectedIndexChanged event procedure.

- To perform one or more tasks when the value in a check box's Checked property changes:

  Enter the appropriate code in the check box's CheckedChanged event procedure.

- To have a radio button list control automatically trigger a postback when the selected radio button changes:

  Change the control's AutoPostBack property to True.

- To have a check box automatically trigger a postback when the value in its Checked property changes:

  Change the check box's AutoPostBack property to True.

Lesson C Key Terms

AutoPostBack property—determines whether a control triggers an automatic postback

Check box—provides an option that can be selected or unselected

CheckBox tool—used to instantiate (create) a check box

RadioButtonList tool—used to instantiate (create) a radio button list control on a Web page

Radio button list control—groups together related radio buttons on a Web page

Lesson C Review Questions

1. Which of the following tools is used to group related radio buttons on a Web page?

   a. ButtonRadioList

   b. ListRadioButton

   c. RadioButtonList

   d. RadioButtons

2. Which of the following If clauses determines whether the chkTaxable control is selected?

   a. `If chkTaxable = True Then`

   b. `If chkTaxable.Checked Then`

   c. `If chkTaxable.Selected Then`

   d. `If chkTaxable.Selection = True Then`

3. Which of the following determines whether the first radio button in the rblAges control is selected?

   a. `If rblAges.Selected = 0 Then`

   b. `If rblAges(0).Selected Then`

   c. `If rblAges.SelectedIndex = 0 Then`

   d. none of the above

4. Which event procedure contains the code to process when a different radio button is selected in a radio button list control?

   a. CheckedChanged

   b. SelectedIndexChanged

   c. SelectedIndex

   d. SelectionChanged

5. Which event procedure contains the code to process when a check box is selected by the user?

   a. Checked

   b. CheckBoxChanged

   c. CheckedChanged

   d. SelectedCheckBox

6. When a check box's AutoPostBack property is set to _____, the code in its _____ event procedure will be automatically processed by the server when the value in its _____ property changes.

   a. Auto, CheckedChanged, Checked

   b. Post, Checked, CheckChanged

   c. True, Checked, CheckChanged

   d. True, CheckedChanged, Checked

Lesson C Exercises

1. In this exercise, you modify the Satellite Radio application from this lesson. Use Windows to make a copy of the Radio folder. Rename the copy Modified Radio. Open the Modified Radio Web site. Right-click Default.aspx in the Solution Explorer window and then click View Designer. Figure 12-60 shows the company's current offerings and pricing information. Make the appropriate modifications to the interface and the code. (If the customer purchases the Music only package, he or she can purchase only the 12-month Internet listening subscription.)

INTRODUCTORY

Satellite Radio Pricing Sheet

Packages:

Select

    3-month subscription $44.99
    6-month subscription $77.99
    12-month subscription $150.99

Gold

    3-month subscription $55.99
    6-month subscription $95.99
    12-month subscription $166.99

Platinum

    3-month subscription $69.99
    6-month subscription $119.99
    12-month subscription $200.99

Music only

    3-month subscription .... N/A
    6-month subscription .... N/A
    12-month subscription $130.99

Internet listening:

    3-month subscription $14.99
    6-month subscription $24.50
    12-month subscription $45.50

Discount for new customers:

    10% off the package subscription price only; does not apply to Internet listening subscription

Figure 12-60   Satellite Radio company's current offerings and prices

INTRODUCTORY

2. Create an empty Web Site application named Tea and save it in the VB2015\
Chap12 folder. Add a new Web page named Default.aspx to the application. Change
the DOCUMENT object's Title property to Brazilian Tea. Brazilian Tea is a store that
sells both hot and iced tea in three different cup sizes: Small ($2.55), Medium ($3.75),
and Large ($4.50). The store must also charge a 4% sales tax. Use Figure 12-61 as a
guide when designing the Web page. The Calculate button should calculate the total
price of a cup of tea. It then should display (in the lblMessage control) a message that
indicates the cup size, total price, and whether the tea is hot or iced. In the Code Editor
window, enter comments to document the application's name and purpose as well as
your name and the current date. Also enter the appropriate Option statements. Code
the Calculate button's Click event procedure. Display the total price with a dollar sign
and two decimal places. Save the application, and then start and test it. Close the
browser window. Close the Code Editor window and then close the application.

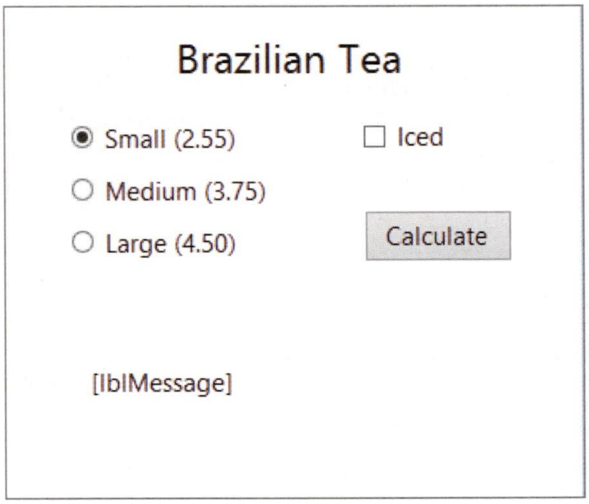

Brazilian Tea

- ◉ Small (2.55)   ☐ Iced
- ○ Medium (3.75)
- ○ Large (4.50)   [Calculate]

[lblMessage]

Figure 12-61   Interface for Exercise 2

INTERMEDIATE

3. Create an empty Web Site application named Willow and save it in the VB2015\
Chap12 folder. Add a new Web page named Default.aspx to the application. Change the
DOCUMENT object's Title property to Willow Hill. Willow Hill Athletic Club offers
personal training sessions to its members. The sessions are either 30 or 60 minutes
in length, and members can sign up to meet either two or three times per week. Each
30-minute session costs $17.50; each 60-minute session costs $30. However, members
signing up for three 60-minute sessions per week receive a 10% discount. Additionally,
members who are at least 60 years old receive a senior discount, which is an additional
5% off the total cost. The application should display the total cost for four weeks of
personal training. Use Figure 12-62 as a guide when designing the Web page. The
image is contained in the VB2015\Chap12\Training.png file. (Hint: The monthly cost
for a member who signs up for three 60-minute sessions per week is $324.00. If the
member is entitled to the senior discount, the cost is $307.80.)

Figure 12-62   Interface for Exercise 3

4. Create an empty Web Site application named Dice. Save the application in the VB2015\ Chap12 folder. Add a new Web page named Default.aspx to the application. Change the DOCUMENT object's Title property to Dice Game. In Chapter 5's Lesson C, you created the Roll 'Em Game application. Review the application's interface, pseudocode, and code, which are shown in Figures 5-64, 5-65, and 5-69, respectively. Create a similar application for the Web. The die images are contained in the VB2015\Chap12 folder. (Hint: Image controls on a Web page have a Visible property.) Save the application, and then start and test it.   INTERMEDIATE

5. Create an empty Web Site application named MacroTech. Save the application in the VB2015\Chap12 folder. Add a new Web page named Default.aspx to the application. Change the DOCUMENT object's Title property to MacroTech. MacroTech sells a software package that is available in three editions. The application should display the price of the edition a customer wants to purchase. The retail prices for the Ultimate, Professional, and Student editions are $775.99, $499.99, and $149.99, respectively. Some customers may have a coupon worth 10% off the price of the Ultimate edition, while others may have a coupon worth 20% off the price of the Student edition. Create an appropriate interface and then code the application. Save the application, and then start and test it.   INTERMEDIATE

6. Create an empty Web Site application named Guessing Game. Save the application in the VB2015\Chap12 folder. Add a new Web page named Default.aspx to the application. Change the DOCUMENT object's Title property to Guessing Game. The application should generate a random integer from 1 through 30, inclusive. It then should give the user as many chances as necessary to guess the integer. Each time the user makes a guess, the application should display one of three messages: "Guess higher", "Guess lower", or "Correct. The random integer is x.", where x is the random integer. The application should also display the number of chances it took to guess the number. Create a suitable interface and then code the application. Save the application, and then start and test it. (Hint: You can store the random integer and counter in hidden labels, or you can use two HiddenField controls.)   ADVANCED

Working with Access Databases and LINQ

Creating the Games Galore Application

In this chapter, you will create an application for the Games Galore store, which sells new and used video games. The video game information is contained in a Microsoft Access database named Games. The Games database is stored in the Games.accdb file and contains one table named tblGames. The application will display the records in a DataGridView control, which you will learn about in Lesson A. It will also allow the store manager to display only the games for a specific platform (Xbox, PlayStation, or Wii) as well as the total value of the games in the store.

Previewing the Games Galore Application

Before you start the first lesson in this chapter, you will preview the completed application contained in the VB2015\Chap13 folder.

START HERE

To preview the completed application:

1. Use Windows to locate and then open the VB2015\Chap13 folder on your computer's hard disk or on the device designated by your instructor. Right-click **Games** (**Games.exe**) in the list of filenames and then click **Open**.

2. First, you will display only the games for the PlayStation platform. Click the **Platform** text box, type **p**, and then click the **Go** button. Thirteen records appear in the DataGridView control, as shown in Figure 13-1.

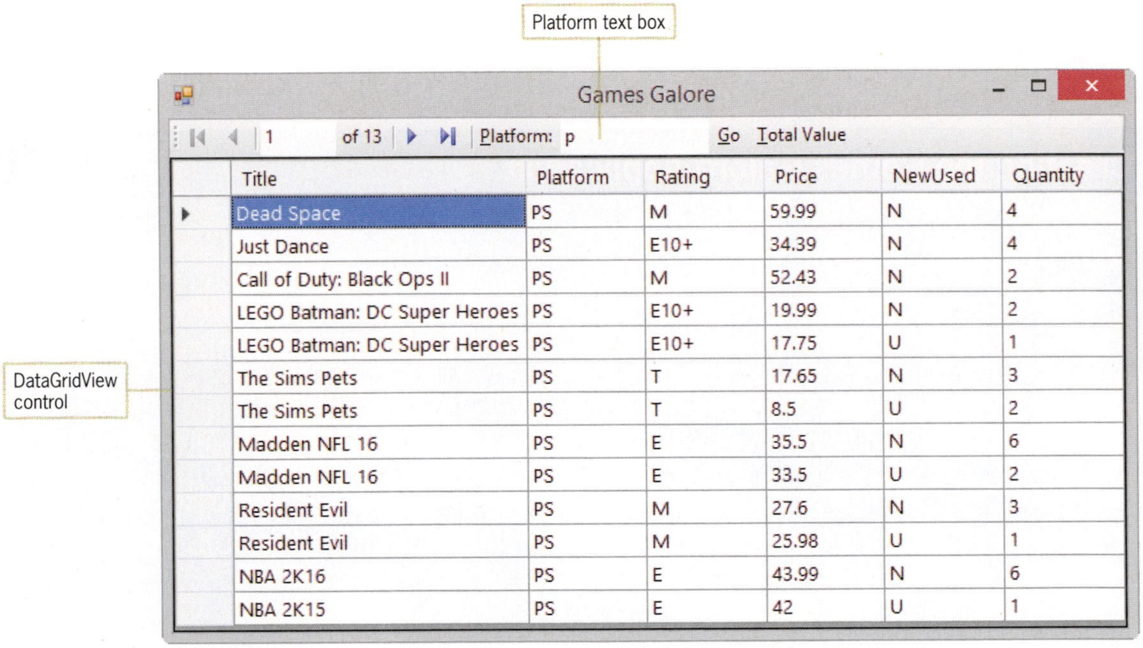

Platform text box

Games Galore

	Title	Platform	Rating	Price	NewUsed	Quantity
▶	Dead Space	PS	M	59.99	N	4
	Just Dance	PS	E10+	34.39	N	4
	Call of Duty: Black Ops II	PS	M	52.43	N	2
	LEGO Batman: DC Super Heroes	PS	E10+	19.99	N	2
	LEGO Batman: DC Super Heroes	PS	E10+	17.75	U	1
	The Sims Pets	PS	T	17.65	N	3
	The Sims Pets	PS	T	8.5	U	2
	Madden NFL 16	PS	E	35.5	N	6
	Madden NFL 16	PS	E	33.5	U	2
	Resident Evil	PS	M	27.6	N	3
	Resident Evil	PS	M	25.98	U	1
	NBA 2K16	PS	E	43.99	N	6
	NBA 2K15	PS	E	42	U	1

DataGridView control

Of 13 | Platform: p | Go Total Value

Figure 13-1   PlayStation games

3. Next, you will display all of the records again. Delete the contents of the Platform text box, and then click the **Go** button to display the 35 records in the DataGridView control.

4. Finally, click the **Total Value** button to display the total value of the games in the store. See Figure 13-2.

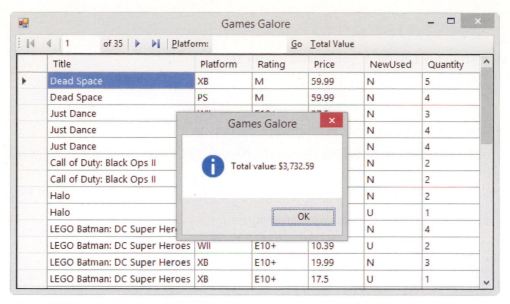

Figure 13-2 Total value of the games

5. Click the **OK** button to close the message box, and then click the **Close** button on the form's title bar to stop the application.

In Lesson A, you will learn how to connect an application to a Microsoft Access database and then display the information in one or more controls in the interface. Lesson B will show you how to query a database using LINQ, which stands for Language-Integrated Query. You will complete the Games Galore application in Lesson C. Be sure to complete each lesson in full and do all of the end-of-lesson questions and several exercises before continuing to the next lesson.

■ LESSON A

After studying Lesson A, you should be able to:

- Define basic database terminology

- Connect an application to a Microsoft Access database

- Bind table and field objects to controls

- Explain the purpose of the DataSet, BindingSource, TableAdapter, TableAdapterManager, and BindingNavigator objects

- Customize a DataGridView control

- Handle errors using the Try…Catch statement

- Format the data displayed in a bound label control

- Position the record pointer in a dataset

Database Terminology

Many people use databases to keep track of their medical records, movie collections, and even golf scores.

In order to maintain accurate records, most businesses store information about their employees, customers, and inventory in computer databases. A **computer database** is an electronic file that contains an organized collection of related information. Many products exist for creating computer databases; such products are called database management systems (or DBMSs). Some of the most popular database management systems are Microsoft Access, Microsoft SQL Server, and Oracle. You can use Visual Basic to access the data stored in databases created by these database management systems. As a result, companies can use Visual Basic to create a standard interface that allows employees to access information stored in a variety of database formats. Instead of learning each DBMS's user interface, the employee needs to know only one interface. The actual format of the database is unimportant and will be transparent to the user.

In this chapter, you will learn how to access the data stored in Microsoft Access databases. Databases created using Microsoft Access are relational databases. A **relational database** stores information in tables composed of columns and rows, similar to the format used in a spreadsheet. The databases are called relational because the information in the tables can be related in different ways.

Each column in a relational database's table represents a field, and each row represents a record. A **field** is a single item of information about a person, place, or thing—such as a name, a salary amount, a Social Security number, or a price. A **record** is a group of related fields that contain all of the necessary data about a specific person, place, or thing. The college you are attending keeps a student record on you. Examples of fields contained in your student record include your Social Security number, name, address, phone number, credits earned, and grades earned.

A group of related records is called a **table**. Each record in a table pertains to the same topic and contains the same type of information. In other words, each record in a table contains the same fields.

A relational database can contain one or more tables. A one-table database would be a good choice for storing information about the college courses you have taken. An example of such a table is shown in Figure 13-3. Each record in the table contains four fields: an ID field that indicates the department name and course number, a course title field, a field listing the number of credit hours, and a grade field.

ID	Title	Hours	Grade
ACC110	Accounting Procedures	3	A
ENG101	English Composition I	3	B
CIS110	Introduction to Programming	3	A
BIO111	Environmental Biology	3	C

Figure 13-3 Example of a one-table relational database

Most tables have a **primary key**, which is a field that uniquely identifies each record. In the table shown in Figure 13-3, you could use either the ID field or the Title field as the primary key because the data in those fields will be unique for each record.

You might use a two-table database to store information about a CD (compact disc) collection. You would store the general information about each CD, such as the CD's name and the artist's name, in the first table. The information about the songs on each CD, such as their title and track number, would be stored in the second table. You would need to use a common field—for example, a CD number—to relate the records contained in both tables.

Figure 13-4 shows an example of a two-table database that stores CD information. The first table is referred to as the **parent table**, and the second table is referred to as the **child table**. The CdNum field is the primary key in the parent table because it uniquely identifies each record in the table. The CdNum field in the child table is used solely to link the song title and track information to the appropriate CD in the parent table. In the child table, the CdNum field is called the **foreign key**.

the two tables are related by the CdNum field

CdNum	Name	Artist
01	For You	Selena Gomez
02	1989	Taylor Swift

CdNum	SongTitle	Track
01	The Heart Wants What It Wants	1
01	Come & Get It	2
01	Love You Like a Love Song	3
02	Welcome To New York	1
02	Blank Space	2
02	Style	3

Parent and child tables are also referred to as master and detail tables, respectively.

Figure 13-4 Example of a two-table relational database

Storing data in a relational database offers many advantages. The computer can retrieve data stored in a relational format both quickly and easily, and the data can be displayed in any order. The information in the CD database, for example, can be arranged by artist name, song title, and so on. You also can control the amount of information you want to view from a relational database. You can view all of the information in the CD database, only the information pertaining to a certain artist, or only the names of the songs contained on a specific CD.

Connecting an Application to a Microsoft Access Database

Ch13A

In this lesson, you will use a Microsoft Access database named Stores. The database contains one table, which is named tblStores. The table data is shown in Figure 13-5. The table contains five fields and 20 records. The StoreNum field is the primary key because it uniquely identifies each record in the table. The Ownership field indicates whether the store is company-owned (C) or a franchisee (F).

	StoreNum	City	State	Sales	Ownership
field names	100	San Francisco	CA	236,700	C
	101	San Diego	CA	125,900	C
	102	Burbank	CA	96,575	F
	103	Chicago	IL	135,400	C
	104	Chicago	IL	108,000	F
	105	Denver	CO	212,600	C
	106	Atlanta	GA	123,500	C
	107	Louisville	KY	178,500	C
	108	Lexington	KY	167,450	F
	109	Nashville	TN	205,625	C
records	110	Atlanta	GA	198,600	F
	111	Denver	CO	45,900	F
	112	Miami	FL	175,300	C
	113	Las Vegas	NV	245,675	C
	114	New Orleans	LA	213,400	C
	115	Louisville	KY	68,900	F
	116	Las Vegas	NV	110,340	F
	117	Indianapolis	IN	97,500	C
	118	Raleigh	NC	86,400	C
	119	San Francisco	CA	65,975	F

Figure 13-5 Data contained in the tblStores table

Before an application can access the data stored in a database, it needs to be connected to the database. You can make the connection using the Data Source Configuration Wizard. The wizard allows you to specify the data you want to access. The computer makes a copy of the specified data and stores the copy in its internal memory. The copy of the data you want to access is called a **dataset**. In the following set of steps, you will connect the Adalene Fashions application to the Stores database.

START HERE

To connect the Adalene Fashions application to the Stores database:

1. If necessary, start Visual Studio 2015. Open the Adalene Solution (Adalene Solution.sln) file contained in the VB2015\Chap13\Adalene Solution-DataGridView folder. Auto-hide the Properties and Toolbox windows, and permanently display the Solution Explorer window.

2. If the Data Sources window is not open, click **View** on the menu bar, point to **Other Windows**, and then click **Data Sources**. If necessary, click the **Auto Hide** button to permanently display the window.

3. Click **Add New Data Source** in the Data Sources window to start the Data Source Configuration Wizard. If necessary, click **Database** on the Choose a Data Source Type screen. See Figure 13-6. (If you want to display the Wizard's access keys, press the Alt key.)

Figure 13-6   Choose a Data Source Type screen

4. Click the **Next** button to display the Choose a Database Model screen. If necessary, click **Dataset**.

5. Click the **Next** button to display the Choose Your Data Connection screen. Click the **New Connection** button. At this point, either the Choose Data Source window or the Add Connection dialog box will open. If the Choose Data Source window opens, click **Microsoft Access Database File** in the Data source box, and then click the **Continue** button to open the Add Connection dialog box.

6. In the Add Connection dialog box, verify that Microsoft Access Database File (OLE DB) appears in the Data source box. If it doesn't, click the **Change** button to open the Change Data Source dialog box, click **Microsoft Access Database File**, and then click the **OK** button.

7. Click the **Browse** button in the Add Connection dialog box to open the Select Microsoft Access Database File dialog box. Open the VB2015\Chap13\Access Databases folder, and then click **Stores.accdb** in the list of filenames. Click the **Open** button. Figure 13-7 shows the completed Add Connection dialog box.

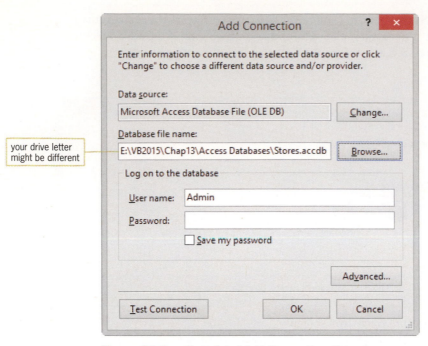

your drive letter
might be different

Figure 13-7 Completed Add Connection dialog box

8. Click the **Test Connection** button. The "Test connection succeeded." message appears in a message box. Close the message box.

9. Click the **OK** button to close the Add Connection dialog box. Stores.accdb appears in the Choose Your Data Connection screen. Click the **Next** button. The message box shown in Figure 13-8 opens. The message asks whether you want to include the database file in the current project. By including the file in the current project, you can more easily copy the application and its database to another computer.

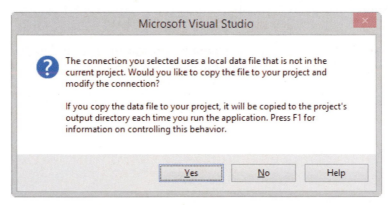

Figure 13-8 Message regarding copying the database file

10. Click the **Yes** button to add the Stores.accdb file to the application's project folder. (You can verify that the file was added to the project folder by viewing the Solution Explorer window.) The Save the Connection String to the Application Configuration File screen appears next and displays the name of the connection string, StoresConnectionString. If necessary, select the **Yes, save the connection as** check box.

11. Click the **Next** button to display the Choose Your Database Objects screen. You use this screen to select the table and/or field objects to include in the dataset, which is automatically named StoresDataSet.

12. Expand the **Tables** node, and then expand the **tblStores** node. In this application, you need the dataset to include all of the fields in the table. Click the **empty box** next to tblStores. Doing this selects the table and field check boxes, as shown in Figure 13-9.

Figure 13-9 Objects selected in the Choose Your Database Objects screen

13. Click the **Finish** button. The computer adds the StoresDataSet to the Data Sources and Solution Explorer windows. Expand the **tblStores** node in the Data Sources window. The dataset contains one table object and five field objects, as shown in Figure 13-10.

Figure 13-10 Result of running the Data Source Configuration Wizard

Previewing the Contents of a Dataset

You can view the fields and records contained in a dataset by right-clicking the dataset's name in the Data Sources window and then clicking Preview Data.

To view the contents of the StoresDataSet:

1. Right-click **StoresDataSet** in the Data Sources window, click **Preview Data**, and then click the **Preview** button. As Figure 13-11 shows, the StoresDataSet contains 20 records (rows), each having five fields (columns). Notice the information that appears in the Select an object to preview box. StoresDataSet is the name of the dataset in the application, and tblStores is the name of the table included in the dataset. Fill and GetData are methods. The Fill method populates an existing table with data, while the GetData method creates a new table and populates it with data.

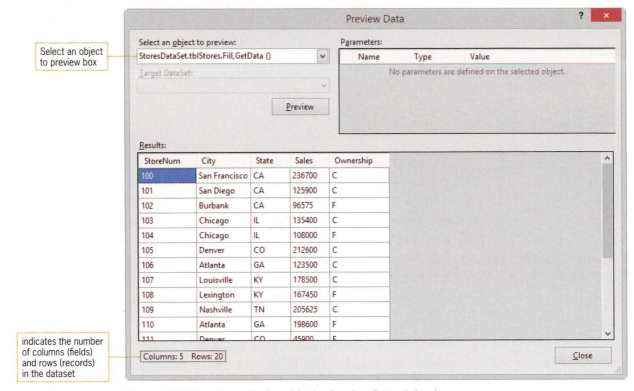

Figure 13-11   Data displayed in the Preview Data dialog box

2. Click the **Close** button to close the Preview Data dialog box, and then auto-hide the Solution Explorer window.

Binding the Objects in a Dataset

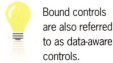

Bound controls are also referred to as data-aware controls.

For the user to view the contents of a dataset while an application is running, you need to connect one or more objects in the dataset to one or more controls in the interface. Connecting an object to a control is called **binding**, and the connected controls are called **bound controls**. As indicated in Figure 13-12, you can bind the object either to a control that the computer creates for you or to an existing control in the interface. First, you will learn how to have the computer create a bound control.

> **Binding an Object in a Dataset**
>
> *To have the computer create a control and then bind an object to it:*
> In the Data Sources window, click the object you want to bind. If necessary, use the object's list arrow to change the control type. Drag the object to an empty area on the form, and then release the mouse button.
>
> *To bind an object to an existing control:*
> In the Data Sources window, click the object you want to bind. Drag the object to the control on the form, and then release the mouse button. Alternatively, you can click the control on the form and then use the Properties window to set the appropriate property or properties. (Refer to the *Binding to an Existing Control* section later in this lesson.)

Figure 13-12   Ways to bind an object in a dataset

Having the Computer Create a Bound Control

When you drag an object from a dataset to an empty area on the form, the computer creates a control and automatically binds the object to it. The icon that appears before the object's name in the Data Sources window indicates the type of control the computer will create. The icon next to tblStores in Figure 13-13 indicates that a DataGridView control will be created when you drag the tblStores table object to the form. A DataGridView control displays the table data in a row and column format, similar to a spreadsheet. You will learn more about the DataGridView control in the next section. The icon next to each of the five field objects, on the other hand, indicates that the computer creates a text box when a field object is dragged to the form.

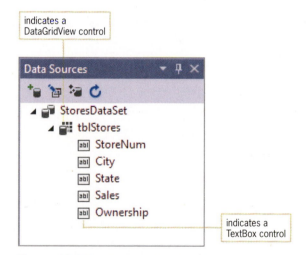

Figure 13-13   Icons in the Data Sources window

When an object is selected in the Data Sources window, you can use the list arrow that appears next to the object's name to change the type of control the computer creates. For example, to display the table data in separate text boxes rather than in a DataGridView control, you click tblStores in the Data Sources window and then click the tblStores list arrow, as shown in Figure 13-14. Clicking Details in the list tells the computer to create a separate control for each field in the table.

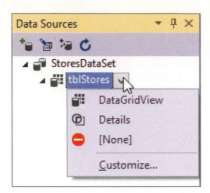

Figure 13-14   Result of clicking the tblStores object's list arrow

Similarly, to display the City field's data in a label control rather than in a text box, you first click City in the Data Sources window. You then click the field's list arrow, as shown in Figure 13-15, and then click Label in the list.

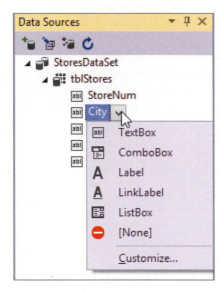

Figure 13-15   Result of clicking the City object's list arrow

In the following set of steps, you will drag the tblStores object from the Data Sources window to the form, using the default control type for a table.

START HERE

To bind the tblStores object to a DataGridView control:

1. If necessary, click **tblStores** in the Data Sources window to select the tblStores object. Drag the object from the Data Sources window to the form, and then release the mouse button. The computer adds a DataGridView control to the form, and it binds the tblStores object to the control. See Figure 13-16.

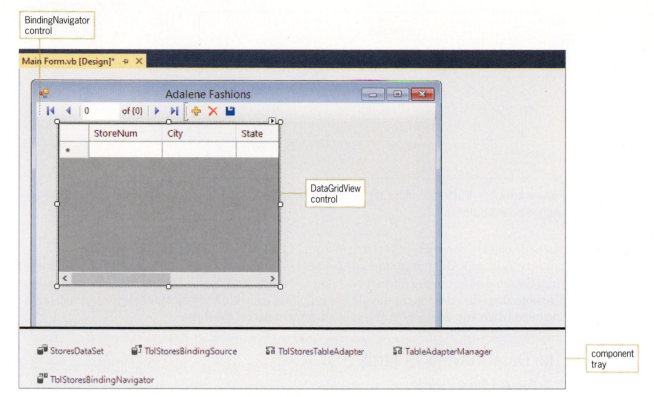

Figure 13-16   Result of dragging the table object to the form

Besides adding a DataGridView control to the form, the computer also adds a BindingNavigator control. When an application is running, you can use the **BindingNavigator control** to move from one record to the next in the dataset, as well as to add or delete a record and save any changes made to the dataset. The computer also places five objects in the component tray: a DataSet, BindingSource, TableAdapter, TableAdapterManager, and BindingNavigator. As you learned in Chapter 1, the component tray stores objects that do not appear in the user interface while an application is running. An exception to this is the BindingNavigator object, which appears as the BindingNavigator control during both design time and run time.

The **TableAdapter object** connects the database to the **DataSet object**, which stores the information you want to access from the database. The TableAdapter is responsible for retrieving the appropriate information from the database and storing it in the DataSet. It also can be used to save to the database any changes made to the data contained in the DataSet. However, in most cases, you will use the **TableAdapterManager object** to save the changes because it can handle saving data to multiple tables in the DataSet.

The **BindingSource object** provides the connection between the DataSet and the bound controls on the form. The TblStoresBindingSource in Figure 13-16, for example, connects the StoresDataSet to two bound controls: a DataGridView control and a BindingNavigator control. The TblStoresBindingSource allows the DataGridView control to display the data contained in the StoresDataSet. It also allows the BindingNavigator control to access the records stored in the StoresDataSet. Figure 13-17 illustrates the relationships among the database, the objects in the component tray, and the bound controls on the form.

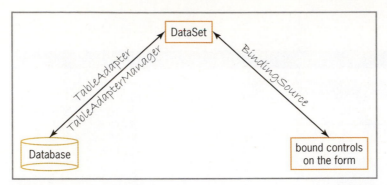

Figure 13-17 Illustration of the relationships among the database, the objects in the component tray, and the bound controls

If a table object's control type is changed from DataGridView to Details, the computer automatically provides the appropriate controls (such as text boxes, labels, and so on) when you drag the table object to the form. It also adds the BindingNavigator control to the form and the five objects to the component tray. The appropriate controls and objects are also automatically included when you drag a field object to an empty area on the form.

The DataGridView Control

The **DataGridView control** is one of the most popular controls for displaying table data because it allows you to view a great deal of information at the same time. The control displays the data in a row and column format, similar to a spreadsheet. Each row represents a record, and each column represents a field. The intersection of a row and a column in a DataGridView control is called a **cell**.

The control's **AutoSizeColumnsMode property**, which has seven different settings, determines the way the column widths are sized in the control. The Fill setting automatically adjusts the column widths so that all of the columns exactly fill the display area of the control. The ColumnHeader setting, on the other hand, adjusts the column widths based on the header text.

Like the PictureBox control, the DataGridView control has a task list. The task list is shown in Figure 13-18 along with a description of each task.

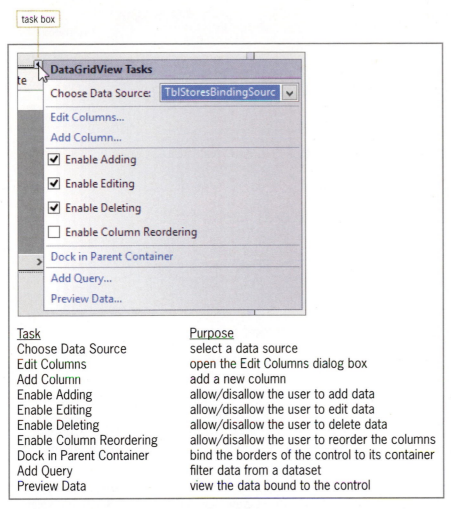

task box

DataGridView Tasks

Choose Data Source: TblStoresBindingSourc ⌄

Edit Columns...

Add Column...

☑ Enable Adding

☑ Enable Editing

☑ Enable Deleting

☐ Enable Column Reordering

Dock in Parent Container

Add Query...

Preview Data...

Task	Purpose
Choose Data Source	select a data source
Edit Columns	open the Edit Columns dialog box
Add Column	add a new column
Enable Adding	allow/disallow the user to add data
Enable Editing	allow/disallow the user to edit data
Enable Deleting	allow/disallow the user to delete data
Enable Column Reordering	allow/disallow the user to reorder the columns
Dock in Parent Container	bind the borders of the control to its container
Add Query	filter data from a dataset
Preview Data	view the data bound to the control

Figure 13-18   DataGridView control's task list

Figure 13-19 shows the Edit Columns dialog box, which opens when you click Edit Columns on the DataGridView control's task list. You can use the Edit Columns dialog box during design time to add columns to the control, remove columns from the control, and reorder the columns. You also can use it to set the properties of the bound columns. For example, you can use a column's DefaultCellStyle property to format the column's data as well as to change the column's width and alignment. You can use a column's HeaderText property to change a column's heading.

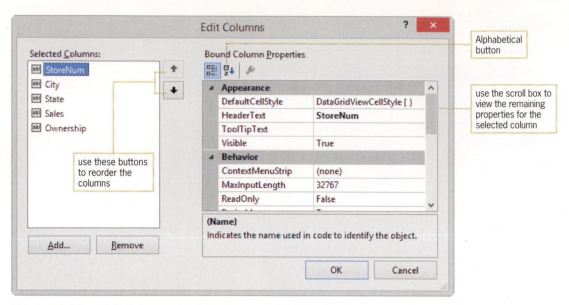

Figure 13-19   Edit Columns dialog box

START HERE

To improve the appearance of the DataGridView control:

1. Temporarily display the Properties window. Click **AutoSizeColumnsMode** in the Properties list, and then set the property to **Fill**.

2. Click the **TblStoresDataGridView control** to close the Properties window. Click the control's **task box**, and then click **Dock in Parent Container**. The DataGridView control expands to the size of the form. This is because the Dock in Parent Container option anchors the control's borders to the borders of its container, which (in this case) is the form.

3. Next, you will change the header text on one of the columns. Click **Edit Columns** in the task list. Click the **Alphabetical** button (shown earlier in Figure 13-19) to display the property names in alphabetical order. StoreNum is currently selected in the Selected Columns list. Change the column's HeaderText property to **Store**.

4. Now you will format the sales amounts to include a dollar sign and (if appropriate) a thousands separator. Click **Sales**, click **DefaultCellStyle**, and then click the **...** (ellipsis) button to open the CellStyle Builder dialog box. Click **Format**, and then click the **...** (ellipsis) button to open the Format String Dialog box. Click **Currency** in the Format type list, and then change the number of decimal places to **0**. See Figure 13-20.

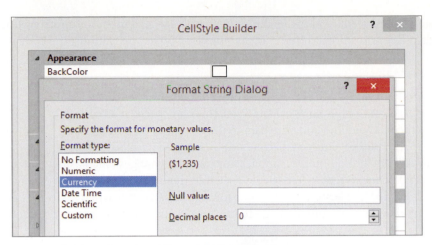

Figure 13-20 Completed Format String Dialog box

5. Click the **OK** button to close the Format String Dialog box. You are returned to the CellStyle Builder dialog box.

6. Finally, you will right-align the sales amounts. Change the Sales column's Alignment property to **MiddleRight**. Click the **OK** button to close the CellStyle Builder dialog box, and then click the **OK** button to close the Edit Columns dialog box.

7. Click the **DataGridView** control to close its task list. Auto-hide the Data Sources window and then save the solution.

Visual Basic Code

In addition to adding the appropriate controls and objects to the application when a table or field object is dragged to the form, Visual Basic also enters some code in the Code Editor window.

To view the code automatically entered in the Code Editor window:

1. Open the Code Editor window. Replace <your name> and <current date> in the comments with your name and the current date, respectively.

2. The two procedures shown in Figure 13-21 were automatically entered when the tblStores object was dragged to the form. (In your Code Editor window, the first procedure header and the comments in the second procedure will appear on one line.)

As you learned in Chapter 1, the keyword Me refers to the current form.

```vb
Private Sub TblStoresBindingNavigatorSaveItem_Click(sender As Object, e As EventArgs
        ) Handles TblStoresBindingNavigatorSaveItem.Click
    Me.Validate()
    Me.TblStoresBindingSource.EndEdit()
    Me.TableAdapterManager.UpdateAll(Me.StoresDataSet)

End Sub


Private Sub frmMain_Load(sender As Object, e As EventArgs) Handles MyBase.Load
    'TODO: This line of code loads data into the
    'StoresDataSet.tblStores' table. You can move, or remove it, as needed.
    Me.TblStoresTableAdapter.Fill(Me.StoresDataSet.tblStores)

End Sub
```

Figure 13-21 Code automatically entered in the Code Editor window

The form's Load event procedure uses the TableAdapter object's Fill method to retrieve the data from the database and store it in the DataSet object. In most applications, the code to fill a dataset belongs in this procedure. However, as the comments in the procedure indicate, you can either move or delete the code.

The TblStoresBindingNavigatorSaveItem_Click procedure is processed when you click the Save Data button (the disk) on the BindingNavigator control. The procedure's code validates the changes made to the data before saving the data to the database. Two methods are involved in the save operation: the BindingSource object's EndEdit method and the TableAdapterManager's UpdateAll method. The EndEdit method applies any pending changes (such as new records, deleted records, and changed records) to the dataset, and the UpdateAll method commits the changes to the database. Because it is possible for an error to occur when saving data to a database, you should add error-handling code to the Save Data button's Click event procedure.

Handling Errors in the Code

When an error occurs in a procedure's code during run time, programmers say that the procedure "threw an exception."

An error that occurs while an application is running is called an **exception**. If your code does not contain specific instructions for handling the exceptions that may occur, Visual Basic handles them for you. Typically, it does this by displaying an error message and then abruptly terminating the application. You can prevent your application from behaving in such an unfriendly manner by taking control of the exception handling in your code; you can do this by using the **Try...Catch statement**.

Figure 13-22 shows the basic syntax of the Try...Catch statement and includes examples of using the syntax. The basic syntax contains only a Try block and a Catch block. Within the Try block, you place the code that could possibly generate an exception. When an exception occurs in the Try block's code, the computer processes the code contained in the Catch block and then skips to the code following the End Try clause. A description of the exception that occurred is stored in the Message property of the Catch block's `ex` parameter. You can access the description using the code `ex.Message`, as shown in Example 1 in the figure; or you can display your own message, as shown in Example 2.

The Try...Catch statement can also include a Finally block, whose code is processed whether or not an exception is thrown within the Try block.

```
Try...Catch Statement
Basic syntax
Try
        one or more statements that might generate an exception
Catch ex As Exception
        one or more statements to execute when an exception occurs
End Try


Example 1
Private Sub TblStoresBindingNavigatorSaveItem_Click(
sender As Object, e As EventArgs
) Handles TblStoresBindingNavigatorSaveItem.Click
    Try
        Me.Validate()
        Me.TblStoresBindingSource.EndEdit()
        Me.TableAdapterManager.UpdateAll(Me.StoresDataSet)
    Catch ex As Exception
        MessageBox.Show(ex.Message, "Adalene Fashions",
                        MessageBoxButtons.OK,
                        MessageBoxIcon.Information)
    End Try
End Sub
```

Figure 13-22   Basic syntax and examples of the Try...Catch statement *(continues)*

(continued)

```
Example 2
Private Sub btnDisplay_Click(sender As Object, e As EventArgs
) Handles btnDisplay.Click
    Dim inFile As IO.StreamReader
    Dim strLine As String

    Try
        inFile = IO.File.OpenText("names.txt")
        Do Until inFile.Peek = -1
            strLine = inFile.ReadLine
            lstNames.Items.Add(strLine)
        Loop
        inFile.Close()
    Catch ex As Exception
        MessageBox.Show("Sequential file error", "JK's",
                    MessageBoxButtons.OK,
                    MessageBoxIcon.Information)
    End Try
End Sub
```

Figure 13-22 Basic syntax and examples of the Try...Catch statement

To include a Try...Catch statement in the Save Data button's Click event procedure:

START HERE

1. Insert a blank line above the `Me.Validate()` statement in the TblStoresBindingNavigatorSaveItem_Click procedure. Type **Try** and press **Enter**. The Code Editor automatically enters the `Catch ex As Exception` and `End Try` clauses for you.

2. Move the three statements that appear below the End Try clause, as well as the blank line below the statements, into the Try block.

3. If the three statements in the Try block do not produce (throw) an exception, the Try block should display the "Changes saved" message; otherwise, the Catch block should display a description of the exception. Enter the two MessageBox.Show methods indicated in Figure 13-23.

```
Private Sub TblStoresBindingNavigatorSaveItem_Click(sender As Object, e As
    Try
        Me.Validate()
        Me.TblStoresBindingSource.EndEdit()
        Me.TableAdapterManager.UpdateAll(Me.StoresDataSet)
        MessageBox.Show("Changes saved", "Adalene Fashions",          ┐ enter this
                    MessageBoxButtons.OK, MessageBoxIcon.Information)  ┘ MessageBox.Show
                                                                        method
    Catch ex As Exception
        MessageBox.Show(ex.Message, "Adalene Fashions",               ┐ enter this
                    MessageBoxButtons.OK, MessageBoxIcon.Information)  ┘ MessageBox.Show
                                                                        method
    End Try

End Sub
```

Figure 13-23 Completed Click event procedure for the Save Data button

4. Save the solution and then start the application. The statement in the frmMain_Load procedure (shown earlier in Figure 13-21) retrieves the appropriate data from the Stores database and loads the data into the StoresDataSet. The data is displayed in the DataGridView control, which is bound to the tblStores table contained in the dataset. See Figure 13-24.

TblStoresBindingNavigator control

TblStoresDataGridView control

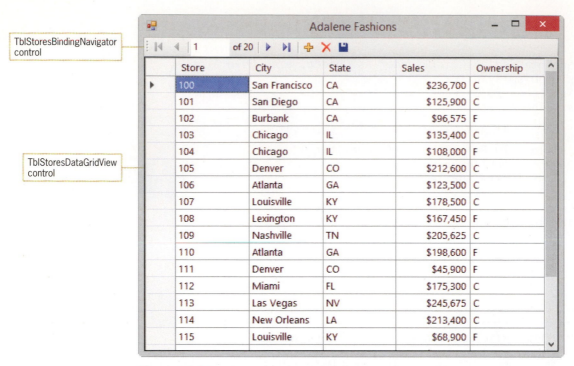

Figure 13-24 Data displayed in the DataGridView control

5. You can use the arrow keys on your keyboard to move the highlight to a different cell in the DataGridView control. When a cell is highlighted, you can modify its contents by simply typing the new data. Press the ↓ key to move the highlight to the next record, and then press the → key to move the highlight to the next field.

6. The BindingNavigator control provides buttons for accessing the first, last, previous, and next records in the dataset. When you rest your mouse pointer on one of these buttons, a tooltip appears and indicates the button's purpose. Rest your mouse pointer on the Move last button, as shown in Figure 13-25.

Move first Move previous Move next

Move last

Figure 13-25 Tooltip for the Move last button

7. Click the **Move last** button to move the highlight to the last record, and then click the **Move first** button to move the highlight to the first record.

8. You can also use the BindingNavigator control to access a record by its record number. The records are numbered 1, 2, 3, and so on. Click the **Current position** box, which contains the number 1. Replace the 1 with a **6** and then press **Enter**. The highlight moves to Store 105's record, which is the sixth record.

9. Click the **Close** button on the form's title bar to stop the application.

The BindingNavigator control also provides buttons for adding a new record to the dataset, deleting a record from the dataset, and saving the changes made to the dataset. You can add additional items (such as buttons and text boxes) to a BindingNavigator control and also delete items from the control. You will learn how to add items to and delete items from a BindingNavigator control in the *Customizing a BindingNavigator Control* section in Lesson B.

The Copy to Output Directory Property

When the Data Source Configuration Wizard connected the Adalene Fashions application to the Stores database, it added the database file (Stores.accdb) to the application's project folder. (You can verify that the file was added to the project folder by viewing the Solution Explorer window.) A database file contained in a project is referred to as a local database file. The way Visual Basic saves changes to a local database file is determined by the file's **Copy to Output Directory property**. Figure 13-26 lists the values that can be assigned to the property.

Copy to Output Directory Property	
Property setting	Meaning
Do not copy	The file in the project folder is not copied to the bin\Debug folder when the application is started.
Copy always	The file in the project folder is copied to the bin\Debug folder each time the application is started.
Copy if newer	When an application is started, the computer compares the date on the file in the project folder with the date on the file in the bin\Debug folder. The file from the project folder is copied to the bin\Debug folder only when its date is newer.

Figure 13-26   Settings for the Copy to Output Directory property

When a file's Copy to Output Directory property is set to its default setting, Copy always, the file is copied from the project folder to the project folder's bin\Debug folder each time you start the application. In this case, the Stores.accdb file is copied from the Adalene Project folder to the Adalene Project\bin\Debug folder. As a result, the file will appear in two different folders in the solution. When you click the Save Data button on the BindingNavigator control, any changes made in the DataGridView control are recorded only in the file stored in the bin\Debug folder; the file stored in the project folder is not changed. The next time you start the application, the file in the project folder is copied to the bin\Debug folder, overwriting the file that contains the changes. You can change this behavior by setting the database file's Copy to Output Directory property to Copy if newer. The Copy if newer setting tells the computer to compare the dates on both files to determine which file has the newer (i.e., more current) date. If the database file in the project folder has a newer date, the computer should copy it to the bin\Debug folder; otherwise, it shouldn't copy it.

To change the Stores.accdb file's Copy to Output Directory property:

START HERE

1.   Temporarily display the Solution Explorer window. Right-click **Stores.accdb** and then click **Properties**. Change the file's Copy to Output Directory property to **Copy if newer**.

2.   Save the solution and then start the application.

3. Click the **Add new** button (the plus sign) to add a new record to the end of the DataGridView control. Type **120** as the store number, press **Tab**, and then type **Miami** as the city. Now, enter **FL**, **84600**, and **F** in the State, Sales, and Ownership fields, respectively. Press **Enter** after typing the letter F.

4. Click the **Move first** button to move the highlight to the Ownership field in the first record. When a cell is highlighted, you can modify its existing data by simply typing the new data. Type **F** and press **Enter** to change the entry in Store 100's Ownership field.

5. Click the **Save Data** button (the disk). The "Changes saved" message appears in a message box. Close the message box and then stop the application.

6. Start the application again. The DataGridView control contains the change you made to Store 100's Ownership field. Scroll down the control to verify that it also contains the record you added.

7. Click **120** in the Store field, and then click the **Delete** button (the X) to delete the record. Now, click the **Move first** button to move the highlight to the first record, and then change Store 100's Ownership field from F to **C**.

8. Click the **Save Data** button. The "Changes saved" message appears in a message box. Close the message box and then stop the application.

9. Start the application again to verify that your changes were saved, and then stop the application. Close the Code Editor window and then close the solution.

YOU DO IT 1!

Create an application named YouDoIt 1 and save it in the VB2015\Chap13 folder. Connect the application to the CD database, which is stored in the VB2015\Chap13\ Access Databases\CD.accdb file. The database contains one table named tblCds. The table contains 13 records. Each record contains three fields: CdName, Artist, and Price. Display the records in a DataGridView control. Include the Try...Catch statement in the Save Data button's Click event procedure. Also, change the database file's Copy to Output Directory property as appropriate. Save the solution and then start and test the application. Close the Code Editor window and then close the solution.

Binding to an Existing Control

As indicated earlier in Figure 13-12, you can bind an object in a dataset to an existing control on a form. The easiest way to do this is by dragging the object from the Data Sources window to the control. However, you also can click the control and then set one or more properties in the Properties window. The appropriate property (or properties) to set depends on the control you are binding. To bind a DataGridView control, you use the DataSource property. However, you use the DataSource and DisplayMember properties to bind a ListBox control. To bind label and text box controls, you use the DataBindings/Text property.

When you drag an object from the Data Sources window to an existing control, the computer does not create a new control; instead, it binds the object to the existing control. Because a new control does not need to be created, the computer ignores the control type specified for the object in the Data Sources window. Therefore, it is not necessary to change the control type in the Data Sources window to match the existing control's type. In other words, you can drag an object that is associated with a text box in the Data Sources window to a label control on the form. The computer will bind the object to the label, but it will not change the label to a text box.

In the next set of steps, you will connect a different version of the Adalene Fashions application to the Stores database. You will then begin binding objects from the dataset to existing label controls in the interface. In this version of the application, you will not need to change the database file's Copy to Output Directory property to Copy if newer because the user will not be adding, deleting, or editing the records in the dataset.

To connect an application to a database and then bind an object to an existing control: START HERE

1. Open the Adalene Solution (Adalene Solution.sln) file contained in the VB2015\ Chap13\Adalene Solution-Labels folder. See Figure 13-27.

Figure 13-27   A different version of the Adalene Fashions application

2. Permanently display the Data Sources window, and then click **Add New Data Source** to start the Data Source Configuration Wizard. If necessary, click **Database** on the Choose a Data Source Type screen.

3. Click the **Next** button to display the Choose a Database Model screen. If necessary, click **Dataset**.

4. Click the **Next** button to display the Choose Your Data Connection screen. Click the **New Connection** button to open the Add Connection dialog box. If Microsoft Access Database File (OLE DB) does not appear in the Data source box, click the **Change** button to open the Change Data Source dialog box, click **Microsoft Access Database File**, and then click the **OK** button.

5. Click the **Browse** button in the Add Connection dialog box. Open the VB2015\Chap13\ Access Databases folder, and then click **Stores.accdb** in the list of filenames. Click the **Open** button. Click the **Test Connection** button in the Add Connection dialog box. The "Test connection succeeded." message appears in a message box. Close the message box.

6. Click the **OK** button to close the Add Connection dialog box. Click the **Next** button on the Choose Your Data Connection screen, and then click the **Yes** button to add the Stores.accdb file to the application's project folder.

7. If necessary, select the **Yes, save the connection as** check box on the Save the Connection String to the Application Configuration File screen. Click the **Next** button to display the Choose Your Database Objects screen.

8. Expand the **Tables** node and then expand the **tblStores** node. In this application, you will include only three fields in the dataset. Click the **empty box** that appears next to each of the following field names: StoreNum, Sales, and Ownership. Click the **Finish** button. The computer adds the StoresDataSet to the Data Sources window. Expand the tblStores node in the Data Sources window. The dataset contains one table object and three field objects.

9. Click **StoreNum** in the Data Sources window, and then drag the field object to the lblStore control. Release the mouse button. The computer binds the control and adds the DataSet, BindingSource, TableAdapter, and TableAdapterManager objects to the component tray. See Figure 13-28.

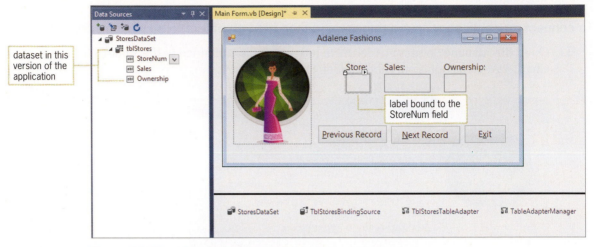

Figure 13-28 Result of binding a field to an existing control

Notice that when you drag an object from the Data Sources window to an existing control, the computer does not add a BindingNavigator object to the component tray, nor does it add a BindingNavigator control to the form. You can use the BindingNavigator tool, which is located in the Data section of the toolbox, to add a BindingNavigator control and object to the application. You then would set the control's DataSource property to the name of the BindingSource object (in this case, TblStoresBindingSource).

Besides adding the objects shown in Figure 13-28 to the component tray, the computer also enters (in the Code Editor window) the Load event procedure shown earlier in Figure 13-21. Recall that the procedure uses the TableAdapter object's Fill method to retrieve the data from the database and store it in the DataSet object.

START HERE **To bind the remaining objects in the dataset to existing controls:**

1. On your own, drag the **Sales** and **Ownership** field objects to the lblSales and lblOwner controls, respectively.

2. Auto-hide the Data Sources window and then save the solution. Start the application. Only the first record in the dataset appears in the interface. See Figure 13-29.

Figure 13-29 First record displayed in the interface

3. Because the interface does not contain a BindingNavigator control, which would allow you to move from one record to the next, you will need to code the Next Record and Previous Record buttons to view the remaining records. Click the **Exit** button to stop the application.

Coding the Next Record and Previous Record Buttons

The BindingSource object uses an invisible record pointer to keep track of the current record in the dataset. It stores the position of the record pointer in its **Position property**. The first record is in position 0, the second is in position 1, and so on. Figure 13-30 shows the Position property's syntax and includes examples of using the property.

BindingSource Object's Position Property

Syntax
bindingSourceName.**Position**

Example 1
`intRecordNum = TblStoresBindingSource.Position`
assigns the current record's position to the `intRecordNum` variable

Example 2
`TblStoresBindingSource.Position = 4`
moves the record pointer to the fifth record in the dataset

Example 3
`TblStoresBindingSource.Position += 1`
moves the record pointer to the next record in the dataset

Figure 13-30   Syntax and examples of the BindingSource object's Position property

Rather than using the Position property to position the record pointer in a dataset, you can use the BindingSource object's **Move methods** to move the record pointer to the first, last, next, or previous record in the dataset. Figure 13-31 shows each Move method's syntax and includes examples of using two of the methods.

BindingSource Object's Move Methods

Syntax
bindingSourceName.**MoveFirst()**
bindingSourceName.**MoveLast()**
bindingSourceName.**MoveNext()**
bindingSourceName.**MovePrevious()**

Example 1
`TblStoresBindingSource.MoveFirst()`
moves the record pointer to the first record in the dataset

Example 2
`TblStoresBindingSource.MoveNext()`
moves the record pointer to the next record in the dataset

Figure 13-31   Syntax and examples of the BindingSource object's Move methods

START HERE **To code and then test the Next Record and Previous Record buttons:**

1. Open the Code Editor window. Replace <your name> and <current date> in the comments with your name and the current date, respectively.

2. Open the code template for the btnNext_Click procedure, and then enter the following statement:

   TblStoresBindingSource.MoveNext()

3. Open the code template for the btnPrevious_Click procedure, and then enter the following statement:

   TblStoresBindingSource.MovePrevious()

4. Save the solution and then start the application. Click the **Next Record** button to display the second record. Continue clicking the **Next Record** button until the last record appears in the interface.

5. Click the **Previous Record** button until the first record appears in the interface.

6. Click the **Exit** button and then close the Code Editor window.

Formatting the Data Displayed in a Bound Label Control

The sales amounts displayed in the lblSales control would be easier to read if they included a thousands separator.

START HERE **To display the sales amounts with a thousands separator:**

1. Click the **lblSales** control. Temporarily display the Properties window. Click **(DataBindings)**, which appears at the top of the properties list. Click the **plus box** that appears next to the property, and then click **(Advanced)**. Click the **...** (ellipsis) button to open the Formatting and Advanced Binding dialog box. Click **Numeric** in the Format type box, and then change the number of decimal places to **0**. See Figure 13-32.

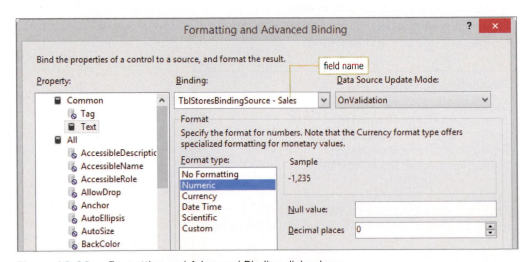

Figure 13-32 Formatting and Advanced Binding dialog box

2. Click the **OK** button to close the dialog box. Save the solution and then start the application. The sales amount now appears with a thousands separator.

3. Click the **Exit** button and then close the solution.

YOU DO IT 2!

Create an application named YouDoIt 2 and save it in the VB2015\Chap13 folder. Add three labels and two buttons to the form. Connect the application to the CD database, which is stored in the VB2015\Chap13\Access Databases\CD.accdb file. The database contains one table named tblCds. The table contains 13 records. Each record contains three fields: CdName, Artist, and Price. Display the records, one at a time, in the labels. (One of the CD names contains an ampersand. To display the &, you will need to set the UseMnemonic property of the label that displays the names to False.) Display the Price field with a dollar sign and two decimal places. Use the buttons to display the next and previous records. Save the solution, and then start and test the application. Close the Code Editor window and then close the solution.

Lesson A Summary

- To connect an application to a database:

  Use the Data Source Configuration Wizard. To start the wizard, open the Data Sources window by clicking View on the menu bar, pointing to Other Windows, and then clicking Data Sources. Then click Add New Data Source in the Data Sources window.

- To preview the data contained in a dataset:

  Right-click the dataset's name in the Data Sources window, click Preview Data, and then click the Preview button in the Preview Data dialog box.

- To have the computer create a control and then bind an object to it:

  In the Data Sources window, click the object you want to bind. If necessary, use the object's list arrow to change the control type. Drag the object to an empty area on the form, and then release the mouse button.

- To bind an object to an existing control:

  In the Data Sources window, click the object you want to bind. Drag the object to the control on the form, and then release the mouse button. Alternatively, you can click the control on the form and then use the Properties window to set the appropriate property or properties. (Refer to the *Binding to an Existing Control* section in this lesson.)

- To have the columns exactly fill the display area in a DataGridView control:

  Set the DataGridView control's AutoSizeColumnsMode property to Fill.

- To anchor the DataGridView control to the borders of its container:

  Click the Dock in Parent Container option in the DataGridView control's task list. You can also set the DataGridView control's Dock property in the Properties window.

- To handle exceptions (errors) that occur during run time:

  Use the Try...Catch statement.

- To move the record pointer in a dataset during run time:

  You can use a BindingNavigator control. You also can use either the BindingSource object's Position property or one of its Move methods.

- To format the data displayed in a bound label control:

  Click the label control, click the plus box next to the (DataBindings) property in the properties list, click (Advanced), and then click the ... (ellipsis) button to open the Formatting and Advanced Binding dialog box.

Lesson A Key Terms

AutoSizeColumnsMode property—determines the way the column widths are sized in a DataGridView control

Binding—the process of connecting an object in a dataset to a control on a form

BindingNavigator control—can be used to add, delete, and save records and also to move the record pointer from one record to another in a dataset

BindingSource object—connects a DataSet object to the bound controls on a form

Bound controls—the controls connected to an object in a dataset

Cell—the intersection of a row and a column in a DataGridView control

Child table—a table linked to a parent table

Computer database—an electronic file that contains an organized collection of related information

Copy to Output Directory property—a property of a database file; determines both when and if the file is copied from the project folder to the project folder's bin\Debug folder

DataGridView control—displays data in a row and column format

Dataset—a copy of the data (database fields and records) that can be accessed by an application

DataSet object—stores the information you want to access from a database

Exception—an error that occurs while an application is running

Field—a single item of information about a person, place, or thing

Foreign key—the field used to link a child table to a parent table

Move methods—methods of a BindingSource object; used to move the record pointer to the first, last, next, or previous record in a dataset

Parent table—a table linked to a child table

Position property—a property of a BindingSource object; stores the position of the record pointer

Primary key—a field that uniquely identifies each record in a table

Record—a group of related fields that contain all of the necessary data about a specific person, place, or thing

Relational database—a database that stores information in tables composed of columns (fields) and rows (records)

Table—a group of related records

TableAdapter object—connects a database to a DataSet object

TableAdapterManager object—handles saving data to multiple tables in a dataset

Try...Catch statement—used for exception handling in a procedure

Lesson A Review Questions

1. Which of the following objects connects a database to a DataSet object?

   a. BindingSource

   b. DataBase

   c. DataGridView

   d. TableAdapter

2. The _____ property stores an integer that represents the location of the record pointer in a dataset.

   a. BindingNavigator object's Position

   b. BindingSource object's Position

   c. TableAdapter object's Position

   d. none of the above

3. If the record pointer is positioned on record number 7 in a dataset, which of the following will move the record pointer to record number 8?

   a. `TblBooksBindingSource.GoNext()`

   b. `TblBooksBindingSource.Move(8)`

   c. `TblBooksBindingSource.MoveNext()`

   d. `TblBooksBindingSource.PositionNext`

4. A _____ is an organized collection of related information stored in a computer file.

   a. database

   b. dataset

   c. field

   d. record

5. The information in a _____ database is stored in tables.

   a. columnar

   b. relational

   c. sorted

   d. tabular

6. Which of the following objects provides the connection between a DataSet object and a control on a form?

   a. Bound

   b. Binding

   c. BindingSource

   d. Connecting

7. Which of the following statements retrieves data from the Friends database and stores it in the FriendsDataSet?

   a. `Me.FriendsDataSet.Fill(Friends.accdb)`

   b. `Me.TblNamesBindingSource.Fill(Me.FriendsDataSet)`

   c. `Me.TblNamesBindingNavigator.Fill(Me.FriendsDataSet.tblNames)`

   d. `Me.TblNamesTableAdapter.Fill(Me.FriendsDataSet.tblNames)`

8. If an application contains the `Catch ex As Exception` clause, which of the following can be used to access the exception's description?

    a. `ex.Description`   c. `ex.Message`

    b. `ex.Exception`   d. `Exception.Description`

9. If the current record is the ninth record in a dataset that contains 10 records, which of the following statements will position the record pointer on the tenth record?

    a. `TblEmployBindingSource.Position = 9`

    b. `TblEmployBindingSource.Position += 1`

    c. `TblEmployBindingSource.MoveLast()`

    d. all of the above

10. The field that links a child table to a parent table is called the _____ .

    a. foreign key in the child table   c. link key in the parent table

    b. foreign key in the parent table   d. primary key in the child table

11. The process of connecting a control to an object in a dataset is called _____ .

    a. assigning   c. joining

    b. binding   d. none of the above

12. Which of the following is true?

    a. Data stored in a relational database can be retrieved both quickly and easily by the computer.

    b. Data stored in a relational database can be displayed in any order.

    c. A relational database stores data in a column and row format.

    d. all of the above

Lesson A Exercises

INTRODUCTORY

1. In this exercise, you modify one of the Adalene Fashions applications from this lesson. Use Windows to make a copy of the Adalene Solution-Labels folder. Rename the copy Modified Adalene Solution-Labels. Open the Adalene Solution (Adalene Solution.sln) file contained in the Modified Adalene Solution-Labels folder. Modify the btnNext_Click and btnPrevious_Click procedures to use the Position property rather than the MoveNext and MovePrevious methods. Test the application appropriately

INTRODUCTORY

2. Diamond Spa records the ID, name, and price of each of its services in a database named Services. The Services database, which is stored in the VB2015\Chap13\Access Databases\Services.accdb file, contains a table named tblServices. Open the Diamond Solution (Diamond Solution.sln) file contained in the VB2015\Chap13\Diamond Solution-DataGridView folder. Connect the application to the Services database. Change the database file's Copy to Output Directory property to Copy if newer. Bind the table to a DataGridView control, and then make the necessary modifications to the control. Enter the Try... Catch statement in the Save Data button's Click event procedure; include appropriate messages. Test the application appropriately.

3. Diamond Spa records the ID, name, and price of each of its services in a database named Services. The Services database, which is stored in the VB2015\Chap13\ Access Databases\Services.accdb file, contains a table named tblServices. Open the Diamond Solution (Diamond Solution.sln) file contained in the VB2015\Chap13\ Diamond Solution-Labels folder. Connect the application to the Services database. Bind the appropriate objects to the existing label controls. Code the btnNext_Click and btnPrevious_Click procedures. Test the application appropriately.

INTRODUCTORY

4. Open the MusicBox Solution (MusicBox Solution.sln) file contained in the VB2015\ Chap13\MusicBox Solution-DataGridView folder. Connect the application to the MusicBox database. The database, which is stored in the VB2015\Chap13\Access Databases\MusicBox.accdb file, contains a table named tblBox. Change the database file's Copy to Output Directory property to Copy if newer. Bind the table to a DataGridView control, and then make the necessary modifications to the control. Enter the Try...Catch statement in the Save Data button's Click event procedure; include appropriate messages. Test the application appropriately.

INTRODUCTORY

5. Open the MusicBox Solution (MusicBox Solution.sln) file contained in the VB2015\ Chap13\MusicBox Solution-Labels folder. Connect the application to the MusicBox database. The database, which is stored in the VB2015\Chap13\Access Databases\ MusicBox.accdb file, contains a table named tblBox. Bind the appropriate objects to the existing label controls. Code the btnNext_Click and btnPrevious_Click procedures. Test the application appropriately.

INTRODUCTORY

6. Open the MusicBox Solution (MusicBox Solution.sln) file contained in the VB2015\ Chap13\MusicBox Solution-ListBox folder. Connect the application to the MusicBox database. The database, which is stored in the VB2015\Chap13\Access Databases\ MusicBox.accdb file, contains a table named tblBox. Bind the Shape, Source, and Song field objects to the existing label controls. Then set the lstId control's DataSource and DisplayMember properties to TblBoxBindingSource and ID, respectively. Test the application by clicking each entry in the list box.

INTERMEDIATE

7. In this exercise, you modify one of the Adalene Fashions applications from this lesson.

INTERMEDIATE

   a. Use Windows to make a copy of the Adalene Solution-Labels folder. Rename the copy Adalene Solution-ListBox. Open the Adalene Solution (Adalene Solution.sln) file contained in the Adalene Solution-ListBox folder.

   b. Unlock the controls, and then delete the lblStore control from the form. Also delete the Previous Record and Next Record buttons and their Click event procedures.

   c. Add a list box to the form. Change the list box's name to lstStore. Assign an access key to the list box. Make any needed modifications to the interface. Lock the controls, and then set the tab order as appropriate.

   d. Set the lstStore control's DataSource and DisplayMember properties as appropriate. Test the application appropriately.

▌ LESSON B

After studying Lesson B, you should be able to:

- Query a dataset using LINQ
- Customize a BindingNavigator control
- Use the LINQ aggregate operators

Creating a Query

The records in the StoresDataSet from Lesson A can be arranged in any order, such as by store number, city name, and so on. You can also control the number of records you want to view at any one time. You can view all of the records in the StoresDataSet, or you can choose to view only the records for the company-owned stores. You use a **query** to specify both the records to select and the order in which to arrange the records. You can create a query in Visual Basic 2015 using a language feature called **Language-Integrated Query** or, more simply, **LINQ**.

Figure 13-33 shows the basic syntax of LINQ when used to select and arrange records in a dataset. In the syntax, *variableName* and *elementName* can be any names you choose as long as the name follows the naming rules for variables. In other words, there is nothing special about the `records` and `store` names used in the examples. The Where and Order By clauses are optional parts of the syntax. You use the **Where clause**, which contains a *condition*, to limit the records you want to view. Similar to the condition in the If...Then...Else and Do...Loop statements, the condition in a Where clause specifies a requirement that must be met for a record to be selected. The **Order By clause** is used to arrange (sort) the records in either ascending (the default) or descending order by one or more fields.

Ch13B-LINQ

Using LINQ to Select and Arrange Records in a Dataset

<u>Basic syntax</u>
Dim *variableName* = **From** *elementName* **In** *dataset.table*
      [Where *condition***]**
      [Order By *elementName.fieldName1* **[Ascending | Descending]**
            [, *elementName.fieldNameN* **[Ascending | Descending]]]**
      Select *elementName*

<u>Example 1</u>
```
Dim records = From store In StoresDataSet.tblStores
              Select store
```
selects all of the records from the dataset

<u>Example 2</u>
```
Dim records = From store In StoresDataSet.tblStores
              Order By store.Sales
              Select store
```
selects all of the records from the dataset and arranges them in ascending order by the Sales field

---

Figure 13-33   Basic LINQ syntax and examples for selecting and arranging records in a dataset *(continues)*

(continued)

```
Example 3
Dim records = From store In StoresDataSet.tblStores
              Where store.Ownership.ToUpper = "F"
              Select store
selects only the franchisees' records from the dataset


Example 4
Dim records = From store In StoresDataSet.tblStores
              Where store.Sales > 100000
              Select store
selects from the dataset only the records for stores having sales of more than $100,000


Example 5
Dim records = From store In StoresDataSet.tblStores
              Where store.State.ToUpper Like "C*"
              Order By store.City Descending
              Select store
selects from the dataset only the records whose State field begins with the letter C and
arranges them in descending order by the City field
```

Figure 13-33   Basic LINQ syntax and examples for selecting and arranging records in a dataset

Notice that the syntax shown in Figure 13-33 does not require you to specify the data type of the variable in the Dim statement. Instead, the syntax allows the computer to infer the data type from the value being assigned to the variable. However, for this inference to take place, you must set Option Infer to On (rather than to Off, as you have been doing) in the General Declarations section of the Code Editor window.

Figure 13-33 also includes examples of using the LINQ syntax. The statement in Example 1 selects all of the records from the dataset and assigns them to the `records` variable. The statement in Example 2 performs the same task; however, the records are assigned in ascending order by the Sales field. If you are sorting records in ascending order, you do not need to include the keyword `Ascending` in the Order By clause because `Ascending` is the default sort order. The statement in Example 3 assigns only the franchisees' records to the `records` variable. The statement in Example 4 assigns only the records for stores having sales of more than $100,000. The statement in Example 5 uses the Like operator and the asterisk pattern-matching character to select only records whose State field begins with the letter C. (You learned about the Like operator and pattern-matching characters in Chapter 8.) The records are then arranged in descending order by the City field.

The syntax and examples in Figure 13-33 merely assign the selected and/or arranged records to a variable. To actually view the records, you need to assign the variable's contents to the DataSource property of a BindingSource object. The syntax for doing this is shown in Figure 13-34 along with an example of using the syntax. Any control that is bound to the BindingSource object will display the appropriate field(s) when the application is started.

> **Assigning a LINQ Variable's Contents to a BindingSource Object**
>
> Basic syntax
> *bindingSource*.**DataSource** = *variableName*.**AsDataView**
>
> Example
> `TblStoresBindingSource.DataSource = records.AsDataView`
> assigns the contents of the `records` variable (from Figure 13-33) to the TblStoresBindingSource
> object

Figure 13-34 Syntax and an example of assigning a LINQ variable's contents to a BindingSource object

START HERE ▶

To use LINQ to select specific records in the Adalene Fashions application:

1. If necessary, start Visual Studio 2015. Open the Adalene Solution (Adalene Solution.sln) file contained in the VB2015\Chap13\Adalene Solution-LINQ folder. The Find State button in the interface will display records whose State field begins with one or more characters entered by the user.

2. Open the Code Editor window. Replace <your name> and <current date> in the comments with your name and the current date, respectively.

3. The btnFind_Click procedure will use LINQ to select the appropriate records. Therefore, you will change the Option Infer setting from Off to On. Locate the `Option Infer Off` statement, and then change Off to **On**. Press the **Tab** key twice, and then type ' **using LINQ**.

4. Locate the btnFind_Click procedure. The InputBox function prompts the user either to enter the first letter(s) in the state ID or to leave the input area empty. The user's response is converted to uppercase and assigned to the `strState` variable. Click the **blank line** above the procedure's End Sub clause.

5. First, you will enter the LINQ statement to select the appropriate records. The condition in the statement's Where clause will use the Like operator and the asterisk pattern-matching character to compare the contents of each record's State field with the user's entry followed by zero or more characters. Enter the following lines of code:

   Dim records = From store In StoresDataSet.tblStores
            Where store.State.ToUpper Like strState & "*"
            Select store

6. Next, you will display the contents of the `records` variable in the DataGridView control. You do this by assigning the variable to the TblStoresBindingSource object's DataSource property. Enter the following assignment statement:

   TblStoresBindingSource.DataSource = records.AsDataView

Figure 13-35 shows the code entered in the General Declarations section and the btnFind_Click procedure.

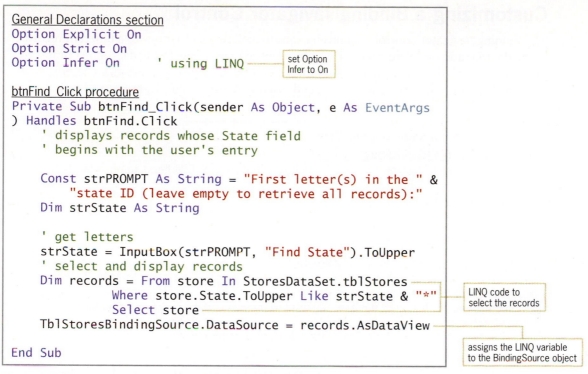

Figure 13-35 Code entered in the General Declarations section and btnFind_Click procedure

To test the btnFind_Click procedure:

START HERE

1. Save the solution and then start the application. The 20 records in the dataset appear in the DataGridView control.

2. Click the **Find State** button. First, you will find all of the records whose State field begins with the letter I. Type **i** and press **Enter**. Three records appear in the DataGridView control: two for Illinois (IL) and one for Indiana (IN). See Figure 13-36.

Figure 13-36 Records whose State field begins with the letter I

3. Next, you will display only the Indiana record. Click the **Find State** button, type **in** and then press **Enter**. The Indiana (IN) record appears in the DataGridView control.

4. Finally, you will display all of the records. Click the **Find State** button and then press **Enter**.

5. You can click a column header to sort the records in order by the associated field. Click **State** to display the records in ascending order by the State field. Now click **State** again to display the records in descending order by the State field.

6. Click the **Exit** button. Close the Code Editor window and then close the solution.

Customizing a BindingNavigator Control

The BindingNavigator control contains buttons that allow you to move to a different record in the dataset, add or delete a record, and save any changes made to the dataset. At times, you may want to include additional items on the control, such as another button, a text box, or a drop-down button. The steps for adding and deleting items are shown in Figure 13-37.

Customizing a BindingNavigator Control

To add an item to a BindingNavigator control:
1. Click the BindingNavigator control's task box, and then click Edit Items to open the Items Collection Editor window.
2. If necessary, click the "Select item and add to list below" arrow.
3. Click the item you want to add to the BindingNavigator control, and then click the Add button.
4. If necessary, you can use the up and down arrows to reposition the item.

To delete an item from a BindingNavigator control:
1. Click the BindingNavigator control's task box, and then click Edit Items to open the Items Collection Editor window.
2. In the Members list, click the item you want to remove and then click the X button.

Figure 13-37 Instructions for customizing a BindingNavigator control

In the following set of steps, you will add a DropDownButton to the BindingNavigator control in the Adalene Fashions application. The DropDownButton will display a menu that contains three options: All Stores, Company-Owned, and Franchisee. The All Stores option will display the total sales for all stores. The Company-Owned and Franchisee options will display the total sales for company-owned stores and franchisees, respectively.

START HERE

To add a DropDownButton to the BindingNavigator control:

1. Open the Adalene Solution (Adalene Solution.sln) file contained in the VB2015\ Chap13\Adalene Solution-Aggregate folder.

2. Click an **empty area** on the TblStoresBindingNavigator control, and then click the control's **task box**.

3. Click **Edit Items** in the task list to open the Items Collection Editor dialog box. Click the **down arrow** in the "Select item and add to list below" box, and then click **DropDownButton** in the list. Click the **Add** button. See Figure 13-38.

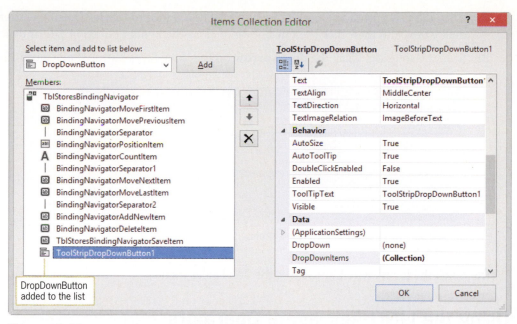

Figure 13-38   Items Collection Editor dialog box

4. Click the **Alphabetical** button to display the property names in alphabetical order. Click **(Name)** in the properties list, and then type **ddbSales** and press **Enter**. Change the DisplayStyle and Text properties to **Text** and **&Total Sales**, respectively.

5. Click **DropDownItems** in the Properties list, and then click the **...** (ellipsis) button. Click the **Add** button to add a menu item to the DropDownButton's menu. Click the **Alphabetical** button to display the property names in alphabetical order. Change the menu item's Name, DisplayStyle, and Text properties to **mnuAll**, **Text**, and **&All Stores**, respectively. See Figure 13-39.

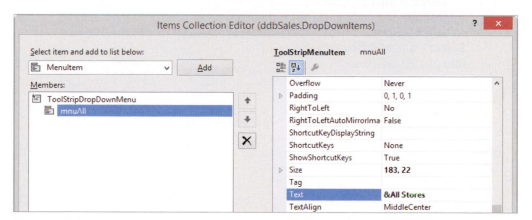

Figure 13-39   First drop-down menu item added to the menu

6. Click the **Add** button to add another menu item to the menu. Change the menu item's Name, DisplayStyle, and Text properties to **mnuCompany**, **Text**, and **&Company-Owned**, respectively.

7. Click the **Add** button once again. Change the menu item's Name, DisplayStyle, and Text properties to **mnuFranchisee**, **Text**, and **&Franchisee**, respectively.

8. Click the **OK** button to close the Items Collection Editor (ddbSales.DropDownItems) dialog box, and then click the **OK** button to close the Items Collection Editor dialog box.

9. Save the solution. Click the **down arrow** on the Total Sales button. See Figure 13-40.

Figure 13-40 DropDownButton's menu

10. Click the form's **title bar** to close the Total Sales menu.

Using the LINQ Aggregate Operators

LINQ provides several aggregate operators—such as Average, Count, Max, Min, and Sum—that you can use when querying a dataset. An **aggregate operator** returns a single value from a group of values. The Sum operator, for example, returns the sum of the values in the group, whereas the Min operator returns the smallest value in the group. You include an aggregate operator in a LINQ statement using the syntax shown in Figure 13-41. The figure also includes examples of using the syntax.

Ch13B-Aggregate

LINQ aggregate operators

Syntax
[**Dim**] *variableName* [**As** *dataType*] =
    Aggregate *elementName* **In** *dataset.table*
    [**Where** *condition*]
    Select *elementName.fieldName*
    Into *aggregateOperator*

Example 1
```
Dim intTotal As Integer =
      Aggregate store In StoresDataSet.tblStores
      Select store.Sales Into Sum
```
calculates the total of the sales amount contained in the dataset and assigns the result to the `intTotal` variable

Example 2
```
Dim intHighestCoOwned As Integer
intHighestCoOwned =
      Aggregate store In StoresDataSet.tblStores
      Where store.Ownership.ToUpper = "C"
      Select store.Sales Into Max
```
finds the highest sales amount for a company-owned store and assigns the result to the `intHighestCoOwned` variable

---

Figure 13-41 Syntax and examples of the LINQ aggregate operators *(continues)*

(continued)

Example 3
```
Dim dblAvg As Double =
      Aggregate store In StoresDataSet.tblStores
      Where store.State.ToUpper = "GA"
      Select store.Sales Into Average
```
calculates the average of the sales amounts for stores in Georgia and assigns the result to the dblAvg variable

Example 4
```
Dim intCounter As Integer =
      Aggregate store In StoresDataSet.tblStores
      Where store.City.ToUpper = "CHICAGO"
      Into Count
```
counts the number of stores in the city of Chicago and assigns the result to the intCounter variable (The Count operator is the only operator that does not need the Select clause.)

Figure 13-41   Syntax and examples of the LINQ aggregate operators

START HERE

To use the Sum aggregate operator to code the DropDownButton's menu items:

1. Open the Code Editor window. Replace <your name> and <current date> in the comments with your name and the current date, respectively.

2. Open the code templates for the mnuAll_Click, mnuCompany_Click, and mnuFranchisee_Click procedures. Type the three comments, three Dim statements, and three MessageBox.Show methods shown in Figure 13-42.

```
Private Sub mnuAll_Click(sender As Object, e As EventArgs
) Handles mnuAll.Click
    ' displays the total sales for all stores

    Dim intTotal As Integer =
        Aggregate store In StoresDataSet.tblStores
        Select store.Sales Into Sum

    MessageBox.Show("Total sales for all stores: " &
                    intTotal.ToString("C0"),
                    "Adalene Fashions",
                    MessageBoxButtons.OK,
                    MessageBoxIcon.Information)
End Sub

Private Sub mnuCompany_Click(sender As Object, e As EventArgs
) Handles mnuCompany.Click
    ' displays the total sales for company-owned stores

    Dim intTotal As Integer =
        Aggregate store In StoresDataSet.tblStores
        Where store.Ownership.ToUpper = "C"
        Select store.Sales Into Sum
```

Figure 13-42   Completed Click event procedures for the three menu items *(continues)*

(continued)

```
        MessageBox.Show("Total sales for company-owned stores: " &
                        intTotal.ToString("C0"),
                        "Adalene Fashions",
                        MessageBoxButtons.OK,
                        MessageBoxIcon.Information)
    End Sub

    Private Sub mnuFranchisee_Click(sender As Object, e As EventArgs
    ) Handles mnuFranchisee.Click
        ' displays the total sales for franchisees

        Dim intTotal As Integer =
            Aggregate store In StoresDataSet.tblStores
            Where store.Ownership.ToUpper = "F"
            Select store.Sales Into Sum

        MessageBox.Show("Total sales for franchisees: " &
                        intTotal.ToString("C0"),
                        "Adalene Fashions",
                        MessageBoxButtons.OK,
                        MessageBoxIcon.Information)
    End Sub
```

Figure 13-42 Completed Click event procedures for the three menu items

Note: Instead of using the Dim statement to both declare and assign a LINQ value to a variable, you can declare the variable in the Dim statement and then use an assignment statement to assign the LINQ value to it. For example, you can replace the Dim statement in the mnuAll_Click procedure in Figure 13-42 with the following two statements:

```
Dim intTotal As Integer
intTotal =
    Aggregate store In StoresDataSet.tblStores
    Select store.Sales Into Sum
```

START HERE

To test the code in each menu item's Click event procedure:

1. Save the solution and then start the application. Click the **down arrow** on the Total Sales button and then click **All Stores** (or you can press **Alt+t** and then type the letter **a**). The total sales for all stores appears in a message box. See Figure 13-43.

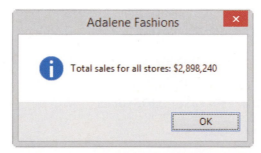

Figure 13-43 Message box showing the total sales for all stores

2. Close the message box. On your own, display the total sales for company-owned stores and for franchisees; the total sales amounts should be $2,036,500 and $861,740, respectively.

3. Close the message box and then stop the application. Close the Code Editor window and then close the solution.

Lesson B Summary

- To use LINQ (with Option Infer set to On) to select and arrange records in a dataset:

  Use the following syntax:

  ```
  Dim variableName = From elementName In dataset.table
      [Where condition]
      [Order By elementName.fieldName1 [Ascending | Descending]
      [, elementName.fieldNameN [Ascending | Descending]]]
      Select elementName
  ```

- To assign a LINQ variable's contents to a BindingSource object:

  Use the following syntax: *bindingSource*.**DataSource** = *variableName*.**AsDataView**

- To either add items to or delete items from a BindingNavigator control:

  Follow the instructions shown in Figure 13-37 in this chapter.

- To use the LINQ aggregate operators:

  Use the following syntax:

  ```
  [Dim] variableName [As dataType] =
      Aggregate elementName In dataset.table
      [Where condition]
      Select elementName.fieldName
      Into aggregateOperator
  ```

Lesson B Key Terms

Aggregate operator—an operator that returns a single value from a group of values; LINQ provides the Average, Count, Max, Min, and Sum aggregate operators

Language-Integrated Query—LINQ; the query language built into Visual Basic 2015

LINQ—an acronym for Language-Integrated Query

Order By clause—used in LINQ to arrange the records in a dataset

Query—specifies the records to select in a dataset and the order in which to arrange the records

Where clause—used in LINQ to limit the records you want to view in a dataset

Lesson B Review Questions

1. Which of the following will select only records whose City field begins with the letter L?

   a. ```
      Dim records = From StoresDataSet.tblStores
          Select City.ToUpper Like "L*"
      ```
   b. ```
      Dim records = From tblStores
          Where tblStores.City.ToUpper Like "L*"
          Select city
      ```
   c. ```
      Dim records =
          From store In StoresDataSet.tblStores
          Where store.City.ToUpper Like "L*"
          Select store
      ```
   d. ```
      Dim records =
          From store In StoresDataSet.tblStores
          Where tblStores.City.ToUpper Like "L*"
          Select store
      ```

2. Which of the following calculates the average of the values stored in a numeric field named Population?

   a. ```
      Dim dblAvg As Double =
          Aggregate city In CitiesDataSet.tblCities
          Select city.Population
          Into Average
      ```
   b. ```
      Dim dblAvg As Double =
          From city In CitiesDataSet.tblCities
          Select city.Population
          Into Average
      ```
   c. ```
      Dim dblAvg As Double =
          From city In CitiesDataSet.tblCities
          Aggregate city.Population
          Into Average
      ```
   d. ```
      Dim dblAvg As Double =
          From city In CitiesDataSet.tblCities
          Average city.Population
      ```

3. Which of the following statements selects all of the records in the tblCities table?

   a. ```
      Dim records =
          From city In CitiesDataSet.tblCities
          Select All city
      ```
   b. ```
      Dim records =
          From city In CitiesDataSet.tblCities
          Select city
      ```
   c. ```
      Dim records =
          Select city From CitiesDataSet.tblCities
      ```
   d. ```
      Dim records = From CitiesDataSet.tblCities
          Select tblCities.city
      ```

4. The tblInventory table contains a numeric field named InStock. Which of the following statements selects all records having at least 500 of the item in stock?

a. ```
Dim records =
    From item In InventoryDataSet.tblInventory
    Where item >= 500
    Select item.InStock
```

b. ```
Dim records =
    From item In InventoryDataSet.tblInventory
    Select item.InStock >= 500
```

c. ```
Dim records =
    From item In InventoryDataSet.tblInventory
    Where item.InStock >= 500
    Select item
```

d. ```
Dim records =
    Select item.InStock >= 500
    From tblInventory
```

5. The tblInventory table contains a numeric field named InStock. Which of the following statements calculates the total of the items in inventory?

a. ```
Dim intTotal As Integer =
    Aggregate item In InventoryDataSet.tblInventory
    Select item.InStock
    Into Sum
```

b. ```
Dim intTotal As Integer =
    Sum item In InventoryDataSet.tblInventory
    Select item.InStock
    Into Total
```

c. ```
Dim intTotal As Integer =
    Aggregate InventoryDataSet.tblInventory.item
    Select item.InStock
    Into Sum
```

d. ```
Dim intTotal As Integer =
    Sum item In InventoryDataSet.tblInventory.InStock
```

6. In a LINQ statement, which clause limits the records that will be selected?

a. Limit   c. Select

b. Order By   d. Where

Lesson B Exercises

1. The tblBooks table contains five fields. The BookNum, Price, and QuantityInStock fields are numeric; the Title and Author fields contain text. The dataset's name is BooksDataSet.

   INTRODUCTORY

   a. Write a LINQ statement that arranges the records in ascending order by the Author field.
   b. Write a LINQ statement that selects records having a price of at least $12.75.
   c. Write a LINQ statement that selects records having more than 100 books in inventory.
   d. Write a LINQ statement that selects the books written by George Marten and arranges the books in descending order by the book's price.

2. In this exercise, you modify one of the Adalene Fashions applications from this lesson. Use Windows to make a copy of the Adalene Solution-Aggregate folder. Rename the copy Modified Adalene Solution-Aggregate. Open the Adalene Solution (Adalene Solution.sln) file contained in the Modified Adalene Solution-Aggregate folder. Add a DropDownButton to the TblStoresBindingNavigator control. Change the DropDownButton's name to ddbOwned. Change its DisplayStyle and Text properties to Text and &Owned, respectively. Use the DropDownItems property to add two menu items to the DropDownButton's menu: Company-Owned and Franchisee. Be sure to change each menu item's name as well as its DisplayStyle and Text properties. The Company-Owned menu item should display (in a message box) the number of company-owned stores; the Franchisee menu item should display (in a message box) the number of franchisees. Code each menu item's Click event procedure. Test the application appropriately.

3. Open the Magazine Solution (Magazine Solution.sln) file contained in the VB2015\ Chap13\Magazine Solution-Introductory folder. The application is connected to the Magazines database, which is stored in the Magazines.accdb file. The database contains a table named tblMagazine. The table's Cost field is numeric; its Code and MagName fields contain text. Start the application to view the records contained in the dataset, and then stop the application. Open the Code Editor window. The btnCode_Click procedure should display the record whose Code field exactly matches the user's entry. The btnName_Click procedure should display the records whose MagName field begins with the one or more characters entered by the user. The btnAll_Click procedure should display all of the records. Code the procedures and then test the application appropriately.

4. The tblCds table contains three fields. The CdNum and Price fields are numeric; the Title field contains text. The dataset's name is CdsDataSet. Write a LINQ statement that selects records having titles that begin with the word "The" (in either uppercase or lowercase). Then write a LINQ statement that calculates the average price of a CD.

5. Open the Magazine Solution (Magazine Solution.sln) file contained in the VB2015\ Chap13\Magazine Solution-Intermediate folder. The application is connected to the Magazines database, which is stored in the Magazines.accdb file. The database contains a table named tblMagazine. The table's Cost field is numeric; its Code and MagName fields contain text. Start the application to view the records contained in the dataset, and then stop the application. Open the Code Editor window. Code the btnAll_Click procedure so that it displays all of the records. Code the btnCost_Click procedure so that it displays records having a cost equal to or greater than the amount entered by the user. Code the btnAverage_Click procedure so that it displays (in a message box) the average cost of a magazine. Test the application appropriately.

6. Open the MusicBox Solution (MusicBox Solution.sln) file contained in the VB2015\ Chap13\MusicBox Solution-LINQ folder. The application is connected to the MusicBox database, which is stored in the MusicBox.accdb file. The tblBox table in the database contains four text fields. Start the application to view the records contained in the dataset, and then stop the application. Open the Code Editor window. Code the btnAll_Click procedure so that it displays all of the records. Code the btnShape_Click procedure so that it displays the records for music boxes having the shape selected by the user. Code the btnSource_Click procedure so that it displays the records for music boxes either received as gifts or purchased by the user. Code the btnCount_Click procedure to display the number of music boxes in the dataset. Test the application appropriately.

LESSON C

After studying Lesson C, you should be able to:

- Prevent the user from adding and deleting records
- Remove buttons from a BindingNavigator control
- Add a label, a text box, and a button to a BindingNavigator control

Completing the Games Galore Application

Your task in this chapter is to create an application for the Games Galore store, which sells new and used video games. The video game information is contained in a Microsoft Access database named Games. The Games database is stored in the Games.accdb file and contains one table named tblGames. The table has seven fields and 35 records. Figure 13-44 shows only the first 10 records. The ID, Price, and Quantity fields are numeric; the remaining fields contain text.

ID	Title	Platform	Rating	Price	NewUsed	Quantity
1	Dead Space	XB	M	$59.99	N	5
2	Dead Space	PS	M	$59.99	N	4
3	Just Dance	WII	E10+	$37.50	N	3
4	Just Dance	XB	E10+	$37.35	N	4
5	Just Dance	PS	E10+	$34.39	N	4
6	Call of Duty: Black Ops II	XB	M	$49.44	N	2
7	Call of Duty: Black Ops II	PS	M	$52.43	N	2
8	Halo	XB	M	$39.99	N	2
9	Halo	XB	M	$33.55	U	1
10	LEGO Batman: DC Super Heroes	WII	E10+	$19.99	N	4

Figure 13-44 First 10 records in the tblGames table

The Games Galore application will display the records in a DataGridView control. It will also allow the store manager to display only the games for a specific platform (Xbox, PlayStation, or Wii) as well as the total value of the games in the store.

To begin modifying the Games Galore application:

START HERE

1. If necessary, start Visual Studio 2015. Open the VB2015\Chap13\Games Solution (Games Solution.sln) file.

2. In this application, the user will not be allowed to add, edit, or delete records. If necessary, click the **TblGamesDataGridView** control to select it. Click the control's **task box** to open its task list. Deselect the **Enable Adding**, **Enable Editing**, and **Enable Deleting** check boxes. Click the form's **title bar** to close the task list.

3. Click the **TblGamesBindingNavigator** control, and then click its **task box**. Click **Edit Items** on the task list. Click **BindingNavigatorAddNewItem** in the Members list, and then click the **X** button to remove the item from the list. This also removes the Add new button (the plus sign) from the TblGamesBindingNavigator control.

4. The BindingNavigatorDeleteItem member should be selected in the Members list. Click the **X** button to remove the item from the list. This also removes the Delete button (the letter *X*) from the TblGamesBindingNavigator control.

5. Click the **X** button again to remove the TblGamesBindingNavigatorSaveItem member. This also removes the Save Data button (the disk) from the TblGamesBindingNavigator control.

6. Next, you will add a label and a text box for entering the platform designation. Click the **down arrow** in the "Select item and add to list below" box, and then click **Label** in the list. Click the **Add** button. Click the **Alphabetical** button to display the property names in alphabetical order. Click **Text** in the properties list (if necessary), and then type **&Platform:** and press **Enter**.

7. Click the **down arrow** in the "Select item and add to list below" box, and then click **TextBox** in the list. Click the **Add** button. Change the text box's name to **txtPlatform**.

8. Next, you will add a button that, when clicked, will display the games whose platform designation is entered in the text box. Click the **down arrow** in the "Select item and add to list below" box, and then click **Button** in the list. Click the **Add** button. Change the button's name to **btnGo**. Also change its DisplayStyle and Text properties to **Text** and **&Go**, respectively.

9. Finally, you will add a button for displaying the total value of the games. Click the **Add** button again to add another button to the BindingNavigator control. Change the button's name to **btnTotal**. Also change its DisplayStyle and Text properties to **Text** and **&Total Value**, respectively. See Figure 13-45.

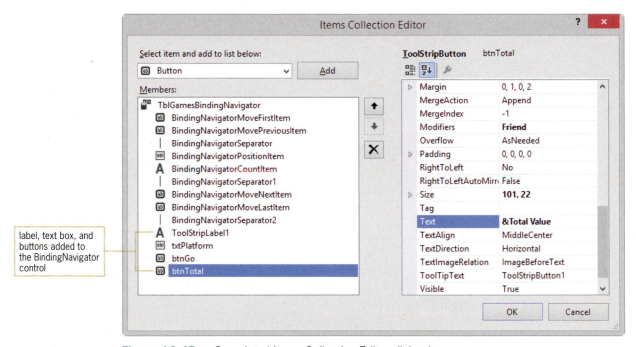

Figure 13-45   Completed Items Collection Editor dialog box

10. Click the **OK** button to close the dialog box, and then click the form's **title bar**. See Figure 13-46.

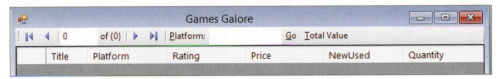

Figure 13-46 Completed TblGamesBindingNavigator control

Coding the Games Galore Application

The btnGo_Click procedure should display only records whose Platform field begins with the one or more characters entered in the txtPlatform control. If the text box is empty, the procedure should display all of the records.

To code and then test the btnGo_Click procedure:

START HERE

1. Open the Code Editor window. Replace <your name> and <current date> in the comments with your name and the current date, respectively.

2. Delete the TblGamesBindingNavigatorSaveItem_Click procedure.

3. Open the code template for the btnGo_Click procedure. Type the comment and code shown in Figure 13-47.

```
Private Sub btnGo_Click(sender As Object, e As EventArgs) Ha
        ' display records for a specific platform

    Dim records = From game In GamesDataSet.tblGames
                  Where game.Platform.ToUpper Like
                     txtPlatform.Text.ToUpper & "*"
                  Select game
    TblGamesBindingSource.DataSource = records.AsDataView

End Sub
```

Figure 13-47 btnGo_Click procedure

4. Save the solution and then start the application. The 35 records appear in the DataGridView control.

5. Click the **Platform** text box (or press **Alt+p**), and then type the letter **w**. Click the **Go** button (or press **Alt+g**). The DataGridView control shows only the seven games for the Wii. See Figure 13-48.

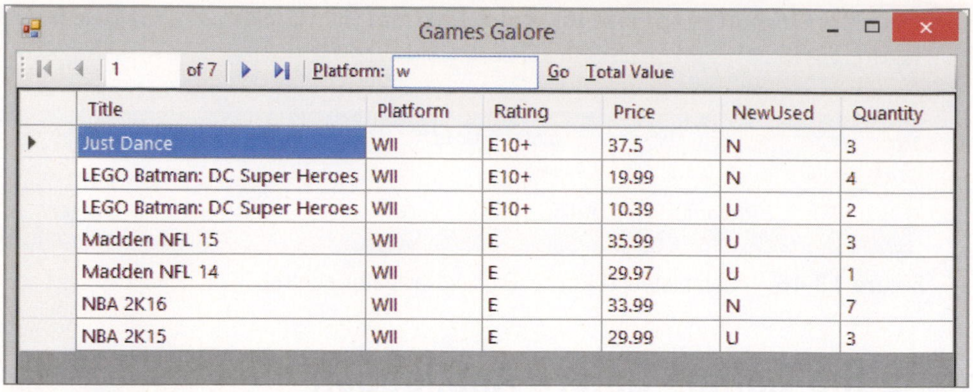

Title	Platform	Rating	Price	NewUsed	Quantity
Just Dance	WII	E10+	37.5	N	3
LEGO Batman: DC Super Heroes	WII	E10+	19.99	N	4
LEGO Batman: DC Super Heroes	WII	E10+	10.39	U	2
Madden NFL 15	WII	E	35.99	U	3
Madden NFL 14	WII	E	29.97	U	1
NBA 2K16	WII	E	33.99	N	7
NBA 2K15	WII	E	29.99	U	3

Figure 13-48 Games for the Wii

6. Delete the letter w from the Platform text box, and then click the **Go** button. The 35 records appear in the DataGridView control.
7. Click the **Close** button on the form's title bar to stop the application.

The btnTotal_Click procedure should display the total value of the games in the store. The total value is calculated by multiplying the value in each game's Quantity field by the value in its Price field, using the Sum aggregate operator to accumulate the results.

START HERE

To code and then test the btnTotal_Click procedure:

1. Open the code template for the btnTotal_Click procedure. Type the comment and code shown in Figure 13-49.

```
Private Sub btnTotal_Click(sender As Object, e As EventArgs
    ' display the total value of the games

    Dim dblTotal As Double =
        Aggregate game In GamesDataSet.tblGames
        Select game.Quantity * game.Price
        Into Sum

    MessageBox.Show("Total value: " &
                    dblTotal.ToString("C2"),
                    "Games Galore",
                    MessageBoxButtons.OK,
                    MessageBoxIcon.Information)

End Sub
```

Figure 13-49 btnTotal_Click procedure

2. Save the solution and then start the application. Click the **Total Value** button (or press **Alt+t**). The total value of the games appears in a message box. See Figure 13-50.

Figure 13-50   Message box showing the total value of the games

3. Close the message box and then stop the application. Close the Code Editor window and then close the solution.

Lesson C Summary

- To prevent the user from adding, editing, or deleting records in a DataGridView control:

  Click the DataGridView control's task box, and then deselect the Enable Adding, Enable Editing, and Enable Deleting check boxes.

- To delete items from a BindingNavigator control:

  Click the BindingNavigator control's task box, and then click Edit Items. In the Members list, click the item you want to remove. Click the X button.

- To add controls to a BindingNavigator control:

  Click the BindingNavigator control's task box, and then click Edit Items. Use the "Select item and add to list below" box and the Add button to add the appropriate control.

Lesson C Key Terms

There are no key terms in Lesson C.

Lesson C Review Questions

1. The Enable Deleting check box in a _____ control's task list determines whether a record can be deleted from the control.

   a. BindingNavigator

   b. BindingSource

   c. DataBindingNavigator

   d. DataGridView

2. The tblBooks table in the Books database contains a numeric field named BookNumber. Which of the following will select book number 401 from the BooksDataSet?

   a. ```
   Dim records = From book In BooksDataSet.tblBooks
       Where book.BookNumber = "401" Select book
   ```

   b. ```
   Dim records = From book In BooksDataSet.tblBooks
       Select book.BookNumber = 401
   ```

c. Dim records = From book In BooksDataSet.tblBooks
     Where book.BookNumber = 401
     Select book

d. Dim records = From book In BooksDataSet.tblBooks
     Select BookNumber = 401

3. Which of the following determines the number of records in the BooksDataSet?

a. Dim intNum As Integer =
     Aggregate book In BooksDataSet.tblBooks
     In Counter

b. Dim intNum As Integer =
     Aggregate book In BooksDataSet.tblBooks
     Into Count

c. Dim intNum As Integer =
     Aggregate book In BooksDataSet.tblBooks
     Into Sum

d. Dim intNum As Integer =
     Aggregate book In BooksDataSet.tblBooks
     Into Total

4. The tblBooks table in the Books database contains a numeric field named Quantity. Which of the following determines the total number of books in the BooksDataSet?

a. Dim intNumBooks As Integer =
         Aggregate book In BooksDataSet.tblBooks
         Into Count

b. Dim intNumBooks As Integer =
         Aggregate book In BooksDataSet.tblBooks
         Select book.Quantity
         Into Sum

c. Dim intNumBooks As Integer =
         Aggregate book In BooksDataSet.tblBooks
         Into Sum

d. Dim intNumBooks As Integer =
         Aggregate book In BooksDataSet.tblBooks
         Into Total

5. The tblBooks table in the Books database contains a numeric field named Price. Which of the following determines the number of books whose price is at least $20? The dataset's name is BooksDataSet.

a. Dim intNum As Integer =
         Aggregate book In BooksDataSet.tblBooks
         Where book.Price > 20
         Into Count

b. Dim intNum As Integer =
         Aggregate book In BooksDataSet.tblBooks
         Where book.Price >= 20
         Into Sum

```
c.  Dim intNum As Integer =
        Aggregate book In BooksDataSet.tblBooks
        Where book.Price >= 20
        Select book
d.  Dim intNum As Integer =
        Aggregate book In BooksDataSet.tblBooks
        Where book.Price >= 20
        Into Count
```

Lesson C Exercises

1. In this exercise, you modify the Games Galore application from this lesson. Use Windows to make a copy of the Games Solution folder. Rename the copy Games Solution-Rating. Open the Games Solution (Games Solution.sln) file contained in the VB2015\Chap13\Games Solution-Rating folder. Add a DropDownButton to the TblGamesBindingNavigator. The DropDownButton should allow the user to display only the games for a specific rating: M, E10+, T, or E. The ratings are stored in the Rating field. (The M, E10+, T, and E stand for Mature, Everyone 10 and over, Teen, and Everyone, respectively.) Test the application appropriately.

INTRODUCTORY

2. In this exercise, you modify the Games Galore application from this lesson. Use Windows to make a copy of the Games Solution folder. Rename the copy Games Solution-NewUsed. Open the Games Solution (Games Solution.sln) file contained in the VB2015\Chap13\Games Solution-NewUsed folder. Add a DropDownButton to the TblGamesBindingNavigator. The DropDownButton should allow the user to display either new games or used games. The game's status (new or used) is stored in its NewUsed field. Test the application appropriately.

INTRODUCTORY

3. In this exercise, you modify the Games Galore application from this lesson. Use Windows to make a copy of the Games Solution folder. Rename the copy Games Solution-TotalGames. Open the Games Solution (Games Solution.sln) file contained in the VB2015\Chap13\Games Solution-TotalGames folder. Add a button to the TblGamesBindingNavigator. The button should display three values in a message box: the number of new games available for sale, the number of used games available for sale, and the total number of games available for sale. The quantity of each game is stored in its Quantity field. Test the application appropriately.

INTRODUCTORY

4. Open the Playhouse Solution (Playhouse Solution.sln) file contained in the VB2015\Chap13\Playhouse Solution folder. Connect the application to a Microsoft Access database named Play. The database is stored in the VB2015\Chap13\Access Databases\Play.accdb file. The database contains one table named tblReservations. Each record has three fields: a numeric field named Seat and two text fields named Patron and Phone. The application should display the contents of the Play database in a DataGridView control. It should also allow the user to add, delete, modify, and save records. Enter the Try...Catch statement in the Save Data button's Click event procedure. Test the application appropriately.

INTRODUCTORY

5. Open the Sports Action Solution (Sports Action Solution.sln) file contained in the VB2015\Chap13\Sports Action Solution folder. Connect the application to a Microsoft Access database named Sports. The database is stored in the VB2015\Chap13\Access Databases\Sports.accdb file. The database contains one table named tblScores. Each

INTRODUCTORY

record has five fields that store the following information: a unique number that identifies the game, the date the game was played, the name of the opposing team, the home team's score, and the opposing team's score. The application should display each record contained in the Sports database, one at a time, in label controls. (Hint: First, change each field object's control type to Label in the Data Sources window. Then, change the table object's control type to Details before dragging it to the form.) The user should not be allowed to add, delete, edit, or save records. Include a button on a BindingNavigator control to allow the user to display the average of the home team's scores. Code the application and then test it appropriately.

INTERMEDIATE ▶   6.   In this exercise, you use a Microsoft Access database named Courses. The database is stored in the VB2015\Chap13\Access Databases\Courses.accdb file. The database contains one table named tblCourses. Each record has the following four fields: ID, Title, CreditHours, and Grade. The CreditHours field is numeric; the other fields contain text.

    a. Open the Courses Solution (Courses Solution.sln) file contained in the VB2015\Chap13\Courses Solution folder. Connect the application to the Courses database. Drag the table into the group box control, and then dock the DataGridView control in its parent container. (In this case, the parent container is the group box control.) Use the task list to disable Adding, Editing, and Deleting. Change the DataGridView control's AutoSizeColumnsMode property to Fill. Change its RowHeadersVisible and Enabled properties to False. Also change its SelectionMode property to FullRowSelect.

    b. Remove the BindingNavigator control from the form by deleting the BindingNavigator object from the component tray.

    c. Open the Code Editor window. Delete the Save Data button's Click event procedure. Code the btnNext_Click and btnPrevious_Click procedures. Code the btnDisplay_Click procedure to display either all the records or only the records matching a specific grade. Test the application appropriately.

INTERMEDIATE ▶   7.   In this exercise, you use a Microsoft Access database named Trips. The database, which is stored in the VB2015\Chap13\Access Databases\Trips.accdb file, keeps track of a person's business and pleasure trips. The database contains one table named tblTrips. Each record has the following four text fields: TripDate, Origin, Destination, BusinessPleasure. The user should be able to display the number of trips from a specific origin to a specific destination, such as from Chicago to Atlanta. He or she should also be able to display the total number of business trips and the total number of pleasure trips.

    a. Create an application, using the following names for the solution and project, respectively: Trips Solution and Trips Project. Save the application in the VB2015\Chap13 folder.

    b. Connect the application to the Trips database, and then drag the tblTrips object to the form. Make the appropriate modifications to the DataGridView control. The user should not be able to add, edit, delete, or save records.

    c. Code the application. (Hint: You can use a logical operator in the Where clause.) Use the application to answer the following questions:

        How many trips were made from Chicago to Nashville?

        How many trips were made from Atlanta to Los Angeles?

        How many business trips were taken?

        How many pleasure trips were taken?

8. In this exercise, you use a Microsoft Access database named Calories. The database, which is stored in the VB2015\Chap13\Access Databases\Calories.accdb file, keeps track of the calories consumed during the day. The database contains one table named tblCalories. Each record has the following six fields: Day, Breakfast, Lunch, Dinner, Dessert, and Snack. The Day field is a text field; the other fields are numeric. The user should be able to display the total number of calories consumed in the entire dataset. He or she should also be able to display the total calories consumed for a specific meal, such as the total calories consumed for breakfasts, lunches, dinners, desserts, or snacks. In addition, the user should be able to display the total calories consumed on a specific day, the number of days in which more than 1,200 calories were consumed, and the average number of calories consumed per day. ADVANCED

   a. Create an application, using the following names for the solution and project, respectively: Calorie Counter Solution and Calorie Counter Project. Save the application in the VB2015\Chap13 folder.

   b. Connect the application to the Calories database, and then drag the tblCalories object to the form. Make the appropriate modifications to the DataGridView control. The user should not be able to add, edit, delete, or save records.

   c. Code the application. Use the application to answer the following questions:
   How many calories were consumed in the entire dataset?
   How many calories were consumed for desserts?
   How many calories were consumed on 12/21/2017?
   On how many days were more than 1,200 calories consumed?
   What is the average number of calories consumed per day?

9. In this exercise, you modify the College Courses application from Exercise 6. Use Windows to make a copy of the Courses Solution folder. Rename the copy Modified Courses Solution. Open the Courses Solution (Courses Solution.sln) file contained in the Modified Courses Solution folder. Add a Calculate GPA button to the form. Code the button's Click event procedure so that it displays the student's GPA. (An A grade is worth 4 points, a B is worth 3 points, and so on.) Display the GPA in a message box. Test the application appropriately. ADVANCED

10. Open the VB2015\Chap13\Debug Solution\Debug Solution (Debug Solution.sln) file. The application is connected to the Friends database stored in the Friends.accdb file. The database contains one table named tblFriends. The table contains nine records. Open the Code Editor window and review the existing code. Correct the code to remove the jagged line that appears below one of the lines of code. Save the solution and then start the application. Click the Fill button, and then click the Next and Previous buttons. Notice that the application is not working correctly. Correct the application's code, and then test it appropriately. SWAT THE BUGS

Access Databases and SQL

Creating the Oscar Winners Application

In this chapter, you will create the Oscar Winners application, which uses a Microsoft Access database named Oscars. The database keeps track of the annual Oscar winners in the following four categories: Actor in a Leading Role, Actress in a Leading Role, Best Picture, and Animated Feature Film. The application will display the records in a DataGridView control, which you learned about in Chapter 13. It will also allow the user to both add records to and delete records from the database.

Previewing the Oscar Winners Application

Before you start the first lesson in this chapter, you will preview the completed application contained in the VB2015\Chap14 folder.

START HERE

To preview the completed application:

1. Use Windows to locate and then open the VB2015\Chap14 folder on your computer's hard disk or on the device designated by your instructor. Right-click **Oscars (Oscars.exe)** in the list of filenames and then click **Open**. Eight records appear in a DataGridView control. As Figure 14-1 indicates, the record for the year 2010 is missing.

the record for year 2010 is missing

Figure 14-1   Oscar Winners application

2. Click the **Year** box in the Add new record section of the interface. Type **2010** and press **Tab**. Type **Jeff Bridges**, **Sandra Bullock**, **The Hurt Locker**, and **Up** in the Actor, Actress, Picture, and Animated boxes, respectively. Click the **Add** button. The record you added appears in numerical order by the year. See Figure 14-2.

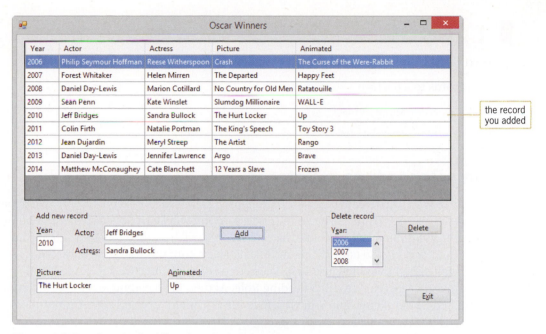

Figure 14-2   Result of adding the missing record

3. Next, you'll verify that the record was saved to the database. Click the **Exit** button to end the application, and then run the Oscars (Oscars.exe) file again. The record for the year 2010 appears in the DataGridView control.

4. Now, you'll delete the record. Click **2010** in the first column of the DataGridView control; doing this highlights (selects) the entire record. It also selects the 2010 value in the Delete record section's list box. Click the **Delete** button. The "Delete record for year 2010?" message appears in a message box. Click the **Yes** button to delete the record. The computer removes the record from the DataGridView control, the dataset, and the database.

5. Click **2009** in the first column of the DataGridView control, and then click the **Delete** button. This time, click the **No** button in the Confirm Delete message box. The record remains in the DataGridView control, the dataset, and the database.

6. Click the **Exit** button to end the application, and then run the Oscars (Oscars.exe) file again. Notice that the 2010 record, which you deleted in Step 4, does not appear in the DataGridView control.

7. Click the **Exit** button.

In Lesson A, you will learn how to add records to a dataset, delete records from a dataset, and sort the records in a dataset. You will also learn how to save (to a database) the changes made to a dataset. Lessons B and C cover SQL, which stands for Structured Query Language. You will create the Oscar Winners application in Lesson C. Be sure to complete each lesson in full and do all of the end-of-lesson questions and several exercises before continuing to the next lesson.

▌ LESSON A

After studying Lesson A, you should be able to:

- Add records to a dataset

- Delete records from a dataset

- Sort the records in a dataset

Adding Records to a Dataset

In Chapter 13, you learned how to use a BindingNavigator control to add records to a dataset and also delete records from a dataset. In this lesson, you will learn how to perform both tasks without using a BindingNavigator control. The records will be added to and deleted from a Microsoft Access database named Oscars. The database contains one table named tblOscars. The table, which is shown in Figure 14-3, keeps track of the annual Oscar winners in the following four categories: Actor in a Leading Role, Actress in a Leading Role, Best Picture, and Animated Feature Film. The YearWon field is the primary key and contains numbers; the remaining fields contain text.

YearWon	Actor	Actress	Picture	Animated
2006	Philip Seymour Hoffman	Reese Witherspoon	Crash	The Curse of the Were-Rabbit
2007	Forest Whitaker	Helen Mirren	The Departed	Happy Feet
2008	Daniel Day-Lewis	Marion Cotillard	No Country for Old Men	Ratatouille
2009	Sean Penn	Kate Winslet	Slumdog Millionaire	WALL-E
2010	Jeff Bridges	Sandra Bullock	The Hurt Locker	Up
2011	Colin Firth	Natalie Portman	The King's Speech	Toy Story 3
2012	Jean Dujardin	Meryl Streep	The Artist	Rango
2013	Daniel Day-Lewis	Jennifer Lawrence	Argo	Brave
2014	Matthew McConaughey	Cate Blanchett	12 Years a Slave	Frozen

Figure 14-3   Data contained in the tblOscars table

START HERE

To open the Oscar Winners application:

1. If necessary, start Visual Studio 2015. Open the VB2015\Chap14\Oscars Solution\ Oscars Solution (Oscars Solution.sln) file. The Oscar Winners application is already connected to the Oscars database, and the Oscars.accdb file's Copy to Output Directory property is set to Copy if newer.

2. Start the application. The lstDeleteYear control is bound to the YearWon field in the dataset. This is accomplished by setting the control's DataSource and DisplayMember properties to TblOscarsBindingSource and YearWon, respectively. The text boxes in the interface are named txtAddYear, txtActor, txtActress, txtPicture, and txtAnimated. See Figure 14-4.

Figure 14-4   Records displayed in the TblOscarsDataGridView control

3. Press the **down arrow** key on your keyboard, slowly, several times. Each time the highlight moves to a different row in the DataGridView control, the value in the current row's YearWon field is highlighted in the lstDeleteYear control.

4. Click the **Exit** button to end the application.

The btnAdd_Click procedure should add the record entered in the five text boxes to the OscarsDataSet. Visual Basic provides several ways of adding records to a dataset. In this lesson, you will use the syntax shown in Figure 14-5. The figure also includes examples of using the syntax.

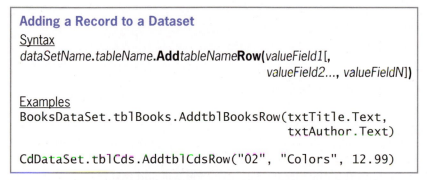

Adding a Record to a Dataset

Syntax
dataSetName.*tableName*.**Add***tableName***Row**(*valueField1*[,
                                    valueField2..., valueFieldN])

Examples
```
BooksDataSet.tblBooks.AddtblBooksRow(txtTitle.Text,
                              txtAuthor.Text)

CdDataSet.tblCds.AddtblCdsRow("02", "Colors", 12.99)
```

Figure 14-5   Syntax and examples of adding a record to a dataset

To begin coding the btnAdd_Click procedure:

1. Open the Code Editor window. Replace <your name> and <current date> in the comments with your name and the current date, respectively.

2. Locate the btnAdd_Click procedure, and then click the **blank line** above the End Sub clause.

3. The YearWon field in the dataset is numeric. Therefore, the procedure will need to convert the value entered in the txtAddYear control to a number before storing it in the YearWon field. Enter the following two statements. Press **Enter** twice after typing the second statement.

   Dim intYear As Integer
   Integer.TryParse(txtAddYear.Text, intYear)

4. Next, the procedure will add the record to the OscarsDataSet. Enter the following statement:

   OscarsDataSet.tblOscars.AddtblOscarsRow(intYear,
                                       txtActor.Text,
                                       txtActress.Text,
                                       txtPicture.Text,
                                       txtAnimated.Text)

5. Save the solution and then start the application. In the Add new record section of the interface, type **2015** in the Year box, **Eddie Redmayne** in the Actor box, **Julianne Moore** in the Actress box, **Birdman** in the Picture box, and **Big Hero 6** in the Animated box. Click the **Add** button. The new record appears as the last record in the DataGridView control. See Figure 14-6.

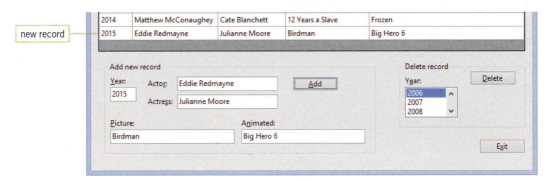

Figure 14-6   New record added to the DataGridView control

6. Click the **Exit** button, and then start the application again. Notice that the new record is missing from the DataGridView control. This is because the btnAdd_Click procedure contains only the code for adding a record to a dataset. It does not yet contain the code for actually saving the record to the Oscars database. You will add that code in the next set of steps. Click the **Exit** button.

For the changes made to a dataset to be permanent, you need to save the changes to the database associated with the dataset. You can accomplish this task using the Validate, EndEdit, and Update methods, as shown in Figure 14-7. Because it is possible for an error to occur when saving data to a database, you should place the methods within the Try block of a Try...Catch statement, as shown in the figure. (The code in Figure 14-7 is similar to the code entered in the Save Data button in Chapter 13's Figure 13-23.)

Saving Dataset Changes to a Database

Syntax

Try
  Validate()
  bindingSourceName.**EndEdit()**
  tableAdapterName.**Update(***dataSetName.tableName***)**
  [*optional message*]
Catch ex As Exception
  [*optional message*]
End Try

Example

```
Try
    Validate()
    TblBooksBindingSource.EndEdit()
    TblBooksTableAdapter.Update(BooksDataSet.tblBooks)
    MessageBox.Show("Saved", "Books",
         MessageBoxButtons.OK, MessageBoxIcon.Information)
Catch ex As Exception
    MessageBox.Show(ex.Message, "Books",
         MessageBoxButtons.OK, MessageBoxIcon.Information)
End Try
```

Figure 14-7 Syntax and an example of saving dataset changes to a database

To complete the btnAdd_Click procedure and then test it: START HERE

  1. Enter the entire Try...Catch statement shown in Figure 14-8.

```
Try
    Validate()
    TblOscarsBindingSource.EndEdit()
    TblOscarsTableAdapter.Update(OscarsDataSet.tblOscars)
    MessageBox.Show("Record saved", "Oscar Winners",
                   MessageBoxButtons.OK,
                   MessageBoxIcon.Information)
Catch ex As Exception
    MessageBox.Show(ex.Message, "Oscar Winners",
                   MessageBoxButtons.OK,
                   MessageBoxIcon.Information)
    End Try
End Sub
```

Figure 14-8 Try...Catch statement entered in the btnAdd_Click procedure

  2. Save the solution and then start the application. In the Add new record section of the interface, type **2015**, **Eddie Redmayne**, **Julianne Moore**, **Birdman**, and **Big Hero 6** in the appropriate boxes. Click the **Add** button. The new record is added to the end of the records in the DataGridView control, and the "Record saved" message appears in a message box.

3. Close the message box. Now observe what happens when you try to add a duplicate record to the dataset. In this case, a duplicate record is a record whose YearWon field value is already in the dataset. (Recall that the YearWon field is the primary key in the tblOscars table.) Click the **Add** button again. A run time error occurs when the computer attempts to process the AddtblOscarsRow function. The run time error occurs because the 2015 value is already present in the dataset. See Figure 14-9.

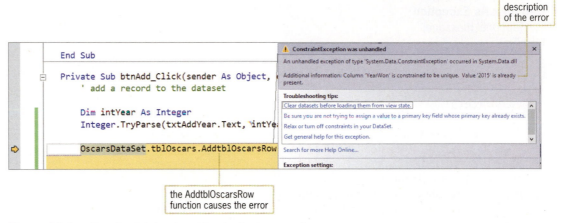

Figure 14-9 Result of trying to add a duplicate record

4. Click **Debug** on the menu bar and then click **Stop Debugging**. You can fix this problem by placing the AddtblOscarsRow function in a Try...Catch statement. Click the **blank line** above the statement containing the AddtblOscarsRow function, and then press **Enter**. Type **Try** and press **Enter**.

5. Move the statement containing the AddtblOscarsRow function, as well as the existing Try...Catch statement, into the Try section of the new Try...Catch statement.

6. Enter the additional MessageBox.Show method in the second Catch section. See Figure 14-10.

```
            End Try
        Catch ex As Exception
            MessageBox.Show("Duplicate record", "Oscar Winners",
                            MessageBoxButtons.OK,
                            MessageBoxIcon.Information)
        End Try
    End Sub
```

enter this MessageBox.Show method

Figure 14-10 Additional code entered in the btnAdd_Click procedure

7. Save the solution and then start the application. In the Add new record section of the interface, type **2015** in the Year box and then click the **Add** button. The "Duplicate record" message appears in a message box. Close the message box.

8. Next, enter the following new record: **2005, Jamie Foxx, Hilary Swank, Million Dollar Baby, The Incredibles**. Click the **Add** button and then close the message box. The 2005 record appears as the last record in the DataGridView control.

9. Click the **Year** header in the DataGridView control. The records now appear in numerical order by the YearWon field. As a result, the 2005 record appears first in the DataGridView control.

10. Click the **Exit** button and then start the application again. Notice that the record for the year 2005 is, once again, at the bottom of the list. This is because the records are displayed in the order they appear in the tblOscars table. The record for the year 2005 was the last record entered into the table, so it appears as the last record in the DataGridView control. You will fix this problem in the next section.

11. Click the **Exit** button.

Sorting the Records in a Dataset

As you observed in the previous set of steps, you can sort the records in a DataGridView control by clicking the appropriate header while the application is running. You also can use the BindingSource object's **Sort method** in code. The method's syntax is shown in Figure 14-11 along with an example of using the syntax. If you want the records in a dataset to appear in a particular order when the application is started, you enter the Sort method in the form's Load event procedure.

Sorting the Records in a Dataset

Syntax
bindingSourceName.**Sort** = *fieldName*

Example – sorts records by the Author field
`TblBooksBindingSource.Sort = "Author"`

Figure 14-11 Syntax and an example of sorting the records in a dataset

To sort the records by the YearWon field:

START HERE

1. Locate the frmMain_Load procedure. Click the **blank line** above the End Sub clause, and then enter the following line of code:

   TblOscarsBindingSource.Sort = "YearWon"

2. Save the solution and then start the application. The records appear in numerical order by the YearWon field. Click the **Exit** button.

YOU DO IT 1!

Close the Oscar Winners solution. Open the YouDoIt 1 (YouDoIt 1.sln) file contained in the VB2015\Chap14\YouDoIt 1 folder. The application is connected to the Names database, which contains one table named tblNames. The table contains five records, each having three fields: ID (the primary key), FirstName, and LastName. When the application starts, the records should be displayed in order by the LastName field. Add three text boxes and a button to the form. The button's Click event procedure should add the information entered in the text boxes to the dataset and then save the record in the database. The procedure should not add a record unless all of the text boxes contain data, and it shouldn't allow duplicate records to be entered. Save the solution and then start the application. Add your name to the database, and then try to add a duplicate record. Close the Code Editor window and then close the solution.

Deleting Records from a Dataset

The btnDelete_Click procedure should search the dataset for the record whose YearWon field contains the value selected in the lstDeleteYear control. Before deleting the record, the procedure will ask the user to confirm the deletion.

START HERE

To begin coding the btnDelete_Click procedure:

1. If necessary, open the Oscar Winners solution. Locate the btnDelete_Click procedure, and then click the **blank line** above the End Sub clause. Enter the Dim statement and MessageBox.Show method shown in Figure 14-12, and then position the insertion point as indicated in the figure.

```
                  Dim dlgButton As DialogResult
                  dlgButton =
enter these six       MessageBox.Show("Delete record for year " &
lines of code                         lstDeleteYear.Text & "?", "Confirm Delete",
                                       MessageBoxButtons.YesNo,
                                       MessageBoxIcon.Exclamation)

                          position the
                          insertion point here
              End Sub
```

Figure 14-12   Code entered in the btnDelete_Click procedure

2. The procedure will delete the record only when the user selects the Yes button in the message box. Enter the following If clause:

   If dlgButton = DialogResult.Yes Then

3. Save the solution.

Before the btnDelete_Click procedure can delete the record from the dataset, it first must locate the record. Visual Basic provides several ways of locating records in a dataset. In this lesson, you will use the syntax shown in Figure 14-13. The figure also includes examples of using the syntax.

Locating a Record in a Dataset

Syntax
dataRowVariable = *dataSetName*.*tableName*.**FindBy***fieldName*(*value*)

Example 1
```
Dim row As DataRow
row = BooksDataSet.tblBooks.FindById(123)
```
The assignment statement searches the dataset for the record whose Id field contains 123 and then assigns the record to the row variable.

Example 2
```
Dim findRow As DataRow
findRow = CdDataSet.tblCds.FindByArtist("Cher")
```
The assignment statement searches the dataset for the record whose Artist field contains "Cher" and then assigns the record to the findRow variable.

Figure 14-13   Syntax and examples of locating a record in a dataset

START HERE

To continue coding the btnDelete_Click procedure:

1. Enter the following declaration statement below the If clause:

    Dim row As DataRow

2. Recall that the YearWon field in the dataset is numeric. Therefore, the procedure will need to convert the year selected in the lstDeleteYear control to a number before searching for the record in the dataset. You can determine the selected item in the list box using either its SelectedItem property (which you learned about in Chapter 6) or its Text property. Enter the following statements:

    Dim intYear As Integer
    Integer.TryParse(lstDeleteYear.Text, intYear)

3. Next, the procedure will locate the appropriate record. Enter the following statement:

    row = OscarsDataSet.tblOscars.FindByYearWon(intYear)

4. Save the solution.

After locating the appropriate record and assigning it to a DataRow variable, you can use the variable's **Delete method** to delete the record. Figure 14-14 shows the method's syntax and includes an example of using the method.

Deleting a Record from a Dataset

Syntax
dataRowVariable.**Delete()**

Example – deletes the record associated with the row variable
```
Dim row As DataRow
row = BooksDataSet.tblBooks.FindByTitle("Money")
row.Delete()
```

Figure 14-14 Syntax and an example of deleting a record from a dataset

To finish coding the btnDelete_Click procedure:

START HERE

1. Type **row.Delete()** and press **Enter**.

2. As you learned earlier, the changes made to a dataset are not permanent until they are saved to the database associated with the dataset. Enter the Try...Catch statement shown in Figure 14-15.

```
            row.Delete()
        Try
            Validate()
            TblOscarsBindingSource.EndEdit()
            TblOscarsTableAdapter.Update(OscarsDataSet.tblOscars)
            MessageBox.Show("Record deleted", "Oscar Winners",
                            MessageBoxButtons.OK,
                            MessageBoxIcon.Information)
        Catch ex As Exception
            MessageBox.Show(ex.Message, "Oscar Winners",
                            MessageBoxButtons.OK,
                            MessageBoxIcon.Information)
        End Try
    End If
```

enter this Try...Catch statement

Figure 14-15 Try...Catch statement entered in the btnDelete_Click procedure

3. Save the solution and then start the application. The first record is highlighted in the DataGridView control, and the value of the record's YearWon field (2005) is highlighted in the list box.

4. Click the **Delete** button. The "Delete record for year 2005?" message appears in a message box. Click the **Yes** button. The computer deletes the record from the dataset, the DataGridView control, and the database. It also deletes the 2005 entry from the list box. The "Record deleted" message now appears in a message box. Click the **OK** button.

5. Next, click **2014** in the Year Won column. The record for the year 2014 is highlighted in the DataGridView control, and the value of the record's YearWon field (2014) is highlighted in the list box. Click the **Delete** button, and then click the **No** button in the message box. The record remains in the dataset, the DataGridView control, and the database. The 2014 entry also remains in the list box.

6. Finally, click **2015** in the list. Click the **Delete** button and then click the **Yes** button. The computer deletes the record from the dataset, the DataGridView control, and the database. It also deletes the 2015 entry from the list box. Click the **OK** button.

7. Click the **Exit** button and then start the application again. Notice that the 2014 record remains in the dataset, but the 2005 and 2015 records were deleted.

8. Click the **Exit** button to end the application. Close the Code Editor window and then close the solution.

Figure 14-20 shows the frmMain_Load, btnAdd_Click, and btnDelete_Click procedures. Notice that you can nest the Try...Catch statement.

```
Private Sub frmMain_Load(sender As Object, e As EventArgs
) Handles MyBase.Load
    'TODO: This line of code loads data into the
    'OscarsDataSet.tblOscars' table. You can move, or remove it,
    as needed.
    Me.TblOscarsTableAdapter.Fill(Me.OscarsDataSet.tblOscars)
    TblOscarsBindingSource.Sort = "YearWon"

End Sub

Private Sub btnAdd_Click(sender As Object, e As EventArgs
) Handles btnAdd.Click
    ' add a record to the dataset

    Dim intYear As Integer
    Integer.TryParse(txtAddYear.Text, intYear)

    Try
        OscarsDataSet.tblOscars.AddtblOscarsRow(intYear,
                                        txtActor.Text,
                                        txtActress.Text,
                                        txtPicture.Text,
                                        txtAnimated.Text)

        Try
            Validate()
            TblOscarsBindingSource.EndEdit()
            TblOscarsTableAdapter.Update(OscarsDataSet.tblOscars)
            MessageBox.Show("Record saved", "Oscar Winners",
                        MessageBoxButtons.OK,
                        MessageBoxIcon.Information)
        Catch ex As Exception
            MessageBox.Show(ex.Message, "Oscar Winners",
                        MessageBoxButtons.OK,
                        MessageBoxIcon.Information)
        End Try
    Catch ex As Exception
        MessageBox.Show("Duplicate record", "Oscar Winners",
                    MessageBoxButtons.OK,
                    MessageBoxIcon.Information)
    End Try
End Sub

Private Sub btnDelete_Click(sender As Object, e As EventArgs
) Handles btnDelete.Click
    ' delete a record from the dataset

    Dim dlgButton As DialogResult
    dlgButton =
        MessageBox.Show("Delete record for year " &
                    lstDeleteYear.Text & "?", "Confirm Delete",
                    MessageBoxButtons.YesNo,
                    MessageBoxIcon.Exclamation)
```

Figure 14-16   frmMain_Load, btnAdd_Click, and btnDelete_Click procedures *(continues)*

(continued)

```
    If dlgButton = DialogResult.Yes Then
        Dim row As DataRow
        Dim intYear As Integer
        Integer.TryParse(lstDeleteYear.Text, intYear)
        row = OscarsDataSet.tblOscars.FindByYearWon(intYear)
        row.Delete()
        Try
            Validate()
            TblOscarsBindingSource.EndEdit()
            TblOscarsTableAdapter.Update(OscarsDataSet.tblOscars)
            MessageBox.Show("Record deleted", "Oscar Winners",
                            MessageBoxButtons.OK,
                            MessageBoxIcon.Information)
        Catch ex As Exception
            MessageBox.Show(ex.Message, "Oscar Winners",
                            MessageBoxButtons.OK,
                            MessageBoxIcon.Information)

        End Try
    End If
End Sub
```

Figure 14-16   frmMain_Load, btnAdd_Click, and btnDelete_Click procedures

Lesson A Summary

- To add a record to a dataset:

  Use the following syntax:

  dataSetName . *tableName* . Add*tableName*Row(*valueField1*[, *valueField2...*, *valueFieldN*])

- To save dataset changes to a database:

  Use the code shown in Figure 14-7 in this lesson.

- To sort the records in a dataset:

  Use the BindingSource object's Sort method. The method's syntax is:

  bindingSourceName . Sort = *fieldName*

- To locate a record in a dataset:

  Use the following syntax:

  dataRowVariable = *dataSetName* . *tableName* . FindBy*fieldName*(*value*)

- To delete a record from a dataset:

  Use the following syntax:

  dataRowVariable . Delete()

Lesson A Key Terms

Delete method—a method of a DataRow variable; used to delete a record from a dataset

Sort method—a method of the BindingSource object; used to sort a dataset in order by a specific field

Lesson A Review Questions

1. The StatesDataSet contains a table named tblStates. The table contains two text fields named State and Capital. Which of the following will add a new record to the dataset?

    a. `StatesDataSet.tblStates.AddStatesRow(strS, strC)`

    b. `StatesDataSet.tblStates.AddRowToStates(strS, strC)`

    c. `StatesDataSet.tblStates.AddtblStatesRow(strS, strC)`

    d. `StatesDataSet.AddtblStatesRow(strS, strC)`

2. Two records were added to the StatesDataSet from Review Question 1. Which of the following will save the records in the States database?

    a. `TblStatesBindingSource.Save(StatesDataSet.tblStates)`

    b. `TblStatesBindingSource.Update(StatesDataSet.tblStates)`

    c. `TblStatesTableAdapter.Save(StatesDataSet.tblStates)`

    d. `TblStatesTableAdapter.Update(StatesDataSet.tblStates)`

3. The StatesDataSet from Review Question 1 is associated with the TblStatesBindingSource and TblStatesTableAdapter objects. Which of the following will sort the records by the Capital field?

    a. `TblStatesBindingSource.Sort = "Capital"`

    b. `TblStatesBindingSource.Sort("Capital")`

    c. `TblStatesTableAdapter.Sort = "Capital"`

    d. `TblStatesTableAdapter.Sort("Capital")`

4. Using the StatesDataSet from Review Question 1, which of the following will assign the Atlanta record to the **row** variable?

    a. `row =`
        `StatesDataSet.tblStates.FindCapital("Atlanta")`

    b. `row =`
        `StatesDataSet.tblStates.FindByCapital("Atlanta")`

    c. `row =`
        `StatesDataSet.tblStates.FindByState("Georgia")`

    d. both b and c

5. Which of the following will delete the record associated with a DataRow variable named `findRow`?

    a. `findRow.Delete()`   c. `delete(findRow)`

    b. `findRow.Remove()`   d. none of the above

Lesson A Exercises

INTRODUCTORY

1. In this exercise, you modify the Oscar Winners application from this lesson. Use Windows to make a copy of the Oscars Solution folder. Rename the copy Modified Oscars Solution. Open the Oscars Solution (Oscars Solution.sln) file contained in the Modified Oscars Solution folder. Modify the btnAdd_Click procedure so that it adds a record only when the five text boxes contain data. In addition, save the entries in the txtActor, txtActress, txtPicture, and txtAnimated controls without any leading or trailing spaces. Test the application appropriately.

INTRODUCTORY

2. Open the VB2015\Chap14\Jacoby Solution\Jacoby Solution (Jacoby Solution.sln) file. The application is connected to the Sales database, which contains a table named tblSales. Each record in the table has four numeric fields named RecordNum (the primary key), YearNum, MonthNum, and Sales. The btnAdd_Click procedure should allow the user to add records to the database, but only when the four text boxes contain data. The record numbers in the database must be unique. The records should appear in numerical order by the record number. Code the application and then test it appropriately.

INTRODUCTORY

3. Open the VB2015\Chap14\Fashions Solution\Fashions Solution (Fashions Solution.sln) file. The application is connected to the Stores database, which contains a table named tblStores. Each record in the table contains five fields. The StoreNum (primary key) and Sales fields contain numbers; the remaining fields contain text. The btnAdd_Click procedure should allow the user to add records to the database, but only when the five text boxes contain data. All of the records in the database must be unique. The btnDelete_Click procedure should allow the user to delete records from the database. The records should appear in order by the store number when the application is started. Code the application and then test it appropriately.

INTERMEDIATE

4. Open the VB2015\Chap14\Valentia Solution\Valentia Solution (Valentia Solution.sln) file. The application is connected to the Employees database, which contains a table named tblEmploy. Each record in the table contains seven fields. The EmpNum field is the primary key. The Status field contains the employment status, which is either the letter F (for full time) or the letter P (for part time). The Code field identifies the employee's department: 1 for Accounting, 2 for Advertising, 3 for Personnel, and 4 for Inventory. The btnAdd_Click procedure should allow the user to add records to the database, but only when the user provides all of the employee information. All of the records in the database must be unique. The btnDelete_Click procedure should allow the user to delete records from the database. The records should appear in order by the employee number when the application is started. Code the application. Be sure to code each text box's Enter event procedure. Also code the KeyPress event procedures for the Number, Rate, Status, and Code text boxes. Test the application appropriately.

INTERMEDIATE

5. In this exercise, you modify the application from Exercise 2. Use Windows to make a copy of the Jacoby Solution folder. Rename the copy Jacoby Solution-LINQ. Open the Jacoby Solution (Jacoby Solution.sln) file contained in the Jacoby Solution-LINQ folder. Add a button named btnTotal to the form. Change the button's Text property to &Total Sales. The button's Click event procedure should display the total sales amount in a message box. (Hint: Use one of the LINQ aggregate operators, which you learned about in Chapter 13.) Test the application appropriately.

6. In this exercise, you modify the Oscar Winners application from this lesson. Use Windows to make a copy of the Oscars Solution folder. Rename the copy Oscars Solution-Advanced. Open the Oscars Solution (Oscars Solution.sln) file contained in the Oscars Solution-Advanced folder. Use the Delete button, followed by the Yes and OK buttons, to delete all of the records from the dataset, and then click the Delete button again. The "Delete record for year ?" message appears. Notice that the message does not specify a year. Click the Yes button. A run time error occurs because the procedure is attempting to delete a record that does not exist. Click Debug on the menu bar and then click Stop Debugging. The btnDelete_Click procedure should ask the user to confirm the deletion of only existing records. In addition, it should not attempt to delete a record that does not exist. Modify the procedure, and then test it appropriately.

ADVANCED

7. Open the Adalene Solution (Adalene Solution.sln) file contained in the VB2015\Chap14\Adalene Solution-Sort folder. The btnSort_Click procedure should sort the records in alphabetical order by city name within state name. Code the procedure and then test the application appropriately.

DISCOVERY

LESSON B

After studying Lesson B, you should be able to:

- Query a database using the SQL SELECT statement
- Create queries using the Query Builder dialog box

Structured Query Language

As you learned in Chapter 13, you use a query to specify both the records to select from a database and the order in which to arrange the records. In Chapter 13, you created the queries using LINQ (Language-Integrated Query). In this chapter, you will use a different query language called SQL. You can pronounce SQL either as *ess-cue-el* or as *sequel*.

SQL, which stands for **Structured Query Language**, is a set of statements that allows you to access and manipulate the data stored in many database management systems on computers of all sizes, from large mainframes to small microcomputers. You can use SQL statements—such as SELECT, INSERT, and DELETE—to perform common database tasks. Examples of these tasks include storing, retrieving, updating, deleting, and sorting data.

In this lesson, you will use the SQL SELECT statement to query the Oscars database from Lesson A. The tblOscars table in the database contains the nine records shown in Figure 14-17. The YearWon field is numeric; the remaining fields contain text.

YearWon	Actor	Actress	Picture	Animated
2006	Philip Seymour Hoffman	Reese Witherspoon	Crash	The Curse of the Were-Rabbit
2007	Forest Whitaker	Helen Mirren	The Departed	Happy Feet
2008	Daniel Day-Lewis	Marion Cotillard	No Country for Old Men	Ratatouille
2009	Sean Penn	Kate Winslet	Slumdog Millionaire	WALL-E
2010	Jeff Bridges	Sandra Bullock	The Hurt Locker	Up
2011	Colin Firth	Natalie Portman	The King's Speech	Toy Story 3
2012	Jean Dujardin	Meryl Streep	The Artist	Rango
2013	Daniel Day-Lewis	Jennifer Lawrence	Argo	Brave
2014	Matthew McConaughey	Cate Blanchett	12 Years a Slave	Frozen

Figure 14-17   Contents of the tblOscars table

The SELECT Statement

The **SELECT statement** is the most commonly used statement in SQL. You can use it to specify the fields and records you want to view as well as to control the order in which the fields and records appear when they are displayed. The statement's basic syntax is shown in Figure 14-18. In the syntax, *fieldList* is one or more field names separated by commas, and *tableName* is the name of the table containing the fields. The WHERE and ORDER BY clauses are optional parts of the syntax. You use the **WHERE clause**, which contains a *condition*, to limit the records you want to view. Similar to the condition in the If...Then...Else and Do...Loop statements, the condition in a WHERE clause specifies a requirement that must be met for a record to be selected. The **ORDER BY clause** is used to arrange the records in either ascending (the default) or descending order by one or more fields. Although you do not have to capitalize the boldfaced keywords in a SELECT statement, many programmers do so for clarity.

SELECT Statement

<u>Basic syntax</u>
SELECT *fieldList* **FROM** *tableName*
        [**WHERE** *condition*]
        [**ORDER BY** *fieldName* [**DESC**]]

<u>Example 1</u>
SELECT YearWon, Actor, Actress, Picture, Animated FROM tblOscars
selects all of the fields and records in the table

<u>Example 2</u>
SELECT YearWon, Actor, Actress, Picture, Animated FROM tblOscars
        WHERE YearWon >= 2011
selects all of the fields from records for the year 2011 and later

<u>Example 3</u>
SELECT YearWon FROM tblOscars WHERE Picture = 'Argo'
selects the YearWon field for the Argo record

<u>Example 4</u>
SELECT Actor, Actress, Picture FROM tblOscars ORDER BY Picture
selects the Actor, Actress, and Picture fields for all of the records in the table, arranging the records
in ascending order by the Picture field

<u>Example 5</u>
SELECT YearWon, Picture FROM tblOscars
        WHERE Picture LIKE 'The %'
        ORDER BY Picture DESC
selects the YearWon and Picture fields for all records whose Picture field begins with the word "The"
followed by a space and zero or more characters, and then arranges the records in descending
order by the Picture field

Figure 14-18   Syntax and examples of the SELECT statement

The SELECT statement in Example 1 selects all of the fields and records from the tblOscars table. The SELECT statement in Example 2 uses the WHERE clause to limit the selected records to only those for the year 2011 and later. The SELECT statement in Example 3 selects the YearWon field for only the Argo record. Notice that the word *Argo* in Example 3 appears in single quotes, but the number 2011 in Example 2 does not. The single quotes around the value in the WHERE clause's condition are necessary only when you are comparing a text field with a literal constant. Recall that the Picture field contains text, whereas the YearWon field contains numbers. Text comparisons in SQL are not case sensitive. Therefore, you can also write the WHERE clause in Example 3 as WHERE Picture = 'argo'.

The SELECT statement in Example 4 selects each record's Actor, Actress, and Picture fields and then arranges the records in ascending order by the Picture field. The SELECT statement in Example 5 shows how you can use the **LIKE operator** along with the **%** (percent sign) wildcard character in the WHERE clause. The statement tells the computer to select the YearWon and Picture fields for records whose Picture field begins with the word "The" followed by a space and zero or more characters. The ORDER BY clause in the statement will arrange the selected records in descending order by the Picture field.

Creating a Query

In this section, you will use the Oscar Winners application to test the SELECT statements from Figure 14-18.

START HERE

To test the SELECT statements:

1. If necessary, start Visual Studio 2015. Open the Oscars Solution (Oscars Solution.sln) file contained in the VB2015\Chap14\Oscars Solution-SQL folder. The application is already connected to the Oscars database.

2. Right-click **OscarsDataSet.xsd** in the Solution Explorer window. The .xsd file, called the dataset's schema file, contains information about the tables, fields, records, and properties included in the OscarsDataSet. Click **Open** to open the DataSet Designer window. See Figure 14-19.

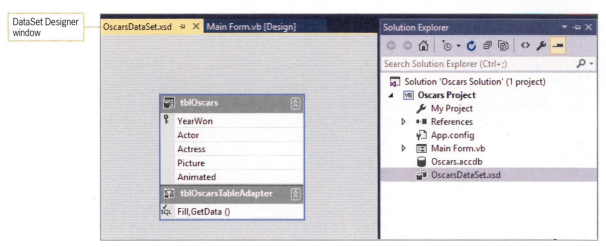

DataSet Designer window

Figure 14-19   DataSet Designer window

3. Right-click **tblOscarsTableAdapter** in the DataSet Designer window. Point to **Add** on the shortcut menu and then click **Query**. (If Add does not appear on the shortcut menu, click Add Query instead.) Doing this starts the TableAdapter Query Configuration Wizard. The "Use SQL statements" radio button should be selected on the Choose a Command Type screen, as shown in Figure 14-20.

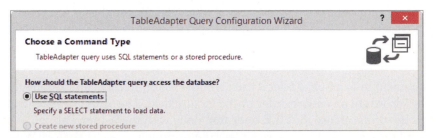

Figure 14-20   Choose a Command Type screen

4. Click the **Next** button to display the Choose a Query Type screen. Verify that the "SELECT which returns rows" radio button is selected.

5. Click the **Next** button to display the Specify a SQL SELECT statement screen. The screen already contains a SELECT statement, as shown in Figure 14-21.

Figure 14-21   Specify a SQL SELECT statement screen

6. You can type a different SELECT statement in the "What data should the table load?" box, or you can use the Query Builder dialog box to construct the statement for you. Click the **Query Builder** button to open the Query Builder dialog box. See Figure 14-22. The table's primary key appears boldfaced in the Diagram pane.

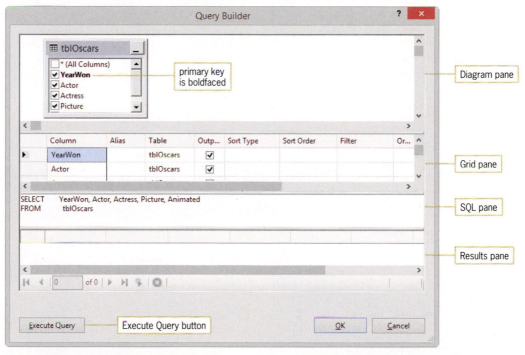

Figure 14-22   Query Builder dialog box

7. The SQL pane contains the same SELECT statement shown in Example 1 in Figure 14-18. The statement selects all of the fields and records from the tblOscars table. Click the **Execute Query** button to run the query. The query results appear in the Results pane, as shown in Figure 14-23. You can use the scroll bar to view the remaining records.

Figure 14-23 Records listed in the Results pane

8. Next, you will create a query that selects all of the fields, but only for records for the year 2011 and later. In the Grid pane, click the **blank cell** in the YearWon field's Filter column. Type >= **2011** and press **Enter**. The Filter column entry tells the Query Builder to include the WHERE (YearWon >= 2011) clause in the SELECT statement. The funnel symbol that appears in the Diagram pane indicates that the YearWon field is used to filter the records. Notice the Query Changed message and icon that appear in the Results pane. The message and icon alert you that the information displayed in the Results pane is not from the current query. See Figure 14-24. (For clarity, the Query Builder places the WHERE clause's condition in parentheses; however, the parentheses are not a requirement of the SELECT statement.)

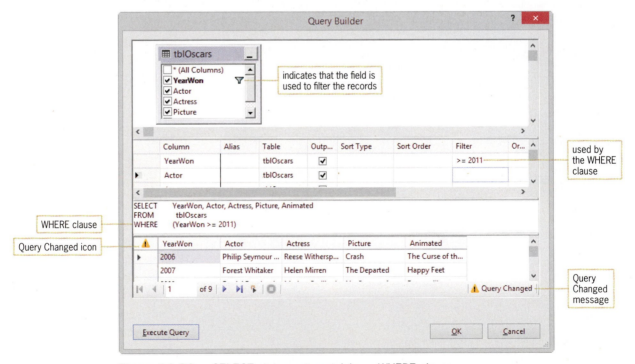

Figure 14-24 SELECT statement containing a WHERE clause

9. Click the **Execute Query** button to run the current query. If necessary, scroll the Results pane to verify that it contains only the records for the years 2011 through 2014.

10. The next query will select only the YearWon field for the Argo record. Delete the **>= 2011** entry from the YearWon field's Filter column. Click the **blank cell** in the Picture field's Filter column. Type **Argo** and press **Enter**. The Query Builder changes the entry in the Filter column to = **'Argo'**. It also enters the WHERE (Picture = 'Argo') clause in the SELECT statement.

11. In the Diagram pane, deselect the **Actor**, **Actress**, **Picture**, and **Animated** check boxes. The Query Builder changes the first line in the SELECT statement to SELECT YearWon. Click the **Execute Query** button. See Figure 14-25.

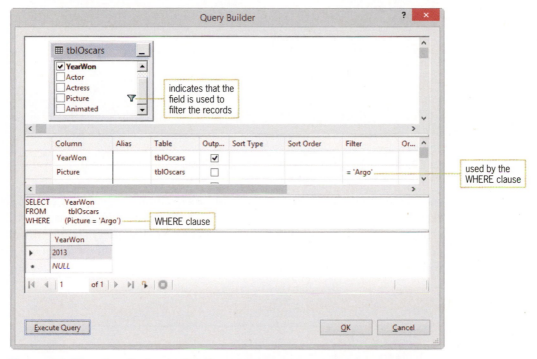

Figure 14-25   Result of executing the current query

12. Next, you will create a query that selects each record's Actor, Actress, and Picture fields and then sorts the records in ascending order by the Picture field. In the Diagram pane, select the **Actor**, **Actress**, and **Picture** check boxes, and then deselect the **YearWon** check box. The Query Builder changes the first line in the SELECT statement to SELECT Actor, Actress, Picture.

13. In the Grid pane, delete the **= 'Argo'** entry and then press **Enter**. The Query Builder removes the WHERE clause from the SELECT statement.

14. Click the **blank cell** in the Picture field's Sort Type column, and then click the **list arrow** in the cell. Click **Ascending** and press **Enter**. The word "Ascending" appears as the Picture field's Sort Type, and the number 1 appears as its Sort Order. The number 1 indicates that the Picture field is the primary field in the sort. Notice that the Query Builder adds the ORDER BY Picture clause to the SELECT statement. Click the **Execute Query** button. See Figure 14-26.

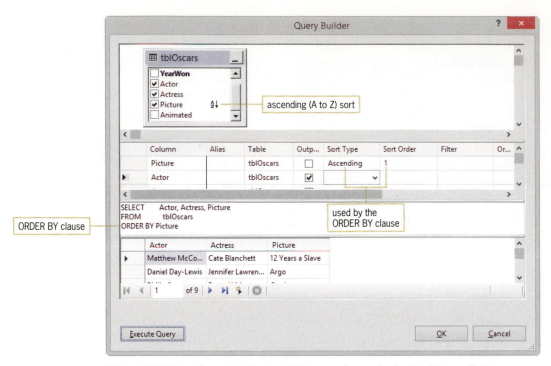

Figure 14-26 Records displayed in ascending order by the Picture field

15. On your own, create the query for Figure 14-18's Example 5. The query should select the YearWon and Picture fields for all records whose Picture field begins with the word "The" followed by a space and zero or more characters. The query should sort the records in descending order by the Picture field. Figure 14-27 shows the query along with the result of executing it.

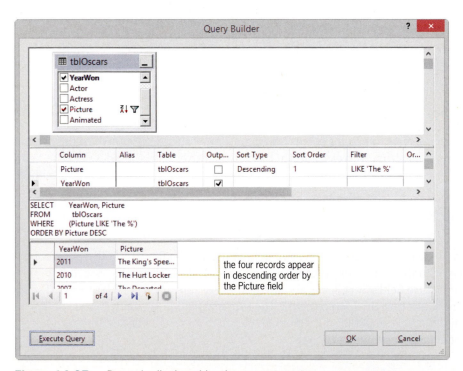

Figure 14-27 Records displayed by the current query

16. Click the **Cancel** button in the Query Builder dialog box, and then click the **Cancel** button in the TableAdapter Query Configuration Wizard dialog box.

17. Save the solution. Close the OscarsDataSet.xsd window and then close the solution.

Lesson B Summary

- To query a database using SQL:

  Use the SELECT statement. The statement's basic syntax is:

  > SELECT *fieldList* FROM *tableName*
  > [WHERE *condition*]
  > [ORDER BY *fieldName* [DESC]]

- To limit the records you want to view:

  Use the SELECT statement's WHERE clause.

- To sort the selected records:

  Use the SELECT statement's ORDER BY clause.

- To open the DataSet Designer window:

  Right-click the name of the dataset's schema file in the Solution Explorer window and then click Open. The schema filename ends with .xsd.

- To start the TableAdapter Query Configuration Wizard:

  Open the DataSet Designer window and then right-click the table adapter's name. Point to Add on the shortcut menu and then click Query. (If Add does not appear on the shortcut menu, click Add Query instead.)

- To open the Query Builder dialog box:

  Start the TableAdapter Query Configuration Wizard. Click the Next button, and then click the Next button again to display the Specify a SQL SELECT statement screen. Click the Query Builder button.

- To represent zero or more characters in the WHERE clause's condition:

  Use the % wildcard.

Lesson B Key Terms

%—a wildcard character used in the condition in a SELECT statement's WHERE clause; represents zero or more characters

LIKE operator—used with a wildcard character in the condition in a SELECT statement's WHERE clause

ORDER BY clause—used in a SELECT statement to sort the selected records

SELECT statement—the SQL statement that allows you to specify the fields and records to select as well as the order in which the fields and records appear when displayed

SQL—an acronym for Structured Query Language

Structured Query Language—SQL; a set of statements that allows you to access and manipulate the data stored in a database

WHERE clause—used in a SELECT statement to limit the records to be selected

Lesson B Review Questions

1. SQL stands for _____.

   a. Select Query Language

   b. Semi-Quick Language

   c. Structured Quick Language

   d. Structured Query Language

2. Which of the following will select the State and Sales fields from the tblStores table?

   a. `SELECT State AND Sales FROM tblStores`

   b. `SELECT State OR Sales FROM tblStores`

   c. `SELECT State, Sales FROM tblStores`

   d. `SELECT ONLY State, Sales FROM tblStores`

3. Which of the following will select the SSN field from the tblPayInfo table and then sort the records in descending order by the SSN field?

   a. `SELECT SSN FROM tblPayInfo DESC`

   b. `SELECT SSN FROM tblPayInfo ORDER BY SSN DESC`

   c. `SELECT SSN FROM tblPayInfo WHERE SSN DESC`

   d. `SELECT SSN FROM tblPayInfo SORT SSN DESC`

4. Which of the following will select the Id and Status fields for records whose Status field contains only the letter F?

   a. `SELECT Id, Status FROM tblEmp WHERE Status = 'F'`

   b. `SELECT Id, Status FROM tblEmp ORDER BY Status = 'F'`

   c. `SELECT Id, Status FROM tblEmp FOR Status = 'F'`

   d. `SELECT Id, Status FROM tblEmp SELECT Status = 'F'`

5. Which of the following will select the State and Capital fields for the Kansas and Kentucky records?

   a. `SELECT State, Capital FROM tblState WHERE State LIKE 'K'`

   b. `SELECT State, Capital FROM tblState WHERE State LIKE 'K*'`

   c. `SELECT State, Capital FROM tblState WHERE State LIKE 'K%'`

   d. `SELECT State, Capital FROM tblState WHERE State LIKE 'K#'`

6. Which of the following will select the State and Capital fields for states with populations that exceed 5,000,000? (The Population field is numeric.)

    a. `SELECT State, Capital FROM tblState WHERE Population > 5000000`

    b. `SELECT State, Capital FROM tblState WHERE Population > '5000000'`

    c. `SELECT State, Capital FROM tblState WHERE Population > "5000000"`

    d. `SELECT State, Capital FROM tblState SELECT Population > 5000000`

7. In a SELECT statement, which clause is used to limit the records that will be selected?

    a. LIMIT   c. ONLY

    b. ORDER BY   d. WHERE

8. If a funnel symbol appears next to a field's name in the Query Builder dialog box, it indicates that the field is _____.

    a. used in an ORDER BY clause in a SELECT statement

    b. used in a WHERE clause in a SELECT statement

    c. the primary key

    d. the foreign key

9. The SQL SELECT statement performs case-sensitive comparisons.

    a. True

    b. False

Lesson B Exercises

1. The tblMagazine table contains three fields. The Cost field is numeric. The Code and MagName fields contain text.

INTRODUCTORY

    a. Write a SQL SELECT statement that arranges the records in descending order by the Cost field.

    b. Write a SQL SELECT statement that selects only the MagName and Cost fields from records having a code of PG10.

    c. Write a SQL SELECT statement that selects only the MagName and Cost fields from records having a cost of $3 or more.

    d. Write a SQL SELECT statement that selects the Visual Basic record.

    e. Write a SQL SELECT statement that selects only the MagName field from records whose magazine name begins with the letter C.

    f. Open the VB2015\Chap14\Magazine Solution\Magazine Solution (Magazine Solution.sln) file. The application is connected to the Magazines database. Start the application to view the records contained in the dataset, and then stop the application. Open the DataSet Designer window and then start the TableAdapter Query Configuration Wizard. Open the Query Builder dialog box. Use the dialog box to test your SELECT statements from Steps a through e.

INTRODUCTORY

2. The tblEmploy table contains seven fields. The EmpNum, Rate, and Code fields are numeric. The LastName, FirstName, Hired, and Status fields contain text. The Status field contains either the letter F (for full time) or the letter P (for part time). The Code field identifies the employee's department: 1 for Accounting, 2 for Advertising, 3 for Personnel, and 4 for Inventory.

    a. Write a SQL SELECT statement that selects all of the fields and records in the table and then sorts the records in ascending order by the Code field.

    b. Write a SQL SELECT statement that selects only the EmpNum, LastName, and FirstName fields from all of the records.

    c. Write a SQL SELECT statement that selects only the records for full-time employees.

    d. Write a SQL SELECT statement that selects the EmpNum and Rate fields for employees in the Personnel department.

    e. Write a SQL SELECT statement that selects the EmpNum and LastName fields for employees having the last name Smith.

    f. Write a SQL SELECT statement that selects the EmpNum and LastName fields for employees having a last name that begins with the letter S.

    g. Write a SQL SELECT statement that selects only the first and last names for part-time employees and then sorts the records in descending order by the LastName field.

    h. Open the Morgan Industries Solution (Morgan Industries Solution.sln) file contained in the VB2015\Chap14\Morgan Industries Solution-SQL folder. The application is connected to the Employees database. Start the application to view the records contained in the dataset, and then stop the application. Open the DataSet Designer window and then start the TableAdapter Query Configuration Wizard. Open the Query Builder dialog box. Which field in the table is the primary key? How can you tell that it is the primary key?

    i. Use the Query Builder dialog box to test your SELECT statements from Steps a through g.

LESSON C

After studying Lesson C, you should be able to:

- Create a parameter query
- Save a query
- Invoke a query from code
- Add records to a dataset using the SQL INSERT statement
- Delete records from a dataset using the SQL DELETE statement

Parameter Queries

In Lesson B, you learned how to create queries that search for records meeting specific criteria, such as `Picture = 'Argo'`. Most times, however, you will not know ahead of time the value to include in the criteria. For example, the next time the user runs the query, he or she may want to view the Slumdog Millionaire record rather than the Argo record. When you don't know the specific value to include in the criteria, you use a parameter query.

A **parameter query** is a query that uses the parameter marker in place of the criteria's value. The **parameter marker** is a question mark (**?**). Figure 14-28 shows examples of parameter queries using the tblOscars table from Lessons A and B.

Parameter Queries

Example 1
```
SELECT YearWon, Actor, Actress, Picture, Animated FROM tblMovies
    WHERE Picture = ?
```
selects all of the fields for the record whose Picture field value is represented by the parameter marker

Example 2
```
SELECT YearWon, Picture FROM tblMovies WHERE YearWon >= ?
```
selects the YearWon and Picture fields for records whose YearWon field contains a value that is greater than or equal to the value represented by the parameter marker

---

Figure 14-28 Examples of parameter queries

In this section, you will use the Oscar Winners application to test the SELECT statements from Figure 14-28.

To test the SELECT statements from Figure 14-28:

START HERE

1. If necessary, start Visual Studio 2015. Open the Oscars Solution (Oscars Solution.sln) file contained in the VB2015\Chap14\Oscars Solution-Parameter Queries folder. The application is already connected to the Oscars database.

2. Right-click **OscarsDataSet.xsd** in the Solution Explorer window, and then click **Open** to open the DataSet Designer window.

3. Right-click **TblOscarsTableAdapter** in the DataSet Designer window. Point to **Add** on the shortcut menu, and then click **Query** to start the TableAdapter Query Configuration Wizard. (If Add does not appear on the shortcut menu, click Add Query instead.)

4. Verify that the Use SQL statements radio button is selected on the Choose a Command Type screen. Click the **Next** button to display the Choose a Query Type screen. Verify that the "SELECT which returns rows" radio button is selected. Click the **Next** button to display the Specify a SQL SELECT statement screen. Click the **Query Builder** button to open the Query Builder dialog box.

5. First, you will create a parameter query that selects a record by the value in the Picture field. In the Grid pane, click the **blank cell** in the Picture field's Filter column. Type **?** and press **Enter**. The Query Builder changes the entry in the Filter column to = ?. It also adds the WHERE (Picture = ?) clause to the SELECT statement.

6. Click the **Execute Query** button to run the query. The Query Parameters dialog box opens. Type **Argo** in the Value column. See Figure 14-29.

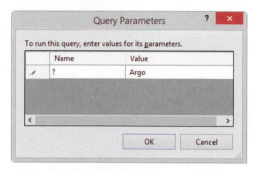

Figure 14-29   Query Parameters dialog box

7. Click the **OK** button to close the Query Parameters dialog box. The Argo record appears in the Results pane.

8. Next, you will use the query to select the Slumdog Millionaire record. Click the **Execute Query** button, type **Slumdog Millionaire** in the Value column, and then click the **OK** button. The Slumdog Millionaire record appears in the Results pane.

9. Next, you will create a query for Example 2 from Figure 14-28. Delete the = ? from the Picture field's Filter column. Type >= **?** in the YearWon field's Filter column, and then press **Enter**. Click the **Execute Query** button to run the query. Type **2011** in the Value column of the Query Parameters dialog box, and then click the **OK** button. The records for years 2011 through 2014 appear in the Results pane. See Figure 14-30.

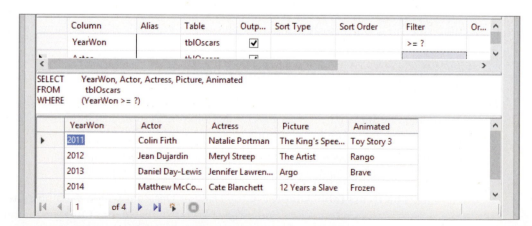

Figure 14-30   Records with a YearWon field value of at least 2011

10. Now you will use the query to select records for the year 2013 and later. Click the **Execute Query** button, type **2013** in the Value column, and then click the **OK** button. This time, only the records for the years 2013 and 2014 appear in the Results pane.

11. Click the **Cancel** button in the Query Builder dialog box, and then click the **Cancel** button in the TableAdapter Query Configuration Wizard dialog box. Save the solution. Close the OscarsDataSet.xsd window and then close the solution.

Saving a Query

For an application to use a query during run time, you will need to save the query and then invoke it from code. You save a query that contains the SELECT statement by associating the query with one or more methods. The TableAdapter Query Configuration Wizard provides an easy way to perform this task.

To save a query:

START HERE

1. Open the Oscars Solution (Oscars Solution.sln) file contained in the VB2015\Chap14\ Oscars Solution-Save Query folder. The application, which is already connected to the Oscars database, allows the user to display either all of the records or only the record for the year entered in the txtYear control.

2. Right-click **OscarsDataSet.xsd** in the Solution Explorer window, and then click **Open** to open the DataSet Designer window.

3. Right-click **tblOscarsTableAdapter** in the DataSet Designer window. Point to **Add** on the shortcut menu, and then click **Query** to start the TableAdapter Query Configuration Wizard. (If Add does not appear on the shortcut menu, click Add Query instead.)

4. Verify that the Use SQL statements radio button is selected. Click the **Next** button to display the Choose a Query Type screen. Verify that the "SELECT which returns rows" radio button is selected. Click the **Next** button to display the Specify a SQL SELECT statement screen. The "What data should the table load?" box contains the default query, which selects all of the fields and records in the table. The default query shown in Figure 14-31 is automatically invoked when you use the TblOscarsTableAdapter object's Fill method.

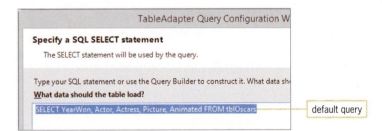

Figure 14-31 Default query in the Specify a SQL SELECT statement screen

5. Click the **Query Builder** button to open the Query Builder dialog box. You will create a parameter query that displays the Oscar winners for the year entered in the txtYear control. In the Grid pane, type **?** in the YearWon field's Filter column, and then press **Enter**. The Query Builder adds the WHERE (YearWon = ?) clause to the SELECT statement.

6. Click the **Execute Query** button to run the query. The Query Parameters dialog box opens. Type **2010** in the Value column, and then click the **OK** button to close the dialog box. The 2010 record appears in the Results pane.

7. Click the **OK** button to close the Query Builder dialog box. The parameter query appears in the "What data should the table load?" box. See Figure 14-32.

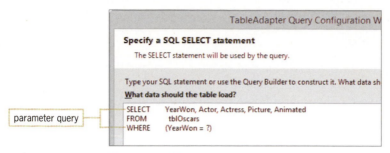

Figure 14-32   Parameter query in the Specify a SQL SELECT statement screen

8. Click the **Next** button to display the Choose Methods to Generate screen. If necessary, select the **Fill a DataTable** and **Return a DataTable** check boxes. Change the Fill a DataTable method's name from FillBy to **FillByYear**. Change the Return a DataTable method's name from GetDataBy to **GetDataByYear**. See Figure 14-33. The FillByYear and GetDataByYear methods are associated with the parameter query you created. Therefore, you can use the methods to invoke the query during run time.

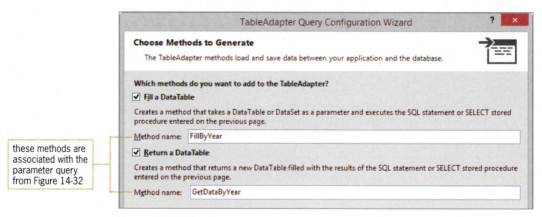

Figure 14-33   Completed Choose Methods to Generate screen

9. Click the **Next** button to display the Wizard Results screen. See Figure 14-34.

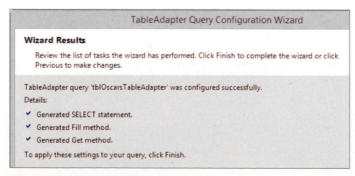

Figure 14-34   Wizard Results screen

10. Click the **Finish** button. The FillByYear and GetDataByYear methods appear in the DataSet Designer window, as shown in Figure 14-35.

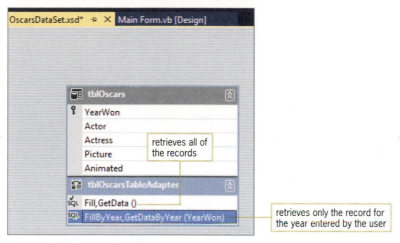

Figure 14-35   Method names included in the DataSet Designer window

11. Save the solution and then close the OscarsDataSet.xsd window.

Invoking a Query from Code

You can invoke a query during run time by entering its associated methods in a procedure.

To have the btnDisplay_Click procedure invoke the appropriate query:

START HERE

1. Open the Code Editor window. Replace <your name> and <current date> in the comments with your name and the current date, respectively.

2. Locate the btnDisplay_Click procedure, and then click the **blank line** above the End Sub clause.

3. If the All radio button is selected in the interface, the procedure will use the TblOscarsTableAdapter object's Fill method to select all of the records. (Recall that the frmMain_Load procedure also uses the Fill method.) Enter the lines of code shown in Figure 14-36.

```
Private Sub btnDisplay_Click(sender As Object, e As EventArgs)
    ' displays a specific record

    If radAll.Checked Then
        TblOscarsTableAdapter.Fill(OscarsDataSet.tblOscars)
    Else

    End If
End Sub
```
enter these lines of code

Figure 14-36   Code entered in the procedure

4. If the Year radio button is selected, the procedure will use the TblOscarsTableAdapter object's FillByYear method to select the record whose YearWon field matches the year number entered in the txtYear control. First, the procedure will determine whether the control contains a value. If it does not contain a value, the procedure will display an appropriate message. Enter the additional lines of code indicated in Figure 14-37.

```
Else
    If txtYear.Text.Trim = String.Empty Then
        MessageBox.Show("Please enter the year.", "Oscar Winners",
                        MessageBoxButtons.OK,
                        MessageBoxIcon.Information)
    Else

    End If
End If
```

enter these lines of code

Figure 14-37   Additional code entered in the procedure

5. The YearWon field is numeric, so the procedure will need to convert the text box entry to a number. Enter the following lines of code:

Dim intYear As Integer
Integer.TryParse(txtYear.Text, intYear)

6. Next, the procedure will invoke the TblOscarsTableAdapter object's FillByYear method. The method is associated with a parameter query, so it will need to include the parameter information. Enter the additional lines of code indicated in Figure 14-38.

```
        Else
            Dim intYear As Integer
            Integer.TryParse(txtYear.Text, intYear)
            TblOscarsTableAdapter.FillByYear(OscarsDataSet.tblOscars,
                                             intYear)
        End If
    End If
```

enter these lines of code

year number for the parameter query

Figure 14-38   FillByYear method entered in the procedure

7. Save the solution and then start the application. Click the **Year** radio button, and then click the **Display** button. The "Please enter the year." message appears in a message box. Close the message box.

8. Click the **text box** located below the Year radio button. Type **2013** and then click the **Display** button. Only the 2013 record appears in the DataGridView control. See Figure 14-39.

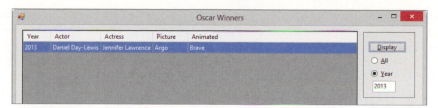

Figure 14-39   2013 record shown in the interface

9. Click the **All** radio button, and then click the **Display** button to display all of the records in the DataGridView control.

10. Click the **Exit** button. Close the Code Editor window and then close the solution.

The INSERT and DELETE Statements

SQL provides the **INSERT statement** for inserting records into a database and the **DELETE statement** for deleting records from a database. The syntax and examples of both statements are shown in Figures 14-40 and 14-41, respectively.

INSERT Statement

Syntax
INSERT INTO *tableName*(*fieldName1*, *fieldName2*, ...*fieldNameN*)
    VALUES (*field1Value*, *field2Value*, ...*fieldNValue*)

Example 1
```
INSERT INTO 'tblOscars' ('YearWon', 'Actor', 'Actress',
                          'Picture', 'Animated')
      VALUES (2005, 'Jamie Foxx', Hilary Swank',
               'Million Dollar Baby', 'The Incredibles')
```

Example 2 – parameter query
```
INSERT INTO 'tblOscars' ('YearWon', 'Actor', 'Actress',
                          'Picture', 'Animated')
      VALUES (?, ?, ?, ?, ?)
```

Figure 14-40   Syntax and examples of the SQL INSERT statement

---

DELETE Statement

Syntax
DELETE FROM *tableName* **WHERE** *condition*

Example 1
```
DELETE FROM tblOscars WHERE YearWon = 2005
```

Example 2
```
DELETE FROM tblOscars WHERE Picture = 'Million Dollar Baby'
```

Example 3 – parameter query
```
DELETE FROM tblOscars WHERE YearWon = ?
```

Figure 14-41   Syntax and examples of the SQL DELETE statement

In the next two sets of steps, you will create Insert and Delete queries for the Oscar Winners application. An **Insert query** uses the INSERT statement to add a record to a database. A **Delete query** uses the DELETE statement to delete a record from a database.

To create an Insert query:

1. Open the Oscars Solution (Oscars Solution.sln) file contained in the VB2015\Chap14\ Oscars Solution-InsertDelete folder. The application is already connected to the Oscars database.

2. Right-click **OscarsDataSet.xsd** in the Solution Explorer window, and then click **Open** to open the DataSet Designer window.

3. Right-click **tblOscarsTableAdapter** in the DataSet Designer window. Point to **Add** on the shortcut menu, and then click **Query** to start the TableAdapter Query Configuration Wizard. (If Add does not appear on the shortcut menu, click Add Query instead.)

4. Verify that the Use SQL statements radio button is selected, and then click the **Next** button to display the Choose a Query Type screen. Click the **INSERT** radio button. See Figure 14-42.

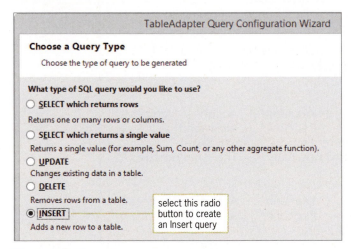

Figure 14-42   Choose a Query Type screen

5. Click the **Next** button to display the Specify a SQL INSERT statement screen, which contains the default INSERT statement for the tblOscars table. See Figure 14-43.

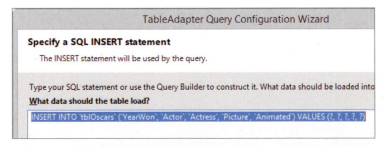

Figure 14-43   Default INSERT statement for the tblOscars table

6. Click the **Next** button to display the Choose Function Name screen. Change the function's name to **InsertRecordQuery**, and then click the **Next** button to display the Wizard Results screen. See Figure 14-44.

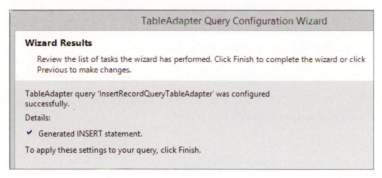

Figure 14-44   Wizard Results screen

7. Click the **Finish** button. The InsertRecordQuery function appears in the DataSet Designer window, as shown in Figure 14-45.

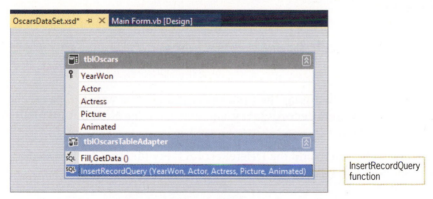

Figure 14-45   InsertRecordQuery function

Next, you will create a Delete query.

To create a Delete query:

START HERE

1. Right-click **tblOscarsTableAdapter** in the DataSet Designer window. Click **Add Query** on the shortcut menu to start the TableAdapter Query Configuration Wizard. (If Add Query does not appear on the shortcut menu, point to Add and then click Query.)

2. Verify that the Use SQL statements radio button is selected. Click the **Next** button to display the Choose a Query Type screen.

3. Click the **DELETE** radio button, and then click the **Next** button to display the Specify a SQL DELETE statement screen, which contains the default DELETE statement for the tblOscars table.

4. Click the **Query Builder** button. Change the WHERE clause in the SQL pane of the Query Builder dialog box as shown in Figure 14-46. (Don't be concerned about the values in the Grid pane.)

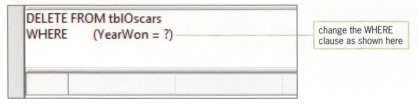

Figure 14-46   SQL pane in the Query Builder dialog box

5. Click the **OK** button. The DELETE statement shown in Figure 14-47 appears in the Specify a SQL DELETE statement screen.

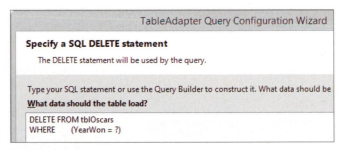

Figure 14-47   SQL DELETE statement

6. Click the **Next** button to display the Choose Function Name screen. Change the function's name to **DeleteRecordQuery**, and then click the **Next** button to display the Wizard Results screen.

7. Click the **Finish** button to add the DeleteRecordQuery function to the DataSet Designer window. See Figure 14-48.

Figure 14-48   DeleteRecordQuery function

8. Save the solution and then close the OscarsDataSet.xsd window.

In the next set of steps, you will code the btnAdd_Click and btnDelete_Click procedures. The btnAdd_Click procedure will use the InsertRecordQuery function to add a record to the Oscars database. The btnDelete_Click procedure will use the DeleteRecordQuery function to delete a record from the database.

To code and then test the btnAdd_Click and btnDelete_Click procedures:

1. Open the Code Editor window. Locate the btnAdd_Click procedure and then click the **blank line** above the End Sub clause. First, the procedure will determine whether the five text boxes contain data. If at least one of the text boxes is empty, the procedure will display an appropriate message. Enter the selection structure shown in Figure 14-49.

```
Private Sub btnAdd_Click(sender As Object, e As EventArgs) Handle
    ' add a record to the dataset

    If txtAddYear.Text.Trim = String.Empty OrElse
            txtActor.Text.Trim = String.Empty OrElse
            txtActress.Text.Trim = String.Empty OrElse
            txtPicture.Text.Trim = String.Empty OrElse
            txtAnimated.Text.Trim = String.Empty Then
        MessageBox.Show("Please enter all of the information.",
                    "Oscar Winners", MessageBoxButtons.OK,
                    MessageBoxIcon.Information)
    Else

    End If
End Sub
```

enter this selection structure

Figure 14-49 Selection structure entered in the btnAdd_Click procedure

2. If all of the text boxes contain data, the procedure can add the data to the database. First, however, it will need to convert the value in the txtAddYear control to a number because the YearWon field in the table is numeric. Enter the following lines of code:

Dim intYear As Integer
Integer.TryParse(txtAddYear.Text, intYear)

3. Now the procedure can use the InsertRecordQuery function to add the data to the database and then use the Fill method to retrieve the appropriate data from the database. However, as you learned in Lesson A, a run time error occurs when a procedure attempts to add a duplicate record to the Oscars database. A duplicate record is one whose YearWon field value is already in the dataset. You can prevent the application from ending abruptly by placing both the InsertRecordQuery function and the Fill method in a Try...Catch statement. Enter the additional lines of code shown in Figure 14-50.

```
        Else
            Dim intYear As Integer
            Integer.TryParse(txtAddYear.Text, intYear)
          ┌─Try
          │     TblOscarsTableAdapter.InsertRecordQuery(intYear,
          │                                             txtActor.Text.Trim,
          │                                             txtActress.Text.Trim,
          │                                             txtPicture.Text.Trim,
          │                                             txtAnimated.Text.Trim)
          │     TblOscarsTableAdapter.Fill(OscarsDataSet.tblOscars)
          │ Catch ex As Exception
          │     MessageBox.Show("Duplicate record", "Oscar Winners",
          │                 MessageBoxButtons.OK, MessageBoxIcon.Information)
          └─End Try
        End If
```

enter these
lines of code

Figure 14-50   Additional lines of code entered in the btnAdd_Click procedure

4. Next, locate the btnDelete_Click procedure, and then click the **blank line** above the End Sub clause. Before the procedure deletes a record, it will ask the user to confirm the deletion. Enter the code indicated in Figure 14-51.

```
Private Sub btnDelete_Click(sender As Object, e As EventArgs) Handles
        ' delete a record from the dataset

      ┌─Dim dlgButton As DialogResult
      │ dlgButton =
      │     MessageBox.Show("Delete record for year " &
      │                 lstDeleteYear.Text & "?", "Confirm Delete",
      │                 MessageBoxButtons.YesNo,
      └─                MessageBoxIcon.Exclamation)

        │
End Sub
```

enter these six
lines of code

Figure 14-51   Code entered in the btnDelete_Click procedure

5. If the user confirms the deletion, the procedure will need to convert the value in the lstDeleteYear control to a number because the YearWon field in the table is numeric. Enter the following lines of code:

    If dlgButton = DialogResult.Yes Then
    Dim intYear As Integer
    Integer.TryParse(lstDeleteYear.Text, intYear)

6. Now the procedure can use the DeleteRecordQuery function to delete the record from the database and then use the Fill method to retrieve the appropriate data from the database. Enter the following lines of code:

    TblOscarsTableAdapter.DeleteRecordQuery(intYear)
    TblOscarsTableAdapter.Fill(OscarsDataSet.tblOscars)

7. Save the solution and then start the application. Click the **Add** button. The "Please enter all of the information." message appears in a message box. Close the message box.

8. Next, try to add a duplicate record. In the Add new record section, type **2010** in the Year box, type **Jamie Foxx** in the Actor box, type **Hilary Swank** in the Actress box, type **Million Dollar Baby** in the Picture box, and type **The Incredibles** in the Animated box. Click the **Add** button. The "Duplicate record" message appears in a message box. Close the message box.

9. In the Year box, change 2010 to **2005**, and then click the **Add** button. The new record appears at the top of the list in the DataGridView control. (The frmMain_Load procedure contains the `TblOscarsBindingSource.Sort = "YearWon"` statement, which you learned about in Lesson A.)

10. Click the **Exit** button to end the application, and then start the application again to verify that the new record appears in the DataGridView control.

11. Next, you will delete the record for the year 2005. The record is already selected in the DataGridView control, and its YearWon value is selected in the lstDeleteYear control. (The list box is bound to the YearWon field in the dataset.) Click the **Delete** button. The "Delete record for year 2005?" message appears in the Confirm Delete message box. Click the **Yes** button to delete the record.

12. Click **2010** in the lstDeleteYear control, and then click the **Delete** button. When the Confirm Delete message box opens, click the **No** button. The record remains in the DataGridView control.

13. Click the **Exit** button to end the application, and then start the application again to verify that only the record for the year 2005 was deleted.

14. Click the **Exit** button to end the application. Close the Code Editor window and then close the solution.

Figure 14-52 shows the code entered in the frmMain_Load, btnAdd_Click, and btnDelete_Click procedures.

```vb
Private Sub frmMain_Load(sender As Object, e As EventArgs
) Handles MyBase.Load
    'TODO: This line of code loads data into the
    'OscarsDataSet.tblOscars' table. You can move, or remove it,
    as needed.
    Me.TblOscarsTableAdapter.Fill(Me.OscarsDataSet.tblOscars)
    TblOscarsBindingSource.Sort = "YearWon"
End Sub

Private Sub btnAdd_Click(sender As Object, e As EventArgs
) Handles btnAdd.Click
    ' add a record to the dataset

    If txtAddYear.Text.Trim = String.Empty OrElse
        txtActor.Text.Trim = String.Empty OrElse
        txtActress.Text.Trim = String.Empty OrElse
        txtPicture.Text.Trim = String.Empty OrElse
        txtAnimated.Text.Trim = String.Empty Then
        MessageBox.Show("Please enter all of the information.",
                "Oscar Winners", MessageBoxButtons.OK,
                MessageBoxIcon.Information)
```

Figure 14-52 Most of the application's code *(continues)*

(continued)

```
        Else
            Dim intYear As Integer
            Integer.TryParse(txtAddYear.Text, intYear)
            Try
            TblOscarsTableAdapter.InsertRecordQuery(intYear,
                                        txtActor.Text.Trim,
                                        txtActress.Text.Trim,
                                        txtPicture.Text.Trim,
                                        txtAnimated.Text.Trim)
            TblOscarsTableAdapter.Fill(OscarsDataSet.tblOscars)
            Catch ex As Exception
                MessageBox.Show("Duplicate record", "Oscar Winners",
                    MessageBoxButtons.OK, MessageBoxIcon.Information)
            End Try
        End If
End Sub

Private Sub btnDelete_Click(sender As Object, e As EventArgs
) Handles btnDelete.Click
    ' delete a record from the dataset

    Dim dlgButton As DialogResult
    dlgButton =
        MessageBox.Show("Delete record for year " &
                    lstDeleteYear.Text & "?", "Confirm Delete",
                    MessageBoxButtons.YesNo,
                    MessageBoxIcon.Exclamation)
    If dlgButton = DialogResult.Yes Then
        Dim intYear As Integer
        Integer.TryParse(lstDeleteYear.Text, intYear)
        TblOscarsTableAdapter.DeleteRecordQuery(intYear)
        TblOscarsTableAdapter.Fill(OscarsDataSet.tblOscars)

    End If
End Sub
```

Figure 14-52   Most of the application's code

Lesson C Summary

- To create a parameter query:

  Use a question mark in place of the criteria's value in the WHERE clause.

- To save a query that contains the SELECT statement:

  Use the TableAdapter Query Configuration Wizard to associate the query with one or more methods.

- To save a query that contains either the INSERT statement or the DELETE statement:

  Use the TableAdapter Query Configuration Wizard to associate the query with a function.

- To invoke a query from code:

  Enter the query's method or function in a procedure.

- To use SQL to insert records into a database:

  Use the INSERT statement.

- To use SQL to delete records from a database:

  Use the DELETE statement.

Lesson C Key Terms

?—the parameter marker in a parameter query

Delete query—a query that uses the DELETE statement to delete a record from a database

DELETE statement—the SQL statement used to delete a record from a database

Insert query—a query that uses the INSERT statement to add a record to a database

INSERT statement—the SQL statement used to insert a record into a database

Parameter marker—a question mark (?)

Parameter query—a query that uses the parameter marker (?) in place of the criteria's value

Lesson C Review Questions

1. When used in a parameter query, which of the following WHERE clauses will allow you to select the records for employees working more than 40 hours?

   a. `WHERE Hours >= 40`   c. `WHERE Hours > #`

   b. `WHERE Hours > ?`   d. `WHERE Hours < ?`

2. The FillByCity method is associated with a parameter query. Which of the following invokes the method, passing it the contents of the txtCity control's Text property?

   a. `TblCityTableAdapter.FillByCity(CityDataSet.tblCity, txtCity.Text)`

   b. `TblCityTableAdapter.FillByCity(txtCity.Text)`

   c. `TblCityBindingSource.FillByCity(CityDataSet.tblCity, txtCity.Text)`

   d. `CityDataSet.FillByCity(txtCity.Text)`

3. You can use the SQL _____ statement to add a record to a database.

   a. ADD   c. APPEND

   b. ADD INTO   d. INSERT

4. You can use the SQL _____ statement to remove a record from a database.

   a. DELETE   c. ERASE

   b. DETACH   d. REMOVE

Lesson C Exercises

1. Open the JM Sales Solution (JM Sales Solution.sln) file contained in the VB2015\Chap14\ JM Sales Solution folder. The application is connected to the AnnualSales database, which contains a table named tblSales. Each record in the table has two numeric fields: YearNum (the primary key) and Sales. The btnAdd_Click procedure should allow the user to add records to the database. The btnDelete_Click procedure should allow the user to delete records (by year number) from the database. Use SQL to code the procedures. Test the application appropriately. Be sure to try adding a record whose year number matches an existing year number.

2. Open the Addison Playhouse Solution (Addison Playhouse Solution.sln) file contained in the VB2015\Chap14\Addison Playhouse Solution folder. The application is connected to the Play database, which contains a table named tblReservations. Each record in the table has three fields: a numeric field named Seat (the primary key) and two text fields named Patron and Phone. The application should allow the user to add records to the database and also delete records (by seat number) from the database. It should also allow the user to enter a seat number and then view the associated record. In addition, it should allow the user to view the records whose Patron field begins with the one or more characters the user enters. (Hint: Use LIKE ? & '%' as the filter.) The records should always appear in order by the seat number. Code the application and then test it appropriately.

3. Open the VB2015\Chap14\Polter Solution\Polter Solution (Polter Solution.sln) file. The application is connected to the Products database, which contains a table named tblProducts. Each record in the table has three fields. The ItemNum (primary key) and ItemName fields contain text; the Price field contains numbers. The application should allow the user to view the record associated with a specific item number. It should also allow the user to enter a price and then view the records whose price is equal to or greater than that amount. The records should appear in order by the item number when the application is started. Code the application and then test it appropriately.

4. Open the Morgan Industries Solution (Morgan Industries Solution.sln) file contained in the VB2015\Chap14\Morgan Industries Solution folder. The application is connected to the Employees database, which contains a table named tblEmploy. Each record in the table contains seven fields. The EmpNum field is the primary key. The Status field contains the employment status, which is either the letter F (for full time) or the letter P (for part time). The Code field identifies the employee's department: 1 for Accounting, 2 for Advertising, 3 for Personnel, and 4 for Inventory. The records should appear in order by the employee number when the application is started. The application should allow the user to display all of the records, only the part-time records, only the full-time records, and only the records for a specific department. Use the InputBox function to get the department code. Code the application and then test it appropriately.

Finding and Fixing Program Errors

After studying Appendix A, you should be able to:

- ◎ Locate syntax errors using the Error List window
- ◎ Locate a logic error by stepping through the code
- ◎ Locate logic errors by using breakpoints
- ◎ Fix syntax and logic errors
- ◎ Identify a run time error

Finding and Fixing Syntax Errors

As you learned in Chapter 2, a syntax error occurs when you break one of a programming language's rules. Most syntax errors are a result of typing errors that occur when entering instructions, such as typing `Intger` instead of `Integer`. The Code Editor detects syntax errors as you enter the instructions. However, if you are not paying close attention to your computer screen, you may not notice the errors. In the next set of steps, you will observe what happens when you start an application that contains a syntax error.

START HERE ► **To start debugging the Total Sales Calculator application:**

1. If necessary, start Visual Studio 2015. Open the Total Sales Solution (Total Sales Solution.sln) file contained in the VB2015\AppA\Total Sales Solution folder. The application calculates and displays the total of the sales amounts entered by the user. See Figure A-1.

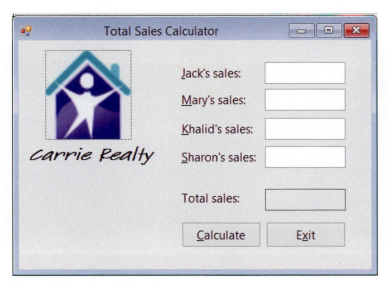

Figure A-1 Total Sales Calculator application

2. Open the Code Editor window. Replace <your name> and <current date> with your name and the current date, respectively. Figure A-2 shows the code entered in the btnCalc_Click procedure. The red jagged lines, called squiggles, alert you that three lines of code contain a syntax error. The green squiggle warns you of a potential problem in your code.

```
Private Sub btnCalc_Click(sender As Object, e As EventArgs
    ' calculates and displays the total sales

    ' declare variables
    Dim intJack As Integer
    Dim intMary As Integer
    Dim intKhalid As Integer
    Dim intSharon As Integer
    Dim intTotal As Intger                              ⟶ syntax error

    ' assign input to variables
    Integer.TryParse(txtJack.Text, intJack             ⟶ syntax error
    Integer.TryParse(txtMary.Text, intMary)
    Integer.TryParse(txtKhalid.Text, intKhalid)
    Integer.TryParse(txtSharon.Text, intSharon)
syntax error
    ' calculate total sales
    inTotal = intJack + intMary + intKhalid + intSharon

    ' display total sales
    lblTotal.Text = intTotal.ToString("C0")
                                                        ⟶ warning
End Sub
```

Figure A-2 btnCalc_Click procedure in the Total Sales Calculator application

3. Press **F5** to start the application. If the dialog box shown in Figure A-3 appears, click the **No** button.

Figure A-3   Dialog box

4. The Error List window opens at the bottom of the IDE. See Figure A-4. The Error List window indicates that the code contains three errors and one warning, and it provides both a description and the location of each in the code. When debugging your code, always correct the syntax errors first because doing so will often remove the warning.

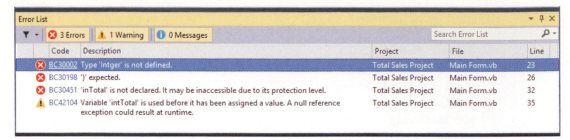

Figure A-4 Error List window

Note: You can change the size of the Error List window by positioning your mouse pointer on the window's top border until the mouse pointer becomes a vertical line with an arrow at the top and bottom. Then press and hold down the left mouse button while you drag the border either up or down.

5. Double-click the **first error's description** in the Error List window. A LightBulb indicator appears in the margin. Hover your mouse pointer over the light bulb until a list arrow appears, and then click the list arrow. A list of suggestions for fixing the error appears. See Figure A-5.

Figure A-5 Result of clicking the LightBulb indicator's list arrow

6. The first error is simply a typing error; the programmer meant to type Integer. You can either type the missing letter e yourself or click the appropriate suggestion in the list. Click **Change 'Intger' to 'Integer'.** in the list. The Code Editor makes the change in the Dim statement and also removes the error, as well as the warning, from the Error List window.

7. The Error List window now indicates that there is a missing parenthesis in the statement on Line 26. Double-click the **first error's description** in the Error List window. The Code Editor places the insertion point at the end of the first TryParse method. Hover your mouse pointer over the jagged red line. See Figure A-6.

```
' assign input to variables
Integer.TryParse(txtJack.Text, intJack|
Integer.TryParse(txtMary.Text, intMary)
Integer.TryParse(txtKhalid.Text, intKha        ● (local variable) intJack As Integer
Integer.TryParse(txtSharon.Text, intSha        ')' expected.────── error
```

Figure A-6   Result of double-clicking the error description for Line 26

8. Type). The Code Editor removes the error from the Error List window.

9. The description of the remaining error indicates that the Code Editor does not recognize the name `inTotal`. Double-click the **error's description**, hover your mouse pointer over the light bulb, and then click the **list arrow**. This error is another typing error; the variable's name is `intTotal`, not `inTotal`. Click **Change 'inTotal' to 'intTotal'.** in the list. The Code Editor removes the error from the Error List window.

10. Close the Error List window. Save the solution and then start the application. Test the application using **125600** as Jack's sales, **98700** as Mary's sales, **165000** as Khalid's sales, and **250400** as Sharon's sales. Click the **Calculate** button. The sales total is $639,700.

11. Click the **Exit** button. Close the Code Editor window and then close the solution.

Finding and Fixing Logic Errors

Unlike syntax errors, logic errors are much more difficult to find because they do not trigger an error message from the Code Editor. A logic error can occur for a variety of reasons, such as forgetting to enter an instruction or entering the instructions in the wrong order. Some logic errors occur as a result of calculation statements that are correct syntactically but incorrect mathematically. For example, consider the statement `dblSum = dblNum1 * dblNum2`, which is supposed to calculate the sum of two numbers. The statement's syntax is correct, but it is incorrect mathematically because it uses the multiplication operator rather than the addition operator. In the next two sections, you will debug two applications that contain logic errors.

To debug the Discount Calculator application:

START HERE

1. Open the VB2015\AppA\Discount Solution\Discount Solution (Discount Solution.sln) file. See Figure A-7. The application calculates and displays three discount amounts, which are based on the price entered by the user.

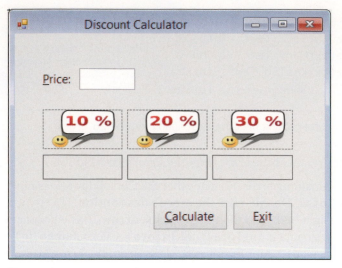

Figure A-7   Discount Calculator application

2. Open the Code Editor window. Figure A-8 shows the btnCalc_Click procedure.

```
Private Sub btnCalc_Click(sender As Object, e As
    ' calculates and displays a 10%, 20%, and
    ' 30% discount on an item's price

    ' declare variables
    Dim decPrice As Decimal
    Dim decDiscount10 As Decimal
    Dim decDiscount20 As Decimal
    Dim decDiscount30 As Decimal

    ' calculate discounts
    decDiscount10 = decPrice * 0.1D
    decDiscount20 = decPrice * 0.2D
    decDiscount30 = decPrice * 0.3D

    ' display discounts
    lbl10.Text = decDiscount10.ToString("N2")
    lbl20.Text = decDiscount20.ToString("N2")
    lbl30.Text = decDiscount30.ToString("N2")
End Sub
```

Figure A-8   btnCalc_Click procedure in the Discount Calculator application

3. Start the application. Type **100** in the Price box and then click the **Calculate** button. The interface shows that each discount is 0.00, which is incorrect. Click the **Exit** button.

4. You will use the Debug menu to run the Visual Basic debugger, which is a tool that helps you locate the logic errors in your code. Click **Debug** on the menu bar. The menu's Step Into option will start your application and allow you to step through your code. It does this by executing the code one statement at a time, pausing immediately before each statement is executed. Click **Step Into**. Type **100** in the Price box and then

click the **Calculate** button. The debugger highlights the first instruction to be executed, which is the btnCalc_Click procedure header. In addition, an arrow points to the instruction, as shown in Figure A-9, and the code's execution is paused.

```
⇨    ⊟ Private Sub btnCalc_Click(sender As Object, e As Eve
              ' calculates and displays a 10%, 20%, and
              ' 30% discount on an item's price

              ' declare variables
```

Figure A-9 Procedure header highlighted

5. You can use either the Debug menu's Step Into option or the F8 key on your keyboard to tell the computer to execute the highlighted instruction. Press the **F8** key. After the computer processes the procedure header, the debugger highlights the next statement to be processed, which is the decDiscount10 = decPrice * 0.1D statement. It then pauses execution of the code. (The Dim statements are skipped over because they are not considered executable by the debugger.)

6. While the execution of a procedure's code is paused, you can view the contents of controls and variables that appear in the highlighted statement and also in the statements above it in the procedure. Before you view the contents of a control or variable, however, you should consider the value you expect to find. Before the highlighted statement is processed, the decDiscount10 variable should contain its initial value, 0. (Recall that the Dim statement initializes numeric variables to 0.) Place your mouse pointer on decDiscount10 in the highlighted statement. The variable's name and current value appear in a small box, as shown in Figure A-10. At this point, the decDiscount10 variable's value is correct.

```
       Dim decPrice As Decimal
       Dim decDiscount10 As Decimal
       Dim decDiscount20 As Decimal
       Dim decDiscount30 As Decimal

       ' calculate discounts
⇨      decDiscount10 = decPrice * 0.1D
       decDiscour● decDiscount10 0 ⊡ te * 0.2D          ┌─────────────┐
       decDiscount30 = decPrice * 0.3D                  │ variable's name │
                                                        │ and value      │
                                                        └─────────────┘
```

Figure A-10 Value stored in the variable before the highlighted statement is executed

7. Now consider the value you expect to find in the decPrice variable. Before the highlighted statement is processed, the variable should contain the number 100, which is the value you entered in the Price box. Place your mouse pointer on decPrice in the highlighted statement. The variable contains 0, which is its initial value. The value is incorrect because no statement above the highlighted statement assigns the Price box's value to the decPrice variable. In other words, a statement is missing from the procedure.

8. Click **Debug** on the menu bar, and then click **Stop Debugging** to stop the debugger. Click the **blank line** below the last Dim statement, and then press **Enter** to insert another blank line. Enter the following comment and TryParse method:

   ' assign price to a variable
   Decimal.TryParse(txtPrice.Text, decPrice)

9. Save the solution. Click **Debug** on the menu bar and then click **Step Into**. Type **100** in the Price box and then click the **Calculate** button. Press **F8** to process the procedure header. The debugger highlights the TryParse method and then pauses execution of the code.

10. Before the TryParse method is processed, the txtPrice control's Text property should contain 100, which is the value you entered in the Price box. Place your mouse pointer on `txtPrice.Text` in the TryParse method. The box shows that the Text property contains the expected value. The 100 is enclosed in quotation marks because it is considered a string.

11. The `decPrice` variable should contain its initial value, 0. Place your mouse pointer on `decPrice` in the TryParse method. The box shows that the variable contains the expected value.

12. Press **F8** to process the TryParse method. The debugger highlights the `decDiscount10 = decPrice * 0.1D` statement before pausing execution of the code. Place your mouse pointer on `decPrice` in the TryParse method, as shown in Figure A-11. Notice that after the method is processed by the computer, the `decPrice` variable contains the number 100, which is correct.

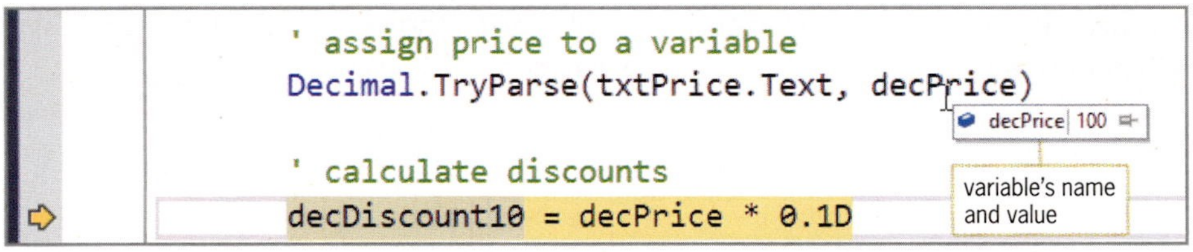

```
    ' assign price to a variable
    Decimal.TryParse(txtPrice.Text, decPrice)
                                         decPrice 100

    ' calculate discounts
⇨   decDiscount10 = decPrice * 0.1D      variable's name
                                         and value
```

Figure A-11   Value stored in the variable after the TryParse method is executed

13. Before the highlighted statement is processed, the `decDiscount10` variable should contain its initial value, and the `decPrice` variable should contain the value assigned to it by the TryParse method. Place your mouse pointer on `decDiscount10` in the highlighted statement. The box shows that the variable contains 0, which is correct. Place your mouse pointer on `decPrice` in the highlighted statement. The box shows that the variable contains 100, which also is correct.

14. After the highlighted statement is processed, the `decPrice` variable should still contain 100. However, the `decDiscount10` variable should contain 10, which is 10% of 100. Press **F8** to execute the highlighted statement, and then place your mouse pointer on `decDiscount10` in the statement. The box shows that the variable contains 10.0, which is correct. On your own, verify that the `decPrice` variable in the statement contains the appropriate value (100).

15. To continue program execution without using the debugger, click **Debug** on the menu bar and then click **Continue**. This time, the correct discount amounts appear in the interface. See Figure A-12.

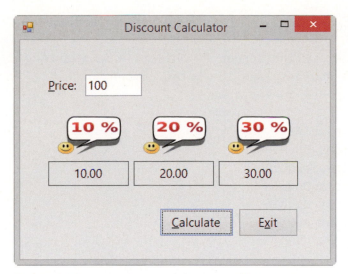

Figure A-12   Sample run of the Discount Calculator application

16. Click the **Exit** button. Close the Code Editor window and then close the solution.

Setting Breakpoints

Stepping through code one line at a time is not the only way to search for logic errors. You can also use a breakpoint to pause execution at a specific line in the code. You will learn how to set a breakpoint in the next set of steps.

To begin debugging the Hours Worked application:

START HERE

1. Open the Hours Worked Solution (Hours Worked Solution.sln) file contained in the VB2015\AppA\Hours Worked Solution folder. See Figure A-13. The application calculates and displays the total number of hours worked in four weeks.

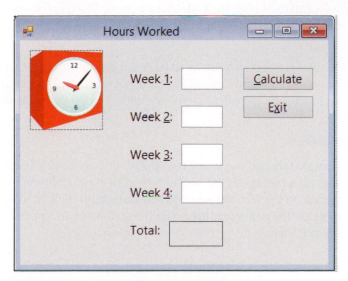

Figure A-13   Hours Worked application

2. Open the Code Editor window. Figure A-14 shows the btnCalc_Click procedure.

```
Private Sub btnCalc_Click(sender As Object, e As EventArgs
    ' calculates and displays the total number
    ' of hours worked during 4 weeks

    ' declare variables
    Dim dblWeek1 As Double
    Dim dblWeek2 As Double
    Dim dblWeek3 As Double
    Dim dblWeek4 As Double
    Dim dblTotal As Double

    ' assign input to variables
    Double.TryParse(txtWeek1.Text, dblWeek1)
    Double.TryParse(txtWeek2.Text, dblWeek2)
    Double.TryParse(txtWeek3.Text, dblWeek2)
    Double.TryParse(txtWeek4.Text, dblWeek4)

    ' calculate total hours worked
    dblTotal = dblWeek1 + dblWeek2 + dblWeek3 + dblWeek4

    ' display total hours worked
    lblTotal.Text = dblTotal.ToString("N1")
End Sub
```

Figure A-14 btnCalc_Click procedure in the Hours Worked application

3. Start the application. Type **10.5**, **25**, **33**, and **40** in the Week 1, Week 2, Week 3, and Week 4 boxes, respectively, and then click the **Calculate** button. The interface shows that the total number of hours is 83.5, which is incorrect; it should be 108.5. Click the **Exit** button.

The statement that calculates the total number of hours worked is not giving the correct result. Rather than having the computer pause before processing each line of code in the procedure, you will have it pause only before processing the calculation statement. You do this by setting a breakpoint on the statement.

START HERE

To finish debugging the application:

1. Right-click the **calculation statement**, point to **Breakpoint**, and then click **Insert Breakpoint**. (You can also set a breakpoint by clicking the statement and then using the Toggle Breakpoint option on the Debug menu, or you can simply click in the gray margin next to the statement.) The debugger highlights the statement and places a circle next to it, as shown in Figure A-15.

```
    ' calculate total hours worked
●   dblTotal = dblWeek1 + dblWeek2 + dblWeek3 + dblWeek4
```

Figure A-15   Breakpoint set in the procedure

2. Start the application. Type **10.5**, **25**, **33**, and **40** in the Week 1, Week 2, Week 3, and Week 4 boxes, respectively, and then click the **Calculate** button. The computer begins processing the code contained in the btnCalc_Click procedure. It stops processing when it reaches the breakpoint statement, which it highlights. The highlighting indicates that the statement is the next one to be processed. Notice that a yellow arrow now appears in the red dot next to the breakpoint. See Figure A-16.

```
    ' calculate total hours worked
⇨   dblTotal = dblWeek1 + dblWeek2 + dblWeek3 + dblWeek4
```

Figure A-16   Result of the computer reaching the breakpoint

3. Before viewing the values contained in each variable in the highlighted statement, consider the values you expect to find. Before the calculation statement is processed, the dblTotal variable should contain its initial value (0). Place your mouse pointer on dblTotal in the highlighted statement. The box shows that the variable's value is 0, which is correct. (You can verify the variable's initial value by placing your mouse pointer on dblTotal in its declaration statement.)

4. The other four variables should contain the numbers 10.5, 25, 33, and 40, which are the values you entered in the text boxes. On your own, view the values contained in the dblWeek1, dblWeek2, dblWeek3, and dblWeek4 variables. Notice that two of the variables (dblWeek1 and dblWeek4) contain the correct values (10.5 and 40). The dblWeek2 variable, however, contains 33 rather than 25, and the dblWeek3 variable contains its initial value (0) rather than the number 33.

5. Two of the TryParse methods are responsible for assigning the text box values to the dblWeek2 and dblWeek3 variables. Looking closely at the four TryParse methods in the procedure, you will notice that the third one is incorrect. After converting the contents of the txtWeek3 control to a number, the method should assign the number to the dblWeek3 variable rather than to the dblWeek2 variable. Click **Debug** on the menu bar and then click **Stop Debugging**.

6. Change dblWeek2 in the third TryParse method to **dblWeek3**.

7. Click the **breakpoint circle** to remove the breakpoint.

8. Save the solution and then start the application. Type **10.5**, **25**, **33**, and **40** in the Week 1, Week 2, Week 3, and Week 4 boxes, respectively, and then click the **Calculate** button. The interface shows that the total number of hours is 108.5, which is correct. See Figure A-17.

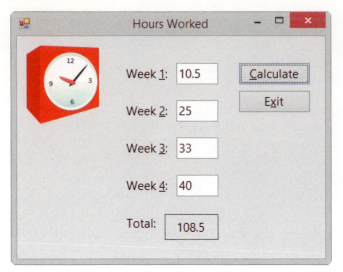

Figure A-17   Sample run of the Hours Worked application

9. On your own, test the application using other values for the hours worked in each week. When you are finished testing, click the **Exit** button. Close the Code Editor window and then close the solution.

Run Time Errors

In addition to syntax and logic errors, programs can also have run time errors. A run time error is an error that occurs while an application is running. As you will observe in the following set of steps, an expression that attempts to divide a value by the number 0 will result in a run time error if the expression's numerator and/or denominator has the Decimal data type.

START HERE

To use the Quotient Calculator application to observe a run time error:

1. Open the VB2015\AppA\Quotient Solution\Quotient Solution (Quotient Solution.sln) file. See Figure A-18. The interface provides two text boxes for the user to enter two numbers. The Calculate button's Click event procedure divides the number in the txtNumerator control by the number in the txtDenominator control and then displays the result, called the quotient, in the lblQuotient control.

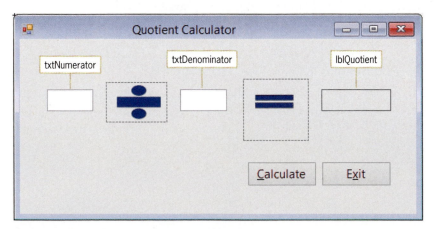

Figure A-18   Quotient Calculator application

2. Open the Code Editor window. Figure A-19 shows the btnCalc_Click procedure.

```
Private Sub btnCalc_Click(sender As Object, e As EventArgs)
    ' display the result of dividing two numbers

    Dim decNumerator As Decimal
    Dim decDenominator As Decimal
    Dim decQuotient As Decimal

    Decimal.TryParse(txtNumerator.Text, decNumerator)
    Decimal.TryParse(txtDenominator.Text, decDenominator)

    decQuotient = decNumerator / decDenominator

    lblQuotient.Text = decQuotient.ToString("N2")
End Sub
```

Figure A-19 btnCalc_Click procedure in the Quotient Calculator application

3. Start the application. Type **100** and **5** in the txtNumerator and txtDenominator controls, respectively, and then click the **Calculate** button. The interface shows that the quotient is 20.00, which is correct.

4. Delete the 5 from the txtDenominator control, and then click the **Calculate** button. A run time error occurs. The Error Correction window indicates that the highlighted statement, which also has an arrow pointing to it, is attempting to divide by 0. The troubleshooting tips section of the window advises you to "Make sure the value of the denominator is not zero before performing a division operation." See Figure A-20.

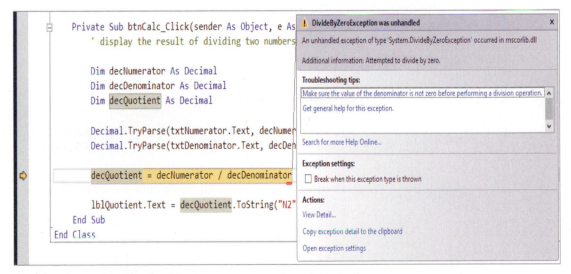

Figure A-20 Run time error caused by attempting to divide by 0

When the txtDenominator control is empty, or when it contains a character that cannot be converted to a number, the second TryParse method in the procedure stores the number 0 in the decDenominator variable. When that variable contains the number 0, the statement that calculates the quotient will produce a run time error because the variable is used as the denominator in the calculation. To prevent this error from occurring, you will need to tell the computer to calculate and display the quotient only when the decDenominator variable does not contain the number 0; otherwise, it should display the "N/A" message. You do this using a selection structure, which is covered in Chapter 4 in this book.

START HERE

To add a selection structure to the btnCalc_Click procedure:

1. Click **Debug** on the menu bar and then click **Stop Debugging**.

2. Enter the selection structure shown in Figure A-21. Be sure to move the statements that calculate and display the quotient into the selection structure's true path as shown in the figure.

```
Private Sub btnCalc_Click(sender As Object, e As EventArgs)
    ' display the result of dividing two numbers

    Dim decNumerator As Decimal
    Dim decDenominator As Decimal
    Dim decQuotient As Decimal

    Decimal.TryParse(txtNumerator.Text, decNumerator)
    Decimal.TryParse(txtDenominator.Text, decDenominator)

    If decDenominator <> 0 Then
        decQuotient = decNumerator / decDenominator
        lblQuotient.Text = decQuotient.ToString("N2")
    Else
        lblQuotient.Text = "N/A"
    End If
End Sub
```

enter this selection structure

Figure A-21 Selection structure entered in the procedure

3. Start the application. Type **100** and **5** in the txtNumerator and txtDenominator controls, respectively, and then click the **Calculate** button. The interface shows that the quotient is 20.00, which is correct.

4. Next, delete the 5 from the txtDenominator control, and then click the **Calculate** button. Instead of a run time error, N/A appears in the interface. See Figure A-22.

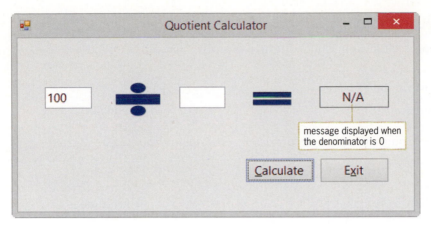

Figure A-22   Result of including the selection structure in the btnCalc_Click procedure

5. Click the **Exit** button. Close the Code Editor window and then close the solution.

Appendix A Summary

- To find the syntax errors in a program:

  Look for squiggles (jagged lines) in the Code Editor window, or start the application and then look in the Error List window.

- To find the logic errors in a program:

  Either step through the code in the Code Editor window or set a breakpoint.

- To step through your code:

  Use either the Step Into option on the Debug menu or the F8 key on your keyboard.

- To set a breakpoint:

  Right-click the line of code on which you want to set the breakpoint. Point to Breakpoint and then click Insert Breakpoint. You can also click the line of code and then use the Toggle Breakpoint option on the Debug menu. In addition, you can click in the gray margin next to the line of code.

- To remove a breakpoint:

  Right-click the line of code containing the breakpoint, point to Breakpoint, and then click Delete Breakpoint. You can also simply click the breakpoint circle in the margin.

- To determine whether a variable contains the number 0:

  Use a selection structure.

Review Questions

1. The process of locating and fixing any errors in a program is called
   _____.

   a. bug-proofing
   b. bug-eliminating
   c. debugging
   d. error removal

2. While stepping through code, the debugger highlights the statement that
   _____.

   a. was just executed
   b. will be executed next
   c. contains the error
   d. none of the above

3. Logic errors are listed in the Error List window.

   a. True
   b. False

4. Which key is used to step through code?

   a. F5
   b. F6
   c. F7
   d. F8

5. While stepping through the code in the Code Editor window, you can view the contents of controls and variables that appear in the highlighted statement only.

   a. True
   b. False

6. You use _____ to pause program execution at a specific line in the code.

   a. a breakpoint
   b. the Error List window
   c. the Step Into option on the DEBUG menu
   d. the Stop Debugging option on the DEBUG menu

7. The statement `Constant dblRATE As Double` is an example of a
   _____.

   a. correct statement
   b. logic error
   c. syntax error
   d. run time error

8. When entered in a procedure, which of the following statements will result in a syntax error?

   a. `Me.Clse()`
   b. `Integer.TryPars(txtHours.Text, intHours)`
   c. `Dim decRate as Decimel`
   d. all of the above

Exercises

1. Open the Commission Calculator Solution (Commission Calculator Solution.sln) file contained in the VB2015\AppA\Commission Calculator Solution folder. Use what you learned in the appendix to debug the application.

INTRODUCTORY

2. Open the New Pay Solution (New Pay Solution.sln) file contained in the VB2015\AppA\New Pay Solution folder. Use what you learned in the appendix to debug the application.

INTRODUCTORY

3. Open the Hawkins Solution (Hawkins Solution.sln) file contained in the VB2015\AppA\Hawkins Solution folder. Use what you learned in the appendix to debug the application.

INTRODUCTORY

4. Open the Allenton Solution (Allenton Solution.sln) file contained in the VB2015\AppA\Allenton Solution folder. Use what you learned in the appendix to debug the application.

INTRODUCTORY

5. Open the Martins Solution (Martins Solution.sln) file contained in the VB2015\AppA\Martins Solution folder. Use what you learned in the appendix to debug the application.

INTERMEDIATE

6. Open the Average Score Solution (Average Score Solution.sln) file contained in the VB2015\AppA\Average Score Solution folder. Use what you learned in the appendix to debug the application.

INTERMEDIATE

7. Open the Beachwood Solution (Beachwood Solution.sln) file contained in the VB2015\AppA\Beachwood Solution folder. Use what you learned in the appendix to debug the application.

ADVANCED

8. Open the Framington Solution (Framington Solution.sln) file contained in the VB2015\AppA\Framington Solution folder. Use what you learned in the appendix to debug the application.

ADVANCED

GUI Design Guidelines

Chapter 1—Lesson C

FormBorderStyle, ControlBox, MaximizeBox, MinimizeBox, and StartPosition Properties

- A splash screen should not have Minimize, Maximize, or Close buttons, and its borders should not be sizable. In most cases, a splash screen's FormBorderStyle property is set to either None or FixedSingle. Its StartPosition property is set to CenterScreen.

- A form that is not a splash screen should always have a Minimize button and a Close button, but you can choose to disable the Maximize button. Typically, the FormBorderStyle property is set to Sizable; however, it can also be set to FixedSingle. The form's StartPosition property is usually set to CenterScreen.

Chapter 2—Lesson A

Layout and Organization of the User Interface

- Organize the user interface so that the information flows either vertically or horizontally, with the most important information always located in the upper-left corner of the interface.

- Group related controls together using either white (empty) space or one of the tools from the Containers section of the toolbox.

- Use a label to identify each text box in the user interface. Also use a label to identify other label controls that display program output. The label text should be meaningful, consist of one to three words only, and appear on one line. Left-align the text within the label and position the label either above or to the left of the control it identifies. Enter the label text using sentence capitalization, and insert a colon (:) following the label text.

- Display a meaningful caption on the face of each button. The caption should indicate the action the button will perform when clicked. Enter the caption using book title capitalization. Place the caption on one line and use from one to three words only.

- When a group of buttons are stacked vertically, all buttons in the group should be the same height and width. When a group of buttons are positioned horizontally, all buttons in the group should be the same height. In a group of buttons, the most commonly used button is typically placed first in the group.

- Align the borders of the controls wherever possible to minimize the number of different margins appearing in the interface.

Chapter 2—Lesson B

Adding Graphics

- Use graphics sparingly. If the graphic is used solely for aesthetics, use a small graphic and place it in a location that will not distract the user.

Selecting Font Types, Styles, and Sizes

- Use only one font type (typically Segoe UI) for all of the text in the interface.
- Use no more than two different font sizes in the interface.
- Avoid using italics and underlining because both font styles make text difficult to read.
- Limit the use of bold text to titles, headings, and key items that you want to emphasize.

Selecting Colors

- Build the interface using black, white, and gray. Only add color if you have a good reason to do so.
- Use white, off-white, or light gray for the background. Use black for the text.
- Never use a dark color for the background or a light color for the text. A dark background is hard on the eyes, and light-colored text can appear blurry.
- Limit the number of colors in an interface to three, not including white, black, and gray. The colors you choose should complement each other.
- Never use color as the only means of identification for an element in the interface.

Setting the BorderStyle Property of a Text Box or Label

- Keep the BorderStyle property of text boxes at the default setting: Fixed3D.
- Keep the BorderStyle property of identifying labels at the default setting: None.
- Use FixedSingle for the BorderStyle property of labels that display program output, such as the result of a calculation.
- Avoid setting a label control's BorderStyle property to Fixed3D because in Windows applications, a control with a three-dimensional appearance implies that it can accept user input.

Setting the AutoSize and TextAlign Properties of a Label

- Keep the AutoSize property of identifying labels at the default setting: True.
- In most cases, use False for the AutoSize property of label controls that display program output.
- Use the TextAlign property to specify the alignment of the text within the label.

Assigning Access Keys

- Assign a unique access key to each control that can accept user input.

- When assigning an access key to a control, use the first letter of the control's caption or identifying label, unless another letter provides a more meaningful association. If you can't use the first letter and no other letter provides a more meaningful association, then use a distinctive consonant. As a last resort, use a vowel or a number.

Using the TabIndex Property to Control the Focus

- Assign a TabIndex value (starting with 0) to each control in the interface, except for controls that do not have a TabIndex property. The TabIndex values should reflect the order in which the user will want to access the controls.

- To allow users to access a text box using the keyboard, assign an access key to the text box's identifying label. Set the identifying label's TabIndex property to a value that is one number less than the value stored in the text box's TabIndex property.

Chapter 3—Lesson B

InputBox Function's Prompt and Title Capitalization

- Use sentence capitalization for the prompt but book title capitalization for the title.

Assigning a Default Button

- The default button should be the button that is most often selected by the user, except in cases where the tasks performed by the button are both destructive and irreversible. If a form contains a default button, it typically is the first button.

Chapter 4—Lesson B

Labeling a Group Box

- Use sentence capitalization for the optional identifying label, which is entered in the group box's Text property.

MessageBox.Show Method

- Use sentence capitalization for the *text* argument, but use book title capitalization for the *caption* argument.

- Display the Exclamation icon to alert the user that he or she must make a decision before the application can continue. You can phrase the message as a question. Message boxes that contain the Exclamation icon typically contain more than one button.

- Display the Information icon along with an OK button in a message box that displays an informational message.

- Display the Stop icon to alert the user of a serious problem that must be corrected before the application can continue.

- The default button in the message box should represent the user's most likely action as long as that action is not destructive.

Chapter 5—Lesson B

Radio Button Standards

- Use radio buttons to limit the user to one choice in a group of related but mutually exclusive choices.

- The minimum number of radio buttons in a group is two, and the recommended maximum number is seven.

- The label in the radio button's Text property should be entered using sentence capitalization.

- Assign a unique access key to each radio button in an interface.

- Use a container (such as a group box) to create separate groups of radio buttons. Only one button in each group can be selected at any one time.

- Designate a default radio button in each group of radio buttons.

Check Box Standards

- Use check boxes to allow the user to select any number of choices from a group of one or more independent and nonexclusive choices.

- The label in the check box's Text property should be entered using sentence capitalization.

- Assign a unique access key to each check box in an interface.

Chapter 6—Lesson C

List Box Standards

- Use a list box only when you need to offer the user at least three different choices.

- Don't overwhelm the user with a lot of choices at the same time; instead, display from three to eight items and let the user employ the scroll bar to view the remaining ones.

- Use a label control to provide keyboard access to the list box. Set the label's TabIndex property to a value that is one number less than the list box's TabIndex value.

- List box items are either arranged by use, with the most used entries appearing first in the list, or sorted in ascending order.

Default List Box Item

- If a list box allows the user to make only one selection, a default item is typically selected when the interface first appears. The default item should be either the item selected most frequently or the first item in the list. However, if a list box allows more than one selection at a time, you do not select a default item.

Chapter 7—Lesson B

Combo Box Standards

- Use a label control to provide keyboard access to a combo box. Set the label's TabIndex property to a value that is one number less than the combo box's TabIndex value.

- Combo box items are either arranged by use, with the most used entries appearing first in the list, or sorted in ascending order.

Chapter 8—Lesson B

Menu Standards

- Menu title captions should be one word, with only the first letter capitalized. Each menu title should have a unique access key.

- Menu item captions can be from one to three words. Use book title capitalization, and assign a unique access key to each menu item on the same menu.

- Assign unique shortcut keys to commonly used menu items.

- If a menu item requires additional information from the user, place an ellipsis (...) at the end of the item's caption, which is entered in the item's Text property.

- Follow the Windows standards for the placement of menu titles and items.

- Use a separator bar to separate groups of related menu items.

Visual Basic Conversion Functions

Syntax	Return data type	Range for *expression*
CBool(expression)	Boolean	Any valid String or numeric expression
CByte(expression)	Byte	0 through 255 (unsigned)
CChar(expression)	Char	Any valid String expression; value can be 0 through 65535 (unsigned); only the first character is converted
CDate(expression)	Date	Any valid representation of a date and time
CDbl(expression)	Double	−1.79769313486231570E+308 through −4.94065645841246544E-324 for negative values; 4.94065645841246544E-324 through 1.79769313486231570E +308 for positive values
CDec(expression)	Decimal	−79,228,162,514,264,337,593,543,950,335 for zero-scaled numbers, that is, numbers with no decimal places; for numbers with 28 decimal places, the range is +/− 7.9228162514264337593543950335; the smallest possible non-zero number is 0.0000000000000000000000000001 (+/−1E-28)
CInt(expression)	Integer	−2,147,483,648 through 2,147,483,647; fractional parts are rounded
CLng(expression)	Long	−9,223,372,036,854,775,808 through 9,223,372,036,854,775,807; fractional parts are rounded
CObj(expression)	Object	Any valid expression
CSByte(expression)	SByte (signed Byte)	−128 through 127; fractional parts are rounded
CShort(expression)	Short	−32,768 through 32,767; fractional parts are rounded
CSng(expression)	Single	−3.402823E+38 through −1.401298E-45 for negative values; 1.401298E-45 through 3.402823E+38 for positive values
CStr(expression)	String	Depends on the expression
CUInt(expression)	UInt	0 through 4,294,967,295 (unsigned)
CULng(expression)	ULng	0 through 18,446,744,073,709,551,615 (unsigned)
CUShort(expression)	UShort	0 through 65,535 (unsigned)

Visual Basic 2015 Cheat Sheet

Statements

Assignment

object.property = expression
variableName = expression

Updating a counter

counterVariable = counterVariable {+ | −} constantValue
counterVariable {+= | −=} constantValue

Updating an accumulator

accumulatorVariable = accumulatorVariable {+ | −} value
accumulatorVariable {+= | −=} value

Option Explicit

when set to On, prevents the computer from creating an undeclared variable:
Option Explicit [On | Off]

Option Strict

when set to On, prevents the computer from making implicit type conversions that may result in a loss of data: **Option Strict [On | Off]**

Option Infer

when set to Off, prevents the computer from inferring a variable's data type:
Option Infer [On | Off]

Do...Loop

Pretest loop

Do {**While** | **Until**} *condition*
    loop body instructions to be processed either while the condition is true or until the condition becomes true
Loop

Posttest loop

Do
    loop body instructions to be processed either while the condition is true or until the condition becomes true
Loop {**While** | **Until**} *condition*

For Each...Next

For Each *elementVariableName* **As** *dataType* **In** *group*
    loop body instructions
Next *elementVariableName*

For...Next

For *counterVariableName* [**As** *dataType*] = *startValue* **To** *endValue* [**Step** *stepValue*]
    loop body instructions
Next *counterVariableName*

stepValue	Loop body processed when	Loop ends when
positive number	counter's value <= *endValue*	counter's value > *endValue*
negative number	counter's value >= *endValue*	counter's value < *endValue*

If...Then...Else

If *condition* **Then**
    statement block to be processed when the condition is true
[**ElseIf** *condition2*
    statement block to be processed when the first condition is false and condition2 is true]
[**Else**
    statement block to be processed when all previous conditions are false]
End If

Logic errors in selection structures

1. using a compound condition rather than a nested selection structure
2. reversing the decisions in the outer and nested selection structures
3. using an unnecessary nested selection structure
4. including an unnecessary comparison in a condition

Select Case

Select Case *selectorExpression*
    Case *expressionList1*
        instructions for the first Case
    [**Case** *expressionList2*
        instructions for the second Case]

[**Case** *expressionListN*
     instructions for the Nth Case]
[**Case Else**
     instructions for when the selectorExpression does not match any of the expressionLists]

End Select
Case *smallest value in the range* **To** *largest value in the range*
Case Is *comparisonOperator value*

Try...Catch

Try
     one or more statements that might generate an exception
Catch ex As Exception
     one or more statements to execute when an exception occurs
End Try

Variable and Named Constant Declaration

{**Dim** | **Private** | **Static**} *variableName* **As** *dataType* [= *initialValue*]

[**Private**] **Const** *constantName* **As** *dataType* = *expression*

Data Types

Boolean	a logical value (True, False)
Char	one Unicode character
Date	date and time information
Decimal	a number with a decimal place
Double	a number with a decimal place
Integer	integer
Long	integer
Object	data of any type
Short	integer
Single	a number with a decimal place
String	text

Rules for Naming Variables

1. The name must begin with a letter or an underscore.
2. The name can contain only letters, numbers, and the underscore character. No punctuation characters, special characters, or spaces are allowed in the name.
3. Although the name can contain thousands of characters, 32 characters is the recommended maximum number of characters to use.
4. The name cannot be a reserved word, such as Sub or Double.

Type Conversion Rules

1. Strings will not be implicitly converted to numbers.
2. Numbers will not be implicitly converted to strings.
3. Wider data types will not be implicitly demoted to narrower data types.
4. Narrower data types will be implicitly promoted to wider data types.

Operators and Precedence

^	exponentiation	1
−	negation	2
*, /	multiplication and division	3
\	integer division	4
Mod	modulus (remainder) arithmetic	5
+, −	addition and subtraction	6
&	concatenation	7
=, <>	equal to, not equal to	8
>, >=	greater than, greater than or equal to	8
<, <=	less than, less than or equal to	8
Not	reverses the truth-value of the condition; True becomes False, and False becomes True	9
And	all subconditions must be true for the compound condition to evaluate to True	10
AndAlso	same as the And operator, except performs short-circuit evaluation	10
Or	only one of the subconditions needs to be true for the compound condition to evaluate to True	11
OrElse	same as the Or operator, except performs short-circuit evaluation	11
Xor	only one of the sub-conditions can be true for the compound condition to evaluate to True	12

Arithmetic Assignment

variableName arithmeticAssignmentOperator value

Operator	Purpose
+=	addition assignment
−=	subtraction assignment
*=	multiplication assignment
/=	division assignment

Printing

Print the interface during design time

Make the designer window the active window. Use the Windows Snipping tool to take a picture of the interface, and then save the picture as a PNG file. Close the Snipping tool. Use Windows to locate the PNG file, right-click the file's name, click Print, select the appropriate printer, and then click the Print button.

You can also tap the Print Screen key while the designer window is open. You then would need to start an application that can display a picture. Open a new document (if necessary), and then press Ctrl+v.

Print the interface during run time

Add a PrintForm control (object) to the component tray. Use the following statements to print:
object.**PrintAction** = **Printing.PrintAction.***destination*
object.**Print()**

destination	Purpose
PrintToPreview	sends the printout to the Print Preview window
PrintToPrinter	sends the printout to the printer

Print the code during design time

Make the Code Editor window the active window. Collapse any code you do not want to print. Click the Print option on the File menu. Select/deselect the Hide collapsed regions and/or Include line numbers check boxes. Click the OK button.

Generate Random Numbers

Integers

Dim *randomObjectName* **As New Random**
randomObjectName.**Next**(*minValue, maxValue*)

Double numbers

Dim *randomObjectName* **As New Random**
(*maxValue – minValue* + **1**) * *randomObjectName*.**NextDouble** + *minValue*

Methods

Convert

converts a number from one data type to another: **Convert.***method*(*value*)

Focus

sends the focus to an object: *object*.**Focus()**

MessageBox.Show

displays a message box
MessageBox.Show(*text, caption, buttons, icon*[, *defaultButton*])
dialogResultVariable = **MessageBox.Show**(*text, caption, buttons, icon*[, *defaultButton*])

SelectAll

selects the contents of a text box: *textbox*.**SelectAll()**

Strings.Space

includes a specific number of spaces in a string: **Strings.Space**(*number*)

ToString

formats a number: *numericVariableName*.**ToString**(*formatString*)

TryParse

converts a string to a number
dataType.**TryParse**(*string, numericVariableName*)
booleanVariable = *dataType*.**TryParse**(*string, numericVariableName*)

Functions

Format

formats a number: **Format**(*expression, style*)

InputBox

gets data from the user: **InputBox**(*prompt*[, *title*][, *defaultResponse*])

Val

converts a string to a Double number: **Val**(*string*)

Independent Sub Procedure

Private Sub *procedureName*([*parameterList*])
      statements
End Sub
Call *procedureName*([*argumentList*])

Function Procedure

Private Function *procedureName*([*parameterList*]) **As** *dataType*
      statements
      Return *expression*
End Function

Internally Document the Code

Start the comment with an apostrophe followed by an optional space.

Control the Characters Accepted by a Text Box

<u>Example</u>

```
Private Sub txtAge_KeyPress(sender As Object,
e As KeyPressEventArgs) Handles txtAge.KeyPress
    ' allows the text box to accept only
    ' numbers and the Backspace key
    If (e.KeyChar < "0" OrElse e.KeyChar > "9") AndAlso
        e.KeyChar <> ControlChars.Back Then
            e.Handled = True
    End If
End Sub
```

Prevent a Form from Closing (FormClosing Event Procedure)

```
e.Cancel = True
```

Working with Strings

Accessing characters

string.**Substring**(*startIndex*[, *numCharsToAccess*])

Aligning the characters

string.**PadLeft**(*totalChars*[, *padCharacter*])
string.**PadRight**(*totalChars*[, *padCharacter*])

Comparing using pattern matching

string **Like** *pattern*

Pattern-matching characters	Matches in *string*
?	any single character
*	zero or more characters
#	any single digit (0 through 9)
[*characterList*]	any single character in the *characterList* (for example, "[A5T]" matches A, 5, or T, whereas "[a–z]" matches any lowercase letter)
[!*characterList*]	any single character *not* in the *characterList* (for example, "[!A5T]" matches any character other than A, 5, or T, whereas "[!a–z]" matches any character that is not a lowercase letter)

Concatenation

string **&** *string* [...**&** *string*]

Converting to uppercase or lowercase

string.**ToUpper**
string.**ToLower**

Determining the number of characters

string.**Length**

Inserting characters

string.**Insert**(*startIndex*, *value*)

Removing characters

string.**Trim**
string.**Remove**(*startIndex*[, *numCharsToRemove*])

Searching

string.**Contains**(*subString*)
string.**IndexOf**(*subString*[, *startIndex*])

List/Combo Boxes

Add items

object.**Items.Add**(*item*)

Clear items

object.**Items.Clear**()

Determine the selected item

object.**SelectedItem**
object.**SelectedIndex**

Perform a task when the selected item changes

Code the SelectedValueChanged or SelectedIndexChanged events.

Remove items

object.**Items.Remove**(*item*)
object.**Items.RemoveAt**(*index*)

Select an item

object.**SelectedItem** = *item*
object.**SelectedIndex** = *itemIndex*

One-Dimensional Arrays

Array declaration

{**Dim** | **Private** | **Static**} *arrayName*(*highestSubscript*) **As** *dataType*
{**Dim** | **Private** | **Static**} *arrayName*() **As** *dataType* = {*initialValues*}

Highest subscript

arrayName.**GetUpperBound(0)**
arrayName.**Length – 1**

Number of elements

arrayName.**Length**
arrayName.**GetUpperBound(0) + 1**

Reversing

Array.Reverse(*arrayName***)**

Sorting (ascending order)

Array.Sort(*arrayName***)**

Traversing

```
Dim strCities() As String = {"Boston", "Chicago",
                             "Louisville", "Tampa"}
```

Example 1 – For...Next

```
Dim intHigh As Integer = strCities.GetUpperBound(0)
For intSub As Integer = 0 To intHigh
    MessageBox.Show(strCities(intSub))
Next intSub
```

Example 2 – Do...Loop

```
Dim intHigh As Integer = strCities.Length - 1
Dim intSub As Integer
Do While intSub <= intHigh
    lstCities.Items.Add(strCities(intSub))
    intSub += 1
Loop
```

Example 3 – For Each...Next

```
For Each strCity As String In strCities
    MessageBox.Show(strCity)
Next strCity
```

Two-Dimensional Arrays

Array declaration

{**Dim** | **Private** | **Static**} *arrayName*(*highestRowSubscript, highestColumnSubscript*) **As** *dataType*
{**Dim** | **Private** | **Static**} *arrayName*(,) **As** *dataType* = {{*initialValues*}, ...{*initialValues*}}

Highest column subscript

arrayName.**GetUpperBound(1)**

Highest row subscript

arrayName.**GetUpperBound(0)**

Traversing

```
Dim strMonths(,) As String = {{"Jan", "31"},
                    {"Feb", "28"},
                    {"Mar", "31"},
                    {"Apr", "30"}}
```

Example 1 – For...Next (displays contents row by row)

```
Dim intHighRow As Integer = strMonths.GetUpperBound(0)
Dim intHighCol As Integer = strMonths.GetUpperBound(1)
For intR As Integer = 0 To intHighRow
    For intC As Integer = 0 To intHighCol
            lstMonths.Items.Add(strMonths(intR, intC))
    Next intC
Next intR
```

Example 2 – Do...Loop (displays contents column by column)

```
Dim intHighRow As Integer = strMonths.GetUpperBound(0)
Dim intHighCol As Integer = strMonths.GetUpperBound(1)
Dim intR As Integer
Dim intC As Integer
Do While intC <= intHighCol
    intR = 0
    Do While intR <= intHighRow
            lstMonths.Items.Add(strMonths(intR, intC))
            intR += 1
    Loop
    intC += 1
Loop
```

Example 3 – For Each...Next (displays contents row by row)

```
For Each strElement As String In strMonths
    lstMonths.Items.Add(strElement)
Next strElement
```

Sequential Access Files

Close a file

streamWriterVariableName.**Close()**
streamReaderVariableName.**Close()**

Create a StreamReader object

IO.File.OpenText(*fileName***)**

Create a StreamWriter object

IO.File.*method*(*fileName*)

method	Description
CreateText	opens a sequential access file for output
AppendText	opens a sequential access file for append

Declare StreamWriter and StreamReader variables

{**Dim** | **Private**} *streamWriterVariableName* **As IO.StreamWriter**
{**Dim** | **Private**} *streamReaderVariableName* **As IO.StreamReader**

Determine whether a file exists

IO.File.Exists(*fileName*)

Read data from a file

*streamReaderVariableName.***ReadLine**

Determine whether a file contains another character to read

*streamReaderVariableName.***Peek**

Write data to a file

*streamWriterVariableName.***Write**(*data*)
*streamWriterVariableName.***WriteLine**(*data*)

Structures

Declare a structure variable

{**Dim** | **Private**} *structureVariableName* **As** *structureName*

Declare an array of structure variables

Use the structureName as the array's dataType.

Definition

Structure *structureName*
    Public *memberVariableName1* **As** *dataType*
    [**Public** *memberVariableNameN* **As** *dataType*]
End Structure

Member variable within a structure variable

structureVariableName.memberVariableName

Member variable within an array of structure variables

arrayName(*subscript*)**.***memberVariableName*

Databases

Connect an application to an Access database

1. Open the application's solution file.
2. If necessary, open the Data Sources window by clicking View on the menu bar, pointing to Other Windows, and then clicking Data Sources.
3. Click Add New Data Source in the Data Sources window to start the Data Source Configuration Wizard, which displays the Choose a Data Source Type screen. If necessary, click Database.
4. Click the Next button, and then continue using the wizard to specify the data source and the name of the database file. The data source for an Access database is Microsoft Access Database File (OLE DB).

Preview the contents of a dataset

1. Right-click the dataset's name in the Data Sources window and then click Preview Data.
2. Click the Preview button.
3. When you are finished previewing the data, close the dialog box.

Bind an object in a dataset

To have the computer create a control and then bind an object to it:

In the Data Sources window, click the object you want to bind. If necessary, use the object's list arrow to change the control type. Drag the object to an empty area on the form and then release the mouse button.

To bind an object to an existing control:

In the Data Sources window, click the object you want to bind. Drag the object to the control on the form and then release the mouse button. Alternatively, you can click the control on the form and then use the Properties window to set the appropriate property or properties.

Customizing a BindingNavigator control

To add an item to a BindingNavigator control:

1. Click the BindingNavigator control's task box, and then click Edit Items to open the Items Collection Editor window.
2. If necessary, click the "Select item and add to list below" arrow.
3. Click the item you want to add to the BindingNavigator control, and then click the Add button.
4. If necessary, you can use the up and down arrows to reposition the item.

To delete an item from a BindingNavigator control:

1. Click the BindingNavigator control's task box, and then click Edit Items to open the Items Collection Editor window.
2. In the Members list, click the item you want to remove and then click the X button.

Determine the location of the record pointer

bindingSourceName.**Position**

Move the record pointer

bindingSourceName.**MoveFirst()**
bindingSourceName.**MoveLast()**
bindingSourceName.**MoveNext()**
bindingSourceName.**MovePrevious()**

Add a record to a dataset

dataSetName.tableName.**Add***tableName***Row(***valueField1*[,
valueField2..., valueFieldN])

Save dataset changes to a database

tableAdapterName.**Update(***dataSetName.tableName***)**

Sort the records in a dataset

bindingSourceName.**Sort** = *fieldName*

Locate a record in a dataset

dataRowVariable =
dataSetName.tableName.**FindBy***fieldName***(***value***)**

Delete a record from a dataset

dataRowVariable.**Delete()**

LINQ

Select and arrange records

Dim *variableName* = **From** *elementName* **In** *dataset.table*
    [**Where** *condition*]
    [**Order By** *elementName.fieldName1* [**Ascending** | **Descending**]
       [, *elementName.fieldName*N [**Ascending** | **Descending**]]]
    Select *elementName*

Assign a LINQ variable's contents to a BindingSource control

bindingSource.**DataSource** = *variableName*.**AsDataView**

LINQ aggregate operators

The aggregate operators are Average, Count, Max, Min, and Sum. The Count operator does not need the Select clause.

Dim *variableName* [**As** *dataType*] =
        Aggregate *elementName* **In** *dataset.table*
        [**Where** *condition*]
        Select *elementName.fieldName*
        Into *aggregateOperator*()

SQL

Selecting fields and records

SELECT *fieldList* **FROM** *tableName*
        [**WHERE** *condition*]
        [**ORDER BY** *fieldName* [**DESC**]]

Add a record to a dataset

INSERT INTO *tableName(fieldName1, fieldName2,...fieldNameN)*
              VALUES (*field1Value, field2Value,...fieldNValue*)

Delete a record from a dataset

DELETE FROM *tableName* **WHERE** *condition*

Classes

Define a class

Public Class *className*
        attributes section
        behaviors section
End Class

Instantiate an object

<u>Syntax – Version 1</u>

{**Dim** | **Private**} *variableName* **As** *className*
variableName = **New** *className*

<u>Syntax – Version 2</u>

{**Dim** | **Private**} *variableName* **As New** *className*

Create a Property procedure

Public [**ReadOnly** | **WriteOnly**] **Property** *propertyName*[(*parameterList*)] **As** *dataType*
   Get
      [*instructions*]
      Return *privateVariable*
   End Get
   Set(value As *dataType*)
      [*instructions*]
      privateVariable = {**value** | *defaultValue*}
   End Set
End Property

Create a constructor

Public Sub New([*parameterList*]**)**
        instructions to initialize the class's Private variables
End Sub

Create a method that is not a constructor

Public {Sub | Function} *methodName*(*[parameterList]*) [**As** *dataType*]
     instructions
End {Sub | Function}

Create an auto-implemented property

Public Property *propertyName* **As** *dataType*

Most Commonly Used Properties

Windows Form

AcceptButton	specify a default button that will be selected when the user presses the Enter key
CancelButton	specify a cancel button that will be selected when the user presses the Esc key
ControlBox	indicate whether the form contains the Control box and Minimize, Maximize, and Close buttons
Font	specify the font to use for text
FormBorderStyle	specify the appearance and behavior of the form's border
MaximizeBox	specify the state of the Maximize button
MinimizeBox	specify the state of the Minimize button
Name	give the form a meaningful name (use frm as the ID)
StartPosition	indicate the starting position of the form
Text	specify the text that appears in the form's title bar and on the taskbar

Button

Enabled	indicate whether the button can respond to the user's actions
Font	specify the font to use for text
Image	specify the image to display on the button's face
ImageAlign	indicate the alignment of the image on the button's face
Name	give the button a meaningful name (use btn as the ID)
TabIndex	indicate the position of the button in the Tab order
Text	specify the text that appears on the button

CheckBox

Checked	indicate whether the check box is selected or unselected
Font	specify the font to use for text
Name	give the check box a meaningful name (use chk as the ID)
TabIndex	indicate the position of the check box in the Tab order
Text	specify the text that appears inside the check box

ComboBox

DropDownStyle	indicate the style of the combo box
Font	specify the font to use for text
Name	give the combo box a meaningful name (use cbo as the ID)
SelectedIndex	get or set the index of the selected item
SelectedItem	get or set the value of the selected item
Sorted	specify whether the items in the list portion are sorted
TabIndex	indicate the position of the combo box in the Tab order
Text	get or set the value that appears in the text portion

DataGridView

AutoSizeColumnsMode	control the way the column widths are sized
DataSource	indicate the source of the data to display in the control
Dock	define which borders of the control are bound to its container
Name	give the data grid view control a meaningful name (use dgv as the ID)

GroupBox

Name	give the group box a meaningful name (use grp as the ID)
Padding	specify the internal space between the edges of the group box and the edges of the controls contained within the group box
Text	specify the text that appears in the upper-left corner of the group box

Label

AutoSize	enable/disable automatic sizing
BorderStyle	specify the appearance of the label's border
Font	specify the font to use for text
Name	give the label a meaningful name (use lbl as the ID)
TabIndex	specify the position of the label in the Tab order
Text	specify the text that appears inside the label
TextAlign	specify the position of the text inside the label

ListBox

Font	specify the font to use for text
Name	give the list box a meaningful name (use lst as the ID)
SelectedIndex	get or set the index of the selected item
SelectedItem	get or set the value of the selected item
SelectionMode	indicate whether the user can select zero choices, one choice, or more than one choice
Sorted	specify whether the items in the list are sorted

PictureBox

Image	specify the image to display
Name	give the picture box a meaningful name (use pic as the ID)
SizeMode	specify how the image should be displayed
Visible	hide/display the picture box

RadioButton

Checked	indicate whether the radio button is selected or unselected
Font	specify the font to use for text
Name	give the radio button a meaningful name (use rad as the ID)
Text	specify the text that appears inside the radio button

TextBox

BackColor	indicate the background color of the text box
CharacterCasing	specify whether the text should remain as is or be converted to either uppercase or lowercase
Font	specify the font to use for text
ForeColor	indicate the color of the text inside the text box
Name	give the text box a meaningful name (use txt as the ID)
MaxLength	specify the maximum number of characters the text box will accept
Multiline	control whether the text can span more than one line
PasswordChar	specify the character to display when entering a password
ReadOnly	specify whether the text can be edited
ScrollBars	indicate whether scroll bars appear on a text box (used with a multiline text box)
TabIndex	specify the position of the text box in the Tab order
TabStop	indicate whether the user can use the Tab key to give focus to the text box
Text	get or set the text that appears inside the text box

Timer

Name	give the timer a meaningful name (use tmr as the ID)
Enabled	stop/start the timer
Interval	indicate the number of milliseconds between each Tick event

Case Projects

Your Special Day Catering (Chapters 1–3)

Create an application for Your Special Day Catering. The interface should allow the user to enter the customer ID, the bride's name, the groom's name, and the date of the wedding reception. It should also allow the user to enter the number of beef dinners, the number of chicken dinners, and the number of vegetarian dinners ordered for the reception. The interface should display the total number of dinners ordered, the total price of the order without sales tax, the sales tax, and the total price of the order with sales tax. Each dinner costs $26.75, and the sales tax rate is 5%. Include an appropriate image in the interface. (Hint: You can find many different images on the Open Clip Art Library Web site at *http://openclipart.org*.)

Crispies Bagels and Bites (Chapters 1–3)

Create an application for Crispies Bagels and Bites. The interface should allow the salesclerk to enter the number of bagels, donuts, and cups of coffee a customer orders. Bagels are 99¢, donuts are 75¢, and coffee is $1.20 per cup. The application should calculate and display the total price of the order without sales tax, the sales tax, and the total price of the order with sales tax. The sales tax rate is 6%. Include an appropriate image in the interface. (Hint: You can find many different images on the Open Clip Art Library Web site at *http://openclipart.org*.)

High Roll Game (Chapters 1–5)

The High Roll game requires two players. When the application is started, it should get each player's name and then display the names in the interface. Each player will roll two dice. The application should calculate the total roll for each player and then compare both totals. The application should display one of the following messages: "Tie", "*player 1's name* wins", or "*player 2's name* wins". The application should keep track of the number of times player 1 wins, the number of times player 2 wins, and the number of ties. You can use either your own die images or the ones contained in the VB2015\AppE folder. (The die images were downloaded from the Open Clip Art Library at *http://openclipart.org*.)

Math Practice (Chapters 1–5)

Create an application that can be used to practice adding, subtracting, multiplying, and dividing numbers. The application should display a math problem on the screen and then allow the student to enter the answer and also verify that the answer is correct. The application should give the student as many chances as necessary to answer the problem correctly. The math problems should use random integers from 1 through 20 only. The subtraction problems should never ask the student to subtract a larger number from a smaller one. The division problems should never ask the student to divide a smaller number by a larger number. Also, the division problems should always result in a whole number. The application should keep track of the number of correct and incorrect responses made by the student.

Mortgage Calculator (Chapters 1–6)

Create an application that calculates and displays three monthly mortgage payments. The application should use the loan amount and annual interest rate provided by the user with terms of 15 years, 25 years, and 30 years. The application should also display the total amount paid at the end of 15 years, 25 years, and 30 years.

Loan Payment Calculator (Chapters 1–7)

Create an application that calculates and displays the monthly payments on a loan. The application should use the loan amount provided by the user, rates of 3% to 7%, and terms of 3, 4, and 5 years. Use either a Sub procedure or a function.

Savings Calculator (Chapters 1–7)

Research Visual Basic's Financial.FV (Future Value) method. Create an application that allows the user to enter the amount a customer plans to deposit in a savings account each month, and whether the money will be deposited at either the beginning or the end of the month. The application should calculate and display the value of the account at the end of 5 years, 10 years, 15 years, 20 years, and 25 years. The interest rate is 3% and is compounded monthly.

Tax-Deductible Calculator (Chapters 1–8)

Create an interface that provides text boxes for entering the following business expenses: lodging, travel, meals, and entertainment. Lodging and travel are 100% tax deductible; meals and entertainment are only 50% tax deductible. The application should calculate and display the total expenses, the amount that is tax deductible, and the percentage that is tax deductible. The text boxes should accept only numbers, the period, and the Backspace key. The application should display an error message if a text box contains more than one period.

State Finder (Chapters 1–8)

Create an interface that provides a text box for the user to enter one or more characters. The interface should also include a list box containing the names of the 50 U.S. states. When the user clicks a button in the interface, the button's Click event procedure should select the first list box item that begins with the character(s) entered by the user. For example, if the user enters the letter K, the procedure should select Kansas in the list box. However, if the user enters the letters Ke, the procedure should select Kentucky.

Shopping Cart (Chapters 1–10)

The shopping cart application should list the names of 10 different DVDs in a list box and store the associated prices in a one-dimensional array. To purchase a DVD, the user needs to click its name in the list box and then click an Add to Cart button. The button's Click event procedure should display the DVD's name and price in another list box, which will represent the shopping cart. The interface should also provide a Remove from Cart button. The application should display the cost of the items in the shopping cart, the sales tax, the shipping charge, and the total cost. The sales tax rate is 4%. The shipping charge is $1 per DVD, up to a maximum shipping charge of $5.

Airplane Seats (Chapters 1–10)

Create an interface that contains 18 controls arranged in six rows and three columns. You can use label controls, picture boxes, or buttons. The seats in the first row are designated 1A, 1B, and 1C. The seats in the second row are designated 2A, 2B, and 2C, and so on. When the user clicks one of the 18 controls, the application should display the passenger's name, seat designation, and ticket price. The application should use a sequential access file for the passenger information, a structure, and an array.

Theater Seats (Chapters 1–11)

Create an interface that contains 10 controls arranged in five rows and two columns. You can use label controls, picture boxes, or buttons. The seats in the first row are designated A1 and B1. The seats in the second row are designated A2 and B2, and so on. When the user clicks one of the 10 controls, the application should display the patron's name, seat designation, and ticket price. The application should use a sequential access file for the patron information, a class, and an array.

Roll 'Em Again (Chapters 1–11)

Code the Roll 'Em Game from Chapter 5's Lesson C using a class for the pair of dice.

Rosette Catering (Chapters 1–12)

Create a Web Site application for Rosette Catering. The interface should allow the user to enter the customer ID, the bride's name, the groom's name, and the date of the wedding reception. It should also allow the user to enter the number of chicken dinners, the number of pasta dinners, and the number of vegetarian dinners ordered for the reception. The interface should display the total number of dinners ordered, the total price of the order without sales tax, the sales tax, and the total price of the order with sales tax. Each dinner costs $21, and the sales tax rate is 3%. Include an appropriate image in the interface. (Hint: You can find many different images on the Open Clip Art Library Web site at *http://openclipart.org*.)

Jefferson Realty (Chapters 1–13)

Create a Microsoft Access database that contains one table named tblHomes. The table should contain 10 records, each having five fields. The ID and ZIP code fields should contain text. Be sure to use several different ZIP codes. The number of bedrooms, number of bathrooms, and price fields should be numeric. Create an application that displays the contents of the database in a DataGridView control. The user should not be allowed to add or delete records. The application should allow the user to display the records for a specific number of bedrooms, a specific number of bathrooms, or a specific ZIP code. It also should allow the user to display the average home price for the entire database and also for a specific ZIP code.

Foxmore Realty (Chapters 1–14)

Create a Microsoft Access database that contains one table named tblHomes. The table should contain 10 records, each having six fields. The ID, city, and state fields should contain text. The number of bedrooms, number of bathrooms, and price fields should be numeric. Create an application that displays the contents of the database in a DataGridView control. If necessary, remove the BindingNavigator control from the application. The application should allow the user to insert and delete records. It should also allow the user to display the records for a specific number of bedrooms, a specific number of bathrooms, a specific ZIP code, and a specific combination of bedrooms and bathrooms.

Index

Note: Page numbers in **boldface** type indicate where key terms are defined.